SOCIOCULTURAL PERSPECTIVES IN SOCIAL PSYCHOLOGY

CURRENT READINGS

Edited by

Letitia Anne Peplau
University of California, Los Angeles

Shelley E. Taylor
University of California, Los Angeles

Prentice Hall, Upper Saddle River, New Jersey 07458

Library of Congress Cataloging-in-Publication Data
Sociocultural perspectives in social psychology: current readings/edited by
   Letitia Anne Peplau and Shelley E. Taylor.
         p.   cm.
      Includes bibliographical references.
      ISBN 0-13-241860-6 (pbk.)
      1. Social psychology.   2. Ethnicity.   3. Minorities.   4. Social
   sciences—Research.   I. Peplau, Letitia Anne.   II. Taylor, Shelley
   E.
   HM251.S68713   1997
   302—dc20   96-36173
                                                                   CIP

Editor-in-Chief: Peter Janzow
Acquisitions Editor: Heidi Freund
Editorial Assistant: Emsal Hasan
Director of Production and Manufacturing: Barbara Kittle
Managing Editor: Bonnie Biller
Project Manager: Karen Trost
Project Liaison: Shelly Kupperman
Manufacturing Manager: Nick Sklitsis
Prepress and Manufacturing Buyer: Tricia Kenny
Marketing Manager: Michael Alread
Marketing Assistant: Aileen Ugural
Interior Design: Meryl Poweski
Cover Director: Jayne Conte

This book was set in 10/12.5 ITC Berkeley OS by Pub-Set and printed and bound by
R.R. Donnelley/Harrisonburg.
The cover was printed by Phoenix.

Acknowledgments for text selections appear as footnotes on the first page of each
selection.

© 1997 by Prentice-Hall, Inc.
Simon & Schuster/A Viacom Company
Upper Saddle River, New Jersey 07458

Printed in the United States of America
10   9   8   7   6   5   4   3   2

ISBN   0-13-241860-6

Prentice-Hall International (UK) Limited, *London*
Prentice-Hall of Australia Pty. Limited, *Sydney*
Prentice-Hall Canada Inc., *Toronto*
Prentice-Hall Hispanoamericana, S.A., *Mexico*
Prentice-Hall of India Private Limited, *New Delhi*
Prentice-Hall of Japan, Inc., *Tokyo*
Simon & Schuster Asia Pte. Ltd., *Singapore*
Editora Prentice-Hall do Brasil, Ltda., *Rio de Janiero*

❖ CONTENTS ❖

❖ PREFACE ❖

This volume brings together the very best contemporary work in social psychology on sociocultural issues. The selections present work by leading scholars and include studies of ethnic minority populations in the United States as well as cross-cultural comparisons. The book is designed for undergraduate and graduate students in psychology and related fields.

Several trends suggest that sociocultural perspectives will become more central to social psychology in coming years. We live in an increasingly diverse, multicultural society. College faculty today teach students from varied ethnic and social backgrounds and face the challenge of incorporating new multicultural research into the traditional academic curriculum. At the same time, psychological researchers are giving increased attention to sociocultural influences on human behavior. In social psychology, some of the most distinguished researchers in the field have begun to investigate cultural influences, and this research now appears in our very best journals. This recent growth in first-rate research makes it possible and timely to compile an edited collection.

The articles included in this volume were selected with several criteria in mind. First, we made every effort to select articles that students will find interesting, readable, and understandable. To this end, we scoured the research literature for relevant articles and had a panel of undergraduates independently evaluate articles being considered for inclusion in the reader.

Second, we picked a set of articles that provide comprehensive and balanced coverage. These articles include the full range of standard topics in social psychology and can easily be used as a supplement to a basic textbook. The chart on page vi indicates which readings address each of 17 basic topics in social psychology. The volume includes both conceptual papers that review a body of literature and new empirical studies. The articles present important work by prominent researchers and consequently expose readers to outstanding examples of diverse research methods. For example, both experimental and correlational designs are included; methods of data collection include questionnaires, interviews, telephone surveys, and daily interaction diaries. Instructors who use primary sources in order to illustrate different research approaches will find that our reader serves this purpose well.

Third, this collection of articles represents a broad spectrum of cultural and ethnic populations. Major emphasis is given to African-American, Asian-American and Latino/Hispanic groups in the United States. In addition, 9 of the selections present cross-cultural research from Brazil, China, India, Iraq, Japan, Korea, and several other countries.

ORGANIZATION AND PEDAGOGICAL FEATURES

We introduce this collection with a section offering student readers guidance about how to use this book effectively. "To the Reader" explains the basic ingredients in a sociocultural perspective, offers advice about reading a research report in psychology, and introduces basic statistical terms that may be unfamiliar to some readers. The following section, "A Guide to Sociocultural Resources in Social Psychology," provides an overview of sources that could be used by instructors and students to delve more deeply into the topics in this book. This guide includes information about relevant journals and recent books. It also of-

COVERAGE OF BASIC TOPICS IN SOCIAL PSYCHOLOGY
Numbers indicate which chapters address each topic.

Aggression/violence—Chapters 15, 17
Attitude change/persuasion—Chapters 2, 9, 16
Attitudes—Chapters 2, 6, 8, 9, 10, 16
Attribution—Chapters 1, 4, 7, 8, 16
Emotion—Chapters 7, 8
Environmental psychology—Chapters 15, 18
Gender—Chapters 6, 12, 13, 17
Groups/intergroup relations—Chapters 2, 4, 5, 8, 9, 10, 11, 14, 16
Health—Chapters 1, 18
Interpersonal attraction—Chapter 13
Person perception—Chapters 4, 5, 7, 8, 9, 10, 16
Personal/intimate relationships—Chapters 4, 6, 8, 9, 12, 13, 17
Prejudice/discrimination—Chapters 11, 15, 16, 17
Prosocial behavior/helping—Chapters 6, 9
Self—Chapters 2, 4, 5, 6, 8, 9, 10, 11, 16
Social cognition—Chapters 2, 4, 5, 6, 7, 8, 9, 10, 16
Social influence—Chapters 2, 4, 6, 8, 9, 10, 11

fers suggestions about films, videos, fiction, and first-person accounts that can enrich an understanding of culture.

The 19 reprinted articles in this collection are organized into 5 sections, but can easily be used in other sequences. Each article is preceded by a paragraph-long introduction written by the editors. The purpose of these introductions is to alert students to the main issues in the article and to indicate how the article uses a sociocultural perspective. Each article is followed by a set of questions designed to stimulate students to examine the arguments, evidence, and methods presented by the author(s), and to consider applications of the research to their own lives. These questions could also be used for classroom discussion.

ACKNOWLEDGMENTS

A team of UCLA undergraduates helped us to evaluate a large pool of articles for possible inclusion in this volume. We greatly appreciate the candid and insightful comments of Talia Barag, Ron Gold, Grace Lee, and Katrina Minck. We are grateful to the authors of the papers collected here for their permission to reprint their work. Garrett Songhawke has provided invaluable assistance in the preparation of this volume. Heidi Freund, Senior Editor at Prentice Hall, has encouraged this project from the outset, and we value her support and advice.

❖ About the Editors ❖

Letitia Anne Peplau is Professor of Psychology at the University of California, Los Angeles. Anne received her B.A. in Psychology from Brown University and her Ph.D. in Social Psychology from Harvard University. Since 1973, she has taught at UCLA, where she has served as chair of the Social Psychology program and acting Co-Director of the Center for the Study of Women. Anne is currently president of the International Society for the Study of Personal Relationships. Her other books include *Loneliness: A Sourcebook of Current Theory, Research and Therapy* (edited with Daniel Perlman), *Close Relationships* (with Harold H. Kelley, et al.), and an introductory text, *Psychology* (with Zick Rubin and Peter Salovey). She has published numerous articles and book chapters on such topics as loneliness and social support, friendship, heterosexual dating, homosexual relationships, and social power.

Shelley E. Taylor is Professor of Psychology at the University of California, Los Angeles. Shelley received her B.A. in Psychology from Connecticut College and her Ph.D. in Social Psychology from Yale University. She taught at Harvard University until 1979, when she joined the faculty at UCLA. She has won a number of awards for her work, including the Donald Campbell Award for Distinguished Scientific Contribution to Social Psychology and the Senior Outstanding Scientific Contribution Award in Health Psychology from the American Psychological Association. She is currently a consulting editor for the *Journal of Personality and Social Psychology* and has served on the editorial boards of many other journals. Her other books include *Social Cognition* (with Susan T. Fiske), *Health Psychology*, and *Positive Illusions*. She has published numerous articles and book chapters in social cognition and health psychology.

❖ To the Reader ❖

This collection of readings invites you to explore the many fascinating ways in which culture affects our daily lives and personal experiences. Consider the pace of life. In some cultures, punctuality and the efficient use of time are valued. In other cultures, people have more casual attitudes about time and a more leisurely approach to life. Robert Levine (1988) asked college students in the United States and Brazil when they would consider a friend late for a lunch appointment. Americans said a friend would be late after 19 minutes, but Brazilians gave the friend nearly twice as long, not considering a friend late until 34 minutes after the time of their appointment. Cultural differences can create problems when we interact with people from different cultural backgrounds. American Peace Corps volunteers reported having more trouble getting used to the relatively slow pace of life and lack of punctuality in other countries than they did in adjusting to unfamiliar foods or different standards of living (Spradley & Phillips, 1972). The pace of life is only one facet of culture, but it reveals one of the many ways in which cultural patterns affect our daily life.

The articles in this volume present new research that uses sociocultural perspectives to understand basic topics in social psychology. Some articles use a cross-cultural approach that compares the experiences of people in the United States and other countries such as Brazil, India, or Japan. Other articles focus on ethnic and racial groups within the United States. We believe that these selections offer an excellent introduction to new research on culture and also provide an exciting glimpse of social psychology researchers in action.

WHAT IS A SOCIOCULTURAL PERSPECTIVE?

Social psychologists study how the thoughts, feelings, and behaviors of individuals are influenced by other people. This focus leads social psychologists to study how people form impressions of each other and interpret other people's behavior, and how people interact with others in dyads and groups. Social psychologists also study specific types of behavior such as altruism, prejudice, conformity, competition, and love. Traditionally, social psychologists have tended to emphasize the immediate social context of behavior and have not examined the larger culture.

A sociocultural perspective encourages us to expand our analysis by examining how membership in a specific cultural group influences social life. In a large and complex society such as the United States, many cultural worlds coexist. The experiences of a White teenager living in an upper-class suburb of Chicago differ markedly from those of an African-American teenager living in rural Georgia or from a teenager who recently immigrated to Los Angeles from Mexico. A sociocultural perspective draws our attention to the importance of culture, and then seeks to understand ways in which specific features of culture affect people's thoughts, feelings, and behavior.

Culture refers to the shared beliefs, values, traditions, and behavior patterns of a particular group. These groups can be nations, ethnic groups, religious communities, or even teenage gangs or college fraternities. Culture is taught by one generation to the next through a process of *socialization*. New fraternity members, for example, are expected to learn the traditions, songs, and secrets of their group from senior members of the fraternity. An important aspect of a culture is its *social norms*—rules and expectations about how group members should behave. Social rules govern a surprisingly broad range of behaviors, including how close we stand when talking to a teacher, how much we reveal about our inner thoughts to our parents, and when we feel obligated to help a stranger in distress.

One goal of cultural research is to identify important ways in which cultures differ. For example, a useful distinction contrasts cultures that emphasize individualism and those that emphasize collectivism (Triandis, 1994). The cultural norms and values of American and European societies emphasize the importance of individualism and personal independence. In an individualistic culture, a person's behavior is guided largely by the individual's goals, rather than the goals of collectives such as the family, work group, or tribe. Further, a person's sense of self is based largely on his or her personal attributes and accomplishments, rather than membership in social groups. In contrast, collectivist cultures emphasize loyalty to the family, adherence to group norms, and the preservation of harmony in social relations with members of one's own group. The cultural norms and values of many African, Asian, and Latin American societies emphasize collectivism. Several papers in this book (Chapters 8, 9, 12, and 13) use this individualist–collectivist distinction to examine the self-concept, social interaction with friends, and the nature of romantic love.

GOALS IN READING THIS BOOK

Before you begin to read this book, it is a good idea to think about what you want to learn from these readings. Here are some things to look for in this collection of research reports.

1. *Specific research findings.* Obviously, a main goal in reading research reports is to learn about important results from social-psychological research. The articles in this book provide a sampling of findings about human behavior on such diverse topics as social identity, moral reasoning, violence, and school achievement.

2. *Sociocultural perspectives.* These articles were selected to provide excellent examples of how cultures vary and how cultural factors affect our thoughts, feelings, and behavior. As you read, try to develop your own ideas about a sociocultural approach and why it is important.

3. *How social psychologists learn about human behavior.* The research methods used by social psychologists are diverse, and the selections in this book illustrate a wide range of approaches. These include laboratory experiments (for example, Chapters 5 and 9) and the use of correlational designs to investigate naturally occurring relationships among variables (for example, Chapters 12 and 15). The many methods of data collection used in these articles include questionnaires, interviews, telephone surveys, and daily interaction diaries. As you read each article, think about the type of research design and methods of data collection that are used.

HOW TO READ A RESEARCH ARTICLE IN PSYCHOLOGY

Some of the articles in this book are literature reviews that provide an overview of research findings on specific topics. Most articles, however, are reports of empirical research conducted by the authors and written for professional colleagues. Reading a journal article in psychology is somewhat different from other reading that you do, and so we want to offer some advice for those of you who are reading research reports in social psychology for the first time. In addition, we have written our own brief introduction to each article in this volume that highlights the importance of the selection. We have also provided several questions at the end of each article about major points raised by the authors.

Most journal articles in psychology are organized in a standard format based on the *Publication Manual of the American Psychological Association* (1994). A typical article has five main sections: abstract, introduction, method, results, and discussion.

Abstract

The abstract provides a quick overview of the research question, the methods used, the main findings, and the conclusions to be drawn from the study. The abstract is probably the single most important paragraph in the article, and deserves special attention. If you read the abstract carefully (and perhaps more than once), it will be easier to follow the rest of the article.

Introduction

The introduction sets the stage for the study by describing the central issue of interest and briefly reviewing previous research on the topic. The introduction also presents the rationale for the research, that is, the reasons for undertaking this particular study. The introduction specifies the goals of the research and the research strategy to be used. In some articles, the research problem will be stated in the form of specific hypotheses. After reading the introduction, you should be able to answer these questions: Why is this study important? What questions will this study answer? How does this study build on previous research?

Method

The method section describes in detail how the study was conducted. This section usually begins with a description of the people who participated in the research. Next, the materials used in the study, such as questionnaires or standardized laboratory tasks, are described. The method section also includes a step-by-step description of the specific procedures used in the research. In reading the method section, try to imagine what it was like to be a participant in the study. After reading the method section, you should be able to describe from start to finish what the researcher did and how he or she did it.

Results

The results section describes the data that were collected and the ways in which the data were analyzed. Statistical analyses are presented here. Because space in professional journals is limited, authors must juggle the need to be clear and detailed against the need to be concise. Tables are often used to summarize information efficiently, and you should be sure to look at them carefully. After reading the results section, you should be able to answer these questions: What were the main findings? Did the results support the original hypotheses? Were there any important but unexpected results?

Discussion

The discussion section evaluates and interprets the results. This is where the researcher can consider the implications of the study and compare these findings to results from previous research. Authors may also comment on limitations or special features of their research that may have affected the results, or they may propose directions for future studies. After reading the discussion section, you should be able to answer these questions: What have we learned from this research? How have these findings helped to understand the original research problem identified in the introduction?

There is no single "right" way to read a journal article. As you read the articles in this book, you will need to develop an approach that works well for you. Some people find it easiest to get a clear overview of a study before tackling the details of methods and statistics. So they carefully read the introduction and conclusion sections first, and then go back to read the methods and results to fill in the details. Others prefer to read an article from front to back in sequence. You may want to try these or other approaches to see which you personally prefer. As you read an article, try to summarize in your own words the research problem or hypotheses, the specific findings for each hypothesis, and the overall conclusions to be drawn. Don't be surprised if you need to read some articles more than once in order to understand them fully.

A FEW WORDS ABOUT STATISTICS

For many people, the most intimidating aspect of reading professional articles in psychology is confronting the statistical analyses of data in the results section. Such terms as "analysis of variance" or "correlation coefficient" may seem mysterious and perplexing. For readers with training in research design and statistics, the articles in this collection provide an opportunity to see how particular techniques are actually put to use in research. But how should students with little or no background in statistics handle this issue?

Readers cannot be expected to understand the specifics of sophisticated data analyses that go beyond their level of training. And this should not be necessary. In an essay on how to write a good journal article, Daryl Bem offers this advice to psychologists:

> No matter how technical or abstruse your article is in its particulars, intelligent nonpsychologists with no expertise in statistics or experimental design should be able to comprehend the broad outlines of what you did and why. They should understand in general terms what was learned. (1987, p. 174)

In other words, even articles with the fanciest statistics should also state the key findings in plain English. Our suggestion is to read the results section carefully. Try to understand what each particular analysis is designed to accomplish and how specific results are interpreted. Some of the basic abbreviations and statistical terms you will encounter are explained in a glossary on page xiii. But do not worry that you need to be a statistician to understand the results reported in professional articles. The goal for readers lacking background in statistics is to be a thoughtful consumer of psychological research.

One reason you can safely overlook the finer points of complex data analysis in reading journal articles is that each article was subjected to a careful professional review before publication. The leading psychology journals require that articles submitted for publication be evaluated by two or three psychologists with expertise in the subject matter. Reviewers are asked to judge both the overall significance of the study and the adequacy of its methodology. Further, the competition to have an article accepted for publication is often fierce. So there is some assurance that articles published in major journals meet the methodological standards of the day.

We hope that these suggestions will help you get started reading the articles in this book. We believe that the research reported here represents some of the most interesting and important new work in social psychology. As you read psychologists' descriptions of their own work, you will also gain a better appreciation of the excitement and the challenges of our quest to understand social behavior in cultural contexts.

REFERENCES

American Psychological Association. (1994). *Publication manual of the American Psychological Association* (4th ed.). Washington, DC: American Psychological Association.

Bem, D. J. (1987). Writing the empirical journal article. In M. P. Zanna & J. M. Darley (Eds.), *The compleat academic: A practical guide for the beginning social scientist* (pp. 171–201). New York: Random House.

Levine, R. V. (1988). The pace of life across cultures. In J. E. McGrath (Ed.), *The social psychology of time: New perspectives* (pp. 39–60). Newbury Park, CA: Sage.

Spradley, J. P., & Phillips, M. (1972). Culture and stress: A quantitative analysis. *American Anthropologist, 74,* 518–529.

Triandis, H. C. (1994). *Individualism and collectivism.* Boulder, CO: Westview Press.

COMMON STATISTICAL TERMS AND ABBREVIATIONS

analysis of variance—A statistical procedure used to compare the mean scores of two or more groups to determine if their scores are significantly different. Analysis of variance (abbreviated as ANOVA) uses an F-test to assess the degree of difference between the mean scores of two or more groups.

ANOVA—Abbreviation for analysis of variance.

Chi square—A statistical way to assess the degree of association between two categorical variables. A categorical variable has named categories, not numerical values; ethnicity is a categorical variable with such categories as Latino or Japanese American. Chi square is abbreviated as χ^2.

correlation—A statistical way to assess the degree of association between two variables with numerical values, such as age and income. A correlation (abbreviated as r) can range between 0 (no relationship between the variables) and 1 (perfect relationship). A negative correlation (such as $r = -.72$) indicates that high scores on one variable are associated with low scores on the other. A positive correlation (such as $r = .72$) indicates that high scores on one measure are associated with high scores on the other.

F-test—A statistical procedure used to assess the degree of difference between the mean scores of two or more groups. (*See also* Analysis of variance)

M—Abbreviation for the mean or average score.

N or n—Abbreviation for the number of subjects in a study or subgroup.

ns—Abbreviation for "not statistically significant."

p—Abbreviation for probability or significance level. This refers to the likelihood that a pattern of results could have occurred by chance; $p = .01$ means that there is only a 1% probability that the observed result occurred by chance.

r—Abbreviation for correlation. (*See also* Correlation)

reliability—The degree to which test scores are reproducible and consistent over time.

S, Ss—Abbreviations for "subject" and "subjects."

SD—Abbreviation for "standard deviation." This refers to how much scores vary around the mean score; a large SD means that there is much variation in scores.

statistical significance—A result, such as a difference in scores between two groups, is said to be statistically significant if it is unlikely to have occurred by chance. For example, if a group difference is significant at the ".05 level," the probability is only 5% that a difference of this size occurred by chance.

t-test—This is a statistical procedure used to assess the degree of difference in mean scores between two groups.

validity—Refers to the degree to which a test or instrument measures what it is intended to measure.

A Guide to Sociocultural Resources in Social Psychology

Rosemary C. Veniegas and Letitia Anne Peplau

As the papers in this book amply demonstrate, there is a growing scientific literature incorporating cultural and ethnic perspectives into research in social psychology. This increased interest in the sociocultural context of social behavior has contributed to the publication of many articles and books relevant to social psychology. This guide provides an overview of some of the resources available to instructors and students interested in learning more about these topics. This guide begins with a listing of professional books on sociocultural issues and journals that publish relevant research. We also include brief descriptions of fiction, autobiographies, and films that vividly illustrate the impact of culture on identity, personal relationships, intergroup relations, and other central topics in social psychology. These resource listings are suggestive rather than exhaustive.

BOOKS

The following selection of books suggests the range of sociocultural topics currently being investigated.

Altman, I. (1984). *Culture and environment.* New York: Cambridge University Press.

Berry, J. W., Poortinga, Y. H., Segall, M. H., & Dasen, P. R. (Eds.). (1992). *Cross-cultural psychology: Research and applications.* London: Methuen.

Bond, M. H. (Ed.). (1988). *The cross-cultural challenge to social psychology.* Newbury Park, CA: Sage.

Brislin, R. W. (Ed.). (1990). *Applied cross-cultural psychology.* Newbury Park, CA: Sage.

Bronstein, P. A., & Quina, K. (Eds.). (1988). *Teaching a psychology of people: Resources for gender and sociocultural awareness.* Washington, DC: American Psychological Association.

Burlew, K. H., Banks, W. C., McAdoo, H. P., & Azibo, D. A. (Eds.). (1992). *African-American psychology.* Thousands Oaks, CA: Sage.

Goodchilds, J. D. (Ed.). (1991). *Psychological perspectives on human diversity in America.* Washington, DC: American Psychological Association.

Jones, J. M. (in press). *Cultural psychology of African Americans.* Boulder, CO: Westview Press.

Kim, U., Triandis, H. C., Kagitcibasi, C., Choi, S., & Yoon, G. (Eds.). (1994). *Individualism and collectivism: Theory, method and applications.* Thousand Oaks, CA: Sage.

Kitayama, S., & Markus, H. R. (Eds.). (1994). *Emotion and culture: Empirical studies of mutual influence.* Washington, DC: American Psychological Association.

Lonner, W. J., & Malpass, R. (Eds.). (1994). *Psychology and culture.* Boston: Allyn & Bacon.

Miller, J. (in press). *Culture and interpersonal morality.* Boulder, CO: Westview Press.

Moghaddam, F. M., Taylor, D. M., & Wright, S. C. (1993). *Social psychology in cross-cultural perspective.* New York: Freeman.

Nisbett, R. E., & Cohen, D. (in press). *Culture of honor. The psycho-economic roots of violence.* Boulder, CO: Westview Press.

Padilla, A. M. (Ed.). (1994). *Hispanic psychology: Critical issues in theory and research.* Thousand Oaks, CA: Sage.

Rosenblatt, P., Karis, T., & Powell, R. (1995). *Multicultural couples: Black and White voices.* Thousand Oaks, CA: Sage.

Segall, M. H., Dasen, P. R., Berry, J. W., & Poortinga, Y. H. (Eds.). (1990). *Human behavior in global perspective: An introduction to cross-cultural psychology.* New York: Pergamon Press.

Smith, P. B., & Bond, M. H. (1993). *Social psychology across cultures: Analysis and perspectives.* Boston: Allyn & Bacon.

Triandis, H. C. (1994). *Culture and social behavior.* New York: McGraw-Hill.

Triandis, H. C. (1994). *Individualism and collectivism.* Boulder, CO: Westview Press.

Trickett, E. J., Watts, R. J., & Birman, D. (Eds.). (1994). *Human diversity: Perspectives on people in context.* San Francisco: Jossey-Bass.

JOURNALS

Articles incorporating a sociocultural perspective now appear in "mainstream" social psychology journals, as well as in journals specializing in cultural and ethnic studies. The following journals are useful resources. The first year of publication for each journal is indicated in parentheses.

Basic and Applied Social Psychology. (1980–). Mahwah, NJ: Erlbaum.

Culture and Psychology. (1995–). Thousand Oaks, CA: Sage Periodicals Press.

European Journal of Social Psychology. (1971–). The Hague, Netherlands: Mouton.

Hispanic Journal of Behavioral Sciences. (1979–). Thousand Oaks, CA: Sage Periodicals Press.

Journal of Applied Social Psychology. (1971–). Silver Spring, MD: Winston.

Journal of Black Psychology. (1974–). Thousand Oaks, CA: Sage Periodicals Press.

Journal of Cross-Cultural Psychology. (1970–). Thousand Oaks, CA: Sage Periodicals Press.

Journal of Cross-Cultural Research. (1993–). Thousand Oaks, CA: Sage Periodicals Press.

Journal of Gender, Culture and Health. (Forthcoming). New York: Plenum.

Journal of Personality and Social Psychology. (1965–). Washington, DC: American Psychological Association.

Personality and Social Psychology Bulletin. (1974–). Thousand Oaks, CA: Sage Periodicals Press.

Psychology of Women Quarterly. (1976–). New York: Cambridge University Press.

Sex Roles. (1975–). New York: Plenum.

FICTION AND AUTOBIOGRAPHY

Our understanding of the experiences of people from diverse cultures and ethnic backgrounds can be enriched by reading stories and first-person accounts. Such descriptions inform abstract discussions of cultural topics with personal illustrations and individual stories. It is not possible for many of us to know what it means to grow up rich, poor, Asian, Chicana/o, or gay. These stories complement scholarly analyses of major topics in social psychology. Titles available in paperback are noted.

Alvarez, J. (1992). *How the Garcia girls lost their accents.* New York: Plume. The story of four sisters and the two cultures they attempt to reconcile. In telling the tale of the women of the Garcia de la Torre family, the author tackles issues of acculturation, cultural conflict, gender roles, and the self-concept. Available in paperback.

Anaya, R. (1974). *Bless me Ultima.* New York: Warner. Ultima, a curandera, comes to live with Antonio and his family in New Mexico. A curandera is a woman who heals with herbs and magic. Through his friendship with Ultima, Antonio explores his family ties and the spiritualism of his Chicano roots. This is a story about close relationships, cultural values, and the search for identity. Available in paperback.

Baranay, I. (1994). *Rascal rain: A year in Papua New Guinea.* Sydney, Australia: Angus & Robertson. An Australian woman volunteers to go to the Enga province of New Guinea to help improve the lives of women there. However, she soon finds that she is neither welcome nor wanted by the locals, women or men. This story addresses the questions of "Should we decide what developing countries need and how women from different cultures define 'oppression'?" The novel is useful for discussions of prosocial behavior, gender, and the environment. Available in paperback.

Barnes, J. (1995). *Letters from London*. New York: Vintage Books. A British journalist takes a humorous insider's look at British culture. He also pokes fun at the tendency toward "American-centrism" in the United States, illustrated by describing other nations in terms of their size compared to American states (e.g., Great Britain is "approximately the size of Oregon"). The book is relevant to such topics as ethnocentrism, cross-cultural contact, and communication. Available in paperback.

Boyd, H., & Allen, R. L. (Eds.). (1995). *Brotherman: The odyssey of Black men in America*. New York: Ballantine. This anthology includes a diverse selection of writings by men such as Frederick Douglass, the Rev. Martin Luther King, Jr., and Duke Ellington. Black men write about fatherhood, discrimination, the Vietnam War, close relationships, and the challenges of maintaining positive identities in the face of racism. Available in paperback.

Brown, R. M. (1973). *Rubyfruit jungle*. This classic novel by Rita Mae Brown is the amazing story of Molly Dock, the child of an unwed mother who is adopted by a poor Southern couple. All of her life, Molly has felt "different." As a girl she beats up the boys. In college she is expelled for her lesbian relationship with another student. She dreams of being a great filmmaker. Molly's story is told with warmth and humor. This is a useful book for discussing nonconformity, sexual orientation, and gender. Available in paperback.

Corcoran, J. (1995). *Bitter harvest: The birth of paramilitary terrorism in the heartland*. New York: Penguin. Gordon Kahl is a farmer, religious man, patriot, and leader of an extremist right-wing paramilitary group. His story shows how American cultural values can lead to violence and hate. The author also discusses social and individual explanations for the 1994 bombing of the Federal Building in Oklahoma City. The book addresses many issues, including violence, prejudice, and the links between attitudes and behavior.

Eisenberg, R. (1995). *Boychiks in the hood*. San Francisco: HarperSanFrancisco. A Jewish man from Omaha, Nebraska, searches for his roots in Orthodox Hasidic culture. The contrast between the traditional practices of the Hasidim (strict observance of religious law, distinctive clothing and dialect, and rejection of contemporary culture) and modern forms of religious practice in Jewish communities provides the backdrop for this man's exploration of his own culture. This book can be used to discuss reference groups, socialization, and social norms.

Growing up Asian-American, Growing up Black, Growing up Chicana/o, Growing up Native American. (1992–93). New York: Avon. Each book in this series features writing and memoirs from well-known Asian, Black, Chicana/o, or Native American writers. Available in paperback.

Hirschfelder, A. (Ed.). (1995). *Native heritage: Personal accounts by American Indians 1790 to the present*. New York: Macmillan. This is a superb selection of writings from nearly 100 Native American tribes, Apache to Yupik Eskimo. The authors discuss cultural values about conserving the environment, family and close relationships, and spirituality.

Holland, D. C., & Eisenhart, M. A. (1990). *Educated in romance: Women, achievement and college culture*. Chicago: University of Chicago Press. This book follows the lives of young Black and White women attending universities in the southern United States. The authors show how the search for romance and a husband gradually erodes the careeer goals of these young women. This book provides an insightful and pointed look at achievement, traditional gender roles, and women in education.

Leavitt, D. (1986). *The lost language of the cranes*. Twenty-five-year-old Philip has his first romance with another man and reveals his sexual orientation to his parents. A novel about sexual awakening and how a family deals with change. Available in paperback. (The film version of this novel is available at video sales/rental outlets).

Lee, J. F. J. (Ed.). (1991). *Asian Americans: Oral histories of first to fourth generation Americans from China, the Philippines, Japan, India, the Pacific Islands, Vietnam and Cambodia*. New York: New Press. This compilation includes an excellent section on interracial dating and marriage. Writers also discuss the pressure to conform to mainstream American culture, family and sex roles across generations, and the importance of familial duty in many Asian cultures. Available in paperback.

Miner, H. (1956). Body ritual among the Nacirema. *American Anthropologist, 58*, 503–507. This classic article examines the body cleansing and healing practices of the Nacirema. It is a humorous and surprising look at the "normal" and "superstitious" facets of body-related behaviors in one culture, which turns out to be our own (*Nacirema* is *American* spelled backwards). This provocative article promotes discussions of socialization, social norms, and person perception.

Morales, A. (1992). *The brick people*. Houston, TX: Arte Public Press. The Simons run a brick factory that employs the Revueltas. Like many people who work in factories, the Revueltas work long, back-breaking hours in hope of a better life. This is the story of the people who made the bricks used to build some of the most beautiful buildings in California. It can be used to discuss discrimination, power, and stress. Available in paperback.

Reid, J. (1976). *The best little boy in the world*. New York: Ballantine Books. This novel tells the story of a young man who was the first in his class, the eternally respectful son, and the best young executive. He was also the most closeted person, never even daring to read anything about being gay. This is the sensitive story of a man who realizes that being the "best little boy" also means being true to oneself. This novel promotes discussion of conformity, masculinity, and sexual orientation. Available in paperback.

Santiago, E. (1995). *When I was Puerto Rican*. New York: Vintage Books. In this insightful and poignant autobiography about coming of age, Santiago's transformation from island child to Harvard scholar illuminates the experience of one immigrant family. Throughout the book she addresses the challenge of having multiple identities—Puerto Rican, American, rural girl, urban adult. Available in paperback.

Schein, V. E. (1995). *Working from the margins: Voices of mothers in poverty*. Ithaca, NY: ILR Press. An industrial psychologist interviewed 30 single mothers living in poverty. Unlike many studies of women in poverty that focus on metropolitan settings, this book examines the lives of women in small towns and rural areas. Topics covered include social support, families, and social class.

Sledge, M. (1995). *Mother and son*. New York: Simon & Schuster. In Texas in the 1970s, a divorced mother finds it difficult to let go of the American dream of a happy, nuclear family. Slowly, both the mother and her son give up their search for the "right man" to head their family, and define new models for their own happiness. A touching story about changing norms for women, men, and close relationships.

Terkel, S. (1995). *Coming of age: The story of our century by those who've lived it*. New York: New Press. Diverse Americans—a farmer in Nebraska, a bank president in New York, a labor unionist, and a gay activist—tell their life stories and reflect on what it means to be an American. Topics include the meaning of work, changing roles for women and men, and protecting the environment.

Wakatsuki-Houston, J., & Houston, J. D. (1973). *Farewell to Manzanar*. New York: Bantam. This is perhaps the best-known novel about the internment of Japanese Americans during World War II. It is the story of a young woman and her family forced to leave their home to live in an isolated camp because the U.S. government believed Japanese-American citizens were a risk to national security. Useful for generating discussion on prejudice, discrimination, and political psychology. Available in paperback. (The film version of this novel is available at video sales/rental outlets.)

Williams, G. H. (1995). *Life on the color line: The true story of a White boy who discovered he was Black*. New York: Penguin. This is the story of the author's journey to understand his Black heritage. This is the real experience of someone who discovers that he is not the person he believed himself to be. It can be used to discuss topics such as the self, personal identity, and the meaning of race.

FILMS/AUDIOVISUAL MATERIAL

This selection includes both wide-release films and instructional media. Several recent popular movies deal with sociocultural topics, including class, social norms, and cultural conflict (e.g., *Jungle Fever*, *Mi Familia*, *The Wedding Banquet*). Many instructional media companies have expanded their sociocultural offerings, and their catalogs are useful resources. We also recommend an excellent video guide entitled *Mediating History: The Media Alternatives Project Guide to Independent Video By and About African American, Asian American, Latino and Native American People* (New York University Press, 1993). This guide describes many videos that are available for rental from independent film distributors. Another useful reference that reviews more than 70 films is *Crossing Cultures Through Film* by Ellen Summerfield (Intercultural Press, 1993).

Aggression. (1995). 30 minutes. Videotape. A look at the physical and social environments that predict violent behavior. It suggests ways for controlling anger and aggression. Available from Insight Media, 2162 Broadway, New York, NY 10024. (212) 721-6316.

Anderson, J. (Producer), & Choy, C. (Director). (1988). *Who killed Vincent Chin?* 82 minutes. Videotape. Vincent Chin, a Chinese American, was murdered by Ron Ebens, an auto worker angry about the impact of Japanese car imports on American car sales. The story of Vincent Chin focuses on the scapegoating of minority groups during economic crises and is relevant to discussions of attitudes, prejudice, and aggression. Available from Filmakers Library, 124 East 40th St., New York, NY 10016. (212) 808-4980.

Arau, A. (Producer/Director). (1992). *Like water for chocolate*. 105 minutes. Videotape. This film, based on Laura Esquivel's best-selling novel, is a story of familial duty and love denied in turn-of-the-century Mexico. Tita is told she cannot marry the man she loves because she must devote the rest of her life to caring for her aging mother. Instead, the man she loves marries her younger sister, and Tita must find other ways to express her love. This is an entertaining film useful for discussing cultural norms regarding close relationships and love. Available at local video sales/rental outlets.

Black and White America. (1995). 26 minutes. Videotape. Five students—two Black, two White, one of mixed ethnicity—talk about trying to maintain positive ethnic identities in the face of racism. It is useful for discussing personal and social identity, the self, and prejudice. Available from Films for the Humanities and Sciences, P.O. Box 2053, Princeton, NJ 08543-2053. (800) 257-5126.

Domino: Interracial people and the search for identity. (1995). 44 minutes. Videotape. The stories of six interracial (mixed ethnicity) people searching for their identity. They talk about the influence of parents, family politics, sex, race, and class in shaping identity. Available from Films for the Humanities and Sciences, P.O. Box 2053, Princeton, NJ 08543-2053. (800) 257-5126.

Emotion. (1995). 30 minutes. Videotape. Psychologist Paul Ekman examines the expression of emotion across cultures, research on facial expressions, and the relationship between emotion and performance. Available from Insight Media, 2162 Broadway, New York, NY 10024. (212) 721-6316.

Faces of the enemy. (1995). 58 minutes. Videotape. This documentary examines the dehumanization of members of out-groups. Footage includes political cartoons, examples of propaganda, and media images used in mass persuasion. Some materials depict graphic violence. It is useful for discussions of dehumanization, deindividuation, attitudes, and political psychology. Available from Insight Media, 2162 Broadway, New York, NY 10024. (212) 721-6316.

Gee, D. (Producer/Director). (1987). *Slaying the dragon*. 60 minutes. Videotape. Using film footage from the 1940s to the late 1980s, the video examines the changing American media stereotypes of Asians as Evil Emperors, Peaceful Farmers, Dragon Ladies, and Geisha Girls. Several Asian-

American women news anchors also discuss their experiences. It is relevant to discussions of gender, stereotypes, the media, and interracial relationships. Available from Crosscurrent Media, 346 9th St., San Francisco, CA 94103. (415) 552-9550.

Heart of the nation. (1995). 58 minutes. Videotape. This video explores the cultures and values of Japan, Germany, and the United States. The individualism and freedom valued in America are contrasted with the emphasis on conformity and nationalism in Japan. Germany is described as the "middle ground," valuing both individualism and social harmony. Styles of education in these countries are used to illustrate these contrasts. Available from Films for the Humanities and Sciences, P.O. Box 2053, Princeton, NJ 08543-2053. (800) 257-5126.

Interracial marriage. (1995). 52 minutes. Videotape. This video examines why interracial relationships form, how these marriages are affected by ethnicity, religion, and skin color, and how friends and family react to interracial couples. It can be used to discuss love, attraction, and commitment. Available from Films for the Humanities and Sciences, P.O. Box 2053, Princeton, NJ 08543-2053. (800) 257-5126.

Koch, H. W., & Bell, D. (Producers), & Pearce, R. (Director). (1991). *The long walk home.* 98 minutes. Videotape. Whoopi Goldberg stars in this story about a Black housekeeper who works for a White homemaker at the very beginning of the civil rights era in the South. The housekeeper honors the bus boycott sparked by Rosa Parks and walks nine miles to and from work. Gradually, she and her employer realize that they can help one another try to erase the racial lines drawn by their families and society. This is an engaging film about interracial friendship, prejudice reduction, and social change. Available at local video sales/rental outlets.

Lee, S. (Producer/Director). (1989). *Do the Right Thing.* 120 minutes. Videotape. An Italian-American shop owner refuses to put pictures of African Americans on the wall of his establishment despite the fact that many of his customers are Black. It is a very hot day and violence erupts in the neighborhood. This popular movie lends itself to discussions on crowding, noise pollution, intergroup relations, and violence. Available at local video sales/rental outlets.

Matsumoto, D. (Director). *A world of difference.* 60 minutes each tape. Videotapes. This two-tape set depicts several interactions between students of different ethnic backgrounds. These examples show how cultural norms for interpersonal behavior can be misinterpreted and lead to conflict. These videos are designed for audiences with little knowledge about diversity issues. We recommend the first tape of this set only, as the second tape repeats much of the same material. Useful for discussing attributions, nonverbal communication, and social perception. Available from Brooks/Cole, Pacific Grove, CA. (408) 373-0728.

Musca, T. (Producer), & Menendez, R. (Director). (1988). *Stand and deliver.* 103 minutes. Videotape. Edward James Olmos portrays Jaime Escalante, the East Los Angeles high school teacher who turned his students into math whizzes. When the barrio kids from Garfield High pass the national Advanced Placement Calculus Exam, the Educational Testing Service attributes their performance to cheating. Escalante's students prove that others' stereotypes cannot keep them from success. Topics covered include achievement, attributions, and stereotyping. Available at local video sales/rental outlets.

Okazaki, S. (Producer/Director). (1991). *Troubled paradise.* 58 minutes. Videotape. Interviews with four Native Hawaiians examine culture and conflict in "paradise." One "hot" topic is the debate over land use, conservation, and ownership. Hawaiian cultural beliefs hold that the land is something held in common among its people but American culture endorses private ownership. The video can stimulate discussions of conservation, leadership, and social change. Available from Crosscurrent Media, 346 9th St., San Francisco, CA 94103. (415) 552-9550.

Redford, R. (Producer/Director), & Esparza, M. (Producer). (1988). *Milagro beanfield war.* 118 minutes. Videotape. A poor Chicano farmer in New Mexico "borrows" some water from a nearby commercial development to irrigate his small field. When the wealthy developers discover this, they brutally trample his sparse plantings. The farmer's friends join him in rebelling against the developers, fighting not only for water but to preserve a way of life. It is useful for discussing group cooperation, conflict, and social dilemmas. Available at local video sales/rental outlets.

Stone, O. (Producer), & Wang, W. (Director). (1994). *The Joy Luck club.* 139 minutes. Videotape. Based on Amy Tan's best-selling book, this is a delightful movie about the ties uniting friends and family. Four aging mothers share their happiness and disappointments regarding their daughters' lives. Their grown daughters also meet to continue the tradition of sharing memories begun by their mothers. This film illustrates cultural norms for achievement, close relationships, and social support. Available at local video sales/rental outlets.

Street gangs of Los Angeles. (1995). 44 minutes. Videotape. The thrills and danger of gang life for young Blacks and Latinos are shown as well as their parents' efforts to keep them out of gangs. Topics covered include violence and group membership. Available from Films for the Humanities and Sciences, P. O. Box 2053, Princeton, NJ 08543-2053. (800) 257-5126.

Sun, S. (Producer), & Wang, P. (Director). *A great wall.* 103 minutes. Videotape. A Chinese-American family visits relatives in mainland China. The teenage son sees himself as an all-American guy and ridicules his family's "Chinese ways." This movie presents the conflict faced by many American-born Chinese: "Am I Chinese or American?" This movie can be used to discuss ethnic identity, cultural norms, and the self. Available at local video sales/rental outlets.

Valuing diversity: Multicultural communication. (1995). 49 minutes. Videotape. This video explores ways to overcome cross-cultural communication barriers such as different interpretations of body language and speaking to people with a nonstandard English accent. It also considers how stereotypes can lead to quick, inaccurate judgments that can affect communication. Available from Insight Media, 2162 Broadway, New York, NY 10024. (212) 721-6316.

PART I

INTRODUCTION

❖ CHAPTER 1 ❖

THE STUDY OF CULTURE, ETHNICITY, AND RACE IN AMERICAN PSYCHOLOGY

Hector Betancourt and Steven Regeser López

Psychologists Betancourt and López consider how psychologists should study culture and behavior. The authors define culture as learned systems of meanings that are shared by members of the cultural group. Culture includes such elements as social norms, roles, beliefs, and values. For psychologists, the goal of a cultural analysis should be to identify how a specific aspect of culture, such as attitudes about competition or the value placed on duty to family, affects specific aspects of human behavior or experience. In this view, it is not sufficient to show that people from two cultures differ in their behavior; rather, researchers need to uncover the specific cultural variables that create the difference. This can be done in two ways. In one approach, researchers first identify an important dimension along which cultures vary, such as beliefs about individualism versus collectivism. Then researchers demonstrate how differences on this dimension affect behavior. Several articles in this book illustrate the value of this approach (see, for example, chapters 8, 9, 12, and 13). In a second approach, researchers begin with a theory developed in a single culture, then test the applicability of the theory to other cultures and modify the theory as needed. The authors illustrate this approach using Weiner's theory of causal attribution. If Americans believe a person succeeds because of something within the person's own control, such as extreme effort, they tend to praise the accomplishment and reward the person. However, beliefs about control do not lead to the same consequences in Chile and Brazil, which raises questions about the universal effects of perceived control. Researchers have proposed that a new cultural dimension, which they call a "control-subjugation value orientation," may modify the theoretical relationship between perceived control and reactions to success. Cultural differences in the psychology of control are discussed further in Chapter 4.

ABSTRACT: *The study of culture and related concepts, such as ethnicity and race, in American psychology are examined in this article. First, the conceptual confusion and ways in which culture, ethnicity, and race are used as explanatory factors for intergroup differences in psychological phenomena are discussed. Second, ways in which to study culture in mainstream psychology and to enhance hypothesis testing and theory in cross-cultural psychology are illustrated. Finally, the importance of examining sociocultural variables and considering theory in ethnic minority research is addressed. In general, it is proposed that by including theory, conceptualizing, and measuring cultural and related variables, mainstream, cross-cultural, and*

Source: Reprinted from *American Psychologist,* 48(6), (1993), 629–637. Copyright © 1993 by the American Psychological Association, Inc. Reprinted by permission.

ethnic research can advance the understanding of culture in psychology as well as the generality of principles and the cultural sensitivity of applications.

Culture and its significant role in human behavior have been recognized for many years, as far back as Hippocrates from the classical Greek era (see Dona, 1991) as well as near the beginning of psychology as a discipline (Wundt, 1921). More recently, a number of authors have questioned the cross-cultural generalizability of psychological theories (e.g., Amir & Sharon, 1987; Bond, 1988; Pepitone & Triandis, 1987), some arguing for the inclusion of culture in psychological theories (e.g., Harkness, 1980; Rokeach, 1979; Smith, 1979; Triandis, 1989). An abundant literature demonstrates cultural variations in many areas of psychology that can guide such theoretical efforts (see handbooks edited by Triandis et al., 1980, and by Munroe, Munroe, & Whiting, 1981; see also Berman, 1990). Most recently, the need to study culture in psychology was highlighted in an American Psychological Association (APA) report on education (McGovern, Furumoto, Halpern, Kimble, & McKeachie, 1991). Because of the changing demographics in the nation as well as in the student population, McGovern et al. indicated that an "important social and ethical responsibility of faculty members is to promote their students' understanding of gender, race, ethnicity, culture, and class issues in psychological theory, research, and practice" (p. 602).

Despite the historical and contemporary awareness concerning the importance of culture among a number of scholars, the study of culture and related variables occupies at best a secondary place in American (mainstream) psychology. It appears to be the domain of cross-cultural psychology and is often associated with the replication of findings in some remote or exotic part of the world. In the United States, it is often associated with the study of ethnic minorities, which is as segregated from mainstream psychology (see Graham, 1992) as is cross-cultural research. There seems to be a widespread assumption that the study of culture or ethnicity contributes little to the understanding of basic psychological processes or to the practice of psychology in the United States.

The general purpose of this article is to share some of our preoccupations and views concerning the status of the study of culture and related concepts, such as race and ethnicity, in psychology. Our main concern is that whereas mainstream investigators do not consider culture in their research and theories, cross-cultural researchers who study cultural differences frequently fail to identify the specific aspects of culture and related variables that are thought to influence behavior. Consequently, we learn that cultural group, race, or ethnicity may be related to a given psychological phenomenon, but we learn little about the specific elements of these group variables that contribute to the proposed relationship. The limited specificity of this research impedes our understanding of the behavior of a group or groups. In addition, it serves to limit the delineation of more universal processes that cut across cultural, ethnic, and racial groups. In this article, we promote the study of culture. This is not to say that culture is the single most important variable in psychology. It is one of many factors that contribute to the complexities of psychological processes, and it is obviously important to the understanding of culturally diverse populations both inside and outside of the United States. In addition, even though the higher uniformity of cultural elements makes it less obvious, cultural factors also play an important role in the behavior of mainstream individuals. Thus, our focus will be on culture, some of the problems that in our opinion preclude progress in our understanding of its role in psychology and some propositions on how to overcome them. To illustrate our points, we draw from research in the social and clinical domains; these reflect our areas of expertise.

As a general approach, we propose that both mainstream and cross-cultural investigators identify and measure directly what about the group variable (e.g., what cultural element) of interest to their research influences behavior. Then, hypothesized relationships between such variables and the psychological phenomenon of interest could be examined and such research could be incorporated within a theoretical framework. We believe that an adherence to this approach will serve to enhance our understanding of both group-specific and group-general (universal) processes as well as contribute to the integration of culture in theory development and the practice of psychology. Our focus is on the general approach rather than on specific methodological issues already treated elsewhere in the literature (see Brislin, Lonner, & Thorndike, 1973; Lonner & Berry, 1988; Triandis et al., 1980, Vol. 2).

Because culture is closely intertwined with concepts such as race, ethnicity, and social class, and because conceptual confusion has been an obstacle for progress in this area, it is important to first define culture and point out its relationship to these related concepts. Hence, we first focus on these definitions and conceptual problems. Then, we address some of the limitations of cross-cultural and mainstream psychology and suggest ways in which to infuse the study of culture in mainstream research and both experimentation and theory in cross-cultural research. Finally, we illustrate ways in which to study cultural variables and discuss the importance of infusing theory in ethnic minority research.

DEFINITIONS

Variations in psychological phenomena observed in the comparative study of groups identified in terms of nationality, race, ethnicity, or socioeconomic status (SES) are often attributed to cultural differences without defining what is meant by culture, and what about culture and to what extent is related to the differences. This is so common, even among cross-cultural psychologists, that it has led to the criticism that little research in cross-cultural psychology actually deals with culture (e.g., Rohner, 1984). Thus, an important problem is the lack of a clear definition and understanding of culture from a psychological perspective.

Culture

A number of psychologists interested in the study of culture agree that the confusion concerning its definition has been an obstacle for progress (e.g., Brislin, 1983; Jahoda, 1984; Rohner, 1984; Triandis et al., 1980). Although it would be desirable to have a definition that everyone agrees upon, as noted by Segall (1984), consensus is not absolutely necessary to advance knowledge. Even without consensus, progress is possible if, as we propose, cultural research specifies what is meant by culture in terms that are amenable to measurement.

After reviewing the elements found in the anthropological and cross-cultural psychology views of culture, Rohner (1984) proposed a conceptualization of culture in terms of "highly variable systems of meanings," which are "learned" and "shared by a people or an identifiable segment of a population." It represents "designs and ways of life" that are normally "transmitted from one generation to another." We consider this conception as equivalent to that proposed by Herkovits (1948), who conceives culture as the human-made part of the environment. Perhaps the most distinctive characteristic of Rohner's formulation is the explicit statement of aspects such as the learned, socially shared, and variable nature of culture.

Within the context of this general conception of culture, we consider Triandis et al.'s (1980) reformulation of Herkovits's (1948) definition as the most practical one for the purpose of our work. In addition to differentiating between the objective and subjective aspects of Herkovits's human-made part of the environment, Triandis's formulation is quite explicit about the psychologically relevant elements that constitute culture. According to Triandis, although physical culture refers to objects such as roads, buildings, and tools, subjective culture includes elements such as social norms, roles, beliefs, and values. These subjective cultural elements include a wide range of topics, such as familial roles, communication patterns, affective styles, and values regarding personal control, individualism, collectivism, spirituality, and religiosity.

When culture (or subjective culture) is defined in terms of psychologically relevant elements, such as roles and values, it becomes amenable to measurement. Moreover, the relationship of the cultural elements to psychological phenomena can be directly assessed. Hence, it is possible to deal with the complexity of the concept and at the same time pursue an understanding of the role of culture in psychology. By incorporating the conceptualization and measurement of specific cultural elements, the comparative study of national, ethnic, or cultural groups is more likely to contribute to the understanding of the role of culture than are the typical comparative studies (see Poortinga & Malpass, 1986).

Race

Scholars and pollsters often use the concept of culture interchangeably with race, ethnicity, or nationality. For example, in surveys or research instruments, individuals are often required to indicate their race by choosing one of a combination of categories including race, ethnicity, and national origin (such as Asian, American Indian, Black, Latino, and White). Latinos, for instance, can be White, Black, Asian, American Indian, or any combination thereof. We are particularly concerned about the loose way in which culture, race, and ethnicity are used to explain differences between groups. This not only limits our understanding of the specific factors that contribute to group differences, but it also leads to interpretations of findings that stimulate or reinforce racist conceptions of human behavior (see Zuckerman, 1990).

Jones (1991) recently argued that the concept of race is fraught with problems for psychology. For example, race is generally defined in terms of physical characteristics, such as skin color, facial features, and hair type, which are common to an inbred, geographically isolated population. However, the classification of people in groups designated as races has been criticized as arbitrary, suggesting that the search for differences between such groups is at best dubious (Zuckerman, 1990). Specifically, there are more within-group differences than between-group differences in the characteristics used to define the three so-called races (Caucasoid, Negroid, and Mongoloid). Also, studies of genetic systems (e.g., blood groups, serum proteins, and enzymes) have found that differences between individuals within the same tribe or nation account for more variance (84%) than do racial groupings (10%; Latter, 1980; Zuckerman, 1990). This indicates that racial groups are more alike than they are different, even in physical and genetic characteristics. Still, too often in the history of psychology, race has been used to explain variations in psychological phenomena between the so-called racial groups, without examining the cultural and social variables likely to be associated with such variations (e.g., Allport, 1924; Barrett & Eysenck, 1984; Jensen, 1985). We agree with Zuckerman (1990) that the study of racial differences in psychological phenomena is of little scientific use without a clear understanding of the variables responsible for the differences observed between the groups classified as races. We consider racial group or identity inadequate as a general explanatory factor of between-group variations in psychological phenomena. We encourage researchers to give greater attention to cultural elements, as discussed earlier, as they may prove fruitful in understanding behavioral differences associated with racial groupings.

Although we focus on the cultural and social variables associated with racial grouping, we do not imply that biological factors associated with such groupings are of no scientific interest. These biological variables are important, for example, in the study of group differences in essential hypertension, for which Afro-Americans are at a higher risk than Anglo-Americans (Anderson, 1989). From our perspective, what is of scientific interest is not the race of these individuals but the relationship between the identified biological factors (e.g., plasma renin levels and sodium excretion) and hypertension. Moreover, even if a cause-effect relationship is demonstrated between these biological variables and hypertension, one cannot attribute this relationship to race because of intraracial variability and inter-racial overlap with regard to the biological variables (Anderson, 1989). Psychological stress or factors such as diet, life-style, and objective and subjective culture could be responsible for the racial-group differences in the biological factors. Also, this difference may not be observed in a group of the same race in another part of the world or under different living conditions.

In summary, we suggest that when behavioral variations are studied in relation to race, the so-called racial variable under study should be defined, measured, and the proposed relationships tested. The role of specific cultural and social variables could be clearly separated from that of biological and other variables. The area of research will determine the relative importance of any one of these variables. The important point is that the research be on the relevant variable and not on racial groupings alone.

Ethnicity

The concept of ethnicity is also associated with culture and is often used interchangeably with culture as well as with race. Usually, ethnicity is used in reference to groups that are characterized in terms of a common nationality, culture, or language. The concept of ethnicity is related to the Greek concept of ethnos, which refers to the people of a nation or tribe, and ethnikos, which stands for national. Hence, ethnicity refers to the ethnic quality or affiliation of a group, which is normally characterized in terms of culture. However, the distinction between these two related concepts is an important one for psychology. Although cultural background can be a determinant of ethnic identity or affiliation, being part of an ethnic group can also determine culture. As members of an ethnic group interact with each other, ethnicity becomes a means by which culture is transmitted. According to Berry (1985), because an ethnic group is likely to interact with other ethnic groups, such interactions should not be ignored as possible sources of cultural influences. Hence, it is important that comparative studies of ethnic groups identify and measure cultural variables assumed to be responsible for observed differences in psychological phenomena before such differences are attributed to culture on the basis of group membership. This issue is particularly important in the United States today because, beyond face-to-face interactions, interethnic communication takes place through the mass media.

We believe that the study of variations in psychological phenomena between ethnic groups is relevant as far as the specific variable of theoretical interest is measured and related to the relevant psychological phenomena. In addition to the specific cultural elements, there are a range of ethnic-related variables, such as ethnic identification, perceived discrimination, and bilingualism. Increased specification with regard to what about ethnicity is of interest could reduce the confusion and conceptual problems in this area (for an illustration of research in this direction, see Sue, 1988; Sue & Zane, 1987).

Social and Related Variables

The effect of variables such as the social system and socioeconomic level on behavior can also be confounded with the influence of culture, race, the ethnicity (for a discussion, see Rohner, 1984). Some authors do control for the effects of socioeconomic variables. For example, Frerichs, Aneshensel, and Clark (1981) found that the prevalence of depressive symptoms was significantly different for Latinos, Anglos, and Afro-American community residents. More Latinos reported significant levels of depressive symptoms than did the other ethnic groups. However, when controlling for SES-related variables (e.g., employment status and family income), the ethnic effect disappeared. This suggests that ethnicity, and possibly culture, are of little or no significance in the prevalence rates of depression, whereas SES, that is, economic strain, is viewed as being more significant.

Although this approach has the advantage of reducing the likelihood of misattributing to culture the influence of SES, the possibility of confusion still exists. It is possible, for instance, that cultural influences are not identified and are wrongly attributed to SES. We see at least two instances in which this can happen. First, in societies with a history of ethnic or racial discrimination, segregation may result in significant overlap between culture and SES. For example, in the United States the majority of Anglos are represented in higher social strata, whereas the majority of Latinos are represented in lower social strata. Thus, by methodologically or statistically controlling for SES, the cultures are also separated, and the variance associated with culture is removed along with the effects of SES. This may then lead one to wrongly assume that culture does not play a role.

Second, even if two social classes are represented in each of the two cultures, the economic, social, or living conditions of a segregated lower class that includes both cultural groups may generate beliefs, norms, or values specific to that social strata. These cultural elements associated with lower SES may become significantly different from that of other groups (e.g., the middle class) of the same ethnic group. Although it is possible that some cultural elements associated with ethnicity are consistent across the different SES levels of a given ethnic group, it is also possible that there are beliefs, norms, and values that are common to an SES level across cultural (ethnic) groups. Hence, even when social classes are compared within the same ethnic group, cultural elements unique to a lower strata may be wrongly attributed to SES—that is, income or educational level—when in fact they reflect cultural or subcultural elements—that is, beliefs and attitudes associated with lower-class reality.

Sobal and Stunkard (1989) illustrated this point with regard to obesity and socioeconomic status. They argued that the prevalence of obesity in developing societies is a function of structural elements in society, such as the availability of food supplies, and "cultural values favoring fat body shapes" (p. 266). The former reflect SES-related variables, whereas the values associated with body shapes may be more cultural in nature, even though the cultural beliefs are associated with social strata. The work of Sobal and Stunkard is consistent with our recommendation to measure the specific proximal variables thought to underlie a given behavioral phenomenon. By doing so, the comparative study of social as well as cultural groups will be able to better identify the specific social variables (e.g., income, educational level) as well as cultural elements (e.g., values, beliefs) that are relevant to the behavioral phenomena of interest.

In summary, we encourage investigators to think carefully about the group of interest, whether it be cultural, racial, ethnical, or social, and go beyond the group category to the specific factors that underlie the group category. By doing so, studies will be able to identify what about culture, race, ethnicity, or social class is related to the psychological phenomenon of interest. We argue that cultural variables, specifically social roles, norms, beliefs, and values, are likely to contribute significantly to the effects of these demographic variables. However, culture is only one dimension. Depending on the research problem and the interests of the investigator, more biological or social variables could also be assessed. The important point is that further specification will likely lead to a greater understanding of the roles of culture, race, ethnicity, and social class in psychological phenomena.

LIMITATIONS OF MAINSTREAM AND CROSS-CULTURAL PSYCHOLOGY

The need to study and understand culture in psychology represents a major challenge to mainstream and cross-cultural psychology. A review of the literature reveals important limitations in the ways both mainstream and cross-cultural psychology have responded to this challenge. On the one hand, the study of culture has largely been ignored in mainstream psychology and is often seen as the domain of cross-cultural psychology. Usually, theories do not include cultural variables and findings or principles are thought to apply to individuals everywhere, suggesting that psychological knowledge developed in the United

States by Anglo-American scholars using Anglo-American subjects is universal. Even in areas such as social psychology, in which the importance of variables such as norms and values is particularly obvious, there is little regard for the cultural nature of such variables (Bond, 1988).

On the other hand, cross-cultural psychology, normally segregated from mainstream psychology, has focused on the comparative (cross-cultural) study of behavioral phenomena, without much regard for the measurement of cultural variables and their implications for theory. Attributing to culture the differences observed between countries or groups assumed to represent different cultures ignores the complexity of culture as well as the cultural heterogeneity of nations or ethnic groups (see Berry, 1985). Moreover, it tells us little about the role of culture in human behavior. Without a theoretical focus, cross-cultural research has little connection to mainstream psychology, thus maintaining its segregation.

Although there is no simple solution to the noted limitations (see Lonner & Berry, 1986; Malpass, 1977; Reyes-Lagunes & Poortinga, 1985), we believe that the following two approaches would help psychologists to enhance the study of culture: (a) Begin with a phenomenon observed in the study of culture and apply it cross-culturally to test theories of human behavior, and (b) begin with a theory, typically one that ignores culture, and incorporate cultural elements to broaden its theoretical domain. The former might be considered a bottom-up approach; one is beginning with an observation from the study of cultures and moving toward its implications for psychological theory. The latter might be considered a top-down approach; one is beginning with theory and moving to observations within as well as between cultures, examining the role of culture and searching for universals.

Triandis and associates' research illustrates a bottom-up approach to cross-cultural research. Drawing from anthropological research that identified dimensions of cultural variations, they proposed the following steps: (a) Develop measures of such dimensions, (b) assess different cultures along the dimensions so that the cultures could be placed on a continuum of a designated dimension, and (c) test predictions relating the cultural dimension and behavioral phenomenon across cultures. These steps are evident in the work of Triandis et al. (1986) on collectivism versus individualism. They first developed a measure; second, they assessed students from Illinois and Puerto Rico along this dimension. Then, as expected, this dimension was found to be related to behaviors such as cooperation and helping (Triandis, Bontempo, Villareal, Asai, & Lucca, 1988). Not only did they find differences between U.S. mainland students and Puerto Rican students with regard to helping and cooperation, they also found that the cultural dimension of collectivism versus individualism accounted in part for these differences. Thus, in line with the bottom-up approach, the observed cultural phenomenon, in this case individualism-collectivism, has served to inform theoretical accounts of helping and cooperation.

The research of Betancourt and his associates serves to illustrate a top-down approach to the study of cultural influences. They began with a theory and took steps to incorporate cultural factors in the theory. In a first study, Betancourt and Weiner (1982) examined the cross-cultural generality of an attribution theory of motivation (see Weiner, 1986), specifically assessing whether the relationships between the dimensional properties of attributions and related psychological consequences differed for Chilean and U.S. college students. Evidence for both cultural generality and cultural specificity was found. The relationship between the perceived stability of a given causal attribution and expectancy of future success was similar for both groups, suggesting that this part of the theory has cross-cultural generality. The influence of perceived controllability of attributions for a person's achievement on interpersonal feelings and reactions was less important for Chilean students than for students from the United States; this part suggested cultural specificity. For example, although Chileans tended to like the person more when success was due to controllable than to uncontrollable causes, the effect of controllability over liking was significantly lower than for the students from the United States. Chileans tended to like the successful individual, regardless of whether the cause of his or her achievement behavior was perceived as controllable (e.g., effort) or uncontrollable (e.g., aptitude). On the other hand, U.S. students more systematically liked the person according to the degree the achievement behavior was perceived as within the person's volitional control.

In explaining these findings, Betancourt and Weiner (1982) suggested that the generality observed in the relationship between perceived stability of causes and expectancy of success was a reflection of the logic of cause-effect relationships (e.g., if A is the cause of B, and A is stable, B should also be stable). They also suggested that when such logic applies, we might expect psychological principles to be fairly universal. However, in the case of perceived controllability and its relation to interpersonal feelings and behavior, elements of the culture such as norms and values are thought to play a role.

Recall that we have criticized comparative studies of cultures as insufficient in that the aspects of culture responsible for the observed differences are not identified or measured, nor are the relationships between these and the corresponding psychological phenomena demonstrated. From this perspective, Betancourt and Weiner's (1982) study was appropriate as a first step, but limited in that cultural variables responsible for observed variations were not identified and measured. Hence, one may not conclusively attribute differences to cultural factors.

To more directly test the specific cultural element that might underlie the noted difference, Betancourt (1985) first reviewed the cross-cultural literature on attribution processes in an effort to identify possible cultural dimensions that might contribute to explaining further these findings. Key studies were identified that suggested that the perception of control and the effects of causal controllability are culturally determined. Specifically, the relationship observed in the United States between controllability for success and failure and reward and punishment (Weiner & Kukla, 1970) was replicated in Germany (Meyer, 1970) but was not fully replicated in Brazil (Rodrigues, 1981). In addition, Salili, Maehr, and Gillmore (1976) only partially replicated in Iran the findings of Weiner and Peter (1973) concerning developmental aspects of the proposed relationship between controllability of attributions and interpersonal judgment.

The findings from these key studies, in conjunction with the work of Kluckhohn and Strodtbeck (1961) on dimensions of cultural variation, suggested that the cultural dimension of "control over nature versus subjugation to nature" (control-subjugation) was potentially relevant. When the results on the control-subjugation value orientation are compared for the countries noted in the cross-cultural attributional research, Germany, a country in which results are replicated, scores high on control, as does the United States, whereas Brazil, Chile, and Iran, where variations are observed, score low on control.

A series of studies was then designed (e.g., Betancourt, Hardin, & Manzi, 1992) to investigate the control-subjugation value orientation and related cultural beliefs in relation to the attributional components of a model of helping behavior (Betancourt, 1990). Although no cross-cultural comparison took place, within-culture measures of the control-subjugation value orientation were used to examine the influence of value orientation on the attribution process, as well as the relationship between controllability of attributions and helping behavior. In addition, the manipulation (activation) of beliefs associated with this value orientation demonstrated how it relates to the other components of the helping behavior model.

The research by Betancourt and associates progresses from mainstream social psychological research and theory to the study of cultural variables relevant to the theory and search for universals. They identify a specific cultural element hypothesized to be related to the cognitive process and behavior under study and then test the relationships. Their findings indicate that value orientation influences attributional processes. Accordingly, attention to values in attribution theory may serve to broaden the scope and universality of the theory. This is an example in which attention to culture may serve to enhance theory development in mainstream research. In addition, the work of Betancourt et al. (1992) has methodological implications. Although these authors could have taken a cross-cultural or between-groups approach by selecting cultures that vary with regard to value orientation, they chose a within-culture approach. Specifically, they measured differences on the theoretically relevant cultural dimension and tested its relationship to helping. This research suggests that cultural variables can be studied within a single culture and that research with mainstream subjects can also examine culture.

The main limitation of mainstream theories is that they ignore culture and therefore lack universality. The limitation of a segregated cross-cultural psychology is that it fails to use experimentation and develop theory. Two approaches were described above (Betancourt et al., 1992; Triandis et al., 1988) to illustrate how these limitations might be overcome. We submit that progress will follow if mainstream investigators include cultural elements in their research and theory and if cross-cultural researchers incorporate the measurement of cultural variables within a theoretical network.

LIMITATIONS OF ETHNIC MINORITY RESEARCH

Ethnic minority research shares conceptual problems similar to those of cross-cultural psychology. Direct measures of cultural elements are frequently not included, yet cultural factors are assumed to underlie ethnic group differences. Furthermore, ethnic minority research often lacks sufficient attention to psychological theory. It appears that investigators of ethnicity are more inclined toward description than testing theoretically derived hypotheses. In this section, we examine ethnic minority research as it pertains to the study of psychopathology. We draw attention to the importance of directly examining the cultural basis of psychopathology and suggest ways to incorporate psychological theory.

Like cross-cultural research, a typical cross-ethnic design compares a given set of variables across samples of two ethnic groups. In the study of ethnic differences in psychopathology, such research is frequently based on community or clinic surveys of psychological distress or rates of mental disorders. Usually, methodological or statistical controls are included to rule out the effects of socioeconomic status, age, and other sociodemographic variables that could possibly be related to the given dependent variable. If group differences are found with these controls in place, then the investigator frequently argues that the differences between Asian Americans and Anglo Americans, for example, reflect cultural influences. In other words, the observed group differences are thought to be the result of differences in the groups' cultural values and beliefs.

Often, researchers will discuss the cultural differences that are thought to contribute to the observed differences. It is important to note that the "cultural differences" thought to underlie the observed group differences are frequently not directly measured or assessed. It is assumed that because the two groups are from two distinct cultural or ethnic groups, they differ from one another on key cultural dimensions. This may or may not be the case. Without directly assessing these cultural dimensions, one cannot be sure whether culture plays a role, nor can one understand the nature of the relationship between cultural variables and psychological processes.

In an attempt to more directly assess cultural influences associated with ethnicity, some investigators have been using measures of acculturation. Acculturation typically refers to the degree to which minority groups adhere to traditional cultural practices (in many cases, those practices that are associated with people from their country of origin) or to U.S. cultural practices (for a review, see Berry, 1990). These efforts represent a step forward as they serve to increase the specificity in measuring cultural influences.

The inclusion of acculturation measures are not without limitations. First of all, such measures are usually based on behavioral indices such as language usage (native language or English) and place of birth (country of origin or the United States). At best, these are indirect measures of cultural values and beliefs. It is assumed that individuals of low acculturation are more likely to adhere to traditional cultural values regarding such variables as sex role orientation and collectivism-individualism. This may not be the case for a given sample.

Another reason why acculturation is a poor measure of cultural influences is that it is confounded with acculturative stress, or the stress experienced in adjusting from one culture to another culture (Berry, 1990). Some investigators have attempted to determine whether certain levels of acculturation are related to psychological adjustment and distress, as well as rates of mental disorders (see Rogler, Cortes, & Malgady, 1991, for a recent review of Latino research). For example, some researchers find that low-acculturated Latinos, in this case Mexican Americans, report more distress than do more acculturated Latinos and Anglos (Vega, Kolody, & Warheit, 1985). It is not reasonable to interpret findings such as these as only reflecting acculturative stress. It seems possible that the results could also reflect the association between level of distress and specific cultural values, indirectly assessed.

Acculturation indices may serve then as indirect measures of adherence to cultural values, but they may also serve as indices of stress associated with adjusting to the Anglo culture. If an investigator is interested in examining cultural influences, he or she would do best to incorporate direct measures of culture-relevant variables rather than a global measure of acculturation. Furthermore, if acculturative stress is the focus of an investigation, a direct measure of this construct should be included (see Cervantes, Padilla, & Salgado de Snyder, 1991). Without directly assessing cultural values and beliefs and without directly assessing acculturative stress, it is difficult to know the meaning of finding significant relationships between acculturation and psychological variables.

In a recent study, López, Hurwicz, Karno, and Telles (1992) attempted to approximate the goal of directly measuring culture in the study of psychopathology. Drawing from the Los Angeles Epidemiologic Catchment Area database, a large epidemiologic study of the prevalence rates of several mental disorders among Mexican-origin Latinos and Anglos (Karno et al., 1987), López et al. took two significant steps to examine possible cultural influences. First, they chose symptoms as the dependent variable rather than disorders, the dependent variable used in past analyses. Influenced by the work of Draguns (1980) and Persons (1986), they argued that symptoms may be more sensitive to possible sociocultural influences.

The second step was to test hypotheses regarding ethnic differences in the report of specific symptoms and counted for the hypothesized ethnic differences. To develop specific hypotheses, they turned to prior descriptive work of a clinical nature. For example, some clinical observers had noted that Latinos may have the experience of hearing voices, which is reflective of a high degree of spirituality or religiosity and not reflective of psychosis (Abad, Ramos, & Boyce, 1977; Torrey, 1972). Religiosity was also implicated in the relative absence of hypersexuality in the symptomatology of Amish with bipolar disorders (Egeland, Hostetter, & Eshleman, 1983). On the basis of these clinical observations, López et al. (1992) hypothesized that, relative to Anglo residents, Mexican-origin residents would report more evidence of auditory hallucinations, a symptom frequently associated with schizophrenia, and less evidence of hypersexuality, a symptom frequently associated with mania. Furthermore, they hypothesized that religiosity would account for these ethnic differences.

Consistent with their hypotheses, there were significant differences in the reporting of these two symptoms among Latinos of Mexican origin (U.S. born and Mexican born) and Anglos. Furthermore, the patterns of findings are consistent with the hypotheses. With regard to auditory hallucinations, more. Mexican-born Latinos reported this symptom (2.3%) than U.S.-born Latinos (1.6%), who reported more such symptoms than Anglos (0.6%). The opposite pattern resulted for hypersexuality: Mexican-born Latinos (2.2%), U.S.-born Latinos (4.3%), and Anglos (6.8%). Although these findings are consistent with cultural hypotheses—that is, there is something about one or both cultures that contributes to these symptom patterns—there is no direct evidence that cultural elements are responsible for the findings.

To more closely approximate a direct cultural test, López et al. (1992) examined the role of religiosity in the report of these symptoms. Regression analyses revealed that ethnicity is an important variable in the reporting of hypersexuality; however, Catholicism accounts for a greater proportion of the variance. Thus, ethnicity appears to be a more distal variable, whereas religious affiliation is a more proximal variable. In contrast to the report of hypersexuality, religiosity was not found to be significantly related to the report of auditory hallucinations. It might be that the report of auditory hallucinations is more related to spiritual beliefs that may exist independent of religious background.

Although the past Los Angeles Epidemiologic Catchment Area research indicates that there are no ethnic differences in the prevalence rates of disorders such as schizophrenia and bipolar disorder (Karno et al., 1987), suggesting that sociocultural factors are unimportant, the López et al. (1992) study indicates that ethnic and socio-cultural factors are related to psychopathology as reflected in the report of specific symptomatology. Their findings are consistent with the notion that cultural elements or the values and beliefs of individuals are likely to shape the manner in which psychological distress and disorder are manifest.

This research goes beyond the typical comparative ethnic study by examining specific sociocultural factors that are related to psychopathology; however, it falls short of the ideal study. For example, although Catholicism may represent a more proximal variable to hypersexuality than ethnicity, it is not a direct measure of values and beliefs. Measuring values and beliefs about sexual relations would have provided a more direct assessment of cultural elements. Another limitations is that the relationship between Catholicism and hypersexuality may reflect the reticence on the part of Catholics to report this symptom and not their relatively less hypersexual behavior. Also, this study lacks a specific theoretical base. To incorporate theory, the authors might have linked conceptual processes thought to underlie the given symptoms. One such theoretical framework is offered by Bentall (1990), who posited that hallucinations are the result of impaired reality discrimination. In spite of the noted limitations, this research serves to illustrate the importance of including more proximal sociocultural variables in the study of ethnic group behavior, in this case psychopathology.

CONCLUSION

We have discussed some of our concerns about the status of culture in American psychology. We have pointed out three areas of concern that in our opinion represent limitations that preclude the advancement of knowledge concerning the role of culture in human behavior and the universality of psychological theories. At the same time we have suggested possible ways in which to deal with some of the limitations in these areas. First, we addressed and tried to clarify some confusion in the understanding and use of the concepts of culture, race, ethnicity, and social variables, all of which are often used as general explanatory factors for intergroup variations in psychological phenomena. Second, addressing the limitations of mainstream psychology, we suggested ways in which to infuse the study of culture in mainstream research and theory as well as ways to enhance experimentation and the use of theory in cross-cultural research. Finally, we illustrated ways in which to study sociocultural variables and to consider theory in ethnic minority research. In general, we propose that by clearly conceptualizing and measuring cultural and related variables and by including theory, cross-cultural, ethnic, and mainstream research, we can advance the understanding of the role of culture as well as contribute to theory development and applications.

We believe that psychology as a discipline will benefit both from efforts to infuse culture in mainstream research and theory and from efforts to study culture and develop theory in cross-cultural and ethnic psychology. Specifically, we believe that the advancement of knowledge in this area is necessary for psychology to enhance its status as a scientific discipline and its standards of ethical and social responsibility as a profession. As a scientific discipline, progress in the understanding of culture and its role in psychology would result in more universal principles and theories. As a profession, it would result in instruments and interventions that are more sensitive to the reality and cultural diversity of society and the world. Our hope is that this article may stimulate attempts to overcome the limitations we have noted and advance the study of culture in psychology.

REFERENCES

Abad, V., Ramos, J., & Boyce, E. (1977). Clinical issues in the psychiatric treatment of Puerto Ricans. In E. Padilla & A. Padilla (Eds.), *Transcultural psychiatry: An Hispanic perspective* (Monograph No. 4, pp. 23–24). Los Angeles: Spanish Speaking Mental Health Research Center.

Allport, F. (1924). *Social psychology*. New York: Houghton Mifflin.

Amir, Y., & Sharon, I. (1987). Are social psychological laws cross-culturally valid? *Journal of Cross-Cultural Psychology, 8,* 383–470.

Anderson, N. B. (1989). Racial differences in stress-induced cardiovascular reactivity and hypertension: Current status and substantive issues. *Psychological Bulletin, 105,* 89–105.

Barrett, P., & Eysenck, S. (1984). The assessment of personality factors across 25 countries. *Personality and Individual Differences, 5,* 615–632.

Bentall, R. P. (1990). The illusion of reality: A review and integration of psychological research on hallucinations. *Psychological Bulletin, 107,* 82–95.

Berman, J. J. (Ed.). (1990). *Nebraska Symposium on Motivation, 1989: Cross-cultural perspectives* (Vol. 37). Lincoln: University of Nebraska Press.

Berry, J. (1985). In I. Reyes-Lagunes & Y. Poortinga (Eds.), *From a different perspective: Studies of behavior across cultures.* Lisse, The Netherlands: Swets & Zeitlinger.

Berry, J. (1990). Psychology of acculturation. In J. J. Berman (Ed.), *Nebraska Symposium on Motivation, 1989: Cross-cultural perspectives* (Vol. 37, pp. 201–234). Lincoln: University of Nebraska Press.

Betancourt, H. (1985, July). *Cultural variations in attribution processes and the universality of psychological principles.* Paper presented at the XX Congress of the Interamerican Society of Psychology, Caracas, Venezuela.

Betancourt, H. (1990). An attribution-empathy model of helping behavior: Behavioral intentions and judgements of help-giving. *Personality and Social Psychology Bulletin, 16,* 573–591.

Betancourt, H., Hardin, C., & Manzi, J. (1992). Beliefs, value orientation, and culture in attribution processes and helping behavior. *Journal of Cross-Cultural Psychology, 23,* 179–195.

Betancourt, H., & Weiner, B. (1982). Attributions for achievement-related events expectancy, and sentiments: A study of success and failure in Chile and the United States. *Journal of Cross-Cultural Psychology, 13*, 362–374.

Bond, M. (Ed.). (1988). *The cross-cultural challenge to social psychology*. Newbury Park, CA: Sage.

Brislin, R. W. (1983). Cross-cultural research in psychology. *Annual Review of Psychology, 34*, 363–400.

Brislin, R., Lonner, W., & Thorndike, R. (1973). *Cross-cultural research methods*. New York: Wiley.

Cervantes, R. C., Padilla, A. M., & Salgado de Snyder, N. (1991). The Hispanic Stress Inventory: A culturally relevant approach to psychosocial assessment. *Psychological Assessment: A Journal of Consulting and Clinical Psychology, 3*, 438–447.

Dona, G. (1991). Cross-cultural psychology as presaged by Hippocrates. *Cross-Cultural Psychology Bulletin, 25*, 2.

Draguns, J. G. (1980). Psychological disorders of clinical severity. In H. C. Triandis & J. G. Draguns (Eds.), *Handbook of cross-cultural psychology: Psychopathology* (Vol. 6, pp. 99–174). Boston: Allyn & Bacon.

Egeland, J. A., Hostetter, A. M., & Eshleman, S. K., III. (1983). Amish study: 3. The impact of cultural factors on diagnosis of bipolar illness. *American Journal of Psychiatry, 140*, 67–71.

Frerichs, R. R., Aneshensel, C. S., & Clark, V. A. (1981). Prevalence of depression in Los Angeles County. *American Journal of Epidemiology, 113*, 691–699.

Graham, S. (1992). Most of the subjects were White and middle class: Trends in published research on African Americans in selected APA journals, 1970–1989. *American Psychologist, 47*, 629–639.

Harkness, S. (1980). Child development theory in anthropological perspective. *New Directions in Child Development, 8*, 7–13.

Herkovits, M. (1948). *Man and his works*. New York: Knopf.

Jahoda, G. (1984). Do we need a concept of culture. *Journal of Cross-Cultural Psychology, 15*, 139–151.

Jensen, A. R. (1985). The nature of the Black-White difference on various psychometric tests: Spearman's hypothesis. *The Behavioral and Brain Sciences, 8*, 193–263.

Jones, J. M. (1991). Psychological models of race: What have they been and what should they be? In J. D. Goodchilds (Ed.), *Psychological perspectives on human diversity in America* (pp. 5–46). Washington, DC: American Psychological Association.

Karno, M., Hough, R. L., Burnam, M. A., Escobar, J. I., Timbers, D. M., Santana, F., & Boyd, J. H. (1987). Lifetime prevalence of specific psychiatric disorders among Mexican Americans and Non-Hispanic Whites in Los Angeles. *Archives of General Psychiatry, 44*, 695–701.

Kluckhohn, F., & Strodtbeck, F. (1961). *Variations in value orientations*. Evanston, IL: Row, Peterson.

Latter, B. (1980). Genetic differences within and between populations of the major human subgroups. *The American Naturalist, 116*, 220–237.

Lonner, W., & Berry, J. (1986). *Field methods in cross-cultural research*. Newbury Park, CA: Sage.

López, S. R., Hurwicz, M., Karno, M., & Telles, C. A. (1992). *Schizophrenic and manic symptoms in a community sample: A sociocultural analysis*. Unpublished manuscript.

Malpass, R. (1977). Theory and method in cross-cultural psychology. *American Psychologist, 32*, 1069–1079.

McGovern, T. V., Furumoto, L., Halpern, D. F., Kimble, G. A., & McKeachie, W. J. (1991). Liberal education, study in depth, and the arts and sciences major—Psychology. *American Psychologist, 46*, 598–605.

Meyer, W. U. (1970). *Selbstverantwortlichkeit und Leistungs-motivation* [Self-concept and achievement motivation]. Unpublished doctoral dissertation, Ruhr Universität, Bochum, Federal Republic of Germany.

Munroe, R. H., Munroe, R. L., & Whiting, B. (Eds.). (1981). *Handbook of cross-cultural human development*. New York: Garland STPM.

Pepitone, A., & Triandis, H. (1987). On the universality of social psychological theories. *Journal of Cross-Cultural Psychology, 18*, 471–498.

Persons, J. B. (1986). The advantages of studying psychological phenomena rather than psychiatric diagnoses. *American Psychologist, 41,* 1252–1260.

Poortinga, Y., & Malpass, R. (1986). In W. Lonner & J. Berry (Eds.), *Fields methods in cross-cultural research* (pp. 17–46). Newbury Park, CA: Sage.

Reyes-Lagunes, I., & Poortinga, Y. (1985). *From a different perspective: Studies of behavior across cultures.* Lisse, The Netherlands: Swets & Zeitlinger.

Rodrigues, A. (1981). Causal ascription and evaluation of achievement related outcomes: A cross-cultural comparison. *International Journal of Intercultural Relations, 4,* 379–389.

Rogler, L. H., Cortes, D. E., & Malgady, R. G. (1991). Acculturation and mental health status among Hispanics: Convergence and new directions for research. *American Psychologist, 46,* 585–597.

Rohner, R. P. (1984). Toward a conception of culture for cross-cultural psychology. *Journal of Cross-Cultural Psychology, 15,* 111–138.

Rokeach, M. (1979). Some unresolved issues in theories of beliefs, attitudes, and values. In *Proceedings of the Nebraska Symposium on Motivation* (pp. 261–304). Lincoln: University of Nebraska Press.

Salili, F., Maehr, M. L., & Gillmore, F. (1976). Achievement and morality: A cross-cultural analysis of causal attribution and evaluation. *Journal of Personality and Social Psychology, 33,* 327–337.

Segall, M. H. (1984). More than we need to know about culture, but are afraid not to ask. *Journal of Cross-Cultural Psychology, 15,* 153–162.

Smith, M. B. (1979). Attitudes, values, and selfhood. In *Proceedings of the Nebraska Symposium on Motivation* (pp. 305–350). Lincoln: University of Nebraska Press.

Sobal, J., & Stunkard, A. J. (1989). Socioeconomic status and obesity: A review of the literature. *Psychological Bulletin, 105,* 260–275.

Sue, S., (1988). Psychotherapeutic services for ethnic minorities: Two decades of research findings. *American Psychologist, 43,* 301–308.

Sue, S., & Zane, N. (1987). The role of culture and cultural technique in psychotherapy: A critique and reformulation. *American Psychologist, 42,* 37–45.

Torrey, E. F. (1972). *The mind game: Witch doctors and psychiatrists.* New York: Emerson Hall.

Triandis, H. (1989). The self and social behavior in differing cultural contexts. *Psychology Review, 96,* 506–520.

Triandis, H., Bontempo, R., Betancourt, H., Bond, M., Leung, K., Brenes, A., Georgas, J., Hui, C. H., Marin, G., Setiadi, B., Sinha, J. B. P., Verma, J., Spangenberg, J., Touzard, H., & de Montmollin, G. (1986). The measurement of the etic aspects of individualism and collectivism across cultures. *Australian Journal of Psychology, 38,* 257–267.

Triandis, H., Bontempo, R., Villareal, M. J., Asai, M., & Lucca, N. (1988). Individualism and collectivism: Cross-cultural perspectives on self-ingroup relationships. *Journal of Personality and Social Psychology, 54,* 323–338.

Triandis, H., Lambert, W., Berry, J., Lonner, W., Heron, A., Brislin, R., & Draguns, J. (Eds.). (1980). *Handbook of cross-cultural psychology: Vols. 1–6.* Boston: Allyn & Bacon.

Vega, W. A., Kolody, B., & Warhett, G. (1985). Psychoneuroses among Mexican Americans and other Whites: Prevalence and caseness. *American Journal of Public Health, 75,* 523–527.

Weiner, B. (1986). *An attribution theory of motivation and emotion.* New York: Springer-Verlag.

Weiner, B., & Kukla, A. (1970). An attributional analysis of achievement motivation. *Journal of Personality and Social Psychology, 15,* 1–20.

Weiner, B., & Peter, N. (1973). A cognitive developmental analysis of achievement and moral judgments. *Developmental Psychology, 9,* 290–309.

Wundt, W. (1921). *Volkerpsychologie: Vols. 1–10.* Leipzig, Germany: Alfred Kroner Verlag.

Zuckerman, M. (1990). Some dubious premises in research and theory on racial differences: Scientific, social, and ethical issues. *American Psychologist, 45,* 1297–1303.

THINKING CRITICALLY AND APPLYING YOUR KNOWLEDGE

1. How do the authors define *culture*? Think about the cultural group or groups you belong to. Give three examples of distinctive elements of your own culture.

2. Compare and contrast the concepts of culture, race, and ethnicity.

3. Betancourt and López distinguish between "mainstream psychology" and "cross-cultural psychology." How do these differ? What do the authors propose to bring these two relatively separate fields of inquiry together?

4. What do the authors believe are the main limitations of typical ethnic minority research? Select an ethnic group that interests you. Then, design a study that avoids the problems identified by Betancourt and López.

5. According to the authors, why is the concept of "race" fraught with problems? What do the authors propose about the study of race by psychologists?

❖ CHAPTER 2 ❖

COLLEGE SOPHOMORES IN THE LABORATORY: INFLUENCES OF A NARROW DATA BASE ON PSYCHOLOGY'S VIEW OF HUMAN NATURE

David O. Sears

If we are to learn about the full range of human experience, our research must include participants from a wide range of backgrounds. Yet, as David Sears documents in this paper, social psychological research suffers from an unusually narrow data base. Using archival data to analyze the typical research practices of social psychologists, Sears concludes that most studies involve college-student subjects who are studied in laboratory experiments. Sears notes that students are not representative of the general population and that the laboratory is an artificial situation. Sears then takes his critique one step further and suggests some specific ways in which social psychology's description of human nature may be biased because of our particular data base. The paper concludes that college students in laboratories are appropriate for some purposes but not for others. Sears argues for the value of using diverse samples and diverse methodologies.

ABSTRACT: *For the 2 decades prior to 1960, published research in social psychology was based on a wide variety of subjects and research sites. Content analyses show that since then such research has overwhelmingly been based on college students tested in academic laboratories on academiclike tasks. How might this heavy dependence on one narrow data base have biased the main substantive conclusions of sociopsychological research in this era? Research on the full life span suggests that, compared with older adults, college students are likely to have less-crystallized attitudes, less-formulated senses of self, stronger cognitive skills, stronger tendencies to comply with authority, and more unstable peer group relationships. The laboratory setting is likely to exaggerate all these differences. These peculiarities of social psychology's predominant data base may have contributed to central elements of its portrait of human nature. According to this view people (a) are quite compliant and their behavior is easily socially influenced, (b) readily change their attitudes and (c) behave inconsistently with them, and (d) do not rest their self-perceptions on introspection. The narrow data base may also contribute to this portrait of human nature's (e) strong emphasis on cognitive processes and to its lack of emphasis on (f) personality dispositions, (g) material self-interest, (h) emotionally based irrationalities, (i) group norms, and (j) stage-specific phenomena. The analysis implies the need*

Source: Reprinted from *Journal of Personality and Social Psychology, 51,* (1986), 515–530. Copyright © 1986 by the American Psychological Association. Reprinted by permission.

both for more careful examination of sociopsychological propositions for systematic biases introduced by dependence on this narrow data base and for increased reliance on adults tested in their natural habitats with materials drawn from ordinary life.

Every science has its own methodological idiosyncracies. Pharmacological research relies heavily on the white rat, research on new birth control techniques is most commonly conducted on non-American women, astronomers use telescopes, and psychoanalysts depend on the self-reports of affluent self-confessed neurotics. Ordinarily, such researchers trust that they have a reasonably good grasp of the biases introduced by their own particular methodological proclivities and that they can correct their conclusions for whatever biases are present. But conclusions can be so corrected only if the direction and magnitude of bias can be estimated on the basis of reliable empirical evidence. Such systematic evidence may not always exist, or it may be hard to find, or it may not even be sought. The danger then is that biases resulting from overreliance on a particular data base may be ignored, and the conclusions of the science may themselves be flawed.

This article suggests that social psychology has risked such biases because of its heavy dependence during the past 25 years on a very narrow data base: college student subjects tested in the academic laboratory with academiclike materials. My concern is that overdependence on this one narrow data base may have unwittingly led us to a portrait of human nature that describes rather accurately the behavior of American college students in an academic context but distorts human social behavior more generally.

This article begins by documenting the growth of social psychology's heavy reliance on this narrow data base. It then proceeds to describe the biases this reliance may have introduced into the central substantive conclusions of the field. These biases could in theory be assessed in two ways. One way is through systematic replication of empirical findings using other populations and situations. In practice, however, these data do not now exist, so this is not a practical approach. The second way involves estimating these biases both from the known differences between our data base and the general population in everyday life, and from the known effects of those differences. That will be my approach, using as examples research on several of the most important topics in the subfields of attitudes and social cognition. This part of the argument is frankly speculative. As a result it should not stimulate wholesale abandonment of our familiar, captive, and largely friendly data base. I would hope, however, that it might generate some serious thought about how this narrow data base has affected our major substantive conclusions. I doubt that they are flat out wrong. But taken together as a cumulative body of knowledge presented by the field of social psychology, they may give quite a distorted portrait of human nature.

A NARROW METHODOLOGICAL BASE

The first great burst of empirical research in social psychology, which occurred in the years surrounding World War II, used a wide variety of subject populations and research sites. Cantril (1940) and Lazarsfeld, Berelson, and Gaudet (1948), for example, investigated radio listeners and voters. Hovland, Lumsdaine, and Sheffield (1949), Merton and Kitt (1950), Shils and Janowitz (1948), and Stouffer, Suchman, De Vinney, Star, and Williams (1949) studied soldiers in training and combat, whereas Lewin (1947) and Cartwright (1949) looked at the civilian end of the war effort, and Bettelheim and Janowitz (1950) at returning veterans. Deutsch and Collins (1951) and Festinger, Schachter, and Back (1950) investigated residents of housing projects, and Coch and French (1948) studied industrial workers in factories. Adorno, Frenkel-Brunswik, Levinson, and Sanford (1950) investigated authoritarianism in a wide range of subjects that included merchant marine officers, veterans, as well as members of unions, the PTA, and the League of Women Voters. Even Leon Festinger, in some ways the godfather of laboratory-based experimental social psychology, based his best-known book, *A Theory of Cognitive Dissonance* (1957), on data bases ranging from the analysis of rumors in India and the participant-observation of a millenial group to carefully crafted laboratory experiments on college students. The conventional methodological wisdom of the era was that the researcher must travel back and forth between field and laboratory (and their differing indigenous populations) in order to bracket properly any sociopsychological phenomenon.

The subsequent generation of social psychologists created the experimental revolution. They were much more thoroughly committed to the laboratory experiment and, inevitably, as thoroughly committed to the use of undergraduate college students (the well-known "college sophomore") as research subjects. By the 1960s, this conjunction of college student subject, laboratory site, and experimental method, usually mixed with some deception, had become the dominant methodology in social psychology, as documented in several systematic content analyses of journal articles (Christie, 1965; Fried, Gumpper, & Allen, 1973; Higbee & Wells, 1972).

Like all revolutions, this one immediately came under attack. There was concern about such internal biases as demand characteristics, experimenter bias, and evaluation apprehension. Others demanded more "relevant" and applied research that would more directly address "real world" problems. Both critiques encouraged broader methodological practice. But the 1970s also witnessed the rapid development of research modeled on work in cognitive psychology that used brief, emotionally neutral laboratory experiments on college students. Paper-and-pencil role-playing studies became especially common.

The net effects of these conflicting developments are best assessed with a systematic inventory of actual methodological practice. Hence we coded, for subject population and research site, articles published during 1980 in the three mainstream outlets for sociopsychological research, *Journal of Personality and Social Psychology* (JPSP), *Personality and Social Psychology Bulletin* (PSPB), and the *Journal of Experimental Social Psychology* (JESP). Subject populations were coded into four categories: (a) recruited directly from a North American undergraduate psychology class; (b) other North American undergraduates; (c) other students (mainly primary and secondary school students or college students in other westernized societies); or (d) adults. The site of the research was coded as either

(a) laboratory or (b) natural habitat. The latter was interpreted quite liberally to include either a physical site in the individual's ordinary life (such as college gymnasiums and dormitories, beaches, military barracks, a voter's living room, or airport waiting rooms) or even self-report questionnaires concerning the individual's daily life and activities (e.g., personality, political and social attitudes, or ongoing interpersonal relationships) no matter where they were administered.[1]

American college undergraduates were overwhelmingly the subject population of choice. In 1980, 75% of the articles in these journals relied solely on undergraduate subjects, almost all from the United States. Most (53%) stated that they used students recruited directly from undergraduate psychology classes, but this is probably an underestimate because many studies relying on undergraduates do not further specify their origin. All totaled, 82% used students of one kind or another. By far the majority (71%) were based on laboratory research. Considering these two dimensions jointly, 85% of the articles used undergraduates and/or a laboratory site; only 15% used adults in their natural habitats or dealt with content concerned with adults' normal lives. All of this is displayed in Table 1.

To provide more current data, all of the issues of these journals were again coded in 1985 (except for the personality section of *JPSP*, because of some dispute over its editorial policies). Table 2 shows that use of undergraduates in the laboratory had diminished only marginally; 83% of the articles coded used students, 74% American undergraduates, 78% the laboratory, and 67% undergraduates in the lab; the latter overwhelmingly remained the data base of choice. The one substantial change occurred in the Interpersonal Relations section of JPSP, which showed an increase in studies of adults in their natural habitats, from 14% to 26%. But even there, the majority (55%) still used undergraduates in the laboratory.[2]

The later discussion of the implications of this pattern will emphasize the areas of attitudes and social cognition, because they are the areas with which I am most familiar. Table 1 shows that articles in the Attitudes and Social Cognition section of *JPSP* relied as much if not more on college students in the lab than did the others. Similarly, Findley and Cooper (1981) reported that the attitude change chapters of social psychology texts were about at the median in use of college students. So research on attitudes and social cognition is as likely as any other area of social psychology to be vulnerable to whatever problems these methodological practices introduce.

[1] Articles relying on more than one study were given a summary rating on the basis of the majority of their studies. In general, ambiguous decisions were biased in the direction of underestimating the use of college students in the laboratory. A reliability check was made by having a second coder (the author) code three issues of *JPSP*. Both coders agreed on subject population and research site in 97% and 88% of the cases, respectively, with no particular pattern to the disagreements. Since reliability was acceptably high, the first coder's judgments were used in all cases.

[2] If the study, rather than the article, is used as the unit of analysis, the codeable N for Table 2 rises from 178 to 268, and the results only become stronger: 84% (rather than 83%) used students; 76% (rather than 74%) American undergraduates, 80% (rather than 78%) the lab, and 69% (rather than 67%) both; only 10% (rather than 13%) used adults in their natural habitats.

TABLE 1
Subject Population and Research Site in Social Psychologists' 1980 Journal Articles

Code category	JPSP							JPSP Authors' Other Articles		
	% Atts. & soc. cog.	% Interp. rels. & grp. proc.	% Pers. proc. & indiv. diffs.	Total %	% PSPB	% JESP	Total %	% In JPSP, PSPB, or JESP	% In other journals	Total %
Subject population										
American undergraduates	85	78	51	70	81	81	75	84	66	72
Psychology classes	56	56	39	52	53	57	53	50	43	46
Other	29	22	12	18	28	24	21	34	23	26
Other students	8	3	19	12	0	8	7	8	12	11
Adults	8	19	30	18	19	11	18	8	22	17
Research site										
Laboratory	88	69	44	64	75	95	71	97	78	85
Natural habitat	12	31	56	36	25	5	29	3	22	15
Combined										
Undergraduates/lab	83	64	32	58	73	78	64	84	59	68
Adults/natural habitat	8	14	28	17	16	3	15	3	11	9
Number of articles										
Total	53	36	59	198	93	42	333	75	162	237
Empirical and codeable	52	36	57	191	73	37	301	62	116	178

Note. JPSP = Journal of Personality and Social Psychology. The three sections of *JPSP* are Attitudes and Social Cognition, Interpersonal Relations and Group Processes, and Personality and Individual Differences. *PSPB = Personality and Social Psychology Bulletin. JESP = Journal of Experimental Social Psychology.* The base for all percentages includes only articles shown in the last row (empirical, codeable, and available in the library). Columns 4 and 5–7 include all such 1980 journal articles; columns 1–3 include all such journal articles for April through December 1980, the first nine months of the tripartite division of the journal; and columns 8–10 are based on all such articles obtained from entries given in the 1980 *Psychological Abstracts.* Some articles could not be located (8%), others could not be coded (3%), and still others were nonempirical articles (15%). The percentages presented exclude all these from the base.

TABLE 2
**Subject Population and Research Site in Social Psychologists' 1985
Journal Articles**

	JPSP				
	% Atts. & soc. cog.	% Interp. rels. & grp. proc.	% PSPB	% JESP	Total %
Subject population					
American undergraduates	81	58	79	82	74
Psychology classes	55	40	61	53	51
Other	26	19	18	29	23
Other students	8	9	6	12	8
Adults	11	32	16	6	17
Research site					
Laboratory	75	66	84	91	78
Natural habitat	25	34	16	9	22
Combined					
Undergraduates/lab	70	55	71	76	67
Adults/natural habitat	8	26	11	3	13
Number of articles					
Total	58	54	40	35	187
Empirical and codeable	53	33	38	34	178

Note. JPSP = Journal of Personality and Social Psychology. The two sections of *JPSP* are Attitudes and Social Cognition and Interpersonal Relations and Group Processes. *PSPB = Personality and Social Psychology Bulletin. JESP = Journal of Experimental and Social Psychology.* The base for all percentages includes only articles shown in the last row.

A Flight From Mainstream Journals?

This reliance on laboratory studies of college students might, however, only describe these mainstream journals and not social psychologists' general research practice. Perhaps the editorial policies of these particular journals are dominated by a conformist in-group wedded to this "traditional" mode of research. Or, these journals are known to be the most selective, and so they might tend to reject the somewhat "softer" research that is done in real-world settings on less captive (and less compliant) subject populations. Or perhaps researchers wishing to communicate with colleagues who also conduct nonmainstream research might reach them more directly through more specialized journals; for example, it may be easier to reach public opinion researchers through *Public Opinion Quarterly* than through *JPSP*. It is possible therefore that social psychologists' research published elsewhere actually uses a broader range of methodologies than is apparent from inspecting these three journals.

To check this, we canvassed articles written by social psychologists that had been published in other journals. We drew a representative sample of social psychologists who had published in *JPSP*, consisting of the one individual listed in each 1980 *JPSP* article as the person to be contacted for reprints (on the grounds that he or she would be the one most likely to have a research career). We then coded the methodological characteristics of all the articles these social psychologists had published elsewhere in a comparable time frame—specifically, all articles listed for each such 1980 *JPSP* "reprint author" in the 1980 *Psychological Abstracts.*

At first glance, these other articles seem to display social psychologists at work in quite a different manner, because *JPSP* authors also publish in a spectacular variety of other journals. In the 1980 *Psychological Abstracts*, they generated no fewer than 237 other entries that appeared in no fewer than 128 different journals. These ranged from such fraternal outlets as the *European Journal of Social Psychology* to distant relatives, arguably even of the same species, such as *Behavior and Neural Biology* or the *Journal of Altered States of Consciousness.* This variety alone might suggest that, once away from the staid scrutiny or narrow conformity pressures of their peers, social psychologists may be using strange and wonderfully different kinds of data bases.

In fact, however, even in their research published in these more distant outlets, social psychologists mainly used college student subjects in laboratory settings. The last column of Table 1 shows that 72% of these other articles used North American undergraduates as subjects, a figure slightly higher than the 70% that held in the original sample of the same authors' articles in *JPSP* (column 4). Use of both college student subjects and the laboratory setting was more common in these social psychologists' other articles (68%) than in their original *JPSP* articles (58%). Viewed from the opposite perspective, only 9% of their other articles used adults in their natural habitat, whereas 17% of their *JPSP*, articles had.

This continuity of methodological practice could simply reflect the fact that many of these other articles themselves had appeared in mainstream outlets. Indeed half of these other articles had appeared in the basic social-personality journals (mostly in *JPSP*, *JESP* and *PSPB*, with the rest scattered through 11 other journals of similar focus). Another 21% appeared in basic psychological journals outside of the social-personality area (in experimental psychology, psychobiology, and developmental). Only 11% appeared in applied social psychology journals (on health, the environment, public opinion, women's issues, and politics), and 17% in other applied psychology journals (including educational and clinical psychology). But the other articles published outside of the basic social psychology journals also relied primarily on undergraduate subjects in the laboratory (78%); only 11% investigated adults in their natural habitat (Table 1, column 9).

In short, wherever they publish, social psychologists seem to publish laboratory research on college students. A dispositional, rather than a situational, attribution seems most appropriate for social psychologists' methodological proclivities.[3]

Historical Trends

Content analyses show that articles published in mainstream social psychology journals during the immediate postwar years relied heavily on adults. But the proportion of articles published in the *Journal of Abnormal and Social Psychology* that relied on college student subjects more than doubled from 1949 to 1959 (Christie, 1965). And it has held steady

---

[3]These data do not rule out the possibility that a wholly different set of social psychologists publishes research using more representative subject populations and more realistic settings outside of the mainstream journals. Hence these data should be understood as describing the behavior of social psychologists who publish at least some of the time in the mainstream journals.

ever since. American college students have been the primary subject population for at least 70% of the articles in *JPSP* in every sounding done since the early 1960s, without much variation: 73% in 1962–1964, 70% in 1966–1967, 76% in 1969, 77% in 1970–1972, 72% in 1979, 70% in 1980, and 70% in 1985 (see Higbee, Lott, & Graves, 1976; Higbee, Millard, & Folkman, 1982; Higbee & Wells, 1972; Schultz, 1969; Smart, 1966; and Tables 1 and 2). In *JESP*, 80% of the articles in 1969, 81% in 1980, and 82% in 1985 relied on American college students (see Higbee et al., 1976; and Tables 1 and 2).

Also, there has not been any drop in the use of the other aspects of this now traditional methodology in social psychology. About three fourths of the articles in *JPSP* were using the laboratory by the late 1960s (Fried et al., 1973). As Tables 1 and 2 show, this remains true today: Of mainstream journal articles in 1980, 71% used the lab; also, 85% of *JPSP* authors' other articles and even 78% of their articles published in nonmainstream journals were laboratory based. In 1985, 78% of the articles coded were laboratory based. Potter (1981) reported the same constancy in laboratory use in British journal articles.

Prestigious Research

These data only describe the subjects used in representative samples of social psychological research articles, not those used in the research generally regarded as most central to our accumulated knowledge. It could be that much of the research that really has a lasting impact is more likely to have been conducted on adults and/or in more realistic settings.

One index of prestigious research is that cited in social psychology textbooks. Findley and Cooper (1981) coded the articles cited in nine widely used textbooks in social psychology for reliance on college students; the median, across content areas, was 73%, very close to the field as a whole at the time (75% of the 1980 articles in mainstream journals and 72% of the other articles used college students, as shown in Table 2.1).

A second index of prestige is appearance in books of readings. In social psychology, the reader market was dominated from World War II through the early 1960s by the Society for the Psychological Study of Social Issues (SPSSI) series, originally titled *Readings in Social Psychology*. Subsequently the market, such as it was, was dispersed among other books. The articles reprinted in the pre-1960 readers used adult subjects considerably more often than they did college students, as shown in Table 3. After 1960, however, college student subjects took over, both in readers with a social problems focus (e.g., Brigham & Wrightsman, 1982) and those focusing more on basic research (Aronson, 1981; Freedman et al., 1971).

This transition around 1960 to college student subjects is aptly illustrated within the SPSSI reader series itself. In 1965, in lieu of a fourth edition of a general reader, two volumes were issued. *Basic Studies in Social Psychology* was intended to emphasize the "classics" (Proshansky & Seidenberg, 1965) and consisted almost exclusively of articles published prior to 1958 (the median year was actually 1952). *Current Studies in Social Psychology* was intended to represent current research (Steiner & Fishbein, 1965) and consisted exclusively of post-1958 articles (the median publication year was actually 1962). As shown in Table 3, adult subjects predominated in the pre-1958 *Basic Studies*, whereas college students were by far the dominant subject population in the post-1958 *Current Studies*.

TABLE 3
Subject Populations in Selected Books of Readings in Social Psychology

Editors and pub. date	Title	Subjects			No. of codeable articles
		% College students	% Other preadults	% Adults	
	Pre-1960 research				
Swanson, Newcomb, & Hartley (1952)	*Readings in Social Psychology* (2nd ed.)	28	23	49	61
Proshansky & Seidenberg (1965)	*Basic Studies in Social Psychology*	35	18	47	60
	Post-1960 research				
Steiner & Fishbein (1965)	*Current Studies in Social Psychology*	64	12	24	42
Freedman, Carlsmith, & Sears (1971)	*Readings in Social Psychology*	69	13	18	39
Wrightsman & Brigham (1973)	*Contemporary Issues in Social Psychology* (2nd ed.)	57	24	19	21
Brigham & Wrightsman (1977)	*Contemporary Issues in Social Psychology* (3rd ed.)	73	0	27	15
Aronson (1981)	*Readings About the Social Animal* (3rd ed.)	55	16	29	31
Brigham & Wrightsman (1982)	*Contemporary Issues in Social Psychology* (4th ed.)	59	6	35	17

A third way to index the most prestigeful research in the field is to select that done by the most frequent contributors to mainstream journals. And those who publish most regularly in the mainstream journals turn out also to be the most likely to use college students in the lab. The other articles of *JPSP* authors that appear in mainstream social psychology journals relied heavily on undergraduate subjects (84%), were almost exclusively based on laboratory studies (97%), and so almost never considered adults in their natural habitats (3%). This is shown in column 8 of Table 1. Prestige in our field therefore seems to be linked closely to the use of college student subjects in laboratory settings.

Summary

In short, (a) social psychologists during the late 1940s and 1950s commonly conducted research on adults in their natural habitats, but (b) since the early 1960s the great majority of social psychological studies have relied exclusively on college students tested in the laboratory, (c) at a level that has held quite steady over the past 25 years. Indeed, (d) in the current era, the most prestigious research, as indicated by textbook citations, by inclusion in books of readings, or by having been conducted by the most prolific publishers in the most mainstream journals is, if anything, the most likely to be based on laboratory research with college students. This reliance on undergraduates in the lab (e) seems not to be a product of journal policy or peer review, because it emerges wherever social psychologists publish.

WHAT DIFFERENCE DOES IT MAKE?

That sociopsychological research overwhelmingly uses one rather narrow subject population and artificial laboratory settings does not necessarily mean its results are invalid. Much biomedical research does the same, and few would question the cumulative value of that work. There should be little reason for concern unless it can be shown that such choices threaten the validity of the research.

The Consensus: Little or None

The consensus of the field certainly appears to be that such a heavy reliance on college student subjects does not have major negative consequences. It has typically been assumed that the phenomena under investigation by social psychologists are so ubiquitous and universal that it does not matter much what subjects are used; one might as well use those cheapest and easiest to obtain. As a result, social psychologists have, by and large, ignored the question of subject population and thus have not discussed its possible consequences. Without going into detail, a careful perusal of the most widely used textbooks in the field, the major books and handbook chapters on methodology, the major handbook and review chapters on attitudes and social cognition, the most recent texts on attitude change or social cognition, and even the several articles in the 1970s expressing concern about a crisis in social psychology reveals that subject selection is generally not mentioned at all. Only a few mention it even in passing, and none express any particular concern about it.

A few critical articles have been published recording the particular characteristics of sociopsychological methodology, most of them cited above in the discussion of historical trends. In general, however, they have not attempted to specify the consequences of these patterns. And in any case they seem to me to have had little impact so far, either upon researchers' practices or on researchers' attitudes toward their practices.

The Potential Hazards of a Narrow Data Base

What kinds of mischief might this narrow data base do? Presumably the principal goal of research in social psychology is to establish a body of causal propositions of the general form $y = a + bx$. Problems could arise when a narrow data base disturbs functional relationships and misrepresents them in some way. But some possibilities seem more threatening than others. Conceivably, the nature of the relationship may be wrongly described, in that either the sign or the shape of the b term may be wrong. However, I doubt that either of these is a major problem in social psychology. Incentives for discovering incorrect signs are quite lavish and usually motivate a great deal of research when they are suspected, as happened following the classic Festinger and Carlsmith (1959) study of forced compliance. And our propositions are usually too crude to invoke subtly shaped relationships.

More likely is that the strength of the relationship may be wrongly described. A test conducted under artificial circumstances is best at telling us whether or not x can cause y under favorable circumstances. Having established that it can, the criterion of success shifts to the validity of the proposition in everyday life: Is x in general a major cause of y in everyday life? And here, as Converse (1970) has pointed out, the absence of research on the general population in natural situations can leave the experimental social psychologist ignorant of the actuarial mainstream, unaware of what the critical sources of variation are, or are not, in "natural" social processes.

The strength of the relationship can be misestimated in at least three different ways. First, the size of b may be incorrectly estimated from the artificial data base: x may, in everyday life, not influence y much, and/or other variables may influence it more strongly. It would be a serious matter if some seemingly strong functional relationships were in fact limited only to college students in the laboratory or had very small (even if statistically significant) effects elsewhere. A vast amount of research and textbook space might be devoted to variables (or processes) that are simply not very important in general. Conversely, some relationships might hold with ordinary adults in everyday life but not to any visible degree among college students in the laboratory. Our research would fail to detect them, and some key aspects of human nature might thereby be omitted from theories in social psychology.

Second, the range of the x values used in our research may not map well onto their range in ordinary life. This seems to me a particular hazard. The x values in an artificial data base are likely to be set at some ecologically unrepresentative level. For example, laboratory research on media violence usually presents much higher and more concentrated doses of filmed violence than do the everyday mass media; for example, showing only an intensely violent segment of a prize fight as opposed to the occasional violent episode of a typical 1-hr TV show.

Finally, the effort to get pure laboratory conditions is likely to result in testing a narrow and/or atypical sample of possibly interacting conditions. For example, in most aggression experiments, the reigning authority either approves or actually encourages aggression (e.g., with the Buss shock machine), certainly an atypical condition for antisocial aggression in everyday life. Moreover, they do not even enter the range of the threatened punishments for antisocial aggression that in fact control much of its variance in everyday life.[4]

Assessment of Risk

How can one assess the threat to the validity of research findings posed by heavy reliance on this one narrow data base? Two strategies seem evident. Most obviously, one could repeat tests of various cause-and-effect propositions on subject populations of various ages and social locations and in a representative sample of everyday situations. This is the *ecological validity* strategy advocated by Bronfenbrenner (1977) and Brunswik (1955). If some propositions prove to hold for college students in the laboratory but not for ordinary people in everyday life (or vice versa) there would be reason for concern. Although systematic comparisons across subject populations and research sites would provide the most certain evidence of external validity, they have not, to my knowledge, been attempted in any area of social psychology.[5]

Hence a more realistic (and less expensive) strategy would be to extrapolate from existing information. This would require several steps: identifying the ways in which college students in the laboratory differ from the general population in everyday life, estimating the effects of those factors on the basis of other research, and then making some informed guesses about how this biased data base might affect the resulting substantive generalizations. This was essentially Hovland's (1959) strategy in accounting for the differences between survey and experimental studies of attitude change. This second strategy appears to me to be the only feasible one at the present time, given the very limited amount of evidence available on ordinary people in ordinary life. Presumably if it gives cause for concern, it should be followed by more precisely focused replications using a broader range of subject populations, research sites, and research materials.

---

[4]Berkowitz and Donnerstein (1982), and many others, argued that experimental, rather than mundane, realism is sufficient to test causal hypotheses. This seems less obvious to me than it does to them. Although usually intended to test causal hypotheses, experiments are frequently interpreted as making population estimates (e.g., the important studies by Asch, Bem, Milgram, and those on cognitive heuristics, attributional biases, and attitude-behavior inconsistency). Testing functional relationships may also require more ecological validity than is usually assumed, for the reasons given in the text above. And even experimental realism is rarely assessed in much detail beyond, at most, a relatively narrowly focused manipulation check.

[5]Some have replicated studies with nonstudent populations and/or in sites other than academic laboratories, of course. But the effects of subject characteristic and site variables have not been assessed systematically. For example, Crutchfield (1955) did use some adult subjects in his laboratory studies of conformity, though he made no explicit age comparisons. Similarly, Milgram (1974) took great pains to replicate his findings on obedience to authority with nonstudent subjects of varying age and social class and in a nonuniversity setting. I hope it will not seem churlish to point out that, nevertheless, the effects of age and class were not assessed; that the nonuniversity context did produce a significant reduction in obedience (though it remained at very high levels); and that Milgram felt the laboratory context was crucial in producing the phenomenon. The critical question here is one Milgram speculated extensively about: how common are such settings in ordinary people's natural habitats?

How Is the College Student in the Laboratory Unusual?

How might American undergraduates, enrolled in introductory psychology classes and tested in academic laboratories on academiclike tasks, differ systematically from the general population in everyday life in ways that might lead us to mistaken conclusions about human nature in general?

Most obviously, undergraduates usually come from a very narrow age range and are concentrated at the upper levels of educational background. Those who work extensively with survey data on the general population are accustomed to finding that age and education are the two most powerful demographic factors influencing attitudes and attitudinal processes. This alone leads us to suspect that those at the tails of those distributions will be a shaky foundation upon which to generalize to the population as a whole. But it is possible to be more specific.

Introductory psychology tends to be one of the first classes taken by college freshmen: It is usually an easy, popular course that satisfies breadth requirements and has no prerequisites. Hence the students tend to be 17 to 19 years old and thus concentrated in a narrow band of late adolescence. Persons in this particular life stage tend to have a number of quite unique characteristics, as described in the standard texts on adolescence (see Atwater, 1983; Conger, 1977; and Douvan & Adelson, 1966; see also Rubenstein, 1983). At an intrapsychic level, they tend to have (a) a less than fully formulated sense of self, manifested variously in mercurial self-esteem, identity confusion and diffusion, inadequate integration of past, present, and future selves, feelings of insecurity, and depression. One important consequence is that (b) their social and political attitudes tend to be considerably less crystallized at this stage than later in life. They also tend to be (c) substantially more egocentric than older adults. They differ from adults in their interpersonal relationships, as well, having (d) a stronger need for peer approval, manifested in dependency, conformity, and overidentification with peers. However, this need tends to be mixed with (e) highly unstable peer relationships and especially highly unstable peer *group* relationships.

But college students also differ systematically from other late adolescents in general: (f) They have been carefully preselected for having unusually adept cognitive skills, and (g) they have also been selected for compliance to authority; few can successfully navigate 13 years of primary and secondary schooling and obtain good grades and positive letters of recommendation while fighting authority at every turn. (h) College students would also seem likely to have more unstable peer (and peer group) relationships than other later adolescents because of their greater geographical and social mobility and later entry into the work force and family life.[6]

The use of college students as a subject population cannot be disentangled completely from the equally widespread reliance on the laboratory setting and the academiclike task. Laboratory studies in social psychology would seem likely to induce (i) a considerably

---

[6]The fact that these college students almost all are from the American middle class or other westernized middle-classes and educational systems no doubt has other ramifications, but thorough consideration of such cultural factors would take this article too far afield (see Miller, 1984, for a recent foray into that territory).

more cognitive set than the other sites of ordinary life. They are usually conducted as part of a course requirement in an academic setting, such as a laboratory or classroom, and usually use paper-and-pencil materials that resemble academic tests. They would also seem likely to induce (j) a set to comply with authority, for some of the same reasons: the academic setting, the course requirement, the testlike material, with an older authority—the experimenter—giving authoritative instructions and controlling the awarding of credit. Finally, most laboratory situations deliberately (k) sever students from whatever close peer (and peer group) relationships they have, in order to minimize contamination of individuals' responses.

The critical question is whether or not these unusual characteristics of college students tested in the laboratory are likely to produce misleading or mistaken substantive conclusions about social behavior. Unfortunately, one cannot extrapolate very well from research in experimental social psychology, because it provides very little direct evidence on these variables. For example, the excellent review of attitude change research by Petty and Cacioppo (1981) refers to age and intelligence only once each, and not at all to educational level or to Hovland's (1959) compelling paper on research site.

On the other hand, we may be able to make such informed guesses if we turn to evidence gathered within other disciplines that have researched persons from the full life span and from a wider variety of ecological locations. Using such sources of evidence and focusing especially on attitudes and social cognition, the remainder of this article attempts to identify major features of our account of human nature which may be misleading as a result of our narrow data base.

WEAK SELF-DEFINITION

There is much current research on the self. One of its major themes is that people have a rather wobbly definition or sense of the self. For example, the central observation of the social comparison literature (Festinger, 1954) is that people arrive at perceptions of their own attitudes and abilities not through introspection but by comparing themselves with others. The extensive literature on the self-perception of attitudes (Bem, 1972), preferences (Nisbett & Wilson, 1977), and emotions (Schachter & Singer, 1962) also argues that people have relatively impoverished introspective access to their own subjective states. In commonsense language, people do not know their own minds. In a related vein, research on objective self-awareness (Duval & Wicklund, 1972) asserts that self-esteem is highly fragile. It can be significantly lowered by minimal levels of self-reflection, which, it is argued, confronts the individual with the discrepancy between internal standards and reality.

The consensus among developmental psychologists is that adolescents do not have as firm a sense of self, or self-definition, as do older adults. As Erikson (1963) and many others have noted, they frequently do not have a clearly crystallized identity. They are quite uncertain about many of their values, preferences, abilities, and emotions, and for good reason. Many of these dispositions are still developing, many are quite volatile as yet, and the stability that may ultimately come to internal dispositions simply has not yet had time or experience to develop.

It is possible that people of all ages are in fact rather uncertain about their own true attitudes, emotions, and abilities. But research in the areas of social comparison, self-perception, and objective self-awareness has relied almost exclusively on college student subjects. The reliance for empirical data on a subpopulation that is particularly uncertain about its own dispositions could quite naturally, but possibly misleadingly, lead to a view of the whole species as equally uncertain about its own internal states.

UNCRYSTALLIZED ATTITUDES

One important consequence of this wobbly sense of self is that late adolescents and young adults tend to have less crystallized social and political attitudes than do older people. This has been demonstrated with at least four different methodologies (see Glenn, 1980; Sears, 1983). Panel studies have consistently shown that older adults have more stable social and political attitudes than do late adolescents or young adults (Jennings & Niemi, 1981; also see Jennings & Markus, 1984). Second, young people change attitudes more than older persons in response to political events. In Mueller's (1973) terms, "the public swerves to follow" sudden switches in official foreign policy (such as that concerning the Korean and Vietnam wars), and the young swerve most (also see Sears, 1969, pp. 351–353). The racial conflicts of the 1960s and the Vietnam War influenced basic party preferences more for young adults than for their parents (Markus, 1979). Similarly, the young were the first to jump on the bandwagons of such right-wing extremists as Adolf Hitler and George Wallace (see Lipset & Raab, 1978; Loewenberg, 1971), as well as on those of the radical leftist movements that swept the campuses in the late 1960s and early 1970s. Third, cohort analyses have generally shown younger cohorts to be more responsive to strong long-term period pressures, such as those of the late 1960s and 1970s toward more distrust of government and weaker party identification (Glenn, 1980) and those of the early 1980s toward Reagan and the Republican party (Shanks & Miller, 1985). Converse's (1976) cohort analyses also showed party identification to strengthen with age, especially in "steady state" eras with only weak period effects. Fourth, Kirkpatrick (1976) has shown that older cohorts in the late 1950s and 1960s had more consistent attitudes on social welfare issues than did younger ones, and consistency increased within cohorts as they aged.

In short, four quite different lines of research have shown late adolescents and young adults to have more unstable, changeable, weak, and inconsistent attitudes than older adults. This lesser crystallization of their attitudes may be partially responsible for three important conclusions that social psychologists have generally drawn about human nature primarily on the basis of their research on college students in the laboratory.

Easily Influenced

One core conclusion of modern social psychology is that people are easily influenced. Almost every textbook has chapters on attitudes and attitude change. Almost always the message is that judgments and attitudes are readily changed and that social psychology provides an extensive roster of successful change techniques. Similarly, most textbooks have chapters on conformity and compliance, which are illustrated by the well-known studies by Asch, Milgram, and many others, that document the many ways in which psychologists have shown behavior to be easily controlled through social influence. At this very general level, social psychologists stand somewhat apart from social scientists in some other disciplines who have often found human preferences and behavior to be quite refractory. According to these individuals, mass communications frequently are found to have minimal effects, racial prejudice resists the most painstaking interventions, expensive desegregation programs and other educational reforms do not substantially improve minority children's performance, neuroses fail to succumb to elaborate psychological therapies, and alcohol and other drug dependencies are resistant to all but the most draconian treatment.

The conclusion of relatively easy influence may stem from the unusual data base from which it emerges. Attitude change research generally involves exposing captive college student subjects, with their relatively uncrystallized attitudes, to authoritative communications in an academic atmosphere. Moreover, college students are probably unusually compliant to authority, inasmuch as they are sufficiently well socialized (or conformist) to have successfully followed the arcane directions of dozens, if not hundreds, of teachers, school administrators, parents, and test-givers over the prior 2 decades of their lives.[7] Use of such subjects and research sites, perhaps not surprisingly, thus produces data indicating that attitudes are easily changed and that the independent variables of the laboratory experience are powerful levers on that influence.[8]

Similarly, studies of conformity and obedience conducted with college students in the laboratory may give the false impression that behavior is also generally easily influenced. But their subject population is predisposed to be more compliant, and their atmosphere more authoritative, than is usually true for the general population in its many natural habitats. Distortions here might be of even more consequence inasmuch as the conformity studies of Asch, Milgram, Zimbardo, and others have been among the most widely publicized of all sociopsychological findings.[9]

Attitude-Behavior Inconsistency

Another widely accepted contention is that attitudes only weakly control behavior. However, much evidence indicates that attitude-behavior consistency is substantially enhanced when attitudinal preferences are strong or nonconflicted (Kelley & Mirer, 1974; Norman, 1975), when the attitude is based on relatively more information (Davidson, Yantis, Norwood, & Montano, 1985) or direct experience with the attitude object (Fazio & Zanna, 1981), or when the subject has a vested interest in the issue (Sivacek & Crano, 1982).

Focusing research attention on students, whose attitudinal dispositions, among other

[7]A most useful earlier review of research on "the subject role" in psychological experiments, by Weber and Cook (1972), similarly singles out the *faithful subject* and *apprehensive subject* roles as threats to the validity of laboratory experiments. Their discussion touches on subject selection biases only in passing.

[8]Hovland (1959) earlier noted a number of features of laboratory situations that made attitude change much easier to accomplish there than in the field. The present article should be viewed as following in the same vein, developing certain implications of his argument in greater detail, and adding the fcous on subject selection in particular.

[9]Replications by Crutchfield (1955) and Milgram (1974) put some boundaries on this point. See note 5.

things, are not yet at full strength because they are still developing and are based in relatively poor information and little direct experience, is bound therefore to underestimate the general level of consistency between attitudes and behavior. Moreover, for the reasons given earlier, the environmental press may be stronger in an academic laboratory situation than in most natural habitats, further diminishing the role of such predispositions as attitudes. This is not to argue that attitudes and behavior are invariably highly consistent. But the conventional wisdom has been, I think, that attitudes and behavior are generally not consistent, which is probably overdrawn because of unrepresentative subject populations and research settings (among others, see Schuman & Johnson, 1976).

Self-Perception

Self-perception research has suggested that people frequently arrive at judgments about their own attitudes on the basis of external cues (the situation and their overt behavior), rather than on the basis of introspective access to their true internal attitudes. Sometimes this conclusion has been tempered by suggesting that this process may occur primarily when internal cues are weak (e.g., Bem, 1972). This qualification has, however, received much less attention than assertions that the self-perception process is quite general. As anyone who has lectured on this material knows, the strong form of the assertion is usually received as quite startlingly fresh and original, probably because it so completely violates our own subjective experience of acting on the basis of our introspection.

There is now substantial evidence, however, that these self-perception effects may occur only when the subject has very weak prior attitudes. Chaiken and Baldwin (1981) found that significant self-perception effects occurred only among subjects with poorly defined prior attitudes; Wood (1982) found the same among those who had engaged in relatively few prior relevant behaviors; and Taylor (1975) found the same when the behavior had no important consequences. According to this research, then, the self-perception phenomenon may occur mainly when people have relatively uncrystallized prior attitudes on the issue in question. Its ubiquity in everyday life may not be as great as it might seem from social psychological experiments, then. These are conducted almost exclusively on students who have generally rather uncrystallized attitudes. They also ordinarily use attitude objects that elicit only mild preferences, presenting alternatives that are novel, artificial, or quite similar.

Drawing subjects from such a narrow age range also prevents our investigating the determinants of life stage differences in attitude crystallization. For example, informational mass, information-processing skills and social support all are likely to vary systematically with life stage (see Sears, 1981, 1983), but assessing their effects would require sampling quite different life stages.

UNINTEGRATED ATTITUDES

If late adolescents' attitudes tend to be relatively uncrystallized and if they have a less than fully formulated self in other respects as well, it is also likely that these attitudes will not be as integrated into other aspects of their personalities as they will prove to be later in life. Early postwar research on anti-Semitism, racial prejudice, and attitude change, heavily influenced by psychoanalytic theory, often viewed these as firmly rooted in chronic personality predispositions (Adorno et al., 1950; Allport, 1954; Sarnoff, 1960). Data for the most extensive work, on authoritarianism and anti-Semitism, came from adults who were given depth interviews in the psychoanalytic mode, both in treatment itself (Ackerman & Jahoda, 1950) and in extended research interviews (Adorno et al., 1950; Bettelheim & Janowitz, 1950; also see Lane, 1962; Smith, Bruner, & White, 1956). The psychodynamic insights thus generated led to the development of questionnaire measures of personality, which were initially administered to college students, because they were, as Adorno et al. (1950, pp. 21–22) explicitly acknowledged, the most available, cooperative, and easily retested of possible subjects. However, their research soon moved on to a wide variety of adult subject populations, including veterans, union members, professional women, and so on.

This research received several damaging critiques. Some criticized even this modest pilot use of college student subjects as part of a broader uneasiness about unexamined confounds of educational level with the supposed measures of personality and ethnocentrism (Hyman & Sheatsley, 1954). However, complaints that the research had neglected response sets and authoritarianism of the left demanded more controlled research. This, not surprisingly, led to a virtual avalanche of research on college students, which soon evolved into rather arid and esoteric methodological debates and, as Kirscht and Dillehay pointed out in their excellent review, simply exacerbated the sampling inadequacies of the original work: "that problem is still with us. Its crux is the use of college students for research samples . . . the results are no closer to proper generalization than ten years ago" (1967, pp. 31–32).

The same psychodynamic reasoning led also to intervention programs. Brief insight-therapy experiences were administered, mainly to student subjects to break down ego-defensive support for their prejudice (e.g., Katz, Sarnoff, & McClintock, 1956). These studies generated rather mixed findings, along with more complaints about lack of rigor (see Kiesler, Collins, & Miller, 1969).

Today personality predispositions are no longer portrayed as central determinants of social and political attitudes, either social psychology or in neighboring disciplines (see Kinder & Sears, 1985; McGuire, 1985). There are clearly several reasons for this. Whatever the merits of other considerations, it seems to me that both research and intervention on personality determinants of attitudes were doomed to failure once the move to students in the laboratory took place. Most late adolescents focus on the world of public affairs only in passing if at all. Their personalities, like their attitudes and other aspects of their selves, have not yet fully crystallized. And if passionately held social attitudes are to become imbedded in the individual's deepest personality needs, it seems most unlikely that that time-consuming and complex psychological task will ordinarily have been completed by the age of 18 or 19. Special cultural and historical circumstances may speed it up, as in Berkeley in the 1960s or in Beirut in the 1980s. But most American college sophomores, in most eras, are far from Berkeley and Beirut.

Are we content with an account of the origins of political and social attitudes that omits the role of personality dynamics? If we believe that they do play a role, is it likely that we could discover it with research on American college students in a laboratory setting?

THE ABSENCE OF SELF-INTEREST

Some potentially powerful determinants of attitudes are nearly absent in late adolescence. Limiting research to that life stage risks omitting those processes from our accounts of human nature. For example, material self-interest has been a dominant factor in many social scientists' theories of attitude formation and change, from Smith, Bentham, and Marx to today's public choice crowd. But it is even touched on by only the most comprehensively taxonomic social psychologists (see Katz, 1960) and almost never researched. Why not? Both the mean and variability of the independent variable, material self-interest, are generally very low in a college student population. Very few social and political issues bear directly on college students' lives, with the occasional exceptions of military issues or the costs and funding of higher education (e.g., Sears, Steck, Lau, & Gahart, 1983). A process that usually cannot be studied with college students probably will not prove very central to social psychologists' theories of human nature. Among adults, self-interest may not have the universal importance some claim, but it is crucial at certain important junctures (e.g., Sears & Allen, 1984; Sears & Citrin, 1985).

GROUP NORMS AND SOCIAL SUPPORT

Much early empirical research in social psychology demonstrated the great power of group norms over the individual's judgments and attitudes. Sherif's early work on social norms (1936), Newcomb's Bennington study (1943), Kurt Lewin's discussion of group decision (1947), Shils and Janowitz' (1948) research on military morale, Festinger's (1950) and associates' work on small group influence, Berelson, Lazarsfeld, and McPhee (1954) and Converse and Campbell's (1960) treatments of voting behavior, and Kelley's fine work (e.g., 1955) on the role of group loyalties in influence by mass communications, all underlined the powerful effects of primary group loyalties in everything from novel laboratory tasks to the most important political decisions.

Certainly groups remain powerful determinants of sociopolitical attitudes, as witnessed by passionate ethnic and religious rivalries in Northern Ireland and throughout the Mideast, the response of the Afghans to Russian domination and the resistance of Afrikaners to black demands, and black bloc voting in the United States. But social psychologists' accounts of attitude change today generally ignore the role of groups in attitudinal processes and, indeed, rarely even cite the important early studies just mentioned (for examples, see the excellent reviews by Petty and Cacioppo, 1981; McGuire, 1985). Even the numerous accounts of extensive direct interpersonal influence among college students alluded to earlier, such as laboratory studies of conformity, tend to describe influence by unaffiliated strangers rather than by fellow members of ongoing groups. The image of the human being is of a social isolated, atomized individual—an odd portrayal by a "social" psychology.

One reason may be that groups are peculiarly unimportant to an individual undergraduate filling out a questionnaire in an artificial laboratory situation. Partly, life stage plays a role here. Adolescents' dependency on their peer groups is well known, but their group affiliations are in fact notoriously unstable and changeable and provide very little of the long-term social support and anchorage for their judgments and attitudes that they do for more mature individuals. Disruptive changes in primary groups are more common in late adolescence and early adulthood than at any other stage of life, owing to high rates of geographical mobility, entering and/or changing work environments, status mobility, higher education, beginning a marriage or other intimate relationships, and military service (Brown, 1981; Carlsson & Karlsson, 1970). Moreover, since attitude similarity is a powerful determinant of interpersonal attraction (Byrne, 1971), people prove to be increasingly able, as they get older, to assemble attitudinally supportive family, work, and friendship groups (Newcomb, Koenig, Flacks, & Warwick, 1967; Berelson et al., 1954). Thus groups should, with age, become increasingly important sources of social support and resistance to change.

College students may be even less thoroughly tied to stable primary groups than are other late adolescents because they are more likely to have become detached from the groups of their earlier life, and they have not yet become fully embedded in the group relationships of their adulthood, such as in marriage, the workplace, neighborhood, or in recreational, fraternal, and solidarity groups. Further, the laboratory setting usually deliberately severs college students from their close friends and other group ties in order to avoid any contamination as a result of influence by them. They are usually tested individually, or at least individuated (by being given individual questionnaires in a mass testing situation), and on artificial tasks that are irrelevant to peer-group norms, again to minimize group-based resistance.

In short, group norms are very powerful influences on individuals' attitudes but probably considerably more for mature adults in their natural habitats than for college students in the laboratory. Moreover, the nature of that impact most likely also varies systematically across the life span, probably increasingly supporting resistance to change with age. So laboratory research on college students is bound to underemphasize the role of the group, in terms of both influence and social support, and overemphasize the role of purely individual factors.

STAGE-SPECIFIC ATTITUDES

Reliance on this data base may also lead to problems concerning dispositions or processes that vary substantially with life stage. For instance, life-stage or life-cycle theories of attitudes suggest that people tend to adopt certain specific attitudes at specific life stages and to reject them at other stages. The aged are thought to be especially attracted to conservatism because of their material and cognitive stake in maintaining the status quo. The middle-aged are thought to be especially self-interested, because they have hard-earned "stakes" to protect. And late adolescents are thought to be especially attracted to political radicalism, because it serves their stage-specific needs for autonomy and/or rebellion against parents and parent-surrogates, their youthful idealism, or their lack of economic responsibilities (see Glenn, 1980; Sears, 1975).

These stage-specific theories of attitudes simply cannot be assessed in a student population because of its narrow age range. Hence such life-stage theories are rarely mentioned in the standard sociopsychological treatments of attitudes, even though they are fairly common in other social sciences. To be sure, many cohort analyses have found that age differences in attitudes are more likely to be caused by generational than stage-specific factors (see Glenn, 1980; Sears, 1975). Nevertheless, these are potentially important determinants of attitude formation and change and cannot be investigated in a college student population.

COGNITIVE PROCESSES AND RATIONALITY

The oldest and most recurrent debates about attitudes and decision making revolve around the normative question: How good are they? This in turn usually breaks down into two separate questions, about the rationality of attitudes and decisions and about the relative roles of cognitive, as opposed to affective, processes. Both provoke endless definitional controversies. At a commonsensical level, though, there is probably general agreement that rationality is marked by scanning all available relevant information in an unbiased manner and combining it according to some logical decision rule. Similarly, most would probably agree that emphasizing cognitive processes leads us to focus on perception, memory, and thinking, whereas emphasizing affective processes leads us to focus on emotion, motivation (or need or drive), value, and preference.

Changing Theoretical Emphases

In my view (and certainly to oversimplify), theory and research in social psychology have shifted from a rather strong emphasis on affectively based irrationality in the immediate postwar years to today's emphasis on cognitive processes, though in both rational and irrational forms. In the social psychology of the 1940s and 1950s, attitudes were blindly learned in childhood from parents and schoolmates (Hyman, 1959; Proshansky, 1966) or were driven by powerful psychodynamic forces (Adorno et al., 1950), and they could be changed by such emotions as fear, aggression, and sexual arousal (Hovland, Janis, & Kelley, 1953; Sarnoff, 1960).

During the 1960s, as psychoanalytic and conditioning theories were losing favor, theories based on "rational" processing became more popular, but it still had a strong affective emphasis. Congruity theory (Osgood & Tannenbaum, 1955), Abelson and Rosenberg's (1958) "psycho-logic," Anderson's integration theory (1971), and linear decision-making models (Slovic, Fischoff, & Lichtenstein, 1977) all described the decision maker as combining a broad and unbiased sample of informational inputs into a decision (or attitude) using a simple and straightforward decision rule, usually a linear model. At the same time, they all described the inputs as coded in evaluative terms and did not invoke configural combinatorial principles or intervening perceptual or cognitive variables. In these senses they depicted rational decision making on the basis of affective, rather than cognitive, processes.

Today social psychology generally portrays people as dominated by cognitive processes. In some cases they process rationally as well. In the pure form of Kelley's covariance model of attribution (1967), the individual thoroughly scans available information and uses a statistical algorithm to arrive at a logical attribution. Cognitive response theory (Petty, Ostrom, & Brock, 1981) views attitude change as a simple function of the number of favorable or unfavorable cognitive responses the individual has to a persuasive communication. Ajzen and Fishbein's (1980) theory of reasoned action holds that behavior follows in a straightforward, rational way from its perceived costs and benefits. Expectancy-value or subjective expected utility theories (e.g., Feather, 1982) view the individual as scanning different possible utilities and, using a simple statistical rule, combining them according to their probabilities of occurrence to produce a rational decision. In each case, thoughtful, deliberate, self-conscious, and thus rational processing is assumed along with such cognitive variables as expectancies or subjective probabilities.

Other contemporary work is equally cognitive, but it emphasizes "irrational" errors and biases, using such concepts as salience, availability, illusory correlation, misattribution, categorization, schemas, and mindlessness (see Fiske & Taylor, 1984; Kahneman, Slovic, & Tversky, 1982; Nisbett & Ross, 1980). This approach shares a focus on judgments that are erroneous from a normative standpont and biased as a result of cognitive processes; hence, it emphasizes both cognitive and irrational processes.

In short, I would argue that the emphasis in social psychology has shifted from irrational, affective, evaluative processes to cognitive processing with a renewed interest in rational models. To be sure, there remains a lively debate within the cognitive camp, pitting rational theories against biases in information processing. Some approaches encompass both (e.g., Kelley, 1967; Taylor & Fiske, 1978). But this very controversy yields a net shift away from the irrational. In all, social psychology's portrait of the human being has changed quite markedly: no longer driven by primary drives, unconscious motives, stale repetition of childhood learning, and blind conformity, but thinking, perceiving, remembering, aware, reasoning, and often reasonable.[10]

The Role of the Data Base

Why did these changes occur? In part, no doubt, for several reasons that have nothing at all to do with social psychology's unique data base. In recent years the pendulum of intellectual fashion throughout all the behavioral sciences has cycled away from emotion-laden theories of human irrationality, such as psychoanalytic theory and behaviorism, toward more cognitive and economically rational theories. Also, because of heightened ethical sensibilities and more extensive ethical monitoring systems, many investigators have no doubt shied away from research on emotion-laden, upsetting, "hot" processes and have been en-

---

[10]Perlman (1984) has presented data documenting these shifts, based on the Social Science Citation index and research citations in textbooks. There is a recent renewal of interest in affect (e.g., Clark & Fiske, 1982; Roseman, Abelson, & Ewing, 1986; Ross & Sicoly, 1979; Smith & Ellsworth, 1985; Weiner, 1982; Zajonc, 1980). Some of these are genuine exceptions to the dominant focus on cognition, whereas others analyze affect from a cognitive point of view.

couraged to do research on safer, less controversial and troublesome, "cool" cognitive processes.

Nevertheless, I would argue that the shift to more cognitive theories has been at least abetted by the increased dependence upon college students tested in the laboratory. Here the students' life stage is probably less relevant than their unusual cognitive skills. They have been carefully preselected for these, usually by some combination of prior performance at the cognitive tasks in high school courses and cognitive tests like the Scholastic Aptitude Test (SAT). As a result, information-processing skills of the kind emphasized on academiclike tests are considerably stronger among those attending college. Similarly, the complex cognitive structures that are relevant to sociopolitical attitudes are much more common among persons with a college education (Converse, 1964).

Moreover, customary procedures in laboratory studies should produce a strongly cognitive set. Almost all studies are conducted in an actual classroom or in a rather artificial, sterile, official-seeming laboratory on a college campus. The student usually participates as a requirement for some college course. And the studies themselves resemble standard college tests, with paper-and-pencil question-and-answer formats and complex, authoritative directions. A college student in a testlike situation knows not to respond with simple evaluative preferences; rather, what is called for is paying close attention, dispassionate judgment, a search for the "right" answer, critical thinking, and close attention. Many studies use artificial or novel content, or role-playing techniques. Others have cover stories presenting them as studies of perception or learning, not of prejudice or idiosyncratic emotion. Social psychology's use of relatively well-educated subjects, selected for their superior cognitive skills, along with research sites, procedures, and tasks that promote dispassionate, academiclike information processing, should help produce empirical evidence that portrays humans as dominated by cognitive processes, rather than by strong evaluative predispositions.

These same conditions seem to me likely to allow the cognitively oriented researcher to make a fairly strong case for either rational or biased processing, depending on theoretical proclivity. On the one hand, the conditions of most psychology experiments encourage "cognitive miser"-like behavior. The incentives for participating in experiments are minimal, and students generally try to get through the task as quickly and painlessly as possible. Haste and meager incentive are likely to produce shortcuts of all kinds, among them presumably cognitive errors and biases.

On the other hand, college students are selected for their ability to be rational. They are taught the habits of rational thought quite explicitly, to treat evidence objectively and to develop conclusions from it in a logical fashion. Rational thinking is a prerequisite for success in the academic, grade-oriented world. So it should not be difficult to set up conditions in which students process information in a logical, rational way.

Some tests of the cognitive response, reasoned action, and expectancy-value theories adduce evidence of rationality from the reasons subjects give for their actions, before or after the behavior itself. But college students in particular have been exquisitely trained to rationalize conclusions when they can recall little or no real information. One of their most common tasks is to make up and write down plausible-sounding reasons for something they know they are supposed to believe but usually cannot remember in detail the reasons why. Indeed Nisbett and Wilson (1977) suggested that asking a person to give "reasons" may lead to a falsely rational portrait of the determinants of the decision because people provide the most available plausible causal schema for their behavior rather than the *real* reasons. Such highly trained confabulators would seem to provide a particularly apt subject population from which to gather data that demonstrate rational decision-making processes, or at least reasonable-sounding reasons for decisions.

EGOCENTRIC BIASES

Finally, late adolescents are considerably more egocentric and preoccupied with their own needs and desires, often overwhelmed by their own emotions, and less empathic with others than they are likely to be later in life. In parallel fashion, recent research has dramatically underlined the egocentricity of social perception. It is given to egocentric biases, such that both members of a dyad claim most responsibility for joint activities (Ross & Sicoly, 1979; Thompson & Kelley, 1981), and to self-based consensus or false consensus effects in which one's own behavior or attitudes are seen as typical of everyone else's (Ross, Greene, & House, 1977). It is possible that indeed these should be explained as cognitive biases on the grounds that the self is most salient and/or available in memory. On the other hand, virtually all this research has been done on college students (see Mullen et al., 1985). Again, humans in general are described in terms that particularly characterize the late adolescent life stage.

CONCLUSIONS

The questions raised here are twofold: How heavily has research in social psychology relied on American college students tested in artificial laboratory settings during the past 25 years? And, to what extent might primary reliance on this particular data base have led to biased substantive conclusions about human social behavior? Does social psychology's portrait of human nature match American college student's behavior in a laboratory better than the general population's behavior in its natural habitats?

Social psychology has indeed, since about 1960, relied primarily on a very narrow data base: young American college students tested in the academic laboratory. This data base is unusual in a number of respects. Such students tend, among other things, to have incompletely formulated senses of self, rather uncrystallized sociopolitical attitudes, unusually strong cognitive skills, strong needs for peer approval, tendencies to be compliant to authority, quite unstable group relationships, little material self-interest in public affairs, and unusual egocentricity. The sociopsychological laboratory also has its idiosyncracies, being a rather authoritative, academic, test-oriented setting that isolates subjects from their normal interpersonal relationships.

Some of the main emphases and conclusions of contemporary social psychology parallel these unusual features of its data base. Four examples have been presented above. First,

modern social psychology tends, in a variety of respects, to view people in general as having a weak sense of their own preferences, emotions, and abilities: They have easily dam-
aged self-esteem; they are quite compliant behaviorally; their attitudes and judgments are
easily changed; their attitudes have a minor effect on their behavior; they are ignorant of
or insensitive to their own true attitudes; and their long-standing personality predispositions are not important determinants of their sociopolitical attitudes. Second, material self-
interest, group norms, reference group identification, and social support play little role in
current research on attitudes and social cognition. Nor do stage-specific theories of attitudes, which assert that the individual's particular life stage may powerfully affect attitude
formation and change. Third, contemporary social psychology views humans as dominated
by cognitive rather than affective processes, especially emotionally based irrationalities.
And, finally, sociopsychological theories tend to treat people as highly egocentric.

In all these respects, the idiosyncracies of social psychology's rather narrow data base parallel the portrait of human nature with which it emerges. To caricature the point, contemporary social psychology, on the basis of young students preselected for special cognitive
skills and tested in isolation in an academic setting on academic tasks, presents the human
race as composed of lone, bland, compliant wimps who specialize in paper-and-pencil tests.
The human being of strong and irrational passions, of intractable prejudices, who is solidly
embedded in tightly knit family and ethnic groups, who develops and matures with age, is
not that of contemporary social psychology; it does not provide much room for such as
Palestinian guerrillas, southern Italian peasants, Winston Churchill, Idi Amin, Florence
Nightingale, Archie Bunker, Ma Joad, Clarence Darrow, or Martin Luther King.

The effects of this narrow data base on our portrait of human nature is nicely illustrated
by Steele and Southwick's (1985) meta-analysis of the effects of alcohol consumption. They
predicted, and found, that higher blood alcohol levels produced more impulsive social behavior (aggression, gambling, sexuality, etc.) when inhibitory conflict was strongest, presumably because intoxication's disinhibiting effect has its most potent effects when the
individual is most conflicted about the behavior in question. But the strongest predictor of
extremely impulsive behavior, after conflict and blood alcohol level, was subject type: Non-
college student populations produced larger alcohol effects. The difference was a major
one: Conflict and blood alcohol level (and their interaction) accounted for 20% of the variance; subject type accounted for 9% (the equivalent of a partial correlation of .30). This
study reveals that subject effects are of the nature suggested above: College students in laboratory studies behave less emotionally and impulsively than the general population. And
it indicates that the effects are potentially of major importance.

What is the recommendation? We have developed an impressive corpus of scientific
knowledge and, indeed, have learned a great deal from studying college sophomores in the
laboratory. But it may be appropriate to be somewhat more tentative about the portrait of
human nature we have developed from this data base. The specific examples given in this
article perhaps will serve to illustrate the point and raise the larger question and, in that
way, point to a research agenda that might examine the question more directly.

Most obviously, a greater effort must be made to conduct research on persons from life stages other than late adolescence. But simply testing samples of a broader age range, in my view, would not by itself be sufficient. Other changes in our conventional methodologies would have to be made. Everyone has been to school, and I suspect that even middle-aged people, separated from family and friends and confronted with testlike materials on novel and artificial topics in an academic laboratory, would often behave like college students do. Any parents who have sat at their child's desk in a third-grade classroom on Parents-Back-to-School Night can testify to the power of that situation. However, that is not how a truck driver and his cronies behave at a Teamsters meeting. Even "genuine" courtroom judges behave in an artificially rational and normative manner when tested with artificial paper-and-pencil materials by a student doing a class project, as Ebbesen and Konecni (1975) have compellingly demonstrated. My suspicion is that the biases introduced by reliance on the college sophomore in the laboratory reflect a genuine interaction of subject characteristics with the many unusual features of the academic laboratory method. Very different people, in very different behavioral settings, would need to be studied.

On a cost-benefit basis, it would not pay to convert all sociopsychological research to adult populations in more representative settings or to replicate all past findings on them. Rather, selective conversion and replication is called for, when there is reason to believe that the findings might be biased by our peculiar data base. Much is already known about the life-span trajectory of social processes, and knowledge is rapidly accumulating as various disciplines recognize the value of a life-span perspective. The question of the ecological representativeness of research behavior settings has been raised explicitly in developmental psychology, and analogous questions have been raised in cross-cultural and comparative psychology. Enough is known to allow some good guesses about where the laboratory study of college students is likely to mislead us and where it is likely not to. This article has offered a few examples, but a wider canvass, both of the life span and the full breadth of social psychology, would surely present a more complete picture.

This would require more vigilance to the possible limitations of student and/or laboratory-based data than most social psychologists have practiced in recent years. My guess, as developed above, is that such a strategy would open some of the more interesting developments of recent years to question, perhaps partly because their interest value is due to their contradicting our everyday experience (and perhaps, therefore, valid only within some rather narrow conditions). At the very least, it would lead to more complete and ecologically valid substantive conclusions. And, for the future, it might bring back into the purview of social psychology a broad range of important human phenomena, presently largely ignored, whose inclusion would allow social psychologists to speak with more authority to the full range of human social experience.

REFERENCES

Abelson, R. P., & Rosenberg, M. J. (1958). Symbolic psychologic: A model of attitudinal cognition. *Behavioral Science, 3,* 1–13.

Ackerman, N. W., & Jahoda, M. (1950). *Anti-Semitism and emotional disorder: A psychoanalytic interpretation.* New York: Harper.

Adorno, T. W., Frenkel-Brunswik, E., Levinson, D. J., & Sanford, R. N., (1950). *The authoritarian personality.* New York: Harper & Row.

Ajzen, I., & Fishbein, M. (1980). *Understanding attitudes and predicting social behavior.* Englewood Cliffs, NJ: Prentice-Hall.

Allport, G. W, (1954). *The nature of prejudice.* Garden City, NY: Doubleday Anchor.

Anderson, N. H. (1971). Integration theory and attitude change. *Psychological Review, 78,* 171–206.

Aronson, E. (Ed.). (1981). *Readings about the social animal* (3rd ed.). San Francisco: Freeman.

Atwater, E. (1983). *Adolescence.* Englewood Cliffs, NJ: Prentice-Hall.

Bem, D. J. (1972). Self-perception theory. In L. Berkowitz (Ed.), *Advances in experimental social psychology* (pp. 1–62). New York: Academic Press.

Berelson, B. R., Lazarsfeld, P. F., & McPhee, W. N. (1954). *Voting: A study of opinion formation in a presidential campaign.* Chicago: University of Chicago Press.

Berkowitz, L., & Donnerstein, E. (1982). External validity is more than skin deep: Some answers to criticisms of laboratory experiments. *American Psychologist, 37,* 245–257.

Bettelheim, B., & Janowitz, M. (1950). *Dynamics of prejudice.* New York: Harper.

Brigham, J. C., & Wrightsman, L. S. (Eds.). (1982). *Contemporary issues in social psychology* (4th ed.). Monterey, CA: Brooks/Cole.

Bronfenbrenner, U. (1977). Toward an experimental ecology of human development. *American Psychologist, 32,* 513–531.

Brown, T. (1981). On contextual change and partisan attitudes. *British Journal of Political Science, 11,* 427–447.

Brunswik, E. (1955). Representative design and probabilistic theory in a functional psychology. *Psychological Review, 62,* 193–217.

Byrne, D. (1971). *The attraction paradigm.* New York: Academic Press.

Cantril, H. (1940). *The invasion from Mars.* Princeton, NJ: Princeton University Press.

Carlsson, G., & Karlsson, K. (1970). Age, cohorts, and the generation of generations. *American Sociological Review, 35,* 710–718.

Cartwright, D. (1949). Some principles of mass persuasion: Selected findings of research on the sale of United States war bonds. *Human Relations, 2,* 253–267.

Chaiken, S., & Baldwin, M. W. (1981). Affective-cognitive consistency and the effect of salient behavioral information on the self-perception of attitudes. *Journal of Personality and Social Psychology, 41,* 1–12.

Christie, R. (1965). Some implications of research trends in social psychology. In O. Klineberg & R. Christie (Eds.), *Perspectives in social psychology* (pp. 141–152). New York: Holt, Rinehart & Winston.

Clark, M. S., & Fiske, S. T. (Eds.). (1982). *Affect and cognition: The Seventeenth Annual Carnegie Symposium on Cognition.* Hillsdale, NJ: Erlbaum.

Coch, L., & French, J. R., Jr. (1948). Overcoming resistance to change. *Human Relations, 11,* 512–532.

Conger, T. (1977). *Adolescence and youth: Psychological development.* New York: Harper & Row.

Converse, P. E. (1964). The nature of belief systems in mass publics. In D. E. Apter (Ed.), *Ideology and discontent* (pp. 206–261). New York: Free Press of Glencoe.

Converse, P. E. (1970). Attitudes and non-attitudes: Continuation of a dialogue. In E. R. Tufte (Ed.), *The quantitative analysis of social problems* (pp. 168–189). Reading, MA: Addison-Wesley.

Converse, P. E. (1976). *The dynamics of party support: Cohort-analyzing party identification.* Beverly Hills, CA: Sage.

Converse, P. E., & Campbell, A. (1960). Political standards in secondary groups. In D. Cartwright & A. Zander (Eds.), *Group dynamics* (2nd ed., pp. 300–318). Evanston, IL: Row, Peterson.

Crutchfield, R. S. (1955). Conformity and character. *American Psychologist, 10,* 191–198.

Davidson, A. R., Yantis, S., Norwood, M., & Montano, D. E. (1985). Amount of information about the attitude object and attitude-behavior consistency. *Journal of Personality and Social Psychology, 49,* 1184–1198.

Deutsch, M., & Collins, M. E. (1951). *Interracial housing: A psychological evaluation of a social experiment.* Minneapolis: University of Minnesota Press.

Douvan, E., & Adelson, J. (1966). *The adolescent experience.* New York: Wiley.

Duval, S., & Wicklund, R. A. (1972). *A theory of objective self-awareness.* New York: Academic Press.

Ebbesen, E. B., & Konecni, V. J. (1975). Decision making and information integration in the courts: The setting of bail. *Journal of Personality and Social Psychology, 32,* 805–821.

Erikson, E. H. (1963). *Childhood and society* (2nd ed.). New York: Norton.

Fazio, R. H., & Zanna, M. P. (1981). Direct experience and attitude-behavior consistency. In L. Berkowitz (Ed.), *Advances in experimental social psychology* (Vol. 14). New York: Academic Press.

Feather, N. T. (Ed.). (1982). *Expectations and actions in expectancy-value models in psychology.* Hillsdale, NJ: Erlbaum.

Festinger, L. (1950). Informal social communication. *Psychological Review, 57,* 271–282.

Festinger, L. (1954). A theory of social comparison processes. *Human Relations, 7,* 117–140.

Festinger, L. (1957). *A theory of cognitive dissonance.* Evanston, IL: Row, Peterson.

Festinger, L., & Carlsmith, J. M. (1959). Cognitive consequences of forced compliance. *Journal of Abnormal and Social Psychology, 58,* 203–210.

Festinger, L., Schachter, S., & Back, K. (1950). *Social pressures in informal groups: A study of a housing project.* New York: Harper.

Findley, M., & Cooper, H. (1981). Introductory social psychology testbook citations: A comparison in five research areas. *Personality and Social Psychology Bulletin, 7,* 173–176.

Fiske, S., & Taylor, S. (1984). *Social cognition.* Reading, MA: Addison-Wesley.

Freedman, J. L., Carlsmith, J. M., & Sears, D. O. (Eds.). (1971). *Readings in social psychology.* Englewood Cliffs, NJ: Prentice-Hall.

Fried, S. B., Gumpper, D. C. & Allen, J. C. (1973). Ten years of social psychology: Is there a growing commitment to field research? *American Psychologist, 28,* 155–156.

Glenn, N. D. (1980). Values, attitudes, and beliefs. In O. G. Brim, Jr., & J. Kagan (Eds.), *Constancy and change in human development* (pp. 596–640). Cambridge, MA: Harvard University Press.

Higbee, K. L., Lott, W. J., & Graves, J. P. (1976). Experimentation and college students in social-personality research. *Personality and Social Psychology Bulletin, 2,* 239–241.

Higbee, K. L., Millard, R. J., & Folkman, J. R. (1982). Social psychology research during the 1970s: Predominance of experimentation and college students. *Personality and Social Psychology Bulletin, 8,* 180–183.

Higbee, K. L., & Wells, M. G. (1972). Some research trends in social psychology during the 1960s. *American Psychologist, 27,* 963–966.

Hovland, C. I. (1959). Reconciling conflicting results derived from experimental and survey studies of attitude change. *American Psychologist, 14,* 8–17.

Hovland, C. I., Janis, I. L., & Kelley, H. H. (1953). *Communication and persuasion.* New Haven, CT: Yale University Press.

Hovland, C. I., Lumsdaine, A. A., & Sheffield, F. D. (1949). *Experiments on mass communication.* Princeton, NJ: Princeton University Press.

Hyman, H. (1959). *Political socialization.* Glencoe, IL: Free Press.

Hyman, H. H., & Sheatsley, P. B. (1954). The authoritarian personality: A methodological critique. In R. Christie & M. Jahoda (Eds.), *Studies in the scope and method of the authoritarian personality* (pp. 50–122). Glencoe, IL: Free Press.

Jennings, M. K., & Markus, G. B. (1984). Partisan orientations over the long haul: Results from the three-wave political socialization panel study. *American Political Science Review, 78,* 1000–1018.

Jennings, M. K., & Niemi, R. G. (1981). *Generations and politics.* Princeton, NJ: Princeton University Press.

Kahneman, D., Slovic, P., & Tversky, A. (Eds.). (1982). *Judgment under uncertainty: Heuristics and biases.* New York: Cambridge University Press.

Katz, D. (1960). The functional approach to the study of attitudes. *Public Opinion Quarterly, 24,* 163–204.

Katz, D., Sarnoff, I., & McClintock, C. (1956). Ego defense and attitude change. *Human Relations, 9,* 27–46.

Kelley, H. H. (1955). Salience of membership and resistance to change of group-anchored attitudes. *Human Relations, 8,* 275–289.

Kelley, H. H. (1967). Attribution theory in social psychology. In D. Levine (Ed.), *Nebraska Symposium on Motivation* (pp. 192–238). Lincoln: University of Nebraska Press.

Kelley, S., Jr., & Mirer, T. W. (1974). The simple act of voting. *American Political Science Review, 68,* 572–591.

Kiesler, C. A., Collins, B. E., & Miller, N. (1969). *Attitude change: A critical analysis of theoretical approaches.* New York: Wiley.

Kinder, D. R., & Sears, D. O. (1985). Public opinion and political action. In G. Lindzey & E. Aronson (Eds.), *Handbook of social psychology* (3rd ed., pp. 659–741). New York: Random House.

Kirkpatrick, S. A. (1976). Aging effects and generational differences in social welfare attitude constraint in the mass public. *Western Political Quarterly, 29,* 43–58.

Kirscht, J. P., & Dillehay, R. C. (1967). *Dimensions of authoritarianism.* Lexington: University of Kentucky Press.

Lane, R. E. (1962). *Political ideology: Why the American common man believes what he does.* New York: Free Press.

Lazarsfeld, P. F., Berelson, B., & Gaudet, H. (1948). *The people's choice* (2nd ed.). New York: Columbia University Press.

Lewin, K. (1947). Group decision and social change. In T. M. Newcomb & E. L. Hartley (Eds.), *Readings in social psychology* (pp. 459–473). New York: Holt.

Lipset, S. M., & Raab, E. (1978). *The politics of unreason* (2nd ed.). Chicago: The University of Chicago Press.

Loewenberg, P. (1971). The psychohistorical origins of the Nazi youth cohort. *The American Historical Review, 76,* 1457–1502.

Markus, G. B. (1979). The political environment and the dynamics of public attitudes: A panel study. *American Journal of Political Science, 23,* 338–359.

McGuire, W. J. (1985). Attitudes and attitude change. In G. Lindzey & E. Aronson (Eds.), *Handbook of social psychology, Vol. II* (3rd ed., pp. 223–346). New York: Random House.

Merton, R. K., & Kitt, A. S. (1950). Contributions to the theory of reference-group behavior. In R. K. Merton & P. F. Lazarsfeld (Eds.), *Continuities in social research: Studies in the scope and method of "The American soldier"* (pp. 40–105). Glencoe, IL: Free Press.

Milgram, S. (1974). *Obedience to authority.* New York: Harper & Row.

Miller, J. G. (1984). Culture and the development of everyday social explanation. *Journal of Personality and Social Psychology, 46,* 961–978.

Mueller, J. E. (1973). *War, presidents, and public opinion.* New York: Wiley.

Mullen, B., Atkins, J. L., Champion, D. S. Edwards, D. H., Hardy, D., Story, J. E., & Vanderklok, M. (1985). The false consensus effect: A meta-analysis of 115 hypothesis tests. *Journal of Experimental Social Psychology, 21,* 262–283.

Newcomb, T. M. (1943). *Personality and social change*. New York: Dryden Press.

Newcomb, T. M., Koenig, K. E. Flacks, R., & Warwick, D. P. (1967). *Persistence and change: Bennington College and its students after 25 years*. New York: Wiley.

Nisbett, R., & Ross, L. (1980). *Human inference: Strategies and shortcomings of social judgment*. Englewood Cliffs, NJ: Prentice-Hall.

Nisbett, R. E., & Wilson, T. D. (1977). Telling more than we can know: Verbal reports on mental processes. *Psychological Review, 84*, 231–259.

Norman, R. (1975). Affective-cognitive consistency, attitudes, conformity, and behavior. *Journal of Personality and Social Psychology, 32*, 83–91.

Osgood, C. E., & Tannenbaum, P. (1955). The principle of congruity and the prediction of attitude change. *Psychological Review, 62*, 42–55.

Perlman, D. (1984). Recent developments in personality and social psychology: A citation analysis. *Personality and Social Psychology Bulletin, 10*, 493–501.

Petty, R. E., & Cacioppo, J. T. (1981). *Attitudes and persuasion: Classic and contemporary approaches*. Dubuque, IA: Wm. C. Brown.

Petty, R. E., Ostrom, T. M., & Brock, T. C. (1981). Historical foundations of the cognitive response approach to attitudes and persuasion. In R. E. Petty, T. M. Ostrom, & T. C. Brock (Eds.), *Cognitive responses in persuasion* (pp. 5–29), Hillsdale, NJ: Erlbaum.

Potter, J. (1981). The development of social psychology: Consensus, theory and methodology in the *British Journal of Social and Clinical Psychology*. *British Journal of Social Psychology, 20*, 249–258.

Proshansky, H. M. (1966). The development of intergroup attitudes. In L. W. Hoffman & M. L. Hoffman (Eds.), *Review of child development research* (Vol. 2, pp. 311–371). New York: Russell Sage Foundation.

Proshansky, H. M., & Seidenberg, B. (Eds.). (1965). *Basic studies in social psychology*. New York: Holt, Rinehart & Winston.

Roseman, I., Abelson, R. P., & Ewing, M. F. (1986). Emotion and political cognition: Emotional political communication. In R. R. Lau & D. O. Sears (Eds.), *Political cognition: The 19th Annual Carnegie Symposium on Cognition* (pp. 279–294). Hillsdale, NJ: Erlbaum.

Ross, L., Greene, D., & House, P. (1977). The "false consensus effect": An egocentric bias in social perception and attribution processes. *Journal of Experimental Social Psychology, 13*, 279–301.

Ross, M., & Sicoly, F. (1979). Egocentric biases in availability and attribution. *Journal of Personality and Social Psychology, 37*, 322–336.

Rubenstein, C. (1983, July). Psychology's fruit flies. *Psychology Today*, pp. 83–84.

Sarnoff, I. (1960). Reaction formation and cynicism. *Journal of Personality, 28*, 129–143.

Schachter, S., & Singer, J. E. (1962). Cognitive, social and physiological determinants of emotional state. *Psychological Review, 69*, 379–399.

Schultz, D. D. (1969). The human subject in psychology research. *Psychological Bulletin, 72*, 214–228.

Schuman, H., & Johnson, M. P. (1976). Attitudes and behavior. *Annual Review of Sociology, 2*, 161–207.

Sears, D. O. (1969). Political behavior. In G. Lindzey & E. Aronson (Eds.), *Handbook of social psychology* (Vol. 5, rev. ed., pp. 315–458). Reading, MA: Addison-Wesley.

Sears, D. O. (1975). Political socialization. In F. I. Greenstein & N. W. Polsby (Eds.), *Handbook of political science* (Vol. 2, pp. 92–153). Reading, MA: Addison-Wesley.

Sears, D. O. (1981). Life stage effects upon attitude change, especially among the elderly. In S. B. Kiesler, J. N. Morgan, & V. K. Oppenheimer (Eds.), *Aging: Social change* (pp. 183–204). New York: Academic Press.

Sears, D. O. (1983). The persistence of early political predispositions: The roles of attitude object and life stage. In L. Wheeler & P. Shaver (Eds.), *Review of personality and social psychology* (Vol. 4, pp. 79–116). Beverly Hills: Sage.

Sears, D. O., & Allen, H. M., Jr. (1984). The trajectory of local desegregation controversies and Whites' opposition to busing. In N. Miller & M. B. Brewer (Eds.), *Groups in contact: The psychology of desegregation* (pp. 123–151). Orlando, FL: Academic Press.

Sears, D. O., & Citrin, J. (1985). *Tax revolt: Something for nothing in California* (Enlarged ed.). Cambridge, MA: Harvard University Press.

Sears, D. O., Steck, L., Lau, R. R., & Gahart, M. T. (1983). *Attitudes of the post-Vietnam generation toward the draft and American military policy*. Paper presented at the annual meeting of the International Society of Political Psychology, Oxford, England.

Shanks, J. M., & Miller, W. E. (1985). *Policy direction and performance evaluation: Complementary explanations of the Reagan elections*. Paper presented at the annual meeting of the American Political Science Association, New Orleans, LA.

Sherif, M. (1936). *The psychology of social norms*. New York: Harper.

Shils, E. A., & Janowitz, M. (1948). Cohesion and disintegration in the Wehrmacht in World War II. *Public Opinion Quarterly, 12,* 280–315.

Sivacek, J., & Crano, W. D. (1982). Vested interest as a moderator of attitude-behavior consistency. *Journal of Personality and Social Psychology, 43,* 210–221.

Slovic, P., Fischhoff, B., & Lichtenstein, S. (1977). Behavioral decision theory. *Annual Review of Psychology, 28,* 1–39.

Smart, R. G. (1966). Subject selection bias in psychological research. *The Canadian Psychologist, 7a,* 115–121.

Smith, C. A., & Ellsworth, P. C. (1985). Patterns of cognitive appraisal in emotion. *Journal of Personality and Social Psychology, 48,* 813–838.

Smith, M. B., Bruner, J. S., & White, R. W. (1956). *Opinions and personality*. New York: Wiley.

Steele, C. M., & Southwick, L. (1985). Alcohol and social behavior I: The psychology of drunken excess. *Journal of Personality and Social Psychology, 48,* 18–34.

Steiner, I. D., & Fishbein, M. (Eds.). (1965). *Current studies in social psychology*. New York: Holt, Rinehart.

Stouffer, S. A., Suchman, E. A., DeVinney, L. C., Star, S. A., & Williams, R. M., Jr. (1949). *The American soldier: Adjustment during army life*. New York: Wiley.

Swanson, G. E., Newcomb, T. M., & Hartley, E. L. (Eds.). (1952). *Readings in social psychology* (rev. ed.). New York: Holt.

Taylor, S. E. (1975). On inferring one's attitudes from one's behavior: Some delimiting conditions. *Journal of Personality and Social Psychology, 31,* 126–131.

Taylor, S. E., & Fiske, S. T. (1978). Salience, attention, and attribution: Top of the head phenomena. In L. Berkowitz (Ed.), *Advances in experimental social psychology* (Vol. II, pp. 249–288). New York: Academic Press.

Thompson, S. C., & Kelley, H. H. (1981). Judgments of responsibility for activities in close relationships. *Journal of Personality and Social Psychology, 41,* 469–477.

Weber, S. J., & Cook, T. D. (1972). Subject effects in laboratory research: An examination of subject roles, demand characteristics, and valid inferences. *Psychological Bulletin, 77,* 273–295.

Weiner, B. (1982). The emotional consequences of causal attributions. In M. S. Clark & S. T. Fiske (Eds.), *Affect and cognition: The Seventeenth Annual Carnegie Symposium on Cognition* (pp. 185–209). Hillsdale, NJ: Erlbaum.

Wood, W. (1982). Retrieval of attitude-relevant information from memory: Effects on susceptibility to persuasion and on intrinsic motivation. *Journal of Personality and Social Psychology, 42,* 798–810.

Wrightsman, L. S., & Brigham, J. C. (Eds.). (1973). *Contemporary issues in social psychology* (2nd ed.). Monterey, CA: Brooks/Cole.

Zajonc, R. B. (1980). Feeling and thinking: Preferences need no inferences. *American Psychologist, 35,* 151–175.

THINKING CRITICALLY AND APPLYING YOUR KNOWLEDGE

1. How does Sears characterize American undergraduates enrolled in introductory psychology classes? Based on your experience in psychology classes, how accurate is Sears's description of college students? Are there any elements of Sears's description that you disagree with? If so, why?

2. Sears suggests that college students are appropriate subjects for studying some topics and inappropriate for other topics. What are two research topics that could reasonably be studied with college students? What are two topics that require non-college students as subjects? Explain your answers.

3. According to Sears, what are some of the problems of studying human behavior in laboratory settings rather than in "natural" settings? Give specific examples.

4. If you have ever been a participant in a psychology experiment, describe that experience. How did you feel when you were in the research room? Did you answer questions fully and honestly? Did you wonder what the researcher was trying to find out? Do you think your behavior as a "subject" was characteristic of your behavior in other settings? Do you think your parents or other older adults would have responded as you did?

5. We are all consumers of psychological research: We often hear studies described in the news or read about research findings in magazines. But unless we pay attention to the research methods used, we may fail to distinguish between solid research and "pop psychology." Based on the Sears article, what issues should you consider in evaluating the quality or usefulness of a psychology study?

CHAPTER 3

"MOST OF THE SUBJECTS WERE WHITE AND MIDDLE CLASS": TRENDS IN PUBLISHED RESEARCH ON AFRICAN AMERICANS IN SELECTED APA JOURNALS, 1970–1989

Sandra Graham

Psychologists who study the impact of culture on human experience recognize the importance of basing psychological theory on diverse samples. It appears, however, that researchers often fall short of this goal. In the previous chapter, Sears warned about the dangers of basing social psychological research on college students studied in laboratory settings. In this more recent article, Sandra Graham raises concerns about research based almost exclusively on White, middle-class people. Graham analyzed the racial background of participants in all psychological research published in six major psychology journals during the 1970s and 1980s. Graham concludes that only a very small percentage of all articles (3.6%) include African-American subjects, and the representation of African Americans in psychology journals has actually declined from 1970 to the present.

ABSTRACT: *Six APA journals* (Developmental Psychology, Journal of Applied Psychology, Journal of Consulting and Clinical Psychology, Journal of Counseling Psychology, Journal of Educational Psychology, *and* Journal of Personality and Social Psychology) *were content analyzed for the presence of empirical articles on African Americans during the 1970–1989 publication period. The analysis revealed a declining representation of African-American research in the six journals. In addition, the empirical literature that does exist was found to be lacking in methodological rigor, as defined by characteristics such as the reporting of the socioeconomic status of subjects and experimenter race. Explanations for the decline were suggested, and recommendations were proposed for alleviating the growing marginalization of African-American research in the journals of mainstream psychology.*

With regard to the study of African Americans, academic psychologists face serious challenges as the 1990s unfold. This is a time when social concerns demand increased understanding of the psychological functioning of Black Americans, and pedagog-

Source: Reprinted from *American Psychologist, 47*(5), (1992), 629–639. Copyright © 1992 by the American Psychological Association. Reprinted by permission.

ical needs call for cultural diversity in our academic curricula. As difficult and complex as these challenges are, they are not likely to be met without a strong empirical literature on African Americans from which psychologists can draw. It therefore seems appropriate to stop and take stock of the status of African-American research in the journals of mainstream psychology.

In this article, I will argue that there has been a growing exclusion of research on African Americans in some of the major journals of our discipline, and this has resulted in a shrinking empirical base from which to pursue the challenges stated above. Just as mainstream psychology was once accused of being "womanless" (see Crawford & Marecek, 1989), so too in the 1990s it is in danger of becoming "raceless." This state of affairs has serious intellectual and pedagogical implications for the discipline that have not, in my judgment, been adequately acknowledged.

To document the status of African-American research in mainstream psychology, I conducted a content analysis of six American Psychological Association (APA) journals for the presence of empirical articles on African Americans. Four journals publishing primarily basic research were first selected, each representative of one of the subdisciplines of psychology most likely to have sustained an intellectual focus and supported empirical literature on issues of race. These subdisciplines are clinical, developmental, educational, and social/personality (Evans & Whitfield, 1988; Hall, Evans, & Selice, 1989). From these fields, the publications chosen for analysis were *Journal of Consulting and Clinical Psychology* (*JCCP*), *Developmental Psychology* (*DP*), *Journal of Educational Psychology* (*JEP*), and *Journal of Personality and Social Psychology* (*JPSP*). Because these journals are among the most respected in their respective subdisciplines (e.g., J. M. Jones, 1983; Peery & Adams, 1981), they represent good sources for examining both the visibility and credibility of empirical research on a given topic. Although skeptics may question whether empirical journals are the best indicator of a discipline's intellectual focus, there can be little doubt that these journals depict the current zeitgeist, mirror the scholarly interests of our academic leadership, and disseminate the products of what funding agencies deem worthy of support.

It could be argued, of course, that basic research journals concerned with so-called universal principles of human behavior might be less likely to publish research on African Americans than those oriented more toward application. To examine this possibility and to ensure a broader sampling of journals, two APA publications with a more applied research focus were included in the analysis. Selected from this category were *Journal of Counseling Psychology* (*JCP*), which publishes clinical research specific to the field of counseling process and intervention, and *Journal of Applied Psychology* (*JAP*), which is devoted to applied work in any subdiscipline of psychology except clinical.

The APA publishes 16 journals devoted to the reporting of empirical research in particular subdisciplines, and the 6 selected here represent approximately 50% of the APA's annual empirical output, measured in terms of total articles and pages published ("Summary Report of Journal Operations," 1991). Although there are many non-APA publications that feature research on ethnic minorities and therefore might well have been included in a content analysis of African-American research, I chose to focus on the journals of psychology's major organization, whose members are the intended audience for this article. Thus the analysis is a representative rather than exhaustive survey of the status of African-American research in mainstream psychology.

The representation of research on African Americans in the six APA journals was explored in two ways. The journals were first examined for the presence of studies on African-American subjects, and total counts were tabulated. Because my interest was in publication *trends*, as well as the current status of research, the journals were examined over a 20-year period beginning in 1970. This appeared to be a reasonable starting point inasmuch as the social unrest of the 1960s stimulated psychologists to turn their attention toward the study of socially relevant topics, particularly ethnic minority groups (see Caplan & Nelson, 1973).

Next, studies on African Americans were further examined for specific content and for selected methodological features that are pertinent to empirical research on Blacks, yet general enough for an analysis covering the range of journals and topics of psychology sampled here. Specifically, I was interested in how many studies were conducted within a comparative racial framework and whether or not socioeconomic status (SES) of subjects and race of experimenter (E; examiner, therapist) were reported. Whether such investigations take place, for example, in the laboratory or in the workplace or entail basic versus applied issues, questions can be raised about their methodological soundness and the validity of their findings if African Americans are studied only in terms of how they compare with Whites, if SES is confounded with race, or if Black subjects are tested only by White experimenters. (These issues will be further elaborated in the Results section.) In sum, the two broad goals of the journal content analysis were based on the belief that understanding the status of African-American research in mainstream psychology involves issues of both quantity (e.g., How large is the literature?) and quality (e.g., How can we ascertain its relative merit?).

Before launching into the specifics of the analysis, it might be useful to anchor our expectations about quantity by considering what would constitute an adequate representation of research on African Americans in APA journals. More specifically, if one were to calculate the percentage of African-American articles relative to the total empirical output of the six target journals during the past 20 years, within what range of values would this percentage be expected to fall? Perhaps the best source of information for answering this question can be found in the results of prior journal content analyses on this topic. J. M. Jones (1983) analyzed seven social psychology journals, including *JPSP*, for the presence of race-relevant articles during the 1968–1980 publication period, and McLoyd and Randolph (1984) surveyed 21 journals, including *DP*, *JEP*, and *JPSP*, for empirical articles on African-American children between 1973 and 1975. McLoyd and Randolph (1985) conducted a similar analysis of articles published in *Child Development* from 1936 to 1980. In addition, Ponterotto (1988) examined the *Journal of Counseling Psychology* for ethnic minority research over the 1976–1986 decade. Extrapolating from data reported by J. M. Jones (1983, Table 2), roughly 5% of the articles published in *JPSP* between 1968 and 1980 were race relevant. About the same percentages emerge for research on African-American children in

DP and JEP during the 1973–1975 time period (McLoyd & Randolph, 1984, Table 2). Similarly, Ponterotto (1988, Table 1) reported that close to 6% of the articles in *JCP* dealt with ethnic minority research, with African Americans being the most frequently studied ethnic group. Thus if we are guided by prior quantitative summaries of trends in published research, we might expect at least 5% of the articles published in four of the six target journals to be about African Americans.

This estimate assumes that there have been no discernible changes in publication trends in recent years. One might ask, however, whether the representation of African Americans in mainstream psychology has increased, decreased, or remained relatively constant over the past decade or so. The 20-year time period over which the journals were examined allowed this question to be explored.

METHOD

The data for this study consisted of the empirical articles published in *Developmental Psychology*, *Journal of Applied Psychology*, *Journal of Consulting and Clinical Psychology*, *Journal of Counseling Psychology*, *Journal of Educational Psychology*, and *Journal of Personality and Social Psychology* between 1970 and 1989. Excluded from consideration were monographs, review articles, essays, commentaries, rejoinders, or other non-data-analytic reports. Because the goal of this article was to examine research specifically *about* African Americans, two additional selection criteria were imposed. First, empirical articles that addressed race-relevant issues (i.e., prejudice, stereotyping) were discounted if the subjects were not African American. Thus, for example, a number of articles on the racial attitudes of Whites toward Blacks, published largely in *JPSP* during the time period under review, were not included in the total count. Although one could certainly argue that studies of racial attitudes and prejudice are pertinent to understanding the psychological functioning of African Americans, they were deemed less central to this analysis, which focused on the subjective experiences of Black research participants. Second, articles that included African Americans as subjects were not counted unless (a) the researchers specifically stated that Blacks were the population of interest or (b) the data were analyzed by race. These selection criteria are somewhat more conservative than those adopted by J. M. Jones (1983) in his survey of seven social psychological journals and by McLoyd and Randolph (1984, 1985) in their content analyses of journals publishing research on African-American children. J. M. Jones included any journal article that was concerned with racial issues, even when all of the subjects were White, and McLoyd and Randolph counted all articles in which at least 10% of the sample was African American, whether or not the racial variable was analyzed.

To identify those articles that fit these criteria, I read the titles and abstracts and scanned the method sections of all empirical articles published in the six journals during the 20 years under review. Articles about African Americans, identified on the basis of these criteria, were then retrieved, read in detail, and coded for content (topics covered) as well as for selected methodological characteristics (number of comparative racial studies, SES of subjects, and experimenter race). To ensure reliability of the selection and coding procedures, five randomly selected volumes of each journal were evaluated by a graduate research assistant trained to code the articles according to the same criteria. Following the procedures of McLoyd and Randolph (1984, 1985), reliabilities were calculated as the number of studies (characteristics) identified by both coders, divided by the number identified by either coder. For selection of empirical articles on African Americans, interrater agreement exceeded .95. Reliabilities for coding of the topics covered and methodological characteristics ranged from .86 to .98, indicating substantial agreement between the two raters.

RESULTS AND DISCUSSION

A total of 14,542 empirical articles were published in the six target journals between 1970 and 1989 (see Table 1). With 12 issues a year, *JPSP* produced the greatest number of articles (4,037), followed by *JCCP* (2,946) and *DP* (2,399), the two bimonthly publications. The three remaining journals began as bimonthlies but became quarterly publications in the mid-1980s and therefore accounted for the fewest empirical articles: *JAP* (1,810), JEP (1,768), and *JCP* (1,582).[1]

Table 1 displays the number and percentage of articles on African Americans in each journal across four 5-year publication periods. Turning first to overall patterns in the bottom rows, the entries in the column of totals show that 526 articles on African Americans were published between 1970 and 1989, or 3.6% of these journals' entire empirical output. This is not altogether surprising, in light of the less conservatively based estimates in the range of 5% inferred from the earlier journal content analyses by J. M. Jones (1983), McLoyd and Randolph (1984), and Ponterotto (1988). It nonetheless remains disheartening to uncover such a poor representation of studies on African Americans across this range of APA journals and particular time period sampled.

Rise and Fall of Research on African Americans

It has been documented that the overall percentage of studies on African Americans is low (3.6%). But how has this percentage fluctuated during the past 20 years, both within and across journals? Here the data in Table 1 are particularly revealing. Most striking is the steady decrease in both the number and percentage of African-American articles across the four publication periods: from 203 articles (5.2%) in 1970–1974 to 65 articles (2.0%) in 1985–1989. Furthermore, this pattern of decline is evident in all of the target journals except *JCP*, in which there appeared to be some recovery by the fourth publication period. Chi-square tests confirmed that there were significant variations in the frequency of African-American articles across the four publication periods for five of the six journals: JEP, χ^2 (3, N = 108) = 16.74; JAP, χ^2 (3, N = 77) = 16.56; DP, χ^2 (3, N = 111) = 46.87; JCCP, χ^2 (3, N = 90) = 13.64; and JPSP, χ^2 (3, N = 65) = 22.93 (all *ps* < .01).

---

[1] *Journal of Applied Psychology* resumed its status as a bimonthly publication in 1989.

TABLE 1

Number and Percentage of Empirical Articles on African Americans in Six APA Journals, Across Four Publication Periods

Journal	Publication period				
	1970–1974	1975–1979	1980–1984	1985–1989	Total
JCP					
No. of articles	446	474	363	299	1,582
No. African-American articles	26	21	12	16	75
%	5.8	4.4	3.3	5.3	4.7
JEP					
No. of articles	470	538	438	322	1,768
No. African-American articles	38	36	22	12	108
%	8.1	6.7	5.0	3.7	6.1
JAP					
No. of articles	488	532	392	398	1,810
No. African-American articles	26	30	12	9	77
%	5.3	5.6	3.1	2.3	4.3
DP					
No. of articles	724	625	521	529	2,399
No. African-American articles	58	25	14	14	111
%	8.0	4.0	2.7	2.6	4.6
JCCP					
No. of articles	816	946	626	558	2,946
No. African-American articles	25	35	19	11	90
%	3.1	3.7	3.0	2.0	3.1
JPSP					
No. of articles	969	881	1,057	1,130	4,037
No. African-American articles	30	18	14	3	65
%	3.1	2.0	1.3	0.3	1.6
Total					
Articles	3,913	3,996	3,397	3,236	14,542
African-American articles	203	165	93	65	526
%	5.2	4.1	2.7	2.0	3.6

Note. JCP = Journal of Counseling Psychology; JEP = Journal of Educational Psychology; JAP = Journal of Applied Psychology; DP = Developmental Psychology; JCCP = Journal of Consulting and Clinical Psychology; JPSP = Journal of Personality and Social Psychology.

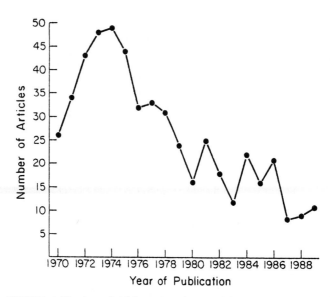

FIGURE 1 Number of African-American articles as a function of publication year, combined across six APA journals

This trend is perhaps more clearly illustrated in Figure 1, which displays the number of African-American articles in each of the 20 years between 1970 and 1989, combined over all six journals. (The same trend is exhibited when the numbers are expressed as percentages.) Figure 1 reveals a linear increase from 1970 to 1974, the year in which the greatest number (49) and percentage (5.5%) of articles were published. Thereafter these numbers and percentages steadily drop. In 1989 the six journals combined published only 11 articles (1.8%) on African Americans. This pattern of increase through the early 1970s followed by decline is similar to what J. M. Jones (1983) reported for seven social psychology journals and McLoyd and Randolph (1985) documented for *Child Development* up to 1980. Despite some increased activity in the early part of the last decade, the decrease in mainstream published research on African Americans that began in the mid-1970s has continued unabated through the 1980s.

Having documented the declining status of published research on African Americans, relative to the total empirical output in six target APA journals, I will now attend to the 526 articles that compose this African-American empirical literature. What are these studies about, and how have they been conducted? In the analyses that address these questions, my intent is to describe general topical and methodological trends in this literature, not to analyze the research findings in any particular area. There are complex issues associated with the study of specific psychological variables among African Americans that cannot (and should not) be addressed in an article of this scope. Furthermore, in the descriptive analyses that follow, the data are examined by journal but combined across publication period, inasmuch as the numbers are too small in the most recent time period to permit meaningful comparisons.

African-American Empirical Literature: Topics Covered

Among the six journals sampled, *Journal of Applied Psychology* and *Journal of Counseling Psychology* were the most specialized and therefore published articles specific to particular topical domains. Most of the 77 African-American articles in *JAP* were concerned with job training and performance (26%); occupational and vocational attitudes (21%); test bias, particularly in instruments for employment selection (17%); or leadership and managerial styles (9%). These topics are consistent with the general emphasis in *JAP* on organizational behavior. With its focus on the practice of counseling, *JCP* published 75 African-American empirical articles that dealt primarily with counselor characteristics, such as their perceived trustworthiness (35%), vocational aspirations (16%), evaluations of counseling interventions (16%), or general attitudes toward counseling (9%).

The African-American articles published in the four basic research journals, on the other hand, were concerned with the more molar topics of psychology and could therefore be classified into general content areas. The number and percentage of articles in *DP*, *JEP*, *JCCP*, and *JPSP* that dealt with these various topics are shown in Table 2.

Again, some topics appeared to be specific to particular journals. For example, African-American research on infant development was published only in *DP*, academic achievement and teacher-student interaction were topics of interest mostly to *JEP*, and studies involving clinical diagnosis or treatment of African Americans were logically the purview of *JCCP*. Within the more general topics of psychology, the most popular domains of inquiry and those represented in all of the journals, have been social behavior, particularly aggression and interracial cooperation and competition; intelligence, as assessed by standardized measures of IQ; and personality, largely studied as individual differences in locus of control, self-esteem, and psychopathology.

Because studies of intelligence and personality represent a substantial share of the research, I want to offer one general observation about these two literatures. The study of intelligence among African Americans in APA journals has almost exclusively focused on the psychometrics of IQ tests. Of the 22 articles in *JCCP*, for example, 15 (68%) were either reliability or validity studies of the Wechsler Adult Intelligence Scale (WAIS) or the Wechsler Intelligence Scale for Children (WISC). There has been a similar pattern in the study of personality. The most popular individual difference examined has been psychopathology and the instrument of choice has been the Minnesota Multiphasic Personality Inventory (MMPI). But again, the majority of this research has been psychometric in nature: Of the 31 personality studies in *JPSP* and *JCCP* combined, 17 (55%) were directly concerned with the validity and reliability of the MMPI. It is not my intent to question the importance of studies that carefully examine the psychometric properties of the WAIS, WISC, or MMPI. The research focus on measurement issues, however, has its own set of costs. Although readers of APA journals may have now been alerted to the complexities of using standardized instruments with ethnic minority populations, they have not learned very much about

TABLE 2
Number and Percentage of African-American Articles Covering a Designated Topic in Four APA Journals

	Journal							
	DP (n = 111)		JEP (n = 108)		JCCP (n = 90)		JPSP (n = 65)	
Topic	No.	%	No.	%	No.	%	No.	%
Social behavior	24	21.6	19	17.6	8	8.9	24	36.9
Intelligence	8	7.2	23	21.2	22	24.4	0	0.0
Personality	11	9.9	6	5.6	21	23.3	10	15.4
Cognition/learning	17	15.3	11	10.2	3	3.3	2	3.1
Language	11	9.9	10	9.3	0	0.0	0	0.0
Attitudes	16	14.4	1	0.9	3	3.3	14	21.5
Motivation	8	7.2	5	4.6	5	5.6	5	7.6
Anxiety/stress/coping	1	0.9	1	0.9	7	7.8	6	9.2
Infant development	9	8.1	0	0.0	0	0.0	0	0.0
Academic achievement	2	1.8	18	16.7	1	1.1	0	0.0
Teacher-student interaction	0	0.0	10	9.3	0	0.0	0	0.0
Clinical diagnosis/ treatment	0	0.0	0	0.0	15	16.7	0	0.0
Miscellaneous	4	3.6	4	3.7	5	5.6	4	6.2

Note. DP = Developmental Psychology; JEP = Journal of Educational Psychology; JCCP = Journal of Consulting and Clinical Psychology; JPSP = Journal of Personality and Social Psychology.

the processes underlying healthy personality development and competent intellectual functioning among African Americans.

Methodological Factors

How have these topics been studied in the 526 articles sampled across six APA journals? In terms of subject population, empirical studies of African Americans are typically one of two types: A psychological variable such as intelligence might be examined among Black subjects only. Thus, for example, Moore (1986) examined IQ (WISC) performance of young African-American children who had been either traditionally or transracially adopted. Such studies are labeled *intrasubcultural* by J. M. Jones (1983) and *race homogeneous* by McLoyd and Randolph (1984, 1985). Alternatively, Black subjects can be contrasted on the relevant variable with one or more other racial groups, typically Whites. Reynolds and Jensen (1983), for example, compared the subscale scores of African-American and White school-aged children on the revised WISC. This type of investigation has been classified as *cross subcultural* by J. M. Jones (1983) and *race comparative* by McLoyd and Randolph (1984, 1985).

The social and developmental journals surveyed in the earlier content analyses by J. M. Jones (1983) and McLoyd and Randolph (1984, 1985) revealed a preponderance of race-comparative studies. The same pattern prevailed for the six APA publications examined here. The first panel of data in Table 3 shows the number and percentage of African-American articles in each journal that were race comparative. Note that in all cases comparative investigations predominated, and in four of the six journals, there were about three times as many race-comparative as race-homogeneous studies.

Much criticism has been voiced about this comparative approach. Quite a few years ago, Donald Campbell (1967) warned psychologists about the risks of ethnic stereotyping, if the field were to become inundated with racial comparisons. And a number of African-American psychologists have been particularly critical of the scientific basis of a comparative racial paradigm that both reinforces interpretations of African-American behavior as deviant and ignores within-group variation (e.g., Azibo, 1988). Considering the topics examined in the APA journals sampled here and their reliance on the comparative approach, it is not at all clear, for example, that psychologists have achieved better understanding of the intellectual potential of Black children or their repertoires of adaptive social behaviors by relying on empirical literatures that simply chart their gains and losses relative to those of a White comparison group. This is further evidenced when we turn to two other methodological features relating to the quality of the research: socioeconomic status of subjects and race of experimenter.

TABLE 3
Selected Methodological Characteristics of the Articles on African Americans in Six APA Journals

		Characteristic							
		Race comp[a]		SES measure[b]		Race of E[c]		African American E[d]	
Journal	No.	No.	%	No.	%	No.	%	No.	%
DP	111	72	64.9	40	36.0	39	35.1	24	21.6
JEP	108	84	77.8	44	40.7	24	22.2	18	16.7
JCCP	90	67	74.4	20	22.2	10	11.1	9	10.0
JAP	77	60	77.9	27	35.1	13	16.9	9	11.7
JCP	75	40	53.3	29	38.7	28	37.3	26	34.7
JPSP	65	58	89.2	16	27.6	27	41.5	21	32.3
Total	526	381	72.4	176	33.5	141	26.8	107	20.3

Note: SES = socioeconomic status; E = experimenter; *DP* = *Developmental Psychology*, *JEP* = *Journal of Educational Psychology*; *JCCP* = *Journal of Consulting and Clinical Psychology*; *JAP* = *Journal of Applied Psychology*; *JCP* = *Journal of Counseling Psychology*; *JPSP* = *Journal of Personality and Social Psychology*.
[a]Number and percentage of articles that were race comparative. [b]Number and percentage of articles that reported a measure of subject SES. [c]Number and percentage of articles that reported experimenter race. [d]Number and percentage of articles including African-American experimenters.

Socioeconomic Status of Subjects. Because African Americans are overrepresented among economically disadvantaged groups in this society, researchers who make Black-White comparisons need to incorporate SES in their designs in order to disentangle race and social class effects. Furthermore, with the growing gap between the affluent and the impoverished within the population of American Blacks, it is just as important that race-homogeneous studies not err in the direction of ignoring socioeconomic distinctions between African-American subjects. Despite these obvious (and oft-stated) potential confoundings, empirical studies involving African Americans have remained remarkably insensitive to the complexities of race and social class in this society. It is evident that this is true for research published in APA journals as well, when we turn to the second panel of data in Table 3. These findings show the number and percentage of studies (race homogeneous and race comparative) in the six target journals that included a measure of subject SES. Acceptable measures included not only the standard social class indices (e.g., Hollingshead, Warner, and Duncan scales), but also indirect measures such as census data, information contained in school records, or participation in a compensatory education program, such as Headstart. Not acceptable were statements by researchers assigning social class designation based simply on their own subjective impressions about the communities from which subjects were drawn.

As Table 3 shows, fewer than one half of the African-American articles appearing in *DP*, *JEP*, *JAP*, and *JCP*, and fewer than one third of those in *JCCP* and *JPSP*, specified SES of participants in an acceptable manner. Note that *JPSP*, the journal with the greatest percentage of comparative racial articles, had the second worst showing with regard to the percentage including an SES variable.

Even among those studies that did measure SES, it was not necessarily the case that this variable was appropriately examined as a factor in the analyses. For example, in *DP* and *JEP*, in which larger percentages of studies satisfied the SES criteria, 10 of the 40 articles (25%) in *DP* and 16 of the 44 studies (36%) in *JEP* compared low-SES Blacks with either middle-SES Whites alone or to samples consisting of both low- and middle-SES Whites. There is nothing ambiguous about this pattern of findings: Race and social class have been seriously confounded in much of the African-American empirical literature published in prestigious APA journals.

Experimenter race. Yet another important methodological concern in this literature is the race of the experimenter (examiner, interviewer, therapist). By experimenter I mean the individual who actually participates in data collection, as opposed to a study's authors, whose racial identity cannot ordinarily be ascertained from the information accompanying a published article. Are these studies telling us whether African-American subjects were tested by Black or White experimenters? The third panel of data in Table 3 displays the number and percentage of studies that reported the race of the experimenter. In terms of percentages, *JPSP* and *JCP* fared somewhat better than did the other journals in this category; a number of *JPSP*'s comparative racial articles were studies of race-of-examiner effects, as were *JCP*'s studies on race of counselor. But in none of the journals did even one half of the studies mention experimenter race.

Acknowledging race of E can still pose a problem if all of the experimenters testing Black subjects are White. The data in the final panel of Table 3 show the number and percentage of articles reporting that one or more of the experimenters were African American. Comparing the third and fourth panels shows, for example, that only 22% rather than 35% of the *DP* articles, and only 32% rather than 42% of the *JPSP* studies, reported that at least some of the Black subjects were tested by Black experimenters.

Failure to take into account experimenter race is certainly an issue, whether an article is race homogeneous or race comparative. The problem is not so much that White experimenters have well-documented negative effects on African-American subjects. In fact, two reviews indicate that White experimenters do *not* negatively influence Black subjects' intellectual performance, the domain in which most of the criticism of White experimenters and examiners has been voiced (Graziano, Varca, & Levy, 1982; Sattler & Gwynne, 1982). The crux of the problem is really the unknown—given the range of experimental contexts, some novel but some frankly threatening—to which African-American subjects have been exposed. In the absence of careful controls on race of E, we simply do not know what effect a White experimenter has on an African-American child who is required, for example, to read a passage in perfect Standard English, choose between a Black and a White doll, solve a puzzle in the wake of induced failure, or realistically estimate the likelihood of going to college.

Race-comparative studies. The data in Table 3 portray particular methodological characteristics of all of the studies that compose the APA empirical literature on African Americans from 1970 through 1989. I will now take a more searching look at the methodological characteristics of those investigations that were race comparative, inasmuch as this has been the preferred mode of inquiry. Table 4 shows the comparative racial studies in each journal, analyzed by whether they met neither of the methodological criteria discussed earlier, one of the criteria (either SES or race of E), or both criteria. Thus, in this analysis, the question is as follows: If a study is race comparative, how likely is it to have systematically measured SES of subjects or included African-American experimenters?

TABLE 4
Race-Comparative Articles in Six APA Journals Meeting 0, 1, or 2 Methodological Criteria

No. of criteria	Journal											
	DP (n = 72)		JEP (n = 84)		JCCP (n = 67)		JAP (n = 60)		JPSP (n = 58)		JCP (n = 40)	
	No.	%	No.	%	No.	%	No.	%	No.	%	No.	%
0	37	51.4	46	54.8	48	71.6	34	56.7	32	55.2	15	37.5
1	32	44.4	34	40.5	19	28.4	22	36.7	21	36.2	21	52.5
2	3	4.2	4	4.8	0	0.0	4	6.7	5	8.6	4	10.0

Note: Criteria are measuring socioeconomic status of subjects and including African-American experimenters. *DP = Developmental Psychology; JEP = Journal of Educational Psychology; JCCP = Journal of Consulting and Clinical Psychology; JAP = Journal of Applied Psychology; JPSP = Journal of Personality and Social Psychology; JCP = Journal of Counseling Psychology.*

Table 4 reveals that more than one third of the race-comparative studies in each target journal failed to meet either of these methodological criteria, and not more than 10% satisfied both. Judged this way, the comparative racial literature on African Americans is lacking in methodological rigor, and this is true for all six APA journals analyzed here.

Brief Reports

One of the implications of the analyses on methodology is that researchers who study African Americans may be more guilty of sins of omission rather than sins of commission, and it is therefore essential that they provide complete descriptions of their designs and procedures. Ironically, this need runs counter to another trend observed in the representation of African-American articles in APA journals. That trend concerns a category of empirical article adopted by some journals, known as Brief Reports.

In the Instructions to Authors, Brief Reports are defined by *JCCP* as "soundly designed studies of *specialized interest or limited importance* [italics added] which cannot now be accepted as regular articles because of lack of space" (similar definitions appear in *DP* and *JEP*). Such an abbreviated article is typically one or two journal pages. No tables or figures are included, and the text consists of one continuous narrative rather than the customary divisions into Introduction, Method, Results, and Discussion. *JCCP* includes Brief Reports in every issue and has for the entire publication period under review. *DP* published them until 1981, and *JEP* began the practice with the third issue of 1987. *JCP* has always included somewhat longer articles in a Brief Reports section, but I was unable to locate any editorial statement about their purpose.[2]

Table 5 shows the number and percentage of African-American articles that have been published as Brief Reports, rather than regular articles, in *JCCP*, *DP*, *JEP*, and *JCP* during the time period in which each journal followed this procedure. One third of all articles on African Americans appearing in *JCCP* were Brief Reports, and almost as large a percentage appeared in *DP* during the 1970–1980 decade. Only eight articles on African Americans have appeared in *JEP* since the establishment of Brief Reports, but of those eight, three were published in the abbreviated format. Even with its unclear stated intent, *JCP* also published almost one fifth of its African-American articles as Brief Reports.

Naturally, I want to be cautious about making inferences concerning the causes of the pattern shown in Table 5. It is not known whether authors initially submitted their manuscripts as Brief Reports or whether they were encouraged by editors to consider this format as part of the regular article review process. But the consequences of this trend are far from ambiguous: African-American research tends to be portrayed as of marginal importance, and the readers of these articles are not able to benefit from full descriptions of methodology.

---

[2] *Journal of Applied Psychology* publishes a similar category of empirical article called Short Notes. However, in the Instructions to Authors, *JAP* defines Short Notes as studies "involving some methodological contribution or important replication." Only six such articles on African Americans were identified during the 1970–1989 publication period.

TABLE 5
Number and Percentage of African-American Articles
Published as Brief Reports

Journal	No. of articles	Brief reports	
		No.	%
JCCP	90	30	33.3
DP[a]	83	22	26.5
JCP	75	13	17.3
JEP[b]	8	3	37.5

Note: JCCP = Journal of Consulting and Clinical Psychology; DP = Developmental Psychology; JCP = Journal of Counseling Psychology; JEP = Journal of Educational Psychology.

[a]DP ceased publishing Brief Reports in 1981. [b]JEP began publishing Brief Reports in 1986 (Vol. 78, No. 3).

GENERAL DISCUSSION

African Americans have been increasingly marginalized in mainstream psychological research, as methodologically sound empirical articles on Blacks have all but vanished from the pages of major APA journals. This trend prevailed across six diverse journals, with both basic and applied research foci and over numerous individual editorships. Thus no single journal or editorial tenure can be singled out as particularly blameworthy. Why has this literature undergone such a steady decline since the early 1970s? Five possible explanations are offered, although in my view the first two are less plausible than the last three.

1. *Diminishing pool of African-American psychologists.* Psychologists often choose research topics based on their own life experiences or personal concerns. Hence, the volume of the research on African Americans might be expected to covary to some degree with the number of same-race investigators. If the number of Black doctoral psychologists has been declining over the past two decades, as popular wisdom seems to suggest, then it logically follows that the empirical fruits of their collective efforts would similarly decline. One flaw in this argument is that the recent past has *not* produced such a diminished pool of African-American doctoral psychologists. According to data compiled by APA (Kohout & Pion, 1990), during the 1977–1987 decade, the percentage of doctorates in psychology earned by African Americans remained relatively constant. In 1977, 95 (3.5%) of the new PhDs in psychology were Black, and in 1987 there were 92 (3.4%) such new graduates.[3]

---

[3] I acknowledge that there are additional complexities underlying this issue. Because clinical psychology continues to be the most popular subdiscipline among Black doctoral psychologists (Kohout & Pion, 1990), it is difficult to estimate how the African-American empirical literature has been influenced by the preferences of Black clinical psychologists to seek nonacademic positions.

Presently, of course, the waning enrollment of African-American students in all levels of higher education is well documented (see Thomas, 1987). This declining participation in the educational pipeline represents the *current* state of affairs and portends poorly for the future. But it cannot be considered a very plausible explanation for the 1970–1989 trends discussed earlier.

2. *Preference for non-APA journals.* As journals have arisen that more directly address issues pertinent to African-American psychology, these specialized publications might be viewed as more receptive and thus preferred over the mainstream APA alternatives. If this argument is correct, then one might expect to find a growing empirical focus in, for example, *Journal of Black Psychology*, the publication arm of the Association of Black Psychologists. The journal, which began in 1974, states that one of its primary goals is "to promote psychological research, theory, and writing that is for and about Blacks." Yet, only two issues a year are published, each consisting of from three to five articles. Furthermore, because the journal must serve so many functions, this small sampling of articles includes not only empirical investigations, but also literature reviews, theoretical analyses, and position papers as well. During the past 10 years, a total of 35 empirical articles appeared in the *Journal of Black Psychology*. Thus the overall number of empirical articles found in this journal is now, and always has been, relatively small.

Perhaps other mainstream journals examined in previous content analyses are perceived as more receptive. J. M. Jones (1983) reported that *Journal of Social Psychology* (*JSP*) had published the most race-relevant articles of the seven social psychology journals included in this analysis. To get a sense of whether this is still true, I scanned the titles and in some cases read abstracts of the empirical articles published in *JSP* over the last five years (1985–1989). Although the journal continues to have a strong cross-cultural focus, I identified only 13 articles, or 3.7%, that specifically were concerned with African Americans. Similarly with *Child Development*, the non-APA journal analyzed by McLoyd and Randolph (1985), scanning the titles and abstracts for the same publication period revealed 10 African-American articles, or 1.6% of that journal's total. In sum, African-American research does not appear to have found a more receptive audience in other mainstream journals. My sense is that one has to turn to the more specialized publications with an interdisciplinary focus, such as *Journal of Black Studies*, to find an adequate representation of empirical work on the psychological functioning of African Americans. Needless to say, such journals do not have the readership or the visibility of the more mainstream variety.

3. *Fears associated with conducting socially sensitive research.* There are ethical and moral risks associated with studying the psychological functioning of African Americans. Many researchers are drawn to this topic out of concern for the social problems associated with ethnic minority status in this society. Thus, for example, one may investigate intelligence because of the chronic school failure of many African-American children; aggression due to the higher incidence of violent crimes among urban Black males; helping behavior, given the negative consequences associated with welfare dependency; and so on. Often the study of such phenomena leads to unpopular findings or, even worse, to accusations of "victim blame" (Caplan & Nelson, 1973; Ryan, 1971). Many committed researchers may

be unwilling to risk the kind of reprisal leveled against Jensen (1969), for example, following the publication of his monograph on racial differences in IQ. They may instead opt for the safer alternative of scientifically acceptable, but socially noncontroversial, research topics (see Scarr, 1988; Sieber & Stanley, 1988). More often than not, such choices will foster the decision to avoid or abandon the study of African Americans.

4. *Bandwagon effects.* Over the years, some psychological topics pertinent to African Americans have been subject to "bandwagon" effects (cf. E. E. Jones, 1985). By this I mean the tendency for particular issues to rapidly emerge as timely, to dominate an empirical literature for some period, and to just as quickly fade from view. For example, the study of language in the developmental and educational journals (see Table 2) largely grew from the attention surrounding the use of the Black English Vernacular (BEV). During the early 1970s, a flurry of research studies were conducted to explore whether economically disadvantaged African-American children actually spoke a language that was structurally different from Standard English (Labov, 1972). The study of the BEV also became the rallying cry for psychologists' recognition of the "differences versus deficits" and "performance versus competence" distinctions (e.g., Baratz & Baratz, 1970; Cole & Bruner, 1971). But once these distinctions became part of the conventional wisdom of psychology, and without a strong theoretical basis for conducting the research, studies of the Black English Vernacular faded from the scene.

5. *Changes in the zeitgeist.* As reflected in their journals, the intellectual foci of the subdisciplines of psychology examined here have shifted to topics less relevant to the study of Black Americans. In recent years, developmental psychology's adoption of life-span perspectives has yielded more articles in *DP* on populations at both ends of the life cycle, but this conceptual shift has yet to embrace published research on African-American infants and older adults. Similarly, educational psychology's concern with sociocultural influences on achievement has narrowed of late, with the growing emphasis in *JEP* on the psychology of subject matter.

Perhaps the clearest example of shifts in dominant research themes that undermine the study of African Americans has occurred in social psychology. As social psychology has become increasingly cognitive, the traditional concerns of the discipline—that is, the social influences on psychological functioning—have gradually been displaced. Even a cursory glance at the titles in the Attitudes and Social Cognition section of *JPSP* reveals an increasing emphasis on information-processing metaphors in social psychology that rely on principles and methodologies borrowed from cognitive psychology. For some this may signal progress in the field; others may lament a perceived loss of identity (e.g., Carlson, 1984). But it is clear that as the intellectual focus of the subdiscipline has become the effect of priming, reaction time, or other indicators of process, the traditionally social psychological issues pertinent to the study of African Americans have receded from view. Of course, this need not (and should not) be the case. But academic psychologists in social psychology, as well as those in the other subdisciplines of the field, appear to implicitly assume that the study of basic process transcends the need to examine within- or between-group variation.

Independent of one's preferred causal explanation, the trends documented in this article do not bode well for mainstream psychology in the 1990s. Whether personal research agendas are affected by the demise of an African-American literature, as academic psychologists most of us will have to confront this issue, if for no reason other than the vociferous demands for greater diversity in the undergraduate curriculum. Diversifying the psychology curriculum is interpreted to mean more than the creation of courses for and about ethnic minorities, including African Americans. Substantive changes are also demanded in the discipline's core programs of study to eradicate what often amounts to mere token reference to the psychological functioning of these groups. Yet how will we be able to meet these challenges in the absence of a strong empirical base of research on ethnic minorities from which we can confidently draw? How will we be able to avoid oversimplifying complex topics, citing outdated findings, or perpetuating incorrect beliefs if a relevant database remains so unfamiliar and inaccessible? As an African-American psychologist, I find it disconcerting, for example, to hear and read so often in the popular press that Black children have a unique learning style or that they prefer cooperation to competition, when the empirical evidence supporting these conclusions is so thin. What we need from our major journals is a substantive African-American psychological literature that is both accurate and current. What we have instead are sets of isolated and outdated findings, often of questionable methodological soundness.

What Can Be Done?

Steps must be taken to rectify this perilous state of affairs. Much of what is needed will require major shifts in priorities of the research enterprise, such as greater access to training opportunities for minority scholars, enhanced funding initiatives for minority research, and more sensitivity to the diversity of paths that scholarship can follow, given the enormous complexity underlying the psychological study of ethnic minority populations. Rather than tackle these broad issues, I wish to remain closer to the focus of this article and conclude with some specific recommendations to those who regulate the dissemination of knowledge in APA journals.

First, some of the methodological problems noted for published research on African Americans might be corrected if editors required authors to report complete descriptions of method. These more detailed accounts should then enter into the publication decision. *Any* study in which substantial numbers of the subjects are Black should routinely report the race of the experimenter (examiner, therapist), and investigations that use only White experimenters to interview, test, or otherwise interact with African-American research participants should acknowledge this potential drawback. Socioeconomic information should just as routinely be reported, although I recognize that such data are often difficult to secure, particularly in research with children. But in comparative racial studies, the reporting of SES information should be mandatory, along with analyses or experimental controls that reveal sensitivity to possible interactions.

Second, editors should be more open to alternative (nonexperimental) methodologies when the research pertains to African Americans. Many Black psychologists express dismay that the requirements of a so-called proper scientific psychology (cf. Sampson, 1978) seem to place disproportional value on studies with "control groups" of White subjects and with experimental manipulations in laboratory settings. The well-conducted field investigation of a particular African-American population rarely finds its way into mainstream APA journals.

Third, special issues and special sections of journals are a good forum for enhancing the visibility of particular areas of psychological research, and all of the journals examined here have used this format during the period under review. With a structure already in place, this might be an appropriate time for APA journal editors to initiate a special section or special issue on African-American research. A good model for such an undertaking has recently been provided by *Child Development*, which devoted its entire April 1990 issue to research on ethnic minorities, under the guest editorship of two African-American developmental psychologists.

Finally, APA journal editors must attend to the new generation of African-American psychologists by finding ways to enhance their access to the production of knowledge. In addition to encouraging submission of articles, journal editors should take steps to foster mentorships whereby young Black scholars can benefit from the expertise of established researchers, both Black and White, who have successfully mastered the publication process. Progress along these lines has already been achieved by *JEP*, under the editorship of Robert Calfee, with the establishment in 1987 of its Underrepresented Groups Project (UGP). The UGP sponsors a mentoring program whereby junior minority scholars are "linked with a mentor who will provide substantive or methodological guidance, or both, *before* the manuscript is submitted to the Journal for regular review" (Calfee & Valencia, 1987, p. 362). Although it is evident that the fruits of this labor have yet to be reaped (Calfee, 1990), editors of other APA journals should follow the *JEP* lead so that this kind program can be further nurtured.

Academic psychology cannot maintain its integrity by continuing to allow ethnic minorities to remain so marginalized in mainstream research. In contemporary society, most of the population is not White and middle class. Neither should the subject populations in the journals of our discipline continue to be so disproportionately defined.

REFERENCES

Azibo, D. A. (1988). Understanding the proper and improper usage of the comparative research framework. *Journal of Black Psychology*, *15*, 81–91.

Baratz, S., & Baratz, J. (1970). Early childhood intervention: The social science base of institutional racism. *Harvard Educational Review*, *40*, 29–49.

Calfee, R. C. (1990). Educational psychology: The journal and the discipline. *Journal of Educational Psychology*, *82*, 613–615.

Calfee, R. C., & Valencia, R. R. (1987). Editorial. *Journal of Educational Psychology*, *79*, 362.

Campbell, D. T. (1967). Stereotypes and the perception of group differences. *American Psychologist*, *22*, 817–829.

Caplan, N., & Nelson, S. D. (1973). On being useful: The nature and consequences of psychological research on social problems. *American Psychologist*, *28*, 199–211.

Carlson, R. (1984). What's social about social psychology? Where's the person in personality research? *Journal of Personality and Social Psychology, 47,* 1304–1309.

Cole, M., & Bruner, J. S. (1971). Cultural differences and inferences about psychological processes. *American Psychologist, 26,* 867–876.

Crawford, M., & Marecek, J. (1989). Psychology reconstructs the female. *Psychology of Women Quarterly, 13,* 147–165.

Evans, B. J., & Whitfield, J. R. (Eds.). (1988). *Black males in the United States: An annotated bibliography from 1967 to 1987.* Washington, DC: American Psychological Association.

Graziano, W., Varca, P., & Levy, J. (1982). Race of examiner effects and the validity of intelligence tests. *Review of Educational Research, 52,* 469–498.

Hall, C., Evans, B. J., & Selice, S. (Eds.). (1989). *Black females in the United States: A bibliography from 1967 to 1987.* Washington, DC: American Psychological Association.

Jensen, A. R. (1969). How much can we boost IQ and scholastic achievement? *Harvard Educational Review, 39,* 1–123.

Jones, E. E. (1985). Major developments in social psychology during the past five decades. In G. Lindzey & E. Aronson (Eds.), *The handbook of social psychology* (Vol. 3, pp. 47–107). New York: Random House.

Jones, J. M. (1983). The concept of race in social psychology. In L. Wheeler & P. Shaver (Eds.), *Review of personality and social psychology* (Vol. 4, pp. 117–150). Beverly Hills, CA: Sage.

Kohout, J., & Pion, G. (1990). Participation of ethnic minorities in psychology: Where do we stand today?. In G. Striker, E. Davis-Russell, E. Bourg, E. Duran, W. Hammond, J. McHolland, K. Polite, & B. Vaughn (Eds.), *Toward ethnic diversification in psychology education and training* (pp. 153–165). Washington, DC: American Psychological Association.

Labov, W. (1972). *Language in the inner city: Studies in the Black English Vernacular.* Philadelphia: University of Pennsylvania Press.

McLoyd, V. C., & Randolph, S. M. (1984). The conduct and publication of research on Afro-American children. *Human Development, 27,* 65–75.

McLoyd, V. C., & Randolph, S. M. (1985). Secular trends in the study of Afro-American children: A review of *Child Development,* 1936–1980. *Monographs of the Society for Research in Child Development, 50,* 78–92.

Moore, E. (1986). Family socialization and the IQ test performance of traditionally and transracially adopted Black children. *Developmental Psychology, 22.*

Peery, J. C., & Adams, G. R. (1981). Qualitative ratings of human development journals. *Human Development, 24,* 312–319.

Ponterotto, J. G. (1988). Racial/ethnic minority research in the *Journal of Counseling Psychology:* A content analysis and methodological critique. *Journal of Counseling Psychology, 35,* 410–418.

Reynolds, C. R., & Jensen, A. R. (1983). WISC-R subscale patterns of abilities of Blacks and Whites matched on full scale IQ. *Journal of Educational Psychology, 75,* 207–214.

Ryan, W. (1971). *Blaming the victim.* New York: Pantheon.

Sampson, E. E. (1978). Scientific paradigms and social values: Wanted—A scientific revolution. *Journal of Personality and Social Psychology, 36,* 1332–1343.

Sattler, J. M., & Gwynne, J. (1982). White examiners generally do not impede the intelligence test performance of Black children: To debunk a myth. *Journal of Consulting and Clinical Psychology, 50,* 196–208.

Scarr, S. (1988). Race and gender as psychological variables. *American Psychologist, 43,* 56–59.

Sieber, J. E., & Stanley, B. (1988). Ethical and professional dimensions of socially sensitive research. *American Psychologist, 43,* 49–55.

Summary report of journal operations, 1990. (1991). *American Psychologist, 46,* 769.

Thomas, G. E. (1987). Black students in U. S. graduate and professional schools in the 1980s: A national and institutional assessment. *Harvard Educational Review, 57,* 261–282.

James M. Jones served as action editor for this article. This article was written while the author was a Fellow at the Center for Advanced Study in the Behavioral Sciences, Stanford, CA, 1990-1991. Support during that year was provided by the Spencer Foundation and the Ford Foundation Postdoctoral Minority Scholars Program. Special appreciation is extended to Bernard Weiner and the Attribution "Elders" (Jim Amirkhan, Hector Betancourt, Valerie Folkes, and Steve Lopez) for their comments on the manuscript.

THINKING CRITICALLY AND APPLYING YOUR KNOWLEDGE

1. Graham documents a decline in the percentage of articles about African Americans published in major psychology journals. What explanations does she offer for this decline? What factors do you think may be most important and why?

2. Evaluate this proposition: "Studies of African Americans should always include information about the socioeconomic status of participants." Why might a thoughtful researcher agree with this statement? Can you think of exceptions to this general rule?

3. Graham discusses the possible dangers of race-comparative research. Comparisons of Blacks and Whites may ignore variation within each racial group, may seem to imply that Whites are the standard against which Blacks should be judged, and may not consider factors other than race (e.g., social class) that may differ between Blacks and Whites. Following this general line of reasoning, why might researchers interested in gender be concerned about an exclusive focus on sex-difference research that compares men and women?

4. In designing studies, social psychologists are taught to be careful about experimenter bias, that is, subtle ways in which the behavior or characteristics of the researcher may influence the behavior or responses of research participants. How might the race or ethnic background of a researcher make a difference? What could a researcher studying race or ethnicity do to minimize this potential problem?

5. Graham focuses on the inclusion of Black and White participants in research. What do you think we would find if we did a comparable analysis about research on other ethnic or racial minorities, such as Latinos/Hispanics, Asian Americans, or Native Americans? Analyze the ethnic/racial background of subjects in one of the journals studied by Graham and discuss your findings.

6. In your opinion, what are the implications of the fact that psychological research relies so heavily on White participants? Suggest two or three specific ways in which research involving other racial or ethnic groups might change our conclusions about human behavior.

PART II
PERCEIVING PEOPLE AND EVENTS

❖ CHAPTER 4 ❖

STANDING OUT AND STANDING IN: THE PSYCHOLOGY OF CONTROL IN AMERICA AND JAPAN

John R. Weisz, Fred M. Rothbaum, and Thomas C. Blackburn

Psychologists have long believed that a sense of personal control may be important for coping with daily life. The authors of this article document two paths to a feeling of control. The first is a primary control route through which people enhance their rewards by trying to influence external circumstances and other people directly. In the secondary form of control, individuals enhance their rewards by accommodating to the existing reality and attempting to fit in with other people and circumstances. Weisz and his associates argue that, while the United States and other Western cultures heavily emphasize and value primary control, in Eastern cultures, most notably Japan, secondary control assumes a more central role. They show the importance of this distinction in child-rearing practices, socialization, religion and philosophy, work, and psychotherapy. They conclude that an optimal goal both for individuals and for cultures is a blend of primary and secondary control.

ABSTRACT: *There are at least two general paths to a feeling of control. In primary control, individuals enhance their rewards by influencing existing realities (e.g., other people, circumstances, symptoms, or behavior problems). In secondary control, individuals enhance their rewards by accommodating to existing realities and maximizing satisfaction or goodness of fit with things as they are. American psychologists have written extensively about control, but have generally defined it only in terms of its primary form. This, we argue, reflects a cultural context in which primary control is heavily emphasized and highly valued. In Japan, by contrast, primary control has traditionally been less highly valued and less often anticipated, and secondary control has assumed a more central role in everyday life than in our own culture. To illustrate this cross-cultural difference, we contrast Japanese and American perspectives and practices in child rearing, socialization, religion and philosophy, work, and psychotherapy. These Japanese-American comparisons reveal some key benefits, and some costs, of both primary and secondary approaches to control. In the process, the comparisons reveal the disadvantages of a one-sided pursuit of either form of control. They suggest that an important goal, both for individuals and for cultures, is an optimally adaptive blend of primary and secondary control, a goal best achieved with one's cultural blinders removed.*

Source: Reprinted from *American Psychologist, 39*(9), (1984), 955–969. Copyright © 1984 by the American Psychological Association. Reprinted by permission.

In most American theory and research on the psychology of control, a common theme can be identified: the view that perceived control obtains when individuals shape existing physical, social, or behavioral realities to fit their perceptions, goals, or wishes. According to this view, individuals who do not act to influence such realities may be suffering from learned helplessness (see, e.g., Abramson, Seligman, & Teasdale, 1978), defects in "self-efficacy" (Bandura, 1977), perceptions of self as a "pawn" (deCharms, 1979), or some form of relinquished control (see, e.g., Langer, 1979). Rothbaum, Weisz, and Snyder (1982) recently spelled out a somewhat broader view. They acknowledged that people do often attempt to gain control by influencing existing realities, often via acts involving personal agency, dominance, or even aggression. Rothbaum et al. labeled this process "primary control." But they argued that control is often sought via alternative paths, which they collectively labeled "secondary control." In secondary control, individuals attempt to align themselves with existing realities, leaving them unchanged but exerting control over their personal psychological impact. Table 1 gives an overview of these two forms of control.

Rothbaum et al. reviewed evidence indicating that secondary control often involves behaviors that American investigators have typically classified as signs of relinquished control. For example:

1. Attributing outcomes to low ability combined with behaving in a passive and withdrawn manner is often labeled helplessness; yet, this combination may often represent an attempt to inhibit unfulfillable expectations, thus preparing oneself for future events and thereby gaining *predictive secondary control* (e.g., Averill, 1973; Lazarus, 1966; Miller & Grant, 1980). Lefcourt (1973) has reviewed several studies suggesting that prediction allows people to prepare themselves for future events and thus to gain control over the psychological impact of those events.

2. When people attribute outcomes to powerful others and show submissive behavior, they are often thought to have abandoned the pursuit of perceived control; yet, this pattern may foster enhanced identification with the powerful others and thus promote *vicarious secondary control* (e.g., Hetherington & Frankie, 1967; Johnson & Downing, 1979). Fromm (1941) has written about the human inclination to align oneself with powerful entities (e.g., individuals, groups, or institutions) outside the self in order to enhance one's sense of strength or power.

3. The attribution of outcomes to chance, luck, or fate combined with passivity in or withdrawal from certain competitive skill situations is frequently taken as evidence of relinquished control. However, the combination may often reflect an attempt to be allied with forces of chance or fate so that one may feel a partnership with chance, comfortably accept one's "breaks," and thus experience *illusory secondary control* (e.g., Kahle, 1980; Weisz, 1983). There is evidence, for example, that people who expect little primary control (e.g., people external in locus of control) actively seek to align themselves with chance, showing elevated preferences for chance activities (Ducette & Wolk, 1973) and relying on fortune-tellers and horoscopes (Rotter & Mulry, 1965).

4. All the attributions referred to above may foster *interpretive secondary control*. Individuals often gain a sense of control and mastery over realities in their world by altering their

TABLE 1
Primary and Secondary Control: An Overview

Type of control	General strategy	Typical targets for causal influence	Overall intent
Primary	Influence existing realities	Other people, objects, environmental circumstances, status or standing relative to others, behavior problems	Enhance reward (or reduce punishment) by influencing realities to fit self
Secondary	Accommodate to existing realities	Self's expectations, wishes, goals, perceptions, attitudes, interpretations, attributions	Enhance reward (or reduce punishment) by influencing psychological impact of realities on self

Note: This table represents an extension and refinement of ideas first presented in "Changing the World and Changing Self: A Two-Process Model of Perceived Control," by F. M. Rothbaum, J. R. Weisz, and S. S. Snyder, 1982, *Journal of Personality and Social Psychology, 42,* pp. 5–37. Copyright 1982 by the American Psychological Association.

perspective on those realities so as to derive meaning from them and accept them (see Burgess & Holstrom, 1979; Janoff-Bulman & Brickman, 1980). For example, Bulman and Wortman (1977) found that paralyzed accident victims typically develop explanations for their accidents (e.g., predetermination, "God had a reason") and find in the accidents a sense of purpose (e.g., being forced to slow down, learn about life, or strengthen their faith). Finding reasons and purpose in events that cannot be altered presumably affords the individuals some degree of control over at least the personal psychological impact of those events.

These four forms of secondary control are defined and illustrated in Table 2; the illustrations have been selected for their direct relevance to the present article, and to Japanese behavior in particular.

The evidence reviewed by Rothbaum et al. (1982) indicates that on some occasions people really do relinquish control, but on many other occasions people pursue control, following either of the two general paths outlined above. They may strive for primary control and attempt to influence specific realities, sometimes via acts involving personal agency, dominance, or even aggression. These acts are often intended to express, enhance, or sustain individualism and personal autonomy. Alternatively, individuals may strive for secondary control and attempt to accommodate to existing realities, sometimes via acts that limit individualism and personal autonomy but enhance perceived alignment or goodness of fit with people, objects, or circumstances in their world. Actually, rather than opting exclusively for one form of control or the other, people almost certainly strive for some primary control and some secondary control, thus establishing a kind of primary-secondary ratio.

What determines the relative emphasis that individuals place on primary and secondary control? In addressing this question briefly, Rothbaum et al. (1982) suggested that an in-

TABLE 2
Four Forms of Secondary Control

Form of secondary control	Definition	Examples
Predictive	Attempts to accurately predict events and conditions so as to control their impact on self (e.g., to avoid uncertainty, anxiety, or future disappointment)	Trying to anticipate one's exact status within a social hierarchy, the rules of etiquette that will be followed in a social event, or the sequence of steps by which a corporate decision will be made so as to minimize uncertainty and discomfort in those situations
Vicarious	Attempts to associate or closely align oneself with other individuals, groups, or institutions so as to participate psychologically in the control they exert	Identifying closely with and adapting one's behavior to sustain alignment with one's peer group, supervisor, employer, work group, or family so as to derive feelings of self-esteem and pride from their accomplishments and successes
Illusory	Attempts to associate or get into synchrony with chance so as to enhance comfort with and acceptance of one's fate	Learning to accept streaks of good and bad luck, health and illness, or business success and failure as they come; to avoid fighting bad luck; and to be "at peace with what fate has given me"
Interpretive	Attempts to understand or construe existing realities so as to derive a sense of meaning or purpose from them and thereby enhance one's satisfaction with them	Learning to see the advantages of one's anxiety (e. g., it keeps one alert and makes one prepare work thoroughly), attaining transcendental awareness, and overcoming a desire to make realities better than they are

Note: This table represents an extension and refinement of ideas first presented in Rothbaum et al. (1982, p. 12).

dividual's background and past experience play a role. For example, individuals who have been led to perceive primary control as relatively undesirable or unseemly may emphasize secondary control more than individuals taught to regard primary control as desirable and appropriate. This reasoning suggests an important possibility: The manner in which people blend primary and secondary control may be influenced by their cultural milieu. We believe that cultural differences in the primary-secondary ratio can be found when comparing certain Eastern and Western cultures, particularly when comparing the Japanese and American cultures. Differences in approaches to control have, we believe, stimulated misunderstanding across these cultures; Americans are sometimes perceived by the Japanese as "pushy" or "selfish," and Japanese are sometimes perceived by Americans as "inscrutable" or even "devious." Certainly Japanese and American societies are neither homogeneous nor static. Yet, despite the diversity and flux that characterize both populations, certain central tendencies can be identified that are quite meaningful from the perspective of our expanded theory of control.

In a brief preliminary section, we consider comparative laboratory and questionnaire studies of control-related expectancies and values of Americans and Japanese. This evidence suggests that Japanese, more than Americans, manifest two key correlates of an emphasis on secondary control: a relatively external locus of control and a preference for alignment with others and groups. In the second, more extensive section, we examine diverse evidence from Japanese and American child rearing, socialization, religion and philosophy, work, and psychotherapy. In each area, behavior patterns in Japan appear to reflect a pursuit of secondary control more than do patterns in the United States. In the final section, we discuss implications of our Japanese-American comparisons. The reader should bear in mind that this article is frankly exploratory and speculative; it is not a detailed review and analysis of experimental evidence. We report the experimental evidence we have found, but the bulk of what we report comes from anecdotal, ethnographic, and historical accounts of Japanese and American cultural patterns. By pulling together information from diverse sources, we hope to identify possible relationships that bear systematic, empirical examination in the future. We also caution the reader against assuming that any information reported is characteristic of Japanese or U.S. society as a whole. Our discussion takes little account of the obvious heterogeneity of Japanese and American values and behavior, of such within-culture sources of variance as social class and urban versus rural environment, or of the recently accelerating Americanization of many Japanese and Japanization of many Americans. The information reported should be viewed with appropriate reserve.

PRELIMINARIES: EXPECTANCIES AND VALUES

Rothbaum et al. (1982) maintained that people who seek secondary control are apt to be "characterized by external locus of control" and related expectancies (p. 28). We have found five studies comparing locus of control scores of Japanese and Americans. In all five, the Japanese scored as significantly more external than the Americans (Bond & Tornatzky, 1973; Evans, 1981; McGinnies, Nordholm, Ward, & Bhanthumnavin, 1974; Mahler, 1974; Parsons & Schneider, 1974). Parsons and Schneider (1974) found that Japanese, compared with Americans, (a) saw fate and luck as much more influential, and (b) perceived themselves as less able to alter others' opinions of them. Mahler, Greenberg, and Hayashi (1981) found that Japanese were much more likely than Americans to believe that (a) the world is a capricious place where people do not always produce the outcomes they deserve, (b) individuals can have only limited effectiveness acting alone, and (c) chance and fate play a major role in shaping the outcomes people experience.

To the extent that people are oriented toward secondary control, they should value alignment with others and devalue attempts to shape realities to fit individuals' wishes. Morris and his colleagues (e.g., Morris, 1956; Morris & Jones, 1955) studied values in the

United States, Japan, and elsewhere, asking individuals to rate 13 "ways to live." The Japanese most preferred Way 3, which stressed close alignment with others and discouraged attempts to make realities fit one's own wishes. By contrast, the Americans rated Way 3 lower than did any other national group studied. The way rated highest by the Americans (Way 7) emphasized autonomous pursuit of self-actualization and deemphasized alignment with others. Commenting on some additional values data, Morris (1956) noted, "The relative number of entries for the United States group in the category 'orientation to self' is somewhat stronger than in any other national group, while those in the category 'orientation to society' are somewhat weaker" (p. 47). In characterizing the Japanese pattern of responses, Morris concluded, "The general orientation is clearly to persons and to society" (p. 56).

PATTERNS OF DAILY LIVING: STYLES OF COPING WITH LIFE TASKS

The preceding evidence suggests that the Japanese may perceive primary control as both less attainable (expectancy data) and less desirable (value data) than do Americans. But do Japanese actually seek secondary control more than do Americans? To answer this question, we need to know whether, in their daily activities, Japanese are more likely than Americans to (a) try to accommodate to existing realities in their world and (b) do so for the purpose of achieving control.

We define *control* as causing an intended event (cf. Skinner & Chapman, 1983; Weisz, in press). We emphasize that the "intended event" may involve influencing objective or external realities (primary control) or influencing the personal, psychological impact of those realities (secondary control). Typically, control involves the production of a voluntary response (behavioral, cognitive, or affective) that increases the probability of reward or reduces the probability of punishment. Thus, control may be associated with such a broad range of outcomes as success or mastery, a heightened sense of well-being, or a reduction in aversiveness.

Child Rearing

We begin our survey of everyday, control-relevant behavior at the beginning of the life span, with child rearing. In Japan (as detailed in Befu, 1971; DeVos, 1973; Lebra, 1976; Lebra & Lebra, 1974; and Morsbach, 1980) children are reared in ways that seem to promote what Rothbaum et al. labeled vicarious secondary control. Diverse experiences of satisfaction are repeatedly achieved via physical and psychological alignment with parents and siblings. This training is expected to induce a capacity in the child to participate vicariously in the experiences and feelings of family members, including their experiences and feelings of control and mastery at school or on the job.

The Japanese emphasis on close alignment is illustrated by the importance they attach to "skinship," that is, prolonged body contact between family members. In contrast to Dr. Spock's (1968) account of breast-feeding as a time-limited, task-oriented activity whose main objective is to deliver nutrition, the most prominent Japanese child-care manuals (e.g., Matsuda, 1974) emphasize the mother-child bonding that breastfeeding can promote. Caudill and Weinstein (1974) have documented Japanese-American differences in actual breastfeeding behavior. In Japan, skin-to-skin contact is prolonged well beyond feeding per se and even after the infant has fallen asleep with nipple in mouth. The American mother, by contrast, "is more brisk, and usually gets up and leaves once her baby has fallen asleep" (p. 257). The Japanese infant's experience of control in the feeding situation, that is, gratification of hunger, thus occurs in conjunction with prolonged bodily merger with the mother.

There are also many other occasions for Japanese skinship. For example, an infant often shares a bed with its mother until a new baby is expected (contrast this practice with Dr. Spock's advice "not to take a child into the parents' bed for any reason," 1968, p. 169); mothers and babies may often bathe together, with the baby molding closely to its mother's body. For human infants generally, control typically comes in the form of obtaining desired physical gratifications. For Japanese infants in particular, a large number of such control experiences, for example, those involving such gratifications as feeding, sleeping, and bathing, require that infants adjust themselves to effect a close alignment with persons other than self (e.g., Befu, 1971; Benedict, 1946; Lebra, 1976).[1] Such skinship practices as co-bathing and co-sleeping are extended to family members other than the mother as the child matures (Caudill & Plath, 1966; Dore, 1958).

The Japanese emphasis on close alignment and on vicarious experiencing of others' feelings can be seen in two disciplinary methods that Japanese parents appear to favor. Children are taught to value close alignment with family members by threats to the continuity of that alignment. For example, parents may tell a visitor, "We don't need this boy, so please take him with you" (Lebra, 1976, p. 151), or may simply lock their child out of the house. Vogel and Vogel (1961) have contrasted this latter procedure with the more typical American punishment of "grounding" the child *inside* the house. In Japan, realignment with home and family signifies the end of punishment and the reinstatement of a rewarding state of affairs—hence realignment provides control. In America, by contrast, forced alignment with home and family is the punishment, and thus alignment signifies a loss of control; termination of this alignment means autonomy from family, which implies the end of punishment and a reinstatement of control.

These two alternative paths to a sense of control have been discussed by Fromm (1941). He stresses that establishing independence from parents leads to increased potency in the form of perceived control. Yet, such individuation may lead to increased loneliness and decreased power as the benefits of association with more powerful others are lost. The pro-alignment forms of discipline just described appear to emphasize the aversiveness of individuation and the vicarious potency and control that can be gained through a sustained linkage with family members.

---

[1] The degree of alignment or bonding that Japanese society expects is symbolized by a venerable custom. Japanese hospitals often present mothers of newborns with a preserved portion of the umbilical cord that originally bound mother and infant together. Often mothers keep the cords of all their children in an ornate box in the home; in some regions a child who marries is given his or her cord to take to the new household as a symbol of continuing union with the mother (see Caudill & Weinstein, 1974, p. 266).

Japanese parents also emphasize pro-empathy forms of discipline quite heavily. Conroy, Hess, Azuma, and Kashiwagi (1980) found that American mothers tended to prefer discipline via the assertion of maternal authority and power, whereas Japanese mothers used such empathy-oriented approaches as describing how a child's misbehavior would hurt others' feelings. Lebra (1976) provided an example, "If you don't stop doing that, it is I who will suffer most. Try to put yourself in my place" (p. 153). These Japanese practices evidently provide training in the vicarious experiencing of others' feelings.

Japanese child rearing has been said to foster "a blurring of the boundaries between mother and child" (Caudill & Weinstein, 1974, p. 229) and, eventually, "to eliminate the boundary between self and environment" (Lebra, 1976, p. 168). A valued sign of maturity in Japan is the capacity for *ittaikan*—a feeling of merger or oneness with persons other than self. The capacity for *ittaikan* ideally develops to the point that vicarious experience is virtually reflexive, that is, that "the pride and the shame of an individual are shared by his group, and in turn, the group's pride and shame are shared individually by its members" (Lebra, 1976, p. 36; see also Doi, 1962; Norbeck & DeVos, 1972). When a Japanese youngster's parent, sibling, or peer group member exerts control at work, at school, or elsewhere, that youngster has been prepared by elaborate child-rearing patterns to experience that control vicariously. Certainly this is true of some American children, but the cross-cultural literature (e.g., Befu, 1971; Benedict, 1946; DeVos, 1973; Doi, 1962; Lebra, 1976; Lebra & Lebra, 1974; Vogel & Vogel, 1961) strongly indicates that this capacity for vicarious control runs deeper and broader in Japan.

Socialization

In the United States, child training in social and moral behavior places considerably more primary control in the hands of the individual child than is the case in Japan. Since the time of Hall (1901) and Dewey (1929), the American ideology of child training has emphasized autonomy and individualism. This emphasis is reflected in Kohlberg's (1969) stage theory of moral development. The theory depicts children as maturing in the direction of an ideal state in which individuals rely on principles that they have personally constructed for themselves. At this highest level each individual assumes full primary control over moral decisions, abandoning earlier reliance on others, on conventional social standards, on rules, and on legal authority. Kohlberg favors moral education via open discussion in which leaders do not advocate "right" or "wrong" answers; students are encouraged to develop autonomous moral reasoning in which they control their own moral decisions. Kohlberg's scheme reflects a value central to American research on conformity (e.g., Asch, 1956; Milgram, 1974)—that is, that aligning one's judgments and decisions with influences outside the self is both immature and potentially dangerous (Hogan, 1975).

Japanese socialization in the moral realm contrasts sharply with the American individualism of Kohlberg's scheme. Moral development in Japan involves learning a complex system of societally sanctioned rules. Children are trained to conform to norms for their sex, age, birth order, and position in a group. These norms, in the words of Benedict (1946), "require subordinating one's own will to the ever-increasing duties to neighbors, to family and to country" (p. 273; see also Befu, 1971). In conforming to these norms, individuals give up considerable primary control, but they harness, in exchange, the predictive secondary control that comes with knowing exactly what others expect one to do and exactly how others will respond. The Japanese are also described by several ethnographers (see, e.g., Lebra & Lebra, 1974) as submitting to "shoulds" and "oughts" for the very reasons discussed by Fromm (1941). He attributed such submission to a "tendency to give up the independence of one's individual self and to fuse one's self with somebody or something outside oneself in order to acquire the strength which the individual self is lacking" (p. 141). To the extent that Fromm's analysis applies to Japanese children, their submissive behavior reflects a pursuit of vicarious secondary control.[2]

An overarching theme in Japanese socialization is the cultivation of skills in maintaining harmony or "goodness of fit" with others.[3] Research (e.g., Carmichael & Carmichael, 1972; Seagoe & Murakami, 1961) has shown that, as early as kindergarten and first grade, Japanese youngsters favor cooperative group activities over competition and individual activities, whereas American children favor individual pursuits. (For conflicting findings, see Toda, Shinotsuka, McClintock, & Stech, 1978, discussed in footnote 4.) From his studies of social interaction, Barnlund (1975) concluded that learning group skills in the United States means learning to "stand out," that is, to make one's individuality salient, but that in Japan, by contrast, one learns to "stand in," that is, to become so identified with the group that one's individuality is not noticed. Socially well-educated Japanese can read sub-

---

[2] In contrast to the general patterns described in this section, the Japanese do appear to emphasize primary control in situations involving pressure to achieve, especially in academic pursuits. One study found that Japanese pupils attend school more weeks per year and more hours per week, and spend more time at homework, than do U.S. pupils (Stigler, Lee, Lucker, & Stevenson, 1982). Toda et al. (1978) reported that Japanese elementary-school boys were more competitive than their American agemates in a game designed to pit cooperative against competitive motives. In general, Japanese students appear highly motivated to succeed on exams and to be admitted to the "best" schools. To some extent, these achievement strivings seem to be stimulated by the Japanese propensity to feel that the outcomes they experience personally are experienced vicariously by members of their group and their family (Morsbach, 1980). They strive for success, in part, to enhance the standing of their family (an in-group) vis-à-vis other families (out-groups), and to spare group and family members the "shame" of failure (S. Sukemune, personal communication, 1982). Also, these achievement strivings may be construed as efforts to sustain an alignment with family members by living up to their goals and expectations. Later, admission to the "best" schools may enhance the student's experience of vicarious secondary control; alignment with such schools is presumably more rewarding psychologically than alignment with lesser institutions. Such secondary control objectives, of course, may well coexist with primary control aims involving individual success in school and, ultimately, career.

[3] The ability to maintain a precise alignment with others in social situations is no less important among Japanese adults. This is nicely illustrated by Hsu's (1975) report of a visit with a Japanese friend and some acquaintances near Osaka. The group was picnicking in a secluded spot near a lake. They were sitting in a circle. Hsu reported.

After a while I was attracted by the tiny lake shining in the afternoon sun. Instead of sitting facing the rest of our little group, I turned to the lake. . . . Tired of sitting with my legs folded, I partially stretched them out in front of me. At this point something astonishing happened. My Japanese friend pulled my arm firmly and whispered to me, "Please turn around and sit facing the others." Having already observed Japanese life for several months, I more or less realized the meaning of my friend's corrective gesture. When one is with a group, even temporarily, he should actively participate in the activities of the group and not venture out on his own. But I had not yet learned how very fundamental and widespread this principle of interpersonal relationships is in the Japanese way of life. (p. 14)

tle cues to others' thoughts and feelings, identify areas of agreement, and thus keep their words and deeds carefully attuned to others.[4]

The importance of maintaining harmonious alignment is reflected in Ueda's (1974) description of 16 different strategies Japanese employ to avoid saying "no." Even the Japanese language itself seems designed to maximize interpersonal harmony. Because the verb comes at the end of the sentence, a speaker may state the subject and object, all the while watching the listener's reaction, then adjust the verb to accommodate to the listener. The speaker may also add a negative at the end, "thus reversing the entire meaning of the sentence, but preserving the human relationship" (Morrow, 1983, p. 25). Why this extreme emphasis on maintaining an affirmative, harmonious fit with others? Several writers (e.g., Befu, 1971; Benedict, 1946; Lebra, 1976) imply that it affords a continuing sense of what we have called predictive secondary control to a people taught to fear the unpredictable consequences of deviations from harmony, consensus, and the customary.

Religion and Philosophy

In discussing religion and philosophy in the United States we will focus on Christianity because it figures so prominently in our history, traditions, and culture. For similar reasons our discussion of Japan will focus on Buddhism and, in particular, the Zen tradition. We should note, however, that we use Zen Buddhism only as an example. It is a minority sect in Japan, and only one of many streams of religious and philosophical thought that have influenced cultural patterns there. Many Japanese practice *juso shinke* (multilayered faith) and keep both a Shinto and a Buddhist altar at home. (Note that 98 million are nominal adherents of Shinto and 88 million of Buddhism, but Japan's population is only 119 million.) As is the case with a number of other religions, the influence of Zen is more visible in the history and evolution of Japanese culture than in the everyday behavior of modern mainstream Japanese. However, as we suggest later, there appear to be significant differences between American and Japanese behavior and underlying attitudes that are related to differences between Christianity and Zen Buddhism.

Religion in general has a distinct emphasis on secondary control across sects and cultures. That is, in a variety of religions, adherents are expected to accommodate to powerful cosmic forces, and be rewarded by feelings of vicarious participation in the power, wisdom, or virtue of those forces. Christianity reflects this secondary control emphasis in many respects, but it also emphasizes primary control in a number of ways. A central objective of many Christian sects has been to alter the world to make it fit their own Christian precepts. God is described as having told Adam and Eve, "Have many children, so that your descendants will live all over the earth and bring it under their control" (American Bible Society, 1976, Genesis 1:28). Jesus is said to have instructed his disciples, "Go . . . to all peoples everywhere and make them my disciples: baptize them in the name of the Fa-

---

[4] Lebra (1976) has argued that Japanese show less eye contact during interpersonal interaction than do Americans precisely because people who have refined the art of reading subtle cues find the massive amount of interpersonal information conveyed by direct eye contact almost overwhelming.

ther, the Son, and the Holy Spirit, and teach them to obey everything I have commanded you" (Matthew 28:19–20). Jesus's early disciples preached, baptized many new converts, and established churches all along the northeast Mediterranean. As Christianity grew stronger, dispersing its influence throughout Europe and parts of Asia, many Christians tried to alter the world in violent ways. In the Crusades of the 11th through 14th centuries, Christians battled Moslems and others for control of the Holy Land. Today, most Christian denominations fund large-scale missionary ventures, and many Protestant sects aim to "win the lost" through campaigns like the Billy Graham Crusades. Beyond proselytizing, Christian groups are attempting to alter political realities (e.g., Moral Majority), television programming (e.g., Coalition for Better Television), and the realities of poverty and hunger (e.g., Bread for the World) and racism (e.g., National Council of Churches).

Even when they turn contemplative, Christians often do so in order to change the world, with meditation and prayer often aimed partly at becoming attuned to God and partly at convincing God to alter certain realities. Many regard this as consistent with Jesus's instruction to "Ask, and you will receive; seek, and you will find; knock, and the door will be opened to you" (Luke 11:9). At other times, prayer and meditation are intended to strengthen the prayerful person for social activism aimed at changing the world (see Merton, 1961, 1968, 1971). In summary, Christianity, although it is embedded within the context of secondary control that frames most religions, has a number of important manifestations that appear to reflect an emphasis on primary control.

The history and current practice of Zen Buddhism reflect a considerably heavier emphasis on secondary control than is the case with Christianity. An important objective for Zen Buddhists is to purge themselves of intense desire for realities that do not exist and to achieve a state of bliss, enlightenment, or "transcendental awareness."[5] Zen adherents are trained not to attempt to alter existing realities, even those that appear to provoke misery and suffering. Instead, with enlightenment, Buddhists change their orientation toward those realities. Such acts of interpretation or reorientation in Zen exemplify interpretive secondary control. Whereas Christians are inclined to alter adverse realities, for example, by good deeds, Zen Buddhists are more likely to view good deeds as "not only of little merit in themselves, but often a hindrance to true insight" (Noss, 1966, p. 231). By controlling not realities as such but rather their perspective on those realities, Zen Buddhists obtain what one comparative religion scholar has described as "the ultimate expression of self-power" (Fellows, 1979, p. 187).

---

[5] The enlightenment experience itself involves an altered perception of human realities (e.g., misery), not an attempt to alter those realities. However, one might argue that Buddhists are interested in altering the human situation to the extent that they attempt to show others the path that they believe will lead to an end of suffering. The Bodhisattva is an important figure in this process. The Bodhisattva is an enlightened person who could enter the state of nirvana (cessation of one's personal suffering), but instead vows to remain in the samsaric realm of ordinary human experience in order to help others attain enlightenment. From our perspective, the Bodhisattva's objective appears to be to help others attain a form of interpretive control for themselves. Thus, the Bodhisattva appears to be altering the world, but only by helping people to accommodate to the realities of that world.

Zen culture also allows individuals to exercise vicarious secondary control, via an intense alignment with realities in the world. Such Zen culture forms as flower arrangement, stone gardens, haiku poems, and No theater (the highly stylized classical drama of Japan) are designed to give the perceiver a feeling of complete identification with the focal object or event (Hoover, 1977). Consider this haiku, "An old pond, mirror-still/A quick frog, slanting waterward/A liquid *plop!*" A Zen listener "merges self with pond, then frog, and finally water sound" (Noss, 1966, p. 237). Similarly, in archery, one unites with the arrow spiritually, as it takes flight from the bow (Hoover, 1977). In a number of ways, then, Zen culture emphasizes vicarious control via close alignment with realities in the world.

Another aspect of Japanese philosophy does not reflect Zen Buddhism per se. Although often described as fatalistic, the Japanese are not just passively resigned to fate. Instead, they make active attempts to become allied with fate (*un*). *Un* is generally seen as oscillating between good and bad fortune. The proverb "Fortune and misfortune are like the twisted strands of a rope" is said to mean "good luck and bad luck befall one alternately" (Lebra, 1976, p. 167).[6] This attitude fosters a belief that one can get into synchrony with the rhythm of chance or flow with the tides of fate. There is a strong prohibition against fighting bad luck, and an ability to peacefully accept one's outcomes *arugamama* (as they are) is considered a sign of great maturity and wisdom (Kondo, 1953; Lebra, 1976). One attempts to adjust self to the ebb and flow of fate, and one strives for *akirame*, the sense that "I am at peace with what fate has given me." The objective is evidently not to change fate but to accommodate to it with an acceptance that marks what we have called illusory secondary control.

The World of Work

In contrast to religion, the world of work has a distinct cast of primary control. Across cultures, people work so as to influence such realities as their income and living conditions. However, the emphasis on primary control may be considerably heavier in the United States than in Japan. American work traditions emphasize the value of self-reliance, independence, and individual initiative—all attributes that foster primary control. By several measures, American workers are more aggressive than Japanese workers in altering realities in their working worlds. Americans are more likely than the Japanese to strike, and to do so in ways that inflict real damage on their employers (Ouchi, 1981). Americans also exercise primary control by quitting jobs at much higher rates than do Japanese (Cole, 1979; Hsu, 1975; Whitehall & Takezawa, 1968).

American attitudes reflect a core concept that epitomizes primary control: the self-made man—the "archetypical embodiment of the American dream" (Lasch, 1979, p. 53). Williams (1970) wrote, "The [occupational] 'success story' and the respect accorded to the self-made man are distinctly American if anything is" (pp. 454–455). The quest for primary

---

6 One reason for our exclusion of this line of thought from Zen Buddhism is that the concepts *good* and *bad* are foreign to the nonjudgmental attitude for which many Buddhists strive. A successful practitioner of Buddhism chooses not to judge events as either good or bad, and in making that choice might be seen as achieving a form of interpretive secondary control.

control by the self-made is illustrated by the "MBA phenomenon." The half million Americans who hold Master of Business Administration (MBA) degrees now help to manage many U.S. corporations. They have been described by business experts as creative and hard working, but also as aggressive, controlling, more dedicated to personal advancement than to their companies, and prone to shift companies so as to rise quickly (see, e.g., Friedrich, 1981; Ouchi, 1981). Studies show that workers with MBAs average two job resignations in their first ten years (Ouchi, 1981). Such evidence has contributed to the view that these workers are "arrogant, highly individualistic operators with no patience for team effort" (Nelson Cornelius, quoted in Friedrich, 1981, p. 60) and that "they tend to be more loyal to their personal careers than to any company" (Thomas Hubbard, quoted in Friedrich, 1981, p. 60). If true, this may reflect societally reinforced values. As the dean of Pennsylvania's Wharton School of Business put it, "Our system has a built-in tendency to reward the aggressive loner" (Donald Carroll, quoted in Friedrich, 1981, p. 60). This perception is reflected in such American best sellers as *Looking Out for Number One* (Ringer, 1978) and *Power! How to Get It, How to Use It* (Korda, 1975), and in such ballads as "Take This Job and Shove It" and "I Did It My Way."

Workers in Japan, to a greater extent than in the United States, emphasize the vicarious and predictive forms of secondary control. This is particularly true of the 30% of the work force employed by large, stable, highly successful companies—the employment to which most Japanese workers aspire. In a now all-too-familiar symbol of vicarious control employees of many of these major companies throughout Japan begin each workday by standing to sing their company songs. (A sample first line is "A bright heart overflowing with life linked together Matsushita Electric.") The wearing of company colors reflects what most Japanese regard as lifelong identification with their employers (Hsu, 1975; Ouchi, 1981). Successes achieved by the company are experienced vicariously by the workers as their own (Byron, 1981). A favored slogan is "Your team can win, even if you cannot" (Taniuchi, White, & Pollak, 1981, p. 52). Bellah (1957) and Brown (1974) see in this slogan a traditional Japanese ethical principle: The worker dedicates self to the advancement of the group, and "in this way he manages to achieve a kind of mystical union with his group" (Brown, 1974, p. 186). The strength of this "mystical union" is reflected in Whitehall's (1964) finding that 66% of Japanese workers rated their companies as at least equal in importance to them as their personal lives (compared with 24% of American workers).

Many members of Japanese labor unions appear to agree with the head of the Hitachi Corporation's 70,000-member union that "what is good for the company is good for the union" (quoted in Byron, 1981, p. 59). To strike in a way that weakens the company is to weaken oneself. Thus, most "strikes," as Hsu (1975) and Ouchi (1981) describe them, are brief, symbolic, token affairs, often occuring during lunch hour or after closing time, with workers sometimes even making up lost production at no extra cost. In job actions of this sort, Japanese workers strive for primary control via a strike, but do so in a manner that protects their vicarious secondary control.

Two forms of secondary control may be seen in the *ringi* system that the Japanese use to achieve consensus in business decisions. *Ringi* involves five invariant steps (detailed by Hsu, 1975): (a) a proposal, written up by the middle management group, (b) cautious "horizontal" consideration of the proposal by those at about the middle management level, (c) cautious "vertical" consideration of the proposal by those above and below the middle level, (d) formal affixment of seals to the *ringisho* document containing the proposal, and (e) final, deliberate ambiguity regarding authority and responsibility for the proposal. The five steps permit all participants to feel that the group to which they belong has shaped the final product, but that no individual has. In our terminology, the procedure seems calculated to discourage primary control and foster vicarious secondary control. The fixed nature of the *ringi* steps also ensures considerable predictive secondary control. Each individual foregoes personal, primary control over the final decision, but each gains control in the form of certainty as to how the decision will be reached and certainty that it will be accepted. Thus, uncertainty and risk are minimized for all who participate.

Both predictive and vicarious secondary control can be found within the clear status hierarchy of most Japanese organizations. Clear lines of status and formalized rituals related to status permit a person to unambiguously identify superiors and inferiors and to predict with precision the nature of his or her interactions with others, for example, how deferent each person will be and what forms of address will be used. This minimizes uncertainty, anxiety, and disappointment. Japanese business people and professionals, meeting for the first time, immediately exchange business cards; this instantly clarifies the up and down vectors in their relationship and fixes the language and behavior each will use with the other (Morrow, 1983).

Japanese workers seem surprisingly capable of deriving vicarious secondary control from the status of their superiors. Hsu (1975) described an interview in which a company official of lower-middle rank showed "a gesture of devotion to his office superior which I had never experienced in the Western world" (p. 215). At the end of the interview in the employee's small, sparsely furnished office, the employee said, "Let me show you the office of my Section Chief." He then escorted Hsu to a well-furnished office three times the size of his own, pointed to a large, ornamented desk, "and proudly said, 'This is the desk of my Section Chief' " (p. 215). To achieve such secondary forms of control means that workers must align themselves with their employers and supervisors and relinquish primary control to a degree that most Americans might resist. For example, Whitehall (1964) found that 54% of Japanese workers indicated that they would normally offer their seat on a crowded bus to their immediate supervisor who had just entered; only 4% of the U.S. sample said they would do so. Yet, for people reared to value secondary control as strongly as the Japanese appear to, the gains may be worth the sacrifice.[7]

---

[7] One can find apparent exceptions to the general pattern described here—for example, in the aggressive, competitive style of Japanese marketing. Note, however, that this competitiveness is manifest among corporations often across national boundaries, and thus between groups; it appears to be relatively rare among individual Japanese within the same corporation and even rarer among individual Japanese within the same work group. In Japan, competitive behavior toward out-groups appears more acceptable than competitive behavior toward members of one's own in-group. Individual Japanese do engage in highly competitive behavior on behalf of their employer, but often in ways that seem calculated to minimize attention and credit to themselves as individuals and maximize the power and prestige of their corporation as a whole. From our perspective, it appears that one effect of this behavior may be to enhance vicarious secondary control by enhancing the power of the employer with whom the employee is aligned.

Psychotherapy

Psychotherapy in both Japan and the United States is aimed at helping people change so as to better adapt to their world. Psychotherapists in both cultures treat behavior problems or "symptoms" as realities in the patient's or client's world that require some form of treatment. However, psychotherapies in the two cultures appear to differentially emphasize primary and secondary control. To illustrate, we will focus on two of the most prominent schools of therapy in each culture—the psychoanalytic and behavioral schools in the United States and the Morita and naikan schools in Japan.

Although psychoanalytic and behavioral approaches differ in many ways, they share an important general goal with respect to control of symptoms or problem behaviors. Freud (1916/1963) described psychoanalysis as a "battle" in which "we must make ourselves masters of the symptoms and resolve them" (p. 454). Before analysis could be ended Freud required that "the patient shall no longer be suffering from his symptoms and shall have overcome his anxieties and his inhibitions" (p. 219). Altering symptoms or behavioral problems is also a central objective of behavior therapy, although its precepts and procedures differ markedly from those of psychoanalysis. Despite numerous differences among the various behavioral perspectives, therapists who advocate operant procedures (e.g., Ayllon & Azrin, 1968), respondent methods (e.g., Wolpe & Lazarus, 1966), observational learning approaches (e.g., Bandura, 1977), and cognitive behavior modification strategies (e.g., Meichenbaum, 1977) seem united as to the central importance of identifying, then altering, problem behaviors. By supporting individuals' efforts to modify existing symptoms or problem behaviors to fit their wishes, psychoanalytic and behavioral therapists are emphasizing primary control to a greater extent than many of their Japanese counterparts.

In Japan the Morita approach is a popular method used to treat diverse neurotic and psycho-physiological problems. Morita therapy (described in detail by Lebra, 1976; Miura & Usa, 1970; and Reynolds, 1976, 1980) involves a period of isolated bed rest and structured meditation, then meditation with light manual activity (e.g., sweeping), then heavy manual labor (e.g., chopping wood) combined with meditation and reading of Moritist literature, and finally "life training," that is, a combination of social activities, meditation, reading of Moritist literature, and sessions with the therapist. The principal objective of Morita therapy is not to alter symptoms, but rather to alter the client's perspective on them. Clients are encouraged to perceive their symptoms as a natural part of themselves, to accept the symptoms,[8] and "to work, socialize, and behave normally in spite of them" (Reynolds, 1980, p. 12). Consider anxiety, for example. An American expert on Morita therapy notes that "for almost all Western psychotherapies, anxiety is an intrusive element . . . like a fever or rash, . . . something to be erased," but the client in Morita therapy is encouraged "to see his anxiety as part of himself, not as an appended symptom" (Reynolds, 1980, p. 12). Clients are encouraged "to obey their own nature" (Miura & Usa, 1970, p. 25), and according to a Japanese psychiatrist (quoted in Reynolds, 1980) "a patient is considered cured when he has stopped groping for means to relieve his symptoms" (p. 34).

---

[8] American therapists sometimes give similar suggestions to their clients, but, interestingly, when they do so, the suggestions are often called "paradoxical" interventions.

The Moritist concept of a cure is illustrated by this self-report from a former Moritist client: "I would say that I am completely cured.... I can still pinpoint these conditions which I had thought to be symptoms.... These worries and anxieties make me prepare thoroughly for the daily work I have to do. They prevent me from being careless. They are expressions of the desire to grow and to develop. All I have to do now is to get going, by leaving all my symptoms as they are" (Kora, 1967, pp. 92–98). Here we see the epitome of interpretive secondary control. Rather than attempt to alter existing realities, one alters one's perspective on those realities so as to find purpose or meaning in them and thus accept them as they are. In fact, "the main tenet of Morita therapeutic philosophy is the imperative of accepting things *arugamama*, 'as they are' " (Lebra, 1976, p. 223).

Naikan therapy (described in detail by Lebra, 1976; Murase, 1974; and Reynolds, 1980) also stresses understanding and accepting symptoms via reinterpretation. Naikan (*nai* means "within"; *kan* means "looking") involves guided introspection aimed at attitude change. Lebra (1976) described naikan as the method that "best elucidates the core values of Japanese culture" (p. 201). The procedure involves continuous, carefully structured, solitary meditation, initially in a small enclosed space, from early morning until late at night. The client's *sensei* (guide) hears "confessions" and gives meditation instructions. Meditation topics involve a sequence of significant others in the patient's past, for example, mother, father, siblings, teachers, spouse, employers, friends. Focusing on one person at a time, clients reflect upon (a) kindnesses received from that person during specified periods of their lives, (b) how little they have returned to that person, and (c) how many "troubles and worries" they have caused that person (Murase, 1974).

Ideally, these meditations provoke an emotionally intense "restructuring of the client's view of his past . . . along with a reassessment of his self-image and his current social relationships" (Reynolds, 1980, pp. 47–48). A resultant sense of gratitude to others and a desire to repay those others are expected to generate "joy, new purpose, and new meaning in life" (Reynolds, 1980, p. 48). The specific problems that caused the client to seek treatment may or may not be altered. Changes in behavior problems are considered "merely circumstantial by-products of the working out of naikan's genuine purpose—changing the client's attitude toward his past" (Reynolds, 1980, p. 65). Instead of primary control via symptom elimination, naikan therapy appears to offer its clients a sense of meaning and purpose that will afford interpretive secondary control regardless of whether symptoms have been changed.

A Cautionary Note: Limiting Features of This Survey

The reader should be aware of two limitations of the approach taken in the foregoing discussion. First, we have blended examples from the past and the present for both cultures. We must emphasize that both cultures continue to evolve and that at least some Japanese-American differences that were obvious and profound some years ago appear to be less marked today. This may be due in part to the intense mutual awareness of our two populations in recent years.

A second limitation of our approach is that it has been necessarily selective. We have focused on domains of living that appear to be closely related to core subdisciplines of psychology (i.e., developmental, educational, personality, social-organizational, and clinical). In future work, other domains will need to be examined as well.

We focused our discussion on the primary-secondary control construct, believing that it provides a conceptual framework that can enhance understanding of the cultural differences discussed. It would also be possible to account for at least some of the cross-cultural differences by reference to such important alternative constructs as "internal-external," "individualistic-collectivistic," "achieving-affiliative," "direct action-palliation" (Lazarus, 1976), or "alloplastic-autoplastic" (Hartmann, 1958). However, we believe that the construct of primary-secondary control offers somewhat broader explanatory power. For example, it generates an explanation of cultural differences in behaviors such as prediction and interpretation of events—behaviors that are not quite so readily subsumed by those alternative construct systems. Given this perspective, and space limitations, we have not spelled out how the various alternative construct systems might have dealt with the American-Japan differences. With these limiting features of our analysis in mind, let us now turn our attention to the question of optimum adaptation.

PRIMARY CONTROL, SECONDARY CONTROL, AND THE PURSUIT OF EQUILIBRIUM

As suggested earlier, we construe the relation between primary and secondary control as essentially synergic, with the interplay of both required for optimum adaptation. The relative emphasis placed on the two processes is likely to vary as a function of person, situation, and control objectives. However, across situations, individuals, and even cultures generally, there may be a drift toward such a heavy emphasis on either primary or secondary control that the synergic complement is underemphasized and adaptation is undermined. In this section, we give a few apparent examples of such drift; in the process, we illustrate some benefits and costs of primary and secondary control.

Child Rearing, Socialization, and the "Commons Dilemma"

Japanese patterns of child rearing and socialization seem to foster self-discipline, politeness, attentiveness to others, a strong sense of personal and group identity, and confidence as to appropriate behavior in a variety of situations. As Morrow (1983) said, "Everywhere in Japan, one senses an intricate serenity that comes to a people who know exactly what to expect from each other" (p. 22). Japanese patterns also foster the preservation of traditions and social institutions. However, some argue that the Japanese people's intense capacity for accommodation makes them excessively conforming, overly sensitive to disapproval, prone to read failure not only as a personal humiliation but also as a disgrace to family and in-group members, and even inclined to atone by acts of self-destruction (see Lebra, 1976; Lebra & Lebra, 1974; DeVos, 1973).

The American emphasis on primary control via autonomy and individuation seems to foster self-expression, independent thinking, and creativity. Yet, a number of writers have complained that the trend in America is toward such excessive self-absorption that important social structures are being undermined (Campbell, 1975; Heilbroner, 1974; Hogan, 1975; Milgram, 1974; Schur, 1976; for a conflicting view, see Waterman, 1981) and that individuals are experiencing alienation and loneliness (Kanfer, 1979). This latter argument is quite consistent with Fromm's (1941) view that extremes of freedom lead to loneliness and vacuity. The single-minded pursuit of primary control by individuals within a society can also provoke "commons dilemmas," that is, situations in which community resources are depleted because individual consumers act to satisfy their own wishes without accommodating to the needs of their group as a whole (see Cass & Edney, 1978; Crowe, 1969; Hardin & Baden, 1977). When individuals take more than their fair share of limited community resources or give less than their fair share to preserve or replenish those resources, they threaten the well-being of their community as a whole. In a world of shrinking resources, child rearing and socialization patterns that encourage extremes of primary control may cost our society more than it can afford.

Religion, Philosophy, and Interactions With the World

Christians are known for their zeal to change the world. When this zeal takes the form of efforts to feed the hungry, shelter the needy, or promote justice, few reasonable people can object. But some have argued that, historically, Christians have often let zeal become zealotry and have favored altering the world by military means. There is some evidence that even today those U.S. Christians who consider themselves most devoted are also the most militaristic (McClelland; 1975; Russell, 1971). Christian zeal, according to McClelland's (1975) detailed historical analysis, "often leads to warfare in the long run" (p. 357). Zen Buddhism, by contrast, offers its adherents the peaceful sense of interpretive control that comes with an acceptance of things as they are. Yet, the way of Zen may risk too easy an acceptance of the way things are. Many forms of human misery can be ameliorated by direct intervention. To simply accept suffering as a reality to which one must accommodate may be taking predictive and interpretive control to unnecessary extremes.

Perhaps an optimum balance between primary and secondary control can be found in some sects that manage to significantly alter realities in the world although avoiding excessive militarism. The Quakers, for example, have traditionally enjoyed a rich sense of vicarious participation in God's control; they have stressed "that God is in man" (McClelland, 1975, p. 359) and that the "central part of the human self [is] identical with God" (Russell, 1971, p. 65). The Quakers believe that all human beings are unified with God and that "the divinity in all human beings . . . makes violence against them violence against God" (McClelland, 1975, p. 359). By emphasizing this view, the Quakers have avoided militarism while exerting a high level of primary control in such forms as underground railroads for liberation of slaves in the 1800s and antiwar activism in the 1900s. The Quakers demonstrate that it is possible to balance primary and secondary control within a single religious faith, sustaining a sense of alignment with God while actively promoting humane values in the world.

In addressing this complex issue we must emphasize two key points. First, the heterogeneity and flux of American and Japanese cultures are such that both pacifism and militarism can be found in the histories of both nations. For example, whatever the influence of Zen on the Japanese, it clearly did not prevent a succession of warlords and warriors from attempting to influence events in military ways; nor did it prevent Japan from attacking China in the 1890s and other countries in the first half of the 1900s. As with certain other exceptions to our analysis, these military acts were directed toward "out-groups" and may also have been seen by some of the perpetrators as mere fulfillment of their karma, acceptance of their predetermined fate. A second key point is that the blend of primary and secondary control that is optimally adaptive for one set of circumstances may be quite maladaptive for another set. For example, a number of western European countries are fortunate indeed that the United States did not unilaterally adopt what we have described as the Quaker stance throughout World War II.

Work, Morale, and Innovation

In the world of work, the American emphasis on primary control by the "self-made" has generated such obvious benefits as high salaries and creative technology. However, this emphasis can foster an exploitative, combat mentality, with employees winning concessions in times of high profit, employers winning in recessionary times, and both factions feeling insecure in times of flux. This mentality, as Dore (1973) and Ouchi (1981) have suggested, can seriously undermine both work quality and morale.

The Japanese, by contrast, have the security of predictive and vicarious control, but these benefits come at a cost. For the individual employee, one cost may be immobility. For example, to resign one's first job with a major corporation, regardless of the reasons, is to risk being labeled self-centered and disloyal for most of one's career (Fürstenburg, 1974; Hsu, 1975; Imai, 1975; Ouchi, 1981). At a broader level, the Japanese system seems to have "discouraged individual creativity and, with it, far-reaching product inventions" (Lohr, 1982, p. 1). Critics of the Japanese system underscore this point by noting that Japan has had only four Nobel laureates. One of these four, Leo Esaki, argues that the Japanese lack the American penchant for innovation because they fear losing the security of what we call predictive control. "The Japanese," he has said, "never challenge the unknown" (quoted in Lohr, 1982, p. 6).

Recently, some people have proposed ways of combining the primary control strengths of U.S. practices and the secondary control strengths of Japanese practices (see, e.g., Ouchi, 1981). A number of Japanese corporations establishing U.S. facilities are, in effect, attempting in vivo experiments of this type. One example is the Sony corporation's San Diego plant. Since 1972, the 1,800 Americans who work there have been exposed to an intriguing blend of opportunities for primary control (e.g., they monitor their own work hours) and secondary control (e.g., they frequently meet with company officials to hear about company goals and successes, apparently in order to enhance their identification with their employer). In the years since the introduction of these changes, there has been considerable evidence of close employee alignment with the employer: Resignations have been rare, employees have repeatedly voted down unionization, and productivity has come to rival that of Sony plants in Japan (Coutu, 1981). However, there is as yet little evidence on whether the Sony efforts (or similar efforts by other Japanese firms) have sustained or in-hibited the American penchant for individual innovation and creativity.

Psychotherapy: Changing the Changeable and Accepting the Rest

Finally, we return to the domain of psychotherapy. American approaches, considered to-gether, evidently produce more symptom change than do nontreatment or placebo controls (Landman & Dawes, 1982; Shapiro & Shapiro, 1982; Smith & Glass, 1977; Smith, Glass, & Miller, 1980; but see critiques by Eysenck, 1978; and Frank, 1979). However, nearly all clients have some intransigent problems, and with such problems therapies that focus more or less exclusively on producing change may be of limited value. Japan's Morita and naikan therapists may be of help in these situations, but their prescription of reinterpretation and acceptance is offered for so broad an array of problems that real opportunities to reduce distress in a direct, primary way may often be missed.

The fact is that virtually every client presents a complex mix of problems, some amenable to primary control, but others appropriate targets only for secondary control, par-ticularly in its interpretive form. This may also apply to other candidates for mental health care more broadly construed. Mentally retarded persons, for example, manifest some spe-cific personality and learning problems that seem amenable to primary control (e.g., a ten-dency toward helpless behavior—see Weisz, 1981, 1983; Zigler, 1973); they also have basic cognitive deficits that are difficult to alter, but interpretable in a light that can foster ac-ceptance (i.e., their intellectual abilities tend to meet normal expectations for people of their cognitive developmental level—see Weisz & Zigler, 1979; Weisz & Yeates, 1981).

Similarly, alcoholism evidently involves a combination of alterable factors and factors that one may try only to understand and accept (see Vaillant & Milofsky, 1982). For ex-ample, most reformed alcoholics have achieved understanding and acceptance of certain perceived realities (e.g., "I am an alcoholic") as well as primary control over other realities (e.g., refusing to take "that first drink"). In fact, the serenity prayer adopted by Alcoholics Anonymous evokes precisely the blend of primary and secondary control that we are de-scribing here. It is a plea for "the serenity to accept the things I cannot change, the courage to change the things I can, and the wisdom to know the difference."

CONCLUSIONS: ON THE INTRANSIGENCE OF CULTURAL PATTERNS

In discussing psychotherapy and the other domains, we have addressed the prospects for balancing primary and secondary control in adaptive ways, but we have deliberately made this article more descriptive than prescriptive. One reason is that the cultural patterns de-scribed here appear to be deeply ingrained and resistant to change. These patterns (a) have multiple causes (both historical and contemporary), (b) form interlocking systems, and (c) are enforced by sanctions against alternatives. Moreover, as the ancient proverb has it, "The fish are the last to discover water." People may become so immersed in their styles of achieving control that they are not fully aware of their habitual patterns. Perhaps viewing ourselves through a cross-cultural lens will broaden our array of coping skills, perhaps not. Either way, the experience may give us a clearer view of the water.

REFERENCES

Abramson, L. Y., Seligman, M. E. P., & Teasdale, J. (1978). Learned helplessness in humans: Critique and reformulation. *Journal of Abnormal Psychology, 87,* 49–74.

American Bible Society. (1976). Good news bible. New York: American Bible Society.

Asch, S. E. (1956). Studies of independence and conformity: I. A minority of one against a unanimous majority. *Psychological Monographs, 70* (Whole No. 416).

Averill, J. R. (1973). Personal control over aversive stimuli and its relationship to stress. *Psychological Bulletin, 80,* 286–303.

Ayllon, T., & Azrin, N. H. (1968). *The token economy: A motivational system for therapy and rehabilitation.* New York: Appleton.

Bandura, A. (1977). Self-efficacy: Toward a unifying theory of behavioral change. *Psychological Review, 84,* 191–215.

Barnlund, D. C. (1975). *Public and private self in Japan and the United States.* Tokyo: Simul Press.

Befu, H. (1971). *Japan: An anthropological introduction.* San Francisco: Chandler.

Bellah, R. N. (1957). *Tokugawa religion.* Glencoe, IL: The Free Press.

Benedict, R. (1946). *The chrysanthemum and the sword.* Boston: Houghton Mifflin.

Bond, M. H., & Tornatzky, L. G, (1973). Locus of control in students from Japan and the United States: Dimensions and levels of response. *Psychologia, 16,* 209–213.

Brown, W. (1974). Japanese management: The cultural background. In T. S. Lebra & W. P. Lebra (Eds.), *Japanese culture and behavior* (pp. 174–191). Honolulu: University of Hawaii Press.

Bulman, R. J., & Wortman, C. B. (1977). Attributions of blame and coping in the "real world": Severe accident victims react to their lot. *Journal of Personality and Social Psychology, 35,* 351–363.

Burgess, A. W., & Holstrom, L. L. (1979). Adaptive strategies and recovery from rape. *American Journal of Psychiatry, 136,* 1278–1282.

Byron, C. (1981, March 30). How Japan does it. *Time,* pp. 54–60.

Campbell, D. T. (1975). On the conflicts between biological and social evolution and between psychology and moral tradition. *American Psychologist, 30,* 1103–1126.

Carmichael, L. M., & Carmichael, R. S. (1972). Observations of the behavior of Japanese kindergarten children. *Psychologia, 15,* 46–52.

Cass, R., & Edney, J. J. (1978). The commons dilemma: A simulation testing the effects of resource visibility and territorial division. *Journal of Human Ecology, 6,* 371–386.

Caudill, W., & Plath, D. W. (1966). Who sleeps by whom? Parent-child involvement in urban Japanese families. *Psychiatry, 29,* 344–366.

Caudill, W., & Weinstein, H. (1974). Maternal care and infant behavior in Japan and America. In T. S. Lebra & W. P. Lebra (Eds.), *Japanese culture and behavior* (pp. 226–276). Honolulu: University of Hawaii Press.

Cole, R. E. (1979). *Work, mobility, and participation.* Berkeley, CA: University of California Press.

Conroy, M., Hess, R. D., Azuma, H., & Kashiwagi, K. (1980). Maternal strategies for regulating children's behavior: Japanese and American families. *Journal of Cross-Cultural Psychology, 11,* 153–172.

Coutu, D. L. (1981, March 30). Consensus in San Diego. *Time,* p. 58.

Crowe, B. (1969). The tragedy of the commons revisited. *Science, 166,* 1103–1107.

deCharms, R. (1979). Personal causation and perceived control. In L. C. Perlmuter & R. A. Monty (Eds.), *Choice and perceived control* (pp. 29–40). Hillsdale, NJ: Erlbaum.

DeVos, G. A. (1973). *Socialization for achievement.* Berkeley, CA: University of California Press.

Dewey, J. (1929). *My pedagogical creed.* Washington, DC: The Progressive Education Association.

Doi, L. T. (1962). Amae: A key concept for understanding Japanese personality structure. In R. J. Smith & R. K. Beardsley (Eds.), *Japanese culture: Its development and characteristics* (pp. 61–84). Chicago: Aldine.

Dore, R. P. (1958). *City life in Japan*. Berkeley, CA: University of California Press.

Dore, R. P. (1973). *British factory—Japanese factory*. Berkeley: University of California Press.

Ducette, J., & Wolk, S. (1973). Cognitive and motivational correlates of generalized expectancies for control. *Journal of Personality and Social Psychology, 26*, 420–426.

Evans, H. M. (1981). Internal-external locus of control and word association: Research with Japanese and American students. *Journal of Cross-Cultural Psychology, 12*, 372–382.

Eysenck, H. J. (1978). An exercise in meta-silliness. *American Psychologist, 33*, 517.

Fellows, W. J. (1979). *Religions East and West*. New York: Holt, Rinehart.

Frank, J. (1979). The present status of outcome studies. *Journal of Consulting and Clinical Psychology, 47*, 310–316.

Freud, S. (1963). Introductory lectures on psychoanalysis (Part III). In J. Strachey (Ed. and Trans.), *The standard edition of the complete psychological works of Sigmund Freud* (Vol. 16). London: The Hogarth Press. (Original work published in 1916)

Friedrich, O. (1981, May 4). The money chase. *Time*, pp. 58–69.

Fromm, E. (1941). *Escape from freedom*. New York: Reinhart.

Fürstenburg, F. (1974). *Why the Japanese have been so successful in business*. London, England: Leviathan House.

Hall, G. S. (1901). The ideal school as based on child study. *Forum, 32*, 24–39.

Hardin, G., & Baden, J. (1977). *Managing the commons*. New York: Freeman.

Hartmann, H. (1958). *Ego psychology and the problem of adaptation*. New York: International Press.

Heilbroner, R. L. (1974). The human prospect. *New York Review of Books, 21*, 21–34.

Hetherington, E., & Frankie, G. (1967). Effects of parental dominance, warmth, and conflict on imitation in children. *Journal of Personality and Social Psychology, 6*, 119–125.

Hogan, R. (1975). Theoretical egocentrism and the problem of compliance. *American Psychologist, 30*, 533–540.

Hoover, T. (1977). *Zen culture*. New York: Random House.

Hsu, F. L. K. (1975). *Iemoto: The heart of Japan*. New York: Wiley.

Imai, M. (1975). *Never take yes for an answer: An inside-look at Japanese business for foreign businessmen*. Tokyo: Simul Press.

Janoff-Bulman, R., & Brickman, P. (1980). Expectations and what people learn from failure. In N. T. Feather (Ed.), *Expectancy, incentive and action* (pp. 30–45). Hillsdale, NJ: Erlbaum.

Johnson, R. D., & Downing, L. L. (1979). Deindividuation and valence of cues: Effects on prosocial and antisocial behavior. *Journal of Personality and Social Psychology, 37*, 1523–1538.

Kahle, L. R. (1980). Stimulus condition self-selection by males in the interaction of locus of control and skill-chance situations. *Journal of Personality and Social Psychology, 38*, 50–56.

Kanfer, F. H. (1979). Personal control, social control, and altruism: Can society survive the age of individualism? *American Psychologist, 34*, 231–239.

Kohlberg, L. (1969). *Stages in the development of moral thought and action*. New York: Holt.

Kondo, A. (1953). Morita therapy: A Japanese therapy for neurosis. *American Journal of Psychoanalysis, 13*, 31–37.

Kora, T. (1967, March 6–8). *Jibun wo shiru (Know thyself)*. NHK reprint of radio broadcast.

Korda, M. (1975). *Power! How to get it, how to use it*. New York: Random House.

Landman, J. T., & Dawes, R. M. (1982). Psychotherapy outcome: Smith and Glass' conclusions stand up under scrutiny. *American Psychologist, 37*, 504–516.

Langer, E. J. (1979). The illusion of incompetence. In L. C. Perlmuter & R. A. Monty (Eds.), *Choice and perceived control* (pp. 301–314). Hillsdale, NJ: Erlbaum.

Lasch, C. (1979). *The culture of narcissism: American life in an age of diminishing expectations*. New York: Norton.

Lazarus, R. S. (1966). *Psychological stress and the coping process.* New York: McGraw-Hill.

Lazarus, R. S. (1976). *Patterns of adjustment* (3rd ed.). New York: McGraw-Hill.

Lebra, T. S. (1976). *Japanese patterns of behavior.* Honolulu: University of Hawaii Press.

Lebra, T. S., & Lebra, W. P. (Eds.). (1974). *Japanese culture and behavior.* Honolulu: University of Hawaii Press.

Lefcourt, H. M. (1973). The functions of the illusions of control and freedom. *American Psychologist, 28,* 417–425.

Lohr, S. (1982, June 13). Japan struggling with itself. *New York Times* (Business section), pp. 1–6.

Mahler, I. (1974). A comparative study of locus of control. *Psychologia, 17,* 135–138.

Mahler, I., Greenberg, L., & Hayashi, H. (1981). A comparative study of rules of justice: Japanese versus American. *Psychologia, 24,* 1–8.

Matsuda, M. (1974). *Nihoushiki ikujihō (Child rearing, Japanese style)* (2nd ed.). Tokyo: Kōdansha.

McClelland, D. C. (1975). *Power: The inner experience.* New York: Irvington.

McGinnies, E. I., Nordholm, C., Ward, C. D., & Bhanthumnavin, D. (1974). Sex and cultural differences in perceived locus of control among students in five countries. *Journal of Consulting and Clinical Psychology, 42,* 451–455.

Meichenbaum, D. (1977). *Cognitive behavior modification.* New York: Plenum Press.

Merton, T. (1961). *The new man.* New York: Farrar, Straus & Cudahy.

Merton, T. (1968). *Faith and violence: Christian teaching and Christian practice.* Notre Dame, IN: Notre Dame University Press.

Merton, T. (1971). *Contemplation in a world of action.* Garden City, NY: Doubleday.

Milgram, S. (1974). *Obedience to authority: An experimental view.* New York: Harper & Row.

Miller, S. M., & Grant, R. P. (1980). The blunting hypothesis: A theory of predictability and human stress. In P. O. Sjoder, S. Bates, & W. R. Dockens (Eds.), *Trends in behavior therapy* (pp. 138–151). New York: Academic Press.

Miura, M., & Usa, S. (1970). A psychotherapy of neurosis: Morita therapy. *Psychologia, 13,* 18–35.

Morris, C. W. (1956). *Varieties of human value.* Chicago: University of Chicago Press.

Morris, C., & Jones, L. V. (1955). Value scales and dimensions. *Journal of Abnormal and Social Psychology, 51,* 523–535.

Morrow, L. (1983, August 1). All the hazards and threats of success. *Time,* pp. 20–25.

Morsbach, H. (1980). Major psychological factors influencing Japanese interpersonal relations. In N. Warren (Ed.), *Studies in cross-cultural psychology* (Vol. 2). New York: Academic Press.

Murase, T. (1974). Naikan therapy. In T. S. Lebra & W. P. Lebra (Eds.), *Japanese culture and behavior* (pp. 431–442). Honolulu: University of Hawaii Press.

Norbeck, E., & DeVos, G. A. (1972). Culture and personality: The Japanese. In F. L. K. Hsu (Ed.), *Psychological anthropology* (pp. 21–70). Cambridge, MA: Schenkman Publishing Co.

Noss, J. B. (1966). *Man's religions* (3rd ed.). New York: Macmillan.

Ouchi, W. G. (1981). *Theory Z.* Reading, MA: Addison-Wesley.

Parsons, O. A., & Schneider, J. M. (1974). Locus of control in university students from Eastern and Western societies. *Journal of Consulting and Clinical Psychology, 42,* 456–461.

Reynolds, D. K. (1976). *Morita psychotherapy.* Berkeley, CA: University of California Press.

Reynolds, D. K. (1980). *The quiet therapies: Japanese pathways to personal growth.* Honolulu: The University of Hawaii Press.

Ringer, R. J. (1978). *Looking out for number one.* New York: Fawcett.

Rothbaum, F., Weisz, J. R., & Snyder, S. S. (1982). Changing the world and changing the self: A two-process model of perceived control. *Journal of Personality and Social Psychology, 42,* 5–37.

Rotter, J. B., & Mulry, R. C. (1965). Internal vs. external control of reinforcement and decision time. *Journal of Personality and Social Psychology, 2,* 598–604.

Russell, E. W. (1971). Christianity and militarism. *Peace Research Reviews, 4,* 1–77.

Schur, E. (1976). *The awareness trap.* New York: Quadrangle/The New York Times Book Co.

Seagoe, M. V., & Murakami, K. (1961). A comparative study of children's play in America and Japan. *California Journal of Educational Research, 12,* 124–130.

Shapiro, D. A., & Shapiro, D. (1982). Meta-analysis of comparative therapy outcome studies: A replication and refinement. *Psychological Bulletin, 92,* 581–604.

Skinner, E. A., & Chapman, M. (1983, April). Control beliefs in an action-perspective. Paper presented at the meeting of the Society for Research in Child Development, Detroit, MI.

Smith, M. L., & Glass, G. V. (1977). Meta-analysis of psychotherapy outcome studies. *American Psychologist, 32,* 752–760.

Smith, M. L. Glass, G. V., & Miller, T. I. (1980). *The benefits of psychotherapy.* Baltimore, MD: Johns Hopkins University Press.

Spock, B. (1968). *Baby and child care.* New York: Pocket Books.

Stigler, J. W., Lee, S., Lucker, G. W., & Stevenson, H. W. (1982). Curriculum and achievement in mathematics: A study of elementary school children in Japan, Taiwan, and the United States. *Journal of Educational Psychology, 74,* 315–322.

Taniuchi, L., White, M., & Pollak, S. (1981). *Draft summary of Bernard van Leer Project on human potential workshop on United States and Japanese perspectives on potential.* Unpublished manuscript, Cambridge, MA: Harvard University Graduate School of Education.

Toda, M., Shinotsuka, H., McClintock, C. G., & Stech, F. J. (1978). Development of competitive behavior as a function of culture, age, and social comparison. *Journal of Personality and Social Psychology, 36,* 825–839.

Ueda, K. (1974). Sixteen ways to avoid saying "no" in Japan. In J. Cordon & M. Saito (Eds.), *Intercultural encounters with Japan: Communication, contact and conflict.* Tokyo: Simul Press.

Vaillant, G. E., & Milofsky, E. S. (1982). The etiology of alcoholism: A prospective viewpoint. *American Psychologist, 37,* 504–516.

Vogel, E., & Vogel, S. H. (1961). Family security, personal immaturity, and emotional health in a Japanese sample. *Marriage and Family Living, 23,* 161–166.

Waterman, A. S. (1981). Individualism and interdependence. *American Psychologist, 36,* 762–773.

Weisz, J. R. (1981). Learned helplessness in Black and White children identified by their schools as mentally retarded: Performance deterioration in response to failure. *Developmental Psychology, 17,* 499–508.

Weisz, J. R. (1982). Learned helplessness and the retarded child. In E. Zigler & D. Balla (Eds.), *Mental retardation: The developmental-difference controversy* (pp. 27–40). Hillsdale, NJ: Erlbaum.

Weisz, J. R. (1983). Can I control it? The pursuit of veridical answers across the life span. In P. B. Baltes & O. G. Brim (Eds.), *Life span development and behavior* (Vol. 5, pp. 234–300). New York: Academic Press.

Weisz, J. R. (in press). Understanding the child's developing understanding of control. In M. Perlmutter (Ed.), *Minnesota Symposium on Child Psychology* (Vol. 18). Hillsdale, NJ: Erlbaum.

Weisz, J. R., & Yeates, K. O. (1981). Cognitive development in retarded and nonretarded persons: Piagetian tests of the similar structure hypothesis. *Psychological Bulletin, 90,* 153–178.

Weisz, J. R., & Zigler, E. (1979). Cognitive development in retarded and nonretarded persons: Piagetian tests of the similar sequence hypothesis. *Psychological Bulletin, 86,* 831–851.

Whitehall, A. M. (1964). Cultural values and employee attitudes: United States and Japan. *Journal of Applied Psychology, 48,* 68–72.

Whitehall, A. M., & Takezawa, S. (1968). *The other worker: A comparative study of industrial relations in the United States and Japan.* Honolulu: East-West Center Press.

Williams, R. (1970). *American Society.* New York: Knopf.

Wolpe, J., & Lazarus, A. A. (1966). *Behavior therapy techniques*. New York: Pergamon Press.
Zigler, E. (1973). Motivational factors in the performance of the retarded child. In F. Richardson (Ed.), *Brain and intelligence: The ecology of child development* (pp. 59–69). Hyattsville, MD: National Education Press.

This article was prepared in part while the first author was supported by a grant from the Spencer Foundation and by National Institute of Mental Health grant I RO3 MH38450-01. We are grateful to several people for their thoughtful comments on various sections of the manuscript. In particular, we thank Katherine Bell, Nancy Burks, Geraldine Dawson, Mark Dix, Mary Lynn Eckert, Martha Green, Seisoh Sukemune, Jan Valsiner, John H. Weisz, Virginia Weisz, and Yutaka Yamata. In addition, we thank Robert Glaser and six anonymous reviewers for their many thoughtful contributions to the manuscript.

THINKING CRITICALLY AND APPLYING YOUR KNOWLEDGE

1. Weisz and his colleagues examine the primary versus secondary control distinction in many aspects of Japanese and American life. Can you think of other domains in which the distinction might be important? How might primary versus secondary control be examined in the schools? In romantic relationships? In friendships?

2. The evidence that Weisz and his colleagues use to support the primary versus secondary control distinction and its differential importance in Western versus Eastern societies comes entirely from a survey of other research investigations. What weaknesses does this methodology have? Can you design a small study to test the primary versus secondary control distinction directly and to compare these types of control in the United States versus Japan?

3. Weisz and his colleagues describe four distinct forms of secondary control. Do you think all of these are equally likely to show cultural differences?

4. Weisz and his associates suggest that there are four different types of secondary control, but they describe only one kind of primary control. Do you think there are different types of primary control, and if so, what might they be?

5. The most provocative conclusion reached by Weisz and his associates is that both individuals and cultures may be best served by a blend of primary and secondary control. Do you agree with this conclusion? What are some ways that we in the United States could bring about more emphasis on secondary control in our culture?

❖ CHAPTER 5 ❖

Token Status and Problem-Solving Deficits: Detrimental Effects of Distinctiveness and Performance Monitoring

Delia S. Saenz

Have you ever been the only member of your gender, race, or religion in a social group? How did it make you feel? People who are distinctive in a group, such as the only African American or the only woman, are often subjected to intense scrutiny from others. Consequently, they may feel uncomfortable during their social interactions. In the following experiment, Delia Saenz shows how the distinctiveness of being a token can lead a person to perform more poorly. She argues that this occurs because cognitive resources such as attention and time that could go into striving to perform well are instead channeled into managing how one behaves in the group. This study is important because it shows the potential problems that can arise when one is the only member of one's racial, gender, or ethnic group in a social or academic situation. This is a circumstance in which African Americans, Hispanics, women, and even white men sometimes find themselves, and as Saenz shows, the consequences for performance can be devastating.

ABSTRACT: *The present experiment examined whether extra-task worry is associated with performance deficits in token individuals, and also examined whether deficits occur in the ongoing performance of group members who are distinctive along a nonvisual dimension. Female subjects took turns solving anagrams with three other same-sex participants who were identified as students belonging to the same school as the subject (nontoken condition) or as students from a rival institution (token condition). The three other participants were actually confederates who had been videotaped previously, thus ensuring that all subjects received the same standard treatment. The primary dependent measure of ongoing performance was the percentage of anagrams solved. Extra-task worry was assessed by examining how well subjects monitored the successes/failures of group participants. The principal hypothesis was that, relative to nontokens, tokens would display poorer problem-solving capability and enhanced performance monitoring behavior. The results corroborated past work and demonstrated that even nonperceptual distinctiveness is detrimental to the individual's cognitive capabilities: Token subjects solved significantly fewer anagrams than nontokens. Moreover, the data on the monitoring task*

Source: Reprinted from *Social Cognition*, *12*(1), (1994), 61–74. Copyright © 1994 by Guilford Publications. Reprinted by permission.

revealed that tokens were more adept than nontokens at tracking the performance of group members. Theoretical implications regarding the role of self-presentational concern in promoting cognitive deficits among tokens are discussed.

Distinctive persons, by definition, attract disproportionate attention (Kanter, 1977; Lord & Saenz, 1985; Saenz & Lord, 1989; Taylor, Fiske, Etcoff, & Ruderman, 1978). Under certain conditions, this heightened social attention can lead to improved performance (e.g., Crocker & McGraw, 1984; Mullen & Baumeister, 1987; Ott, 1989). Numerically distinctive male nurses, for example, report receiving special treatment and this, in turn, increases their outcomes and motivation in the work setting (Ott, 1989). Similarly, solo male participants in groups may more readily be accepted as the group leader than female participants, thereby benefitting from their minority status (Crocker & McGraw, 1984). Distinctiveness, however, can also engender negative consequences. Token women and minorities, for example, evince lowered job proficiency relative to their nontoken counterparts, and display diminished levels of involvement and contributions to the central task (Kanter, 1977; Wolman & Frank, 1975).

Often, the nature of differential outcomes that tokens attain is a function of the treatment they receive from majority group members. In some cases, being distinctive is associated with favorable treatment, and not surprisingly these conditions result in positive outcomes for the token person (e.g., Crocker & McGraw, 1984; Ott, 1989). Conversely, unfavorable treatment of the distinctive group member can result in poor outcomes for him/her. Negative expectancies held by employers, for example, may lead them to assign the token to low-responsibility positions (Kanter, 1977); also, prejudicial attitudes can result in biased evaluations of tokens' successes and failures (Garland & Price, 1977). Additionally, resentment on the part of colleagues toward affirmative action initiatives may contribute to a token's isolation (Garcia, Erskine, Hawn, & Casmay, 1981; Yoder, 1985). Any one of these conditions would serve to undermine the token's performance.

Most research on token status suggests that forces external to the distinctive individual are responsible for the nature of outcomes (deficits, surfeits) that the token attains (Yoder, 1991). There is some work, however, which suggests that the performance of tokens may be affected even in the absence of differential treatment from majority group members. In one laboratory study, for example, subjects exchanged opinions with three other group participants who were either of the same gender as the subject or of the opposite gender (Lord & Saenz, 1985). Following the group conversation, tokens remembered less of what was said than their nontoken counterparts. The role of differential expectancies or treatment on the part of majority members was ruled out as a primary mediator of tokens' deficits in this investigation by the fact that each subject actually interacted with three confederates who had been videotaped previously. Thus, tokens were treated no differently from nontokens; subjects were exposed to identical stimuli, and differed only in their awareness of being distinctive within the group.

The investigators suggested that the cognitive deficits incurred by tokens might be due to one of several underlying mechanisms. First, tokens might be influenced by heightened arousal. Specifically, being the token might induce the individual to believe that he/she is the center of attention (cf. Kanter, 1977; Taylor et al., 1978). This awareness might increase arousal and anxiety, which in turn, might narrow the token's range of attention and reduce his/her level of incidental learning (Easterbrook, 1959; Wine, 1971; Zajonc, 1980). Alternatively, token deficits might be due to an increase in self-focused attention (cf. Mullen & Chapman, 1989). Hence, tokens might turn attention inward and pay less attention to environmental information (Wicklund, 1982). Differential attention might impair processing of information relevant to the group task, particularly information relevant to majority members. In parallel fashion, processing of self-relevant information might be enhanced. Finally, it is possible that cognitive deficits might be due to competing demands on the tokens' attentional resources. That is, tokens—like majority members—might be concerned with performing the central group task. This is often the explicit goal of the group interaction. However, and unlike majority members, tokens might also become acutely aware of their own salience relative to the other group members. Their self-perceived distinctiveness might engender heightened self-presentational concern. Ruminations such as: "I'm different." "What do they think of me?" "How am I coming across?" could divert the token's attention from the group task, thereby impairing performance.

Two features of the putative mediators identified by Lord and Saenz (1985) are noteworthy. First, the mechanisms listed might be concomitant effects of distinctiveness. Accordingly, concern with evaluation could engender increased physiological arousal (e.g., Cottrell, 1972; Geen, 1980; Wicklund, 1975), which in turn, might inform the individual about important elements in the environment on which to focus (Bond, 1982; Carver & Scheier, 1981). To the extent that one or more of these processes is activated, tokens' attentional resources might be either narrowed in range or divided between the central task and irrelevant concerns. These attentional consequences, whether produced independently or jointly, would result in the same outcome: impaired performance for the token.

A second feature of the mediators identified above is that they all involve strictly intrapsychic, as compared to interpersonal, processes. That is, the cognitive and motivational reactions of tokens described above are rooted in the tokens' perceptions of their own numerical status, and not in the actions of the majority group members. This line of reasoning suggests that simply knowing that one is distinctive can generate cognitive deficits in tokens, independent of majority members' behavior. Therefore, it may be the case that individual group members who believe they are distinctive but who possess no perceptually distinguishable features might also suffer performance deficits. If sheer distinctiveness leads to disproportionate concern about one's status, then the tokens' mere awareness of their numerical status should be sufficient to generate attention-based deficits.

Related work in the area of marginal status suggests that impression management concerns preoccupy the stigmatized participants of dyadic interactions, even when they possess a nonvisible blemish (Frable, Blackstone, & Scherbaum, 1990; Goffman, 1963; Jones, Farina, Hastorf, Markus, Miller, & Scott, 1984). Although the nonperceptual stigmas that produce such pervasive concern with self-presentation are typically attributes that are inherent in the marginal person and relatively permanent in nature (e.g., emotional handicap, alcohol/drug addiction, crime victim status), it is possible that temporary and situationally induced marginal status may evoke a similar response. Thus, token status—which is a function of the situational configuration, rather than a stable cross-situational condition—may also engender divided attention. The research conducted to date, however, has focused primarily on perceptual operationalizations of distinctiveness such as gender or race (e.g., Crocker & McGraw, 1984; Kanter, 1977; Lord & Saenz, 1985; 1989; Yoder, 1985). Whether or not nonperceptual tokens also incur costs as a function of their nonvisible distinctiveness remains unknown, and is one of the primary purposes for conducting the present experiment.

Ongoing Task Performance

In addition to examining the consequences of nonperceptual distinctiveness, the present research tested whether *ongoing* performance is impaired in token individuals. In previous studies, the primary dependent measure (e.g., memory) has typically been assessed after subjects are no longer in the group (e.g., Lord & Saenz, 1985). Although such measures are expected to parallel the degree of attention directed at the central group task, the possibility remains that token deficits occur at the retrieval, rather than at the encoding of information. The distinction between deficits occurring at either stage is important. If errors occur only at retrieval, for example, token deficits are likely to be temporary. Given sufficient time, tokens might recover from their period of information loss and regain access to information presented previously (cf. Gilbert & Osborne, 1989). By comparison, errors incurred at encoding are likely to have more detrimental and long-term consequences.

It is necessary to assess whether token status affects ongoing performance adversely, particularly if this work is to have any implications for outcomes attained by token women and minorities in the workplace, or for token students in the classroom. After all, their performance-based evaluations will depend primarily on how they perform while the group is intact. In an effort to capture the impact of token status as it occurs during the group interaction, thus, the current study employed a problem-solving activity (to be described below) as the central group task. By measuring ongoing performance while the token is in the "group," the present demonstration was intended to more closely parallel the experience faced by tokens in nonlaboratory situations, relative to previous studies. Additionally, by using a task different from previous demonstrations, the present work would expand the range of performance behaviors affected by the group member's distinctiveness.

Nature of Extra-Task Worry

Finally, the present study also attempted to assess one of the putative mediators of token deficits—distraction due to extra-task worry. If, as Lord and Saenz (1985) suggest, tokens are concerned with how they are coming across, then they should be engaged in cognitive activity that reflects this self-presentational concern. One possibility is that tokens will more actively monitor their performance than nontokens. In the current study, the presence of this type of activity was assessed by examining how well subjects tracked their successes and failures on the problem-solving task. The prediction was that tokens would display greater concern for the level of their performance than nontokens, and that consequently, they would be more accurate in recalling how well and how poorly they performed.

In sum, the present experiment sought to examine whether tokens who are of a different social category, but who *look no different* from the majority group members, display the typical token deficit effect on a problem-solving task. The experiment also attempted to capture the nature of distraction that putatively occupies tokens' attention.

Research Overview

Subjects were led to believe that they would take turns solving anagrams with three other persons, each located in a separate room, and that participants would be able to see and hear each other on television monitors. In reality, the three other participants were not live, but were instead confederates who had been recorded previously on videotape. All subjects "interacted" with the same videotaped female confederates. However, half of the subjects (tokens) believed that the other group participants were from a rival institution, whereas the other half (nontokens) believed that the others were from the same institution as themselves. Because tokens and nontokens saw the same videotaped others, any effects of the manipulation could not be attributed to differential treatment, verbal or nonverbal, on the part of the group members.

After the group interaction, subjects were asked to recall the number of anagrams that each participant had solved correctly. This measure was expected to capture self-presentational concern, in that it represented the extent to which subjects were aware of how they were performing relative to the other participants. "Keeping track" of their own and other participants' performance was expected to interfere with solving the anagrams.

METHOD

Subjects

Eighteen undergraduate women at a private midwestern university were recruited for a study ostensibly investigating problem-solving behavior in groups. The women received course credit for participating in the study. Half of the subjects were randomly assigned to the token condition, the other half to the nontoken condition.

Stimulus Materials

Anagrams. Anagrams were chosen from an initial pool of 150 scrambled words which had been pretested with an independent group of 20 undergraduate students. Of the initial 150, 80 anagrams were designated as being of relatively low difficulty in that they met 2 criteria during pre-testing: (1) they were solved by 75% of pretest subjects, and (2) they were solved in 15 seconds or less. Seventy-two of these 80 anagrams were then randomly chosen and typed on individual index cards. Each group participant was provided with an identical set of these cards.

Videotape. One anagram group session was staged with three female confederates. At the outset of the taped session, the confederates, who wore name tags and were identified by visually prominent room numbers hanging behind them, took turns introducing themselves. They were then called on by the experimenter randomly to solve eighteen individual anagrams. Whenever the experimenter called on a confederate, the camera focused on that participant and she was given 12 seconds to solve the anagram. Eighteen blank spaces of similar duration were left on the tape. This was done so that during the actual group session the subject would have sufficient time to respond when she was prompted by the experimenter.

During the videotaping session, confederates were instructed to solve as many of the anagrams as possible. They were not allowed to view the set of anagrams prior to the taping and no answers were provided by the experimenter. This procedure ensured that their performance would appear spontaneous, and that they would proceed through the session naturally. The confederates were blind to the purpose of the study and the specific hypotheses being tested.

Manipulation of token variable. Different versions of the confederates' interaction were made by splicing one of two "introduction" sections onto the beginning of the tape, prior to the anagram portion. In these introduction sections, the experimenter called on each group participant, in turn, and asked her to state her name, class, major, and hobbies. The information provided by confederates was constant across both sections, except for their stated school affiliation, which was reported along with the participant's major. In the non-token condition, the confederates indicated they were students at the same institution as the subject. In the token condition, confederates indicated they were students at a rival school.[1] Aside from this reference to school affiliation in the introduction of the group interaction, no mention was made, either implicitly or explicitly, of the subject's distinctive status within the group.

Suspicion among actual subjects regarding the ostensible inclusion of rival school students in the experiment was relatively low because the two school campuses are contiguous, and students from the rival institution frequently enroll in classes offered by the school where the study was conducted.

Procedure

Instructions. Upon arriving at the lab, the subject was given a description of the study and informed consent documents. As the subject read these forms, the experimenter left and could be heard opening doors to adjacent rooms and addressing the other participants. After enough time had passed to allow subjects to complete the forms, the experimenter returned and explained that subjects would be participating in a group problem-solving

---

[1] To prevent confederates from being influenced by the school affiliation information, the introduction portions of the videotape were recorded after their anagram-solving session, and later spliced on to the group interaction.

task. They would take turns with three other students introducing themselves and then solving a series of anagrams. Group participants would be seated in separate rooms, each equipped with a camera, monitor, and microphone. They were told that the interaction would take place via closed-circuit TV in order to avoid embarrassment and distractions that might occur if group participants were placed in the same room. Additionally, subjects were told, the use of cameras and monitors would allow the experimenter to have a good view of each participant during the group exchange. In reality, of course, the adjacent rooms were empty and each subject participated individually.

The experimenter handed the subject a name tag and a deck of 72 sequentially numbered index cards—each with a different anagram typed on it. He explained that the group session would be comprised of 72 individual trials. Thus, for trial 1, one of the participants would be called on to solve the anagram on card 1. Regardless of whether she solved the anagram correctly or not, the experimenter would proceed to the next trial and call on a different participant to solve the anagram on card 2. Throughout the 72 trials, participants would be called on in random order and each would be prompted 18 times. The experimenter further indicated that each participant should respond whenever he called out her room number. Hence, because the subject was in Room 3, as designated by a large numeral "3" on the wall behind her, she should respond whenever the experimenter called on Room 3. The other individuals, who were also given name tags, and were identified by room numbers, would be called on in similar fashion.

The experimenter further requested that subjects not jump ahead in looking at subsequent anagrams, but rather that they turn the cards as the experimenter called out the trial number and prompted each participant in turn. Finally, subjects were instructed to look into the camera as they gave their responses, to watch their monitors as the other participants responded, and to refrain from making extraneous remarks. The experimenter explained that each participant's image would appear on the screen for 12 seconds as she attempted to solve the anagram in question, and that whatever image the subject saw on her screen was the same image seen by all participants. At this point, the experimenter responded to inquiries that the subject might have had about the procedure, and indicated that the group session would begin.

Group interaction. The group session began with introductions, and then proceeded to the anagram portion. The experimenter called on each group participant, in turn, and asked her to state her name, class, major, and hobbies. When it was the subject's turn to respond, the experimenter switched from videotape to live. The subject was able to see and hear herself through the monitor, and believed that the other participants could also. When the subject's turn ended, the experimenter switched back to videotape. Introductions were followed by the group interaction, during which the experimenter again switched from videotape to live, as described above. After the anagram-solving task, subjects completed the performance monitoring measure, as well as manipulation checks on the institutional affiliation of the majority members. Then, they were debriefed, thanked, and given credit slips for their participation.

Dependent Measures and Predictions

The primary dependent measure of ongoing cognitive performance was the percentage of anagrams solved. Tokens were expected to solve fewer anagrams than were nontokens. In addition to the anagram performance measure, the experiment included a dependent variable representing self-presentational concern. This measure, presented on a separate questionnaire following the group interaction, asked subjects to recall the number of anagrams that each participant solved correctly. As mentioned previously, the central hypothesis was that tokens were expected to monitor their relative performance more closely than nontokens; hence, in comparison to task performance, tokens were expected to outperform nontokens on this measure.

RESULTS

Manipulation Checks

All subjects correctly identified the institutional affiliation of majority members. Hence, manipulation of token status via the introduction section of the videotape was successful.

Task Performance

A one-way analyses of variance (ANOVA) with two levels of token status (token, nontoken) was conducted to examine the effect of distinctiveness on task performance. The main prediction for problem-solving performance was that tokens would perform more poorly than nontokens. As can be seen in the top panel of Table 1, the data confirmed this prediction: token subjects solved fewer anagrams (55%) than nontoken subjects (75%), $F(1, 16) = 7.64$, $p < .05$.[2] This result replicated the token deficit effect reported in previous

TABLE 1
Percentage of Anagrams Solved Correctly and Performance Monitoring Errors as a Function of Token Status

	Tokens (%)	Nontokens (%)
Anagrams solved	55	75
	(14)	(17)
Monitoring errors	9.1	18.7
	(3)	(11)

Note: Standard deviations appear in parentheses. The n per cell = 9.

[2] Raw anagram scores were 9.9 for tokens, and 13.5 for nontokens, out of a possible score of 18.

work, and demonstrated that being the only one of a social category in an otherwise homogeneous group is detrimental to the subject's ongoing cognitive performance.

Performance Monitoring

If these deficits are associated, as previously argued, with heightened concern over performance, then tokens should have been more inclined to keep track of hits and misses than nontokens. In order to assess this possibility, error scores were derived by examining subjects' estimates of their own and majority members' performance, and the actual performance of each. The absolute differences between the estimated and the actual percentages of anagrams solved for self and for majority (averaged across the 3 group members) were subjected to a 2-way ANOVA with 2 levels of token status (token, nontoken) and 2 levels of participant (self, other).[3]

The results revealed that tokens made fewer errors than nontokens in recalling the performance of both self (token X = 9.5%; nontoken X = 24.1%) and others (token X = 8.6%; nontoken X = 13.4%). As can be seen in the bottom panel of Table 1, overall error scores were 9.1% for tokens and 18.7% for nontokens, $F (1, 14) = 4.81$, $p < .05$. Only the main effect for token status emerged; neither the main effect of participant nor the interaction was statistically reliable.

Relationship Between Monitoring of Errors and Task Performance

Two additional analyses were conducted to assess the relationship between errors in performance monitoring and anagram-solving capability. First, the correlation between these measures was assessed. As might be expected, the association between number of errors in recalling self and other performance and the number of anagrams solved was positive and significant, $r = .51$, $p < .05$. Hence, increased errors—which reflected inattention to performance of the group participants—were associated with better performance in solving anagrams.

In addition to this correlational assessment, the one-way ANOVA reported previously on task performance was repeated. However, monitoring scores were included as a covariate. This analysis of covariance revealed that the main effect of token status on task performance was eliminated ($p < .10$), indicating that the effect of token status on anagram performance was related to the amount of attention directed at monitoring the relative successes/failures of the group participants.

In sum, the pattern of means for the two dependent measures suggested that token subjects direct more attention toward extra-task worries than toward central group tasks, relative to nontoken subjects. Moreover, these performance tracking tendencies appear to be associated with problem-solving deficits.

---

[3] Subjects' estimates were based on raw scores (the number correctly solved by self and majority members). For ease of presentation, these raw scores were transformed into percentages by dividing the actual and the estimated numbers by the total number possible for each group member (18).

DISCUSSION

The current set of results extends previous work on token status in several ways. First, the present study demonstrates that a token need not look different from majority members to incur deficits. Knowing you are different is sufficient to divert your attention from the central task. This finding is in keeping with both classic and recent discussions on the behavioral consequences of marginal status (Frable et al., 1990; Goffman, 1963; Lewin, 1935). It emphasizes the social nature of self-definition and illustrates how one's self-view is often constructed in negotiation with the social context. In group settings, individuals respond not only to the behavior of others, but also to their own expectations of how others will perceive them. In the present study, token subjects were aware of their distinctive status despite the fact that they looked no different from majority members. Their awareness may have induced them to believe that they were being evaluated by the majority outgroup members. This worry, in turn, diverted their attention from the central task. By comparison, nontokens—who were not expected to have competing demands on their attention—did not show the same amount of concern, and consequently solved more anagrams. In general, then, nonperceptual distinctiveness produced deficits that parallel those found in experiments wherein a visible categorization attribute was used as the token variable.

A second contribution of the present work lies in its demonstration that deficits associated with token status are not limited to memory. Ongoing problem-solving capabilities are also impaired in distinctive persons. Previous work measured performance after the individual was no longer in the group (e.g., memory in the Lord & Saenz, 1985 study). The current study, in contrast, captured the impact of token status as it occurred during the group interaction. As predicted, tokens experienced decrements in performance relative to nontokens, suggesting that the detrimental consequences of token status are not limited to cognitive performance as measured via memory.

Finally, and perhaps most importantly, the current set of results provides evidence for the nature of self-preoccupation that diverts the token's attention from the central group task. The measure of performance monitoring indicated that rather than allocating their attention to solving the anagrams, tokens were thinking about how well or how poorly they were doing relative to majority members. The data suggested that they were busy counting hits and misses instead of simply generating solutions to the anagrams; ironically, this preoccupation proved to be detrimental.

It is notable that tokens were attuned not only to their own performance, but also to that of majority members. Such a pattern is consistent with a self-presentational analysis in that social comparison information might be particularly critical to the token's concern with evaluation. After all, "worrying about the image one is projecting" implicates the evaluation of others. When those others are participating in the same exercise as oneself, a natural response would be to compare one's own performance with that of the other group members. The results on the performance-monitoring measure indicate that this is exactly what tokens did—they focused on how well (or poorly) they and the majority members were doing.

Such a tendency, furthermore, might have been intensified in the present study by elements of the methodology. Specifically, tokens believed they were dissimilar along the dimension of school affiliation, and they were asked to find the correct solutions to an objective set of problems. It might have been that these features led them to see the group task as a competition between students of the two institutions. Even though the group interaction was described as simply a "group problem-solving task," and no explicit reference was made to school affiliation, the presence of rival school members could have heightened social comparison processes. This perception of competition would have applied equally to nontokens and tokens, however, the latter may have had the added burden of believing that they were "the sole representative" of their school in the group. Further, given their distinctive status, tokens may have felt the vulnerability associated with worrying that they might represent their ingroup poorly (Steele, 1993). Although no data were collected directly to assess this type of concern, the results were consistent with such an explanation: Token status produced deficits in task performance, along with surfeits in social comparison tendencies.

Interestingly, the putative role of social comparison has not been explicitly highlighted in previous work on token status, possibly because the group tasks which have been employed previously have focused on expression of preferences rather than on objective performance. Nonetheless, deficits emerge across both task domains. It is possible, hence, that token status produces multiple affective and motivational consequences which differ depending upon the nature of both the group task and the categorization variable. The present work underscored the role of one form of extra-task worry that may impair a token's performance—social comparison. Additional work is needed to assess whether this type of distraction is critical across all token situations, as well as to evaluate the role of processes suggested by earlier investigations of token status (e.g., self-focused attention, arousal).

Work is also needed to assess the range of detrimental effects caused by tokenism. Memory deficits appear robust and the present experiment demonstrated that problem-solving decrements are also associated with tokenism. Future efforts should be directed at uncovering whether other areas of performance are likewise impaired. Similarly, different operationalizations of token status should be implemented. The present work was intended to move beyond previous work in testing the limits of distinctiveness, however, there are other attributes on which individuals are marginal outside the laboratory which have not been examined in experimental research. Changing demographic patterns, moreover, suggest that in the near future females and minorities may not be the only ones who occupy the token role in society. In fact, a recent field study suggests that relatively higher stress levels are reported by caucasian employees when their ingroup is in a numerical minority, relative to when they represent the majority in their work unit (Gutierres, Saenz, & Green, in press). Field research in other settings such as the classroom would be valuable in ascertaining the generalizability of laboratory research. Finally, and perhaps most importantly, we need to examine ways that reduce the detrimental consequences of tokenism for the distinctive individual. Inquiry along these myriad dimensions can provide more definitive answers to questions that remain unanswered by past and current work on token status. For now, there is at least one thing that we can be certain of: distinctiveness has its costs.

REFERENCES

Bond, C. F. (1982). Social facilitation: A self-presentational view. *Journal of Personality and Social Psychology, 42,* 1042–1050.

Carver, C. S., & Scheier, M. F. (1981). *Attention and self-regulation: A control theory approach to human behavior.* New York: Springer-Verlag.

Cottrell, N. B. (1972). Social facilitation. In C. G. McClintock (Ed.), *Experimental social psychology.* New York: Holt.

Crocker, J., & McGraw, K. M. (1984). What's good for the goose is not good for the gander. *American Behavioral Scientist, 27,* 357–369.

Easterbrook, J. A. (1959). The effect of emotion on cue utilization and the organization of behavior. *Psychological Review, 66,* 183–199.

Frable, D. E., Blackstone, T., & Scherbaum, C. (1990). Marginal and mindful: Deviants in social interaction. *Journal of Personality and Social Psychology,* 140–149.

Garcia, L. T., Erskine, N., Hawn, K., & Casmay, S. (1981). The effect of affirmative action on attributions about minority group members. *Journal of Personality, 49,* 427–437.

Garland, H. & Price, K. H. (1977). Attributions toward women in management and attributions for their success and failure in managerial positions. *Journal of Applied Psychology, 62,* 29–33.

Geen, R. C. (1980). The effects of being observed on performance. In P. B. Paulus (Ed.), *Psychology of group influence* (pp. 61–98). Hillsdale, NJ: Lawrence Erlbaum Associates.

Gilbert, D. T., & Osborne, R. E. (1989). Thinking backward: Some curable and incurable consequences of cognitive busyness. *Journal of Personality and Social Psychology, 57,* 940–949.

Goffman, E. (1963). *Stigma: Notes on the management of a spoiled identity.* Englewood Cliffs, NJ: Prentice-Hall.

Gutierres, S. E., Saenz, D. S., & Green, B. L. (In press). Job stress and health outcomes among Anglo and Hispanic employees: A test of the person-environment fit model. In G. Keita & S. Sauter (Eds.), *Stress in the 90's.* Washington, DC: American Psychological Association.

Jones, E. E., Farina, A., Hastorf, A. H., Markus, H., Miller, D. T., & Scott, R. A. (1984). *Social stigma: The psychology of marked relationships.* New York: W. H. Freeman.

Kanter, R. M. (1977). *Men and women of the corporation.* New York: Basic Books.

Lewin, K. (1935). Psycho-sociological problems of a minority group. *Character and Personality, 3,* 175–187.

Lord, C. G., & Saenz, D. S. (1985). Memory deficits and memory surfeits: Differential cognitive consequences of tokenism for tokens and observers. *Journal of Personality and Social Psychology, 49,* 918–925.

Mullen, B., & Baumeister, R. F. (1987). Group effects on self-attention and performance: Social loafing, social facilitation, and social impairment. In C. Hendrick (Ed.), *Review of Personality and Social Psychology* (Vol. 9, pp. 189–206). Sage.

Mullen, B., & Chapman, J. G. (1989). Focus of attention in groups: A self-attention perspective. *Journal of Social Psychology, 129,* 807–817.

Ott, E. M. (1989). Effects of the male-female ratio at work. *Psychology of Women Quarterly, 13,* 41–57.

Saenz, D. S., & Lord, C. G. (1989). Reversing roles: A cognitive strategy for undoing memory deficits associated with token status. *Journal of Personality and Social Psychology, 56,* 698–708.

Steele, C. (1993). *Collective prejudice: How stereotypes shape achievement and performance in American schools.* Invited address presented at the Western Psychological Association Convention, Phoenix, AZ.

Taylor, S. E., Fiske, S. T., Etcoff, N. L., & Ruderman, A. J. (1978). Categorical and contextual bases of person memory and stereotyping. *Journal of Personality and Social Psychology, 36,* 778–793.

Wicklund, R. A. (1975). Objective self-awareness. In L. Berkowitz (Ed.), *Advances in experimental social psychology* (Vol. 8, pp. 233–275). New York: Academic Press.

Wicklund, R. A. (1982). How society uses self-awareness. In J. Suls (Ed.), *Psychological perspectives on the self* (Vol. 1, pp. 209–230). Hillsdale, NJ: Erlbaum.

Wine, J. (1971). Test anxiety and direction of attention. *Psychological Bulletin, 76,* 92–104.

Wolman, C., & Frank, H. (1975). The token woman in a professional peer group. *American Journal of Orthopsychiatry, 45,* 164–171.

Yoder, J. D. (1985). An academic woman as a token: A case study. *Journal of Social Issues, 41,* 61–72.

Yoder (1991). Rethinking tokenism: Looking beyond the numbers. *Gender and Society, 5,* 178–192.

Zajonc, R. B. (1980). Co-presence. In P. B. Paulus (Ed.), *Psychology of group influence* (pp. 35–60). Hillsdale, NJ: Erlbaum.

This research was supported in part by a grant from the National Science Foundation (#RII-8812574) to the investigator. I would like to acknowledge the assistance of Robert S. Clark in the data collection, and to thank Steven Neuberg, Jason Newsom, and four anonymous reviewers for their helpful comments on an earlier version of the manuscript.

Thinking Critically and Applying Your Knowledge

1. Have you ever been a token in a group, that is, the only man or woman, or member of your ethnic group? Did you feel uncomfortable in this role? How did it affect your behavior in the group situation? Did you experience any of the problems Saenz describes?

2. Saenz demonstrates that being a token can harm one's performance. The particular task she used was a series of anagram puzzles. Are there other ways in which performance might be worsened or disrupted when one is a token in a group? Might a token hesitate to speak up or to voice unusual suggestions that might help a group's performance?

3. To create the token situation, Saenz had women solve anagrams with three other women who were said to be either from the same school or from a rival institution. Why did she use this particular method, instead of looking at a token Black in an otherwise White group, or a token White in an otherwise Asian group, for example? In other words, why did she stay clear of race or ethnicity as the manipulation of token status? What does Saenz's experiment tell you about the effects of tokenism that might not be as evident if race or ethnicity had been used?

❖ CHAPTER 6 ❖

PERCEPTIONS OF SOCIAL RESPONSIBILITIES IN INDIA AND IN THE UNITED STATES: MORAL IMPERATIVES OR PERSONAL DECISIONS?

Joan G. Miller, David M. Bersoff, and Robin L. Harwood

What determines how people think about their social responsibilities? Joan Miller and her colleagues suggest that cultures differ in the degree to which they regard social responsibilities as a matter of personal choice or as a moral imperative. Comparing Indian and American moral reasoning about hypothethical situations, Miller and her associates report that Indians tend to regard the failure to help another in moral terms, whereas Americans tend to view such behavior in moral terms only if there is a life-threatening situation or if one's children are in serious need. Cultures, then, vary in the degree to which they encourage a broad versus a narrow view of social responsibilities and the conditions that give rise to them.

ABSTRACT: *Indian and American adults' and children's* (N = 400) *moral reasoning about hypothetical situations in which an agent failed to help someone experiencing either life-threatening, moderately serious, or minor need was compared. For* ⅓ *of Ss, the agent's relationship to the needy other was portrayed as that of parent; for another* ⅓, *as that of best friend; for the rest, as that of stranger. Indians tended to regard the failure to aid another in moral terms in all conditions. In contrast, Americans tended to view it in moral terms only in life-threatening cases or in cases of parents responding to the moderately serious needs of their children. The results imply that Indian culture forwards a broader and more stringent view of social responsibilities than does American culture. Discussion centers on theoretical implications of the various cultural, need, role, and developmental effects observed.*

Moral development theorists have adopted similar formal definitions of morality (Gewirth, 1978; Kohlberg, 1971; Shweder, 1982; Turiel, 1983). In particular, moral concerns are regarded (a) as based on objective obligations, independent of social consensus or personal preference and (b) as legitimately subject to social regulation, rather than as the agent's own business. Moral rules may be seen to differ both from social conventions, which are viewed as legitimately regulated but not as based on objective obligations,

Source: Reprinted from *Journal of Personality and Social Psychology, 58*(1), (1990), 33–47. Copyright © 1990 by the American Psychological Association. Reprinted by permission.

and from matters of personal choice, which are viewed as neither based on objective obligations nor legitimately regulated.

In recent years, research on moral reasoning has focused increased attention on issues involving social responsiveness to the needs of others (e.g., Eisenberg, 1986; Gilligan, 1982; Higgins, Power, & Kohlberg, 1984; Miller & Luthar, 1989). Questions remain, however, regarding whether social responsibilities[1] (a) are imbued with the formal characteristics of moral concerns noted earlier, (b) are based on the magnitude of the recipient's need or on their role relationship with the donor, or on both, and (c) are interpreted similarly across cultural, subcultural, and age groups. In assessing the impact of need and role on reasoning about social responsibilities, the present cross-cultural investigation of American and Indian children and adults addresses these questions.

In the view of Kohlberg and his colleagues (Kohlberg, 1981; Kohlberg, Levine, & Hewer, 1983), social responsibilities obtain full moral force only when they are linked to the preservation of justice or of individual rights. For example, it is argued, in the case of the Heinz dilemma (1981), that Heinz is morally obligated to save his dying wife in order to preserve her right to life. Like other moral duties, this requirement is seen as applying even to strangers, not merely to those who are known to or who are liked by the agent. In contrast, in situations that do not involve justice or rights-based concerns, responding to another's needs is regarded as a supererogatory rather than a fully moral obligation (Higgins et al., 1984; Kohlberg, 1971).

Various social-psychology theorists present an alternative stance in their claims that individuals are guided by norms of helping or of social responsibility (e.g., Berkowitz & Daniels, 1963; Leeds, 1963; Schwartz, 1975). Mandating that individuals should help others who are needy or dependent, such norms are seen as applying even in cases in which the other's right to life is not at stake and cases in which the other is unknown to the agent. However, whereas research has suggested that these norms influence helping behavior (Macaulay & Berkowitz, 1970; Schwartz, 1975), their status as moral requirements is unclear. No effort has been made by theorists in this tradition to assess whether individuals imbue such norms with the formal properties characteristic of moral rules, such as those of being based on objective obligations and of representing legitimate regulations.

Forwarding a third view, Gilligan and her colleagues (Gilligan, 1977, 1982; Murphy & Gilligan, 1980) have maintained that interpersonal responsiveness and care constitute a distinct moral code. In contrast to the morality of justice and the norms of helping and of social responsibility, this morality is seen as relationship based. Thus, for example, a wife's obligation to be sensitive to her husband's welfare is viewed as deriving, in part, from their relationship. The distribution of such a moral code is assumed to be subgroup specific, with girls and women more prone than boys and men to hold the orientation. However, some recent research among American adults has challenged the claim that interpersonal

---

[1] The term *social responsibilities* is used in this article to refer to an individual's obligations to assist a needy other who is dependent on him or her, regardless of whether the individual has received prior assistance from the other.

responsiveness and care are conceptualized in fully moral terms (Higgins et al., 1984; Kohlberg et al., 1983; Nunner-Winkler, 1984). This evidence suggests that although people judge that interpersonal responsiveness and care involve feelings of obligation, they also tend to regard the decision to perform behaviors of this type as personal in nature.

A recent cross-cultural study of Indian and American adult subjects (Miller & Luthar, 1989) provided a cultural perspective on these issues. Comparison was undertaken of American and Hindu Indian adults' reactions to hypothetical incidents in which an agent fails to meet the needs of a dependent other with whom they have an ongoing role relationship, such as a friend. It was demonstrated that whereas Indian subjects tend to categorize such behaviors in moral terms, American subjects tend to regard them as matters of personal choice. Evidence was presented to suggest that these differences arise from the contrasting moral codes emphasized in the two cultures, with Indians' judgments reflecting a moral code that tends to give priority to social duties and Americans' judgments reflecting a moral code that tends to give priority to individual rights (see also Shweder, Mahapahtra, & Miller, 1987).

Although it provided some indication that cultural differences exist in attitudes toward helping dependent others in need, the research left several issues unresolved. It was not clear, for example, whether subjects' interpretations of such issues were based on consideration of the dependent other's need or of the dependent other's role relationship to the agent, or of both. Also, in not sampling a wide range of need and role situations, the research gave little indication of the boundaries of the observed cross-cultural differences. Finally, in discriminating between moral and personal-choice orientations solely on the basis of whether it was legitimate to regulate the behaviors in question, the research may have failed to capture the complexity of Americans' conceptions of social responsibilities. As suggested by Kohlberg et al. (1983), although Americans' views of social responsibilities emphasize individual freedom of choice, they also appear to contain certain moral aspects, such as a notion of obligation.

The present study was designed to investigate these unresolved issues regarding the scope, universality, and moral status of social responsibilities, as well as to examine the development of views regarding social responsibilities among children. To address such concerns, a sample of American and Hindu Indian children and adults were questioned regarding their attitudes toward helping situations. These two groups were selected for comparison because their cultural beliefs and values differ in ways anticipated to affect their attitudes in this domain. Specifically, whereas American culture tends to emphasize individual autonomy and freedom of choice, Hindu Indian culture tends to place greater stress on interpersonal interdependence and social obligations (Dumont, 1970; Kakar, 1978; Lukes, 1973; O'Flaherty & Derrett, 1978).[2]

---

[2] Throughout this article, references are made to global differences in beliefs and values between American and Hindu Indian cultural meaning systems. No attempt is made to characterize the subcultural variation in beliefs and values existing within each society, such as the differences between Hindu Indian and Moslem Indian subcultural orientations.

Attitudes toward social responsibilities were assessed by asking subjects to evaluate hypothetical scenarios, which varied both in magnitude of need and nature of the role relationships portrayed. Specifically, subjects were presented with a set of incidents in which an agent refused to help a dependent other who was experiencing either life-threatening, moderate, or minor need. Control incidents were also included to examine subjects' reactions to noncompliance with another's request in situations not involving need. The control incidents involved agents' refusals to engage in arbitrary unjust behavior or to override their own personal preferences. Role effects were analyzed by means of a between-subjects manipulation that portrayed the relationship between the agent and potential recipient as either (a) parent to a young son or daughter, (b) best friend, or (c) stranger. The roles of parent and best friend were selected as relationships that, in both cultures, entail strong affective bonds as well as ongoing patterns of social interchange (Argyle & Henderson, 1985; Kakar, 1978). In contrast, the relationship of stranger was sampled as one that entails no preexisting affective bonds or patterns of social interchange.

Finally, to provide a sensitive index of subjects' conceptions of social responsibilities, questions were included to assess whether subjects felt that each behavior was (a) governed by objective obligations above rule or law or (b) legitimately regulated, or both. These questions not only made it possible to differentiate among moral, conventional, and personal-choice orientations (Nucci, 1981; Turiel, 1983) but distinguished a fourth category. Referred to here as a *personal-moral* orientation, this category includes behaviors that are seen as governed by objective obligations but not as legitimately regulated.

We hypothesized that Indian subjects would more frequently categorize responsiveness to another's needs as an objective obligation and as legitimately regulated than would American subjects in the cases both of the moderate-need friend and stranger incidents and of all the minor-need incidents. In contrast, no cross-cultural differences on these dimensions were anticipated to occur in categorization either of the extreme-need incidents or of the moderate-need parental incidents. We also hypothesized that whereas Indian subjects' categorizations of the behaviors would remain constant across the various need and role conditions, American subjects' categorizations would vary with the magnitude of need and type of role relationship involved.

Specifically, Indian subjects were expected to view all of the incidents involving responsiveness to another's needs in moral terms (i.e., both as an objective obligation and as legitimately regulated). This effect among Indians was anticipated to reflect the general Hindu cultural emphasis on interdependence and mutual aid. In contrast, it was anticipated that American subjects more frequently would view the incidents in moral terms as the magnitude of the need involved increased and in situations involving parent-child, rather than friend or stranger, role relationships. In particular, it was expected that American subjects would view responsiveness to another's needs in fully moral terms only in cases involving extreme need or in moderate-need parental situations. These trends among Americans were anticipated to reflect the American cultural emphases on both beneficence and maximization of individual liberties. Within such a cultural framework, the desirability of meeting another's needs tends to be weighted against the undesirability of restricting individual freedom of choice.

No cross-cultural differences were hypothesized to occur in reasoning about the control incidents involving agents' refusals (a) to engage in arbitrary unjust behavior or (b) to override their own personal preferences in nonneed situations. In the former cases the agents' behaviors were expected to be categorized both as objective obligations and as legitimately regulated (i.e, in moral terms), whereas in the latter cases the agents' behaviors were expected to be categorized neither as objective obligations nor as legitimately regulated (i.e., as matters of personal choice).

STUDY 1

METHOD

Subjects
Data were collected from American subjects in New Haven, Connecticut, and from Indian subjects in Mysore, a city in Southern India. The sample (N = 360) included 60 American subjects at each of three age levels (college, sixth grade, and second grade) and 60 Hindu Indian subjects at each of the same three age levels. In the United States, college students were recruited from Yale University, and children were recruited from public schools in the New Haven area. In India, college students were recruited from major local colleges (i.e., the University of Mysore and the Regional College of Education), and children were recruited from Mysore schools, conducted in the local language of Kannada. In both cultures, interviews were held in empty classrooms at the educational institutions. An equal number of boys and men, and girls and women were interviewed in all subgroups.

As calculated, using a prestige scale developed by Nam, Powers, and their colleagues (Nam & Terrie, 1982; Powers, 1982), no significant differences were observed in the occupational status of heads of household in the American and Indian samples (M = 65.9). Most of the heads of household were employed in professional occupations, such as medicine, law, academics, or business management. Also, no significant age differences occurred between the American and Indian samples (college M = 20.1 years; sixth-grade M = 10.9 years; second-grade M = 7.0 years). The American sample tended to be of Christian or Jewish background and to maintain liberal social and religious orientations. Although less orthodox than most rural Hindu Indian populations, the Indian sample tended to maintain relatively traditional Hindu beliefs, values, and customs.

Procedures
Interviews with Americans were conducted in English by Yale graduate students. Interviews with Indians were conducted in the local language of Kannada by researchers from the Mysore area, who were native Kannada speakers. Recruited from the University of Mysore and the Regional College of Education, the Indian researchers were fluent in English, held master's degrees either in psychology or education, and had previous experience in psychological interviewing.

Several steps were taken to ensure the cultural appropriateness of the research materials in the Indian context. The protocols were examined for cultural suitability by local Indian scholars and were revised, as necessary, on the basis of their comments. The protocols were also modified, as necessary, on the basis of feedback obtained in pilot work with middle-class and lower-class child and adult populations in Mysore. Finally, two culture-specific versions of the experimental stimuli were prepared for use with the American and Indian samples, respectively. These versions differed only in minor details, such as in substituting Indian for American proper names (e.g., *Rekha* for *Rhonda*) or in referring to culturally appropriate items (e.g., *sari* for *dress*).

The Indian version of the research protocols was translated into Kannada by native Kannada speakers who were fluent in English. The translators were thoroughly instructed regarding the desired connotations of the terms to be used and were directed to use familiar words that would be readily comprehended by subjects. All translated materials were pilot-tested to ensure that they were easily understood. The materials were also subjected to back translation to guarantee that the meaning of the original English version of the forms was preserved.

Stimulus materials. The impact of need on subjects' perceptions of helping behavior was examined in a within-subjects manipulation. Nine stimulus items were prepared: Three concerned an agent refusing to help another person who was experiencing life-threatening need (e.g., the need for mouth-to-mouth resuscitation), three concerned an agent refusing to help another person who was experiencing moderate need (e.g., the need for psychological support before surgery), and three concerned an agent refusing to help another person who was experiencing minor need (e.g., the need for directions to a store). In each case (a) the other was portrayed as dependent on the agent for having his or her needs met in a satisfactory manner, (b) the other was described as explicitly requesting aid from the agent,[3] (c) the cost to the agent of fulfilling the other's request was portrayed as minimal, (d) the agent's motive for refusing the other's request was presented as uncompelling and selfish, and (e) the consequences to the other of the agent's refusal to help were described. Four control incidents were also constructed involving nonneed situations: Two control incidents portrayed agents refusing a person's request to commit an arbitrary unjust act (e.g., to destroy someone else's garden), whereas the remaining two portrayed agents refusing a person's request to override their own personal preferences (e.g., to read a book about sports when they preferred to read a book about current events). An outline of all of the incidents appears in the Appendix.[4]

As a between-subjects manipulation, three versions of each incident were created by varying the role relationship of the hypothetical individuals portrayed in the scenarios: (a)

---

[3] Two exceptions to this rule occurred in cases in which the needy other was unconscious. (a) In the incident involving someone's requiring blood during emergency surgery, a nurse made the explicit request for aid. (b) In the incident involving not administering mouth-to-mouth resuscitation, no explicit request for aid was made because no other persons were present.

[4] Explanations of the concepts *mouth-to-mouth resuscitation* and *migraine headache* were included in the incidents read to child subjects.

One version portrayed parents refusing the requests of their 8–12-year-old children; (b) one version portrayed adults refusing the requests of their same-sex best friends; and (c) one version portrayed adults refusing the requests of strangers, who were of the same age and sex as themselves. In this latter condition, subjects were told to assume that the stranger was nonthreatening and posed no danger to the agent. This information was included in order to prevent suspicion or fear of strangers from influencing subjects' judgments.

Each of the three versions of an incident was presented to one third of the subjects in every age/cultural subgroup. An example of the type of incident used in the study is the following:

(*Low Need Incident—Friend Condition*):
Amy is a 30-year-old woman who likes to draw. One day, she found out that an art store, which was going out of business, was having a big sale. Amy wanted to go to the sale to see if she could get any good bargains there. The art store was on Banyon Street—a street on the other side of town. Amy did not know where Banyon Street was.

So Amy asked her best friend Lisa for directions to Banyon Street. Amy told Lisa that she wanted to get to the sale early, while there were still lots of art supplies left to buy. But Lisa was busy reading an exciting book and did not want to be interrupted. So Lisa refused to give her friend directions to Banyon Street. Because of this, by the time Amy was finally able to get to the art store, there were few art supplies left.

Assessment of rule understandings. A series of probes was devised to assess subjects' understandings of the incidents under consideration. These probes were similar in form to ones developed by Turiel and his colleagues (Turiel, 1983; Turiel, Killen, & Helwig, 1987) to be easily comprehensible by young children. The questions tapped subjects' evaluations of the acceptability and desirability of the behaviors portrayed, as well as subjects' judgments concerning whether the behaviors were (a) governed by objective obligations or (b) legitimately regulated, or both. To provide a check on the experimental division of incidents into the contrasting need categories, assessment was also undertaken of subjects' perceptions of the magnitude of the unmet need experienced by the dependent other in each scenario. The various measures are described next, in order of their administration.

In the initial part of the session, each incident was read to subjects, followed by three interview questions. The first two questions tapped subjects' evaluations of the behavior. Specifically, the first question requested that subjects indicate and explain whether, in their opinion, the agent's behavior was all right or not all right. The second question requested that subjects evaluate the desirability of the agent's action on a 9-point scale, ranging from *extremely undesirable* (1) to *extremely desirable* (9), with a neutral midpoint (5). To promote comprehension, children were requested to give their ratings on a visual form of this scale, consisting of a series of progressively frowning or smiling faces.

The third question tapped subjects' judgments concerning whether the behaviors under consideration are governed by objective obligations. Two versions of this question were prepared. For the control incidents involving an agent's refusal to engage in arbitrary unjust behavior, subjects were asked whether agents are obligated to refuse to undertake the action requested even if they want to undertake it (e.g., "If people want to tear down other people's gardens in situations like this, do you think they still have an obligation to refuse to tear them down anyway?"). In contrast, for the remaining incidents subjects were asked whether agents are obligated to undertake the action requested even if they do not want to undertake it (e.g., "If people do not want to give other people directions in situations like this, do you think they still have an obligation to give them directions anyway?"). In all cases, subjects were told that the question referred to an objective obligation (i.e., "more than an obligation that exists just because of a rule or law").

Although the concept of objectivity is abstract, past research has shown that this concept (i.e., nonrule contingency) is readily understood by children as young as preschool age (Smetana, 1981) and by at least some non-Western cultural populations (Song, Smetana, & Kim, 1987). For example (Nucci, 1981), it has been demonstrated that elementary-school-age children can discriminate between behaviors on the basis of whether they are "wrong, regardless of the presence or absence of a governing rule."

The final portion of the interview consisted of two sorting tasks. These were undertaken using 3-in. × 5-in. (7.5 cm × 12.5 cm) index cards that contained descriptive summaries of each incident. The following summary, for instance, was presented on the card for the low-need friend incident mentioned previously:

A 30-year old woman wants directions to an art store. Her best friend is busy reading an exciting book and so SHE REFUSES TO GIVE THE WOMAN DIRECTIONS TO THE STORE.

The first sorting task assessed subjects' perceptions of whether each behavior (underlined) is legitimately regulated. In this procedure, subjects were asked to group each card under one of the following two descriptions: (a) "It is alright to try to stop or punish, in some way, a person who acts like this" or (b) "This is the person's own business. It is not alright to try to stop or punish, in some way, a person who acts like this."[5] It was explained to subjects that "stop or punish" included not only legal punishment but also nonlegal sanctions, such as shunning or snubbing. Sorting a card under the first category indicated that the subject regarded the action under consideration as legitimately regulated. In contrast, sorting a card under the second category indicated that the subject viewed the action under consideration in personal terms.

The second sorting task and final procedure of the study provided a check on the experimental manipulation of need. The cards were reshuffled, and subjects were requested

[5] The legitimate regulation measure was adapted specifically from a probe developed by Nucci (1981) to assess reasoning about personal issues. The Nucci procedure entailed presenting subjects with a set of behaviors and requiring them to sort into a pile those behaviors "which should be considered the agent's own business or should not have a rule governing them." In the present study, the measure was modified by providing a label for the nonselected alternative (i.e., by providing a definition of what it means for a behavior not to be the agent's own business).

to group them according to the level of need experienced by the dependent other in each scenario. The sorting was done in terms of the following four need categories: "no need (0)," "minor need (1)," "moderate need (2)," and "extreme need (3)."

Data coding. Responses were coded into the various conceptual categories on the basis of subjects' replies to the probes regarding whether the behavior under consideration is governed by an obligation above rule or law, is legitimately regulated, or is both: (a) Behaviors regarded both as governed by an objective obligation and as legitimately regulated were considered moral issues, (b) behaviors regarded as not governed by an objective obligation yet legitimately regulated were considered social conventions, (c) behaviors regarded as governed by an objective obligation but not legitimately regulated were considered personal-moral concerns, and (d) behaviors regarded as neither governed by an objective obligation nor legitimately regulated were considered matters of personal choice.

A five-category coding scheme was constructed to code subjects' open-ended explanations for why they regarded particular behaviors as either all right or not all right. The first category, *welfare considerations*, included references (a) to the needs of the other person (e.g., "Her daughter was very frightened about the operation"), (b) to the fact that the agent did not use resources that he or she had to render help (e.g., "She had plenty of aspirin so she could have given some"), and (c) to the selfishness or unkindness of the agent's failure to help (e.g., "It's a selfish thing to do"). The second category, *personal-choice considerations*, encompassed references (a) to the personal discretion of the agent (e.g., "It's up to her to decide"), (b) to minimal need on the part of the person requesting help (e.g., "It wasn't very important to go sightseeing"), (c) to the other's responsibility for his or her own problems (e.g., "He should bring enough money if he wants to see a movie"), and (d) to the absence of an obligation to render help (e.g., "You don't have to give someone directions, if you don't want to"). The third category, *unjust/harmful*, contained references to the unfairness of the agent's action ("It's unfair to take something without paying for it") and to damages resulting from the agent's action (e.g., "It ruined his garden"). The fourth category, *role duty*, comprised references to obligations deriving from the agent's role status (e.g., "It was part of her obligation as a mother to help"). Finally, the fifth category, *other*, included references to any other factors not accounted for earlier.

Reliability in applying the coding scheme was obtained between an American researcher from New Haven and a Hindu Indian researcher from Mysore on a total of 90 responses, sampled from each cultural/age/role/incident-type condition. Assessed in terms of Cohen's kappa, reliability reached .92, with a range of from .89 for the category of role duty to .96 for the category of personal-choice considerations.

RESULTS

The data were analyzed by means of repeated measures analyses of variance (ANOVAS), with an arcsine transformation applied to proportion scores. The dependent variables in the ANOVAS were calculated using mean scores for each of the five types of incidents contrasted (i.e., extreme need, moderate need, minor need avoidance of injustice, and personal preference). The Scheffé procedure was used to obtain post hoc comparisons of individual means. Preliminary examination revealed no significant effects of sex on subjects' responses; therefore, sex was not included as a variable in subsequent analyses.

Perceptions of Need Portrayed in Stimuli

To determine whether subjects' perceptions of the stimuli were in accordance with the experimentally constructed need divisions, a $2 \times 3 \times 3 \times 5$ (Culture × Age × Role × Incident Type) ANOVA was performed on subjects' need sortings of the incidents. This analysis revealed significant main effects of culture, $F(1, 340) = 14.58$, $p < .01$, age, $F(2, 340) = 8.71$, $p < .01$, and incident type, $F(4, 1,360) = 6,909.67$, $p < .01$, as well as significant interactions of incident type and culture, $F(4, 1,360) = 16.11$, $p < .01$, incident type and age, $F(8, 1,360) = 2.49$, $p < .01$, and incident type and role, $F(8, 1,360) = 2.32$, $p < .05$.

Post hoc analyses revealed that at all ages in both cultures, subjects discriminated between the various levels of need in the expected ways. In particular, the extreme-need incidents tended to be sorted into the extreme-need category ($M = 2.98$) and were judged to be significantly higher in need than were the moderate-need incidents ($p < .01$). These latter incidents, in turn, tended to be sorted into the moderate-need category ($M = 2.07$) and were judged significantly higher in need than were the minor-need incidents ($p < .01$). Also, in accord with the experimental manipulation, the minor-need incidents tended to be grouped in the minor-need category ($M = 1.16$) and were viewed as significantly higher in need than were the two sets of control incidents involving either avoidance of injustice ($M = .04$) or personal-preference considerations ($M = .09$, $p < .01$). These control incidents, as designed, were appraised as nonneed situations.

Various cultural, age, and role effects, however, were also observed. Specifically, Indians perceived both the moderate-need incidents and the minor-need incidents (moderate $M = 2.16$; minor $M = 1.26$) as significantly higher in need than did Americans (moderate $M = 1.98$; minor $M = 1.05$; $p < .01$). Also, in both cultures second graders ($M = 2.14$) and sixth graders ($M = 2.10$) viewed the moderate-need incidents as significantly higher in need than did college students ($M = 1.97$; $p < .01$), and second graders ($M = 1.25$) viewed the minor-need incidents as significantly higher in need than did college students ($M = 1.06$; $p < .01$). Finally, all of the subjects in both cultures viewed the personal-preference incidents as significantly higher in need in the case of parent-child relationships ($M = .17$) than in the case of friendship relationships ($M = .06$) or stranger relationships ($M = .07$; $p < .05$).

In summary, the results indicate that the experimental stimuli were perceived in the intended ways, in that all subgroups judged them to embody four distinct degrees of need: extreme need, moderate need, minor need, and no need. The only unanticipated results occurred in the interactions of perceived need with culture, age, and role. To control for these interactions, the variable of perceived need was included as a covariate in all subsequent analyses.

Evaluations of Incidents

To compare subjects' evaluations of the incidents, a $2 \times 3 \times 3 \times 5$ (Culture × Age × Role × Incident Type) ANOVA was performed on subjects' ratings of incident desirability. (As noted in the previous paragraph, in this and all subsequent analyses, perceived need was included as a covariate.) The analysis revealed significant main effects of role, $F(2, 338) =$

67.85, $p < .01$, and of incident type, $F(4, 1,355) = 791.63$, $p < .01$, as well as a significant interaction of incident type and role, $F(8, 1,355) = 7.13$ $p < .01$.

Post hoc comparisons indicated that desirability ratings differed significantly among each type of incident ($p < .01$). The extreme-need incidents were rated as most undesirable ($M = 1.36$), followed in turn by the moderate-need incidents ($M = 2.44$) and finally by the minor-need incidents ($M = 3.41$). In contrast, the personal-preference incidents were viewed as somewhat desirable ($M = 6.45$), and the avoidance of injustice incidents were viewed as extremely desirable ($M = 8.27$). In each case, the incidents were rated as more undesirable in the parent and friend conditions ($M = 4.22$) than in the stranger condition ($M = 4.72$).

The results demonstrate striking commonalities in subjects' evaluations of incident desirability. No significant cultural or age differences occurred in subjects' evaluations of the incidents.

Categorization of Behaviors

Preliminary frequency analyses revealed that subjects rarely used the social convention category (with an average usage of only 2% in any culture/age/role/incident-type condition). The personal-moral category was also found to be content and culture specific. In particular, the category tended to be used only in relation to the incidents involving nonresponsiveness to another's needs and only by Americans.[6]

On the basis of these findings, a decision was made to analyze subjects' categorizations of the incidents in two ways: (a) To assess the specific locus of any cross-cultural differences in moral reasoning, analyses were performed separately on the two criteria examined (i.e., whether the given behavior is governed by an objective obligation and the legitimacy of regulating the given behavior); and (b) to provide descriptive information regarding American subjects' usage of the personal-moral category, comparison was undertaken of Americans' categorizations of the need incidents in personal-moral, as contrasted with moral or personal-choice, terms.

Perceptions of objective obligations. To examine subjects' views of objective obligation, a $2 \times 3 \times 3 \times 5$ (Culture × Age × Role × Incident Type) ANOVA was performed on subjects' judgments concerning whether the behaviors under consideration are governed by obligations above rule or law. Results revealed significant main effects of culture, $F(1, 339) = 67.76$, $p < .01$; age $F(2, 339) = 7.74$, $p < .01$; role, $F(2, 339) = 20.46$, $p < .01$, and incident type, $F(4, 1,359) = 1,592.15$, $p < .01$, as well as significant interactions of culture and age, $F(2, 339) = 4.35$, $p < .05$, culture and role, $F(2, 339) = 9.18$, $p < .01$, age and role, $F(4, 339) = 3.04$, $p < .05$, incident type and culture, $F(4, 1,359) = 81.13$, $p < .01$, incident type and age, $F(8, 1,359) = 9.85$, $p < .01$, incident type and role, $F(8, 1,359) = 9.74$, $p < .01$,

---

[6] In regard to the control incidents involving avoidance of injustice, the personal-moral category was used, on average, by 4% of the Americans in each age/role condition and by no Indians. In regard to the control incidents involving personal preference considerations, the personal-moral category was used, on average, by 2% of the Americans and by 1% of the Indians in each age/role condition. No Indian used the personal-moral category in relation to the need incidents.

incident type, culture, and role, $F(8, 1,359) = 8.91$, $p < .01$, and of incident type, culture, age, and role $F(16, 1,359) = 1.88$, $p < .05$. The percentage of subjects categorizing the behaviors as objective obligations appears in Table 1.

The results, it may be seen, are in accord with the hypothesized tendency of the Indian subjects to categorize responsiveness to another's needs as objective obligations more frequently than do the American subjects in the cases of the moderate-need friend and stranger incidents and of all the minor-need incidents. No cross-cultural differences occurred in categorization either of the extreme-need incidents or of the moderate-need parental incidents. In contrast, Indians, more frequently than Americans ($p < .01$), categorized all the other need incidents as objective obligations.

As hypothesized, need and role had marked impact only on Americans' judgments. In terms of need effects, Americans more frequently classified behaviors as objective obligations as the need portrayed increased: (a) In the friend and stranger conditions, extreme-need behaviors were most frequently classified as objective obligations, followed in turn by moderate-need behaviors and finally by minor-need behaviors ($p < .01$); and (b) in the parent condition, both extreme-need and moderate-need behaviors were more frequently classified as objective obligations than were minor-need behaviors ($p < .01$). In terms of role effects, under the moderate- and minor-need conditions American second graders and college students classified parental behaviors most frequently as objective obligations, followed in turn by friend behaviors and finally by stranger behaviors ($p < .01$). By comparison, American sixth graders showed a contrasting pattern of role effects, with friend behaviors considered objective obligations as frequently as parental behaviors in the moderate-need condition and more frequently than parental behaviors in the minor-need condition ($p < .01$). Like second graders and college students, however, sixth graders less frequently categorized stranger behaviors as objective obligations than either parental or friend behaviors in the moderate- and minor-need conditions ($p < .01$). Only one localized effect of need and role occurred among Indians: Indian college students classified the minor-need stranger incidents as objective obligations less frequently than they did the other need incidents ($p < .01$).

Results observed in the control conditions conformed to the predicted patterns: Virtually all of the subjects classified the avoidance of injustice incidents as objective obligations, whereas virtually no subjects categorized the personal-preference incidents as objective obligations.

In terms of developmental effects, the responses of American children tended to differ from those of American college students in the same direction as the responses of Indians differed from those of Americans. Whereas no developmental differences occurred in evaluation either of the extreme-need behaviors or of the moderate-need parental behaviors, American children tended to categorize all the other need behaviors as objective obligations more frequently than did American college students. This age trend followed a linear pattern in the parental (minor-need) and stranger (moderate- and minor-need) conditions, second graders classified the breaches as objective obligations most frequently, followed in turn by sixth graders and finally by college students ($p < .01$). In contrast, in the friend

TABLE 1
Percentage of Subjects Categorizing Behaviors as Objective Obligations

Incident type	Parent (to young child)			Friend			Stranger		
	Second grade	Sixth grade	College	Second grade	Sixth grade	College	Second grade	Sixth grade	College
				India					
Extreme need	98	100	98	98	98	100	100	100	100
Moderate need	100	98	97	100	100	100	100	97	100
Minor need	97	98	92	98	100	93	95	97	73
Avoidance of injustice	100	98	100	100	98	100	100	100	100
Personal preference	15	5	10	0	8	8	0	3	0
				United States					
Extreme need	100	100	100	98	100	97	97	95	97
Moderate need	95	94	95	78	92	65	65	53	47
Minor need	75	63	44	58	85	33	53	47	23
Avoidance of injustice	100	95	100	98	100	98	98	100	100
Personal preference	3	5	5	3	0	0	0	0	0

(moderate- and minor-need) condition, a curvilinear age trend was observed; sixth graders classified the behaviors as objective obligations most frequently, followed in turn by second graders and finally by college students ($p < .01$). Among Indians, the only significant age effect occurred in the minor-need stranger condition; children classified these behaviors as objective obligations more frequently than did college students ($p < .01$).

In summary, subjects' perceptions of the behaviors as objective obligations (one aspect of a moral orientation) conformed to the predicted patterns. Specifically Indians more frequently viewed responsiveness to another's needs as an objective obligation than did Americans in all cases involving minor need and under the stranger and friend role conditions in cases involving moderate need. By comparison, no cross-cultural differences occurred in reasoning about extreme-need situations or about moderate-need situations involving parent-child role relationships. Also, as expected, whereas Americans' judgments varied markedly with need and role, Indians' judgments tended to remain constant across the various need and role conditions.

Perceptions of legitimate regulation. To examine subjects' views of legitimate regulation, a $2 \times 3 \times 3 \times 5$ (Culture × Age × Role × Incident Type) ANOVA was undertaken on subjects' judgments concerning whether the behaviors under consideration are legitimately regulated. Results revealed significant main effects of culture, $F(1, 339) = 456.33$, $p < .01$; role $F(2, 339) = 11.72$, $p < .01$, and incident type, $F(4, 1359) = 1,147.46$, $p < .01$, as well as significant interactions of culture and role, $F(2, 339) = 8.62$, $p < .01$, incident type and culture, $F(4, 1359) = 199.20$, $p < .01$, incident type and age, $F(8, 1359) = 2.71$, $p < .01$, incident type and role $F(8, 1359) = 5.18$, $p < .01$, and of incident type, culture, and role, $F(8, 1359) = 8.49$, $p < .01$. The percentage of subjects categorizing the behaviors as legitimately regulated appears in Table 2.

A comparison of Tables 1 and 2 reveals that a higher percentage of Americans regarded the need behaviors as objective obligations than viewed them as legitimately regulated. In contrast, all of the Indians who categorized the need behaviors as objective obligations also categorized them as legitimately regulated. These contrasting patterns reflect the phenomenon, revealed in the earlier frequency analysis, that only Americans categorized the need incidents in personal-moral terms (i.e., as objective obligations but not as legitimately regulated).

Cross-cultural differences in perceptions of legitimate regulation were more extensive than those observed in perceptions of objective obligation. With the exception of extreme-need parental situations, Indians, more frequently than Americans ($p < .01$), regarded all of the need situations as legitimately regulated. Results also revealed that need and role again had greater impact on Americans' than on Indians' judgments. Americans most frequently regarded extreme-need incidents as legitimately regulated, followed in turn by moderate-need incidents and finally by low-need incidents ($p < .01$). Also, Americans more frequently classified parental-need incidents as legitimately regulated than they did either friend- or stranger-need incidents ($p < .01$). In contrast, need and role again had only one effect on Indians' judgments, that is, college students less frequently viewed stranger minor-need incidents as legitimately regulated than all other need incidents ($p < .01$).

TABLE 2
Percentage of Subjects Categorizing Behaviors as Legitimately Regulated

Incident type	Parent (to young child)			Friend			Stranger		
	Second grade	Sixth grade	College	Second grade	Sixth grade	College	Second grade	Sixth grade	College
India									
Extreme need	98	100	98	98	98	100	100	100	100
Moderate need	100	98	97	100	100	100	100	97	100
Minor need	97	98	92	98	100	93	95	97	73
Avoidance of injustice	100	98	100	100	98	100	100	100	100
Personal preference	15	5	8	0	5	8	0	0	0
United States									
Extreme need	100	100	97	87	93	92	87	87	92
Moderate need	79	67	70	42	37	42	32	30	40
Minor need	47	30	18	22	22	18	32	12	22
Avoidance of injustice	100	85	95	93	90	92	100	95	95
Personal preference	0	0	0	0	0	0	0	0	0

Judgments regarding the control incidents conformed to the study predictions. Virtually all of the subjects viewed the avoidance of injustice incidents, but not the personal-preference incidents, as legitimately regulated. Together with the results observed in perceptions of objective obligation, these findings indicate that as hypothesized, the avoidance of injustice incidents were viewed in moral terms, whereas the personal preference incidents were categorized as matters of personal choice.

Finally, only one age effect occurred in perceptions of legitimate regulation. In both cultures, children, more frequently than college students ($p < .01$), viewed minor-need incidents as legitimately regulated.

In summary, the results indicate that extensive cross-cultural differences occurred in perceptions of legitimate regulation. With the exception of extreme-need parental incidents, Indians, more frequently than Americans, viewed all of the need incidents as legitimately regulated. Also, Americans' judgments again varied more by need and role than did those of Indians.

In conjunction with the findings on perceptions of objective obligation, the findings on perceptions of legitimate regulation clarify the locus of cross-cultural commonalities and differences in moral reasoning. In particular, the results indicate that cross-cultural differences were more extensive in judgments of legitimate regulation than in judgments of objective obligation. They also indicate that it was only in the case of extreme-need parental breaches that Indians and Americans fully agreed in viewing the need incidents in moral terms (i.e., as both objective obligations and as legitimately regulated). In contrast, in the case of friend and stranger extreme-need breaches and of parental moderate-need breaches, Indians and Americans agreed in their perceptions of the behaviors as objective obligations but differed in their perceptions of whether the behaviors are legitimately regulated. In the remaining need and role conditions, Indians' and Americans' categorizations differed along both the dimensions of objective obligation and legitimate regulation.

Americans' usage of the personal-moral category. To compare Americans' usage of the personal-moral category with their usage of the moral and personal choice categories, a $3 \times 3 \times 3 \times 3$ (Age × Role × Incident Type × Rule Category) ANOVA was undertaken on the proportion of Americans categorizing the need incidents in moral, personal-moral, or personal-choice terms.[7] Results revealed a significant main effect of rule category, $F(2, 340) = 93.56$, $p < .01$, as well as significant interactions of rule category and age, $F(4, 340) = 5.30$, $p < .01$; rule category and incident type, $F(4, 680) = 189.19$, $p < .01$; rule category and role, $F(4, 340) = 12.70$, $p < .01$; rule category, incident type, and age, $F(8, 680) = 4.67$, $p < .01$; and rule category, incident type, and role, $F(8, 680) = 6.36$, $p < .01$.

Table 3 contrasts Americans' usage of the moral, personal-moral, and personal-choice categories. In terms of role effects, in the moderate-need condition the moral category

---

[7] The social convention category was omitted from this analysis because of its extremely low frequency of usage. Also, as noted earlier, because the personal-moral category was never used by Indians in regard to the need incidents and rarely used by either cultural group in relation to the control incidents, this analysis was undertaken only on Americans' categorizations of the need incidents.

TABLE 3

Percentage of Moral, Personal-Moral, and Personal-Choice Responses Used by Americans in Relation to Need Incidents

Need incident type	Parent (to young child)			Friend			Stranger		
	Second grade	Sixth grade	College	Second grade	Sixth grade	College	Second grade	Sixth grade	College
Extreme need									
Moral	100	100	97	87	93	92	87	87	92
Personal-moral	0	0	3	11	7	5	10	8	5
Personal choice	0	0	0	0	0	3	3	3	3
Moderate need									
Moral	79	67	68	41	37	42	32	30	37
Personal-moral	16	27	27	37	55	23	33	23	10
Personal choice	5	6	3	21	8	35	30	45	50
Minor need									
Moral	47	30	18	18	22	18	31	12	18
Personal-moral	28	33	26	40	63	15	22	35	5
Personal choice	23	33	55	38	12	67	46	50	72

tended to be used most frequently in relation to parental breaches, and the personal-choice category tended to be used most frequently in relation to stranger breaches, whereas the personal-moral category tended to be used most frequently in relation to friend breaches ($p < .01$). Similar role effects were observed in the minor-need condition; the personal-choice category was used most frequently in relation to stranger breaches, and the personal-moral category was used most frequently in relation to friend breaches ($p < .01$). In terms of need effects, the moral category tended to be used most frequently in relation to extreme-need breaches, and the personal-choice category tended to be used most frequently in regard to minor-need breaches ($p < .01$). In contrast, the personal-moral category was used as frequently in relation to moderate-need breaches as in relation to minor-need breaches. Finally, results revealed that the personal-moral category tended to be used more by children than by college students, whereas the reverse developmental trend was observed in usage of the personal-choice category ($p < .01$).

In summary, the personal-moral category tended to be used most frequently in relation to breaches falling in an intermediate range between those categorized as moral issues and those categorized as matters of personal choice. Americans used the category most frequently in relation to friend behaviors and to behaviors in an intermediate range of need extremity.

Justification Responses

Finally, to compare the factors mentioned by subjects in explaining why they evaluated the incidents as all right or not all right, a $2 \times 3 \times 3 \times 5 \times 5$ (Culture × Age × Role × Incident Type × Justification) *ANOVA* was undertaken on subjects' justification responses, which had previously been scored in terms of the five coding categories (i.e., welfare, personal-choice considerations, harmful, role duty, and other). This analysis revealed significant main effects of incident type, $F(4, 1291) = 34.92$, $p < .01$, and of justification, $F(4, 1292) = 2,945.36$, $p < .01$, as well as significant interactions of incident type and culture, $F(4, 1291) = 3.54$. $p < .01$; justification and culture, $F(4, 1292) = 100.63$, $p < .01$; justification and age, $F(8, 1292) = 17.23$, $p < .01$; justification and role, $F(8, 1292) = 15.30$, $p < .01$; justification, culture, and role, $F(8, 1292) = 5.78$, $p < .01$; justification, age, and role, $F(16, 1292) = 3.95$, $p < .01$; justification and incident type, $F(16, 5168) = 2,880.90$, $p < .01$; justification, incident type, and culture, $F(16, 5168) = 57.27$, $p < .01$; justification, incident type, and age, $F(32, 5168) = 8.66$, $p < .01$; justification, incident type, and role, $F(32, 5168) = 9.89$, $p < .01$; justification, incident type, culture, and role, $F(32, 5168) = 5.40$, $p < .01$; justification, incident type, age, and role, $F(64, 5168) = 2.41$, $p < .01$; and of justification, incident type, culture, age, and role, $F(64, 5168) = 1.94$, ($p < .01$).

Post hoc comparisons[8] revealed that cultural differences in references to welfare tended to be in the same direction as those observed in perceptions of objective obligation. Specif-

---

[8] Because of its relatively low frequency of usage, no post hoc analyses were conducted on the "other" justification category. The "other" category was used on average by only 2% of the subjects in any culture/age/role/incident-type condition, with a frequency of usage no greater than 4% in any culture/age/role/incident-type condition.

ically, with the exception of the parent moderate-need condition among college students, Indians made greater reference to welfare considerations than did Americans in the cases of all the moderate- and all the minor-need breaches ($p < .01$). The reverse pattern of cross-cultural differences was observed among college students in the extreme-need parent and friend conditions ($p < .01$), an effect that arose from approximately one fifth of Indian college students' justifications in these conditions referring to role duty.[9] Subjects' references to welfare considerations are presented in Table 4.

As may be seen in Table 5, effects observed in reference to personal-choice considerations tended to be the inverse of those occurring in reference to welfare considerations. Specifically, with the exception of the parent moderate-need condition among sixth graders and college students, Americans made greater reference to personal-choice considerations than did Indians in the cases of all moderate- and all minor-need breaches ($p < .01$). Also, as expected, all of the subjects justified their reactions to the personal-preference control incidents almost exclusively by reference to personal-choice considerations.

No significant group differences occurred in reference to the category of unjust/harmful. All of the subjects used this category almost exclusively in relation to the avoidance of injustice control incidents (overall $M = 93\%$).

DISCUSSION

Support was obtained for the study hypotheses regarding cross-cultural differences in the conceptualization of social responsibilities. Indians more frequently viewed responsiveness to another's needs as an objective obligation than did Americans in all cases that involved minor needs or the moderately serious needs of friends or strangers. Cross-cultural differences in perceptions of legitimate regulation were observed to be even more pervasive— with Indians more frequently viewing behaviors as legitimately regulated than did Americans also in cases involving the moderately serious needs of children or the extreme needs of friends or strangers.

Results call into question an interpretation of such cross-cultural differences on the basis of variation in subjects' evaluations of the behaviors under consideration. The cross-cultural effects were found to occur even when controlling for differences in subjects' perceptions of the need portrayed in the stimuli. Also, the finding that Indians and Americans agreed in their ratings of the desirability of the behaviors indicates that the behaviors were equally salient to both cultural groups.

Indian subjects' reasoning about the control incidents provides evidence that the results also cannot be explained in terms of a general inclination on the part of Indians to be compliant to others' requests or in terms of cultural differences in comprehension of the probes. Indians' tendencies to judge that it is morally obligatory to refuse unjust requests demon-

---

[9] Cross-cultural differences in references to role duty occurred only among adults. Specifically, Indian adults made significantly greater reference to role duty than did American adults in the extreme-need parent (India $M = 22\%$; U.S $M = 11\%$) and friend (India $M = 21\%$; U.S. $M = 9\%$) conditions, as well as in the minor-need parent condition (India $M = 26\%$; U.S. $M = 8\%$; $p < .01$).

TABLE 4

Percentage of Subjects' Justifications Referring to Welfare Considerations

Incident type	Parent (to young child)			Friend			Stranger		
	Second grade	Sixth grade	College	Second grade	Sixth grade	College	Second grade	Sixth grade	College
India									
Extreme need	97	96	78	95	95	79	98	98	96
Moderate need	99	99	73	95	84	88	99	94	94
Minor need	96	99	69	96	91	73	95	92	75
Avoidance of injustice	3	9	7	3	6	4	8	4	20
Personal preference	12	5	4	0	3	3	0	0	0
United States									
Extreme need	93	96	89	93	91	88	100	97	94
Moderate need	88	93	72	79	73	73	70	69	55
Minor need	68	49	48	58	73	65	54	46	28
Avoidance of injustice	1	8	1	1	5	13	4	14	14
Personal preference	3	0	0	0	0	0	0	0	0

132

TABLE 5
Percentage of Subjects' Justifications Referring to Personal-Choice Considerations

	Parent (to young child)			Friend			Stranger		
Incident type	Second grade	Sixth grade	College	Second grade	Sixth grade	College	Second grade	Sixth grade	College
India									
Extreme need	0	0	0	0	0	0	0	0	0
Moderate need	0	0	0	0	0	1	0	3	0
Minor need	0	0	5	0	0	6	5	3	22
Avoidance of injustice	0	0	3	0	0	0	0	0	3
Personal preference	88	95	93	100	97	95	100	100	99
United States									
Extreme need	0	0	0	0	0	3	0	3	2
Moderate need	7	3	2	13	12	7	26	29	42
Minor need	24	45	42	32	17	18	43	54	69
Avoidance of injustice	3	0	7	1	1	3	1	7	4
Personal preference	95	99	93	97	98	100	100	100	95

strate that they regard conforming indiscriminantly to any demand made by another as undesirable. Equally, the absence of cross-cultural differences in response to the personal-preference control incidents provides evidence that the objective obligation and legitimate regulation probes were understood in similar ways in both cultures. In particular, no age or cultural differences occurred in the tendencies to categorize the personal-preference incidents as matters of personal choice (i.e., as neither governed by objective obligations nor legitimately regulated) and to refer to personal-choice considerations in evaluating these incidents. Such findings indicate that Indians possess a concept of personal choice, which they were able to express through their responses to the probes.

STUDY 2

Although the results of the first study conformed to the patterns predicted on the basis of the contrasting cultural beliefs and values emphasized in the United States and India, it also appears possible that they may reflect socioeconomic effects. Living in a more technologically developed society, Americans generally have greater access to economic resources than do Indians. They thus may experience less functional need for a social system that promotes mutual interdependence than do Indians and, thereby, may be less prone to regard social responsibilities in moral terms (Muir & Weinstein, 1962).

To evaluate this alternative explanation of the results, the research was repeated among Hindu Indian adults from different socioeconomic groups. Subjects were sampled from a middle-aged, rather than a college-aged, population in order to obtain subjects whose lifestyles tend to vary more with their socioeconomic status than is the case among students attending college.

METHOD

Subjects

Data was obtained from a sample of 20 middle-class and 20 lower-class adults. The middle-class sample was recruited from among the academic staff of the University of Mysore and from among residents of the middle-class community surrounding the university. The lower-class sample was recruited from among persons employed as sweepers in the university dormitories or as laborers in a nearby factory. Interviews were conducted either in subjects' homes or places of work.

Comparisons revealed that the occupational prestige scores of household heads in the middle-class sample ($M = 68.2$) were significantly higher than those of household heads in the lower-class sample ($M = 33.1$). There was no significant age difference between subjects in the two socioeconomic groups ($M = 43.4$ years).

Procedures

The same measures used in the first study were administered to the middle- and lower-class Indian adult samples. In contrast to the first study, however, subjects were only assessed in the stranger role condition. This condition was selected as the one in which the greatest cross-cultural differences in social domain categorization had been observed in Study I. It was reasoned that if socioeconomic factors affected the cross-cultural results, their influence would be most apparent in the stranger role condition.

RESULTS

Perceptions of Need Portrayed in Stimuli and Evaluations of Incidents

When 2×5 (Socioeconomic Group $\times$ Incident Type) ANOVAs were undertaken on subjects' need ratings of the experimental stimuli and on subjects' ratings of the desirability of the behaviors portrayed, respectively, they revealed only main effects of incident type, $F(4, 152) = 2,654.74$, $p < .01$, and $F(4, 152) = 1,257.81$, $p < .01$. Subjects distinguished levels of need and evaluated the incidents in the same manner as in Study 1. Socioeconomic status was observed to have no effect on subjects' perceptions.

Categorization of Incidents

Preliminary frequency analyses revealed that, as in the first study, Indians made no use of either the personal-moral or social convention categories in appraising the incidents involving nonresponsiveness to another's needs. Rather, all behaviors regarded as objective obligations were also regarded as legitimately regulated. Given such results, a decision was made not to analyze the dimensions of objective obligation and legitimate regulation separately. Instead, an analysis was performed on the category of moral obligation (i.e., on the view that a behavior is both governed by an objective obligation and legitimately regulated).

To assess subjects' classifications of the incidents in moral terms, a 2×5 (Socioeconomic Group $\times$ Incident Type) ANOVA was undertaken. This analysis revealed significant main effects of socioeconomic group, $F(1, 38) = 6.20$, $p < .05$, and of incident type, $F(4, 152) = 395.58$, $p < .01$, as well as a significant interaction of socioeconomic group and incident type, $F(4, 152) = 3.18$, $p < .05$.

Post hoc analyses indicated that socioeconomic status affected only subjects' categorizations of the minor-need incidents. Specifically, lower-class subjects ($M = 83\%$) more frequently categorized minor-need incidents in moral terms than did middle-class subjects ($M = 65\%$; $p < .05$).

Justification Responses

To compare subjects' justification responses, a $2 \times 5 \times 5$ ANOVA (Socioeconomic Group $\times$ Incident Type $\times$ Justification) was performed on the proportion of references made by subjects to the various justification categories. This analysis showed significant main effects of incident type, $F(4, 144) = 5.49$, $p < .01$, and of justification, $F(4, 144) = 785.61$, $p < .01$, as well as significant interactions of justification and socioeconomic group, $F(4, 144) = 6.44$, $p < .01$; incident type and justification, $F(16, 576) = 602.13$, $p < .01$; and of incident type, justification, and socioeconomic group, $F(16, 576) = 2.79$, $p < .01$.

Subgroup differences occurred only in justifying reactions to the minor-need incidents. Consonant with their greater tendency to categorize the minor-need incidents in moral, as contrasted with personal-choice, terms, lower-class subjects made significantly greater reference to welfare considerations (lower-class $M = 84\%$; middle-class $M = 68\%$) and significantly less reference to personal-choice considerations than did middle-class subjects (lower-class $M = 14\%$; middle-class $M = 29\%$; $p < .01$).

In summary, socioeconomic status affected only subjects' categorizations and justifications of the minor-need incidents. As compared with middle-class adults, lower-class adults more frequently categorized minor-need incidents as moral matters, rather than as matters of personal choice, and justified their reactions in terms of welfare rather than personal-choice considerations. No socioeconomic effects occurred in the categorization of the extreme- or moderate-need incidents.

Discussion

The results provide evidence that socioeconomic status may have contributed, in part, to the differences in moral reasoning observed among Indian and American subjects in the first study. It was demonstrated that in the stranger condition, middle-class Hindu Indian adults categorized the low-need issues in moral terms significantly less frequently than did lower-class Hindu Indian adults. Such trends imply that higher socioeconomic status may be associated with a change in orientation toward social responsibilities, from a moral to a personal-choice perspective.

Note, however, that whereas the cross-cultural differences observed in Study 1 may have been enhanced to some degree by the differential socioeconomic status of the American and Indian samples, socioeconomic effects do not appear substantial enough to be the basis of these differences. In particular, no socioeconomic effects were observed either in the extreme- or moderate-need stranger conditions—conditions on which significant cross-cultural variation occurred in the first study. Also, the number of middle-class Indian adult subjects who categorized the minor-need stranger incidents in moral terms was observed to be more than 3 times as great as the number of American adult subjects who did so.

GENERAL DISCUSSION

CULTURAL INFLUENCES ON MORAL REASONING ABOUT SOCIAL RESPONSIBILITIES

The results demonstrate that Americans and Indians hold a common view of social responsibilities in regard to certain types of helping situations. It is documented that in both the Indian and the American samples, the vast majority of subjects viewed social responsibilities involving life-threatening need in moral terms (i.e., as both governed by an objective obligation and legitimately regulated). Also, in both samples subjects referred primarily to nonjustice concerns (i.e., welfare considerations) in justifying their reactions to social responsibilities that they considered to be moral issues.

The evidence also reveals, however, that marked cross-cultural variation exists in the scope of social responsibilities considered as moral and in the criteria applied in judging that such issues constitute moral obligations. Specifically, Indian subjects were found to maintain an extremely broad view of interpersonal moral duties. The primary criterion for categorizing social responsibilities in moral terms was the existence of some unmet need; the magnitude of this need and the nature of the role relationships involved had virtually no effect on Indian subjects' judgments. In contrast, we observed that American subjects considered a smaller domain of social responsibilities as moral obligations, and their judgments were affected both by need and role considerations. With the exception of moderately serious parental breaches, the majority of American subjects viewed non-life-threatening breaches of social responsibilities in personal-moral or personal-choice, rather than in moral, terms.

The findings may be seen to support the view that cultural meaning systems influence the development of moral codes. The wide scope of interpersonal moral obligations observed among the Hindu Indian sample, for example, appears to reflect the sociocentric emphasis of Hindu Indian cultural conceptions and practices (Dumont, 1970; Kakar, 1978; O'Flaherty & Derrett, 1978). In such a cultural framework, the starting point of morality is the social whole, of which the individual forms an interdependent part. Obligations to serve the social whole through responsiveness to the needs of dependent others, then, tend to be regarded as fundamental moral commitments. In contrast, the more narrow scope of interpersonal moral obligations observed among American subjects may be seen to reflect the cultural premise that the autonomous individual constitutes the fundamental social unit (Dumont, 1965). Such a perspective is evidenced, for example, in the high cultural value placed on independence and privacy and in the Western philosophical assumption that individuals exist prior to social institutions (Locke, 1966; Rawls, 1971). Within this cultural system, individual freedom of choice tends to be weighed against the highly desirable, but competing, value of beneficence.

One implication of the present results would be to challenge assertions that the content of moral codes is universal (e.g., Kohlberg, 1981). Contrary to Kohlberg's claim that social responsibilities are supererogatory, our results demonstrate that Indians accord such responsibilities full moral status. Such trends imply that the content of moral codes is not limited to questions of justice but may extend as well to issues of social responsibility.

A further implication of the findings would be to highlight the need to pay greater attention to cultural factors in explaining the distribution and origins of prosocial moral reasoning. No evidence was found to support Gilligan's (1977, 1982) claims that the moral status of interpersonal responsiveness and care is gender based. Rather, the tendency to categorize social responsibilities in moral terms was found to be related to cultural background; Hindu Indians maintained a more fully moral view of social responsibilities than did Americans of either sex. Such results suggest that attitudes toward helping needy others may be most fully explained by reference to culturally variable social beliefs and practices, rather than by reference to universal processes of gender differentiation.

NEED AND ROLE EFFECTS ON PERCEPTIONS OF SOCIAL RESPONSIBILITIES

The observed effects of need on American subjects' moral judgments may be seen to derive, at least in part, from Americans' weighing of their contrasting commitments to personal liberties and to beneficence. Americans' moral judgments showed a linear relationship to need; extreme-need situations were most frequently categorized in moral terms, followed in turn by moderate-need situations and finally by minor-need situations. This pattern of judgment does not appear fully explicable in terms of a tendency to differentiate between scenarios on the basis of whether they involve rights-based concerns (Kohlberg, 1971). Rather, the linear relation found between need magnitude and moral judgment suggests that Americans weighed welfare concerns against personal-choice considerations—the two factors given most emphasis in their justifications. In particular, it appears that in non-life-threatening need situations Americans appraised helping others in moral terms only in cases in which they judged that the negative welfare consequences ensuing from an agent's nonresponsiveness were serious enough to warrant curtailing the agent's freedom of choice.

Contrasting factors may underlie the role effects observed among Americans. As predicted, Americans categorized moderate-need breaches in moral terms more frequently in cases involving parent-child relationships than in cases involving friend or stranger relationships. It appears possible that such trends reflect the somewhat unique status of the parent–young child role relationship in American culture. Specifically, anthropological evidence indicates that compared to other role obligations in the culture, parental obligations to ensure their young children's welfare are seen as based, at least in part, on natural law, rather than solely on contract and consent (Schneider, 1968). It may follow then that lesser degrees of need are required for Americans to regard parental obligations as moral than are required for Americans to make such an assessment of other role obligations. In particular, in the case of parental obligations, personal-choice considerations appear to be weighed not merely against the negative welfare consequences of nonresponsiveness but also against the perceived natural order of things.

It also appears possible that such role effects reflect, at least in part, individual interest considerations related to social group membership (Tajfel, 1978). Americans may judge that there is a stronger moral obligation to help offspring than to help friends or strangers because offspring are members of the family in-group. The welfare of one's offspring then has more self-relevance than does the welfare of persons such as friends or strangers, who are more remotely related. Further evidence in support of this interpretation may be seen in the tendency of American subjects to categorize social responsibilities to known others (i.e., to one's own children and friends) as objective obligations more frequently than social responsibilities to unknown others (i.e., to strangers).

These results imply that Americans' judgments of objective obligation reflect, in part, the personal salience that they accord a needy other. Note, however, that whereas perceptions of objective obligations may thus be linked to affective factors such as self-relevance, the obligations themselves are regarded in impersonal terms. In all cases subjects maintained that agents were obligated to undertake the actions under consideration, even if undertaking such actions violated the agents' personal preferences.

The results also indicate that social group membership effects among Hindu Indians are weaker than those observed among Americans in regard to the types of issues under consideration. Only one significant role effect occurred among Indian subjects: Adults categorized minor-need stranger obligations in moral terms less frequently than all other obligations. Unlike in the American case, no role-related variation in moral judgment was observed either in relation to the extreme- or moderate-need incidents or among children. These results contradict what might be expected to be the general trend for Hindu Indians, their emphasis being on hierarchically structured social obligations, to maintain a more role-based moral perspective than do Americans, their emphasis being on individual rights (see also Triandis, 1989). It may be argued, however, that this contradiction arises from the somewhat distinctive ways Hindu Indians and Americans conceptualize social responsibilities in relation to other moral obligations or rights. In particular, Hindu Indians appear to consider social responsibilities as fundamental obligations inherent in all interpersonal relationships. Although regarding many other moral duties as role based (Shweder et al., 1987), Hindu Indians then tend to treat social responsibilities as absolute. Also, Americans appear to hold a more conflicting attitude toward social responsibilities than they do toward many other types of personal issues. Reflecting this ambivalence, Americans treat the freedom to decide whether to help someone in non-life-threatening need as a role-dependent rather than an absolute right.

Future research is needed that will examine judgments regarding a wider range of role relationships and helping situations to more completely understand the present patterns of role-related differences. Whatever their specific sources, however, the effects support claims that moral obligations are not invariably considered as generalizable across all agents (Gilligan, 1982). Rather, the trends indicate that in non-life-threatening cases, obligations to be responsive to another's needs may be seen as generalizable only across agents in particular types of role relationships.

PERSONAL-MORAL: A CULTURE-SPECIFIC CATEGORY

The results also document the need to expand current views of possible social domain conceptualizations to include the personal-moral category. This orientation merges the notion of an objective obligation, characteristic of the moral domain, with the notion of individual freedom of choice, characteristic of the personal domain.

The findings indicate that the personal-moral category is culture- and content-specific. The category was used only by Americans and only in relation to social responsibilities that fell in an intermediate range between those viewed in moral terms and those viewed as matters of personal choice.

The tendency for the personal-moral category to be applied exclusively by Americans appears to reflect Americans' ambivalent attitudes toward social responsibilities. Although maintaining that it is highly desirable to fulfill social responsibilities, Americans, as noted, also tend to experience such responsibilities as in conflict with individual freedom of choice. The personal-moral category may be seen to express this ambivalence. In particular, in using such a category, Americans simultaneously express (a) a commitment to meet the needs of dependent others through claims that social responsibilities are objective and (b) a commitment to personal liberties through assertions that it is the agent's own business whether to fulfill social responsibilities.

Although this investigation demonstrated use of the personal-moral category only in relation to social responsibilities, it appears likely that such a category is used in relation to other content domains as well. For example, findings that Americans categorize issues such as abortion or certain sex role practices as the agent's own business, yet regard these issues as highly serious, suggest that such culturally salient matters may also be categorized in personal-moral terms (Smetana, 1982; Stoddart & Turiel, 1985). Further study is required to better understand the range of application of the personal-moral category as well as to examine whether other types of hybrid rule conceptualizations exist (see Shweder, Mahapahtra, & Miller, 1987).

DEVELOPMENTAL TRENDS IN VIEWS OF INTERPERSONAL RESPONSIBILITIES

The developmental trends observed in perceptions of objective obligation highlight the need to recognize that both self-construction and social communication processes occur in the ontogenesis of moral reasoning (Dunn, 1987; Edwards, 1987; Miller, 1986). Although marked cross-cultural differences in moral reasoning were present at all ages, somewhat greater cross-cultural commonality was observed among children than among college students. Specifically, American children more frequently classified the minor-need breaches and the friend and stranger moderate-need breaches as objective obligations than did American adults. In this respect, then, American children's responses were more similar to those of Indians than were the responses of American adults.

It appears likely that American and Indian children's similar tendencies to categorize social responsibilities as objective obligations reflect certain common cognitive and affective experiences of human infancy. In all cultures, infants' earliest relationships are with caregivers, on whom they are dependent to fulfill their needs. Such a universal experience of dependency and need fulfillment may result in very young children's forming an impression that mandatory obligations exist to help others in need. This process may account for the finding that commonalities occurred in American and Indian children's views, despite marked cross-cultural differences in Indian and American socialization practices and conceptions of the child (Kakar, 1978).

The results also imply, however, that over development, as children gain increased exposure to the beliefs and values of their culture, these initial self-constructions may be modified (Miller, 1984, 1987). Specifically, in India such initial constructions appear to be supported as children acquire cultural conceptions that treat paternalistic familial relationships as the prototype for many other relationships (Shweder et al., 1987). In contrast, in the United States such initial constructions appear to be narrowed in scope as children acquire cultural conceptions that stress the voluntary aspects of interpersonal commitments.

REFERENCES

Argyle, M., & Henderson, M. (1985). *The anatomy of relationships.* London: Heinemann.

Berkowitz, L., & Daniels, L. (1963). Responsibility and dependency. *Journal of Abnormal and Social Psychology, 66,* 429–436.

Dumont, L. (1965). The modern conception of the individual: Notes on its genesis. *Contributions to Indian Sociology, 8,* 13–61.

Dumont, L. (1970). *Homo hierarchicus.* Chicago: University of Chicago Press.

Dunn, J. (1987). The beginnings of moral understanding: Development in the second year. In J. Kagan & S. Lamb (Eds.), *The emergence of morality in young children* (pp. 91–112). Chicago: University of Chicago Press.

Edwards, C. P. (1987). Culture and the construction of moral values: A comparative ethnography of moral encounters in two cultural settings. In J. Kagan & S. Lamb (Eds.), *The emergence of morality in young children* (pp. 123–151). Chicago: University of Chicago Press.

Eisenberg, N. (1986). *Altruistic emotion, cognition and behavior.* Hillsdale, NJ: Erlbaum.

Gewirth, A. (1978). *Reason and morality.* Chicago: University of Chicago Press.

Gilligan, C. (1977). In a different voice: Women's conceptions of the self and of morality. *Harvard Educational Review, 47,* 481–517.

Gilligan, C. (1982). *In a different voice: Psychological theory and women's development.* Cambridge, MA: Harvard University Press.

Higgins, A., Power, C., & Kohlberg, L. (1984). In W. M. Kurtines & J. L. Gewirtz (Eds.), *Morality, moral behavior and moral development* (pp. 74–106). New York: Wiley.

Kakar, S. (1978). *The inner world: A psychoanalytic study of childhood and society in India.* Oxford, England: Oxford University Press.

Kohlberg, L. (1971). From is to ought: How to commit the naturalistic fallacy and get away with it in the study of moral development. In T. Mischel (Ed.), *Cognitive development and epistemology* (pp. 151–235). New York: Academic Press.

Kohlberg, L. (1981). *The philosophy of moral development: Moral stages and the idea of justice: Vol 1. Essays on moral development.* New York: Harper & Row.

Kohlberg, L., Levine, C., & Hewer, A. (1983). Moral stages: A current formulation and a response to critics. In J. A. Meacham (Ed.), *Contributions to human development.* Basel, Switzerland: Karger.

Leeds, R. (1963). Altruism and the norm of giving. *Merrill-Palmer Quarterly, 9,* 226–232.

Locke, J. (1966). *Two treatises of civil government.* New York: Dutton. (Original work published 1690)

Lukes, S. (1973). *Individualism.* Oxford, England: Basil Blackwell.

Macaulay, J., & Berkowitz, L. (1970). *Altruism and helping behavior.* New York: Academic Press.

Miller, J. G. (1984). Culture and the development of everyday social explanation. *Journal of Personality and Social Psychology, 46,* 961–978.

Miller, J. G. (1986). Early cross-cultural commonalities in social explanation. *Developmental Psychology, 22,* 514–520.

Miller, J. G. (1987). Cultural influences on the development of conceptual differentiation in person description. *British Journal of Developmental Psychology, 5,* 309–319.

Miller, J. G., & Luthar, S. (1989). Issues of interpersonal responsibility and accountability: A comparison of Indians' and Americans' moral judgments. *Social Cognition, 3,* 237–261.

Muir, D. E., & Weinstein, E. A. (1962). The social debt: An investigation of lower class and middle class norms of social obligation. *American Sociological Review, 27,* 532–539.

Murphy, J. M., & Gilligan, C. (1980). Moral development in late adolescence and adulthood: A critique and reconstruction of Kohlberg's theory. *Human Development, 23,* 77–104.

Nam, C. B., & Terrie, E. W. (1982). Measurement of socioeconomic status from United States census data. In M. G. Powers (Ed.), *Measures of socioeconomic status: Current issues* (pp. 29–42). Boulder, CO: Westview Press.

Nucci, L. P. (1981). Conceptions of personal concepts: A domain distinct from moral or societal concepts. *Child Development, 52,* 114–121.

Nunner-Winkler, G. (1984). Two moralities? A critical discussion of an ethic of care and responsibility versus an ethic of rights and justice. In W. M. Kurtines & J. L. Gewirtz (Eds.), *Morality, moral behavior and moral development* (pp. 348–361). New York: Wiley.

O'Flaherty, W., & Derrett, J. (Eds.). (1978). *The concept of duty in South Asia.* Delhi, India: Vikas.

Powers, M. G. (Ed.). (1982). Measures of socioeconomic status: An introduction. In M. G. Powers (Ed.), *Measures of socioeconomic status: Current issues* (pp. 1–28). Boulder, CO: Westview Press.

Rawls, J. (1971). *A theory of justice.* Cambridge, MA: Harvard University Press.

Schneider, D. M. (1968). *American kinship: A cultural account.* Chicago: University of Chicago Press.

Schwartz, S. (1975). The justice of need and the activation of humanitarian norms. *Journal of Social Issues, 31,* 111–136.

Shweder, R. A. (1982). Beyond self-constructed knowledge: The study of culture and morality. *Merrill-Palmer Quarterly, 28,* 41–69.

Shweder, R. A., Mahapahtra, M., & Miller, J. G. (1987). Cultural and moral development in India and the United States. In J. Kagan & S. Lamb (Eds.), *The emergence of morality in young children* (pp. 1–89). Chicago: University of Chicago Press.

Smetana, J. (1981). Preschool children's conceptions of moral and social rules. *Child Development, 52,* 1333–1336.

Smetana, J. (1982). *Concepts of self and morality: Women's reasoning about abortion.* New York: Praeger.

Song, M. J., Smetana, J., & Kim, S. Y. (1987). Korean children's conceptions of moral and conventional transgressions. *Developmental Psychology, 23,* 577–582.

Stoddart, T., & Turiel, E. (1985). Children's concepts of cross-gender activities. *Child Development, 56,* 1241–1252.

Tajfel, H. (1978). *Differentiation between social groups.* London: Academic Press.

Triandis, H. C. (1989). The self and social behavior in differing cultural contexts. *Psychological Review, 96,* 506–520.

Turiel, E. (1983). *The development of social knowledge: Morality and convention.* Cambridge, England: Cambridge University Press.

Turiel, E., Killen, M., & Helwig, C. (1987). Morality: Its structure, functions and vagaries. In J. Kagan & S. Lamb (Eds.), *The emergence of morality in young children* (pp. 155–243). Chicago: University of Chicago Press.

This research was funded by National Institute of Mental Health Grant MH 42940 to Joan G. Miller. Appreciation is expressed to D. P. Pattanayak, E. Annamalai, and B. B. Rajapurohit of the Central Institute of Indian Languages, as well as to R. Indira of the University of Mysore, for their support of the project.

APPENDIX

OUTLINE OF INCIDENTS USED

Failure to Respond to Extreme Need

1. NOT DONATING BLOOD to someone who requires it during emergency surgery, because you have plans to go to a movie and do not want to get tired.
2. NOT ADMINISTERING MOUTH-TO-MOUTH RESUSCITATION to someone who has stopped breathing, because you might get dirty administering the procedure.
3. NOT DRIVING SOMEONE TO THE HOSPITAL who is bleeding uncontrollably, because you are concerned that some blood might get on your car.

Failure to Respond to Moderate Need

1. NOT GIVING ASPIRIN to someone who is suffering from a painful migraine headache on a bus ride, because you do not want to bother looking for the bottle of aspirin you are carrying.
2. NOT PROVIDING COMFORT to someone who is about to undergo knee surgery, because you do not want to get up early in the morning when the surgery begins.
3. NOT PROVIDING A RIDE to someone who needs to get to a ceremony in which he or she is one of the main speakers, because you feel that providing the ride would be uninteresting.

Failure to Respond to Minor Need

1. NOT LOANING MONEY to someone so that they can attend a movie, because you feel like keeping the extra money you have brought yourself.
2. NOT GIVING SOMEONE DIRECTIONS concerning how to get to an art supply shop, because you are busy reading an exciting book and do not want to be interrupted.
3. NOT PROVIDING A RIDE TO THE TRAIN STATION to someone going sightseeing, because you feel that giving the ride might be boring.

Control Incidents: Failure to Engage in Unjust Act

1. NOT STEALING A SHIRT for someone who does not want to pay for it.
2. NOT DESTROYING A FLOWER GARDEN for someone who is jealous of the garden owners and wants to hurt them.

Control Incidents: Failure to Override One's Own Personal Preferences

1. NOT BUYING YOURSELF A DRESS OF A DISLIKED COLOR, even though someone suggests buying a dress of that color.

2. NOT CHOOSING TO READ FOR PLEASURE A BOOK ON AN UNINTERESTING TOPIC, even though someone suggests that you read a book on that topic.

THINKING CRITICALLY AND APPLYING YOUR KNOWLEDGE

1. Miller and her colleagues found that Indians, more frequently than Americans, viewed themselves as having a moral obligation to help another under a wide range of conditions. What reason or reasons do Miller and her associates offer for these differences?

2. Miller and her colleagues argue that the differences between Indians and Americans in their willingness to help in a variety of situations cannot be explained by a general inclination on the part of Indians to comply with others' requests. What condition in the study did Miller and colleagues use to rule out this alternative explanation? Why does this evidence essentially put to rest this alternative explanation?

3. The most prominent theory of moral reasoning is that of Kohlberg (1971), who argues that there is an objective, universal moral code. Do the results obtained by Miller and her associates challenge this assumption? What conclusions would you draw about the cultural bases of moral reasoning?

4. Miller and her associates found that whereas American and Indian *adults* have quite different perceptions of social responsibilities, American and Indian *children's* views of social responsibilities were quite similar. What explanation do Miller and her colleagues offer for this difference? Do you find their explanation convincing?

5. Imagine that you are staying in a hotel in a large city, and you hear someone in the street cry out for help. Would you be likely to help that individual? Would someone from India be likely to help that individual? Why or why not?

CHAPTER 7

Universals and Cultural Differences in the Judgments of Facial Expressions of Emotions

Paul Ekman, Wallace V. Friesen, Maureen O'Sullivan, Anthony Chan,
Irene Diacoyanni-Tarlatzis, Karl Heider, Rainer Krause,
William Ayhan LeCompte, Tom Pitcairn, Pio E. Ricci-Bitti,
Klaus Scherer, Masotoshi Tomita, and Athanase Tzavaras

Often, we can tell what a person is feeling just by looking at the expression on his or her face. This seems to be true whether the person is someone familiar to us or someone from a completely different culture. Why is this the case? Paul Ekman and emotion researchers believe that facial expressions for certain basic emotions are universal. They argue that people looking at faces can recognize such basic emotions as happiness, fear, anger, or disgust, regardless of their own culture and the culture of the person expressing the emotion. The following article, which includes contributions by researchers from eight different countries, presents new evidence about the interpretation of facial expressions in 10 cultures, including Greece, Hong Kong, Japan, Turkey, Sumatra, and the United States. The investigators found that, although there are cultural differences in judgments of the intensity of emotional experience, agreement is very high across cultures regarding which emotion is most intensely expressed by facial features.

ABSTRACT: *We present here new evidence of cross-cultural agreement in the judgment of facial expression. Subjects in ten cultures performed a more complex judgment task than has been used in previous cross-cultural studies. Instead of limiting the subjects to selecting only one emotion term for each expression, this task allowed them to indicate that multiple emotions were evident and the intensity of each emotion. Agreement was very high across cultures about which emotion was the most intense. The ten cultures also agreed about the second most intense emotion signaled by an expression and about the relative intensity among expressions of the same emotion. However, cultural differences were found in judgments of the absolute level of emotional intensity.*

In the last 10 years, opinion has shifted about whether facial expressions of emotion are universal. The earlier view that what a facial expression signifies is completely different from culture to culture (Birdwhistell, 1970; LaBarre, 1947; Leach, 1972) is no longer ac-

Source: Reprinted from *Journal of Personality and Social Psychology, 53*(4), (1987), 712–717. Copyright © 1987 by the American Psychological Association. Reprinted by permission.

cepted within psychology, although it is still maintained by some anthropologists (Howell, 1985). Those who have become persuaded by the evidence of universal facial expressions of emotion can cite consistent findings across three quite different types of research. Those who remain skeptical, however, can cite flaws in each. Our study was designed to remedy some of these flaws. We will consider the strengths and weaknesses in each type of research on the universality of facial expressions of emotion.

In one type of investigation (Ekman & Friesen, 1971), members of one culture were asked to show how their face would look if they were the person in each of a number of different emotional contexts (e.g., "you feel sad because your child died," "you are angry and about to fight"). Universality was demonstrated when observers in another culture did far better than chance in identifying which emotional contexts the expressions were intended to portray. This finding had unusual import because the persons displaying the expressions were members of a visually isolated New Guinea culture (the South Fore). The ability of Americans to understand these New Guinean expressions could not be attributed to prior contact between these groups or to both having learned their expressions from mass media models.

Three problems limit these findings. First, there has been only one such study. It has not been repeated in another preliterate, visually isolated culture, nor for that matter in a literate, non-Western or Western culture. Second, not all six emotions portrayed were accurately recognized. Anger, disgust, happiness, and sadness were distinguished from each other and from fear and surprise, but the American observers could not distinguish the New Guineans portrayals of fear and surprise. Third, the facial expressions were posed, and Mead (1975) argued that establishing that posed expressions are universal need not imply that spontaneous facial expressions of emotion are universal. The next type of research design answered this criticism.

Facial expressions shown by Japanese and by Americans while they watched stress-inducing films (bodily mutilation) and neutral films (nature scenes) were measured. When the subjects in each culture watched the films alone, unaware of a hidden camera, virtually the same facial responses were emitted regardless of culture (Ekman, 1972). However, when a scientist was present when they watched the films, the Japanese more than the Americans masked negative expressions with smiles (Friesen, 1972). In addition to examining spontaneous facial expressions, this study was the first to show how cultural differences in the management of facial expressions (what Ekman & Friesen, 1969, had termed *display rules*) can mask universal facial expressions.

Two problems limit these findings. First, again it is but a single study; no one has yet attempted to replicate it. Also, the mutilation films elicited only a few emotions (disgust and fear), not allowing determination of whether the full range of spontaneous emotional expressions is universal. The next type of research met these two criticisms.

Photographs of facial expressions were shown to observers who were asked to judge the emotion displayed. Very high agreement was found across 12 literate cultures in the specific emotions attributed to facial expressions. The strength of this evidence is its many replications. Unlike the first two kinds of research, this type of study has been repeated in many cultures, by different researchers (Ekman, Sorenson, & Friesen, 1969; Izard, 1971), and with different photographs of facial expression.

Four questions can be raised about the value of such judgment studies in which the same set of faces is shown to observers in different cultures. First, the observers were shown posed rather than spontaneous expressions. This criticism is at least partially met by the fact that universality was also found in one other judgment study (Ekman, 1972) in which the observers saw spontaneous facial behavior. The expressions of the Japanese and American subjects in the study described earlier, in which subjects had watched body mutilation and neutral films, were shown to Japanese and American observers. These observers were asked to judge whether each person's expressions occurred in reaction to a stressful or a neutral film. The judgments made by the Japanese and American observers were highly correlated and did not differ as a function of whether they were interpreting the expressions of their own or the other culture.

Second, all the cultures had some contact either with each other or with media presentations of facial expressions, and therefore their similar judgments could be the consequence of having learned a common set of facial expressions. This criticism is met by judgment studies in two different, visually isolated, preliterate New Guinean cultures, the South Fore and the Dani. The New Guineans discriminated most but not all of the emotions distinguished by the literate-culture observers. In both New Guinean cultures, happiness, sadness, disgust, and surprise were discriminated from each other and from anger and fear. In the South Fore, fear was not distinguished from surprise (Ekman & Friesen, 1971), but this discrimination was made by the other New Guinean culture, the Dani (Heider & Rosch, reported in Ekman, 1973). The Dani did not discriminate anger from disgust, but the South Fore did.

The next two criticisms raise questions due to limitations in the judgment task that the observers used to register their impressions. The third one is that the judgment tasks might have concealed cultural differences in the perception of secondary blended emotions. Many students of emotion have noted that facial expressions may contain more than one message (Ekman & Friesen, 1969; Izard, 1971; Plutchik, 1962; Tomkins, 1963). The two emotions in a blend may be of similar strength, or one emotion may be primary, much more salient than the other secondary emotion. In prior cross-cultural studies, the investigators presumed that the expressions they showed displayed a single emotion rather than a blend and therefore did not provide those who observed the expressions the opportunity to choose more than one emotion for each expression. Without such data, however, it is not possible to ascertain whether an expression conveys a single emotion or a blend, and if there is blend, whether cultures agree in their judgment of the secondary emotion. Prior evidence of cross-cultural agreement in the judgment of expressions might be limited just to the primary message, not to the secondary blended emotions.

Fourth, despite agreement about which emotion is depicted, there might be differences in the strength of the perceived emotion. Only one cross-cultural judgment study (Ekman, 1972) obtained intensity judgments, and no differences were found. Further investigation is warranted as only five cultures were examined.

To summarize, there has been no cross-cultural study of whether cultures differ in the perception of secondary blended emotions. To do so requires that the observers be allowed to indicate that an expression shows multiple emotions. Our study was designed to fill this gap and also to replicate the finding that the intensity ascribed to an emotional expression is also universal. Observers were asked to judge the emotions shown in each photograph twice, once restricted to a single choice for each expression and once allowed to register up to seven emotions and the relative strength of each.

Hypothesis 1: There will be agreement across cultures about which emotion is shown in each expression when observers are limited to a single choice. This hypothesis simply predicts that earlier findings with a single-choice judgment task will be replicated.

Hypothesis 2: There will be agreement across cultures about which emotion is the strongest one shown in each expression when observers are allowed to register the presence of up to seven emotions. This hypothesis predicts that allowing multiple-emotion judgments will not eliminate cross-cultural agreement.

Hypothesis 3: There will be agreement across cultures about which emotion is perceived as the second strongest emotion in each expression. This prediction is more tenuous, for whether or not there will be universality about the secondary emotion is not implied by the prior evidence. We make this prediction extrapolating from Ekman and Friesen's (1975) finding on Americans that the muscular display in the expression predicted the secondary emotion that was attributed to the expression.

Hypothesis 4: There will be agreement across cultures in the judgment of the strength of an emotional expression. Whereas Ekman and Friesen (1969) described how cultural differences in display rules could lead to differences in the judgment of emotional intensity, Hypothesis 4 is based on their finding (Ekman, 1972) of cross-cultural agreement in intensity judgments.

METHOD

Facial Expressions Judged

The facial expressions shown to the observers were drawn from three sources: posed emotions, spontaneous expressions, and photographs in which models followed instructions about which muscles to contract. A large pool of photographs were scored with Ekman Friesen's (1978) Facial Action Coding System to determine the muscular actions that produced each expression. Three pictures were selected for each of six emotions: anger, disgust, fear, happiness, sadness, and surprise. The pictures selected were the best examples of Ekman and Friesen's description of the muscular configurations that universally signal those emotions. The eighteen photographs were black-and-white, head-on views showing only the face of Caucasian adult men (5) and women (4) between the ages of 30 and 40. Three of the women contributed expressions to two emotions, and the fourth woman provided one expression. Two of the men contributed expressions for three emotions, one provided expressions for two emotions, and the other two men contributed one expression each.

Observers

Ekman and Friesen sought to include a broad range of diverse cultures. Although the selection finally depended on opportunities where interested scientists volunteered to participate in the study, the 10 countries in which the study was conducted did include eight
languages and both Western and non-Western countries. Two of these—Japan and Sumatra (the Minangkabau)—are known (Ekman, 1972; Heider, 1984) to differ considerably
from Western cultures in their attitudes about emotional expression. In every country, the
observers were of equivalent age and education (college students). The samples were from
the Estonian S.S.R. (N = 85), Germany (67), Greece (61), Hong Kong (29), Italy (40),
Japan (98), Scotland (42), Sumatra (36), Turkey (64), and the United States (30).

Judgment Tasks and Procedure

In each language, the seven English emotion terms were translated into the native language
by one person and then translated back by an other to verify accurate translation. With
two exceptions, the scientist who made the initial translation and who then collected the
data was a member of the culture in which the study was run. The exceptions were the
Sumatra data gathered by Karl Heider in the Indonesian language from bilingual Minangkabau in Padang, West Sumatra, and the Turkish data gathered by William LeCompte
in the Turkish language from subjects in Ankara.

The seven English emotion terms included a single word for each type of expression
shown (anger, disgust, fear, happiness, sadness, and surprise) plus contempt. Although previous studies had either not allowed contempt as a response alternative or combined it with
disgust, here it was provided as a separate alternative because of other interest in whether
contempt can be distinguished from disgust expressions (Ekman & Friesen, 1986).

The photographs were prepared as 35-mm slides so they could be shown to groups of
observers. The same random order of presentation was used in every culture. The first time
the observers saw the slides, each picture was shown for 10 s, during which the observers
were instructed to check on their answer sheets one of the seven emotion terms to register their judgement of each expression. Before observers saw the expressions a second time,
the instructions explained that some expressions might show many emotions at the same
or different strength, whereas other expressions might show only one emotion. In their second viewing, observers were instructed to rate each of the seven emotions in terms of
whether it was absent or present, and if it was present to indicate its strength on an 8-point
scale from *slight* (1) through *moderate* (4) to *strong* (8). This time the slides were shown
for 30 s each, during which the observers made judgements about all seven emotions for
each expression.

RESULTS

Replicating the Findings of Universality

Because there were 3 expressions for each of 6 emotions judged by members of 10 cultures, there were 180 opportunities for the cultures to agree with Ekman and Friesen's predictions and with each other about which emotions are universally signaled by each facial

expression. Considering first the single-choice judgments, the emotion term chosen by the majority of the subjects in each culture was, as predicted, 172 of 180 times. This high level of agreement across cultures supports Hypothesis 1, replicating previous findings that also used a single-choice judgment task.

Table 1 summarizes the results collapsed across the three expressions for each type of emotion, listing the percentage within each culture who gave the predicted emotional judgments. The figures in Table 1 are within a few points of what was reported 15 years ago with different photographs and observers (Ekman et al., 1969; Izard, 1971). Although there is some variation in the extent of agreement, what is most relevant to Hypothesis 1 is that the majority of the observers in every culture judged the emotions as predicted.

Although these descriptive data very strongly support Hypothesis 1, we also computed kappa coefficients (Hubert, 1977) to obtain a test of significance. Kappa evaluates the extent to which the judgments were as predicted. We prepared 7 × 7 tables for each culture, plotting for each of the seven emotions the distribution of obtained against predicted judgments and pooling the judgments across the three photographs depicting each emotion. In all 10 cultures, the kappas were significant beyond the .001 significance level. These are shown in the first column of Table 2. To be certain that pooling results across photographs did not conceal disagreements in the judgment of some of the facial expressions intended to signal a particular emotion, kappas were also computed separately for every photograph for all 10 cultures. Of the 180 kappas (18 photographs × 10 cultures), 178 were significant beyond the .01 level.

Hypothesis 2 predicted the same findings even when observers were allowed to choose more than one emotion, judging the intensity of every emotion. To test Hypothesis 2, we determined whether the emotion with the most intense rating was the emotion predicted by Ekman and Friesen and was the same across cultures. Hypothesis 2 was supported; in 177 of 180 times, the emotion rated strongest by the largest number of observers in each

TABLE 1

Single-Emotion Judgment Task: Percentage of Subjects Within Each Culture Who Chose the Predicted Emotion

Nation	Happiness	Surprise	Sadness	Fear	Disgust	Anger
Estonia	90	94	86	91	71	67
Germany	93	87	83	86	61	71
Greece	93	91	80	74	77	77
Hong Kong	92	91	91	84	65	73
Italy	97	92	81	82	89	72
Japan	90	94	87	65	60	67
Scotland	98	88	86	86	79	84
Sumatra	69	78	91	70	70	70
Turkey	87	90	76	76	74	79
United States	95	92	92	84	86	81

TABLE 2
Kappa Coefficients

Nation	Single judgments	Multiple judgments
Estonia	.790	.744
Germany	.736	.739
Greece	.762	.789
Hong Kong	.763	.718
Italy	.800	.783
Japan	.693	.678
Scotland	.815	.809
Sumatra	.657	.541
Turkey	.729	.738
United States	.835	.607

Note: All figures are significant beyond .001.

culture was the predicted emotion. This is the first evidence of cross-cultural agreement about the most intense emotion when observers can choose more than one emotion.

Kappa coefficients were also computed for the judgments made on the intensity scales. For each observer, the score used was the emotion scale rated as strongest. Again, all 10 kappa coefficients were significant. Table 2 lists the kappa coefficients computed on the single judgment data and the multiple judgment data.

Is There Agreement About the Second Most Intense Emotion?

Hypothesis 3, which predicted universality in the secondary emotion, could be tested only with those expressions that the observers had judged as showing more than one emotion (i.e., that were blends rather than single-emotion expressions). Although the selection of photographs had followed Ekman and Friesen's (1978) guidelines for excluding blends in which two emotions are signaled with equal strength, those guidelines were not designed to exclude blends in which a secondary emotion is conveyed with less strength than is the primary emotion. Only judgment data in which the observers were allowed to record the presence of more than one emotion and the relative strength of each emotion can reveal whether an expression conveys a single emotion or a blend.

We set the following criteria for classifying an expression as a blend, pertinent to testing Hypothesis 3: (a) The second strongest emotion had to have a mean of at least 1.5 on the *absent* (0) to *strong* (8) intensity scale; (b) at least half of the judges within a culture had to contribute to that rating; and (c) at least two cultures had to meet the first two criteria. There were 180 opportunities for the judgments (18 expressions × 10 cultures) to meet these criteria.

Our criteria were met 98 times, involving the judgments of 13 of the 18 expressions. None of the photographs selected to signal happiness met the criteria for signaling a secondary blended emotion. The judgments of the sadness and the surprise photographs met the criteria for signaling a secondary blended emotion too infrequently for inclusion in the analysis of Hypothesis 3 (for sadness, only 5 of 30 opportunities; for surprise, only 8 of 30). There was complete agreement across the 10 cultures about the secondary emotion signaled by the disgust and by the fear expressions. In every culture on every expression of disgust, the secondary emotion was contempt. In every culture on every expression of fear, the secondary emotion was surprise. Whereas all three anger expressions met the criteria for signaling secondary blended emotions in nearly every culture, the secondary emotion varied with the expression. Disgust was the blended emotion on one anger expression, surprise on another anger expression, and on the third expression the cultures disagreed about the secondary blended emotion (four judged it to be contempt, four judged it to he disgust, and two did not see any secondary emotion).

Cultural Differences in the Intensity of the Judged Emotion

To test Hypothesis 4's prediction of universality in intensity of emotion judgments, we computed a one-way multivariate analysis of variance (MANOVA) with culture as the independent variable and the mean intensity of the six emotions as the six dependent variables. SPSSX MANOVA was used for the analysis. By use of Wilks's criterion, there was an overall effect for culture, $F(54,2743) = 3.95$, $p < .001$. The results reflected a moderate association between culture and the intensity judgments of emotion ($\eta^2 = .32$; Tabachnick & Fidell, 1983). Six univariate F tests ($dfs = 9, 542$) ranged from 2.93 ($p < .002$) for sadness to 6.66 ($p < .000$) for surprise, indicating significant differences among cultures for each of the six emotions.

Rather than examining all the cell means on an atheoretical, pair-wise basis, we used post hoc comparisons to address two possible explanations for the significant overall and univariate Fs. The first possibility was that people will judge a foreigner's expressions to be less intense than expressions shown by members of their own culture. Attributions of less intense emotions to foreigners might be due to politeness or to greater uncertainty about the emotional state of a person from a culture with which one is less familiar. In our experiment, the three Asian cultures could clearly recognize that the Caucasians in the photographs were not from their own culture. In the first post hoc comparison, therefore, we used Scheffé's procedures to contrast the mean intensity ratings of the three Asian cultures with the mean intensity ratings of the other seven cultures for each of the six emotions. Table 3 shows that the intensity ratings made by the Asian and non-Asian cultures were significantly different for fear, happiness, and surprise. Although the Scheffé test was performed on the separate cell means for each culture, Table 3 gives the average intensity ratings for the two contrasting cultures to clarify the differences between them. Even those that were statistically significant are numerically small. None of the differences were as great as a full point on the 9-point intensity scale.

A second explanation of the significant MANOVA is that observers who made their judgments in languages other than English would give different intensity judgments than would those making their judgments in English. The mean intensity ratings of the English-speaking cultures (Scotland and the United States) were compared with those of the other eight countries by using Sheffé's procedures. None of these Fs ($dfs = 9, 542$) was signifi-

TABLE 3
Post Hoc Analyses of Intensity Ratings When Judging Foreigners and Nonforeigners

Emotion	Asian countries	Non-Asian countries	F	p
Happiness			19.63	<.05
M	6.20	6.68		
SD	1.46	1.19		
Surprise			35.25	<.01
M	5.22	6.01		
SD	1.66	1.54		
Sadness			0.61	ns
M	5.69	5.93		
SD	1.63	1.66		
Fear			42.22	<.01
M	5.73	6.70		
SD	2.00	1.47		
Disgust			9.23	ns
M	5.64	6.14		
SD	1.73	1.56		
Anger			5.76	ns
M	5.80	6.04		
SD	1.66	1.61		

Note: Grouped means for the Asian and non-Asian cultures are provided for ease of comparison. In the post hoc analyses, we used Scheffé's procedures to contrast the separate cell means of the three Asian cultures with those from the seven non-Asian cultures. The F values were evaluated using $F' = (k - 1) F_c$, with $k = 10$. Degrees of freedom were 9, 542.

cant, suggesting that language differences among cultures is unimportant in judging the intensity of emotional expressions.

Another way to search for cultural differences in intensity judgments was to look for any disagreements about which of two expressions showing the same emotion was the most intense. We set the following criteria for including expressions in this analysis: Two expressions of the same emotion had to be judged as differing in mean intensity (a) by at least one point and (b) in at least two cultures. When that happened, we determined whether the direction of that difference was the same in those two cultures and in all the other cultures. Although we tallied the results across all cultures if our criteria were met, rarely did we find that the mean intensity difference was greater than a point in more than 3 of the 10 cultures. For example, on two of the faces the mean intensity ratings on the anger scale was 6.6 and 7.7 for the Scots and 5.9 and 7.5 for the Italians. We therefore determined whether the face that was rated as most intense was the same for the Scots and the Italians and for the other 8 cultures, even though in these other 8 cultures the ratings of these two pictures did not differ by as much as one full point. Whenever the mean intensity ratings for a pair of expressions depicting a particular emotion differed by less than a point in every culture, the pair of expressions was considered one in which the faces were rated as the same intensity across cultures.

There were 130 opportunities for disagreement about which of a pair of expressions showing the same emotion is the most intense (13 pairs of photographs in which the mean ratings for a pair of expressions differed by at least a point for 2 cultures × 10 cultures = 130). The 10 cultures agreed about which was the most intense expression 119 of 130 times (binomial test, $z = 9.47$, $p < .0001$).

DISCUSSION

The main, consistent, and robust finding was agreement across cultures in their interpretation of facial expressions of emotion. Three new findings support the view that there are universal facial expressions of emotion. First, cross-cultural agreement is not dependent on limiting observers to choosing only one emotion for each expression. Even when observers were allowed to indicate that an expression showed many emotions, agreement was very high about which emotion was the strongest. Second, cross-cultural agreement is not limited to just the strongest emotion expressed by a face. There was very high agreement across cultures about the second strongest emotion signaled by an expression. Third, cross-cultural agreement is not just about which emotion an expression displays but also about the relative strength of expressions of the same emotion. With few exceptions, the cultures agreed about which of two different expressions of the same emotion was the most intense.

One possible limit on these findings, however, is that all of the observers were college students, all of whom had been exposed to some of the same mass media depictions of facial expressions. Nearly 20 years ago, concerned that their findings of universal facial expressions might be attributed to the opportunity to learn the meaning of expressions from mass media examples rather than as a consequence of evolution, Ekman and Friesen (1971) examined observers in a visually isolated, preliterate culture. They found that judgments of anger, disgust, fear, sadness, and happiness made by these preliterate people were no different than judgments made by college students in eight literate cultures. Given this data base, it is quite unlikely that less educated persons in the cultures we studied would provide different judgments. Nevertheless, data on such observers would make our findings more conclusive.

Further research is needed also to explore alternative explanations of why secondary emotions were perceived for the disgust, fear, and anger expressions but not for the happy expressions and very few for either the sadness or surprise expressions. This difference among emotions might be due to greater similarities among some emotions in appearance or semantic connotations or, less interestingly, to nonreplicable idiosyncracies in the samplings of expressions in this particular study. The secondary emotions found for the disgust and fear expressions were consistent with past studies in which either a single-emotion choice or ratings were obtained (see Ekman, Friesen, & Ellsworth, 1972, chapters 13 and 14, for a review of more than a dozen earlier studies and Russell & Bullock, 1985, for more recent work). However, the failure to find secondary emotions for the expressions of happiness and many secondary emotions for either the sad or the surprise expressions was not consistent with these past studies.

There was also some evidence of cultural differences in intensity judgments. There was some support for the idea that observers attributed less intense emotions to expressions that they could tell were shown by foreigners. The Asians obviously knew that the Caucasians shown in the photographs were members of a foreign culture. Without showing Asian expressions to Caucasians, we cannot know if making less intense emotion attributions to the expressions shown by a foreigner is common across all the cultures studied or unique to the Asian cultures. And without showing Asian faces to Asians, we cannot know if making less intense emotion attributions is general to the Asians judgments of anyone or just of foreigners. In any case, the fact that the Asian and Caucasian ratings did not differ significantly on anger, disgust, or sadness casts some doubt on this line of reasoning. There is no obvious reason that these three emotions would not be influenced by any general tendency to underestimate the strength of emotional expressions shown by a foreigner. The possibility must be considered that the cultural differences in intensity judgments we found are not of real significance despite their statistical significance. Although some differences were statistically significant, even they were very small.

We (Ekman & Friesen, 1969) have always maintained that facial expressions of emotion are both universal (in the evolved muscular displays for each emotion) and culturally variable (in the display rules, some of the antecedents, coping, memories, etc.). The evidence now for universality is overwhelming, whereas that for cultural differences is sparse. Three changes in the research design might help to reveal cultural differences: (a) Each facial expression of emotion should be shown by people who vary in race, sex, and age; (b) facial expressions should be studied in which the muscular signs of the emotion are registered in only one part of the face; and (c) cultures selected for study should be those in which ethnographic investigations have revealed differing attitudes about the experience or expression of specific emotions.

It is possible, however, that despite such changes, the research design itself is not a sensible one for revealing cultural differences. Taking a facial expression out of social context; eliminating the simultaneous speech, vocal clues, and body movements; freezing the expression in a still photograph; forcing attention to it; and asking for judgments by a detached uninvolved observer may remove many of the sources of cultural differences in the interpretation of facial expression. When we sought to demonstrate how cultural differences in display rules produce different facial expressions (Ekman, 1972; Friesen, 1972), we did not ask people to judge photographs but instead observed how facial expressions change in different social contexts. That study may provide a model for the methods needed to reveal further cultural differences in facial expressions of emotion.

REFERENCES

Birdwhistell, R. L. (1970). *Kenesics and context*. Philadelphia: University of Pennsylvania Press.

Ekman, P. (1972). Universals and cultural differences in facial expressions of emotion. In J. Cole (Ed.), *Nebraska Symposium on Motivation, 1971* (Vol. 19, pp. 207–282). Lincoln: University of Nebraska Press.

Ekman, P. (1973). Cross-cultural studies of emotion. In P. Ekman (Ed.), *Darwin and facial expression: A century of research in review* (pp. 169–222). New York: Academic Press.

Ekman, P., & Friesen, W. V. (1969). The repertoire of nonverbal behavior: Categories, origins, usage, and coding. *Semicotica, 1*, 49–98.

Ekman, P., & Friesen, W. V. (1971). Constants across cultures in the face and emotion. *Journal of Personality and Social Psychology, 17*, 124–129.

Ekman, P., & Friesen, W. V. (1975). *Unmasking the face: A guide to recognizing emotions from facial clues.* Englewood Cliffs, NJ: Prentice-Hall.

Ekman, P., & Friesen, W. V. (1978). *Facial Action Coding System: A technique for the measurement of facial movement.* Palo Alto, CA: Consulting Psychologists Press.

Ekman, P., & Friesen, W. V. (1986). A new pan-cultural expression of emotion. *Motivation and Emotion, 10*, 159–168.

Ekman, P., Friesen, W. V., & Ellsworth, P. (1972). *Emotion in the human face: Guidelines for research and an integration of findings.* New York: Pergamon Press.

Ekman, P., Sorenson, E. R., & Friesen, W. V. (1969). Pan-cultural elements in facial displays of emotions. *Science, 164* (3875), 86–88.

Friesen, W. V. (1972). *Cultural differences in facial expressions in a social situation: An experimental test of the concept of display rules.* Unpublished doctoral dissertation, University of California, San Francisco.

Heider, K. G. (1984, November). *Emotion: Inner state versus interaction.* Paper presented at the meeting of the American Anthropological Association, Denver, CO.

Howell, S. (1985, June). *The face as social fact.* Paper presented at British Psychological Society Conference on the Meaning of Faces, Cardiff, Wales.

Hubert, L. (1977). Kappa revisited. *Psychological Bulletin, 84*, 289–297.

Izard, C. E. (1971). *The face of emotion.* New York: Appleton-Century-Crofts.

LaBarre, W. (1947). The cultural basis of emotions and gestures. *Journal of Personality, 16*, 49–68.

Leach, E. (1972). The influence of the cultural context on nonverbal communication in man. In R. Hinde (Ed.), *Nonverbal communication* (pp. 315–344). London: Cambridge University Press.

Mead, M. (1975). Review of *Darwin and facial expression* P. Ekman (Ed.). *Journal of Communication, 25*(1), 209–213.

Plutchik, R. (1962). *The emotions: Faces, theories, and a new model.* New York: Random House.

Russell, J. A., & Bullock, M. (1985). Multidimensional scaling of emotional facial expressions: Similarity from preschoolers to adults. *Journal of Personality and Social Psychology, 48*, 1290–1298.

Tabachnick, B. G., & Fidell, L. S. (1983). *Using multivariate statistics.* New York: Harper & Row.

Tomkins, S. S. (1963). *Affect, imagery, consciousness* (Vol. 2). New York: Springer Publishing.

Paul Ekman's work is supported by Research Scientist Award MH 06092 from the National Institute of Mental Health.

THINKING CRITICALLY AND APPLYING YOUR KNOWLEDGE

1. According to Ekman and his colleagues, certain emotions are more easily recognized than others. Which emotions are these? Why do you think this might be the case?

2. Ekman and his associates describe several ways in which the research methods they used go beyond previous studies of universalities in the recognition of human emotion. Identify *two* methodological features of this study that enable the authors to generalize their evidence for the universality of human emotions beyond that found in previous investigations.

3. Emotional expression is complex. It appears to be influenced by universal factors, but also by factors that vary from culture to culture. What are some of the cultural factors?

4. Think of some factors in your culture that might influence whether you express the happiness, sadness, or anger that you are feeling.

PART III
THE SOCIAL SELF

❖ CHAPTER 8 ❖

CULTURE AND THE SELF: IMPLICATIONS FOR COGNITION, EMOTION, AND MOTIVATION

Hazel Rose Markus and Shinobu Kitayama

How do think about yourself? Do you see yourself as an independent and largely self-directed individual? Or do you perceive yourself as part of a social group whose responsibility it is to work toward shared goals? The two conceptions of self suggested by these questions vary substantially from culture to culture, as Markus and Kitayama show in this highly influential paper. Western cultures, such as the United States, favor a view of the self as independent—people seek to maintain their independence from others and try to discover and make use of their unique inner personal qualities and talents. In contrast, many Southern European and Asian cultures, such as Japan, emphasize the individual as related to others, and stress the importance of fitting in with social groups and achieving harmonious interdependence. Markus and Kitayama show how these different views of the self have important implications for such fundamental processes as social cognition, emotion, and motivation. Though long, this article is well worth the effort, for it conveys insights about culture that go to the very heart of individual experience.

ABSTRACT: *People in different cultures have strikingly different construals of the self, of others, and of the interdependence of the 2. These construals can influence, and in many cases determine, the very nature of individual experience, including cognition, emotion, and motivation. Many Asian cultures have distinct conceptions of individuality that insist on the fundamental relatedness of individuals to each other. The emphasis is on attending to others, fitting in, and harmonious interdependence with them. American culture neither assumes nor values such an overt connectedness among individuals. In contrast, individuals seek to maintain their independence from others by attending to the self and by discovering and expressing their unique inner attributes. As proposed herein, these construals are even more powerful than previously imagined. Theories of the self from both psychology and anthropology are integrated to define in detail the difference between a construal of the self as independent and a construal of the self as interdependent. Each of these divergent construals should have a set of specific consequences for cognition, emotion, and motivation; these consequences are proposed and relevant empirical literature is reviewed. Focusing on differences in self-construals enables apparently inconsistent empirical findings to be reconciled, and raises questions about what have been thought to be culture-free aspects of cognition, emotion, and motivation.*

Source: Reprinted from *Psychological Review, 98,* (1991), 224–253. Copyright © 1991 by the American Psychological Association. Reprinted by permission.

In America, "the squeaky wheel gets the grease." In Japan, "the nail that stands out gets pounded down." American parents who are trying to induce their children to eat their suppers are fond of saying "think of the starving kids in Ethiopia, and appreciate how lucky you are to be different from them." Japanese parents are likely to say "Think about the farmer who worked so hard to produce this rice for you; if you don't eat it, he will feel bad, for his efforts will have been in vain" (H. Yamada, February 16, 1989). A small Texas corporation seeking to elevate productivity told its employees to look in the mirror and say "I am beautiful" 100 times before coming to work each day. Employees of a Japanese supermarket that was recently opened in New Jersey were instructed to begin the day by holding hands and telling each other that "he" or "she is beautiful" ("A Japanese Supermarket," 1989).

Such anecdotes suggest that people in Japan and America may hold strikingly divergent construals of the self, others, and the interdependence of the two. The American examples stress attending to the self, the appreciation of one's difference from others, and the importance of asserting the self. The Japanese examples emphasize attending to and fitting in with others and the importance of harmonious interdependence with them. These construals of the self and others are tied to the implicit, normative tasks that various cultures hold for what people should be doing in their lives (cf. Cantor & Kihlstrom, 1987; Erikson, 1950; Veroff, 1983). Anthropologists and psychologists assume that such construals can influence, and in many cases determine, the very nature of individual experience (Chodorow, 1978; Dumont, 1970; Geertz, 1975; Gergen, 1968; Gilligan, 1982; Holland & Quinn, 1987; Lykes, 1985; Marsella, De Vos, & Hsu, 1985; Sampson, 1985, 1988, 1989; Shweder & LeVine, 1984; Smith, 1985; Triandis, 1989; Weisz, Rothbaum, & Blackburn, 1984; White & Kirkpatrick, 1985).

Despite the growing body of psychological and anthropological evidence that people hold divergent views about the self, most of what psychologists currently know about human nature is based on one particular view—the so-called Western view of the individual as an independent, self-contained, autonomous entity who (a) comprises a unique configuration of internal attributes (e.g., traits, abilities, motives, and values) and (b) behaves primarily as a consequence of these internal attributes (Geertz, 1975; Sampson, 1988, 1989; Shweder & LeVine, 1984). As a result of this monocultural approach to the self (see Kennedy, Scheier, & Rogers, 1984), psychologists' understanding of those phenomena that are linked in one way or another to the self may be unnecessarily restricted (for some important exceptions, see Bond, 1986, 1988; Cousins, 1989; Fiske, in press; Maehr & Nicholls, 1980; Stevenson, Azuma, & Hakuta, 1986; Triandis, 1989; Triandis, Bontempo, Villareal, Asai, & Lucca, 1988). In this article, we suggest that construals of the self, of others, and of the relationship between the self and others may be even more powerful than previously suggested and that their influence is clearly reflected in differences among cultures. In particular, we compare an *independent* view of the self with one other, very different view, an *interdependent* view. The independent view is most clearly exemplified in some sizable segment of American culture, as well as in many Western European cultures. The interdependent view is exemplified in Japanese culture as well as in other Asian cultures. But it is also characteristic of African cultures, Latin-American cultures, and many southern European cultures. We delineate how these divergent views of the self—the independent and the interdependent—can have a systematic influence on various aspects of cognition, emotion, and motivation.

We suggest that for many cultures of the world, the Western notion of the self as an entity containing significant dispositional attributes, and as detached from context, is simply not an adequate description of selfhood. Rather, in many construals, the self is viewed as *inter*dependent with the surrounding context, and it is the "other" or the "self-in-relation-to-other" that is focal in individual experience. One general consequence of this divergence in self-construal is that when psychological processes (e.g., cognition, emotion, and motivation) explicitly, or even quite implicitly, implicate the self as a target or as a referent, the nature of these processes will vary according to the exact form or organization of self inherent in a given construal. With respect to cognition, for example, for those with interdependent selves, in contrast to those with independent selves, some aspects of knowledge representation and some of the processes involved in social and nonsocial thinking alike are influenced by a pervasive attentiveness to the relevant *others* in the social context. Thus, one's actions are more likely to be seen as situationally bound, and characterizations of the individual will include this context. Furthermore, for those with interdependent construals of the self, both the expression and the experience of emotions and motives may be significantly shaped and governed by a consideration of the reactions of others. Specifically, for example, some emotions, like anger, that derive from and promote an independent view of the self may be less prevalent among those with interdependent selves, and self-serving motives may be replaced by what appear as other-serving motives. An examination of cultural variation in some aspects of cognition, emotion, and motivation will allow psychologists to ask exactly what is universal in these processes, and it has the potential to provide some new insights for theories of these psychological processes.

In this analysis, we draw on recent research efforts devoted to characterizing the general differences between American or Western views of personhood and Eastern or Asian perspectives (e.g., Heelas & Lock, 1981; Hofstede, 1980; Marsella et al., 1985; Roland, 1988; Schwartz & Bilsky, 1990; Shweder, 1990; Shweder & LeVine, 1984; Stigler, Shweder, & Herdt, 1990; Triandis, 1989; Triandis & Brislin, 1980; Weisz et al., 1984). We extract from these descriptions many important differences that may exist in the specific content, structure, and functioning of the self-systems of people of different cultural backgrounds. The distinctions that we make between independent and interdependent construals must be regarded as general tendencies that may emerge when the members of the culture are considered as a whole. The prototypical American view of the self, for example, may prove to be most characteristic of White, middle-class men with a Western European ethnic background. It may be somewhat less descriptive of women in general, or of men and women from other ethnic groups or social classes.[1] Moreover, we realize that there may well be important distinctions

---

[1] The prototypical American view may also be further restricted to a particular point in history. It may be primarily a product of late, industrial capitalism (see Baumeister, 1987). For an analysis of the origins of the independent view, see Bellah, Madsen, Sullivan, Swidler, & Tipton (1985) and Weber (1958).

among those views we discuss as similar and that there may be views of the self and others that cannot easily be classified as either independent or interdependent.

Our intention is not to catalog all types of self-construals, but rather to highlight a view of the self that is often assumed to be universal but that may be quite specific to some segments of Western culture. We argue that self-construals play a major role in regulating various psychological processes. Understanding the nature of divergent self-construals has two important consequences. On the one hand, it allows us to organize several apparently inconsistent empirical findings and to pose questions about the universality assumed for many aspects of cognition, emotion, and motivation (see Shweder, 1990). On the other hand, it permits us to better specify the precise role of the self in mediating and regulating behavior.

THE SELF: A DELICATE CATEGORY

Universal Aspects of the Self

In exploring the possibility of different types of self-construals, we begin with Hallowell's (1955) notion that people everywhere are likely to develop an understanding of themselves as physically distinct and separable from others. Head (1920), for example, claimed the existence of a universal schema of the body that provided one with an anchor in time and space. Similarly, Allport (1937) suggested that there must exist an aspect of personality that allows one, when awakening each morning, to be sure that he or she is the same person who went to sleep the night before. Most recently, Neisser (1988) referred to this aspect of self as the *ecological self*, which he defined as "the self as perceived with respect to the physical environment: 'I' am the person here in this place, engaged in this particular activity" (p. 3). Beyond a physical or ecological sense of self, each person probably has some awareness of internal activity, such as dreams, and of the continuous flow of thoughts and feelings, which are private to the extent that they cannot be directly known by others. The awareness of this unshared experience will lead the person to some sense of an inner, private self.

Divergent Aspects of the Self

Some understanding and some representation of the private, inner aspects of the self may well be universal, but many other aspects of the self may be quite specific to particular cultures. People are capable of believing an astonishing variety of things about themselves (cf. Heelas & Lock, 1981; Marsella et al., 1985; Shweder & LeVine, 1984; Triandis, 1989). The self can be construed, framed, or conceptually represented in multiple ways. A cross-cultural survey of the self lends support to Durkheim's (1912/1968) early notion that the category of the self is primarily the product of social factors, and to Mauss's (1938/1985) claim that as a social category, the self is a "delicate" one, subject to quite substantial, if not infinite, variation.

The exact content and structure of the inner self may differ considerably by culture. Furthermore, the nature of the outer or public self that derives from one's relations with other people and social institutions may also vary markedly by culture. And, as suggested by Triandis (1989), the significance assigned to the private, inner aspects versus the public, relational aspects in regulating behavior will vary accordingly. In fact, it may not be unreasonable to suppose, as did numerous earlier anthropologists (see Allen, 1985), that in some cultures, on certain occasions, the *individual*, in the sense of a set of significant inner attributes of the person, may cease to be the primary unit of consciousness. Instead, the sense of belongingness to a social relation may become so strong that it makes better sense to think of the *relationship* as the functional unit of conscious reflection.

The current analysis focuses on just one variation in what people in different cultures can come to believe about themselves. This one variation concerns what they believe about the relationship between the self and *others* and, especially, the degree to which they see themselves as *separate* from others or as *connected* with others. We suggest that the significance and the exact functional role that the person assigns to the other when defining the self depend on the culturally shared assumptions about the separation or connectedness between the self and others.

TWO CONSTRUALS OF THE SELF: INDEPENDENT AND INTERDEPENDENT

The Independent Construal

In many Western cultures, there is a faith in the inherent separateness of distinct persons. The normative imperative of this culture is to become independent from others and to discover and express one's unique attributes (Johnson, 1985; Marsella et al., 1985; J. G. Miller, 1988; Shweder & Bourne, 1984). Achieving the cultural goal of independence requires construing oneself as an individual whose behavior is organized and made meaningful primarily by reference to one's own internal repertoire of thoughts, feelings, and actions, rather than by reference to the thoughts, feelings, and actions of others. According to this construal of self, to borrow Geertz's (1975) often quoted phrase, the person is viewed as "a bounded, unique, more or less integrated motivational and cognitive universe, a dynamic center of awareness, emotion, judgment, and action organized into a distinctive whole and set contrastively both against other such wholes and against a social and natural background" (p. 48).

This view of the self derives from a belief in the wholeness and uniqueness of each person's configuration of internal attributes (Johnson, 1985; Sampson, 1985, 1988, 1989; Waterman, 1981). It gives rise to processes like "self-actualization," "realizing oneself," "expressing one's unique configuration of needs, rights, and capacities," or "developing one's distinct potential." The essential aspect of this view involves a conception of the self as an autonomous, independent person; we thus refer to it as the *independent construal of the self*. Other similar labels include *individualist, egocentric, separate, autonomous, idiocentric*, and *self-contained*. We assume that, on average, relatively more individuals in Western cultures will hold this view than will individuals in non-Western cultures. Within a given culture, however, individuals will vary in the extent to which they are good cultural representatives and construe the self in the mandated way.

The independent self must, of course, be responsive to the social environment (Fiske, in press). This responsiveness, however, is fostered not so much for the sake of the responsiveness itself. Rather, social responsiveness often, if not always, derives from the need to strategically determine the best way to express or assert the internal attributes of the self. Others, or the social situation in general, are important, but primarily as standards of reflected appraisal, or as sources that can verify and affirm the inner core of the self.

The Western, independent view of the self is illustrated in Figure 1A. The large circle represents the self, and the smaller circles represent specific others. The Xs are representations of the various aspects of the self or the others. In some cases, the larger circle and the small circle intersect, and there is an X in the intersection. This refers to a representation of the self-in-relation-to-others or to a particular social relation (e.g., "I am very polite in front of my professor"). An X within the self circle but outside of the intersection represents an aspect of the self perceived to be relatively independent of specific others and, thus, invariant over time and context. These self-representations usually have as their referent some individual desire, preference, attribute, or ability (e.g., "I am creative"). For those with independent construals of the self, it is these inner attributes that are most significant in regulating behavior and that are assumed, both by the actor and by the observer

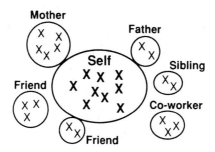

A. Independent View of Self

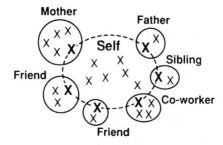

B. Interdependent View of Self

FIGURE 1. Conceptual representations of the self. (A: Independent construal. B: Interdependent construal.)

alike, to be diagnostic of the actor. Such representations of the inner self are thus the most elaborated in memory and the most accessible when thinking of the self (as indicated by Xs in Figure 1A). They can be called *core conceptions*, *salient identities*, or *self-schemata* (e.g., Gergen, 1968; Markus, 1977; Stryker, 1986).

The Interdependent Construal

In contrast, many non-Western cultures insist, in Kondo's (1982) terms, on the fundamental *connectedness* of human beings to each other. A normative imperative of these cultures is to maintain this interdependence among individuals (De Vos, 1985; Hsu, 1985; Miller, 1988; Shweder & Bourne, 1984). Experiencing interdependence entails seeing oneself as part of an encompassing social relationship and recognizing that one's behavior is determined, contingent on, and, to a large extent organized by what the actor perceives to be the thoughts, feelings, and actions of *others* in the relationship. The Japanese experience of the self, therefore, includes a sense of interdependence and of one's status as a participant in a larger social unit (Sampson, 1988). Within such a construal, the self becomes most meaningful and complete when it is cast in the appropriate social relationship. According to Lebra (1976) the Japanese are most fully human in the context of others.

This view of the self and the relationship between the self and others features the person not as separate from the social context but as more connected and less differentiated from others. People are motivated to find a way to fit in with relevant others, to fulfill and create obligation, and in general to become part of various interpersonal relationships. Unlike the independent self, the significant features of the self according to this construal are to be found in the interdependent and thus, in the more public components of the self. We therefore call this view the *interdependent construal of the self*. The same notion has been variously referred to, with somewhat different connotations, as *sociocentric*, *holistic*, *collective*, *allocentric*, *ensembled*, *constitutive*, *contextualist*, *connected*, and *relational*. As with the independent self, others are critical for social comparison and self-validation, yet in an interdependent formulation of the self, these others become an integral part of the setting, situation, or context to which the self is connected, fitted, and assimilated. The exact manner in which one achieves the task of connection, therefore, depends crucially on the nature of the context, particularly the others present in the context. Others thus participate actively and continuously in the definition of the interdependent self.

The interdependent self also possesses and expresses a set of internal attributes, such as abilities, opinions, judgments, and personality characteristics. However, these internal attributes are understood as situation specific, and thus as sometimes elusive and unreliable. And, as such, they are unlikely to assume a powerful role in regulating overt behavior, especially if this behavior implicates significant others. In many domains of social life, one's opinions, abilities, and characteristics are assigned only secondary roles—they must instead be constantly controlled and regulated to come to terms with the primary task of interdependence. Such voluntary control of the inner attributes constitutes the core of the cultural ideal of becoming mature. The understanding of one's autonomy as secondary to, and constrained by, the primary task of interdependence distinguishes interdependent selves from independent selves, for whom autonomy and its expression is often afforded primary significance. An independent behavior (e.g., asserting an opinion) exhibited by a person in an interdependent culture is likely to be based on the premise of underlying interdependence and thus may have a somewhat different significance than it has for a person from an independent culture.

The interdependent self is illustrated in Figure 1B. For those with interdependent selves, the significant self-representations (the *X*s) are those in relationship to specific others. Interdependent selves certainly include representations of invariant personal attributes and abilities, and these representations can become phenomenologically quite salient, but in many circumstances they are less important in regulating observable behavior and are not assumed to be particularly diagnostic of the self.[2] Instead, the self-knowledge that guides behavior is of the self-in-relation to specific others in particular contexts. The fundamental units of the self-system, the core conceptions, or self-schemata are thus predicated on significant interpersonal relationships.

An interdependent self cannot be properly characterized as a bounded whole, for it changes structure with the nature of the particular social context. Within each particular social situation, the self can be differently instantiated. The uniqueness of such a self derives from the specific configuration of relationships that each person has developed. What is focal and objectified in an interdependent self, then, is not the inner self, but the *relationships* of the person to other actors (Hamaguchi, 1985).

The notion of an interdependent self is linked with a monistic philosophical tradition in which the person is thought to be of the same substance as the rest of nature (see Bond, 1986; Phillips, 1976; Roland, 1988; Sass, 1988). As a consequence, the relationship between the self and other, or between subject and object, is assumed to be much closer. Thus, many non-Western cultures insist on the inseparability of basic elements (Galtung, 1981), including self and other, and person and situation. In Chinese culture, for instance, there is an emphasis on synthesizing the constituent parts of any problem or situation into an integrated or harmonious whole (Moore, 1967; Northrop, 1946). Thus, persons are only parts that when separated from the larger social whole cannot be fully understood (Phillips, 1976; Shweder, 1984). Such a holistic view is in opposition to the Cartesian, dualistic tradition that characterizes Western thinking and in which the self is separated from the object and from the natural world.

Examples of the interdependent self. An interdependent view of the self is common to many of the otherwise highly diverse cultures of the world. Studies of the mainland Chinese, for example, summarized in a recent book by Bond (1986), show that even among the most rapidly modernizing segments of the Chinese population, there is a tendency for people to act primarily in accordance with the anticipated expectations of others and social norms rather than with internal wishes or personal attributes (Yang, 1981 b). A premium is placed on emphasizing collective welfare and on showing a sympathetic concern

---

[2] For a discussion of how interdependent selves strive to maintain a balance between internal (private) and extensive (public) representations, see T. Doi (1986).

for others. Throughout the studies of the Chinese reported by Bond, one can see the clear imprint of the Confucian emphasis on interrelatedness and kindness. According to Hsu (1985), the supreme Chinese virtue, *jen*, implies the person's capability to interact with fellow human beings in a sincere, polite, and decent fashion (see also Elvin, 1985).

Numerous other examples of cultures in which people are likely to have some version of an interdependent self can also be identified. For example, Triandis, Marin, Lisansky, and Betancourt (1984) have described the importance of simpatico among Hispanics. This quality refers to the ability to both respect and share others' feelings. In characterizing the psychology of Filipinos, Church (1987) described the importance that people attribute to smooth interpersonal relations and to being "agreeable even under difficult circumstances, sensitive to what others are feeling and willing to adjust one's behavior accordingly." Similarly, Weisz (in press) reported that Thais place a premium on self-effacement, humility, deference, and on trying to avoid disturbing others. Among the Japanese, it is similarly crucial not to disturb the *wa*, or the harmonious ebb and flow of interpersonal relations (see also Geertz, 1974, for characterizations of similar imperatives among the Balinese and Moroccans).

Beattie (1980) claimed that Africans are also extremely sensitive to the interdependencies among people and view the world and others in it as extensions of one another. The self is viewed not as a hedged closure but as an open field. Similarly, Marriott (1976) argued that Hindu conceptions assume that the self is an open entity that is given shape by the social context. In his insightful book, Kakar (1978) described the Hindu's ideal of interpersonal fusion and how it is accompanied by a personal, cultural sense of hell, which is separation from others. In fact, Miller, Bersoff, and Harwood (1990), in a recent, carefully controlled study on moral reasoning, found that Indians regard responsiveness to the needs of others as an objective moral obligation to a far greater extent than do Americans. Although the self-systems of people from these cultures are markedly different in many other important respects, they appear to be alike in the greater value (when compared with Americans) that is attached to proper relations with others, and in the requirement to flexibly change one's own behavior in accordance with the nature of the relationship.

Even in American culture, there is a strong theme of interdependence that is reflected in the values and activities of many of its subcultures. Religious groups, such as the Quakers, explicitly value and promote interdependence, as do many small towns and rural communities (e.g., Bellah, Madsen, Sullivan, Swidler, & Tipton, 1985). Some notion of a more connected, ensembled, interdependent self, as opposed to a self-contained, independent self, is also being developed by several of what Sampson (1989) calls "postmodern" theorists. These theorists are questioning the sovereignty of the American view of the mature person as autonomous, self-determined, and unencumbered. They argue that psychology is currently dominated by a view of the person that does not adequately reflect the extent to which people everywhere are created by, constrained by, and responsive to their various interpersonal contexts (see Gergen & Gergen, 1988; Gilligan, 1982; Miller, 1986; Tajfel, 1984).

Further definition of the interdependent self. Theorists of Japanese culture are beginning to characterize the interdependent self much more specifically than was previously attempted.

These descriptions offer some more refined ideas of how an interdependent view of self can depart markedly from an independent view of self (see Nakane, 1970; Plath, 1980; R. J. Smith, 1983). For example, building on a study of L. T. Doi (1973), Bachnik (1986) wrote

> (in Japanese society) rather than there being a single social reality, a number of possible perspectives of both self and social life are acknowledged. Interaction in Japanese society then focuses on the definition of the appropriate choice, out of all the various possibilities. This means that what one says and does will be different in different situations, depending on how one defines one's particular perspective versus the social other. (p. 69)

In Japan, the word for self, *jibun*, refers to "one's share of the shared life space" (Hamaguchi, 1985). The self, Kimura (cited in Hamaguchi, 1985) claimed, is "neither a substance nor an attribute having a constant oneness" (p. 302). According to Hamaguchi (1985), for the Japanese, "a sense of identification with others (sometimes including conflict) pre-exists and selfness is confirmed only through interpersonal relationships. . . . Selfness is not a constant like the ego but denotes a fluid concept which changes through time and situations according to interpersonal relationships" (p. 302).

The Japanese anthropologist Lebra (1976) defined the essence of Japanese culture as an "ethos of social relativism." This translates into a constant concern for belongingness, reliance, dependency, empathy, occupying one's proper place, and reciprocity. She claimed the Japanese nightmare is exclusion, meaning that one is failing at the normative goal of connecting to others. This is in sharp contrast to the American nightmare, which is to fail at separating from others, as can occur when one is unduly influenced by others, or does not stand up for what one believes, or when one goes unnoticed or undistinguished.

An interdependent view of self does not result in a merging of self and other, nor does it imply that one must always be in the company of others to function effectively, or that people do not have a sense of themselves as agents who are the origins of their own actions. On the contrary, it takes a high degree of self-control and agency to effectively adjust oneself to various interpersonal contingencies. Agentic exercise of control, however, is directed primarily to the inside and to those inner attributes, such as desires, personal goals, and private emotions, that can disturb the harmonious equilibrium of interpersonal transaction. This can be contrasted with the Western notion of control, which primarily implies an assertion of the inner attributes and a consequent attempt to change the outer aspects, such as one's public behaviors and the social situation (see also Weisz et al., 1984).

Given the Japanese notion of control that is inwardly directed, the ability to effectively adjust in the interpersonal domain may form an important basis of self-esteem, and individualized styles of such adjustment to social contingencies may contribute to the sense of self-uniqueness. Thus, Hamaguchi (1985), for example, reported that for the Japanese, "the straightforward claim of the naked ego" (p. 303) is experienced as childish. Self-assertion is not viewed as being authentic, but instead as being immature. This point is echoed in M. White and LeVine's (1986) description of the meaning of *sunao*, a term used by Japanese parents to characterize what they value in their children:

A child that is *sunao* has not yielded his or her personal autonomy for the sake of co-operation; cooperation does not suggest giving up the self, as it may in the West, it implies that working with others is the appropriate way of expressing and enhancing the self. Engagement and harmony with others is, then, a positively valued goal and the bridge—to open-hearted cooperation, as in *sunao*—is through sensitivity, reiterated by the mother's example and encouragement. (p. 58)

Kumagai (1981) said *sunao* "assumes cooperation to be an act of affirmation of the self" (p. 261). Giving in is not a sign of weakness; rather, it reflects tolerance, self-control, flexibility, and maturity.

The role of the other in the interdependent self. In an interdependent view, in contrast to an independent view, others will be assigned much more importance, will carry more weight, and will be relatively focal in one's own behavior. There are several direct consequences of an interdependent construal of the self. First, relationships, rather than being means for realizing various individual goals, will often be ends in and of themselves. Although people everywhere must maintain some relatedness with others, an appreciation and a need for people will be more important for those with an interdependent self than for those with an independent self. Second, maintaining a connection to others will mean being constantly aware of others and focusing on their needs, desires, and goals. In some cases, the goals of others may become so focal in consciousness that the goals of others may be experienced as personal goals. In other cases, fulfilling one's own goals may be quite distinct from those of others, but meeting another's goals, needs, and desires will be a necessary requirement for satisfying one's own goals, needs, and desires. The assumption is that while promoting the goals of others, one's own goals will be attended to by the person with whom one is interdependent. Hence, people may actively work to fulfill the others' goals while passively monitoring the reciprocal contributions from these others for one's own goal-fulfillment. Yamagishi (1988), in fact, suggested that the Japanese feel extremely uncomfortable, much more so than Americans, when the opportunity for such passive monitoring of others' actions is denied.

From the standpoint of an independent, "self-ish" self, one might be led to romanticize the interdependent self, who is ever attuned to the concerns of others. Yet in many cases, responsive and cooperative actions are exercised only when there is a reasonable assurance of the "good-intentions" of others, namely their commitment to continue to engage in reciprocal interaction and mutual support. Clearly, interdependent selves do not attend to the needs, desires, and goals of *all* others. Attention to others is not indiscriminate; it is highly selective and will be most characteristic of relationships with "in-group" members. These are others with whom one shares a common fate, such as family members or members of the same lasting social group, such as the work group. Out-group members are typically treated quite differently and are unlikely to experience either the advantages or disadvantages of interdependence. Independent selves are also selective in their association with others but not to the extent of interdependent selves because much less of their behavior is directly contingent on the actions of others. Given the importance of others in constructing reality and regulating behavior, the in-group–out-group distinction is a vital one for interdependent selves, and the subjective boundary of one's "in-group" may tend to be narrower for the interdependent selves than for the independent selves (Triandis, 1989).

To illustrate the reciprocal nature of interaction among those with interdependent views, imagine that one has a friend over for lunch and has decided to make a sandwich for him. The conversation might be: "Hey, Tom, what do you want in your sandwich? I have turkey, salami, and cheese." Tom responds, "Oh, I like turkey." Note that the friend is given a choice because the host assumes that friend has a right, if not a duty, to make a choice reflecting his inner attributes, such as preferences or desires. And the friend makes his choice exactly because of the belief in the same assumption. This script is "natural," however, only within the independent view of self. What would happen if the friend were a visitor from Japan? A likely response to the question "Hey, Tomio, what do you want?" would be a little moment of bewilderment and then a noncommital utterance like "I don't know." This happens because under the assumptions of an interdependent self, it is the responsibility of the host to be able to "read" the mind of the friend and offer what the host perceives to be the best for the friend. And the duty of the guest, on the other hand, is to receive the favor with grace and to be prepared to return the favor in the near future, if not right at the next moment. A likely, interdependent script for the same situation would be: "Hey, Tomio, I made you a turkey sandwich because I remember that last week you said you like turkey more than beef." And Tomio will respond, "Oh, thank you, I really like turkey."

The reciprocal interdependence with others that is the sign of the interdependent self seems to require constant engagement of what Mead (1934) meant by taking the role of the other. It involves the willingness and ability to feel and think what others are feeling and thinking, to absorb this information without being told, and then to help others satisfy their wishes and realize their goals. Maintaining connection requires inhibiting the "I" perspective and processing instead from the "thou" perspective (Hsu, 1981). The requirement is to "read" the other's mind and thus to know what the other is thinking or feeling. In contrast, with an independent self, it is the individual's responsibility to "say what's on one's mind" if one expects to be attended to or understood.

CONSEQUENCES OF AN INDEPENDENT OR AN INTERDEPENDENT VIEW OF THE SELF

Table 1 presents a brief, highly simplified summary of some of the hypothesized differences between independent and interdependent construals of the self. These construals of self and other are conceptualized as part of a repertoire of self-relevant schemata used to evaluate, organize, and regulate one's experience and action. As schemata, they are patterns of one's past behaviors as well as patterns for one's current and future behaviors (Neisser, 1976). Markus and Wurf (1987) called this assortment of self-regulatory schemata the *self-system*. Whenever a task, an event, or a situation is self-relevant, the ensuing processes and consequences are likely to be influenced by the nature of the self-system. The self-system has been shown to be instrumental in the regulation of intrapersonal processes such as self-relevant information processing, affect regulation, and motivation and in the regulation of interpersonal processes such as person perception, social comparison, and the seeking and shaping of social interaction (see Cantor & Kihlstrom, 1987; Greenwald & Pratkanis, 1984;

TABLE 1
Summary of Key Differences Between an Independent and an Interdependent Construal of Self

Feature compared	Independent	Interdependent
Definition	Separate From social context	Connected with social context
Structure	Bounded, unitary, stable	Flexible, variable
Important features	Internal, private (abilities, thoughts, feelings)	External, public (statuses, roles, relationships)
Tasks	Be unique	Belong, fit-in
	Express self	Occupy one's proof place
	Realize internal attributes	Engage in appropriate action
	Promote own goals	Promote others' goals
	Be direct; "say what's on your mind"	Be indirect; "read other's mind"
Role of others	*Self-evaluation:* others important for social comparison, reflected appraisal	*Self-definition:* relationships with others in specific contexts define the self
Basis of self-esteem[a]	Ability to express self, validate internal attributes	Ability to adjust, restrain self, maintain harmony with social context

[a]Esteeming the self may be primarily a Western phenomenon, and the concept of self-esteem should perhaps be replaced by self-satisfaction, or by a term that reflects the realization that one is fulfilling the culturally mandated task.

Markus & Wurf, 1987, for reviews). The goal of this article is to further specify the role of the self-system in behavior by examining how these divergent cultural self-shemata influence individual experience.

In the current analysis, we hypothesize that the independent versus interdependent construals of self are among the most general and overarching schemata of the individual's self-system. These construals recruit and organize the more specific self-regulatory schemata.[3] We are suggesting here, therefore, that the exact organization of many self-relevant

---

[3] What these very general cultural self-schemata of independence or interdependence mean for a given individual's articulated view of self cannot be specified, however. The self-concept derives not only from the cultural self-schema that is the focus herein but from the complete configuration of self-schemata, including those that are a product of gender, race, religion, social class, and one's particular social and developmental history. Not all people who are part of an independent culture will thus characterize themselves as independent, nor will all those who live as part of an interdependent culture claim to be interdependent. Within independent and interdependent cultures, there is great diversity in individual self-definition, and there can also be strong similarities across cultures. For example, many artists, whether Japanese or American, may describe themselves as nonconformist, innovative, and breaking with tradition. And many aspects of their behavior are indeed very similar. Yet, nonconformity Japanese-style and nonconformity American-style, although similar in some respects, will not, because of the differences in their supporting cultural contexts, be identical. For Japanese, nonconformity is a privilege afforded only to selected, talented individuals whose deviance from the norm of interdependence is implicitly sanctioned by the rest of society. For Americans, nonconformity is regarded as every individual's birthright.

processes and their outcomes depend crucially on whether these processes are rooted in an independent construal of the self or whether they are based primarily on an interdependent construal of the self. For example, in the process of lending meaning and coherence to the social world, we know that people will show a heightened sensitivity to self-relevant stimuli. For those with an independent view of self, this includes information relevant to one's self-defining attributes. For one with an interdependent view of self, such stimuli would include information about significant others with whom the person has a relationship or information about the self in relation to another person.

Affect regulation involves seeking positive states and avoiding negative ones. Positive states are those that enhance or promote one's view of the self, and negative states are those that challenge this view. For a person with an independent view of self, this involves seeking information that confirms or enhances one's internal, private attributes. The most desirable situations are those that allow one to verify and express those important internal attributes and that convey the sense that one is appropriately autonomous. In contrast, for a person with an interdependent view of self, one might expect the most desirable states to be those that allow one to be responsive to one's immediate context or that convey the sense that one is succeeding in his or her interdependent relationships or statuses.

A third important function of the self-concept suggested by Markus and Wurf (1987) is that of motivating persons, of moving them to action. The person with an independent view of self should be motivated to those actions that allow expression of one's important self-defining, inner attributes (e.g., hardworking, caring, independent, and powerful), whereas the person with an interdependent view of self should be motivated to those actions that enhance or foster one's relatedness or connection to others. On the surface, such actions could look remarkably similar (e.g., working incredibly hard to gain admission to a desirable college), but the exact source, or etiology, of the energizing motivation may be powerfully different (De Vos, 1973; Maehr & Nicholls, 1980).

In the following sections, we discuss these ideas in further detail and review the empirical literature, which suggests that there are significant cognitive, emotional, and motivational consequences of holding an independent or an interdependent view of the self.

Consequences for Cognition

If a cognitive activity implicates the self, the outcome of this activity will depend on the nature of the self-system. Specifically, there are three important consequences of these divergent self-systems for cognition. First, we may expect those with interdependent selves to be more attentive and sensitive to others than those with independent selves. The attentiveness and sensitivity to others, characterizing the interdependent selves, will result in a relatively greater cognitive elaboration of the other or of the self-in-relation-to-other. Second, among those with interdependent selves, the unit of representation of both the self and the other will include a relatively specific social context in which the self and the other are embedded. This means that knowledge about persons, either the self or others, will not be abstract and generalized across contexts, but instead will remain specific to the focal context. Third, a consideration of the social context and the reactions of others may also shape some basic, nonsocial cognitive activities such as categorizing and counterfactual thinking.

In exploring the impact of divergent cultural construals on thinking, we assume that how people think (the process) in a social situation cannot be easily separated from what they think about (the content; Shweder, 1990; Shweder & Bourne, 1984). Extensive research on social cognition in the past decade has suggested the power of content in social inference (e.g., see Fiske & Taylor, 1984; Markus & Zajonc, 1985, for reviews). It is the nature of the representation (e.g., self, another person, a weed, or clam chowder) that guides attention, and that determines what other relevant information will be retrieved to fill in the gap of available sense data. For example, investigations by D'Andrade (1981) and Johnson-Laird (1983) indicate that the greater the familiarity with the stimulus materials, the more elaborate the schemata for framing the problem, and the better the problem solving. In general, then, how a given object is culturally construed and represented in memory should importantly influence and even determine how one thinks about the object. Accordingly, the divergent representations of the self we describe should be expected to have various consequences for all cognition relevant to self, others, or social relationships.

More interpersonal knowledge. If the most significant elements of the interdependent self are the self-in-relation-to-others elements, there will be a need, as well as a strong normative demand, for knowing and understanding the social surrounding, particularly others in direct interaction with the self. That is, if people conceive of themselves as interdependent parts of larger social wholes, it is important for them to be sensitive to and knowledgeable about the others who are the coparticipants in various relationships, and about the social situations that enable these relationships. Maintaining one's relationships and ensuring a harmonious social interaction requires a full understanding of these others, that is, knowing how they are feeling, thinking, and likely to act in the context of one's relationships to them. It follows that those with interdependent selves may develop a dense and richly elaborated store of information about others or of the self in relation.

Kitayama, Markus, Tummala, Kurokawa, and Kato (1990) examined this idea in a study requiring similarity judgments between self and other. A typical American finding is that the self is judged to be more dissimilar to other than other is to the self (Holyoak & Gordon, 1983; Srull & Gaelick, 1983). This finding has been interpreted to indicate that for the typical American subject, the representation of the self is more elaborated and distinctive in memory than the representation of another person. As a result, the similarity between self and other is judged to be less when the question is posed about a more distinctive object (Is *self* similar to other?) than when the question is posed about a less distinctive object (Is *other* similar to self?). If, however, those with interdependent selves have at least as much knowledge about some others as they have about themselves, this American pattern of findings may not be found.

To test these predictions, Kitayama et al. (1990) compared students from Eastern cultural backgrounds (students from India) with those from Western cultural backgrounds (American students). As shown in Figure 2, for the Western subjects, Kitayama et al. replicated the prior findings in which the self is perceived as significantly more dissimilar to the other than is the other to the self. Such a finding is consistent with a broad range of studies showing that for individuals with a Western background, supposedly those with independent selves, self-knowledge is more distinctive and densely elaborated than knowl-

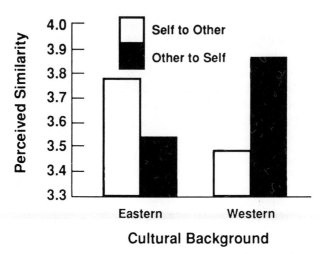

FIGURE 2. Mean perceived similarity of self to other and other to self by subjects with Eastern and Western cultural backgrounds.

edge about other people (e.g., Greenwald & Pratkanis, 1984). This pattern, however, was nonsignificantly reversed for the Indian subjects, who judged the self to be somewhat more similar to the other than is the other to the self. It appears, then, that for the latter, more interdependent subjects, knowledge about others is relatively more elaborated and distinctive than knowledge about the self. Asymmetry in similarity judgments is an indirect way to evaluate knowledge accessibility, but a more direct measure of cross-cultural differences in knowledge of the other should reveal that those with interdependent selves have more readily accessible knowledge of the other.

Context-specific knowledge of self and other. A second consequence of having an interdependent self as opposed to an independent self concerns the ways in which knowledge about self and other is processed, organized, and retrieved from memory. For example, given an interdependent self, knowledge about the self may not be organized into a hierarchical structure with the person's characteristic attributes (e.g., intelligent, competent, and athletic) as the superordinate nodes, as is often assumed in characterizations of the independent self. In other words, those with interdependent selves are less likely to organize knowledge about the "self in general" or about the "other in general." Specific social situations are more likely to serve as the unit of representation than are attributes of separate persons. One learns about the self with respect to a specific other in a particular context and, conversely, about the other with respect to the self in a particular context.

In exploring variations in the nature of person knowledge, Shweder and Bourne (1984) asked respondents in India and America to describe several close acquaintances. The descriptions provided by the Indians were more situationally specific and more relational than those of Americans. Indian descriptions focused on behavior; they described what was done, where it was done, and to whom or with whom it was done. The Indian respondents said, "He has no land to cultivate but likes to cultivate the land of others," or "When a quarrel arises, he cannot resist the temptation of saying a word," or "He behaves properly with guests but feels sorry if money is spent on them." It is the behavior itself that is focal and significant rather than the inner attribute that supposedly underlies it. Notably this tendency to provide the specific situational or interpersonal context when providing a description was reported to characterize the free descriptions of Indians regardless of social class, education, or literacy level. It appears, then, that the concreteness in person description is not due to a lack of skill in abstracting concrete instances to form a general proposition, but rather a consequence of the fact that global inferences about persons are typically regarded as not meaningful or informative.

Americans also describe other people in terms of the specifics of their behavior, but typically this occurs only at the beginning of relationships when the other is relatively unknown, or if the behavior is somehow distinctive and does not readily lend itself to a trait characterization. Rather than saying "He does not disclose secrets," Americans are more likely to say "He is discreet or principled." Rather than "He is hesitant to give his money away," Americans say "He is tight or selfish." Shweder and Bourne (1984) found that 46% of American descriptions were of the context-free variety, whereas this was true of only 20% from the Indian sample.

A study by J. G. Miller (1984) on patterns of explanation among Indian Hindus and Americans revealed the same tendency for contextual and relational descriptions of behavior among Indian respondents. In the first phase of her study, respondents generated two prosocial behaviors and two deviant behaviors and then explained why each behavior was undertaken. For example, in the prosocial case, respondents were asked to "describe something a person you know well did recently that you considered good for someone else." Miller coded the explanations for reference to dispositional explanations; for reference to social, spatial, temporal location; and for reference to specific acts or occurrences. Like Shweder and Bourne (1984), she found that on average, 40% of the reasons given by American respondents referred to the general dispositions of the actor. For the Hindu respondents, dispositional explanations constituted less than 20% of their responses.

In a second phase of the study, Miller (1984) asked both American and Indian respondents to explain several accounts of the deviant behaviors generated by the Indian respondents. For example, a Hindu subject narrated the following incident:

This concerns a motorcycle accident. The back wheel burst on the motorcycle. The passenger sitting in the rear jumped. The moment the passenger fell, he struck his head on the pavement. The driver of the motorcycle—who is an attorney—as he was on his way to court for some work, just took the passenger to a local hospital and went on and attended to his court work. I personally feel the motorcycle driver did a wrong thing. The driver left the passenger there without consulting the doctor concerning the seriousness of the injury—the gravity of the situation—whether the passenger should be shifted immediately—and he went on to the court. So ultimately the passenger died. (p. 972)

Respondents were asked why the driver left the passenger at the hospital without staying to consult about the seriousness of the passenger's injury. On average, Americans made 36% of their attributions to dispositions of the actors (e.g., irresponsible, pursuing success) and 17% of their attributions to contextual factors (driver's duty to be in court). In comparison, only 15% of the attributions of the Indians referred to dispositions, whereas 32% referred to contextual reasons. Both the American and the Indian subjects focused on the state of the driver at the time of the accident, but in the Indian accounts, the social role of the driver appears to be very important to understanding the events. He is obligated to his role, he has a job to perform. Actions are viewed as arising from relations or interactions with others; they are a product of obligations, responsibilities, or commitments to others and are thus best understood with respect to these interpersonal relations. This preference for contextual explanations has also been documented by Dalal, Sharma, and Bisht (1983).

These results call into question the exact nature of the fundamental attribution error (Ross, 1977). In this error, people, in their efforts to understand the causes of behavior, suffer from an inescapable tendency to perceive behavior as a consequence of the internal, personal attributes of the person. Miller's (1984) Indian respondents also explained events in terms of properties or features of the person, yet these properties were their role relationships—their socially determined relations to specific others or groups. Because role relationships necessarily implicate the social situation that embeds the actor, it is unclear whether the explanations of the Indian respondents can be viewed as instances of the fundamental attribution error. It may be that the fundamental attribution error is only characteristic of those with an independent view of the self.

The tendency to describe a person in terms of his or her specific behavior and to specify the context for a given behavior is also evidenced when those with interdependent selves provide self-descriptions. Cousins (1989) compared the self-descriptions of American high school and college students with the self-descriptions of Japanese high school and college students. He used two types of free-response formats, the original Twenty Statements Test (TST; Kuhn & McPartland, 1954), which simply asks "Who Am I?" 20 consecutive times, and a modified TST, which asks subjects to describe themselves in several specific situations (me at home, me with friends, and me at school). When responding to the original TST, the Japanese self-descriptions were like those of the Indians in the Shweder and Bourne (1984) study. They were more concrete and role-specific ("I play tennis on the weekend"). In contrast, the American descriptions included more psychological trait or attribute characterizations ("I am optimistic," and "I am friendly"). However, in the modified TST, where a specific interpersonal context was provided so that respondents could envision the situation (e.g., me at home) and presumably who was there and what was being done to whom or by whom, this pattern of results was reversed. As shown in Figure 3, the Japanese showed a stronger tendency to characterize themselves in psychological trait or attribute terms than did Americans. In contrast, Americans tended to qualify their self-descriptions, claiming, for example, "I am sometimes lazy at home."

Cousins (1989) argued that the original TST essentially isolates or disembeds the "I" from the relational or situational context, and thus self-description becomes artificial for

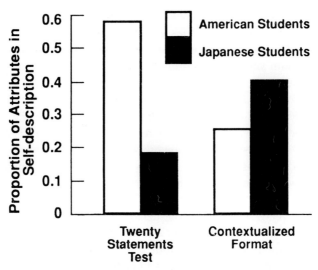

FIGURE 3. Mean proportion of psychological attributes endorsed by American and Japanese students in two self-description tasks.

the Japanese respondents, who are more accustomed to thinking about themselves within specific social situations. For these respondents, the contextualized format "Describe yourself as you are with your family" was more "natural" because it locates the self in a habitual unit of representation, namely in a particular interpersonal situation. Once a defining context was specified, the Japanese respondents were decidedly more willing to make generalizations about their behavior and to describe themselves abstractly using trait or attribute characterizations.

American students, in contrast to their Japanese counterparts, were more at home with the original TST because this test elicits the type of abstract, situation-free self-descriptions that form the core of the American, independent self-concept. Such abstract or global characterizations, according to Cousins (1989), reflect a claim of being a separate individual whose nature is not bound by a specific situation. When responding to the contextualized self-description questions, the American students qualified their descriptions as if to say "This is how I am at home, but don't assume this is the way I am everywhere." For American respondents, selfness, pure and simple, seems to transcend any particular interpersonal relationships.

Basic cognition in an interpersonal context. One's view of self can have an impact even on some evidently nonsocial cognitive activities. I. Liu (1986) described the emphasis that the Chinese place on being loyal and pious to their superiors and obedience to them, whether they are parents, employers, or government officials. He claimed that most Chinese adhere to a specific rule that states "If your superiors are present, or indirectly involved, in any situation, then you are to respect and obey them" (I. Liu, 1986, p. 78). The power and the influence of this rule appear to go considerably beyond that provided by the American admonition to "respect one's elders." I. Liu (1986) argued that the standard of self-regulation that involves the attention and consideration of others is so pervasive that it may actually constrain verbal and ideational fluency. He reasoned that taking account of others in every situation is often at odds with individual assertion or with attempts at innovation or unique expression. This means, for example, that in an unstructured creativity task in which the goal is to generate as many ideas as possible, Chinese subjects may be at a relative disadvantage. In a similar vein, T. Y. Liu and Hsu (1974) suggested that consideration of the rule "respect and obey others" uses up cognitive capacity that might otherwise be devoted to a task, and this may be the reason that Chinese norms for some creativity tasks fall below American norms.

Charting the differences between an independent self and interdependent self may also illuminate the controversy surrounding the debate between Bloom (1981, 1984) and Au (1983, 1984) over whether the Chinese can reason counterfactually (for a thorough review of this debate, see Moser, 1989). Bloom's studies (1981) on the counterfactual began when he asked Chinese-speaking subjects questions like "If the Hong Kong government were to pass a law requiring that all citizens born outside of Hong Kong make weekly reports of their activities to the police, how would you react?" Bloom noted that his respondents consistently answered "But the government hasn't," "It can't," or "It won't." Pressed to think about it anyway, the respondents became frustrated, claiming that it was unnatural or un-Chinese to think in this way. American and French respondents answered similar questions readily and without complaint. From this and subsequent studies, Bloom (1981, 1984) concluded that Chinese speakers "might be expected typically to encounter difficulty in maintaining a counterfactual perspective as an active point of orientation for guiding their cognitive activities" (1984, p. 21).

Au (1983) challenged Bloom's conclusions. Using different stimulus materials and also different translations of the same stimulus materials, she reported that Chinese subjects performed no differently from their Western counterparts. The controversy continues, however, and many investigators remain unconvinced that the differences Bloom and others have observed in a large number of studies on counterfactual reasoning are solely a function of awkward or improper translations of stimulus materials.

Moser (1989), for example, discussed several of Bloom's (1981, 1984) findings that are not easily explained away. He described the following question that Bloom (1981, pp. 53–54) gave to Taiwanese, Hong Kong, and American subjects in their native language.

Everyone has his or her own method for teaching children to respect morality. Some people punish the child for immoral behavior, thereby leading him to fear the consequences of such behavior. Others reward the child for moral behavior, thereby leading him to want to behave morally. Even though both of these methods lead the child to respect morality, the first method can lead to some negative psychological consequences—it may lower the child's self-esteem.

According to the above paragraph, what do the two methods have in common? Please select only one answer.

A. Both methods are useless.
B. They have nothing in common, because the first leads to negative psychological consequences.
C. Both can reach the goal of leading the child to respect morality.
D. It is better to use the second.
E. None of the above answers makes sense. (If you choose this answer, please explain.)

Bloom (1984) reported that 97% of American subjects responded C, but that only 55% of the Taiwanese and 65% of the Hong Kong respondents answered C. In explaining his results, he wrote:

Most of the remaining Chinese-speaking subjects chose D or E and then went on to explain, based on their own experience and often at great length and evidently after much reflection, why, for instance, the second method might be better, or why neither method works, or why both methods have to be used in conjunction with each other, or perhaps, why some other specified means is preferable. For the majority of these subjects, as was evident from later interviewing, it was not that they did not see the paragraph as stating that both methods lead the child to respect morality, but they felt that choosing that alternative and leaving it at that would be misleading since in their experience that response was untrue. As they saw it, what was expected, desired, must be at a minimum an answer reflecting their personal considered opinion, if not a more elaborated explanation of their own experiences relevant to the matter at hand. Why else would anyone ask the question? American subjects, by contrast, readily accepted the question as a purely "theoretical" exercise to be responded to according to the assumptions of the world it creates rather than in terms of their own experiences with the actual world. (Bloom, 1981, p. 54)

It is our view that the differences in response between the Americans and the Chinese may be related to whether the respondent has an independent or interdependent construal of the self. If one's actions are contingent on, determined by, or made meaningful by one's relationships and social situations, it is reasonable to expect that respondents with interdependent selves might focus on the motivation of the person administering the question and on the nature of their current relationship with this person. Consequently, in the process of responding, they might ask themselves, "What is being asked of me here? What does this question expect of me or require from me? What are potential ramifications of answering in one way or another in respect to my relationship with this person?" In Lebra's (1976) terms, what is "my proper place?" in this social interaction [i.e., me and the interviewer], and what are the "obligations attached to [it?]" (p. 67). To immediately respond to the question as a purely abstract or theoretical exercise would require ignoring the currently constituted social situation and the nature of one's relationship with the other. This, of course, can be done, but it does not mean that it will be easily, effortlessly, or automatically done. And this is especially true when the pragmatics of a given context appears to require just the opposite. It requires ignoring the other's perspective and a lack of attention to what the other must be thinking or feeling to ask such a question. One's actions are made meaningful by reference to a particular set of contextual factors. If these are ignored or changed, then the self that is determined by them changes also. Those with relatively unencumbered, self-contained, independent selves can readily, and without hesitation, entertain any of a thousand fanciful possible worlds because there are fewer personal consequences—the bounded, autonomous self remains essentially inviolate.

One important implication of this analysis is that people with interdependent selves should have no disadvantage in counterfactual reasoning if the intent of the questioner and the demand of the situation is simply to test the theoretical reasoning capacities of the person. One such situation would involve an aptitude test such as the Scholastic Aptitude Test (SAT). Indeed, on the quantitative portion of the SAT that requires substantial hypothetical and counterfactual reasoning (e.g., "If Tom walked 2 miles per hour, then how far will he have walked in 4 hours?"), both Taiwanese and Japanese children perform considerably better than their American peers (Stevenson et al., 1986).

It would appear important, therefore, to distinguish between competence and performance or between the presence of particular inference skills and the application of these skills in a particular pragmatic context (see also Laboratory of Comparative Human Cognition, 1982). The discussion thus far implies that regardless of the nature of the self-system, most people with an adequate level of education possess the skills of hypothetical reasoning and the ability to think in a counterfactual fashion. Yet, the application of these skills in a particular situation varies considerably with the nature of the self-system. Some people may invoke these skills much more selectively. For those with interdependent selves, in contrast to those with independent selves, a relatively greater proportion of all inferences will be contingent on the pragmatic implications of a given situation, such as the perceived demands of the interviewer, the convention of the situation, and the rules of conversation.

Do styles of thinking and inference vary above and beyond those that derive from the pragmatic considerations of particular social situations? This question has yet to be more carefully addressed. However, given the tendency to see people, events, and objects as embedded within particular situations and relationships, the possibility seems genuine. Chiu (1972), for example, claimed that the reasoning of American children is characterized by an inferential-categorical style, whereas the reasoning of Taiwanese Chinese subjects displays a relational-contextual style. When American children described why two objects of a set of three objects went together, they were likely to say "because they both live on a farm." In contrast, Chinese children were more likely to display a relational-contextual style, putting two human figures together and claiming the two go together "because the mother takes care of the baby." In the latter case, the emphasis is on synthesizing features into an organized whole. Bruner (1986) referred to such differences as arising from a paradigmatic versus a narrative mode of thought. In the former, the goal is abstraction and analyzing common features, in the latter, establishing a connection or an interdependence among the elements.

Consequences for Emotion

In psychology, emotion is often viewed as a universal set of largely prewired internal processes of self-maintenance and self-regulation (Buck, 1988; Darwin, 1896; Ekman, 1972; LeDoux, 1987). This does not mean, though, that emotional experience is also universal. On the contrary, as suggested by anthropologists Rosaldo (1984), Lutz (1988), and Solomon (1984), culture can play a central role in shaping emotional experience. As with cognition, if an emotional activity or reaction implicates the self, the outcome of this activity will depend on the nature of the self-system. And apart from the fear induced by bright lights and loud sounds, or the pleasure produced by a sweet taste, there are likely to be few emotions that do not directly implicate one's view of the self. Thus, Rosaldo (1984) contended "feelings are not substances to be discovered in our blood but social practices organized by stories that we both enact and tell. They are structured by our forms of understanding" (p. 143), and we would add, specifically, by one's construal of the self. In an extension of these ideas, Lutz (1988) argued that although most emotions are viewed as universally experienced "natural" human phenomena, emotions are anything but natural. Emotion, she contended, "can be viewed as cultural and interpersonal products of naming, justifying, and persuading by people in relationship to each other. Emotional meaning is then a social rather than an individual achievement—an emergent product of social life" (Lutz, 1988, p. 5).

Among psychologists, several cognitively oriented theorists of emotion have suggested that emotion is importantly implicated and embedded in an actual social situation as construed by the person (e.g., De Rivera, 1984; Roseman, 1984; Scherer, 1984). Accordingly, not only does the experience of an emotion depend on the current construal of the social situation (e.g., Frijda, Kuipers, & ter Schure, 1989; Shaver, Schwartz, Kirson, & O'Connor, 1987; C. Smith & Ellsworth, 1987), but the experienced emotion in turn plays a pivotal role in changing and transforming the very nature of the social situation by allowing a new construal of the situation to emerge and, furthermore, by instigating the person to engage in certain actions. From the current perspective, construals of the social situation are constrained by, and largely derived from, construals of the self, others, and the relationship between the two. Thus, emotional experience should vary systematically with the construal of the self.

The present analysis suggests several ways in which emotional processes may differ with the nature of the self-system. First, the predominant eliciting conditions of many emotions may differ markedly according to one's construal of the self. Second, and more important, which emotions will be expressed or experienced, and with what intensity and frequency, may also vary dramatically.

Ego-focused versus other-focused emotions. The emotions systematically vary according to the extent to which they follow from, and also foster and reinforce, an independent or an interdependent construal of the self. This is a dimension that has largely been ignored in the literature. Some emotions, such as anger, frustration, and pride, have the individual's internal attributes (his or her own needs, goals, desires, or abilities) as the primary referent. Such emotions may be called *ego focused*. They result most typically from the blocking (e.g., "I was treated unfairly"), the satisfaction, or the confirmation (e.g., "I performed better than others") of one's internal attributes. Experiencing and expressing these emotions further highlights these self-defining, internal attributes and leads to additional attempts to assert in public and confirm them in private. As a consequence, for those with independent selves to operate effectively, they have to be "experts" in the expression and experience of these emotions. They will manage the expression, and even the experience, of these emotions so that they maintain, affirm, and bolster the construal of the self as an autonomous entity. The public display of one's own internal attributes can be at odds with the maintenance of interdependent, cooperative social interaction, and when unchecked can result in interpersonal confrontation, conflict, and possibly even overt aggression. These negative consequences, however, are not as severe as they might be for interdependent selves because the expression of one's internal attributes is the culturally sanctioned task of the independent self. In short, the current analysis suggests that, in contrast to those with more interdependent selves, the ego-focused emotions will be more frequently expressed, and perhaps experienced, by those with independent selves.

In contrast to the ego-focused emotions, some other emotions, such as sympathy, feelings of interpersonal communion, and shame, have another person, rather than one's internal attributes, as the primary referent. Such emotions may be called *other focused*. They typically result from being sensitive to the other, taking the perspective of the other, and attempting to promote interdependence. Experiencing these emotions highlights one's interdependence, facilitates the reciprocal exchanges of well-intended actions, leads to further cooperative social behavior, and thus provides a significant form of self-validation for interdependent selves. As a consequence, for those with interdependent selves to operate effectively, they will have to be "experts" in the expression and experience of these emotions. They will manage the expression, and even the experience, of these emotions so that they maintain, affirm, and reinforce the construal of the self as an interdependent entity. The other-focused emotions often discourage the autonomous expression of one's internal attributes and may lead to inhibition and ambivalence. Although among independent selves these consequences are experienced negatively (e.g., as timidity) and can, in fact, have a negative impact, they are tolerated, among interdependent selves, as the "business of living" (Kakar, 1978, p. 34). Creating and maintaining a connection to others is the primary task of the interdependent self. In short, this analysis suggests that, in contrast to those with more independent selves, these other-focused emotions will be more frequently expressed and perhaps even experienced among those with interdependent selves.

Ego-focused emotions—emotions that foster and create independence. In a comparison of American and Japanese undergraduates, Matsumoto, Kudoh, Scherer, and Wallbott (1988) found that American subjects reported experiencing their emotions *longer* than did Japanese subjects, even though the two groups agreed in their ordering of which emotions were experienced longest (i.e., joy = sad > anger = guilt > fear = shame = disgust). Americans also reported feeling these emotions more intensely than the Japanese and reported more bodily symptoms (e.g., lump in throat, change in breathing, more expressive reactions, and more verbal reactions) than did the Japanese. Finally, when asked what they would do to cope with the consequences of various emotional events, significantly more of the Japanese students reported that no action was necessary.

One interpretation of this pattern of findings may assume that most of the emotions examined, with the exception of shame and possibly guilt, are what we have called ego-focused emotions. Thus, people with independent selves will attend more to these feelings and act on the basis of them, because these feelings are regarded as diagnostic of the independent self. Not to attend to one's inner feelings is often viewed as being inauthentic or even as denying the "real" self, In contrast, among those with more interdependent selves, one's inner feelings may be less important in determining one's consequent actions. Ego-focused feelings may be regarded as by-products of interpersonal relationships, but they may not be accorded privileged status as regulators of behavior. For those with interdependent selves, it is the interpersonal context that assumes priority over the inner attributes, such as private feelings. The latter may need to be controlled or de-emphasized so as to effectively fit into the interpersonal context.

Given these differences in emotional processes, people with divergent selves may develop very different assumptions about the etiology of emotional expressions for ego-focused emotions. For those with independent selves, emotional expressions may literally "express" or reveal the inner feelings such as anger, sadness, and fear. For those with interdependent selves, however, an emotional expression may be more often regarded as a public instrumental action that may or may not be related directly to the inner feelings. Consistent with this analysis, Matsumoto (1989), using data from 15 cultures, reported that individuals from hierarchical cultures (that we would classify as being generally interdependent; see Hofstede, 1980), when asked to rate the intensity of an angry, sad, or fearful emotion displayed by an individual in a photograph, gave lower intensity ratings than those from less hierarchical cultures. Notably, although the degree of hierarchy inherent in one's cultures was strongly related to the intensity ratings given to those emotions, it was not related to the correct identification of these emotions. The one exception to this finding was that people from more hierarchical cultures (those with more interdependent selves) were less likely to correctly identify emotional expressions of happiness. Among those with interdependent selves (often those from hierarchical cultures), positive emotional expressions are most frequently used as public actions in the service of maintaining interpersonal harmony and, thus, are not regarded as particularly diagnostic of the actor's inner feelings or happiness.

For those with interdependent selves (composed primarily of relationships with others instead of inner attributes), it may be very important not to have intense experiences of ego-focused emotions, and this may be particularly true for negative emotions like anger. Anger may seriously threaten an interdependent self and thus may be highly dysfunctional. In fact, some anthropologists explicitly challenge the universalist view that all people experience the same negative emotions. Thus, in Tahiti, anger is highly feared, and various anthropological accounts claim that there is no expression of anger in this culture (see Levy, 1973; Solomon, 1984). It is not that these people have learned to inhibit or suppress their "real" anger but that they have learned the importance of attending to others, considering others, and being gentle in all situations, and as a consequence very little anger is elicited. In other words, the social reality is construed and actually constructed in such a way that it does not lend itself to the strong experience, let alone the outburst, of negative ego-focused emotions such as anger. The same is claimed for Ukta Eskimos (Briggs, 1970). They are said not to feel anger, not to express anger, and not even to talk about anger. The claim is that they do not show anger even in those circumstances that would certainly produce complete outrage in Americans. These Eskimos use a word that means "childish" to label angry behavior when it is observed in foreigners.

Among the Japanese, there is a similar concern with averting anger and avoiding a disruption of the harmony of the social situation. As a consequence, experiencing anger or receiving anger signals may be relatively rare events. A study by Miyake, Campos, Kagan, and Bradshaw (1986), which compared Japanese and American infants of 11 months of age, provides suggestive evidence for this claim. These investigators showed each infant an interesting toy and paired it with a mother's vocal expression of joy, anger, or fear. Then they measured the child's latency to resume locomotion toward the toy after the mother's utterance. The two groups of infants did not differ in their reactions to expressions of joy or fear. But, after an angry vocal expression of the mother, there was a striking difference between the two groups. The Japanese children resumed locomotion toward the toy after 48s, American children after only 18s. It may be that the Japanese children are relatively more traumatized by their mother's anger expressions because these are such rare events.

Notably, in the West, a controversy exists about the need, the desirability, and the importance of expressing one's anger. Assuming a hydraulic model of anger, some argue that it is necessary to express anger so as to avoid boiling over or blowing up at a later point (Pennebaker, 1982). Others argue for the importance of controlling one's anger so as not to risk losing control. No such controversy appears to exist among those in predominantly interdependent cultures, where a seemingly unchallenged norm directs individuals to restrain their inner feelings and particularly the overt expression of these feelings. Indeed, many interdependent cultures have well-developed strategies that render them expert at avoiding the expression of negative emotions. For example, Bond (1986) reported that in China discussions have a clear structure that is explicitly designed to prevent conflict from erupting. To begin with, discussants present their common problems and identify all the constraints that all the participants must meet. Only then do they state their own views. To Westerners, such a pattern appears as vague, beating around the bush, and not getting to the heart of the matter, but it is part of a carefully executed strategy of avoiding conflict, and thus perhaps the experience of negative emotions. Bond, in fact, noted that among schoolchildren in Hong Kong and Taiwan, there is a tendency to cooperate with opponents even in a competitive reward structure and to rate future opponents more positively than others who will not be opponents (Li, Cheung, & Kau, 1979, 1982).

In a recent cross-cultural comparison of the eliciting conditions of several emotions, Matsumoto et al. (1988) also found that Japanese respondents appear to be avoiding anger in close relations. Specifically, for the Japanese, closely related others were rarely implicated in the experience of anger. The Japanese reported feeling anger primarily in the presence of strangers. It thus appears that not only the expression but also the experience of such an ego-focused emotion as anger is effectively averted within an interdependent structure of relation. When anger arises, it happens outside of the existing interdependence, as in confrontation with out-groups (e.g, Samurai warfare in feudal Japan). In contrast, Americans and Western Europeans report experiencing anger primarily in the presence of closely related others. This is not surprising, given that expressing and experiencing ego-focused, even negative emotions, is one viable way to assert and affirm the status of the self as an independent entity. Consistent with this analysis, Stipek, Weiner, and Li (1989) found that when describing situations that produce anger, Chinese subjects were much more likely than American subjects to describe a situation that happened to someone else ("a guy on a bus did not give up a seat to an old woman"). For Americans, the major stimulus to anger was the situation where the individual was the victim ("a friend broke a promise to me").

Other emotions, such as pride or guilt, may also differ according to the nature of the mediating self-system. As with anger, these expressions may be avoided, or they will assume a somewhat different form. For example, if defined as being proud of one's *own* individual attributes, *pride* may mean hubris, and its expression may need to be avoided for those with interdependent selves.[4] Consistent with the idea that pride in one's own performance may be inhibited among those with interdependent selves, Stipek et al. (1989) found that the Chinese were decidedly less likely to claim their own successful efforts as a source of pride than were Americans. These investigators also reported that the emotion of guilt takes on somewhat different connotations as well. Among those with independent selves, who are more likely to hold stable, cross-situational beliefs and to consider them self-definitional, "violating a law or a moral principle" was the most frequently mentioned cause of guilt. Among Chinese. however, the most commonly reported source of guilt was "hurting others psychologically."

Other-focused emotions—emotions that create and foster interdependence. Those with interdependent selves may inhibit the experience, or at least the expression, of some ego-

---

[4] In interdependent cultures, if pride is overtly expressed, it may often be directed to a collective, of which the self is a part. For example, the Chinese anthropologist Hsu (1975) described an event in which a Japanese company official showed a "gesture of devotion to his office superior which I had never experienced in the Western world" (p. 215). After talking to Hsu in his own small, plain office, the employee said. "Let me show you the office of my section chief." He then took Hsu to a large, elaborately furnished office, pointed to a large desk, and said proudly, "This is the desk of my section chief." Hsu's account makes clear that this was not veiled cynicism from the employee, just complete, unabashed pride in the accomplishments of his boss. Americans with independent self-systems can perhaps understand this type of pride in another's accomplishment if the other involved is one's relative, but it is typically unfathomable in the case of one's immediate supervisor. Without an understanding of the close alignment and interdependence that occurs between employees and supervisors, the emotion experienced by the employee that prompted him to show off his supervisor's office would be incomprehensible.

focused emotions, but they may have a heightened capacity for the experience and expression of those emotions that derive primarily from focusing on the other. In Japan and China, for example, there is a much greater incidence of cosleeping, cobathing, and physical contact between mother and child than is typically true in most Western countries. The traditional Japanese mother carries the child on her back for a large part of the first 2 years. Lebra (1976) claimed that Japanese mothers teach their children to fear the pain of loneliness, whereas Westerners teach children how to be alone. Japanese and Chinese socialization practices may help the child develop an interdependent self in the first place, and at the same time, the capacity for the experience of a relatively greater variety of other-focused emotions.

The greater interdependence that results between mothers and their children in Japan is reflected in the finding that the classification of infants according to the nature of their attachments to their mothers (i.e., secure, ambivalent, and avoidant) departs markedly from the pattern typically observed in Western data. Specifically, many more Japanese infants are classified as "ambivalently attached" because they seem to experience decidedly more stress following a brief separation from the mother than do American infants (Ainsworth, Bell, & Stayton, 1974; Miyake, Chen, & Campos, in press). This finding also indicates that a paradigm like the typical stranger situation is inherently linked to an independent view of self and, thus, may not be appropriate for gauging attachment in non-Western cultures.

In Japan, socialization practices that foster an intense closeness between mother and child give rise to the feeling of *amae*. *Amae* is typically defined as the sense of, or the accompanying hope for, being lovingly cared for and involves depending on and presuming another's indulgence. Although, as detailed by Kumagai and Kumagai (1985), the exact meaning of *amae* is open to some debate, it is clear that "the other" is essential. When a person experiences *amae*, she or he "feels the freedom to do whatever he or she wills" while being accepted and cared for by others with few strings attached. Some say *amae* is a type of complete acceptance, a phenomenal replication of the ideal mother-infant bond (L. T. Doi, 1973). From our point of view, experiencing *amae* with respect to another person may be inherent in the formation and maintenance of a mutually reciprocal, interdependent relationship with another person. If the other person accepts one's *amae*, the reciprocal relationship is symbolically completed, leading to a significant form of self-validation. If, however, the other person rejects one's *amae*, the relationship will be in jeopardy.

For the purpose of comparing indigenous feelings, such as *amae*, with the more universal ones, such as anger and happiness, Kitayama and Markus (1990) used a multidimensional scaling technique, which allows the identification of the dimensions that individuals habitually or spontaneously use when they make judgments about similarities among various emotions. Recent studies have demonstrated that people are capable of distinguishing among various emotions on as many as seven or eight cognitive dimensions (Mauro, Sato, & Tucker, 1989; C. Smith & Ellsworth, 1987). In these studies, however, the dimensions have been specified a priori by the experimenter and given explicitly to the respondents to use in describing the emotions. When the dimensions are not provided but allowed to emerge in multidimensional scaling studies, only two dimensions are typically identified: activation (or excitement) and pleasantness (e.g., Russell, 1980). And it appears that most Western emotions can be readily located on a circumplex plane defined by these two dimensions. Thus, although people are capable of discriminating among emotions on a substantial number of dimensions, they habitually categorize the emotions only on the dimensions of activation and pleasantness.

More recently, Russell (1983; Russell, Lewicka, & Niit, 1989) applied the same technique to several non-Western cultural groups and replicated the American findings. He thus argued that the lay understanding of emotional experience may indeed be universal. Russell used, however, only those terms that have clear counterparts in the non-Western groups he studied. He did not include any emotion terms indigenous to the non-Western groups such as *amae*. It is possible that once terms for such indigenous feeling states are included in the analysis, a new dimension, or dimensions, may emerge. To explore this possibility, Kitayama and Markus (1990) sampled 20 emotions from the Japanese language. Half of these terms were also found in English and were sampled so that they evenly covered the circumplex space identified by Russell. The remaining terms were those indigenous to Japanese culture and those that presuppose the presence of others. Some (e.g., *fureai* [feeling a close connection with someone else]) refer primarily to a positive association with others (rather than events that happen within the individual, such as success), whereas others refer to interpersonal isolation and conflict (e.g., *oime* [the feeling of indebtedness]). Japanese college students rated the similarity between 2 emotions for each of the 190 pairs that could be made from the 20 emotions. The mean perceived similarity ratings for these pairs were then submitted to a multidimensional scaling.

Replicating past research, Kitayama and Markus (1990) identified two dimensions that closely correspond to the activation and the pleasantness dimensions. In addition, however, a new dimension emerged. This third dimension represented the extent to which the person is engaged in or disengaged from an interpersonal relationship. At the interpersonal engagement end were what we have called other-focused emotions, such as shame, *fureai* [feeling a close connection with somebody else], and *shitashimi* [feeling familiar], whereas at the disengagement end were found some ego-centered emotions, such as pride and *tukeagari* [feeling puffed up with the sense of self-importance], along with sleepiness and boredom. This interpersonal engagement—disengagement dimension also differentiated between otherwise very similar emotions. Thus, pride and elation were equally positive and high in activation, yet pride was perceived as considerably less interpersonally engaged than elation. Furthermore, anger and shame were very similar in terms of activation and pleasantness, but shame was much higher than anger in the extent of interpersonal engagement.

More important, this study located the indigenous emotions within the three-dimensional structure, permitting us to understand the nature of these emotions in reference to more universal emotions. For instance, *amae* was low in activation, and neither positive nor negative, fairly akin to sleepiness, except that the former was much more interpersonally engaged than the latter. This may indicate the passive nature of *amae*, involving the hopeful expectation of another person's favor and indulgence without any active, agentic solicitation of them. Completion of *amae* depends entirely on the other person, and, therefore, *amae* is uniquely ambivalent in its connotation on the pleasantness dimension. Another indigenous emotion, *oime*, involves the feeling of being psychologically indebted to somebody else. *Oime* was located at the very negative end of the pleasantness dimension, perceived even more negatively than such universal negative emotions as anger and sadness. The extreme unpleasantness of *oime* suggests the aversive nature of unmet obligations and the press of the need to fulfill one's obligations to others and to return favors. It also underscores the significance of balanced and harmonious relationships in the emotional life of those with interdependent selves.

The finding that the Japanese respondents clearly and reliably discriminated between ego-focused emotions and other-focused emotions on the dimension of interpersonal engagement versus disengagement strongly suggests the validity of this distinction as an essential component of emotional experience at least among Japanese and, perhaps, among people from other cultures as well. In a more recent study, Kitayama and Markus (1990) further tested whether this theoretical dimension of emotion also underlies and even determines how frequently people may experience various emotions and whether the frequency of emotional experience varies with their dominant construal of self as independent or interdependent.

Kitayama and Markus (1990) first sampled three emotions common in Japanese culture that were expected to fall under one of the five types theoretically derived from the current analysis. These types are listed in Table 2. Ego-focused positive emotions (*yuetukan* [feeling superior], pride, and *tukeagari* [feeling puffed up] are those that are most typically associated with the confirmation or fulfillment of one's internal attributes, such as abilities, desires, and needs. Ego-focused, negative emotions (anger, *futekusare* [sulky feeling], and *yokyufuman* [frustration]) occur primarily when such internal attributes are blocked or threatened. Also included were those correspondingly positive or negative emotions associated with the maintenance or enhancement of interdependence. Thus, three emotions are commonly associated with the affirmation or the completion of interdependent relationships (*fureai* [feeling of connection with someone], *shitashimi* [feeling of familiarity to someone], *sonkei* [feeling of respect for someone]) and thus were designated as positive and other focused. In contrast, some negative emotions are typically derived from one's failure to offer or reciprocate favors to relevant others and thus to fully participate in the relationship. They are thus closely linked to disturbance to interdependence and a consequent desire to repair the disturbance. They include *oime* [feeling of indebtedness], shame, and guilt. Finally, as noted before, interdependent selves are likely to tolerate ambivalence regarding one's interdependent status with some relevant others. Interestingly, some emotions are uniquely linked to this interpersonal ambivalence. Three such emotions (*amae* [hopeful expectation of others' indulgence or favor], *tanomi* [feeling like relying on someone], and *sugari* [feeling like leaning on someone]) were examined.

Japanese respondents reported how frequently they experienced each of the 15 emotions listed in Table 2. The five-factor structure implied by the theoretical designation of the 15 emotions to one of the five types was verified in a confirmatory factor analysis (Jöreskog,

TABLE 2
The Fifteen Emotions and Their Meaning

Emotion type (factor)	Emotion	Meaning
Ego-focused		
Positive	*Yuetukan*	Feeling superior
	Tukeagari	Feeling puffed up with the sense of self-importance
	Pride	
Negative	*Futekusare*	Sulky feeling
	Yokyufuman	Frustration
	Anger	
Other-focused		
Positive	*Fureai*	Feeling of connection with someone
	Shitashimi	Feeling of familiarity to someone
	Sonkei	Feeling of respect for someone
Ambivalent	*Amae*	Hopeful expectation of someone's indulgence and favor
	Tanomi	Feeling like relying on someone
	Sugari	Feeling like leaning on someone
Negative	*Oime*	Feeling of indebtedness
	Shame	
	Guilt	

1969). A correlation matrix for the five types is given in Table 3. There was a strong correlation between positive and negative ego-focused emotions, as may be expected if both of them are derived from and also foster and reinforce an independent construal of self. Furthermore, these ego-focused emotions are clearly distinct from the other-focused emotions. Thus, neither positive nor negative ego-focused emotions had any significant relationship with other-focused, positive emotions. Interestingly, however, these ego-focused emotions were significantly associated with the ambivalent and, to a larger extent, with the negative other-focused emotions, suggesting that the experience of ego-focused emotions, either positive or negative, is readily accompanied, at least in Japanese culture, by the felt disturbance of a relationship and, thus, by a strong need to restore harmony. Alternatively, being embedded in a highly reciprocal relation and feeling obliged to contribute to the relationship may sometimes be perceived as a burden or pressure, hence rendering salient some of the ego-focused emotions.[5] Finally, the three types of other-focused emotions (positive, ambivalent, and negative) are all positively correlated (see Table 3).

---

[5] On these occasions, perhaps interdependent selves are most clearly aware of their internal attributes. Such awareness (the *honne* in Japanese) may be typically accompanied by a situational demand (the *tatemae* in Japanese).

TABLE 3
Correlations Among the Five Types of Emotions

Emotion	1	2	3	4	5
Ego-focused					
1. Positive	—				
2. Negative	.70	—			
Other-focused					
3. Positive	−.05	−.18	—		
4. Ambivalent	.35	.63	.40	—	
5. Negative	.49	.69	.18	.43	—

Can the frequency of experiencing the five types of emotions be predicted by one's predominant construal of self as independent or interdependent? To address this issue, Kitayama and Markus (1990) also asked the same respondents eight questions designed to measure the extent to which they endorse an independent construal of self (e.g., "Are you a kind of person who holds on to one's own view?"; "How important is it to hold on to one's own view?") and eight corresponding questions designed to measure the extent to which they endorse an interdependent construal of self (e.g., "Are you the kind of person who never forgets a favor provided by others?"; "How important is it to never forget a favor provided by others?"). Consistent with the current analysis, the frequency of experiencing both positive and negative ego-focused emotions significantly increased with the independent construal of self. They were, however, either negatively related (for positive emotions) or unrelated (for negative emotions) to the interdependent construal of self. In marked contrast to this pattern for the ego-focused emotions, all three types of other-focused emotions were significantly more frequently experienced by those with more interdependent construals of self. These emotions, however, were either unrelated (for positive and negative other-focused emotions) or negatively related (for the ambivalent emotions) to the independent construal of self.

Consequences for Motivation

The study of motivation centers on the question of why people initiate, terminate, and persist in specific actions in particular circumstances (e.g., Atkinson, 1958; Mook, 1986). The answer given to this question in the West usually involves some type of internal, individually rooted need or motive—the motive to enhance one's self-esteem, the motive to achieve, the motive to affiliate, the motive to avoid cognitive conflict, or the motive to self-actualize. These motives are assumed to be part of the unique, internal core of a person's self-system. But what is the nature of motivation for those with interdependent self-systems? What form does it take? How does the ever-present need to attend to others and to gain their acceptance influence the form of these internal, individual motives? Are the motives identified in Western psychology the universal instigators of behavior?

As with cognition and emotion, those motivational processes that implicate the self depend on the nature of the self-system. If we assume that *others* will be relatively more focal in the motivation of those with interdependent selves, various implications follow. First, those with interdependent selves should express, and perhaps experience, more of those motives that are social or that have the other as referent. Second, as we have noted previously for those with independent selves, agency will be experienced as an effort to express one's internal needs, rights, and capacities and to withstand undue social pressure, whereas among those with interdependent selves, agency will be experienced as an effort to be receptive to others, to adjust to their needs and demands, and to restrain one's own inner needs or desires. Motives related to the need to express one's agency or competency (e.g., the achievement motive) are typically assumed to be common to all individuals. Yet among those with interdependent selves, striving to excel or accomplish challenging tasks may not be in the service of achieving separateness and autonomy, as is usually assumed for those with independent selves, but instead in the service of more fully realizing one's connectedness or interdependence. Third, motives that are linked to the self, such as self-enhancement, self-consistency, self-verification, self-affirmation, and self-actualization, may assume a very different form depending on the nature of the self that is being enhanced, verified, or actualized.

More interdependent motives? Murray (1938) assembled what he believed to be a comprehensive list of human motivations (see also Hilgard, 1953, 1987). Many of these motives seem most relevant for those with independent selves, but the list also includes some motives that should have particular salience for those with interdependent selves. These include *deference*, the need to admire and willingly follow a superior, to serve gladly; *similance*, the need to imitate or emulate others, to agree and believe; *affiliation*, the need to form friendships and associations; *nurturance*, the need to nourish, aid, or protect another; *succorance*, the need to seek aid, projection, or sympathy and to be dependent; *avoidance of blame*, the need to avoid blame, ostracism, or punishment by inhibiting unconventional impulses and to be well behaved and obey the law; and *abasement*, the need to comply and accept punishment or self-deprecation. Many of the social motives suggested by Murray seem to capture the types of strivings that should characterize those with interdependent selves. When the cultural imperative is to seek connectedness, social integration, and interpersonal harmony, most of these motives should be typically experienced by the individual as positive and desirable. In contrast, when the cultural task centers on maintaining independence and separateness, holding any of these motives too strongly (e.g., similance and succorance) often indicates a weak or troubled personality. Thus, Murray, for example, gave the need to comply the pejorative label of *need for abasement*.

The limited evidence for the idea that those with interdependent selves will experience more of the social or interdependent motives comes from Bond (1986), who summarized several studies exploring the motive patterns of the Chinese (see also McClelland, 1961). He found that the level of various motives are a fairly direct reflection of the collectivist or group-oriented tradition of the Chinese. Thus, Chinese respondents show relatively high levels of need for abasement, socially oriented achievement, change, endurance, intraception, nurturance, and order; moderate levels of autonomy, deference, and dominance, and succorance; and low levels of individually oriented achievement, affiliation, aggression, exhibition, heterosexuality, and power. The socially oriented achievement motive has, as its ultimate goal, a desire to meet expectations of significant others, whereas the individually oriented achievement motive implies a striving for achievement for its own sake (discussed later). Hwang (1976) found, however, that with continuing rapid social change in China, there is an increase in levels of exhibition, autonomy, intraception, and heterosexuality and a decrease in levels of deference, order, nurturance, and endurance. Interestingly, it appears that those with interdependent selves do not show a greater need for affiliation, as might at first be thought, but instead they exhibit higher levels of those motives that reflect a concern with adjusting oneself so as to occupy a proper place with respect to others.

The motive for cognitive consistency. Another powerful motive assumed to fuel the behavior of Westerners is the need to avoid or reduce cognitive conflict or dissonance. Classic dissonance occurs when one says one thing publicly and feels another, quite contrasting thing privately (Festinger & Carlsmith, 1959). And such a configuration produces particular difficulty when the private attitude is a self-defining one (Greenwald, 1980). One might argue, however, that the state of cognitive dissonance arising from counterattitudinal behavior is not likely to be experienced by those with interdependent selves. First it is the individuals' roles, statuses, or positions, and the commitments, obligations, and responsibilities they confer, that are the constituents of the self, and in that sense they are self-defining. As outlined in Figure 1, one's internal attributes (e.g., private attitudes or opinions) are not regarded as the significant attributes of the self. Furthermore, one's private feelings are to be regulated in accordance with the requirements of the situation. Restraint over the inner self is assigned a much higher value than is expression of the inner self. Thus, Kiefer (1976) wrote:

> Although Japanese are often acutely aware of discrepancies between inner feelings and outward role demands, they think of the latter . . . as the really important center of the self. Regarding feelings as highly idiosyncratic and hard to control, and therefore less reliable as sources of self-respect than statuses and roles, the Japanese tends to include within the boundaries of the concept of self much of the quality of the intimate social group of which he is a member. (R. J. Smith, 1985, p. 28)

More recently, T. Doi (1986) has argued that Americans are decidedly more concerned with consistency between feelings and actions than are the Japanese. In Japan there is a virtue in controlling the expression of one's innermost feelings; no virtue accrues from expressing them. Triandis (1989), for example, reported a study by Iwao (1988), who gave respondents a series of scenarios and asked them to judge which responses would be appropriate for the person described in the scenario. In one scenario, the daughter brings home a person from another race. One of the possible responses given was "thought that he would never allow them to marry but told them he was in favor of their marriage." This answer was rated as best by only 2% of Americans. In sharp contrast, however, it was rated as best by 44% of the Japanese. Among the Americans, 48% thought it was the worst response, whereas only 7% of the Japanese rated it as the worst.

Common motives in an interdependent context. Of those motives assumed by Murray (1938) and Hilgard (1987) to be universally significant, the achievement motive is the most well-documented example. Variously defined as the desire to overcome obstacles, to exert power, to do something as well as possible, or to master, manipulate, or organize physical objects, human beings, or ideas (Hall & Lindzey, 1957; Hilgard, 1987), the achievement motive is thought to be a fundamental human characteristic. However, the drive for achievement in an interdependent context may have some very different aspects from the motive for achievement in an independent cultural context. In a recent analysis of the content and structure of values in seven cultures (i.e., Australia, United States, Spain, Finland, Germany, Israel, and Hong Kong), S. H. Schwartz and Bilsky (1990) found a conflict between values that emphasize independent thought and action and those that emphasize restraining of one's own impulses in all samples except Hong Kong. In the Hong Kong sample, self-restraint appeared to be quite compatible with independent thought and action.

Although all individuals may have some desire for agency or control over their own actions, this agency can be accomplished in various ways (Maehr, 1974). Pushing oneself ahead of others and actively seeking success does not appear to be universally valued. An illuminating analysis of control motivation by Weisz et al. (1984) suggests that acting on the world and altering the world may not be the control strategy of choice for all people. Instead, people in many Asian cultures appear to use what is termed *secondary control*. This involves accommodating to existing realities "sometimes via acts that limit individualism and personal autonomy but that enhance perceived alignment or goodness of fit with people, objects, or circumstances" (Weisz et al., 1984, p. 956).

The American notion of achievement involves breaking away, pushing ahead, and gaining control over surroundings. How do selves concerned with fitting in and accommodating to existing realities achieve? The question of achievement motive in an interdependent context is all the more compelling because many of the most collective societies of the world currently appear extremely preoccupied with achievement. In an analysis of Chinese children's stories, for example, Blumenthal (1977) found that the most common behavior was achievement-oriented in nature, the second most frequent was altruism, and the third was social and personal responsibility. Among junior high school students in Japan, the motto "pass with four, fail with five" is now common. This refers to the fact that if one is sleeping 5 hr a night, he or she is probably not studying hard enough to pass exams. It appears, however, that this strong emphasis on achievement motivation is, in part, other-motivated. It is motivated by a desire to fit into the group and to meet the expectations of the group. In the child's case, the group is the family, and the child's mission is to enhance the social standing of the family by gaining admission to one of the top universities. The motive to achieve need not necessarily reflect a motive to achieve for "me" personally (Maehr & Nicholls, 1980). It can have social or collective origins. Children are striving to achieve the goals of others, such as family and teachers, with whom they are reciprocally interdependent. Consistent with this notion, Yu (1974) reported that the strength of achievement motivation was correlated positively with familism and filial piety. Striving for excellence necessarily involves some distancing or separating from some others, but the separation allows the child to properly accomplish the task of the student and thus to fulfill his or her role within the family.

Several studies by Yang (Yang, 1982/1985; Yang & Liang, 1973) have sought to distinguish between two types of achievement motivation: individually oriented and socially oriented. Individually oriented achievement motivation is viewed as a functionally autonomous desire in which the individual strives to achieve some internalized standards of excellence. In contrast, socially oriented achievement motivation is not functionally autonomous; rather, individuals persevere to fulfill the expectations of significant others, typically the family (Bond, 1986). With socially oriented achievement, when the specific achievement goal is met, the intense achievement motivation formerly evident may appear to vanish. This analysis indeed fits many anecdotal reports indicating that once admitted into the college of their choice, or hired by their preferred company, Japanese high school and college students are no longer particularly interested in achievement.

Once a new goal is established, of course, the socially oriented achievement motive may be easily reengaged by any figure who can serve as a symbolic substitute for family members. A longitudinal survey conducted in Japan over the last 30 years (Hayashi, 1988) has repeatedly shown that approximately 80% of the Japanese, regardless of sex, age, education, and social class, prefer a manager with a fatherlike character (who demands a lot more than officially required in the work, yet extends his care for the person's personal matters even outside of work) over a more Western-type, task-oriented manager (who separates personal matters from work and demands as much as, yet no more than, officially required). In a large number of surveys and experiments, Misumi and his colleagues (summarized in Misumi, 1985) have demonstrated that in Japan a leader who is both demanding and personally caring is most effective regardless of the task or the population examined (e.g., college students, white-collar workers, and blue-collar workers). This is in marked contrast to the major conclusion reached in the leadership literature in the United States, which suggests that leadership effectiveness depends on a complex interaction between characteristics of leaders, characteristics of followers, and, most important, on the nature of the task (Fiedler, 1978; Hollander, 1985). According to our analysis, in Japan as well as in other interdependent cultures, it is the personal attachment to the leader and the ensuing obligation to him or her that most strongly motivate people to do their work. Motivation mediated by a strong personal relationship, then, is unlikely to be contingent on factors associated with the specific task or environment.

The self-related motives. The motive to maintain a positive view of the self is one motive that psychologists since James (1890) through Greenwald (1980), Harter (1983), Steele (1988), and Tesser (1986) have assumed to be universally true. What constitutes a positive view of self depends, however, on one's construal of the self.[6] For those with inde-

---

[6] For a compelling analysis of how self-esteem is related to culture, see Solomon, Greenberg, and Pyszczynski (in press).

pendent selves, feeling good about oneself typically requires fulfilling the tasks associated with being an independent self; that is, being unique, expressing one's inner attributes, and asserting oneself (see Table 1). Although not uncontested, a reasonable empirical generalization from the research on self-related motives is that Westerners, particularly those with high self-esteem, try to enhance themselves whenever possible, and this tendency results in a pervasive self-serving bias. Studies with American subjects demonstrate that they take credit for their successes, explain away their failures, and in various ways try to aggrandize themselves (e.g., Gilovich, 1983; Lau, 1984; J. B. Miller, 1986; Whitley & Frieze, 1985; Zuckerman, 1979). Maintaining self-esteem requires separating oneself from others and seeing oneself as different from and better than others. At 4 years old, children already show a clear self-favorability bias (Harter, 1989). When asked to compare themselves with others with respect to intelligence, friendliness, or any skill, most children think they are better than most others. Wylie (1979) reported that American adults also consider themselves to be more intelligent and more attractive than average, and Myers (1987), in a national survey of American students, found that 70% of students believe they are above average in leadership ability, and with respect to the "ability to get along with others," 0% thought they were below average, 60% thought they were in the top 10%, and 25% thought they were in the top 1%. Moreover, as documented by Taylor and Brown (1988), among Americans, most people feel that they are more in control and have more positive expectations for themselves and their future than they have for other people. This tendency toward false uniqueness presumably derives from efforts of those with independent selves to maintain a positive view of themselves.

The motive to maintain a positive view of the self may assume a somewhat different form, however, for those with interdependent selves. Feeling good about one's interdependent self may not be achieved through enhancement of the value attached to one's internal attributes and the attendant self-serving bias. Instead, positive feelings about the self should derive from fulfilling the tasks associated with being interdependent with relevant others: belonging, fitting in, occupying one's proper place, engaging in appropriate action, promoting others' goals, and maintaining harmony (see Table 1). This follows for at least two reasons. First, people with interdependent selves are likely to be motivated by other-focused emotions, such as empathy and *oime* (i.e., the feeling of psychological indebtedness) and to act in accordance with the perceived needs and desires of their partners in social relations, and this may produce a social dynamic where individuals strive to enhance each other's self-esteem. In such reciprocal relationships, *other* enhancement could be more instrumental to self-enhancement than direct attempts at self-enhancement because the latter are likely to isolate the individual from the network of reciprocal relationships. Second, self-esteem among those with interdependent selves may be based in some large measure on their capacity to exert control over their own desires and needs so that they can indeed belong and fit in. As noted earlier (see also Weisz et al., 1984), such self-control and self-restraint are instrumental to the ability to flexibly adjust to social contingencies and thus are highly valued in interdependent cultures. Indeed, self-restraint together with flexible adjustment is often regarded as an important sign of the moral maturity of the person.

A developmental study by Yoshida, Kojo, and Kaku (1982, Study 1) has documented that self-enhancement or self-promotion are perceived quite negatively in Japanese culture. Second (7–8 years old), third (8–9 years old), and fifth graders (10–11 years old) at a Japanese elementary school were asked how their classmates (including themselves) would evaluate a hypothetical peer who commented on his own superb athletic performance either in a modest, self-restrained way or in a self-enhancing way. The evaluation was solicited on the dimension of personality ("Is he a good person?") and on the dimension of ability ("Is he good at [the relevant athletic domain]?"). As shown in Figure 4A, the personality of the modest peer was perceived much more positively than was that of the self-enhancing peer. Furthermore, this difference became more pronounced as the age (grade) of the respondents increased. A similar finding also has been reported for Chinese college students in Hong Kong by Bond, Leung, and Wan (1982), who found that individuals giving humble or self-effacing attributions following success were liked better than those giving self-enhancing attribution. The most intriguing aspect of the Yoshida et al. (1982) study, however, is their finding for the ability evaluation, which showed a complete crossover interaction (see Figure 4B). Whereas the second graders took the comment of the peer at face value, perceiving the self-enhancing peer to be more competent than the modest peer, this trend disappeared for the third graders, and then completely reversed for the fifth graders. Thus, the fifth graders perceived that the modest peer was more competent than the self-enhancing peer. These findings indicate that as children are socialized in an interdependent cultural context, they begin to appreciate the cultural value of self-restraint and, furthermore, to believe in a positive association between self-restraint and other favorable attributes of the person not only in the social, emotional domains but also in the domains of ability and competence. Although it is certainly possible for those with independent selves

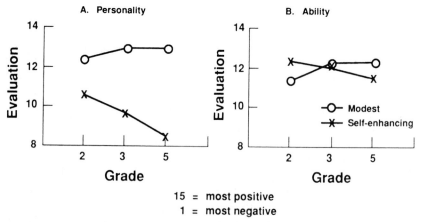

FIGURE 4. Mean evaluations by second, third, and fifth graders. (A: Personality of target person. B: Ability of target person. Drawn from results reported by Yoshida, Kojo, and Kaku, 1982.)

to overdo their self-enhancement (see Schlenker & Leary, 1982), for the most part, the American prescription is to confidently display and express one's strengths, and those who do so are evaluated positively (e.g., Greenwald, 1980; Mullen & Riordan, 1988).

Self- or other-serving bias. Given the appreciation that those with interdependent selves have for self-restraint and self-control, the various, self-enhancing biases that are common in Western culture may not be prevalent in many Asian cultures. In an initial examination of potential cultural variation in the tendency to see oneself as different from others, Markus and Kitayama (in press) administered questionnaires containing a series of false-uniqueness items to large classes of Japanese college students in Japan and to large classes of American college students in the United States. In both cases, the classes were chosen to be representative of university students as a whole. They asked a series of questions of the form "What proportion of students in this university have higher intellectual abilities than yourself?" There were marked differences between the Japanese and the American students in their estimations of their own uniqueness; the Americans displayed significantly more false uniqueness than the Japanese. American students assumed that only 30% of people on average would be better than themselves on various traits and abilities (e.g., memory, athletic ability, independence, and sympathy), whereas the Japanese students showed almost no evidence of this false uniqueness. In most cases, the Japanese estimated that about 50% of students would be better than they were or have more of a given trait or ability. This is, of course, the expected finding if a representative sample of college students were evaluating themselves in a relatively nonbiased manner.

In a recent series of studies conducted in Japan with Japanese college students, Takata (1987) showed that there is no self-enhancing bias in social comparison. In fact, he found just the opposite—a strong bias in the self-effacing direction. Participants performed several anagram problems that were alleged to measure memory ability. After completion of the task, the participants were presented with their actual performance on some of the trials and also the performance of another person picked at random from the pool of subjects who had allegedly completed the study. The direction of the self—other difference was manipulated to be either favorable or unfavorable to the subject. The dependent measures were collected in a private situation to minimize self-presentational concerns. Furthermore, because it was considered possible that the subjects might still believe they had a chance of seeing the other person afterward, in a followup study the "other person" was replaced with a computer program that allegedly simulated the task performance of the average college student.

Several studies (e.g., Goethals, 1989; Marks, 1984; Wylie, 1979) reveal that with respect to abilities, Americans typically give themselves higher ratings than they give to others. Thus, when a comparison with another is unfavorable to the self, the self-enhancement hypothesis predicts that Americans should show little confidence in this estimate of their ability and seek further information. This, in fact, was the case in an American study by J. M. Schwartz and Smith (1976), which used a procedure very similar to Takata's (1987). When subjects performed poorly relative to another person, they had very little confidence in their own score. These American data contrast sharply with the Japanese data. Takata's study shows a tendency exactly the opposite of self-enhancement. Furthermore, the pattern did not depend on whether the comparison was made with another person or with the computer program. The Japanese subjects felt greater confidence in their self-evaluation and were less interested in seeking further information when they had unfavorable self-evaluations than when they had favorable ones. Similarly, Wada (1988) also reported that Japanese college students were convinced of their level of ability on a novel, information-integration task after failure feedback, but not after success feedback. These data suggest what might be called a modesty bias or an other-enhancement bias in social comparison.

A similar modesty bias among those with interdependent selves has also been suggested by Shikanai (1978), who studied the causal attribution for one's own success or failure in an ability task. Typically, American subjects believe that their internal attributes such as ability or competence are extremely important to their performance, and this is particularly the case when they have succeeded (e.g., Davis & Stephan, 1980; Gilmor & Reid, 1979; Greenberg, Pyszczynski, & Solomon, 1982; Weiner, 1986). In the Shikanai study, Japanese college students performed an anagram task. Half of them were subsequently led to believe that they scored better than the average and thus "succeeded," whereas the other half were led to believe that they scored worse than the average and thus "failed." Subjects were then asked to choose the most important factor in explaining the success or the failure for each of 10 pairs made from the 5 possible causes for performance (i.e., ability, effort, task difficulty [or ease], luck, and mental-physical "shape" of the day). Shikanai analyzed the average number of times each cause was picked as most important (possible minimum of 0 and maximum of 4). As shown in Figure 5, a modesty bias was again obtained, especially after success. Whereas failure was attributed mainly to the lack of effort, success was attributed primarily to the ease of the task. Furthermore, the potential role of ability in explaining success was very much downplayed. Indeed, ability was perceived to be more important after a failure than after a success, whereas task difficulty (or its ease) was regarded to be more important after a success than after a failure. Subsequent studies by Shikanai that examined attribution of success and failure of others did not find this pattern (Shikanai, 1983, 1984). Thus, the pattern of "modest" appraisal seems to be specific to the perception and the presentation of the self and does not derive from a more general causal schema applicable to both self and others. For others, ability is important in explaining success. Yoshida et al. (1982, Studies 2 and 3), who studied explanations of performance in a Japanese elementary school, found the tendency to de-emphasize the role of ability in explaining success as early as the second grade.

Observations of a tendency to self-efface, and not to reveal the typical American pattern of blaming others or the situation when explaining failure, have been made outside of the experimental laboratory as well. In a study by Hess et al. (1986), Japanese mothers explained poor performance among their fifth graders by claiming a lack of effort. In marked contrast, American mothers implicated effort in their explanations but viewed ability and the quality of the training in the school as equally important. This study also required the children to explain their own poor performance by assigning 10 points to each of five alternatives (ability, effort, training at school, bad luck, and difficulty of math). Japanese chil-

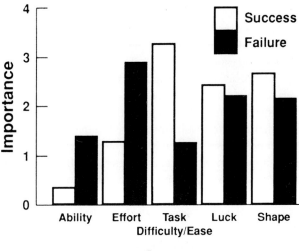

FIGURE 5. Mean importance rating given to each of five causes following success and failure. (Drawn from results reported by Shikanai, 1978.)

dren gave 5.6 points to lack of effort, but American children gave 1.98 points. H. Stevenson (personal communication, September 19, 1989) noted that in observations of elementary school classrooms, Japanese teachers, in contrast to American teachers, rarely refer to differences in ability among their students as an explanation for performance differences, even though the range of ability as assessed by standardized tests is approximately the same. Those with interdependent selves thus seem more likely to view intellectual achievement not as a fixed attribute that one has a certain amount of, but instead as a product that can be produced by individual effort in a given social context.[7]

The nature of modesty. The exact nature of these modesty, self-effacing, or other-enhancing biases has yet to be specified. Perhaps those from interdependent cultures have simply learned that humility is the desired response, or the culturally appropriate response, and that it is wise not to gloat over their performance or to express confidence in their ability. This interpretation implies that the modesty biases observed in the studies described herein are primarily the result of impression management and that the subjects involved

---

[7] Of course, because those in Asian cultures believe high ability to be a result of effort does not mean that they do not differentiate between ability and effort. In all likelihood, they believe that effort and ability are related in a multiplicative fashion to determine performance. Thus, for instance, in a recent study by Stipek, Weiner, and Li (1989), Chinese respondents reasoned, just as their American counterparts did, that if a person shows the same level of performance with much less effort expended on the task, the person must have a high level of the relevant ability. Our point is simply that those in Asian cultures believe that abilities are relatively more changeable over a long span of time through the effort the person expends.

actually could have held different, perhaps opposite, beliefs about themselves and their ability. However, it is also possible that these other-enhancement biases reflect, or are accompanied by, psychologically authentic self-perceptions. There are two related possibilities consistent with this suggestion.

First, given the press not to stand out and to fit in, people in interdependent cultures may acquire through socialization a habitual modest-response tendency. In large part, it may be a function of the need to pay more attention to the other than to the self, just as the self-serving bias is believed to result from a predominant focus on the self (see Ross & Fletcher, 1985). Consequently, for those with interdependent selves, whenever certain aspects of self need to be appraised in public, a modest, self-effacing pattern of responses may occur spontaneously. Furthermore, this modesty can be motivated by many other-focused emotions that are central to the construal of self as an interdependent entity. From an independent viewpoint, such modesty seems false and the result of suppressing a "natural" pride in one's attributes. Yet, such pride is only natural within a view of the self as an independent entity. From an interdependent view, modest responses may be experienced quite positively and engender the pleasant, other-focused feelings that are associated with connecting and maintaining interdependence.

Such positive, other-focused feelings also may be responsible for the finding that Japanese students are more convinced of and more confident in their ability after failure than success. The satisfaction of doing well that can accompany good performance on a novel, decontextualized task may be mitigated by the threat of potential uniqueness and uncertainty over how to respond to it. Moreover, if a predominant basis of self-esteem is how well one fits in and preserves relationships and interpersonal harmony, then failing to distinguish oneself with a highly successful performance may not be particularly devastating.[8] Certainly it will not be as devastating as it is to the person whose self-esteem rests primarily on doing well individually and on separating oneself from others.

Second, among those with interdependent selves, there may not be an awareness of one's own ability in general or in the abstract. Instead, one's own ability in a given task under a given condition may be inferred from whatever cues are available in the specific situation in which the task is performed. And whatever is inferred in this way may be experienced as authentic and genuine. For example, upon receipt of feedback about their ability, interdependent selves may first attend and think not so much about their ability as about the approval or disapproval of the person who gives the feedback. If approval or disapproval can be strongly and unambiguously inferred, then the perception of approval or disapproval may provide a strong heuristic clue about ability; if one receives approval, one must have high ability in this situation, whereas if one receives disapproval, then one must have low ability in this situation. In the absence of a strong, enduring belief about one's ability in the abstract, such a heuristic may provide a subjectively genuine self-appraisal. This analy-

---

[8] As noted, achievement may sometimes be construed as a means to complete one's interdependence, as may well be the case for a Japanese high school student who studies hard to gain admission to a prestigious college. In this case, failure may well be extremely troubling for those with interdependent selves.

sis also suggests why those with interdependent selves may be convinced of their low abil-ity after a failure feedback to a much greater extent than they are convinced of their high ability after a success feedback. Because of the prevalent social norms for polite behavior in interdependent cultures, disapproval can be more unequivocally inferred from negative feedback than approval can be inferred from positive feedback.

These suggestions about the source of a modest self-appraisal have yet to be empirically tested, but they are worthy of careful inquiry because these forms of self-appraisal may be quite unique to interdependent cultures. On the basis of empirical evidence, however, this much seems clear: Those with interdependent selves will typically not claim that they are better than others, will not express pleasure in the state of feeling superior to others, and indeed may not enjoy it. A strong, pervasive motive for self-enhancement through taking personal credit for success, denying personal responsibility for failure, and believing one-self to be better than average may be primarily a Western phenomenon. It is akin to being the nail that stands out.

So far, the empirical evidence on cultural variation in self-related motives is limited largely to differences in self-enhancement versus other enhancement. However, other self-related motives, such as self-affirmation (Steele, 1988), self-verification (Swann & Read, 1981), and self-actualization (Maslow, 1954), may also differ across cultures in similar ways. A series of studies by Steele has shown that the negative psychological impact of one's own misdeed, blunder, or public embarrassment can be reduced once another, significant aspect of the self is activated and affirmed. Thus, one's threatened self-worth can be restored by a reminder of another, unthreatened aspect of the self (e.g., "I may not be athletic, but at least I'm creative"). To the extent that very different aspects of self are highly valued among those with interdependent selves, this process of self-affirmation may also differ. For those with independent selves it will be the internal attributes of self that may most effectively offset each other and reestablish threatened self-esteem, whereas for those with interdependent selves it may be the more public aspects of the self, like one's significant social roles, sta-tuses, and important interpersonal relations, that must be focal in self-esteem maintenance. Thus, self-affirmation for an interdependent self will require an opportunity to ensure that one is fitting in and engaging in proper action in a given situation.

In a similar vein, exactly what is verified in self-verification and what is actualized in self-actualization may also differ considerably across cultures. Currently, it is common to assume that individuals are motivated to verify and actualize an internally coherent set of attributes that they regard as significant. Our present analysis would imply, however, that people with interdependent selves may strive to verify and actualize the more public qual-ities of the self—the ones that allow them to conceive of themselves as respectable and de-cent participants in significant interpersonal relationships.

Furthermore, among those with interdependent selves, self-verification and self-actual-ization may even be achieved through the realization of some more general, abstract forms of relation, that is, one's relationship to or one's role in society or even in the natural or cosmic system. The self-description studies reviewed earlier suggest this possibility. In gen-eral, the self-descriptions of those with interdependent selves have been found to be quite concrete and situation specific (see Cousins, 1989). There is, however, one interesting, reliable exception to this. Subjects from Asian cultural backgrounds (presumably those with predominantly interdependent selves) often provide extremely global self-descriptions, such as "I am a unique creation," "I am a human being," "I am an organic form," and "I am a product of my environment." It could appear that these statements are too abstract to be informative in any pragmatic sense (Rosch, 1978). The lack of information contained in these descriptions, however, may be more apparent than real. Note that these global statements presuppose a view of the world as an encompassing whole in which these subjects perceive themselves to be a part or a participant. And for these subjects, it may be these relationships that must be verified and actualized.

We have suggested the different forms that some self-related motives might assume if they are based in an interdependent rather than an independent construal of self. Further empirical work is required to determine whether the types of self-related motives described herein are indeed as prevalent in Eastern interdependent cultures as they have been found to be in Western, particularly American, cultures. It could be that these self-relevant motives are not part of the set of universal individual strivings,[9] but instead an outgrowth of an independent self-system rooted in the press for separation and individuation.

CONCLUSIONS

We have described two divergent construals of the self—an *independent* view and an interdependent view. The most significant differences between these two construals is in the role that is assigned to the other in self-definition. Others and the surrounding social context are important in both construals, but for the interdependent self, others are included *within* the boundaries of the self because relations with others in specific contexts are the defining features of the self. In the words of Lebra (1976), the individual is in some respects "a fraction" and becomes whole when fitting into or occupying one's proper place in a social unit. The sense of individuality that accompanies an interdependent self includes an attentiveness and responsiveness to others that one either explicitly or implicitly assumes will be reciprocated by these others, as well as the willful management of one's other-focused feelings and desires so as to maintain and further the reciprocal interpersonal relationship. One is conscious of where one belongs with respect to others and assumes a receptive stance toward these others, continually adjusting and accommodating to these others in many aspects of behavior (Azuma, 1984; Weisz et al., 1984). Such acts of fitting in and accommodating are often intrinsically rewarding, because they give rise to pleasant, other-focused emotions (e.g., feeling of connection) while diminishing unpleasant ones (e.g., shame) and, furthermore, because the self-restraint required in doing so forms an important basis of self-esteem. Typically, then, it is others rather than the self that serve as the referent for organizing one's experiences.

With an independent construal of the self, others are less centrally implicated in one's current self-definition or identity. Certainly, others are important for social comparison, for

---

[9] It is intriguing that Murray's (1938) original study of motives, as well as Hilgard's (1953, 1987) update of it, did not include any of the self-focused motives that are so central to current research on the self.

reflected appraisal, and in their role as the targets of one's actions, yet at any given moment, the self is assumed to be a complete, whole, autonomous entity, without the others. The defining features of an independent self are attributes, abilities, traits, desires, and motives that may have been social products but that have become the "property" of the self-contained individual (see Sampson, 1989) and that are assumed to be the source of the individual's behavior. The sense of individuality that accompanies this construal of the self includes a sense of oneself as an agent, as a producer of one's actions. One is conscious of being in control over the surrounding situation, and of the need to express one's own thoughts, feelings, and actions to others, and is relatively less conscious of the need to receive the thoughts, feelings, and actions of others. Such acts of standing out are often intrinsically rewarding because they elicit pleasant, ego-focused emotions (e.g., pride) and also reduce unpleasant ones (e.g., frustration). Furthermore, the acts of standing out, themselves, form an important basis of self-esteem.

The Role of the Self

The relative importance that is accorded to others in these two construals has a wide range of psychological implications. In this article, we have outlined some of the cognitive, emotional, and motivational consequences of holding a view of the self that includes others and that requires others to define the self. Although a rapidly expanding volume of studies suggest that some aspects of cognitive functioning are relatively hardwired, many features of the way people perceive, categorize, or assign causality are probably not basic processes that derive in any straightforward way from the functioning of the human machinery or "hardware." Rather, these processes are to a large extent personal, reflecting the nature of the self that anchors them. Thus, they reflect all of those factors, including cultural aspects, that jointly determine the self. If one perceives oneself as embedded within a larger context of which one is an interdependent part, it is likely that other objects or events will be perceived in a similar way. For example, a given event involving a particular actor will be perceived as arising from the situational context of which this actor is an interdependent part, rather than as stemming solely from the attributes of the actor. Or, in answering any question, one's first tendency may be to consider the particular social situation that is defined by the current interaction (e.g., teacher-student, worker-coworker, and younger-elder) and then to gauge the range of responses that are most appropriate to this situation. These construals of self are probably abstracted through early patterns of direct interactions with parents and peers. The way people initially, and thus thereafter, most naturally or effortlessly perceive and understand the world is rooted in their self-perceptions and self-understandings, understandings that are themselves constrained by the patterns of social interactions characteristic of the given culture.

Consequences for Self-Processes

Our discussion of the cognitive, emotional, or motivational consequences has by no means exhausted the range of potential consequences of holding an independent or interdependent construal of the self. Consider first the set of processes connected by a hyphen to the self. It is reasonable to assume that all of these phenomena (e.g., self-affirmation [Steele,

1988], self-verification [Swann, 1983], self-consciousness [Fenigstein, Scheier, & Buss, 1975], self-control [Carver & Scheier, 1981], self-actualization [Maslow, 1954], or self-handicapping [Jones & Berglas, 1978]) could assume a somewhat different form depending on how interdependent the self is with others.

Self-esteem for those with an independent construal of the self depends on one's abilities, attributes, and achievements. The most widely used measure of self-esteem, the Rosenberg Self-Esteem Scale, requires the endorsement of items like "I am a person of worth" or "I am proud of my abilities." Self-esteem associated with an interdependent self could include endorsement of similar items, although what it means to be, for example, a person of worth could well have a different meaning. Or high self-esteem may be more strongly associated with an endorsement of items that gauge one's ability to read the situation and to respond as required. If this is the case, a threat or a challenge to the self may not come in the form of feedback that one is unlike a cherished conception of the inner or dispositional self (dumb instead of smart; submissive rather than dominant) but instead in terms of a threat of a disruption of, or a disconnection from, the relation or set of relations with which one forms an interdependent whole.

The focus on the distinction between independent versus interdependent selves has the potential to provide a means of integrating research on a large number of separate personality constructs. One of the significant distinctions that appears repeatedly throughout Western psychology reflects a variation among individuals in how tuned in, sensitive to, oriented toward, focused on, or concerned they are with others. The introversion-extraversion dimension reflects this difference, as does the inner-directed–outer-directed distinction (Reisman, Denney, & Glazer, 1950). Other related distinctions include high versus low self-monitoring (Snyder, 1979), personal identity versus social identity (Cheek, 1989; Hogan, 1975), public versus private self-consciousness (Fenigstein, 1984), social orientation versus individual orientation (Greenwald, 1980), collectivism-individualism (Hui, 1988; Triandis, 1989), and field independence–field dependence (Witkin & Goodenough, 1977). In fact, Witkin and his colleagues described a field-dependent person as one who includes others within the boundaries of the self and who does not make a sharp distinction between the self and others. Many of the empirical findings (described in Witkin & Goodenough, 1977; Witkin, Goodenough, & Oltman, 1979) about the interpersonal expertise and sensitivities of field-dependent people are similar to those described herein for people with interdependent selves.

Consequences for Social Psychological Phenomena

Other social behaviors may also depend on one's mediating model of the self (see Triandis, 1989, for a recent analysis of some of these effects). Thus, for one with an interdependent self, conformity may not reflect an inability to resist social pressure and to stick by one's own perceptions, attitudes, or beliefs (the defining features of the self). Instead, conformity to particular others with whom the other is interdependent can be a highly valued end state. It can signify a willingness to be responsive to others and to adjust one's own demands and desires so as to maintain the ever-important relation. The conformity observed for these subjects with interdependent selves when surrounded with others who form part of an important social unit, could well be much higher than typically observed. However, conformity to the desires and demands of those outside the important social unit or the self-defining in-group may not be required at all. Thus, for those with interdependent selves, a typical Asch-type conformity paradigm involving subjects and strangers as confederates may result in less conformity than typically observed in American studies.

Studies of other phenomena such as social facilitation or social loafing could also produce differential effects, depending on the self-systems of the subjects. Should those with interdependent construals of the self show pronounced social facilitation compared with those with individual selves? Or should those with interdependent selves be less susceptible to social loafing (decrements in performance when one's individual contribution to the group product cannot be identified; see Harkins, Latané, & Williams, 1980)? Our analysis is also relevant to two of the central problems in Western psychology—the inconsistency between attitudes and behavior and the inconsistency between personality and behavior. As we have noted, interdependent selves do not prescribe or require such a consistency between one's internal attributes and one's actions. Consequently, the press for consistency should be much less important and much less bemoaned when not observed. In fact, consistency from an interdependent perspective may reflect a lack of flexibility, insensitivity to the context, rigidity, or immaturity.

Further analysis of the consequences of different construals of the self may also prove fruitful in understanding some basic social psychological questions. Social psychologists report that people are enormously influenced by others, often to an extent that the investigators and certainly individuals themselves, find unbelievable. People conform, obey, diffuse responsibility in a group, allow themselves to be easily persuaded about all manner of things, and become hopelessly committed to others on the basis of minimal action (e.g., see Myers, 1989). Even within highly individualist Western culture, most people are still much less self-reliant, self-contained, or self-sufficient than the prevailing cultural ideology suggests that they should be. Perhaps Western models of the self are quite at odds with actual individual social behavior and should be reformulated to reflect the substantial interdependence that characterizes even Western individualists. Sampson (1989) has recently argued that the reality of globalization and a shrinking world will force just such a rethinking of the nature of the individual.

Construals of the Self and Gender

Many important gender differences may also be linked to divergent construals of the self. Recent feminist theory on empathy suggests that relations have a power and a significance in women's lives that have gone largely unrecognized (e.g., Belenky, Clinchy, Goldberger, & Tarule, 1986; Jordan & Surrey, 1986; J. B. Miller, 1986; Stewart & Lykes, 1985). An awareness of and sensitivity to others is described as one of most significant features of the psychology of women. If this is the case, then self-esteem and self-validation should depend not only on being able to do a job well, but on fostering and sustaining relationships. As Gilligan (1986) claimed, a willingness and an ability to care are standards of self-evaluation for many women. This theoretical work is forging a new vision of dependence, one that is similar in many ways to some Eastern views. Being dependent does not invariably mean being helpless, powerless, or without control. It often means being interdependent. It thus signifies a conviction that one is able to have an effect on others and is willing to be responsive to others and to become engaged with them. In other words, there is an alternative to selfishness (which implies the exclusion of others) besides selflessness (which is to imply the exclusion of the self or self-sacrifice): There is a self defined in relationship to others (see Chodorow, 1978; Gilligan, 1982; Markus & Oyserman, 1988).

Difficult Questions

Carrying out the research necessary to systematically investigate the range of basic consequences of having one or another construal of the self raises several complex questions. Some of these we have only touched on. For example, a persistent issue is how deep or pervasive are these cultural differences? Are the observed differences primarily a reflection of differences in styles of behavioral expression, or do they also reflect differences in the phenomenology accompanying the behavior? If there are norms against the display or expression of anger, what happens to the nature of the felt anger? In other words, is it the case, as we suggest here, that these norms can sometimes be internalized to the extent that they determine the nature of one's experience? For example, a recent study by Bontempo, Lobel, and Triandis (1989) compared the public and private responses of individuals from a collectivist culture with those of individuals from an individualist culture. The researchers asked respondents to indicate how enjoyable it would be to engage in a time-consuming, individually costly behavior such as visiting a friend in the hospital. Only in the public condition did individualists claim that the behavior would be enjoyable. The collectivists, in contrast, claimed that the behavior would be enjoyable even when their responses were private.

The view that altruistic behaviors are only seemingly altruistic and that they are public actions without any subjective, private foundation can perhaps be traced to the insistence of Western psychologists on the internal attributes (feeling, thought, and traits) as the universal referents for behavior. They have thus understandably failed to attend to the possibility of the other as a referent for behavior, and thus to the possibility of other-focused emotions. There is, however, the possibility that such emotions can motivate genuine, other-oriented, altruistic behaviors, without any conscious, or even unconscious, calculation of individual payoff, and as such serve as the important glue of interdependent relationships.

Another thorny issue centers on the assessment of cultural differences. The use of introspective reports, for example, which are typically quite useful in the study of cognition, emotion, and motivation, may be problematic in cross-cultural research because within a given cultural context, people have little access to the absolute extent of their attention or responsiveness to others. This may explain, for example, why Triandis et al. (1988) found that those with collective selves do not report a greater than average awareness of or concern for the demands of others. Another persistent issue is that of translation and equating stimuli and questionnaires. Can psychologists readily assume that when an American and a Japanese use the word *embarrass* it indicates a similar emotional experience? Can they hypothesize, for example, that those with interdependent selves should show more high self-monitoring (i.e., attention to the behavior of others) than those with independent selves, and then assume that a translation of Snyder's (1979) scale into Japanese or Chinese will be sufficient to reflect these differences? One may even ask to what extent a construct such as self-monitoring can be unequivocally defined across different cultures with remarkably different construals of self.

In sum, we have argued that the view one holds of the self is critical in understanding individual behavior and also in understanding the full nature of those phenomena that implicate the self. A failure to replicate certain findings in different cultural contexts should not lead to immediate despair over the lack of generality of various psychological principles or to the conclusion of some anthropologists that culturally divergent individuals inhabit incomparably different worlds. Instead, it is necessary to identify the theoretical elements or processes that explain these differences. We suggest that how the self is construed may be one such powerful theoretical element.

REFERENCES

Ainsworth, M. D. S., Bell, S. M., & Stayton, D. (1974). Infant–mother attachment and social development. In M. P. Richards (Eds.), *The introduction of the child into a social world* (pp. 95–135). London: Cambridge University Press.

Allen, N. J. (1985). The category of the person: A reading of Mauss's last essay. In M. Carrithers, S. Collins, & S. Lukes (Eds.), *The category of the person: Anthropology, philosophy, history* (pp. 26–35). Cambridge, England: Cambridge University Press.

Allport, G. W. (1937). *Personality: A psychological interpretation.* New York: Holt.

Atkinson, J. (Ed.). (1958). *Motives in fantasy, action and society.* New York: Van Nostrand.

Au, T. K. (1983). Chinese and English counterfactuals: The Sapir-Whorf hypothesis revisited. *Cognition, 15,* 162–163.

Au, T. K. (1984). Counterfactuals: In reply to Alfred Bloom. *Cognition, 17,* 289–302.

Azuma, H. (1984). Secondary control as a heterogeneous category. *American Psychologist, 39,* 970–971.

Bachnik, J. M. (1986). Time, space and person in Japanese relationships. In J. Hendry & J. Webber (Eds.), *Interpreting Japanese society: Anthropological approaches* (pp. 49–75). New York: Oxford University Press.

Baumeister, R. F. (1987). How the self became a problem: A psychological review of historical research. *Journal of Personality and Social Psychology, 52,* 163–176.

Beattie, J. (1980). Representations of the self in traditional Africa. *Africa, 50,* 313–320.

Belenky, M. F., Clinchy, B. M., Goldberger, N. R., & Tarule, J. M. (1986). *Women's ways of knowing: The development of self, voice, and mind.* New York: Basic Books.

Bellah, R. N., Madsen, R., Sullivan, W. M., Swidler, A., & Tipton, S. M. (1985). *Habits of the heart: Individualism and commitment in American life.* Berkeley, CA: University of California Press.

Bloom, A. (1981). *The linguistic shaping of thought.* Hillsdale, NJ: Erlbaum.

Bloom, A. (1984). Caution—the words you use may effect what you say: A response to Au. *Cognition, 17,* 281.

Blumenthal, E. P. (1977). Models in Chinese moral education: Perspectives from children's books. *Dissertation Abstracts International, 37*(10-A), 6357–6358.

Bond, M. H. (1986). *The psychology of the Chinese people.* New York: Oxford University Press.

Bond, M. H. (Ed.). (1988). *The cross-cultural challenge to social psychology.* Beverly Hills, CA: Sage.

Bond, M., Leung, K., & Wan, K.-C. (1982). The social impact of self-effacing attributions: The Chinese case. *Journal of Social Psychology, 118,* 157–166.

Bontempo, R., Lobel, S. A., & Triandis, H. C. (1989). *Compliance and value internalization among Brazilian and U.S. students.* Unpublished manuscript.

Briggs, J. (1970). *Never in anger.* Cambridge, MA: Harvard University Press.

Bruner, J. (1986). *Actual minds, possible worlds.* New York: Plenum Press.

Buck, R. (1988). *Human motivation and emotion* (2nd ed.). New York: Wiley.

Cantor, N., & Kihlstrom, J. (1987). *Personality and social intelligence.* Englewood Cliffs, NJ: Prentice-Hall.

Carver, C. S., & Scheier, M. F. (1981). *Attention and self-regulation: A control theory approach to human behavior.* New York: Springer-Verlag.

Cheek, J. M. (1989). Identity orientations and self-interpretation. In D. M. Buss & N. Cantor (Eds.), *Personality psychology: Recent trends and emerging directions* (pp. 275–285). New York: Springer-Verlag.

Chiu, L. H. (1972). A cross-cultural comparison of cognitive styles in Chinese and American children. *International Journal of Psychology, 7,* 235–242.

Chodorow, N. (1978). *The reproduction of mothering: Psychoanalysis and the sociology of gender.* Berkeley, CA: University of California Press.

Church, A. T. (1987). Personality research in a non-Western culture: The Philippines. *Psychological Bulletin, 102,* 272–292.

Cousins, S. (1989). Culture and selfhood in Japan and the U.S. *Journal of Personality and Social Psychology, 56,* 124–131.

Dalal, A. K., Sharma, R., & Bisht, S. (1983). Causal attributions of ex-criminal tribal and urban children in India. *Journal of Social Psychology, 119,* 163–171.

D'Andrade, R. (1981). The cultural part of cognition. *Cognitive Science, 5,* 179–185.

Darwin, C. R. (1896). *The expression of emotions in man and animals.* New York: Philosophical Library.

Davis, M. H., & Stephan, W. G. (1980). Attributions for exam performance. *Journal of Applied Social Psychology, 10,* 235–248.

De Rivera, J. (1984). The structure of emotional relationships. In P. Shaver (Ed.), *Review of personality and social psychology: Emotions, relationships, and health* (pp. 116–145). Beverly Hills, CA: Sage.

De Vos, G. A. (1973). *Socialization for achievement: Essays on the cultural psychology of the Japanese.* Berkeley: University of California Press.

De Vos, G. (1985). Dimensions of the self in Japanese culture. In A. Marsella, G. De Vos, & F. L. K. Hsu (Eds.), *Culture and self* (pp. 149–184). London: Tavistock.

Doi, L. T. (1973). *The anatomy of dependence.* Tokyo: Kodansha.

Doi, T. (1986). *The anatomy of self: The individual versus society.* Tokyo: Kodansha.

Dumont, L. (1970). *Homo hierarchicus.* Chicago: University of Chicago Press.

Durkheim, E. (1968). *Les formes elementaires de la vie religieuse* [Basic forms of religious belief] (6th ed.). Paris: Presses Universitarires de France. (Original work published 1912)

Ekman, P. (1972). Universals and cultural differences in facial expression of emotion. In J. K. Cole (Ed.), *Nebraska symposium on motivation* (pp. 207–283). Lincoln: University of Nebraska Press.

Elvin, M. (1985). Between the earth and heaven: Conceptions of the self in China. In M. Carrithers, S. Collins, & S. Lukes (Eds.), *The category of the person: Anthropology, philosophy, history* (pp. 156–189). New York: Cambridge University Press.

Erikson, E. (1950). Identification as the basis for a theory of motivation. *American Psychological Review, 26,* 14–21.

Fenigstein, A. (1984). Self-consciousness and the overperception of self as a target. *Journal of Personality and Social Psychology, 47,* 860–870.

Fenigstein, A., Scheier, M. F., & Buss, A. H. (1975). Public and private self-consciousness: Assessment and theory. *Journal of Consulting and Clinical Psychology, 43,* 522–527.

Festinger, L., & Carlsmith, J. M. (1959). Cognitive consequences of forced compliance. *Journal of Abnormal and Social Psychology, 58,* 203–210.

Fiedler, F. E. (1978). Recent development in research on the contingency model. In L. Berkowitz (Ed.), *Group processes* (pp. 209–225). New York: Academic Press.

Fiske, A. P. (in press). *Making up society: The four elementary relational structures.* New York: Free Press.

Fiske, S. T., & Taylor, S. E. (1984). *Social cognition.* Reading, MA: Addison-Wesley.

Frijda, N. H., Kuipers, P., & ter Schure, E. (1989). Relations among emotion appraisal and emotional action readiness. *Journal of Personality and Social Psychology, 57,* 212–228.

Galtung, J. (1981). Structure, culture, and intellectual style: An essay comparing Saxonic, Teutonic, Gallic and Nipponic approaches. *Social Science Information, 20,* 817–856.

Geertz, C. (1974). From the native's point of view: On the nature of anthropological understanding. In K. Basso & H. Selby (Eds.), *Meaning in anthropology* (pp. 221–237). Albuquerque: University of New Mexico Press.

Geertz, C. (1975). On the nature of anthropological understanding. *American Scientist, 63,* 47–53.

Gergen, K. J. (1968). Personal consistency and the presentation of self. In C. Gordon & K. J. Gergen (Eds.), *The self in social interaction: Classic and contemporary perspectives* (Vol. 1, pp. 299–308). New York: Wiley.

Gergen, K. J., & Gergen, M. M. (1988). Narrative and the self as relationship. In L. Berkowitz (Ed.), *Advances in experimental social psychology* (Vol. 21, pp. 17–56). New York: Academic Press.

Gilligan, C. (1982). *In a different voice: Psychological theory and women's development.* Cambridge, MA: Harvard University Press.

Gilligan, C. (1986). Remapping the moral domain: New images of the self in relationship. In T. C. Heller, M. Sosna, & D. E. Wellbery (Eds.), *Reconstructing individualism: Autonomy, individuality, and the self in Western thought* (pp. 237–252). Stanford, CA: Stanford University Press.

Gilmor, T. M., & Reid, D. W. (1979). Locus of control and causal attribution for positive and negative outcomes on university examinations. *Journal of Research in Personality, 13,* 154–160.

Gilovich, T. (1983). Biased evaluation and persistence in gambling. *Journal of Personality and Social Psychology, 40,* 797–808.

Goethals, A. (1989, April). *Studies of false uniqueness.* Paper presented at the Research Center for Group Dynamics Seminar, Institute for Social Research, University of Michigan, Ann Arbor, MI.

Greenberg, J., Pyszczynski, T., & Solomon, S. (1982). The self-serving attributional bias: Beyond self-presentation. *Journal of Experimental Social Psychology, 18,* 56–67.

Greenwald, A. G. (1980). The totalitarian ego: Fabrication and revision of personal history. *American Psychologist, 35,* 603–618.

Greenwald, A. G., & Pratkanis, A. R. (1984). The self. In R. S. Wyer & T. K. Srull (Eds.), *Handbook of social cognition* (Vol. 3, pp. 129–178). Hillsdale, NJ: Erlbaum.

Hall, C. S., & Lindzey, G. (1957). *Theories of personality.* New York: Wiley.

Hallowell, A. I. (1955). *Culture and experience.* Philadelphia: University of Pennsylvania Press.

Hamaguchi, E. (1985). A contextual model of the Japanese: Toward a methodological innovation in Japan studies. *Journal of Japanese Studies, 11,* 289–321.

Harkins, S. G., Latané, B., & Williams, K. (1980). Social loafing: Allocating effort or taking it easy? *Journal of Experimental Social Psychology, 16,* 457–465.

Harter, S. (1983). The development of the self-system. In E. M. Hetherington (Ed.), *Handbook of child psychology: Vol. 4. Socialization, personality, and social development* (4th ed.). New York: Wiley.

Harter, S. (1990). Causes, correlates and the functional role of global self-worth: A life span perspective. In R. J. Sternberg & J. Kolligian, Jr. (Eds.), *Competence considered* (pp. 67–97). New Haven, CT: Yale University Press.

Hayashi, C. (1988). *National character of the Japanese.* Tokyo: Statistical Bureau, Japan.

Head, H. (1920). *Studies in neurology.* London: Oxford University Press.

Heelas, P. L. F., & Lock, A. J. (Eds.). (1981). *Indigenous psychologies: The anthropology of the self.* London: Academic Press.

Hess, R., Azuma, H., Kashiwagi, K., Dickson, W. P., Nagano, S., Holloway, S., Miyake, K., Price, G., Hatano, G., & McDevitt, T. (1986). Family influences on school readiness and achievement in Japan and the United States: An overview of a longitudinal study. In H. Stevenson, H. Azuma, & K. Hakuta (Eds.), *Child development and education in Japan* (pp. 147–166). New York: Freeman.

Hilgard, E. R. (1953). *Introduction to psychology.* New York: Harcourt, Brace.

Hilgard, E. R. (1987). *Psychology in American: A historical survey.* New York: Harcourt Brace Jovanovich.

Hofstede, G. (1980). *Culture's consequences: International differences in work-related values.* Beverly Hills, CA: Sage.

Hogan, R. (1975). Theoretical egocentrism and the problem of compliance. *American Psychologist, 30,* 533–540.

Holland, D., & Quinn, N. (1987). *Cultural models in language and thought.* Cambridge, England: Cambridge University Press.

Hollander, E. P. (1985). Leadership and power. In G. Lindzey & E. Aronson (Eds.), *Handbook of social psychology* (Vol. 2, pp. 485–537). New York: Random House.

Holyoak, K. J., & Gordon, P. C. (1983). Social reference points. *Journal of Personality and Social Psychology, 44,* 881–887.

Hsu, F. L. K. (1975). *Iemoto: The heart of Japan.* New York: Wiley.

Hsu, F. L. K. (1981). *American and Chinese: Passage to differences.* Honolulu: University of Hawaii Press.

Hsu, F. L. K. (1985). The self in cross-cultural perspective. In A. J. Marsella, G. De Vos, & F. L. K. Hsu (Eds.), *Culture and self* (pp. 24–55). London: Tavistock.

Hui, C. H. (1988). Measurement of individualism–collectivism. *Journal of Research in Personality, 22,* 17–36.

Hwang, C. H. (1976). Change of psychological needs over thirteen years. *Bulletin of Educational Psychology* (Taipei), 9, 85–94.

Iwao, S. (1988, August). *Social psychology's models of man: Isn't it time for East to meet West?* Invited address to the International Congress of Scientific Psychology, Sydney, Australia.

James, W. (1890). *Principles of psychology.* New York: Holt.

A Japanese supermarket in New Jersey. (1989, April 6). *New York Times,* p. 4.

Johnson, F. (1985). The Western concept of self. In A. Marsella, G. De Vos, & F. L. K. Hsu (Eds.), *Culture and self.* London: Tavistock.

Johnson-Laird, P. N. (1983). *Mental models: Towards a cognitive science of language, inference, and consciousness.* Cambridge, MA: Harvard University Press.

Jones, E. E., & Berglas, S. (1978). Control of attributions about the self through self-handicapping strategies: The appeal of alcohol and the role of underachievement. *Personality and Social Psychology Bulletin, 4,* 200–206.

Jordan, J. V., & Surrey, J. L. (1986). The self-in-relation: Empathy and the mother-daughter relationship. In T. Bernay & D. W. Cantor (Eds.), *The psychology of today's women* (pp. 81–104). Cambridge, MA: Harvard University Press.

Jöreskog, K. G. (1969). A general approach to confirmatory maximum likelihood factor analysis. *Psychometrika, 34,* 183–202.

Kakar, S. (1978). *The inner world: A psychoanalytic study of childhood and society in India.* Delhi, India: Oxford University Press.

Kennedy, S., Scheier, J., & Rogers, A. (1984). The price of success: Our monocultural science. *American Psychologist, 39,* 996–997.

Kiefer, C. W. (1976). The *danchi zoku* and the evolution of metropolitan mind. In L. Austin (Ed.), *The paradox of progress* (pp. 279–300). New Haven, CT: Yale University Press.

Kitayama, S., & Markus, H. (1990, August). *Culture and emotion: The role of other-focused emotions.* Paper presented at the 98th Annual Convention of the American Psychological Association, Boston.

Kitayama, S., Markus, H., Tummala, P., Kurokawa, M., & Kato, K. (1990). *Culture and self-cognition*. Unpublished manuscript.

Kondo, D. (1982). *Work, family and the self: A cultural analysis of Japanese family enterprise*. Unpublished doctoral dissertation, Harvard University.

Kuhn, M. H., & McPartland, T. S. (1954). An empirical investigation of self-attitudes. *American Sociological Review, 19*, 68–76.

Kumagai, H. A. (1981). A dissection of intimacy: A study of "bipolar posturing" in Japanese social interaction—*amaeru* and *amayakasu*, indulgence and deference. *Culture, Medicine, and Psychiatry, 5*, 249–272.

Kumagai, H. A., & Kumagai, A. K. (1985). The hidden "I" in *amae*: "Passive love" and Japanese social perception. *Ethos, 14*, 305–321.

Laboratory of Comparative Human Cognition. (1982). Culture and intelligence. In R. J. Sternberg (Ed.), *Handbook of human intelligence* (pp. 642–719). London: Cambridge University Press.

Lau, R. R. (1984). Dynamics of the attribution process. *Journal of Personality and Social Psychology, 46*, 1017–1028.

Lebra, T. S. (1976). *Japanese patterns of behavior*. Honolulu: University of Hawaii Press.

LeDoux, J. E. (1987). Emotion. In V. Mount Castle (Ed.), *Handbook of physiology: Vol. 1. The nervous system* (pp. 419–459). Bethesda, MD: American Physiological Society.

Levy, R. (1973). *The Tahitians*. Chicago: University of Chicago Press.

Li, M.-C., Cheung, S.-F., & Kau, S.-M. (1979). Competitive and cooperative behavior of Chinese children in Taiwan and Hong Kong. *Acta Psychologica Taiwanica, 21*, 27–33. (From *Psychological Abstracts*, 1982, *67*, Abstract No. 11922)

Liu, I. (1986). Chinese cognition. In M. H. Bond (Ed.), *The psychology of the Chinese people* (pp. 73–105). New York: Oxford University Press.

Liu, T. Y., & Hsu, M. (1974). Measuring creative thinking in Taiwan by the Torrance test. *Testing and Guidance, 2*, 108–109.

Lutz, C. (1988). *Unnatural emotions: Everyday sentiments on a Micronesian atoll and their challenge to Western theory*. Chicago: University of Chicago Press.

Lykes, M. B. (1985). Gender and individualistic vs. collectivist bases for notions about the self. In A. J. Stewart & M. B. Lykes (Eds.), *Gender and personality: Current perspectives on theory and research* (pp. 268–295). Durham, NC: Duke University Press.

Maehr, M. (1974). Culture and achievement motivation. *American Psychologist, 29*, 887–896.

Maehr, M., & Nicholls, J. (1980). Culture and achievement motivation: A second look. In N. Warren (Ed.), *Studies in cross-cultural psychology* (Vol. 2, pp. 221–267). New York: Academic Press.

Marks, G. (1984). Thinking one's abilities are unique and one's opinions are common. *Personality and Social Psychology Bulletin, 10*, 203–208.

Markus, H. (1977). Self-schemas and processing information about the self. *Journal of Personality and Social Psychology, 35*, 63–78.

Markus, H., & Kitayama, S. (in press). Cultural variation in the self-concept. In G. R. Goethals & J. Strauss (Eds.), *Multidisciplinary perspectives on the self*. New York: Springer-Verlag.

Markus, H., & Oyserman, D. (1988). Gender and thought: The role of the self-concept. In M. Crawford & M. Hamilton (Eds.), *Gender and thought* (pp. 100–127). New York: Springer-Verlag.

Markus, H., & Wurf, E. (1987). The dynamic self-concept: A social psychological perspective. *Annual Review of Psychology, 38*, 299–337.

Markus, H., & Zajonc, R. B. (1985). The cognitive perspective in social psychology. In G. Lindzey & E. Aronson (Eds.), *Handbook of social psychology* (3rd ed., pp. 137–230). New York: Random House.

Marriott, M. (1976). Hindu transactions: Diversity without dualism. In B. Kapferer (Ed.), *Transaction and meaning* (pp. 109–142). Philadelphia: Institute for Study of Human Issues.

Marsella, A., De Vos, G., & Hsu, F. L. K. (1985). *Culture and self*. London: Tavistock.

Maslow, A. H. (1954). *Motivation and personality*. New York: Harper.

Matsumoto, D. (1989). Cultural influences on the perception of emotion. *Journal of Cross-Cultural Psychology, 20*, 92–105.

Matsumoto, D., Kudoh, T., Scherer, K., & Wallbott, H. (1988). Antecedents of and reactions to emotions in the United States and Japan. *Journal of Cross-Cultural Psychology, 19*, 267–286.

Mauro, R., Sato, K., & Tucker, J. (1989). *A cross-cultural analysis of the cognitive dimensions of human emotion*. Unpublished manuscript, University of Oregon, Eugene, OR.

Mauss, M. (1985). A category of the human mind: The notion of person; the notion of self [W. D. Halls, Trans.]. In M Carrithers, S. Collins, & S. Lukes (Eds.), *The category of the person: Anthropology, philosophy, history* (pp. 1–25). Cambridge, England: Cambridge University Press. (Original work published 1938)

McClelland, D. C. (1961). *The achieving society*. New York: Free Press.

Mead, G. H. (1934). *Mind, self and society*. Chicago: University of Chicago Press.

Miller, J. B. (1986). *Toward a new psychology of women* (2nd ed.). Boston: Beacon Press.

Miller, J. G. (1984). Culture and the development of everyday social explanation. *Journal of Personality and Social Psychology, 46*, 961–978.

Miller, J. G. (1988). Bridging the content–structure dichotomy: Culture and the self. In M. H. Bond (Ed.), *The cross-cultural challenge to social psychology* (pp. 266–281). Beverly Hills, CA: Sage.

Miller, J. G., Bersoff, D. M., & Harwood, R. L. (1990) Perceptions of social responsibilities in India and in the United States: Moral imperatives or personal decisions? *Journal of Personality and Social Psychology, 58*, 33–47.

Misumi, J. (1985). *The behavioral science of leadership: An interdisciplinary Japanese research program*. Ann Arbor, MI: University of Michigan Press.

Miyake, K., Campos, J., Kagan, J., & Bradshaw, D. L. (1986). Issues in socioemotional development. In H. Stevenson, H. Azuma, & K. Hakuta (Eds.), *Child development and education in Japan* (pp. 239–261). New York: Freeman.

Miyake, K., Chen, S., & Campos, J. J. (in press). Infant temperament, mother's mode of interaction, and attachment in Japan: An interim report. In I. Bretherton & E. Waters (Eds.), *Growing points of attachment theory and research. Monographs of the Society for Research in Child Development*. Chicago: University of Chicago Press.

Mook, D. G. (1986). *Motivation: The organization of action*. New York: Norton.

Moore, C. A. (Ed.). (1967). Introduction: The humanistic Chinese mind. In *The Chinese mind: Essentials of Chinese philosophy and culture* (pp. 1–10). Honolulu: University of Hawaii Press.

Moser, D. (1989). *If this paper were in Chinese, would Chinese people understand the title?* Unpublished manuscript, Indiana University.

Mullen, B., & Riordan, C. A. (1988). Self-serving attributions in naturalistic settings: A meta-analytic review. *Journal of Applied Social Psychology, 18*, 3–22.

Murray, H. A. (1938). *Explorations in personality*. New York: Oxford University Press.

Myers, D. (1987). *Social psychology* (2nd ed.). New York: McGraw-Hill.

Myers, D. (1989). *Social psychology* (3rd ed.). New York: McGraw-Hill.

Nakane, C. (1970). *Japanese society*. Berkeley: University of California Press.

Neisser, U. (1976). *Cognition and reality: Principles and implications of cognitive psychology*. San Francisco: Freeman.

Neisser, U. (1988). Five kinds of self-knowledge. *Philosophical Psychology, 1*, 35–59.

Northrop, F. S. C. (1946). *The meeting of East and West*. New York: Macmillan.

Pennebaker, J. W. (1982). *The psychology of physical symptoms*. New York: Springer-Verlag.

Phillips, D. C. (1976). *Holistic thought in social science*. Stanford, CA: Stanford University Press.

Plath, D. W. (1980). *Long engagements: Maturity in modern Japan.* Stanford, CA: Stanford University Press.

Reisman, D., Denney, R., & Glazer, N. (1950). *The lonely crowd: A study of the changing American culture.* New Haven, CT: Yale University Press.

Roland, A. (1988). *In search of self in India and Japan: Toward a cross-cultural psychology.* Princeton, NJ: Princeton University Press.

Rosaldo, M. Z. (1984). Toward an anthropology of self and feeling. In R. A. Shweder & R. A. LeVine (Eds.), *Culture theory: Essays on mind, self, and emotion* (pp. 137–157). Cambridge, England: Cambridge University Press.

Rosch, E. (1978) Principles of categorization. In E. Rosch & B. B. Lloyd (Eds.), *Cognition and categorization.* Hillsdale, NJ: Erlbaum

Roseman, I. J. (1984). Cognitive determinants of emotion: A structural theory. In P. Shaver (Ed.), *Review of personality in social psychology* (Vol. 5, pp. 11–36). Beverly Hills, CA: Sage.

Ross, L. D. (1977). The intuitive psychologist and his shortcomings: Distortions in the attribution process. In L. Berkowitz (Ed.), *Advances in experimental social psychology* (Vol. 10, pp 173–220). New York: Academic Press.

Ross, M., & Fletcher, G. J. O. (1985). Attribution and social perception. In G. Lindzey & E. Aronson (Eds.), *The handbook of social psychology* (3rd ed., Vol. 2, pp. 73–122). New York: Random House.

Russell, J. A. (1980). A circumplex model of affect. *Journal of Personality and Social Psychology, 39,* 1161–1178.

Russell, J. A. (1983). Pancultural aspects of the human conceptual organization of emotions. *Journal of Personality and Social Psychology, 36,* 1152–1168.

Russell, J. A., Lewicka, M., & Niit, T. (1989). A cross-cultural study of a circumplex model of affect. *Journal of Personality and Social Psychology, 57,* 848–856.

Sampson, E. E. (1985). The decentralization of identity: Toward a revised concept of personal and social order. *American Psychologist, 40,* 1203–1211.

Sampson, E. E. (1988). The debate on individualism: Indigenous psychologies of the individual and their role in personal and societal functioning. *American Psychologist, 43,* 15–22.

Sampson, E. E. (1989). The challenge of social change for psychology: Globalization and psychology's theory of the person. *American Psychologist, 44,* 914–921.

Sass, L. A. (1988). The self and its vicissitudes: An "archaeological" study of the psychoanalytic avant-garde. *Social Research, 55,* 551–607.

Scherer, K. R. (1984). Emotions as a multi-component process. A model and some cross-cultural data. In P. Shaver (Ed.), *Review of personality and social psychology: Emotions, relationships, and health* (pp. 37–63). Beverly Hills, CA: Sage.

Schlenker, B. R., & Leary, M. R. (1982). Social anxiety and self-presentation: A conceptualization and model. *Psychological Bulletin, 92,* 641–669.

Schwartz, J. M., & Smith, W. P. (1976). Social comparison and the inference of ability difference. *Journal of Personality and Social Psychology, 34,* 1268–1275.

Schwartz, S. H., & Bilsky, W. (1990). Toward a theory of the universal content and structure of values: Extensions and cross-cultural replications. *Journal of Personality and Social Psychology, 58,* 878–891.

Shaver, P., Schwartz, J., Kirson, D., & O'Connor, C. (1987). Emotion knowledge: Further exploration of a prototype approach. *Journal of Personality and Social Psychology, 52,* 1061–1086.

Shikanai, K. (1978). Effects of self-esteem on attribution of success-failure. *Japanese Journal of Experimental Social Psychology, 18,* 47–55.

Shikanai, K. (1983). Effects of self-esteem on attributions of others' success or failure. *Japanese Journal of Experimental Social Psychology, 23,* 27–37.

Shikanai, K. (1984). Effects of self-esteem and one's own performance on attribution of others' success and failure. *Japanese Journal of Experimental Social Psychology, 24,* 37–46.

Shweder, R. A. (1984). Preview: A colloquy of culture theorists. In R. A. Shweder & R. A. LeVine (Eds.), *Culture theory: Essays on mind, self, and emotion* (pp. 1–24). Cambridge, England: Cambridge University Press.

Shweder, R. A. (1990). Cultural psychology: What is it? In J. W. Stigler, R. A. Shweder, & G. Herdt (Eds.), *Cultural psychology: Essays on comparative human development* (pp. 1–46). Cambridge, England: Cambridge University Press.

Shweder, R. A., & Bourne, E. J. (1984). Does the concept of the person vary cross-culturally? In R. A. Shweder & R. A. LeVine (Eds.), *Culture theory: Essays on mind, self, and emotion* (pp. 158–199). Cambridge, England: Cambridge University Press.

Shweder, R. A., & LeVine, R. A. (Eds.). (1984). *Culture theory: Essays on mind, self, and emotion.* Cambridge, England: Cambridge University Press.

Smith, C., & Ellsworth, P. C. (1987). Patterns of appraisal and emotion related to taking an exam. *Journal of Personality and Social Psychology, 52,* 475–488.

Smith, R. J. (1983). *Japanese society: Tradition, self, and the social order.* Cambridge, England: Cambridge University Press.

Smith, R. J. (1985). A pattern of Japanese society: In society or knowledgement of interdependence? *Journal of Japanese Studies, 11,* 29–45.

Snyder, M. (1979). Self-monitoring process. *Advances in Experimental Social Psychology, 12,* 85–128.

Solomon, R. C. (1984). Getting angry: The Jamesian theory of emotion in anthropology. In R. A. Shweder & R A. LeVine (Eds.), *Culture theory: Essays on mind, self, and emotion* (pp. 238–254). Cambridge, England: Cambridge University Press.

Solomon, S., Greenberg, J., & Pyszczynski, T. (in press). A terror management theory of social behavior: The psychological functions of self-esteem and cultural worldviews. *Advances in Experimental Social Psychology.*

Srull, T. K., & Gaelick, L. (1983). General principles and individual differences in the self as a habitual reference point: An examination of self–other judgments of similarity. *Social Cognition, 2,* 108–121.

Steele, C. (1988). The psychology of self-affirmation: Sustaining the integrity of the self. In L. Berkowitz (Ed.), *Advances in experimental social psychology* (Vol. 21, pp. 181–227). San Diego, CA: Academic Press.

Stevenson, H., Azuma, H., & Hakuta, K. (1986). *Child development and education in Japan.* New York: Freeman.

Stewart, A. J., & Lykes, M. B. (Eds.). (1985). Conceptualizing gender in personality theory and research. In *Gender and personality: Current perspectives on theory and research* (pp. 2–13). Durham, NC: Duke University Press.

Stigler, J. W., Shweder, R. A., & Herdt, G. (Eds.). (1990). *Cultural psychology: Essays on comparative human development.* Cambridge, England: Cambridge University Press.

Stipek, D., Weiner, B., & Li, K. (1989). Testing some attribution–emotion relations in the People's Republic of China. *Journal of Personality and Social Psychology, 56,* 109–116.

Stryker, S. (1986). Identity theory: Developments and extensions. In K. Yardley & T. Honess (Eds.), *Self and identity* (pp. 89–104). New York: Wiley.

Swann, W. B., Jr. (1983). Self-verification: Bringing social reality into harmony with the self. In J. Suls & A. G. Greenwald (Eds.), *Psychological perspectives on the self* (Vol. 2, pp. 33–66). Hillsdale, NJ: Erlbaum.

Swann, W. B., Jr., & Read, S. J. (1981). Self-verification processes: How we sustain our self-conceptions. *Journal of Experimental Social Psychology, 17,* 351–372.

Tajfel, H. (1984). *The social dimension: European developments in social psychology.* Cambridge, England: Cambridge University Press.

Takata, T. (1987). Self-deprecative tendencies in self-evaluation through social comparison. *Japanese Journal of Experimental Social Psychology, 27,* 27–36.

Taylor, S. E., & Brown, J. D. (1988). Illusion and well-being: A social psychological perspective on mental health. *Psychological Bulletin, 103,* 193–210.

Tesser, A. (1986). Some effects of self-evaluation maintenance on cognition and action. In R. M. Sorrentino & E. T. Higgins (Eds.), *Handbook of motivation and cognition: Foundations of social behavior* (pp. 435–464). New York: Guilford Press.

Triandis, H. C. (1989). The self and social behavior in differing cultural contexts. *Psychological Review, 96,* 506–520.

Triandis, H. C., Bontempo, R., Villareal, M. J., Asai, M., & Lucca, N. (1988). Individualism and collectivism: Cross-cultural perspectives on self-ingroup relationships. *Journal of Personality and Social Psychology, 54,* 323–338.

Triandis, H. C., & Brislin, R. W. (Eds.). (1980). *Handbook of cross-cultural social psychology* (Vol. 5). Boston: Allyn & Bacon.

Triandis, H. C., Marin, G., Lisansky, J., & Betancourt, H. (1984). *Simpatía* as a cultural script of Hispanics. *Journal of Personality and Social Psychology, 47,* 1363–1375.

Veroff, J. (1983). Contextual determinants of personality. *Personality and Social Psychology Bulletin, 9,* 331–344.

Wada, M. (1988). Information seeking in self-evaluation of ability [Abstract]. In *Proceedings of Japanese Psychological Association Meeting, 52,* 222.

Waterman, A. S. (1981). Individualism and interdependence. *American Psychologist, 36,* 762–773.

Weber, M. (1958). *The Protestant ethic and the spirit of capitalism* (T. Parsons, Trans.). New York: Scribner.

Weiner, B. (1986). *An attributional theory of emotion and motivation.* New York: Springer-Verlag.

Weisz, J. R. (in press). Culture and the development of child psychopathology: Lessons from Thailand. In D. Cicchetti (Ed.), *Rochester Symposium on Developmental Psychopathology* (Vol. 1). New York: Cambridge University Press.

Weisz, J. R., Rothbaum, F. M., & Blackburn, T. C. (1984). Standing out and standing in: The psychology of control in America and Japan. *American Psychologist, 39,* 955–969.

White, G. M., & Kirkpatrick, J. (Eds.). (1985). *Person, self, and experience: Exploring Pacific ethnopsychologies.* Los Angeles: University of California Press.

White, M., & LeVine, R. A. (1986). What is an *Ii ko* (good child)? In H. Stevenson, H. Azuma, & K. Hakuta (Eds.), *Child development and education in Japan* (pp. 55–62). New York: Freeman.

Whitley, B. E., Jr., & Frieze, I. H. (1985). Children's causal attributions for success and failure in achievement settings: A meta-analysis. *Journal of Educational Psychology, 77,* 608–616.

Witkin, H. A., & Goodenough, D. R. (1977). Field dependence and interpersonal behavior. *Psychological Bulletin, 84,* 661–689.

Witkin, H. A., Goodenough, D. R., & Oltman, P. K. (1979). Psychological differentiation: Current status. *Journal of Personality and Social Psychology, 37,* 1127–1145.

Wylie, R. C. (1979). *The self-concept: Vol 2. Theory and research on selected topics.* Lincoln: University of Nebraska Press.

Yamagishi, T. (1988). Exit from the group as an individualistic solution to the free-rider problem in the United States and Japan. *Journal of Experimental Social Psychology, 24,* 530–542.

Yang, K. S. (1981a). The formation of change of Chinese personality: A cultural–ecological perspective [In Chinese]. *Acta Psychologica Taiwanica, 23,* 39–56.

Yang, K. S. (1981b). Social orientation and individual modernity among Chinese students in Taiwan. *Journal of Social Psychology, 113,* 159–170.

Yang, K. S. (1982). Causal attributions of academic success and failure and their affective consequences. *Acta Psychologica Taiwanica, 24*, 65–83. (From *Psychological Abstracts*, 1985, 72, Abstract No. 13126)

Yang, K. S. (1986). Chinese personality and its change. In M. H. Bond (Ed.), *The psychology of the Chinese people* (pp. 106–170). New York: Oxford University Press.

Yang, K. S., & Liang, W. H. (1973). Some correlates of achievement motivation among Chinese high school boys [In Chinese]. *Acta Psychologica Taiwanica, 15*, 59–67.

Yoshida, T., Kojo, K., & Kaku, H. (1982). A study on the development of self-presentation in children. *Japanese Journal of Educational Psychology, 30*, 30–37.

Yu, E. S. H. (1974). Achievement motive, familism, and *hsiao*: A replication of McClelland-Winterbottom studies. *Dissertation Abstracts International, 35*, 593A. (University Microfilms No. 74-14, 942)

Zuckerman, M. (1979). Attribution of success and failure revisited, or: The motivational bias is alive and well in attribution theory. *Journal of Personality, 47*, 245–287.

Many thanks to Hiroko Akiyama, Nancy Cantor, Steve Cousins, Susan Cross, Alan Fiske, Carol Gilligan, Tom Givon, Lawrence Hirschfeld, Chie Kanagawa, John Kihlstrom, Joan Miller, Richard Nisbett, Jeanne Oggins, Richard Shweder, Mark Snyder, Harry Triandis, Hiroko Yamada, and Robert Zajonc for their extremely helpful comments on earlier versions of this article, and thanks to Debbie Apsley for preparing the manuscript.

THINKING CRITICALLY AND APPLYING YOUR KNOWLEDGE

1. Markus and Kitayama suggest that the independent-interdependent self distinction is important for a wide range of psychological phenomena, including cognition, emotion, and motivation. Their article suggests just a few of what may be many phenomena for which this distinction is important. Can you think of additional life domains in which the independent-interdependent distinction might matter? For example, what predictions would you make for helping behavior or for aggression against another person?

2. Recently, the United States and Japan have been involved in trade negotiations. Does the concept of independence/interdependence help you imagine some of the interpersonal problems that may have arisen as Japanese and American negotiators attempted to see each others' points of view and obtain concessions from each other? What might some of these problems have been?

3. People tend to see their own country, their own religion, and their own customs as better than others. This phenomenon is called in-group favoritism. Drawing on the independence-interdependence distinction, can you make a prediction about whether people in the United States versus Japan would be more likely to show in-group favoritism? How might you test this hypothesis?

❖ CHAPTER 9 ❖

PERSUASION AND CULTURE: ADVERTISING APPEALS IN INDIVIDUALISTIC AND COLLECTIVISTIC SOCIETIES

Sang-Pil Han and Sharon Shavitt

Suppose that you are an advertiser who wants to persuade people to buy a product or use a service. How would you construct a persuasive appeal? If you wanted to market your product internationally, would you use the same message in all countries, or would you vary it depending on aspects of the culture? As we saw in the Markus and Kitayama paper, individualism–collectivism is a basic dimension of culture. In this article, Han and Shavitt suggest that the persuasive appeals used in advertisements often reflect the culture's standing along this dimension. In Korea, a collectivist society, we might expect appeals to collectivist themes to be common (e.g., "For you and your family!"), and these themes should be especially persuasive. In contrast, in the United States, an individualistic society, ads pitched to individualistic themes (e.g., "Take care of number one") should be more common and more persuasive. In a first study, Han and Shavitt showed that Korean and American advertisements differed in the ways predicted. In a second study, they manipulated ads shown to American or Korean college students and showed that ads consistent with the underlying cultural theme were more persuasive. This article shows that core cultural values are reflected in advertising and play an important role in the process of persuasion.

ABSTRACT: *Two studies examined the extent to which a core dimension of cultural variability, individualism–collectivism (Hofstede, 1980, 1983; Triandis, 1990), is reflected in the types of persuasive appeals that tend to be used and that tend to be effective in different countries. Study 1 demonstrated that magazine advertisements in the United States, an individualistic culture, employed appeals to individual benefits and preferences, personal success, and independence to a greater extent than did advertisements in Korea, a collectivistic culture. Korean advertisements employed appeals emphasizing ingroup benefits, harmony, and family integrity to a greater extent than did U.S ads. Study 2, a controlled experiment conducted in the two countries, demonstrated that in the U.S. advertisements emphasizing individualistic benefits were more persuasive, and ads emphasizing family or ingroup benefits were less persuasive than they were in Korea. In both studies, however, product characteristics played a role in moderating these overall differences: Cultural differences*

Source: Reprinted from *Journal of Experimental Social Psychology*, *30*, (1994), 326–350. Copyright © 1994 by Academic Press, Inc. Reprinted by permission.

emerged strongly in Studies 1 and 2 for advertised products that tend to be purchased and used with others, but were much less evident for products that are typically purchased and used individually.

Individualism–collectivism is perhaps the most basic dimension of cultural variability identified in cross-cultural research. Concepts related to this dimension have been employed in several social science domains (cf. Triandis, McCusker, & Hui, 1990), and the individualism–collectivism dimension has come to be regarded as "central to an understanding of cultural values, of work values, of social systems, as well as in the studies of morality, the structure of constitutions, and cultural patterns" (Triandis, Brislin, & Hui, 1988). Several recent studies have suggested that individualism and collectivism are contrasting cultural syndromes that are associated with a broad pattern of differences in individuals' social perceptions and social behavior, including differences in the definition of self and its perceived relation to in-groups and out-groups (Markus & Kitayama, 1991), in the endorsement of values relevant to individual vs group goals (Triandis et al., 1990), and in the pattern and style of social interactions (cf. Triandis, 1990).

However, little is known about the implications of these cultural differences for another social process that is fundamental to every culture: persuasion. Persuasive communications transmit and reflect the values of a culture. Persuasive messages are used to obtain the compliance that achieves the personal, political, and economic ends valued in the culture. Although social influence has always been a central arena of research in social psychology, little is understood about what differences exist in the types of persuasive appeals used in different cultures (see Burgoon, Dillard, Doran, & Miller, 1982; Glenn, Witmeyer, & Stevenson, 1977). Even less is known about the effectiveness of different appeal types in different cultures.

What types of persuasive appeals are prevalent in individualistic versus collectivistic cultures? And how do members of these different cultures differ in the extent to which they are persuaded by these appeals? This paper presents an exploration of these questions.

Our studies focused on cross-cultural differences in advertising, a form of persuasive communication that is highly prevalent in many societies, both individualist and collectivist. The studies examined how this core dimension of cultural variability is reflected in the types of advertising appeals employed in two countries (the United States and Korea) that have been shown to differ greatly on the individualism–collectivism dimension (Hofstede, 1980, 1983). The research also investigated the relative *effectiveness* of individualistic and collectivistic advertising appeals in the United States and Korea. Moreover, the research looks beyond overall cultural differences in advertising content and persuasiveness to identify factors that may moderate these differences.

Individualism and Collectivism

Individualism–collectivism is perhaps the broadest and most widely used dimension of cultural variability for cultural comparison (Gudykunst & Ting-Toomey, 1988). Hofstede (1980) described individualism–collectivism as the relationship between the individual and the collectivity that prevails in a given society. In individualistic cultures, individuals tend to prefer independent relationships to others and to subordinate ingroup goals to their personal goals. In collectivistic cultures, on the other hand, individuals are more likely to have interdependent relationships to their in-groups and to subordinate their personal goals to their in-group goals. Individualistic cultures are associated with emphases on independence, achievement, freedom, high levels of competition, and pleasure. Collectivistic cultures are associated with emphases on interdependence, harmony, family security, social hierarchies, cooperation, and low levels of competition (see Triandis, 1989, 1990; Triandis et al., 1990, for supporting evidence and discussions of the antecedents and consequences of individualism and collectivism).

Individualistic and collectivistic cultures are characterized by important differences in members' social perceptions and social behavior. Members of these cultures have very different construals of the self, of others, and of the interdependence of the two (Markus & Kitayama, 1991). The self is defined in terms of in-group memberships (e.g., family and ethnic identity) to a greater extent in collectivistic cultures than individualistic cultures. Moreover, there is evidence suggesting that members of collectivistic cultures perceive their in-groups to be more homogeneous than their out-groups, whereas the reverse is true among persons in individualistic societies (Triandis et al., 1990). These cultural differences in the perceived relation of the self to others have been shown to have many other cognitive, emotional, and behavioral consequences (see Markus & Kitayama, 1991).

The individualistic cultural pattern is found in most northern and western regions of Europe and in North America, whereas the collectivistic cultural pattern is common in Asia, Africa, Latin America, and the Pacific (Hofstede, 1980, 1983). In the present studies, the United States and Korea were selected to represent individualistic and collectivistic cultures, respectively. These countries were selected based on Hofstede's (1980, 1983) studies of individualism–collectivism in over 50 countries, which indicated that the United States is highly individualistic with a score of 91 on a 100-point individualism scale, whereas Korea is clearly on the collectivistic side with a score of 18.

Persuasion and Culture

We expected that advertisements in the United States and Korea would reflect their indigenous individualistic or collectivistic cultural orientation. We also expected that the persuasiveness of certain types of ad appeals would differ in these two cultures. There are several reasons to hypothesize a link between these cultural patterns and persuasion processes.

First, previous content analyses of advertising have demonstrated differences between countries in the prevalence of various types of ad content, including emotional content, informative content, comparative content, and the use of humor (e.g., Hong, Muderrisoglu, & Zinkhan, 1987; Madden, Caballero, & Matsukubo, 1986; Martenson, 1987; Miracle, 1987; Renforth & Raveed, 1983; Tansey, Hyman, & Zinkhan, 1990; Weinberger & Spotts, 1989; Zandpour, Chang, & Catalano, 1992), although ads have not always been found to reflect their indigenous cultures (e.g., Marquez, 1975; Mueller, 1987). The roles of individualism and collectivism have not been investigated in these content analyses, although the findings have suggested that cultural factors often influence the types of ads employed in different countries.

Furthermore, researchers in the field of communication have argued that the persuasive styles employed by speakers may vary from culture to culture (Burgoon et al., 1982), and that the effectiveness of those strategies may vary, as well (Bronfenbrenner, 1964; Wedge, 1968). For example, research by Glenn et al. (1977) suggested that Americans prefer a persuasive style based on inductive reasoning, Soviets tend to rely on deductive logic and axiomatic principles, and members of the Arab culture tend to use an affective or intuitive style of persuasive communication. As Glenn et al. (1977) argued, it is reasonable to assume that those who are attempting to persuade others will "select approaches consistent with their own past experiences within the cultures to which they belong, and that they are selected, in part, on the basis of their ability to handle a style congruent with the culture" (p. 53).

Research on individualism and collectivism has also suggested a link between culture and attitudinal processes. When asked to endorse attitude statements or to rate the personal importance of values linked to family integrity, welfare of the ingroup, and the importance of personal goals, subjects' ratings tend to correspond with the orientation of their particular culture. In collectivistic cultures, members are less likely to emphasize hedonism and more likely to emphasize in-group obligations than in individualistic societies (Triandis, Bontempo, Betancourt, Bond, Leung, Brenes, Georgas, Hui, Marin, Setiadi, Sinha, Verma, Spangenberg, Touzard, & de Montmollin, 1986; Triandis, Bontempo, Villareal, Asai, & Lucca, 1988; Triandis et al., 1990). Such differences in culturally endorsed attitudes and values may be reflected in the tendency to use, and to accept, persuasive appeals that emphasize these different values.

Finally, research has shown that perceived social norms, roles, and values are major determinants of behavioral intentions in collectivist cultures, whereas individual likes and dislikes as well as perceived costs and benefits are weighted more heavily by individualists (Davidson, Jaccard, Triandis, Morales, & Diaz-Guerrero, 1976). This suggests that persuasive appeals that emphasize social norms and roles versus individual preferences and benefits may be more effective in changing behavioral intentions in collectivistic versus individualistic cultures.

Based on these findings, we expected that different types of advertising appeals would tend to be employed and to be effective in the U.S. and Korea. Specifically, appeals emphasizing family expectations, relations with ingroups, and group benefits—i.e., collectivistic appeals—would be more prevalent in Korean advertising, whereas messages emphasizing a concern with individual benefits, personal success, and independence—i.e., individualistic appeals—would be more prevalent in American advertising. We also expected that ads emphasizing these culturally relevant values would be more persuasive than ads emphasizing other values.

Moderating Factors

Although cultural orientation may be reflected in the prevalence and effectiveness of different types of appeals overall, these cultural differences may be moderated by other factors.

Product characteristics. Products differ in the goals that are associated with them and, therefore, in the types of benefits that are sought from them. As a result, appeals addressing different types of benefits are effective for different types of products (Shavitt, 1990).

Shared versus personal product categories appeared to be potentially important in moderating differences between individualistic and collectivistic cultures. *Shared products* were defined as ones for which the decision making process involved in purchase and the pattern of product usage are likely to include family members or friends (e.g., home appliances, groceries, and furniture). *Personal products*, conversely, were defined as ones for which the purchase decision and product usage are usually done by an individual (e.g., fashion apparel, cosmetics, personal care products).

How would these product characteristics moderate cultural differences in the content and persuasiveness of appeals? Shared products, which offer benefits both for the individual and for the group, could plausibly be advertised both in terms of individualistic and collectivistic appeals. For such products, cultural differences in the value placed on individual versus collective benefits could be manifested in the types of appeals that are typically employed and that are persuasive. In contrast, personal products, which offer primarily personal benefits and are typically used individually, are not likely to be convincingly promoted in terms of group-oriented or collectivistic appeals. Instead, they are likely to be promoted in terms of individual benefits, even in cultures where group benefits are highly valued. Thus, the nature of the product may constrain the degree to which cultural differences in individualism–collectivism are likely to be manifested in advertising (see Shavitt, Lowrey, & Han, 1992, for a similar point about how products constrain individual differences in advertising effectiveness).

Involvement. The concept of involvement has played a central role in theory and research on advertising and persuasion. Involvement has been defined and operationalized in a variety of ways (see Greenwald & Leavitt, 1984; Johnson & Eagly, 1989). The present research focused on involvement as the extent to which the information in a message is potentially important or personally relevant to outcomes desired by the message recipient (e.g., Petty & Cacioppo, 1986). Persuasion processes under conditions of high involvement differ from those under low involvement. Many studies have shown that involvement can moderate the effects of other message factors, including message content, on attitude change (e.g., Kahle & Homer, 1985; Petty & Cacioppo, 1979; Petty, Cacioppo, & Schumann, 1983).

Involvement could also moderate cultural differences in persuasion. Under high involvement conditions, when an ad presents information that is relevant to an anticipated decision (Petty et al., 1983), there may be a greater tendency to evaluate the product in terms of criteria that one considers particularly important, including cultural value standards. Under low involvement, however, one may be responsive to a wider variety of benefits. The possible role of involvement in moderating cultural differences in ad persuasiveness was investigated in Study 2.

STUDY 1

The first study assessed the extent to which advertising content in the U.S. and Korea reflects its indigenous individualistic or collectivistic cultural pattern. By examining the role of product characteristics, the study also attempted to identify conditions under which these cultural differences are most likely to emerge.

METHOD

Sample of Advertisements

One popular news magazine and one women's magazine in each country were chosen for the study. The periodicals selected as being representative of American news and women's magazines were *Newsweek* and *Redbook*, respectively. The comparable magazines for Korea were *Wolgan Chosun* and *Yosong Donga*. In order to achieve sample comparability, the two magazines were selected from each country based on their similarity in format and target audience (Mueller, 1987). The time span studied was January 1987 through December 1988. Every third month's issue was included in the sample. Two hundred product ads from each country were randomly selected from the sample.

Coding of Advertisements

A manual for coding the ads was developed from theory-based factors identified by previous research on individualism–collectivism (Hofstede, 1980; Hui, 1984; Triandis et al. 1986, 1988). The individualistic classification included (1) appeals about individuality or independence, (2) reflections of self-reliance with hedonism or competition, (3) emphasis on self-improvement or self-realization, and (4) emphasis on the benefits of the product to the consumer (you). The collectivistic classification included (1) appeals about family integrity, (2) focus on group integrity or group well-being, (3) concerns about others or support of society, (4) focus on interdependent relationships with others, and (5) focus on group goals. A fuller description of the coding scheme is presented in Appendix A.[1]

The advertisements of each country were evaluated by four judges. For each country's ads, coding was performed by two native speakers from that country (Americans for U.S. ads and Koreans for Korean ads). In addition, two bilingual coders coded both the U.S. and Korean ads. These bilingual coders were native Koreans, who lived in the United States for several years and were fluent in English. Coders were ignorant of the purposes of the study, and independently rated the degree of individualistic or collectivistic content for each of the ads on two 3-point scales [1 = not at all individualistic (collectivistic), 2 = somewhat,

---

[1] It should be noted that the individualistic and collectivistic classifications were generally appropriate to both U.S. and Korean ads. However, direct references to harmony with others did not appear in U.S. ads, only in a small number (<10) of Korean ads.

3 = very].[2] Discrepancies in coding were settled by a fifth judge for the U.S. data, and by discussion among coders for the Korean data. The average correlation between the Korean coders' ratings was $r = .80$, and the average correlation of the American coders' ratings was $r = .84$, which are within acceptable ranges suggested by Kassarjian (1977). Moreover, the bilinguals' coding was highly correlated both with Koreans' coding of Korean ads (mean $r = .85$) and with Americans' coding of U.S. ads (mean $r = .82$), suggesting that possible cross-cultural differences in interpreting the meaning of ad content did not pose a serious threat to the reliability of the coding.

Selection of Personal Versus Shared Products

Personal vs. shared product categories were determined on the basis of a survey in which 24 American students and 24 Korean students rated 44 consumer products and services in terms of (1) the decision making process involved in purchase (1 = never discuss with their family or friends whether to purchase, 5 = always discuss), and (2) usage pattern (1 = used mostly individually, 5 = used mostly with other members of family or friends). The correlations between the two mean scores across all products were high (American data, $r = .81$; Korean data, $r = .74$), and no differences were obtained between countries in the mean rating of the personal products or in the mean rating of the shared products. Thus, an average of the two items across all 48 respondents was used to classify products as personal or shared. Although many products could perhaps be classified as personal in some situations and shared in others, we believe that our classification adequately captured basic differences in the way the products tend to be purchased and used. See Appendix B for a complete listing of these products.

RESULTS

U.S. ads were expected to be rated as more individualistic and less collectivistic than Korean ads. However, product category was expected to moderate these effects such that the differences between countries would be greater for shared than for personal products.

Table 1 shows the mean ratings of individualism and collectivism as a function of country and product category. An analysis of variance with country (United States vs. Korea) and product type (personal vs. shared) as between-subjects factors and rating type (individualism vs. collectivism ratings) as a within-subject factor yielded a significant main

---

[2] In addition to these quantitative ratings, coders also classified the primary emphasis of each advertisement into one of three categories ("individualistic," "collectivistic," or "neither"). 74% of the ads were classified as either individualistic or collectivistic. Thus, the primary emphasis of most of the ads appeared to be captured by the coding categories.

However, one difficulty with these categories is that the use of the labels "individualistic" and "collectivistic" in the coding scheme may have triggered coders' own stereotypes about Korean vs. U.S. culture. Thus, even though coders were unaware of the hypotheses of the study, it is possible that their coding reflected cultural stereotypes that were consistent with those hypotheses. Future use of this coding scheme should ideally avoid use of the terms "individualistic" and "collectivistic" and substitute culture-irrelevant terms or labels.

TABLE 1

Individualism and Collectivism Ratings in U.S. and Korean Advertisements

	U.S. ads[a,b]	Korean ads[a,b]	Overall[c,d]
Individualism ratings			
Personal products	2.07	1.91	1.99
Shared products*	1.88	1.50	1.69
Overall*	1.98	1.70	
Collectivism ratings			
Personal products*	1.11	1.32	1.22
Shared products*	1.25	1.89	1.57
Overall*	1.19	1.61	

Note: Ratings were made on two 3-point scales, where 1 indicated "not at all individualistic (or collectivistic)" and 3 "very."
*Mean ratings for U.S. and Korean ads differed significantly at $p < .005$.
[a]For personal products, individualism and collectivism ratings differed significantly at $p < .005$.
[b]For shared products, individualism and collectivism ratings differed significantly at $p < 005$.
[c]Individualism ratings for personal and shared products differed significantly at $p < .005$.
[d]Collectivism ratings for personal and shared products differed significantly at $p < .005$.

effect of rating type ($F(1, 396) = 72.21$; $p < .0001$) indicating that, overall, ads tended to be rated higher in individualism than in collectivism. More importantly, a significant interaction of country × rating type emerged ($F(1, 396) = 44.69$; $p < .0001$) indicating as expected that the relative ratings of ads on individualism and collectivism differed for U.S. vs. Korean ads. Simple main effects tests demonstrated that U.S. ads were rated significantly higher in individualism than Korean ads ($F(1, 398) = 14.98$; $p < .001$), whereas Korean ads were rated significantly higher in collectivism than U.S. ads ($F(1, 398) = 42.86$; $p < .001$).

The interaction of product category × rating type was also significant ($F(1, 396) = 39.10$; $p < .0001$), indicating that the relative ratings of ads for individualism and collectivism differed for personal vs. shared products. Simple effects tests indicated that ads for personal products were rated significantly higher in individualism than ads for shared products ($F(1, 398) = 17.78$; $p < .0001$), whereas ads for shared products were rated significantly higher in collectivism than ads for personal products ($F(1, 398) = 27.95$; $p < .0001$).

However, as expected, the two-way interactions were qualified by a country × product category × rating type interaction ($F(1, 392) = 11.42$; $p < .001$), indicating as expected that product category moderated the differences in the ratings of Korean vs. U.S. ads. That is, the differences were greater for shared than for personal products. Further analysis revealed that the interaction of country × rating type was significant within each product category, indicating that ratings of U.S. versus Korean ads differed reliably for both product types (personal products: $F(1, 194) = 7.35$; $p < .01$; shared products: $F(1, 202) = 42.76$; $p < .0001$). But within-group comparisons suggested as expected that cultural differences in advertising were much more evident for shared products than for personal products. For personal products, individualism ratings were higher than collectivism ratings for *both* U.S. and Korean ads (U.S. ads: $t(96) = 11.58$; $p < .001$; Korean ads: $t(98) = 5.36$; $p < .001$). In contrast, for shared-products, individualism ratings were higher than collectivism ratings for U.S. ads ($t(102) = 7.73$; $p < .001$), whereas collectivism ratings were higher than individualism ratings for Korean ads ($t(100) = 2.93$; $p < .005$).

DISCUSSION

The data supported the hypothesis that individualism-collectivism, a basic dimension of cultural variability, is reflected in the content of advertising in different cultures. As expected, U.S. ads were rated as more individualistic and less collectivistic than Korean ads. That is, U.S. ads were more likely than Korean ads to emphasize self-reliance, self-improvement, and personal rewards, and less likely to emphasize family well-being, in-group goals, and interdependence.

Importantly, this overall difference was not uniform across products. Cross-cultural differences emerged for both product categories, but were greater for shared than for personal products. The ratings of U.S. and Korean ads suggested that personal products tended to be promoted more in terms of individualistic than collectivistic appeals in both countries. This was as expected, since personal products offer predominantly personal or individually experienced benefits, and thus are unlikely to be promoted with group-oriented appeals. However, shared products tended to be promoted differently in the two countries—more in terms of individualistic appeals in the United States and more in terms of collectivistic appeals in Korea. This may be because shared products, which offer both individual and collective benefits, can be convincingly promoted in terms of either type of benefit, allowing cultural differences in the value placed on these benefits to influence the types of appeals that are employed.

STUDY 2

Study 2 was conducted to investigate cultural differences in the relative *effectiveness* of individualistic and collectivistic appeals. In this experiment, subjects in the United States and in Korea read advertisements that employed individualistic or collectivistic appeals, and completed measures assessing the persuasiveness of those ads. Overall, we expected individualistic appeals to be more persuasive in the United States and collectivistic appeals to be more persuasive in Korea. Additionally, as in Study 1, we examined the role of personal vs shared products in moderating the hypothesized cultural differences. Cultural differences in the persuasiveness of appeals were expected to be greater for shared than for personal products, for the reasons described earlier.

The possible moderating role of ad recipients' level of involvement was also investigated. Based on previous research we reasoned that, under high involvement, when ad information is relevant to an anticipated decision (e.g., Petty et al., 1983), one may be more likely to evaluate products in terms of criteria that are considered highly important, including cultural value standards. Under low involvement, however, one may be responsive to a wider variety of appeals, and thus cultural values may play a more limited role.

Personal and Shared Products

These were chosen from the list of products identified in the Study 1 survey. *Chewing gum* and *running shoes* were chosen as the personal products. *Detergents* and *clothes irons* were selected as the shared products. These products were chosen because (1) they were expected to be equally familiar to subjects in both countries, and (2) appeal types for these products could be readily manipulated.

Involvement

The perceived personal relevance of the ads that subjects read was manipulated. Subjects in the high involvement condition were led to anticipate purchase decisions regarding the advertised products, whereas low involvement subjects were not (see Method).

METHOD

Subjects

American participants were 64 persons between the ages of 18 and 27 recruited through notices placed in University of Illinois campus buildings, promising $4 for participation. Korean participants were 64 persons between the ages of 18 and 27 enrolled in introductory communication and advertising classes at a major university in Seoul.

Involvement Manipulation

Involvement was manipulated in two ways. On subjects' initial instructions sheet, Americans in the high involvement condition were informed that the advertised products were scheduled to be advertised in medium-sized cities throughout the Midwest, including their own city (Champaign–Urbana), whereas subjects in the low involvement condition were informed that the products were scheduled to be advertised only in foreign countries. For Koreans, involvement was manipulated with comparable statements (i.e., products to be advertised in Seoul vs foreign countries). To strengthen the involvement manipulation, all subjects in the high involvement condition were also told that they would be asked to make a purchase decision regarding the advertised products in the study. Subjects in the low involvement condition were not led to anticipate a purchase decision.

These procedures were designed to enhance or reduce the personal relevance of the advertisements. Previous research has consistently found this sort of method to be effective in manipulating outcome-relevant involvement (e.g., Kahle & Homer, 1985; Petty et al., 1983; Sanbonmatsu, Shavitt, & Sherman, 1991).

Materials

All of the advertisements were written first in English. Then, a series of double-translations with decentering (Brislin, 1980) was employed to translate the ads into the Korean versions.[3] Many of the headlines and illustrations for both the individualistic and collectivistic ads were taken from actual magazine ads, enhancing the realism of the stimulus ads. One pair of advertisements (one individualistic and one collectivistic ad) was created for each of the four products. Each ad consisted of only a headline and illustrations. Individualistic ads featured such headlines as "Treat yourself to a breath-freshening experience," and "Easy walking. Easy exercise. Easy weight loss. It's easy when you have the right shoes." Collectivistic ads featured such headlines as, "Share the Freedent breath-freshening experience," and "Easy walking. Easy exercise. The shoes for your family." Individualistic ads generally featured pictures of individuals, whereas collectivistic ads generally featured pictures of groups of people. The product was also pictured in each ad.[4]

Presentation of Ads

Each subject read and responded to all four pairs of ads. The order of the four products subjects read about was counterbalanced in a pairwise balanced Latin-square design. The order of appeals within each pair of ads was also counterbalanced such that an individualistic ad was read first for one personal and one shared product (either for chewing gum and detergent, or for running shoes and iron), and a collectivistic appeal was read first for the other products.

Dependent Measures

Subjects rated their purchase intention for the advertised brand on a 4-point scale, anchored by "I definitely would/would not buy it." They also responded to two attitude measures, each consisting of three semantic differential scales anchored at −4 and +4. The first

---

[3] This type of translation refers to "a process by which one set of materials is not translated with as little change as possible into another language. Rather material in one language is changed so that there will be a smooth, natural-sounding version in the second language . . . decentering means that the research project is not centered around any one culture or language" (Brislin, 1980, p. 433). Double-translation with decentering, in part, enables equivalency of message stimuli (meaning and familiarity) to be achieved between the two cultures.

[4] A pilot study verified that these pairs of ads differed in terms of their individualism-collectivism. Ten native speakers from each country, who were blind to the hypotheses, rated the ads in their native language. They were shown pairs of ads and were asked which one they thought emphasized individualistic and which emphasized collectivistic appeals. All judges in both countries correctly classified all ads into the categories they had been designed to represent.

It was also important to determine whether individualistic and collectivistic ads differed on important dimensions other than their individualism-collectivism, such as their comprehensibility, familiarity of arguments, or readability. To assess the comparability of the ads on these dimensions, the same ten judges from each country evaluated a randomly ordered set of the ads. For each ad, they rated (1) how technically well-written this ad was, (2) how easy it was to understand the ad, and (3) how often they had seen such a set of arguments for purchasing any product (cf. Shavitt, 1990). Their ratings were nearly identical for the individualistic and collectivistic appeals for every product in each country.

measure assessed their attitude toward the ad (scale anchors: bad–good, negative–positive, and disliked–liked). The second assessed their overall impression of the brand (scale anchors: undesirable–desirable, unsatisfactory–satisfactory, and bad–good). Subjects also compared the persuasiveness of the two ads in the pair by responding to a six-item questionnaire, including such items as "Overall, which ad do you think is better?" "Which one appeals to you more?" and "Which ad do you think would be more successful?" Such a measure has been used successfully in previous studies to assess the relative persuasiveness of ads (Snyder & DeBono, 1985, 1987).

As a check on the classification of products as personal vs shared, subjects rated each product in terms of (1) their purchase decision process (1 = never discuss with family or friends prior to purchase, 5 = always), and (2) usage (1 = used mostly individually, 5 = used mostly with family or friends). As a check on the involvement manipulation, subjects completed three 9-point scales (1 = not at all, 9 = very much), on which they rated (1) how much they paid attention to the study, (2) how interesting the study was, and (3) how much attention they paid to the ads.

Procedure

Subjects participated in groups of 12 to 20. They were told that they would evaluate a series of print advertisements currently being studied by researchers at a major advertising firm. Subjects were asked to react to the ads as naturally and spontaneously as possible, the way they would as ordinary consumers. After reading the first ad for the first product, they rated their purchase intention and their attitude toward the ad and the brand. Next, subjects read the second ad for the first product and then completed the questionnaire on which they compared the persuasiveness of the two ads in the pair. In this way, they read and responded to the four pairs of ads in turn. Finally, subjects completed the manipulation checks, and were then debriefed, paid (U.S. subjects), and dismissed.

RESULTS

Manipulation Checks

As a check on the personal–shared classification of products, subjects had rated each product in terms of the involvement of others in their (1) purchase decision and (2) product usage. An average of the two 5-point items was used, with 5 being a highly shared product. Subjects' responses yielded a pattern consistent with *a priori* classifications of the products (and with the results of the same survey conducted for Study 1). Higher ratings were given to products that were classified as shared (United States, $M = 3.17$; Korea, $M = 3.39$) than those classified as personal (United States, $M = 1.89$; Korea, $M = 1.96$). An analysis of variance with product type as a within-subject variable and country as a between-subjects variable indicated that this main effect for product type was significant ($F(1, 124) = 346.56$; $p < .0001$). In addition, when ratings were examined for each product individually, the findings were supportive for all products.

Subjects' levels of attention, interest, and involvement were assessed as a check on the involvement manipulation. Because the three 9-point scales were internally consistent (Cronbach's alpha = .79), an involvement index was created by averaging the items. Subjects' mean ratings in both countries were higher in the high involvement conditions (United States, $M = 7.58$; Korea, $M = 7.33$) than the low involvement conditions (United States, $M = 6.44$; Korea, $M = 6.38$), a significant main effect ($F(1, 95) = 19.17$; $p < .001$). No other effects were significant.

Persuasivenes of Appeals

Attitude index. Subjects had rated their purchase intention and attitudes toward the ad and the brand in response to the first ad they read in each pair of ads for a product. Thus, half of the subjects provided these ratings to one ad for each product, and the other half responded to the other ad. These three ratings were substantially intercorrelated (mean r = .66) and were combined to yield a single attitude index. Because they were made on different scales, the ratings were transformed to z-scores before being averaged. The means of this standardized attitude index showed, as expected, that U.S. subjects were more persuaded overall when the ads presented individualistic ($M = 0.22$) rather than collectivistic ($M = -0.20$) appeals, whereas Koreans were more persuaded overall when the ads presented collectivistic ($M = 0.19$) rather than individualistic ($M = -0.23$) appeals.

Mean attitude index scores are shown in Table 2. These data were submitted to an analysis of variance with appeal type (individualistic vs. collectivistic) and product type (personal vs. shared) as within-subject variables and country (United States vs. Korea), involvement (high vs. low), and counterbalance order of products and of ads as between-subjects variables. This yielded a significant country × appeal type interaction ($F(1, 93)$ = 26.24; $p < .0001$), indicating as predicted that the relative effectiveness of the two appeal types differed in the United States versus Korea. Moreover, pairwise comparisons of the effectiveness of the two appeal types within each country, as well as comparisons of the effectiveness of each appeal type in the United States vs Korea, were all significant (p's < .05).

However, as expected, this effect was moderated by product type. For shared products, U.S. subjects responded more favorably to individualistic appeals than collectivistic appeals, whereas the opposite was the case for Korean subjects (see Table 2). This pattern also emerged for personal products, but less strongly. Although the country × appeal type interaction was significant within each product category (personal products: $F(1, 124) = 4.99$; $p < .05$; shared products: $F(1, 125) = 39.49$; $p < .0001$), there was a significant country × product category × appeal type interaction ($F(1, 93) = 6.42$; $p < .05$), indicating that the magnitude of the overall cultural differences in the persuasiveness of these appeals depended on what type of product was being advertised. Moreover, for personal products, pairwise comparisons of the effectiveness of the two appeal types within each country, as well as comparisons of the effectiveness of each appeal type in the United States vs. Korea, were all nonsignificant. In contrast, for shared products, these comparisons were all significant (p's < .05).

Level of involvement did not moderate how strongly subjects in the United States and Korea differed in their responses to these appeals (see Table 2). The country × involvement × appeal type interaction was nonsignificant ($F(1, 93) = .55$; n.s.). Moreover, the tendency for product category to moderate cultural differences in the persuasiveness of appeals was not itself moderated by subjects' level of involvement. There was no country × product type × involvement × appeal type interaction ($F(1, 93) = 0.31$; n.s.).[5]

Comparative ratings. After reading a pair of ads for a product, subjects had completed a questionnaire on which they compared the persuasiveness of the two ads. Because responses on this six-item questionnaire were internally consistent (Cronbach's alpha coefficients calculated for each product ranged from .71 to .90), an index was created in which a score of 1 was assigned each time subjects favored the collectivistic ad and a 0 each time they favored the individualistic ad. Thus, for each product, a 0–6 ad comparison index was created in which higher scores indicated greater favorability toward collectivistic appeals (see Snyder & DeBono, 1985).

The means on this index suggested that U.S. subjects favored individualistic appeals ($M = 2.30$) more than did Koreans ($M = 3.15$). An analysis of variance with country, involvement, counterbalance order of products and of ads as between-subjects variables and product type as a within-subject variable indicated that this difference between countries was significant ($F(1, 95) = 13.20$; $p < .0001$). Also, comparisons of these ratings to the midpoint (3.0), to determine whether the ratings reflected a significant preference for one type of appeal, indicated that U.S. subjects significantly preferred individualistic ads ($t(63) = 4.43$; $p < .001$), whereas Korean subjects did not show a significant preference ($t(63) = 1.01$; n.s.).

These differences, however, depended on the type of product being advertised. For personal products, both U.S. subjects ($M = 2.12$) and Korean subjects ($M = 2.36$) favored individualistic ads. For shared products, U.S. subjects favored individualistic ads ($M = 2.45$) whereas Koreans favored collectivistic ads ($M = 3.95$). The main effect of product type was significant ($F(1, 95) = 21.40$; $p < .0001$), reflecting the fact that, across countries, comparative ratings of ads were significantly influenced by product category. More importantly, the country × product type interaction was significant ($F(1, 95) = 9.70$; $p < .005$), demonstrating that product category moderated the cultural differences observed in responses to these appeals. In addition, tests comparing these ratings to the midpoint (3.0) indicated that for personal products, the preference for individualistic ads was significant in both countries (United States, $t(62) = 4.25$; $p < .001$; Korea, $t(63) = 2.92$; $p < .01$). For shared products, U.S. subjects significantly preferred individualistic ads ($t(63) = 2.52$; $p < .02$) and Korean subjects significantly favored collectivistic ads ($t(63) = 4.72$; $p < .001$).

[5] Although other effects were also significant in this analysis, none of them were associated with a theoretically meaningful pattern of means. The effects of involvement × product type, country × involvement × product type, counterbalance order of products, product order × involvement, product order × involvement × country, product order × involvement × ad order, and product order × involvement × product type were statistically significant. None of these interactions involve the appeal type factor, and thus none of them have implications for our conclusions regarding the persuasiveness of individualistic versus collectivistic appeals.

TABLE 2
Persuasiveness of Individualistic and Collectivistic Appeals in the United States and Korea

	U.S. subjects	Korean subjects
Low involvement[a]		
Individualistic appeals		
Personal products	.11	−.03
Shared products	.41	−.59
Overall[b]	.26	−.29
Collectivistic appeals		
Personal products	−.11	.09
Shared products	−.24	−.12
Overall	−.17	.01
High involvement[a]		
Individualistic appeals		
Personal products	.09	−.21
Shared products	.32	−.12
Overall[b]	.19	−.17
Collectivistic appeals		
Personal products	−.18	.19
Shared products	−.26	.53
Overall	−.22	.36
Overall[c]		
Individualistic appeals		
Personal products	.10	−.12
Shared products[d]	.34	−.34
Collectivistic appeals		
Personal products	−.13	.14
Shared products[d]	−.25	.25

Note: Tabled values are the standardized scores on the attitude index (the average of standardized scores across three evaluative measures).
[a]Over all products, mean attitude index ratings differed significantly between individualistic and collectivistic appeals for U.S. subjects and for Korean subjects (p's < .05, 2-tailed). (Comparisons within and between product types were not conducted within level of involvement.)
[b]Over all products, mean attitude index ratings differed significantly between countries at $p < .05$, 2-tailed.
[c]For personal products, differences in attitude ratings between individualistic and collectivistic appeals were nonsignificant for U.S. subjects and for Korean subjects. For shared products, these differences were significant for U.S. subjects and for Korean subjects (p's < .0001, 2-tailed).
[d]U.S. and Korean ratings differed significantly at $p < .001$ (2-tailed).

Level of involvement did not appear to moderate substantially the cultural differences in the persuasiveness of individualistic versus collectivistic appeals, as evidenced by a nonsignificant country × involvement interaction ($F(1, 95) = 1.15$; n.s.). Under high involvement, U.S. subjects favored individualistic appeals ($M = 2.34$; $t(31) = 2.66$; $p < .05$), whereas Koreans favored collectivistic appeals ($M = 3.56$; $t(31) = 2.28$; $p < .05$). Under low involvement, U.S. subjects still favored individualistic appeals ($M = 2.26$; $t(30) = 3.66$; $p < .01$), whereas Koreans evidenced no significant preference ($M = 2.83$; $t(31) = .84$; n.s.). Moreover, the country × involvement × product type interaction was nonsignificant ($F(1, 95) = 1.81$; n.s.). The only other significant effect was a country × involvement × product type × counterbalance order of products interaction ($F(3, 95) = 3.57$; $p < .05$), which was not theoretically interpretable.

DISCUSSION

Members of individualistic and collectivistic societies responded differently to ads emphasizing individualistic versus collectivistic appeals. Subjects in the United States were more persuaded overall by ads emphasizing individualistic benefits; whereas subjects in Korea tended to be more persuaded by ads emphasizing collectivistic benefits. This was reflected in more favorable attitude ratings for those products advertised with culturally consistent appeals, and in a preference (significant in the United States) for culturally consistent ads when comparing them with culturally inconsistent appeals.

As expected, however, this cultural difference did not emerge uniformly across products. It emerged strongly for shared products on both the attitude index and the comparative measure. It also emerged, but was diminished, on the attitude index for personal products. However, when making direct comparisons of the persuasiveness of the ads for personal products, both U.S. and Korean subjects favored individualistic appeals as expected (i.e., cultural differences did not emerge). Thus, the type of product advertised moderated cultural differences in the persuasiveness of the ads. It is not clear why comparative evaluations of the ads suggested a stronger moderating role of product category than did the absolute attitude ratings that were taken after the first ad in each pair. One possibility is that when comparing two ads for a product directly, the goals or standards that subjects typically associated with the product became more salient through the contrast between the appeals. That is, for personal products, which offer predominantly personal or individually experienced benefits, standards associated with those benefits became more salient. For shared products, which offer both personal and group benefits, standards or goals valued by the culture became more salient. Previous research has suggested that the goals associated with products are more salient when ad appeals are presented in pairs (rather than separately) prior to evaluating them, heightening the persuasiveness of appeals relevant to those goals (Shavitt, 1990).

We had reasoned that the influence of cultural value standards on product evaluations may be greater under high than low involvement. However, subjects' level of involvement did not significantly moderate cultural differences in the persuasiveness of these appeals. This suggests that cultural value standards may play a role in evaluating certain products regardless of the degree to which the advertisement is personally relevant. That is, such standards may be employed somewhat automatically in product evaluation.

Alternatively, it is possible that other standards would have been used under low involvement if the stimulus ads would have provided some alternative bases for forming evaluations. Recall that the ads in this study consisted of only a headline and illustrations, which focused largely on the individualist or collectivist benefit being touted. Had other types of reasons for purchasing the product also been presented in the ads, low involvement subjects may have been more responsive than high involvement subjects to these other benefits, and involvement may have played a greater role in moderating the cultural differences observed in the persuasiveness of appeals. More research is needed to explore this possibility.

GENERAL DISCUSSION

The present research examined how individualism–collectivism, a core dimension of cultural variability, is reflected in the advertising appeals employed in the United States and Korea, countries that have been shown to differ on this dimension (Hofstede, 1980, 1983). It also investigated the relative effectiveness of ad appeals emphasizing culturally relevant values versus appeals targeting other values. On the basis of the converging pattern of results from a content analysis and an experimental investigation conducted in two countries, it is evident that cultural differences in individualism–collectivism play an important role in persuasion processes both at the societal and the individual level, influencing the prevalence and the effectiveness of different types of advertising appeals.

Study 1, a content analysis of existing magazine advertisements, demonstrated that ads in the U.S. use individualistic appeals to a greater extent, and collectivistic appeals to a lesser extent, than do Korean advertisements. Study 2, an experiment conducted in the United States and Korea, demonstrated that the effectiveness of these types of appeals differed in the two countries. In the United States, advertisements that emphasized individualistic benefits were more persuasive, overall, than ads that emphasized family or ingroup benefits. The reverse was true in Korea.

Although cultural orientation was reflected in the prevalence and effectiveness of different types of appeals overall, the extent to which the advertised products were likely to be purchased and used individually (personal products) or with others (shared products) moderated the cultural differences observed in both studies. For shared products, there were strong differences between the United States and Korea in the prevalence and effectiveness of appeals. For personal products, however, individualistic appeals were generally favored in both countries.

This suggests that product characteristics can constrain the role of cultural differences in the prevalence and persuasiveness of advertising appeals. Personal products, which offer predominantly individually experienced benefits, are unlikely to be convincingly promoted in terms of collectivistic benefits. Thus, such products provide little opportunity for cultural differences in individualism–collectivism to be reflected in advertising use and persuasion. Shared products, however, can be convincingly promoted both in terms of benefits to the individual and to the group, and thus provide an opportunity for these cultural differences to be manifested (for similar findings on the role of product characteristics in constraining individual differences in persuasion, see Shavitt et al. 1992).

Limitations in the Generalizability of the Results

Some limitations must be kept in mind in interpreting these results. First, our research involved only one country from each culture. Although the United States and Korea differ greatly in terms of individualism and collectivism, they do not necessarily represent all aspects of this dimension. Collectivism or individualism can take different forms in different countries (see Triandis et al., 1990). Thus, the present findings should be viewed as preliminary. Further research is needed including other individualistic and collectivistic countries in order to establish further the role of this dimension in persuasion processes.

In Study 1, advertisements from only two magazines in each country were studied. Although these magazines cannot be considered representative of all advertising media in each country, it is important to keep in mind that advertisers as a rule do not produce different ads for different media vehicles. They produce campaigns, in which the same ads highlighting the same product benefits are run in several vehicles (e.g., *Newsweek*, *Harper's*, *The New Yorker*) and even in different media (e.g., magazines, billboards). Thus, if one samples across a number of media and vehicles, one will find overlap in the ads that are run (consider the ubiquitous "Joe Camel" or Absolut Vodka campaigns). It should also be noted that the titles we employed represent mainstream, mass-circulation magazines in two major categories of consumer publications—newsmagazines and women's magazines. Their advertisers include most consumer product categories, from automobiles and appliances to groceries and clothing. Thus, although our sample of magazines was small, the ads that appeared in them are broadly representative of the types of claims made for a wide range of products promoted in mass market campaigns.

In Study 2, only two products were used in each product category. However, the products we selected represent a range of items in each category. For instance, whereas detergents and irons are similar in terms of being shared products, they differ greatly in terms of cost and the length of their purchase cycle. Thus, marketers would classify them into two fundamentally different product categories (packaged goods versus durable goods). Chewing gum and athletic shoes also differ on many dimensions, although they are both personal products. Therefore, although the sample of products employed was small, we believe the products within each category are varied enough to represent a broader range of items in the marketplace.

Our studies examined only print advertisements. As such, they do not provide evidence about the generalizability of the findings to broadcast advertising in individualistic versus collectivistic cultures. Unlike print ads, television ads might be especially likely to feature collectivistic appeals because exposure to TV ads often takes place in family or group contexts. If that is the case, then our research on print ads may have overestimated the differences between American and Korean ads. Still, it should be noted that examinations of television commercials in the United States, Korea, and Japan and have pointed to a number of differences, some of which (e.g., the types of peer groups shown as models) appear consistent with our findings (Bu & Condry, 1991; and see Miracle, 1987, for a relevant nonempirical analysis).

Data collection in our studies focused exclusively on contemporary advertising. Clearly, analyzing advertising usage and effectiveness over a longer period would provide more reliable comparisons between cultures. Another advantage of a longitudinal design would be the information it provides about whether advertising appeals within a culture have changed and whether appeals across cultures have converged (e.g., Tansey et al., 1990). For example, as American "baby boomers" move through their child-bearing years, one might expect U.S. advertising strategies (and their persuasiveness) to reflect the resulting changes in consumers' collectivistic, family-oriented concerns. Research is needed to examine the effects of such demographic changes on cultural differences in the values reflected in advertising.

Further research is also needed to establish the generalizability of our findings to other, noncommercial forms of persuasive appeals. For example, previous studies of cultural differences in persuasive communication (e.g., Bronfenbrenner, 1964; Glenn et al., 1977; Wedge, 1968) often focused on interpersonal communication about political issues. Perhaps individualistic and collectivistic cultures also differ in the persuasive strategies that they favor in political and diplomatic arenas, as well as in commercial communications.

It should be noted that individualistic self-interest tends to be poorly correlated with Americans' social policy attitudes. Instead, there is evidence that Americans often justify their policy attitudes (e g., attitudes toward racial policies) with symbolic arguments about shared social values (Sears & Kinder, 1971; Sears & McConahay, 1973). Among these social values, however, a strong belief in the ethic of individualism and self-reliance has been found to underlie many Americans' attitudes toward racial policies (Sniderman & Hagen, 1985). It is possible, then, that our cross-cultural findings would generalize to the public policy domain in terms of the types of values that are invoked in the policy advocacies of individualistic and collectivistic societies.

Some strengths of these studies should also be noted. First, the procedures minimized potential translation difficulties, which have posed serious problems in cross-cultural research (Brislin, 1980; Miracle, 1990). In Study 1, ads were not translated from one language to another. Instead, both native speakers and bilinguals evaluated all ads. The high correlations between the codings of bilinguals and native speakers (both Americans and Koreans) indicated that possible linguistic or cultural differences in interpretation of the ad content did not pose a serious problem in the coding. In Study 2, where translation of stimulus ads was necessary, a series of double-translations with decentering (Brislin, 1980) was employed to achieve equivalence in meaning and smooth, natural-sounding phrasing in the English and Korean versions of the ads. Thus, the studies minimized language difficulties that can be associated with cross-cultural research.

Moreover, the present research employed multiple methods (content analysis and experimental design) to investigate cultural differences in persuasion processes. Multimethod approaches are deemed highly desirable in cross-cultural research (Hui & Triandis, 1985; Triandis et al., 1990) because each method has inherent limitations.

Content analysis monitors social phenomena unobtrusively as they occur (maximizing external validity), but often does not allow causal relations between variables to be inferred (low internal validity). In contrast, experimental research limits variation to the manipulated factors so that causal relations can be established, maximizing internal validity. But such manipulations may not resemble social phenomena in their natural settings, and thus may be low in external validity (Neuman, 1989). Employing these two complementary methodologies, the present studies converged on the same individualistic and collectivistic categories of advertising appeals, and demonstrated cultural differences in both the prevalence and effectiveness of these types of appeals.

It should also be noted that previous work investigating differences in social behavior and social perceptions in individualistic and collectivistic cultures, reviewed earlier, has yielded results that parallel the present studies (see Markus & Kitayama, 1991; Triandis, 1989, 1990; Triandis et al., 1990). The consistency of our analysis of advertising with several prior studies of self-definitions, ingroup relations, values, and behavioral intentions increases confidence in the validity of the present findings.

APPENDIX A

SCORING CRITERIA FOR CULTURAL VARIATION

1. Criteria for Classification as Individualistic Appeals
   - Appeals about individuality or independence
     "The art of being unique"
     "She's got a style all her own"
   - Reflections of self-reliance with hedonism or competition (mostly expressed in pictures, not in headlines)
     "Alive with pleasure!"
     "Self-esteem"
   - Emphasis on self-improvement or self-realization
     "My own natural color's come back. Only better, much better"
     "You, only better"
   - Emphasis on the benefits of the product to the consumer (you)
     "How to protect the most personal part of the environment. Your skin."
     "A quick return for your investment"
   - Focus on ambition
     "A leader among leaders"
     "Local hero"
   - Focus on personal goals
     "With this new look I'm ready for my new role"
     "Make your way through the crowd"
2. Criteria for Classification as Collectivistic Appeals
   - Appeals about family integrity
     "A more exhilarating way to provide for your family"

- Focus on group integrity or group well-being
  "We have a way of bringing people closer together"
  "Ringing out the news of business friendships that really work"
- Concerns about others or support of society
  "We share our love with seven wonderful children"
  "We devote ourselves to contractors"
- Focus on interdependent relationships to others
  "Successful partnerships"
  "Celebrating a half-century of partnership"
- Focus on group goals
  "The dream of prosperity for all of us"
  "Sharing is beautiful"
- References to harmony with others
  "Your business success: Harmonization with Sunkyong"
- Focus on others' happiness
  "Mom's love—Baby's happiness"
- Paying attention to the views of others
  "Our family agrees with the selection of home-furnishings"

APPENDIX B

Selection of Product Categories

Personal	Shared
Women's sanitary pads	Soft drinks
Cosmetics	Groceries
Haircare (shampoo, mousse)	Baby products (e.g., diapers, cereal)
Lingerie	Coffee/tea
Suntan lotion	Toothpaste
Greeting cards	Laundry products/soap
Gift wrap	Over-the-counter medicines
Kitchen utensils	Baby clothing
Perfume	Batteries
Watches	Corporate advertising
Electric shaver	Insurance
Personal copiers/typewriters	Washer/dryer/iron
Jewelry	Air conditioners
Fashion apparel	Camera/telephone
Credit cards	Television/VCR
Sunglasses	Computer
Jeans	Airline tickets
Wine	Automobiles
	Hotel/resort accommodations
	Home furnishings

REFERENCES

Brislin, R. W. (1980). Translation and content analysis of oral and written material. In H. Triandis & J. W. Berry (Eds.), *Handbook of cross-cultural psychology* (Vol. 2, pp. 389–444). Boston: Allyn and Bacon.

Bronfenbrenner, U. (1964). Allowing for Soviet perceptions. In R. Fisher (Ed.), *International conflict and behavioral science*. New York: Basic Books.

Bu, K. H., & Condry, J. C. (1991, April). *Children's commercials in the U.S. and Korea.* Paper presented at the Biennial Convention of the Society for Research in Child Development, Seattle, April.

Burgoon, M., Dillard, J., Doran, N., & Miller, M. (1982). Cultural and situational influences on the process of persuasive strategy selection. *International Journal of Intercultural Relations, 6*, 85–100.

Davidson, A. R., Jaccard, J. J., Triandis, H. C., Morales, M. L., & Diaz-Guerrero, R. (1976). Cross-cultural model testing: Toward a solution of the emic–etic dilemma. *International Journal of Psychology, 11*, 1–13.

Glenn, E. S., Witmeyer, D., & Stevenson, K. A. (1977). Cultural styles of persuasion. *International Journal of Intercultural Relations, 3*, 52–65.

Greenwald, A. G., & Leavitt, C. (1984). Audience involvement in advertising: Four levels. *Journal of Consumer Research, 11*, 581–592.

Gudykunst, W. B., & Ting-Toomey, S. (1988). *Culture and interpersonal communication.* Newbury Park, CA: Sage.

Hofstede, G. (1980). *Culture's consequences: International differences in work-related values.* Beverly Hills, CA: Sage.

Hofstede, G. (1983). Dimensions of national cultures in fifty countries and three regions. In J. Deregowski et al. (Eds.), *Explications in cross-cultural psychology*. Lisse, The Netherlands: Swets and Zeitlinger.

Hong, J., Muderrisoglu, A., & Zinkhan, G. (1987). Cultural differences and advertising expression: A comparative content analysis of Japanese and U.S. magazine advertising. *Journal of Advertising, 16*(1), 55–62.

Hui, C. H. (1984). *Individualism–collectivism: Theory, measurement and its relation to reward allocation.* Unpublished doctoral dissertation, University of Illinois at Urbana–Champaign.

Hui, C. H., & Triandis, H. C. (1985). Measurement in cross-cultural psychology: A review and comparison of strategies. *Journal of Cross-Cultural Psychology, 16*, 131–152.

Johnson, B. T., & Eagly, A. H. (1989). Effects of involvement on persuasion: A meta-analysis. *Psychological Bulletin, 106*, 290–314.

Kahle, L. R., & Homer, P. M. (1985). Physical attractiveness of the celebrity endorser: A social adaptation perspective. *Journal of Consumer Research, 11*, 954–961.

Kassarjian, H. H. (1977). Content analysis in consumer research. *Journal of Consumer Research, 4*, 8–18.

Madden, C., Caballero, M., & Matsukubo, S. (1986). Analysis of information content in U.S. and Japanese magazine advertising. *Journal of Advertising, 15*(3), 38–45.

Markus, H. R., & Kitayama, S. (1991). Culture and the self: Implications for cognition, emotion, and motivation. *Psychological Review, 98*, 224–253.

Marquez, F. T. (1975). The relationship of advertising and culture in the Philippines. *Journalism Quarterly, 52*(3), 436–442.

Martenson, R. (1987). Advertising strategies and information content in American and Swedish advertising. *International Journal of Advertising, 6*, 133–144.

Miracle, G. (1987). Feel–do–learn: An alternative sequence underlying Japanese response to television commercials. In F. Feasley (Ed.), *Proceedings of the 1987 conference of the American Academy of Advertising* (pp. 73–78).

Miracle, G. (1990). Research methodology to resolve problems of equivalency in cross-cultural advertising research. In P. Stout (Ed.), *Proceedings of the 1990 conference of the American Academy of Advertising* (pp. 197–198).

Mueller, B. (1987). Reflections of culture: An analysis of Japanese and American advertising appeals. *Journal of Advertising Research, 27*, 51–59.

Neuman, W. R. (1989). Parallel content analysis: Old paradigms and new proposals. In G. Comstock (Ed.), *Public communication and behavior*. San Diego: Academic Press.

Petty, R. E., & Cacioppo, J. T. (1979). Issue involvement can increase or decrease persuasion by enhancing message-relevant cognitive responses. *Journal of Personality and Social Psychology, 37*, 1915–1926.

Petty, R. E., & Cacioppo, J. T. (1986). *Communication and persuasion: Central and peripheral routes to attitude change*. New York: Springer-Verlag.

Petty, R. E., Cacioppo, J. T., & Schumann, D. (1983). Central and peripheral routes to advertising effectiveness: The moderating role of involvement. *Journal of Consumer Research, 10*, 134–148.

Renforth, W., & Raveed, S. (1983). Consumer information cues in television advertising: A cross-country analysis. *Journal of the Academy of Marketing Science, 11*(3), 216–225.

Sanbonmatsu, D. M., Shavitt, S., & Sherman, S. J. (1991). The role of personal relevance in the formation of distinctiveness-based illusory correlations. *Personality and Social Psychology Bulletin, 17*, 124–132.

Sears, D. O., & Kinder, D. R. (1971). Racial tensions and voting in Los Angeles. In W. Z. Hirsch (Ed.), *Los Angeles: Viability and prospects for metropolitan leadership*. New York: Praeger.

Sears, D. O., & McConahay, J. (1973). *The new urban Blacks and the Watts riot*. Boston: Houghton Mifflin.

Shavitt, S. (1990). The role of attitude objects in attitude functions. *Journal of Experimental Social Psychology, 26*, 124–148.

Shavitt, S., Lowrey, T. M., & Han, S. (1992). Attitude functions in advertising: The interactive role of products and self-monitoring. *Journal of Consumer Psychology, 1*(4), 337–364.

Sniderman, P. M., & Hagen, M. G. (1985). *Race and inequality: A study in American values*. Chatham, NJ: Chatham House.

Snyder, M., & DeBono, K. (1985). Appeals to image and claims about quality: Understanding the psychology of advertising. *Journal of Personality and Social Psychology, 49*, 586–597.

Snyder, M., & DeBono, K. (1987). A functional approach to attitudes and persuasion. In M. P. Zanna, J. M. Olson, & C. P. Herman (Eds.) *Social influence: The Ontario symposium, Volume 5* (pp. 107–125). Hillsdale, NJ: Erlbaum.

Tansey, R., Hyman, M. R., & Zinkhan, G. M. (1990). Cultural themes in Brazilian and U.S. auto ads: A cross-cultural comparison. *Journal of Advertising, 19*(2), 30–39.

Triandis, H. C., (1989). The self and social behavior in differing cultural contexts. *Psychological Review, 96*(3), 506–520.

Triandis, H. C. (1990). Cross-cultural studies of individualism and collectivism. In J Berman (Ed.), *Nebraska Symposium on Motivation*. Lincoln: University of Nebraska Press.

Triandis, H. C., Bontempo, R., Betancourt, H., Bond, M., Leung, K., Brenes, A., Georgas, J., Hui, C. H., Marin, G., Setiadi, B., Sinha, J. B. P., Verma, J., Spangenberg, J., Touzard, H., & de Montmollin, G. (1986). The measurement of etic aspects of individualism and collectivism across cultures. *Australian Journal of Psychology, 38*(3), 257–267.

Triandis, H. C., Bontempo, R., Villareal, M. J., Asai, M., & Lucca, N. (1988). Individualism and collectivism: Cross-cultural perspectives on self-ingroup relationships. *Journal of Personality and Social Psychology, 54*, 323–338.

Triandis, H. C., Brislin, R., & Hui, C. H. (1988). Cross-cultural training across the individualism-collectivism divide. *International Journal of Intercultural Relations, 12*, 269–289.

Triandis, H. C., McCusker, C., & Hui, C. H. (1990). Multimethod probes of individualism and collectivism. *Journal of Personality and Social Psychology, 59*, 1006–1020.

Wedge, B. (1968). Communication analysis and comprehensive diplomacy. In A. S. Hoffman (Ed.), *International communication and the new diplomacy*. Bloomington: Indiana University Press.

Weinberger, M. B., & Spotts, H. E. (1989). Humor in U.S. versus U.K. TV commercials: A comparison. *Journal of Advertising, 18*(2), 39–44.

Zandpour, F., Chang, C., & Catalano, J. (1992). Stories, symbols, and straight talk: A comparative analysis of French, Taiwanese, and U.S. TV commercials. *Journal of Advertising Research, 32*(1), 25–38.

Portions of this paper are based on a doctoral dissertation conducted by the first author under the direction of the second author. This research was supported by the James Webb Young Fund of the Department of Advertising, and by a Graduate College Dissertation Research Grant, University of Illinois. Thanks are due to James Haefner, Thomas O'Guinn, Harry Triandis, and Charles Whitney for their valuable comments throughout this research.

THINKING CRITICALLY AND APPLYING YOUR KNOWLEDGE

1. Han and Shavitt demonstrated that persuasive appeals, such as those found in advertising, reflect the underlying individualistic or collectivistic values of the culture. Develop a hypothesis about some other form of media or cultural expression, such as movies, television shows, art, or theater, that might reflect these cultural values. Design a small study to test your hypothesis.

2. Han and Shavitt conducted two studies to show that advertising appeals reflect individualistic versus collectivistic cultural themes. One study demonstrated differences in advertisements between the United States and Korea; the other was an experimental investigation demonstrating that ads appealing to individualistic versus collectivistic beliefs are differentially persuasive in the two countries. Why are these two studies together more persuasive than either study alone? What strengths do these two methods have for understanding the relation between persuasive appeals and culture?

3. Han and Shavitt found that the cultural difference in persuasive appeals was greater for products shared with others than for products that were purchased or used on an individual basis. What was their explanation for this effect? Can you think of other reasons why it might occur? Looking back at the study you designed for question 1, could you make a similar prediction in the domain you are investigating?

4. Han and Shavitt used media advertisements to explore the cultural dimension of individualism versus collectivism. What other aspects of culture might be reflected in different advertising appeals? How do advertising appeals differ depending on whether they are pitched to men or women, for example? To younger versus older people? Think about the ethnic group to which you belong. Are there distinctive characteristics of the advertisements that are directed at your ethnic group?

5. Imagine that you have just been made marketing director of a company manufacturing computer software. Your company wants to market the product both in the United States and in Korea. Design advertising campaigns for the two countries. What kinds of slogans and appeals might you use in Korea? Which ones would you use in the United States?

CHAPTER 10

PSYCHOLOGICAL IMPACT OF BICULTURALISM: EVIDENCE AND THEORY

Teresa LaFromboise, Hardin L. K. Coleman, and Jennifer Gerton

Increasingly, the United States is made up of people who are members of two cultures, for instance, a person who is Chinese-American or Mexican-American. In some cases, these individuals were born in another culture and immigrated to the United States, and in other cases, they are of mixed racial heritage. Often, researchers have treated such individuals as marginal and vulnerable to psychological conflict about their identity. LaFromboise and her associates argue that biculturalism is both more complex and more successful than earlier models suggested. The authors review research from diverse American ethnic groups, including Native Americans and Latino/Hispanic Americans to examine the ways individuals become bicultural. They examine the effects of biculturalism on social experiences, psychological processes, and individual challenges. The article emphasizes the importance of gaining competence within both cultures without losing one's primary cultural identity or having to choose one culture over the other.

ABSTRACT: *A vital step in the development of an equal partnership for minorities in the academic, social, and economic life of the United States involves moving away from assumptions of the linear model of cultural acquisition. In this article we review the literature on the psychological impact of being bicultural. Assimilation, acculturation, alternation, multicultural, and fusion models that have been used to describe the psychological processes, social experiences, and individual challenges and obstacles of being bicultural are reviewed and summarized for their contributions and implications for investigations of the psychological impact of biculturalism. Emphasis is given to the alternation model, which posits that an individual is able to gain competence within 2 cultures without losing his or her cultural identity or having to choose one culture over the other. Finally, a hypothetical model outlining the dimensions of bicultural competence is presented.*

Park (1928) and Stonequist (1935) developed the argument that individuals who live at the juncture between two cultures and can lay a claim to belonging to both cultures, either by being of mixed racial heritage or born in one culture and raised in a second, should be considered marginal people. Park suggested that marginality leads to psychological conflict, a divided self, and disjointed person. Stonequist contended that marginality

Source: Reprinted from *Psychological Bulletin, 114*(3), (1993), 395–412. Copyright © 1993 by the American Psychological Association. Reprinted by permission.

has certain social and psychological properties. The social properties include factors of migration and racial (biological) difference and situations in which two or more cultures share the same geographical area, with one culture maintaining a higher status than another. The psychological properties involve a state of what DuBois (1961) labeled *double-consciousness*, or the simultaneous awareness of oneself as being a member and an alien of two or more cultures. This includes a "dual pattern of identification and a divided loyalty . . . [leading to] an ambivalent attitude" (Stonequist, 1935, p. 96).

Words derisively used to describe the marginal person, such as *apple*, *banana*, or *oreo*, reflect the negative stereotype often applied to people who have intimate relationships with two or more cultures. The common assumption, exemplified by the positions of Park (1928) and Stonequist (1935), is that living in two cultures is psychologically undesirable because managing the complexity of dual reference points generates ambiguity, identity confusion, and normlessness. Park also suggested, however, that the history and progress of humankind, starting with the Greeks, has depended on the interface of cultures. He claimed that migration and human movement inevitably lead to intermingling. Park described the individual who is the product of this interaction as the "cosmopile," the independent and wiser person. In other words, even though marginality is psychologically uncomfortable for the individual, it has long-term benefits for society.

Goldberg (1941) and Green (1947), in their responses to the marginal human theory, suggested that people who live within two cultures do not inevitably suffer. Both authors suggested that being a "marginal person" is disconcerting only if the individual internalizes the conflict between the two cultures in which he or she is living. In fact, Goldberg perceived advantages to living at the border between two cultures. According to him, a marginal person may (a) share his or her condition with others of the same original culture; (b) engage in institutional practices that are shared by other "marginal" people; (c) experience no major blockage or frustrations associated with personal, economic, or social expectations; and (d) perceive himself or herself to be a member of a group. Goldberg argued that a person who is part of a subculture that provides norms and a definition of the individual's situation will not suffer from the negative psychological effects of being a marginal person.

The purpose of this article is to review the literature on the psychological impact of being bicultural. We present a definition of cultural competence and discuss models that have been used to describe the psychological processes, social experiences, and individual challenges associated with being bicultural. We identify the various skills we believe are needed to successfully negotiate bicultural challenges and obstacles. Finally, we present a hypothetical model of bicultural competence.

We examined journal articles, books, technical reports, and dissertations from a two-dimensional, level-of-analysis perspective and a subject-matter perspective. Four levels of analysis from the disciplines of psychology, education, sociology, and ethnology were selected for review to support our position that the psychological impact of biculturalism is influenced by an individual's emotional and behavioral characteristics (psychology), relationship with human social structures (education), groups and diverse socioeconomic systems (sociology), and cultural heritage (ethnology). The subject areas reviewed were ones thought to be associated with second-culture acquisition. This included (a) synonyms associated with cultural interactions (e.g., biculturalism, dualism, pluralism, transactionalism, acculturation), (b) descriptors for ethnic group membership, and (c) psychological symptoms (e.g., depression, anxiety, stress) and outcomes (e.g., competence, achievement, health) associated with the process of bicultural adaptation. The time span of this review was unrestricted and yielded theoretical articles dating back to 1929 and empirical articles from around the mid-1960s. Articles not considered for inclusion were ones that were found to be atheoretical, not associated with the major models of dual cultural adaptation, or of questionable quality in terms of research design.

Unfortunately, little empirical research exists in this area and what there is is spread throughout the social sciences. We found that some aspects of the psychological impact of being bicultural have received a great deal of well-designed and controlled study, whereas others have been addressed only along theoretical lines. The result of these inconsistencies is that some of the ideas presented are speculative, whereas others have significant empirical support. We have used this liberal approach because our goal was not merely to report the findings of current empirical research but to provide a model for examining the psychology of biculturalism. At the least, we hope that this article can be used as a springboard for more controlled research on this topic.

CULTURAL COMPETENCE

There is no single definition of culture on which all scholars can agree (Segall, 1986). Attempts to create a satisfactory definition of culture tend to either omit a salient aspect of it or to generalize beyond any real meaning. Despite these problems, there is an abundance of theories available regarding the meaning of the word *culture*. For the purpose of this article, we use a behaviorally focused definition. Like Levine (1982), we believe that human behavior is not just the product of cultural structure, individual cognitive and affective processes, biology, and social environment. Instead, we believe that behavior is a result of the continuous interaction among all of these components. We also ascribe to Bandura's (1978, 1986) concept of reciprocal determinism, which suggests that behavior is influenced by and influences a person's cognition and social environment.

This behavioral model of culture suggests that in order to be culturally competent, an individual would have to (a) possess a strong personal identity, (b) have knowledge of and facility with the beliefs and values of the culture, (c) display sensitivity to the affective processes of the culture, (d) communicate clearly in the language of the given cultural group, (e) perform socially sanctioned behavior, (f) maintain active social relations within the cultural group, and (g) negotiate the institutional structures of that culture.

It is important to note that the length of this list reflects the difficulty involved in developing cultural competence, particularly if one is not raised within a given culture. We do not, however, perceive cultural competence to be a dichotomous construct whereby one is either fully competent or not at all competent. We view cultural competence within a multilevel continuum of social skill and personality development. For example, an individual may be able to perform socially sanctioned behavior in two cultures with great ease but have difficulty negotiating diverse institutional structures. We also recognize that members of groups within different social strata may have differential access to social, occupational, and political roles associated with cultural competence (Ogbu, 1979). We do assume, however, that the more levels in which one is competent, the fewer problems an individual will have functioning effectively within two cultures.

MODELS OF SECOND-CULTURE ACQUISITION

Five models that have been used to understand the process of change that occurs in transitions within, between, and among cultures are assimilation, acculturation, alternation, multiculturalism, and fusion. Although each was created to address group phenomena, they can be used to describe the processes by which an individual from one culture, the culture of origin, develops competence in another culture, often the dominant majority culture. Each model has a slightly different emphasis and set of assumptions and focuses on different outcomes for the individual. We describe each one, identify its underlying assumptions, and review a number of hypotheses about the psychological impact of biculturalism that each appears to generate. We present, when available, examples from research literature that clarify the hypotheses implicit within each model.

Assimilation Model

One model for explaining the psychological state of a person living within two cultures assumes an ongoing process of absorption into the culture that is perceived as dominant or more desirable. Gordon (1964, 1978) outlined a number of sub-processes constituting various stages of the assimilation process: (a) cultural or behavioral assimilation, (b) structural assimilation, (c) marital assimilation, (d) identificational assimilation, (e) attitudinal receptional assimilation, (f) behavioral receptional assimilation, and (g) civic assimilation. Ruiz (1981) emphasized that the goal of the assimilation process is to become socially accepted by members of the target culture as a person moves through these stages. The underlying assumption of all assimilation models is that a member of one culture loses his or her original cultural identity as he or she acquires a new identity in a second culture.

This model leads to the hypothesis that an individual will suffer from a sense of alienation and isolation until he or she has been accepted and perceives that acceptance within the new culture (Johnston, 1976; Sung, 1985). This person will experience more stress, be more anxious, and suffer more acutely from social problems such as school failure or substance abuse than someone who is fully assimilated into that culture (Burnam, Telles, Karno, Hough, & Escobar, 1987; Pasquali, 1985). The gradual loss of support derived from the original culture, combined with the initial inability to use the assets of the newly acquired culture, will cause stress and anxiety.

Kerchoff and McCormick (1955) found that the greatest incidence of marginal personality characteristics (e.g., low self-esteem, impoverished social relationships, negative emotional states) among Ojibwa Indians occurred in individuals who were inclined to identify with the dominant group but encountered a relatively impermeable barrier to assimilation with that group. Chance (1965) found an overall lack of serious psychological impairment in most subjects of either sex during a period of rapidly increasing bicultural contact. However, subjects having relatively little contact with Western society, but who strongly identified with that society, showed more symptoms of personality maladjustment. Neither the contact index nor the identification index alone revealed significant differences with respect to emotional disturbance. Only the combination of the lower contact rank and high identification rank produced a situation conducive to emotional difficulties in the individual. Demographic factors such as age or education failed to delineate consistent differences in emotional disturbance.

Chadwick and Strauss (1975) found that American Indians living in Seattle maintained a strong sense of Indian identity during periods of economic and interpersonal rejection by the majority group. Even though they were able to achieve marital assimilation and perceived an absence of prejudice against them, they experienced value and power conflicts with the dominant power structure over public or civic issues. A substantial number of American Indians living their entire life in the city were perceived by the researchers to be as traditional as those who had recently left the reservation.

By contrast, Fordham's (1988) study of academically successful African-American students identified many of the problems associated with the process of assimilation. According to her findings, successful students felt that they had to reject the values of the African-American community in order to succeed in school. This seemed to be a less psychologically complicated task for women, but both sexes found that they had substantial conflict in their social and academic roles. Those choosing to become "raceless" suffered more stress and personal confusion than did those who maintained their African-American identification. On the other hand, those who did not become raceless failed to meet the standards imposed by the majority group. In this case, social success in the African-American community was associated with school failure, followed by economic failure. According to Fordham, as long as the choice is between one's ethnicity and school success, the latter will be a Pyrrhic victory.

Assimilation is the process by which an individual develops a new cultural identity. Acquiring this new identity, however, involves some loss of awareness and loyalty to one's culture of origin. Three major dangers are associated with assimilation. The first is the possibility of being rejected by members of the majority culture. The second is the likelihood of being rejected by members of the culture of origin. The third is the likelihood of experiencing excessive stress as one attempts to learn the new behaviors associated with the assimilative culture and to shed the inoperable behaviors associated with the culture of origin.

Acculturation Model

The acculturation[1] model of bicultural contact is similar to the assimilation model in three ways. They both (a) focus on the acquisition of the majority group's culture by members of the minority group, (b) emphasize a unidirectional relationship between the two cul-

---

[1] We realize that many individuals will disagree with our use of the term *acculturation*. Many have used the term to refer to the multidimensional phenomena that an individual experiences when he or she lives within or between two or more cultures. This term, when used to describe that phenomena, is not meant to imply a directional relationship. We believe, however, that the term *acculturation* is often used in a manner that does imply a directional relationship. In this work we have labeled the general phenomena of developing competence in another culture *second-culture acquisition* and use the term *acculturation* to identify a particular model of second-culture acquisition.

tures, and (c) assume a hierarchical relationship between the two cultures. What differentiates the two models is that the assimilation approach emphasizes that individuals, their offspring, or their cultural group will eventually become full members of the majority group's culture and lose identification with their culture of origin. By contrast, the acculturation model implies that the individual, while becoming a competent participant in the majority culture, will always be identified as a member of the minority culture.

Smither (1982) stated that one of the distinguishing characteristics of the acculturation process is its involuntary nature. Most often, the member of the minority group is forced to learn the new culture in order to survive economically. Smither presented five models for understanding the process of acculturation. The first is the multivariate model, in which a quantitative approach is used to understand the factors that influence successful acculturation. The focus of this method is on measuring the interactions among premigration characteristics; conditions, such as income; class status; and various situational determinants in the majority society, such as length of stay, education, or occupation. Supposedly, an understanding of new social, political, cultural, and economic patterns, as well as of personal experience such as identification, internalization, and satisfaction, will emerge from this interaction (Pierce, Clark, & Kaufman, 1978).

Using the multivariate model, Prigoff's (1984) study of the self-esteem, ethnic identity, job aspirations, and school stress of Mexican-American youth in a Midwest urban barrio indicated that subjects' use of the Spanish language and ethnic life-style varied inversely with the length of time spent in the United States. He found a significant relationship between ethnic pride and length of stay. In a multivariate study of ethnic migration and adjustment in Toronto, Goldlust, and Richmond (1974) concluded that the influence of ethnicity on acculturation was small compared with length of stay and that level of education had a positive influence on acculturation but was negatively associated with an immigrant's primary cultural identification.

When Richman, Gaviria, Flaherty, Birz, and Wintrob (1987) explored the relationship between acculturation and perceptions of discrimination among migrants in Peru, they found that age at the time of migration was closely associated with both level of acculturation and perceptions of discrimination. The advantage of the multivariate model used in these studies is its flexibility in addressing varying situational and other conditions involved in adapting to a new culture.

The second model of cultural acquisition is the communications theory model developed by Kim (1979), which focuses on four areas of communication: intrapersonal, interpersonal, mass media behavior, and the communication environment. In this model, level of acculturation is determined by the degree of facility one has in these various methods of communication in the language of the majority culture.

The third model, put forth by Szapocznik and his colleagues (Szapocznik & Kurtines, 1980; Szapocznik, Kurtines, & Fernandez, 1980; Szapocznik, Scopetta, Kurtines, & Arandale, 1978; Szapocznik, Santisteban, Kurtines, Perez-Vidal, & Hervis, 1984; Szapocznik et al., 1986), focuses on the behavior and values of the individual to assess his or her level of acculturation. This model suggests that individuals will learn the behaviors needed to survive in a new culture before they acquire the values of the majority group. Like the multivariate model, this one views acculturation as being a function of the time an individual is exposed to the majority culture. Sex and age are other factors. It also assumes that exposure to the majority culture will produce cultural competence.

The fourth model, articulated by Padilla and his colleagues, focuses on the cultural awareness and ethnic loyalty of the individual to determine his or her status of acculturation (Olmedo & Padilla, 1978; Padilla, 1980). This model suggests that an individual's preference for the minority, versus the majority, culture provides a measure of acculturation. It posits that the acculturation process exists in five dimensions: language familiarity, cultural heritage, ethnic pride and identity, interethnic interaction, and interethnic distance. This model argues for a multidimensional understanding of the cultural acquisition process.

Many authors combine these dimensions of the cultural awareness and ethnic loyalty model in their conceptual frameworks for studying acculturation. An example is Thompson's (1948) review of the Dakota Sioux, Northern Ojibwa, Navajo, Tohono O'odham (Papago), and Hopi beliefs in immanent justice. According to this belief, the universe is inherently just and sickness arises in retribution for one's failure to fulfill proper tribal roles or adhere to sacred proscriptions. Notably, regardless of the various kinds of social organization or levels of acculturation, tribal members did not display a significant decrease in the belief in immanent justice. This review did not substantiate the deleterious impact of acculturation on cultural beliefs or values. Spindler's (1952) study of belief in witchcraft among Menomini Indians showed that this belief prevailed among subjects of differing acculturation levels. She described the function of this belief as one supporting a social system invested in retaining traditional culture and providing an adaptive response to the hostilities encountered when interacting with members of the encroaching culture.

In her study of interethnic interaction among American Indians relocated to the San Francisco Bay Area, Ablon (1964) found that most Indian relationships with Anglo-Americans were relatively superficial, consisting of necessary communication with workmates and neighbors. Rather than strive for reciprocal relationships with Anglo-Americans, or positions within Anglo-American organizations, relocated Indians continuously strove to reaffirm their tribal orientation and maintain their identification with other Indians through Pan-Indian organizations. The control these subjects exerted in selecting Anglo-Americans with whom to associate offset the tension surrounding the need to interact with them.

Barger's (1977) comparative study of Inuit (Eskimo) and Cree Indians in Great Whale River, Quebec, Canada, demonstrates the need to consider case-specific factors in the statistical approach to studying the acculturation process. Inuits and Crees who resided in the same town in which Anglos were in the minority for 14 years were compared on a number of behavioral and material integration indexes. It was found that the Inuit demonstrated greater levels of acculturation and became more fully integrated into the town life than did the Crees, who were more selective in their participation in town activities. The association between culture change and presumed deviancy among Cree subjects occurred with certain individuals or families rather than with the tribe as a whole. There were, however, no differences between the two groups in overall psychosocial adjustment.

Similarly, when Boyce and Boyce (1983) studied the relationship between cultural background and the report of illness among Navajo students during their first year at a reservation boarding school (the primary mechanism for acculturating Indian people until the 1970s), they found a significant positive association between the number of clinic visits, referrals for health or psychosocial problems, and the degree of cultural incongruity (dissonance between family and community cultural identities) This finding suggests that externally imposed acculturation does have a deleterious impact on one's health.

Smither (1982) argued that the four models reviewed earlier provide insight into the processes of acculturation at the group level but cannot explain or predict individual differences in acculturation. He supported yet another multidimensional framework, a socioanalytic approach to the study of "the personality processes of the individual which facilitate or retard acculturation" (Smither, 1982, p. 62) to explain individual variation in acculturation. He asserted that an individual must expand his or her role repertoire to meet the demands of the majority culture. In the socioanalytic model, acculturation "is a function of the size of the difference between those qualities of character structure which affect role structure in the majority culture and the same qualities of character structure in the minority compared to the majority role structure" (Smither, 1982, p. 64).

Burnam et al. (1987), in a study of the prevalence of eight psychiatric disorders among Los Angeles adults of Mexican ethnicity, used socioanalytic assumptions to help explain the finding that immigrant Mexican Americans had a lower risk factor for these disorders than their native-born peers. They hypothesized that one of the reasons for the difference between the groups was that the individual who chooses to migrate may have a stronger sense of self (e.g., be more ambitious or capable) and may therefore be better equipped to cope with acculturative stress (defined by Williams & Berry, 1991, as anxiety, depression, feelings of marginality and alienation, heightened psychosomatic symptoms, and identity confusion).

Berry and Annis (1974) applied the socioanalytic approach in their investigation of psychological adaptation to culture change among individuals from the James Bay, Carrier, and Tsimashin communities. They found that the greater the cultural discontinuities between the Indian community and the Anglo communities surrounding them, the greater the acculturation stress on the individual. Individuals attaining a degree of separateness from their fellow tribal members and acquiring an independent cognitive style in interactions with their environment were less susceptible to the stresses of sociocultural change. These studies emphasize the importance of examining the role of individual development when studying the process of second-culture acquisition. However, they do not address the stress associated with any sense of isolation or loss of community ties and approval.

A series of studies by Ekstrand (1978) revealed evidence for the importance of personality factors in the acquisition of bicultural competence. The studies were designed to determine the optimal age for acquisition of a second language. Ekstrand found that personal factors (e.g., motivation, or personal circumstances) were more salient in the acquisition of language than were social factors (e.g., socioeconomic status, immigrant status, teaching method). This supports the assertion that personality factors must be considered in explaining the variation by which individuals develop competence in a new culture.

According to the socioanalytic approach, role structure, character structure, and psychological differentiation need to be understood in relation to constant variables such as age, race, level of education, or degree of cultural discontinuity because they serve to modify expression of personality and role performance. The socioanalytic model of acculturation concentrates on the individual's personality and how it constrains or facilitates learning and the expression of culturally and situationally appropriate behavior.

These studies lend credence to the conclusion that minority individuals attempting to acculturate will often do so antagonistically (Vogt, 1957) or resign themselves to accepting second-class citizenship within the majority group. Most studies of minority groups do seem to indicate that minorities are often relegated to lower status positions within the majority group. This phenomenon seems to hold true for divergent groups such as ethnic minorities in the United States, Finns in Sweden, Turks in Germany, and Koreans in Japan. These studies also suggest that the most active agent in this process may be the discriminatory behavior of the majority culture. However, the role of minority group members' economic resources has been relatively unexplored in acculturation studies, prohibiting conclusions about the role of socioeconomic status in second-culture acquisition.

Collectively, these studies indicate that acculturation can be a stressful experience, reinforcing the second-class citizenship and alienation of the individual acclimating to a new culture. These studies do support the conjecture that the primary feature of the acculturation model rests on the notion that the individual will never be allowed to lose identification with the culture of origin. Furthermore, this can have negative economic and psychological effects on the individual. This observation led Taft (1977) to argue that the detrimental effects of acculturation can be ameliorated by encouraging biculturalism. Taft (1977) suggested that "the mature bicultural individual may rise above both cultures by following superordinate social proscriptions that serve to integrate the individual's behavior relative to each culture" (p. 146). Several of the studies cited support the hypothesis that the more control people have over their relationship with the majority culture, the less likely they are to experience the negative effects of acculturation stress.

Alternation Model

The alternation model of second-culture acquisition assumes that it is possible for an individual to know and understand two different cultures. It also supposes that an individual can alter his or her behavior to fit a particular social context. As Ogbu and Matute-Bianchi (1986) have argued, "it is possible and acceptable to participate in two different cultures or to use two different languages, perhaps for different purposes, by alternating one's behavior according to the situation" (p. 89). Ramirez (1984) also alluded to the use of different problem-solving, coping, human relational, communication, and incentive motivational styles, depending on the demands of the social context. Furthermore, the alternation model assumes that it is possible for an individual to have a sense of belonging in two cultures without compromising his or her sense of cultural identity.

Rashid (1984) defined this type of biculturalism for African Americans as the ability to function effectively and productively within the context of America's core institutions while retaining a sense of self and African ethnic identity. LaFromboise and Rowe (1983) defined this type of biculturalism for American Indians as involving dual modes of social behavior that are appropriately used in different situations.

The alternation model is an additive model of cultural acquisition parallel to the code-switching theories found in the research on bilingualism. Saville-Troike (1981) called this code switching the "sensitive process of signalling different social and contextual relations through language" (p. 3). This hypothesis implies that individuals who can alternate their behavior appropriate to two targeted cultures will be less anxious than a person who is assimilating or undergoing the process of acculturation. Furthermore, some authors (Garcia, 1983; Rashid, 1984; Rogler, Cortes, & Malgady, 1991) have speculated that individuals who have the ability to effectively alternate their use of culturally appropriate behavior may well exhibit higher cognitive functioning and mental health status than people who are monocultural, assimilated, or acculturated. This complements other research (Lambert, 1977; McClure, 1977; Peal & Lambert, 1962) on the positive effects of bilingualism. In similar fashion, Martinez (1987) found that bicultural involvement was the best predictor of esteem and well-being when studying the effects of acculturation and racial identity on self-esteem and psychological well-being among Puerto Rican college students living on the mainland. Although this theoretical perspective still needs to be explored systematically, it may point to the affective or cognitive mechanism that facilitates a bicultural individual's ability to manage the process of alternation.

The alternation model differs from the assimilation and acculturation models in two significant ways. First, it posits a bidirectional and orthogonal relationship between the individual's culture of origin and the second culture in which he or she may be living rather than the linear and unidirectional relationship of the other two models. In fact, the alternation model suggests that it is possible to maintain a positive relationship with both cultures without having to choose between them. Second, this model does not assume a hierarchical relationship between two cultures. Within this framework, it is possible for the individual to assign equal status to the two cultures, even if he or she does not value or prefer them equally.

The alternation model postulates that an individual can choose the degree and manner to which he or she will affiliate with either the second culture or his or her culture of origin. Sodowsky and Carey (1988) described certain dual characteristics of first-generation Asian Indians that appear paradoxical yet support this assumption. Although the groups as a whole reported a high level of proficiency in reading and speaking English, they preferred thinking in an Indian language (e.g., Hindi, Tamil). Many preferred Indian food and dress at home but American food and dress outside of the home.

Early attempts to define American Indian biculturalism, although nonempirical, adhered to the suppositions of the alternation model. Polgar (1960) studied the behavior of gangs of Mesquakie boys in Iowa as they interacted within their own community and the surrounding Anglo-American community. Polgar found that biculturation was most prominent in the area of recreational activities, in which there was a persistent dualism conditioned by geographical location. Subjects were more active when they were in town than when within the Mesquakie community. Bilingual by the age of 7, they had alternative modes of expression available to them to be used as the situation demanded. They also exerted choice in the gangs with which they chose to affiliate. Of the three gangs profiled in Polgar's study, one in particular illustrated the alternation model of biculturalism. When in town, members of this gang adapted to Anglo-American norms, but while they were in the Mesquakie community they adapted to roles expected by the traditional, political, and religious leaders of the community. Polgar found it convenient, and effective, when analyzing the results of biculturation to view the gangs formed by the boys as transitional patterns in a multilineal scheme of cultural change.

McFee (1968), in studying the selective use of roles and situations by tribal members on the Blackfeet reservation, presented two prototypes of bicultural individuals. One type was Indian in psychological orientation and often included full-blood members of the tribe. Subjects in this category knew Blackfeet culture well, having learned it in their childhood homes and practiced it as adults. They were also educated in Anglo-American schools, had a wide range of experiences in various aspects of Anglo culture, and displayed many characteristics required for effective interactions with Anglo-Americans. Their ambition was to remain Indian but to do so by combining the best of the Indian way with the best of the Anglo way. The second type included subjects raised in Anglo-American families but knowledgeable of Blackfeet culture through early experience prior to removal from the home. Subjects in this latter category were situationally Indian oriented, having maintained enough contact with the Blackfeet community to learn and speak the language, know the beliefs and rituals, and appropriately use these skills during Blackfeet events. Even though these individuals retained their involvement with the Anglo-American culture, they also did things with and for the Blackfeet community that gained them respect and acceptance by that community.

As Pertusali (1988) discussed in his study of the Akwasasne Mohawk in both segregated and desegregated schools, the alternation model is nonlinear in its emphasis. The Akwasasne Mohawk reported their attempt to develop bicultural competence in their children through an educational program involving academic segregation in the reservation school up to the fourth grade, then a transfer to a desegregated school that delivered a bicultural academic program. This transition sequence would ideally help Mohawk children to develop a positive sense of cultural identity and build a strong academic foundation prior to attending Anglo-American schools. Data obtained from in-depth interviews with administrators and faculty members at both the segregated and desegregated schools and an analysis of the retention rates indicated that the bicultural curriculum was beneficial for both the Mohawk and non-Indian students. Results revealed that the non-Indian students were differentially and more positively influenced by the bicultural curriculum than the Indian students. Cantrall and Pete (1990) also described a curriculum that was based on the alternation model at Greasewood School entitled "Navajo culture: A bridge to the rest of the world" that emphasized decision-making, problem-solving, reflective and critical thinking, valuing, concept formation, and information-processing skills needed to deal with the social order change occurring on the Navajo reservation and internationally. The focus of both of these programs was not on movement from competence in the minority group to competence in the majority group but on ways students maintain competence in their culture of origin while simultaneously acquiring competence in the majority (or more global) culture.

A study of biculturalism and adjustment of Ramallah-American adolescents by Kazaleh (1986) showed that although identity conflict was indeed present, many of the adolescents had acquired an array of mechanisms for dealing with the dissonance and were adept at alternating between both cultural orientations with minimal anxiety. Those who had more difficulty adjusting were the youth whose parents and clan members reacted with greater anxiety to rapid change and resisted mainstream influences.

The alternation model implies that individuals learning to alternate their behavior to fit into the cultures in which they are involved will be less stressed and less anxious than those who are undergoing the process of acculturation or assimilation. Guzman (1986) emphasized the importance of maintaining a behavior–preference distinction in the assessment of Mexican-American adolescents from a bicultural-model-of-acculturation perspective. Furthermore, Adler (1975) suggested that one outcome of the alternation model may well be an enhanced intuitive, emotional, and cognitive experience. The views are again similar to assertions about the positive effects of bilingualism.

What we see as the essential strength of the alternation model is that it focuses on the cognitive and affective processes that allow an individual to withstand the negative impact of acculturative stress. It also looks at the role the individual has in choosing how he or she will interact with the second culture and the person's culture of origin. This model forces us to consider the bidirectional impact of cultural contact. In other words, it allows us to consider the impact that individuals from both cultures have on each other.

Multicultural Model

The multicultural model promotes a pluralistic approach to understanding the relationship between two or more cultures. This model addresses the feasibility of cultures maintaining distinct identities while individuals from one culture work with those of other cultures to serve common national or economic needs. In this model it is recognized that it may not be geographic or social isolation per se that is the critical factor in sustaining cultural diversity but the manner of multifaceted and multidimensional institutional sharing between cultures. Berry (1986) claimed that a multicultural society encourages all groups to (a) maintain and develop their group identities, (b) develop other-group acceptance and tolerance, (c) engage in intergroup contact and sharing, and (d) learn each other's language.

The multicultural model generates the hypothesis that an individual can maintain a positive identity as a member of his or her culture of origin while simultaneously developing a positive identity by engaging in complex institutional sharing with the larger political entity comprised of other cultural groups. In this model it is assumed that public and private identities need not become fused and that the tension of solving internal conflicts caused by bicultural stress need not have a negative psychological impact but could instead lead to personal and emotional growth. Kelly's (1971) finding, that with little difficulty the Tohono O'odham (Papago) in Tucson could occupy roles in the urban Tohono O'odham community parallel to their status in the wider Tucson social structure, supports the feasibility of this hypothesis.

Berry and his colleagues (Berry, 1984; Berry, Kim, Power, Young, & Bujaki, 1989; Berry, Poortinga, Segall, & Dasen, 1992), in their consideration of the acculturation literature, have developed a model that focuses on the process of group and individual adaptation within plural societies. They argued that there are four choices that the group or individual can make in such a situation: assimilate, integrate, separate, and marginalize. Berry and his colleagues argued that individuals and groups in plural societies have to manage two issues. One involves the decision to maintain one's culture of origin and the other is to engage in intergroup contact. Like Ogbu and Matute-Bianchi (1986), Berry and his colleagues proposed a strategy—the integration approach—that allows the individual or ethnic group to both engage in the activities of one culture while maintaining identity and relationships in another. Where the integration model differs from the alternation model is the former's emphasis on the relationship between the two cultural groups and its implicit assumption that they are tied together within a single social structure. The alternation model addresses this relationship and includes relationships that do not necessarily evolve within a larger multicultural framework.

It is questionable, however, as to whether such a multicultural society can be maintained. As Fishman (1989) suggested, cultural separation of groups demands institutional protection and ethnocultural compartmentalization. He suggested that there is little evidence for such structures surviving more than three generations of cross-cultural contact. Examples of this separation being maintained include groups making that choice for ideological reasons, such as the Old Amish and the Hasidim, or groups actively discriminated against by the majority group, such as American Indians, African Americans, or Australian aborigines. In lieu of active discrimination or self-selected separation, it may be difficult to maintain a truly multicultural society over time (Mallea, 1988). Instead, it is more likely that the various groups will intermingle, leading to the evolution of a new culture.

Fusion Model

The fusion model of second-culture acquisition represents the assumptions behind the melting pot theory. This model suggests that cultures sharing an economic, political, or geographic space will fuse together until they are indistinguishable to form a new culture. The respectful sharing of institutional structures will produce a new common culture. Each culture brings to the melting pot strengths and weaknesses that take on new forms through the interaction of cultures as equal partners. Gleason (1979) argued that cultural pluralism inevitably produces this type of fusion if the various cultures share a common political unit. The fusion model is different from the assimilation or acculturation model in that there is no necessary assumption of cultural superiority. The psychological impact of this model is unclear because there are few successful examples of such a new culture. It seems that minority groups become assimilated into the majority group at the price of their ethnic identity. This would suggest that an individual who is a member of a minority group undergoing fusion would have experiences similar to one undergoing assimilation. Once fused, however, the individual's psychological reality would be indistinguishable from a member of the majority group.

On the other hand, the psychological impact that contact with members of the minority group has on those of the majority group has been rarely discussed. Jung (cited in Hallowell, 1957) alluded to the American Indian influence on the U.S. majority group when he described the American Indian component in the character of some of his American clients. Hallowell also pointed out the need to explore the psychological effects of frontier contacts with American Indians in studying the historical development of the American national character. Weatherford (1988) chronicled how the cultural, social, and political practices of American Indians have influenced the way life is lived throughout the world. The idea that minority groups may have a positive impact on the majority culture also has been discussed in the popular press. For instance, a recent issue of *Ebony* (Bennett, 1991) focused on the African-American contributions to American culture in style, politics, entertainment, sports, gender relations, and religion. This view needs to be explored in greater detail by social scientists.

Summary

Each of these models has its own assumptions concerning what happens to a person as he or she undergoes the process of second-culture acquisition. This does not mean, however, that the models are mutually exclusive. Depending on the situation and person, any one of these models may represent an adequate explanation for a person's experience as he or she acquires competency in a new culture. An example would be of an African-American family that has moved from the rural South to an urban area. One member of the family may assimilate into the dominant Anglo-oriented culture, whereas another's attempt to acquire competence in that culture may better be described using the acculturation model. Yet a third member of the same family may choose to actively alternate between the two cultures, and a fourth may seek to live in an environment in which the two cultures exist side by side as described by the multicultural model or have amalgamated as described in the fusion model.

What separates these models are the aspects of the process that they emphasize in their description of second-culture acquisitions. We assume that there are seven process variables related to second-culture acquisition. We believe that some models more readily facilitate the effective functioning of individuals operating in dual cultures. In Table 1, each of the models described earlier is rated on the emphasis it places on the variables of contact, loyalty, and involvement with one's culture of origin and with the second culture. This table

TABLE 1
Extent of Attention on Select Process Variables Associated with Models of Second-Culture Acquisition

Model	1	2	3	4	5	6	7
Assimilation	Low	Low	Low	Low	High	High	High
Acculturation	Low	Low	Low	High	Low	Low	Low
Alternation	High	High	High	High	High	High	High
Multicultural	High	High	High	High	Moderate	Low	Low
Fusion	Low	Low	Low	Low	High	High	High

Note: 1 = Contact with culture of origin; 2 = loyalty to culture of origin; 3 = involvement with culture of origin; 4 = acceptance by members of culture of origin; 5 = contact with the second culture; 6 = affiliation with the second culture; 7 = acceptance by members of the second culture.

demonstrates that most of the models assume that an individual will lose identification with his or her culture of origin, a process that can be stressful and disorienting. What seems clear from the literature we have reviewed, however, is that the more an individual is able to maintain active and effective relationships through alternation between both cultures, the less difficulty he or she will have in acquiring and maintaining competency in both cultures.

BICULTURAL COMPETENCE

The construct of bicultural competence as a result of living in two cultures grows out of the alternation model. Although there are a number of behaviors involved in the acquisition of bicultural competence (e.g., shifts in cognitive and perceptual processes, acquisition of a new language) the literature on biculturalism consistently assumes that an individual living within two cultures will suffer from various forms of psychological distress. Although it is clear that ethnic minorities in the United States and elsewhere experience high levels of economic and social discrimination as well as other disadvantages, it is inappropriate to assume that this sociological reality produces a predictable negative psychological outcome. Research suggests that individuals living in two cultures may find the experience to be more beneficial than living a monocultural life-style. The key to psychological well-being may well be the ability to develop and maintain competence in both cultures.

Like Schlossberg's (1981) model for analyzing human adaptation to transition, we recognize that there are a number of individual characteristics that may be considered significant in the development of bicultural competence. These include personal and cultural identity, age and life stage, gender and gender role identification, and socioeconomic status, among others. Not all of these characteristics have an equal impact on an individual's ability to develop and refine the necessary skills. The relative influence of each has yet to be determined.

Sameroff (1982) suggested that personal identity is organized around an individual's concept of self and his or her estimates of his or her personal impact in a given social role within particular cultural relationships. He referred to the degree to which an individual has developed a well-formed sense of his or her own identity as distinct from his or her social organization. The potential criticism of this position is that it reflects the individualistic ideology of Anglo-American society. Without promoting this ideology, we suggest that the ability to develop bicultural competence is affected by one's ability to operate with a certain degree of individuation.[2] Furthermore, we suggest that bicultural competence requires a substantial degree of personal integration for one to avoid the negative consequences of a bicultural living situation (Burnam et al., 1987). Triandis (1980) suggested that two factors determining one's effective adjustment to the majority culture are self-

---

[2] See Sampson (1988) for a discussion of the different forms of individualism. We suggest that an ensembled individual, or one who has strong sense of oneself in relation to others, would be able to become biculturally competent. We are arguing that it is the individual who is enmeshed in his or her social context who will have a difficult time developing his or her bicultural competence.

awareness and the ability to analyze social behavior. This points to the importance of individual personality in the development of bicultural competence.

In relation to bicultural competence, it is important to focus on two facets of identity development. The first involves the evolution of an individual's sense of self-sufficiency and ego strength. This identity is the subject of concern for developmentalists such as Erickson (1950, 1968), Spencer, Brookins, and Allen (1985). Except for radical behaviorists, most psychologists theorize an internal sense of self that is separate from a person's environment. This sense develops, in relationship to the individual's psychosocial experience, to the point where a psychologically healthy individual has a secure sense of who he or she is or is not (De La Torre, 1977). This sense of self interacts with the individual's cultural context in a reciprocally deterministic manner to develop an ethnic identity (Mego, 1988). We hypothesize that the strength or weakness of this identity will affect the development of a person's ability to acquire bicultural competence.

The other facet of identity development involves the development of cultural identity. This refers to the evolution of a sense of self in relation to a culture of origin and who one is within and without that cultural context. This type of identity involves the manner in which an individual interprets and internalizes his or her sociological reality. One's cultural identity and the individual's relative commitment to that identity is the focus of the acculturation studies discussed earlier and of those authors (Atkinson, Morten, & Sue, 1989; Cross, 1971; Helms, 1990; Sue & Sue, 1990) who have developed models of ethnic identity development. With some variation, all of these models emphasize a similar process through which a minority individual proceeds in order to develop a coherent and healthy sense of self within a bicultural context.

These models imply that one's stage of ethnic identity development will affect the manner in which the individual will cope with the psychological impact of biculturalism. The more integrated the individual's identity, the better he or she will be able to exhibit healthy coping patterns (Gonzalez, 1986; Murphy, 1977; Rosenthal, 1987). These stage models seem to indicate that the highest level of development includes the ability to be biculturally competent (Gutierrez, 1981). Furthermore, these models generate the hypothesis that a minority individual who is monocultural, either in the minority or majority groups, will experience the negative psychological effects of bicultural contact. However, as that person develops a stronger personal identity, he or she can become biculturally competent, thereby reducing the negative psychological impact of biculturalism (Zuniga, 1988).

Oetting and Beauvais (1990–1991) have recently identified an orthogonal model of cultural identification that includes these four categories: (a) high bicultural identification, (b) high identification with one culture and medium identification with another, (c) low identification with either culture, and (d) monocultural identification. They advocated the independent assessment of identification with multiple cultures (e.g., culture of origin and American Indian, Mexican American, Asian American, African American or Anglo-American). A series of studies with American Indian youth (Beauvais, 1992; Oetting, Edwards, & Beauvais, 1989) indicated that most children and adolescents on reservations showed medium identification with both Anglo and Indian cultures. Their research with Mexican-

American youth living in Southwestern towns and cities containing substantial Hispanic populations, however, showed a different pattern of high Hispanic identification and moderate Anglo identification. This line of research in minority adolescent drug use supports the contention that identification with any culture may serve as an individual's source of personal and social strength and that such an identification will correlate with one's general well-being and positive personal adjustment. Oetting and Beauvais concluded that it is not mixed but weak cultural identification that creates problems.

This component of bicultural competence suggests the need to maintain a distinction between social variables, such as class and ethnicity, and psychological variables, such as identity development and affective processes. It is important to remember that individuals, not groups, become biculturally competent. This suggests that each person will proceed in the process of cultural acquisition at his or her own rate. Researchers can, and should, make group predictions concerning the process, but they must be cautious when applying these findings to individuals (Murphy, 1977; Zuniga, 1988). As such, to understand the psychological impact of becoming or being competent in two cultures, researchers must look at both individual psychological development and the context in which that development occurs (Baker, 1987; LaFromboise, Berman, & Sohi, 1993).

From our reading of the literature, we suggest the following dimensions in which an individual may need to develop competence so as to effectively manage the process of living in two cultures: (a) knowledge of cultural beliefs and values, (b) positive attitudes toward both majority and minority groups, (c) bicultural efficacy, (d) communication ability, (e) role repertoire, and (f) a sense of being grounded.

Knowledge of Cultural Beliefs and Values

Cultural awareness and knowledge involves the degree to which an individual is aware of and knowledgeable about the history, institutions, rituals, and everyday practices of a given culture. This would include an understanding of the basic perspectives a culture has on gender roles, religious practices, and political issues, as well as the rules that govern daily interactions among members of the culture.

A culturally competent person is presumed to be one who knows, appreciates, and internalizes the basic beliefs of a given culture. This would require an acceptance of a particular culture's basic worldview and the ability to act within the constraints of that worldview when interacting with members of that culture. For example, a study of elementary-age Sioux children living on reservations and in a neighboring boarding school (Plas & Bellet, 1983) showed that the older the children were, the more they differed culturally from younger respondents.[3] More pointedly, on the Native American Value-Attitude Scale (NAVAS; Trimble, 1981), younger children tended to provide the expected Indian response, whereas the older children both maintained a preference for the Indian values of community importance and deference to an indirect style of relating yet adopted a more

---

[3] Specific Sioux tribal affiliations and names of reservations were not reported in this study.

Anglicized attitude toward school achievement and interpersonal involvement. This finding suggests that differences in worldview and value conflicts may be primary sources of stress for bicultural individuals. If the values and beliefs of the two cultures are in conflict, the individual may internalize that conflict in an attempt to find an integrated resolution, but the difficulty in finding this resolution may well be what motivates the individual to fuse the two cultures as a stress-reducing solution. Future research on bicultural competence must continue to examine these phenomena as being central to identifying an individual's psychological well-being.

Schiller's (1987) study lends support to considering cultural awareness and knowledge as an important component of cultural competence. In a survey study investigating the impact of biculturalism, she examined the academic, social, psychological, and cultural adjustment of American Indian college students. Schiller found that bicultural Indian students were better adjusted, particularly in the academic and cultural domains, than were their nonbicultural counterparts. They had higher grade point averages (GPAs), more effective study habits, and demonstrated a stronger commitment to using resources for academic success. Participation in cultural activities and enrollment in American-Indian-oriented courses was significantly higher for bicultural students. Finally, these students perceived their Indian heritage to be an advantage, more so than did nonbicultural students. A number of recent studies on the relationship between acculturation and the counseling process (Atkinson & Gim, 1989; Curtis, 1990; Gim, Atkinson, & Whiteley, 1990; Hess & Street, 1991; Hurdle, 1991; Ponce & Atkinson, 1989) support the hypothesis that knowledge of the second culture's values and practices facilitates an ethnic minority's willingness to use available psychological services.

Positive Attitudes Toward Both Groups

This aspect of the construct assumes that the individual recognizes bicultural competence as a desirable goal in its own right, holds each cultural group in positive but not necessarily equal regard, and does not endorse positions that promulgate hierarchical relations between two cultural groups.

The inclusion of this component is based on certain theoretical assumptions. Without positive attitudes toward both groups, an individual will be limited in his or her ability to feel good about interacting with a group that is the target of negative feelings. Arguably, the process of interacting with individuals from a culture one does not respect will result in negative psychological and behavioral outcomes. We hypothesize that one reason for the tremendous rate of conduct disorders among ethnic minority adolescents is a result of the negative attitudes those adolescents have toward the dominant Anglo group. This hypothesis is supported by Palleja's (1987) finding that monocultural-affiliated Hispanic young men exhibited more rebellious behavior than did bicultural or Anglo-affiliated monocultural peers and Golden's (1987) finding that Korean-American high school students practicing biculturalism displayed more positive educational outcomes and self-concepts than monoculturally affiliated Korean-American students. Mullender and Miller (1985) initiated a group for Afro-Caribbean children living in White families who were experiencing discomfort or limited support to help them deal with negative feelings associated with racism from the dominant group. Both the White caregivers and the Afro-Caribbean youth bene-fited from increased knowledge of Caribbean culture and recognition of the importance of the youth having more involvement with the Black community.

One study of Navajo children from five elementary schools in northeastern Arizona by Beuke (1978) did reveal that students in the high Indian–high Anglo cultural identification category had significantly higher self-esteem scores than did those in the low Indian–low Anglo category, regardless of which school they attended. This study on cultural identifi-cation initially supports the hypothesis that positive attitudes toward both groups may be an important component in reducing the stress of bicultural contact.

Contact itself is an essential element in one's ability to develop a positive attitude toward both groups. For example, some American Indians come from tribes that maintained con-siderable autonomy from the encroaching majority culture but then experienced contact at a later point. Individuals from these tribes were less often faced with the contradictions that can result from ongoing contact between different cultures. Of course, there is considerable variation between and within tribal groups regarding the amount and nature of contact with the U.S. majority and other surrounding cultures. Even today, an individual's proximity to a reservation or city influences the bicultural experiences that person has (Little Soldier, 1985). As Berry, Padilla, and Szapocznik and their colleagues have suggested, the length and type of contact individuals from one culture have with the other cultures have a significant impact on their attitudes toward the majority and their own culture.

Information is also an essential element in developing a positive attitude toward both groups. Cultural translators, individuals from a person's own ethnic or cultural group who have successfully undergone the dual socialization experience, can help others in the per-sonal integration process (Brown, 1990). He or she can interpret the values and percep-tions of the majority culture in ways that do not compromise the individual's own ethnic values or norms.

Bicultural Efficacy

Rashid (1984) asserted that "biculturalism is an attribute that all Americans should pos-sess because it creates a sense of efficacy within the institutional structure of society along with a sense of pride and identification with one's ethnic roots" (p. 15). As Bandura (1978) has demonstrated, the belief, or confidence, that an individual can perform an action has a hierarchical relationship to the actual performance of that action. In this article, we posit that bicultural efficacy, or the belief that one can develop and maintain effective interper-sonal relationships in two cultures, is directly related to one's ability to develop bicultural competence.

We define *bicultural efficacy* as the belief, or confidence, that one can live effectively, and in a satisfying manner, within two groups without compromising one's sense of cultural identity. This belief will support an individual through the highly difficult tasks of devel-oping and maintaining effective support groups in both the minority and the majority cul-ture. It will also enable the person to persist through periods when he or she may experience rejection from one or both of the cultures in which he or she is working to de-velop or maintain competence (Rozek, 1980).

A study by Kazaleh (1986) showed that the Ramallah-American youth who were afforded more outlets for social expression, whether in the ethnic community or outside of it, presented the image of being more confident in their abilities and tolerant of the ethnic life-style than did those who were overprotected by their families and restricted in their activities with peer groups. In a study of French Canadian adolescent boys learning English, Clement, Gardner, and Smythe (1977) found two factors that were associated with the motivation to learn English. One involved a positive attitude toward the Anglophone community and the other involved the awareness that learning English had an instrumental function in terms of academic achievement and future job performance. These factors, however, were not as predictive of actual competence in English as a student's confidence in his ability to learn the second language. In a study of Asian-American assertion, Zane, Sue, Hu, and Kwon (1991) found that self-efficacy predicted the ability of Asian Americans to be as assertive, in a situationally appropriate manner, as their Anglo-American peers. These findings support the thesis that efficacy is an important factor in the development of bicultural skills.

We hypothesize that an individual's level of bicultural efficacy will determine his or her ability to (a) develop an effective role repertoire in a second culture, (b) perform effectively within his or her role, (c) acquire adequate communication skills, (d) maintain roles and affiliations within his or her culture of origin, and (e) cope with acculturation stress. Furthermore, encouraging the development of an individual's bicultural efficacy is a vital goal of any program (e.g., therapy or skills training) that is designed to enhance his or her performance in bicultural or multicultural environment. We believe that this statement is as true for ethnic minority people developing competence in a majority culture institution as it is for the majority person developing competence in a bicultural or multicultural environment.

Communication Ability

Communication ability refers to an individual's effectiveness in communicating ideas and feelings to members of a given culture, both verbally and nonverbally.[4] Language competency, in fact, may be a major building block of bicultural competence. As Northover (1988) suggested, "each of a bilingual's languages is the mediator between differing cultural identities within one and the same person" (p. 207). It is vital, however, to distinguish between the language-acquisition processes, which have the goal of transferring competency from the minority group's language to the majority group's language, and processes oriented toward an individual maintaining the language of origin as well as the acquisition of a second language. Bilingual programs that encourage the maintenance, rather than the transfer, of language skills promote bicultural competence rather than assimilation or acculturation (Edwards, 1981; Fishman, 1989; Thomas, 1983).

---

[4] We are not necessarily referring to an individual's ability to communicate in written form. It is certainly possible to be fluent in a language and not be literate.

Fisher's (1974) study is a good example of the potentially positive impact of a maintenance-oriented program. He examined the effects of a bilingual–bicultural program on the self-concepts, self-descriptions, and stimulus-seeking activities of first graders. He found a highly positive effect for the Mexican-American girls on all three measures, no effect on the Mexican-American boys, no effect on the Anglo girls, and a negative effect on the Anglo boys. The drop in self-concept scores among Anglo boys during the school year was attributed to anxiety from having to learn new cultural competencies in addition to their school work. Fisher did not attempt to explain the sex difference among Anglo students in the change of their self-concept scores. The results of this study suggest that communication competency may have a direct effect on self-concept and other nonintellectual attributes. In a comparative study of Hispanic public community college students in a bilingual program and those who received only English as a second language, Tormes (1985) found that those in the bilingual program consistently performed better on most of the criterion measures (e.g., number of credits attempted and earned, GPAs, and progress toward a degree). Therefore, if a program is designed to maintain one's cultural competence, as well as one's language, it will most likely have a positive impact. If the program does not serve in this capacity, it may have a negative effect, as it did for the Anglo boys in the Fisher study and most minority children in mainstream schools or transfer language programs.

Young and Gardner (1990) found that ethnic identification and second-language proficiency were closely related. Their study of ethnic identification, perceptions of language competence, and attitudes toward mainstream and minority cultures among Chinese Canadians highlights the role of attitude in the development of communication competence. They found that the greater a participant's fear of losing his or her cultural identification, the weaker was his or her language proficiency. Participants who had that fear also had more negative attitudes toward language study. These attitudes were bidirectional, meaning that those Chinese who were identified with Canadian culture thought their Chinese language skills were weak and that their desire to improve these skills was also weak. Those who were proficient in Chinese and fearful of assimilation in Canadian culture were not eager to improve their English-language skills. Participants who had a positive attitude toward both cultures or identified with both cultures were proficient in both languages or were eager to improve their skills in the second language. These studies suggest that both attitude and ethnic identification have an impact on the development of communication competence.

McKirnan and Hamayan (1984), in a study of the ways speech norms are used to identify in-group and out-group membership, confirmed the importance of communication ability as a factor in bicultural competence. They found that Anglo in-group members in a Spanish bilingual program ascribed negative characteristics to Hispanic students on the basis of variations in their style of speech. Although the amount of intergroup contact also contributed to the in-group members' attitudes, the Anglo in-group often used the speech pattern as a trigger for making judgments about the Hispanic speaker. This suggests that communication skills are a cue for the majority group in accepting a member of the minority group. Dornic (1985) pointed out that the stress of using the second language inhibits the performance, in a wide variety of roles, of individuals who are recent immigrants to a new culture. The work of McKirnan and Hamayan and of Dornic, although reinforcing the notion that communication ability is an essential building block of bicultural competence, underscores the important function of various contact situations during formative years on acquiring that ability.

In a study of bicultural communication, Simard and Taylor (1973) found that cross-cultural dyads were able to communicate as effectively as were homogeneous dyads. If there was a difference in the effectiveness of communication, it was determined by the nature of the task rather than the cultural composition of the dyad. Those authors used their findings to suggest that cross-cultural communication is a function of both motivation and capability.

LaFromboise and Rowe (1983) evaluated an assertion training program for bicultural competence with urban Indians in Lincoln, Nebraska. The key instructional focus of this program was on the situation-specific nature of assertiveness and language style differences in the assessment of Indian and non-Indian target people prior to delivery of assertive messages. Feedback during training involved the appropriateness of American Indians being assertive with one another and ways for Indians to be succinct and more forceful when being assertive with Anglo-Americans. Behavioral measures of assertiveness, rated by both Indian and Anglo peer observers, revealed a positive training effect. The actual language form (e.g., conventional English, Indian-style English, and bilingual English and Omaha) was not evaluated here; instead, the perceptions of communicative competence derived from message content and sociolinguistic cues were examined. The results of this study reinforce the importance of defining communication competency within the context of specific situations. As such, bicultural communication competency involves one's ability to communicate in a situationally appropriate and effective manner as one interacts in each culture.

In a 1985 study of acculturative stress among 397 high school students in an urban and multiethnic school, Schwarzer, Bowler, and Rauch found that the more acculturated students who spoke English at home had higher levels of self-esteem and less experience with racial tension and interethnic conflict. Other variables (i.e., length of stay in the United States and ethnic group membership) were related to the findings, but the families' facility with the majority group's language appeared to be the primary factor that ameliorated the stress of living in a bicultural environment (see also Bettes, Dusenbury, Kerner, James-Ortiz, & Botvin, 1990).

When Robinson (1985) analyzed census data to determine background characteristics associated with language retention among Canadian Indians, she found that educational advancement reduced the probability of native-language retention but increased the probability of participation in the labor force. This suggests that attempts to improve the economic conditions of Indians by increasing their education may have a detrimental effect on the maintenance of their native-language skills. However, economic and linguistic acculturation, as described by Robinson, does not necessarily imply complete acculturation of Canadian Indian people. It does suggest that gaining majority group language competency may increase majority culture competency, but it does not suggest that majority group language competency ameliorates acculturative stress. In other words, as important as communication competency is in developing cultural competency, it is not the only skill that relieves the stress of becoming biculturally competent.

Role Repertoire

Role repertoire refers to the range of culturally or situationally appropriate behaviors or roles an individual has developed. The greater the range of behaviors or roles, the higher the level of cultural competence.

In a study of individuals who were working and living in Kenya for 2 years, Ruben and Kealey (1979) found that particular interpersonal and social behaviors led to greater effectiveness at role performance and ease in adjustment. The authors looked at (a) displays of respect, (b) interaction posture (e.g., judgmental or not), (c) orientation to knowledge or worldview, (d) empathy, and (e) role behavior. Coinciding with Smither's (1982) assertions, they found that individuals who had the personal resources to use their social skills in a situationally appropriate manner suffered less cultural shock and were more effective in their vocational duties and social interactions than were those whose behavioral repertoire within the second culture was more limited.

In McFee's (1968) study of acculturation among the Blackfeet tribe, he found that individuals knowledgeable about both Blackfeet and Anglo-American cultures and able to interact easily with members of each by applying this knowledge in a situationally appropriate manner had an important role in both cultures. McFee suggested that such individuals perform an important and valued role for both communities as cultural translators, or mediators, as long as they are not perceived by the minority group as being over-identified with the majority group.

In a study of the complexity of parental reasoning about child development in mothers who varied in ethnic background and biculturalism, Gutierrez and Sameroff (1990) found that the bicultural Mexican-American mothers were better skilled at developing an objective understanding of their child's behavior than were monocultural Mexican-American or Anglo-American mothers. Their ability to interpret child development as the result of the dynamic interplay between the child's temperament and his or her environment over time and to see that developmental outcomes could have multiple determinants enhanced their parenting role. Those researchers did not, however, examine how bicultural competence originates or elaborate on the psychological results of this form of biculturalism. Determining the psychological impact of this balancing act is an important area of concern for future research. The processes by which these bicultural skills are developed needs to be delineated, and a close look needs to be taken at the individual psychology of those who have developed these skills.

Cuellar, Harris, and Naron (1981), in a study of Mexican-American psychiatric patients, found that the patient's level of acculturation was highly correlated with diagnosis and treatment outcome. The more acculturated individuals received less severe diagnostic labels than less acculturated individuals. In that study, they were looking at the impact of providing bilingual staff and culturally appropriate decor on treatment outcome. They found that the less acculturated patients in the experimental groups were positively affected by the treatment. The treatment had little effect on more highly acculturated patients. The results of this study support the hypothesis that the minority individual who does not have a sufficient role repertoire in either the majority or minority culture receives differential treatment. It also suggests that treatment keyed to the individual's level of cultural identification is more effective than interventions using a monocultural approach.

Further support for the importance of role repertoire comes from Szapocznik, Kurtines, et al. (1980) and Szapocznik et al. (1984), who determined that the development of bicultural social skills facilitated the adjustment of Hispanic youth. The intervention used with Hispanic families in conflict—bicultural effectiveness training—consisted of the analysis of Hispanic and Anglo cultural conflicts and the presentation of information concerning biculturalism. They found that those who could develop a bicultural repertoire were less likely to experience family or school conflict or become involved in illegal drug use. This line of work reinforces the importance of focusing on bicultural social skills when delivering services to members of the minority group experiencing problems within the majority culture (see also Comer, 1980, 1985; LaFromboise, 1983).

In a study of the psychocultural characteristics of college-bound and non-college-bound Chicanas, Buriel and Saenz (1980) found that the family income and ability to perform masculine behaviors, as measured by the Bem Sex Role Inventory, were the major distinctions between the two groups. The results of this study suggest that knowing the behaviors that have traditionally led to economic success within the American culture, and the ability to be assertive in the majority culture, are aspects of the role repertoire that determine college attendance among Chicanas. Buriel and Saenz also found that family income and sex role identification were positively correlated with biculturalism, defined in their study as "an integration of the competencies and sensitivities associated with two cultures within a single individual" (p. 246). They did not find a causal relation between biculturalism and college attendance; however, they concluded that biculturalism may be an associated factor, particularly as it relates to behavior that leads to college attendance.

When developing programs to facilitate the introduction of ethnic minorities into institutions that are dominated by the majority culture (e.g., universities or corporations), it is vitally important to take the minority individual's dual focus into account (Akao, 1983). Failure to facilitate the maintenance of the minority person's role within his or her culture of origin will lead to either poor retention within the program or aggravate his or her acculturative stress (Fernandez-Barrillas & Morrison, 1984; Lang, Muñoz, Bernal, & Sorensen, 1982; Mendoza, 1981; Van Den Bergh, 1991; Vasquez & McKinley, 1982).

Groundedness

"Every culture provides the individual some sense of identity, some regulation or belonging and some sense of personal place in the school of things" (Adler, 1975, p. 20). The literature indicates that the person most successful at managing a bicultural existence has established some form of stable social networks in both cultures. This suggests that the positive resolution of stress engendered by bicultural living cannot be done on one's own (Hernandez, 1981). One must have the skill to recruit and use external support systems.

We have labeled the experience of having a well-developed social support system "a sense of being grounded."

Baker (1987) supported this position when she argued that African Americans are best able to avoid the major problems that affect mental health facing their communities (e.g., Black-on-Black homicide, teenage pregnancy, attempted suicide, substance abuse, postin-carceration adjustment) when they can call on the resources of the African-American extended family. Both nuclear and extended family models in American Indian communities facilitate this sense of being grounded (Red Horse, 1980). We argue that it is the sense of being grounded in an extensive social network in both cultures that enhances an individual's ability to cope with the pressures of living in a bicultural environment and that acquiring that sense in the second culture is an important outcome of second-culture acquisition (Lewis & Ford, 1991). Murphy (1977) suggested that the ability to become grounded inoculates against the development of psychopathology among immigrants.

Beiser's (1987) study of depression in Southeast Asian refugees underscores the importance of being grounded within one's culture as a coping mechanism for dealing with the psychological impact of entering a new culture. He found that immigrants who either came with other family members, or entered cities with a sizable population of individuals from their home culture, were less depressed after a year's time than were those who came alone or were not involved with people from the home culture. Fraser and Pecora (1985–1986) echoed this finding, discovering that refugees who coped best with the natural reactions to dislocation were those who had "weak ties" in a community. These weak ties are extended family acquaintances, such as an uncle's best friend, who can play an important role in the fabric of daily living by providing support such as child care or employment information. These networks serve to increase an individual's sense of being grounded in time and space.

Porte and Torney-Purta (1987) demonstrated the positive impact that maintaining a bicultural environment had on the academic achievement and level of depression among Indochinese refugee children entering the United States as unaccompanied minors. They found that children placed in foster care with Indochinese families performed better in school and were less depressed than children placed in foster care situations with non-Indochinese families. The results of this study highlight the importance of providing a culturally relevant environment for individuals learning a second culture.

In a study of the impact of the Chinese church on the identity and mental health of Chinese immigrants, Palinkas (1982) reinforced the perspective that a solid social network, one that simultaneously grounds an individual in parts of his or her home culture while facilitating the acquisition of a new culture, sharply reduces the negative impact of acculturation. Topper and Johnson's (1980) study of the effects of relocation on members of the Navajo tribe provides a graphic example of the psychological impact of losing one's groundedness. They found that relocated individuals were eight times more likely to seek mental health services than were Navajos who had not been forced to relocate. They also reported that 70% of the relocatees were found to be suffering from depression or related disorders.

Rodriguez (1975), in a study of the subjective factors affecting assimilation among Puerto Ricans in New York City, found that Puerto Ricans living in the ghetto had more positive attitudes about succeeding in the mainstream economic system than did Puerto Ricans living in Anglo-dominated suburbs. Those living in the ghetto also claimed to experience less discrimination. As Rodriguez (1975) suggested, "the ghetto . . . provides a psychologically more supportive environment than does the middle class area" (p. 77). These findings highlight the role that being grounded plays for the individual living in two cultures. We believe that groundedness joins behavioral effectiveness and personal well-being as key characteristics of mental health.

Summary

Research suggests that there is a way of being bicultural without suffering negative psychological outcomes, assimilating, or retreating from contact with the majority culture. We recognize that bicultural competence requires a difficult set of skills to achieve and maintain. We do not doubt that there will be stress involved in the process of acquiring competence in a second culture while maintaining affiliation with one's culture of origin. The question we have for future research is whether these difficulties lead to personal growth and greater psychological well-being, or inevitably lead to the type of psychological problems posited by Stonequist (1935) and Park (1928).

MODEL OF BICULTURAL COMPETENCE

The goal of this article was to develop an understanding, on the basis of social science research, of the psychological impact of biculturalism. We wanted to understand which factors facilitate a bicultural role and which ones impede the development of that role. We were particularly interested in identifying the skills that would make it possible for an individual to become a socially competent person in a second culture without losing that same competence in the culture of origin. To focus our exploration, we organized our search around a behavioral model of culture that would allow us to better identify the skills of bicultural competence. We also felt that it was important to describe the different models of second-culture acquisition so that our use of the alternation model could be understood in relation to other theories of biculturalism.

Our exploration of the psychological impact of biculturalism was seriously constrained by the fact that research in this area is spread across several disciplines and represents a wide range of methodologies. This fact made it difficult to derive a composite statement about the results of different studies that appeared to be examining similar aspects of biculturalism. The lack of controlled or longitudinal research compounded this difficulty. As a result, our discussion of biculturalism is speculative in nature. We have, however, been able to identify skills that we hypothesize are central to being a socially competent person in two cultures.

At this point, we want to emphasize that we do not know whether these are the only skills of biculturalism, or whether a person needs to be equally competent in all or a particular subset, in order to be biculturally competent. We do think, however, that the dimensions outlined in this article provide a much needed focus to the research on this phenomenon. We believe that identifying these acquirable skills will allow researchers to focus on the relationship between these skills and an individual's sense of psychological well-being, as well as his or her effectiveness in his or her social and work environments. We also believe that these dimensions can be used as the framework for developing programs designed to facilitate the involvement of minority people in majority institutions such as colleges and corporations (Van Den Bergh, 1991).

Initially, each of the skills needs to be subjected to empirical examination. Reliable methods of assessment need to be developed, and construct validity needs to be established (Sundberg, Snowden, & Reynolds, 1978). Subsequently, the relationship between possessing each skill and school and work performance will have to be identified. Finally, the question as to which skills, or set of skills, are necessary in order to be functionally biculturally competent will have to be answered. In other words, these dimensions appear to describe the skills of a biculturally competent individual. Further research using this framework needs to be conducted to determine the degree to which they are normative or optimal for a person involved in two cultures.

To facilitate that process, we have developed a hypothetical model of the relationships among these skills of bicultural competence. After lengthy consideration, we have come to speculate that these skills may have a rational relationship to each other. We believe that some may be more important than others or that some may have to be developed before others. Furthermore, we developed the assumption that one or more of these skills may be the linchpin between monocultural and bicultural competence. In response to these speculations, in the model we have developed it is assumed that there are hierarchical relations among these skills, not linear ones. By this we mean that some of these skills may be developed before others but that the process of skill acquisition does not have an invariant order. Only empirical study can resolve this issue.

The primary emphasis of the model is on the reciprocal relationship between a person and his or her environment. The model becomes complex when considering the acquisition of second-culture competence because one must include two environments, both the culture of origin and the second culture. An individual's personal and cultural identities are primarily developed through the early biosocial learning experiences that an individual has within his or her culture of origin. These identities will also be influenced by the nature and amount of contact the person has with the second culture. For example, if a person lived in rural El Salvador and had no contact with American culture until forced to emigrate in early adulthood, that person's sense of personal and cultural identity would be much different from his or her U.S.-born child, who has attended public schools since kindergarten. It is our contention that in addition to having a strong and stable sense of personal identity, another affective element of bicultural competence is the ability to develop and maintain positive attitudes toward one's culture of origin and the second culture in which he or she is attempting to acquire competence. In addition, we speculate that an individual will also need to acquire knowledge of both cultures in order to develop the belief that he or she can be biculturally competent, which we have labeled *bicultural efficacy*.

We speculate that these attitudes and beliefs about self, what we think of as the affective and cognitive dimension of the model, will facilitate the individual's acquisition of both communication skills and role repertoire, which are the two facets that make up the behavioral aspect of the model. We hypothesize that the individual who has acquired the attitudes and beliefs in the affective and cognitive dimension and the skills of the behavioral aspect of this model will also be able to develop the effective support systems in both cultures that will allow him or her to feel grounded. Being grounded in both cultures will allow the individual to both maintain and enhance his or her personal and cultural identities in a manner that will enable him or her to effectively manage the challenges of a bicultural existence.

This model represents a departure from previous models in that it focuses on the skills that a person needs to acquire in order to be successful at both becoming effective in the new culture and remaining competent in his or her culture of origin. This difference is represented in Table 2, which rates the five models of second-culture acquisition discussed earlier, on the degree to which the assumptions of each model facilitate the acquisition of these skills.

Table 2 shows that the alternation model, on which our model of bicultural competence is based, is the one that best facilitates the acquisition of these skills. It appears that the multicultural model would also be useful in this area, but as mentioned before, there is little evidence of a multicultural perspective being maintained over more than three generations.

CONCLUSION

We suggest that the ethnic minority people who develop these skills will have better physical and psychological health than those who do not. We also think that they will outperform their monoculturally competent peers in vocational and academic endeavors.

There is widespread agreement that failure to achieve equal partnership for minorities in the academic, social, and economic life of the United States will have disastrous effects for this society. A vital step in the development of an effective partnership involves moving away from the assumptions of the linear model of cultural acquisition, which has a negative impact on the minority individual, to a clearer understanding of the process of developing cul-

TABLE 2
Degree to Which Models of Second-Culture Acquisition Facilitate Acquisition of the Skills Related to Bicultural Competence

Model	1	2	3	4	5	6
Assimilation	Low	Low	Low	Low	Low	Low
Acculturation	Low	Low	Moderate	Moderate	Low	Low
Alternation	High	High	High	High	High	High
Multicultural	Moderate	Moderate	Moderate	Moderate	Moderate	Moderate
Fusion	Moderate	Moderate	Moderate	Low	Low	Moderate

Note: 1 = Knowledge of cultural beliefs and values; 2 = positive attitude toward both groups; 3 = bicultural efficacy; 4 = communication competency; 5 = role repertoire; 6 = groundedness.

tural competence as a two-way street. This will require that members of both the minority and majority cultures better understand, appreciate, and become skilled in one another's cultures. We hope that the ideas expressed here will serve to facilitate that process.

REFERENCES

Ablon, G. (1964). Relocated American Indians in the San Francisco Bay area: Social interaction and Indian identity. *Human Organization, 23*, 296–304.

Adler, P. S. (1975). The transitional experience: An alternative view of cultural shock. *Journal of Humanistic Psychology, 15*, 13–23.

Akao, S. F. (1983). Biculturalism and barriers to learning among Michigan Indian adult students. *Dissertation Abstracts International, 44*, 3572A. (University Microfilms No. DA8407162)

Atkinson, D. R., & Gim, R. H. (1989). Asian-American cultural identity and attitudes toward mental health services. *Journal of Counseling Psychology, 36*, 209–212.

Atkinson, D. R., Morten, G., & Sue, D. W. (1989). Proposed minority identity development model. In D. R. Atkinson, G. Morten, & D. W. Sue (Eds.), *Counseling American minorities: A cross-cultural perspective* (pp. 35–52). Dubuque, IA: William C. Brown.

Baker, F. M. (1987). The Afro-American life cycle: Success, failure, and mental health. *Journal of the National Medical Association, 79*, 625–633.

Bandura, A. (1978). The self system in reciprocal determinism. *American Psychologist, 33*, 344–358.

Bandura, A. (1986). *The foundations of social thought and action.* Englewood Cliffs, NJ: Erlbaum.

Barger, W. K. (1977). Culture change and psychological adjustment. *American Ethnologist, 4*, 471–495.

Beauvais, F. (1992). Characteristics of Indian youth and drug use. *American Indian and Alaskan Native Mental Health Research: The Journal of the National Center, 5*(1), 51–67.

Beiser, M. (1987). Influences of time, ethnicity, and attachment on depression in Southeast Asian refugees. *American Journal of Psychiatry, 145*, 46–51.

Bennett, L. (Ed.). (1991). How Black creativity is changing America [Special issue]. *Ebony, 66*(10).

Berry, J. W. (1984). Cultural relations in plural societies: Alternatives to segregation and their sociopsychological implications. In N. Miller & M. Brewer (Eds.), *Groups in contact* (pp. 11–27). San Diego, CA: Academic Press.

Berry, J. W. (1986). Multiculturalism and psychology in plural societies. In L. H. Ekstrand (Ed.), *Ethnic minorities and immigrants in a cross-cultural perspective* (pp. 37–51). Lisse, The Netherlands: Swets & Zeitlinger.

Berry, J. W., & Annis, R. C. (1974). Acculturation stress: The role of ecology, culture and differentiation. *Journal of Cross-Cultural Psychology, 5*, 382–406.

Berry, J. W., Kim, U., Power, S., Young, M., & Bujaki, M. (1989). Acculturation attitudes in plural societies. *Applied Psychology: An International Review, 38*, 185–206.

Berry, J. W., Poortinga, Y. P., Segall, M. H., & Dasen, P. R. (1992). *Cross-cultural psychology: Research and applications.* New York: Cambridge University Press.

Bettes, B. A., Dusenbury, L., Kerner, J., James-Ortiz, S., & Botvin, G. J. (1990). Ethnicity and psychosocial factors in alcohol and tobacco use in adolescence. *Child Development, 61*, 557–565.

Beuke, V. L. (1978). The relationship of cultural identification to personal adjustment of American Indian children in segregated and integrated schools. *Dissertation Abstracts International, 38*, 7203A. (University Microfilms No. 7809310)

Boyce, W., & Boyce, T. (1983). Acculturation and changes in health among Navajo boarding school students. *Social Science and Medicine, 17*, 219–226.

Brown, P. M. (1990). Biracial identity and social marginality. *Child and Adolescent Social Work Journal, 7*, 319–337.

Buriel, R., & Saenz, E. (1980). Psychocultural characteristics of college-bound and noncollege-bound Chicanas. *Journal of Social Psychology, 110,* 245–251.

Burnam, M. A., Telles, C. A., Karno, M., Hough, R. L., & Escobar, J. I. (1987). Measurement of acculturation in a community population of Mexican Americans. *Hispanic Journal of Behavioral Sciences, 9,* 105–130.

Cantrall, B., & Pete, L. (1990, April). *Navajo culture: A bridge to the rest of the world.* Paper presented at the annual meeting of the American Educational Research Association. Boston.

Chadwick, B. A., & Strauss, J. H. (1975). The assimilation of American Indians into urban society: The Seattle case. *Human Organization, 34,* 359–369.

Chance, N. A. (1965). Acculturation, self-identification, and personality adjustment. *American Anthropologist, 67,* 372–393.

Clement, R., Gardner, R. C., & Smythe, P. C. (1977). Motivational variables in second language acquisition: A study of francophones learning English. *Canadian Journal of Behavioral Science, 9,* 123–133.

Comer, J. P. (1980). *School power.* New York: Free Press.

Comer, J. P. (1985). Social policy and mental health of Black children. *Journal of the American Academy of Child Psychiatry, 24,* 175–181.

Cross, W. E. (1971). The Negro-to-Black conversion experience: Toward a psychology of Black liberation. *Black World, 20,* 13–27.

Cuellar, I., Harris, L. C., & Naron, N. (1981). Evaluation of a bilingual treatment program for Mexican American psychiatric inpatients. In A. Barron (Ed.), *Explorations in Chicano psychology* (pp. 165–186). New York: Praeger.

Curtis, P. A. (1990). The consequences of acculturation to service delivery and research with Hispanic families. *Child and Adolescent Social Work, 7,* 147–159.

De La Torre, M. (1977). Towards a definition of Chicano mental disorder: An exploration of the acculturation and ethnic identity process of Chicano psychiatric outpatients. *Dissertation Abstracts International, 39,* 4025B. (University Microfilms No. 7901909)

Dornic, S. M. (1985). Immigrants, language and stress. In L. H. Ekstrand (Ed.), *Ethnic minorities and immigrants in a cross-cultural perspective* (pp. 149–157). Lisse, The Netherlands: Swets & Zeitlinger.

DuBois, W. E. B. (1961). *The soul of black folks: Essays and sketches.* New York: Fawcett.

Edwards, J. R. (1981). The context of bilingual education. *Journal of Multilingual and Multicultural Development, 2,* 25–44.

Ekstrand, L. H. (1978). Bilingual and bicultural adaptation. In *Educational and psychological interactions* (pp. 1–72). Malmo, Sweden: School of Education.

Erickson, E. (1950). *Childhood and society.* New York: Norton.

Erickson, E. (1968). *Identity, youth, and crisis.* New York: Norton.

Fernandez-Barillas, H. J., & Morrison, T. L. (1984). Cultural affiliation and adjustment among male Mexican-American college students. *Psychological Reports, 55,* 855–860.

Fisher, R. I. (1974). A study of non-intellectual attributes of Chicanos in a first grade bilingual-bicultural program. *Journal of Educational Research, 67,* 323–328.

Fishman, J. A. (1989). Bilingualism and biculturalism as individual and societal phenomena. *Journal of Multilingual and Multicultural Development, 1,* 3–15.

Fordham, S. (1988). Racelessness as a factor in Black students' school success: Pragmatic strategy or pyrrhic victory. *Harvard Educational Review, 58,* 54–84.

Fraser, M. W., & Pecora, P. J. (1985–1986). Psychological adaptation among Indochinese refugees. *Journal of Applied Social Sciences, 10,* 20–39.

Garcia, H. S. (1983). Bilingualism, biculturalism and the educational system. *Journal of Non-White Concerns in Personnel and Guidance, 11,* 67–74.

Gim, R. H., Atkinson, D. R., & Whiteley, S. (1990). Asian-American acculturation, severity of concerns, and willingness to see a counselor. *Journal of Counseling Psychology, 37*, 281–285.

Gleason, P. (1979). Confusion compounded: The melting pot in the 1960's and 1970's. *Ethnicity, 6*, 10–20.

Goldberg, M. M. (1941). A qualification of the marginal man theory. *American Sociological Review, 6*, 52–58.

Golden, J. G. (1987). Acculturation, biculturalism and marginality: A study of Korean-American high school students. *Dissertation Abstracts International, 48*, 1135A. (University Microfilms No. DA8716257)

Goldlust, J., & Richmond, A. H. (1974). A multivariate model of immigrant adaptation. *International Migration Review, 8*, 193–225.

Gonzalez, M. (1986). A study of the effects of strength of ethnic identity and amount of contact with the dominant culture on the stress in acculturation. *Dissertation Abstracts International, 47*, 2164B. (University Microfilms No. DA8616648)

Gordon, M. M. (1964). *Assimilation in American life.* New York: Oxford University Press.

Gordon, M. M. (1978). *Human nature, class, and ethnicity.* New York: Oxford University Press.

Green, A. W. (1947). A re-examination of the marginal man concept. *Social Forces, 26*, 167–171.

Gutierrez, F. J. (1981). A process model of bicultural personality development. *Dissertation Abstracts International, 42*, 3871B. (University Microfilms No. DA8203892)

Gutierrez, J., & Sameroff, A. (1990). Determinants of complexity in Mexican-American mother's conceptions of child development. *Child Development, 61*, 384–394.

Guzman, M. E. (1986). Acculturation of Mexican adolescents. *Dissertation Abstracts International, 47*, 2166B. (University Microfilms No. DA8617666)

Hallowell, A. I. (1957). The impact of the American Indian on American culture. *American Anthropologist, 59*, 201–217.

Helms, J. E. (1990). *Black and White racial identity theory, research, and practice.* Westport, CT: Greenwood Press.

Hernandez, S. M. (1981). Acculturation and biculturalism among Puerto Ricans in Lamont, California. *Dissertation Abstracts International, 42*, 428B. (University Microfilms No. 8113419)

Hess, R. S., & Street, E. M. (1991). The effect of acculturation on the relationship of counselor ethnicity and client ratings. *Journal of Counseling Psychology, 38*, 71–75.

Hurdle, D. E. (1991). The ethnic group experience. *Social Work With Groups, 13*, 59–68.

Johnston, R. (1976). The concept of the "marginal man": A refinement of the term. *Australian and New Zealand Journal of Science, 12*, 145–147.

Kazaleh, F. A. (1986). Biculturalism and adjustment: A study of Ramallah-American adolescents in Jacksonville, Florida. *Dissertation Abstracts International, 47*, 448A. (University Microfilms No. DA8609672)

Kelly, M. C. (1971). Las fiestas como reflejo del order social: El caso de San Xavier del Bac. *America Indigena, 31*, 141–161.

Kerchoff, A. C., & McCormick, T. C. (1955). Marginal status and marginal personality. *Social Forces, 34*, 48–55.

Kim, Y. Y. (1979). Toward an interactive theory of communication-acculturation. In D. Nimmo (Ed.), *Communication yearbook 3* (pp. 435–453). New Brunswick, NJ: Transaction Books.

LaFromboise, T. D. (1983). *Assertion training with American Indians.* Las Cruces, NM: ERIC Clearinghouse on Rural Education.

LaFromboise, T. D., Berman, J. S., & Sohi, B. K. (1993). American Indian women. In L. Comas-Diaz & B. Green (Eds.), *Mental health and women of color.* New York: Guilford Press.

LaFromboise, T. D., & Rowe, W. (1983). Skills training for bicultural competence: Rationale and application. *Journal of Counseling Psychology, 30,* 589–595.

Lambert, W. E. (1977). The effects of bilingualism in the individual. In P. W. Hornby (Ed.), *Bilingualism: Psychological, social and educational implications* (pp. 15–27). San Diego, CA: Academic Press.

Lang, J. G., Muñoz, R. F., Bernal, G., & Sorensen, J. L. (1982). Quality of life and psychological well-being in a bicultural Latino community. *Hispanic Journal of Behavioral Sciences, 4,* 433–450.

Levine, R. A. (1982). *Culture, behavior, and personality* (2nd ed.). Chicago: Aldine.

Lewis, E. A., & Ford, B. (1991). The network utilization project: Incorporating traditional strengths of African-American families into group work practice. *Social Work With Groups, 13,* 7–22.

Little Soldier, L. (1985). To soar with the eagles: Enculturation and acculturation of Indian Children. *Childhood Education, 61,* 185–191.

Mallea, J. (1988). Canadian dualism and pluralism: Tensions, contradictions and emerging resolutions. In J. Berry & R. Annis (Eds.), *Ethnic psychology: Research and practice with immigrants, refugees, Native peoples, ethnic groups and sojourners* (pp. 13–37). Berwyn, PA: Swets North America.

Martinez, A. R. (1987). The effects of acculturation and racial identity on self-esteem and psychological well-being among young Puerto Ricans. *Dissertation Abstracts International, 49,* 916B. (University Microfilms No. DA8801737)

McClure, E. (1977). Aspects of code-switching in the discourse of bilingual Mexican-American children. In M. Saville-Troike (Ed.), *Linguistics and anthropology* (pp. 93–115). Washington, DC: Georgetown University Press.

McFee, M. (1968). The 150% man, a product of Blackfeet acculturation. *American Anthropologist, 70,* 1096–1107.

McKirnan, D. J., & Hamayan, E. V. (1984). Speech norms and attitudes toward outgroup members: A test of a model in a bicultural context. *Journal of Language and Social Psychology, 3,* 21–38.

Mego, D. K. (1988). The acculturation, psychosocial development and Jewish identity of Soviet Jewish emigres. *Dissertation Abstracts International, 49,* 4605B. (University Microfilms No. DA8821946)

Mendoza, A. P. (1981). Responding to stress: Ethnic and sex differences in coping behavior. In A. Baron (Ed.), *Explorations in Chicano psychology* (pp. 187–211). New York: Praeger.

Mullender, A., & Miller, D. (1985). The Ebony group: Black children in white foster homes. *Adoption and Fostering, 9*(1), 33–40, 49.

Murphy, H. B. M. (1977). Migration, culture and mental health. *Psychological Medicine, 7,* 677–684.

Northover, M. (1988). Bilingual or "dual linguistic identities"? In J. Berry & R. Annis (Eds.), *Ethnic psychology: Research and practice with immigrants, refugees, Native peoples, ethnic groups and sojourners* (pp. 207–216). Berwyn, PA: Swets North America.

Oetting, E. R., & Beauvais, F. (1990–1991). Orthogonal cultural identification theory: The cultural identification of minority adolescents. *International Journal of the Addictions, 25,* 655–685.

Oetting, E. R., Edwards, R. W., & Beauvais, F. (1989). Drugs and Native American youth. In B. Segal (Ed.), *Perspectives on adolescent drug use* (pp. 1–34). New York: Harworth Press.

Ogbu, J. U. (1979). Social stratification and the socialization of competence. *Anthropology and Education Quarterly, 10,* 3–20.

Ogbu, J. U., & Matute-Bianchi, M. A. (1986). Understanding sociocultural factors: Knowledge, identity, and social adjustment. In California State Department of Education, Bilingual Education Office, *Beyond language: Social and cultural factors in schooling* (pp. 73–142). Sacramento, CA: California State University–Los Angeles, Evaluation, Dissemination and Assessment Center.

Olmedo, E. L., & Padilla, A. M. (1978). Empirical and construct validation of a measure of acculturation for Mexican Americans. *Journal of Social Psychology, 105,* 179–187.

Padilla, A. M. (1980). *Acculturation: Theory, models and some new findings.* Boulder, CO: Westview Press.

Palinkas, L. A. (1982). Ethnicity, identity and mental health: The use of rhetoric in an immigrant Chinese church. *Journal of Psychoanalytic Anthropology, 5,* 235–258.

Palleja, J. (1987). The impact of cultural identification on the behavior of second generation Puerto Rican adolescents. *Dissertation Abstracts International, 48,* 1541A. (University Microfilms No. DA8715043)

Park, R. E. (1928). Human migration and the marginal man. *American Journal of Sociology, 5,* 881–893.

Pasquali, E. A. (1985). The impact of acculturation on the eating habits of elderly immigrants: A Cuban example. *Journal of Nutrition for the Elderly, 5,* 27–36.

Peal, E., & Lambert, W. (1962). The relation of bilingualism to intelligence. *Psychological Monographs, 76*(27).

Pertusali, L. (1988). Beyond segregation or integration: A case study from effective Native American education. *Journal of American Indian Education, 27,* 10–20.

Pierce, R. C., Clark, M., & Kaufman, S. (1978). Generation and ethnic identity: A typological analysis. *International Journal of Aging and Human Development, 9,* 19–29.

Plas, J. M., & Bellet, W. (1983). Assessment of the value-attitude orientations of American Indian children. *Journal of School Psychology, 21,* 57–64.

Polgar, S. (1960). Biculturation of Mesquakie teenage boys. *American Anthropologist, 62,* 217–235.

Ponce, F. Q., & Atkinson, D. R. (1989). Mexican-American acculturation, counselor ethnicity, counseling style, and perceived counselor credibility. *Journal of Counseling Psychology, 36,* 203–208.

Porte, Z., & Torney-Purta, J. (1987). Depression and academic achievement among Indochinese refugee unaccompanied minors in ethnic and nonethnic placements. *American Journal of Orthopsychiatry, 57,* 536–547.

Prigoff, A. W. (1984). Self-esteem, ethnic identity, job aspiration and school stress on Mexican American youth in a Midwest urban barrio. *Dissertation Abstracts International, 45,* 2257A. (University Microfilms No. DA8420403)

Ramirez, M., III. (1984). Assessing and understanding biculturalism—Multiculturalism in Mexican-American adults. In J. L. Martinez & R. H. Mendoza (Eds.), *Chicano psychology* (pp. 77–94). San Diego, CA: Academic Press.

Rashid, H. M. (1984). Promoting biculturalism in young African-American children. *Young Children, 39,* 13–23.

Red Horse, J. (1980). Family structure and value orientation in American Indians. *Social Casework, 61,* 462–467.

Richman, J. A., Gaviria, M., Flaherty, J. A., Birz, S., & Wintrob, R. M. (1987). The process of acculturation: Theoretical perspectives and an empirical investigation in Peru. *Social Science and Medicine, 25,* 839–847.

Robinson, P. (1985). Language retention among Canadian Indians: A simultaneous model with dichotomous endogenous variables. *American Sociological Review, 50,* 515–529.

Rodriguez, C. (1975). A cost-benefit analysis of subjective factors affecting assimilation: Puerto Ricans. *Ethnicity, 2,* 66–80.

Rogler, L. H., Cortes, D. E., & Malgady, R. G. (1991). Acculturation and mental health status among Hispanics. *American Psychologist, 46,* 585–597.

Rosenthal, D. A. (1987). Ethnic identity development in adolescents. In J. S. Phinney & M. J. Rotheram (Eds.), *Children's ethnic socialization* (pp. 156–179). Newbury Park, CA: Sage.

Rozek, F. (1980). The role of internal conflict in the successful acculturation of Russian Jewish immigrants. *Dissertation Abstracts International, 41,* 2778B. (University Microfilms No. 8028799)

Ruben, B. D., & Kealey, D. J. (1979). Behavioral assessment of communication competency and the prediction of cross-cultural adaptation. *International Journal of Intercultural Relations, 3,* 15–47.

Ruiz, R. (1981). Cultural and historical perspectives in counseling Hispanics. In D. Sue (Ed.), *Counseling the culturally different* (pp. 186–215). New York: Wiley.

Sameroff, A. J. (1982). Development and the dialectic: The need for a systems approach. *Minnesota Symposia on Child Psychology, 15*, 83–103.

Sampson, E. E. (1988). The debate on individualism: Indigenous psychologies of the individual and their role in personal and societal functioning. *American Psychologist, 43*, 15–22.

Saville-Troike, M. (1981). *The development of bilingual and bicultural competence in young children.* Urbana, IL: Clearinghouse on Elementary and Early Childhood Education. (ERIC Document Reproduction Service No. ED 206 376)

Schiller, P. M. (1987). Biculturalism and psychosocial adjustment among Native American university students. *Dissertation Abstracts International, 48*, 1542A. (University Microfilms No. DA8720632)

Schlossberg, N. K. (1981). A model for analyzing human adaptation to transition. *The Counseling Psychologist, 9*, 2–36.

Schwarzer, R., Bowler, R., & Rauch, S. (1985). Psychological indicators of acculturation: Self-esteem, racial tension and inter-ethnic contact. In L. Ekstrand (Ed.). *Ethnic minorities and immigrants in a cross-cultural perspective* (pp. 211–229). Lisse, The Netherlands: Swets & Zeitlinger.

Segall, M. M. (1986). Culture and behavior: Psychology in global perspective. *Annual Review of Psychology, 37*, 523–564.

Simard, L. M., & Taylor, D. M. (1973). The potential for bicultural communication in a dyadic situation. *Canadian Journal of Behavioral Science, 5*, 211–255.

Smither, R. (1982). Human migration and the acculturation of minorities. *Human Relations, 35*, 57–68.

Sodowsky, G. R., & Carey, J. C. (1988). Relationship between acculturation-related demographics and cultural attitudes of an Asian-Indian immigrant group. *Journal of Multicultural Counseling and Development, 16*, 117–136.

Spencer, M. B., Brookins, G. K., & Allen, W. R. (Eds.). (1985). *Beginnings: The social and affective development of Black children.* Hillsdale, NJ: Erlbaum.

Spindler, L. S. (1952). Witchcraft in Menomoni acculturation. *American Anthropologist, 54*, 593–602.

Stonequist, E. V. (1935). The problem of marginal man. *American Journal of Sociology, 7*, 1–12.

Sue, D. W., & Sue, D. (1990). *Counseling the culturally different* (2nd ed.). New York: Wiley.

Sundberg, N. D., Snowden, L. R., & Reynolds, W. M. (1978). Toward assessment of personal competence and incompetence in life situations. *American Review of Psychology, 29*, 174–221.

Sung, B. L. (1985). Bicultural conflicts in Chinese immigrant children. *Journal of Comparative Family Studies, 16*, 255–269.

Szapocznik, J., & Kurtines, W. (1980). Acculturation, biculturalism and adjustment among Cuban Americans. In A. M. Padilla (Ed.), *Psychological dimensions on the acculturation process: Theory, models, and some new findings* (pp. 139–159). Boulder, CO: Westview Press.

Szapocznik, J., Kurtines, W., & Fernandez, T. (1980). Bicultural involvement and adjustment in Hispanic-American youths. *International Journal of Intercultural Relations, 4*, 353–365.

Szapocznik, J., Rio, A., Perez-Vidal, A., Kurtines, W., Hervis, O., & Santisteban, D. (1986). Bicultural effectiveness training (BET): An experimental test of an intervention modality for families experiencing intergenerational/intercultural conflict. *Hispanic Journal of Behavioral Sciences, 8*, 303–330.

Szapocznik, J., Santisteban, D., Kurtines, W., Perez-Vidal, A., & Hervis, O. (1984). Bicultural effectiveness training: A treatment intervention for enhancing intercultural adjustment in Cuban American families. *Hispanic Journal of Behavioral Sciences, 6*, 317–344.

Szapocznik, J., Scopetta, M. A., Kurtines, W., & Arandale, M. A. (1978). Theory and measurement of acculturation. *Interamerican Journal of Psychology, 12*, 113–120.

Taft, R. (1977). Coping with unfamiliar cultures. In N. Warren (Ed.), *Studies in cross-cultural psychology* (Vol. 1, pp. 121–153). San Diego, CA: Academic Press.

Thomas, G. E. (1983). The deficit, difference, and bicultural theories of Black dialect and nonstandard English. *Urban Review, 15*, 107–118.

Thompson, L. (1948). Attitudes and acculturation. *American Anthropologist, 50*, 200–215.

Topper, M. D., & Johnson, L. (1980). Effects of forced relocation on Navajo mental patients from the former Navajo-Hopi joint use area. *White Cloud Journal, 2*(1), 3–7.

Tormes, Y. (1985). Bilingual education, English as a second language and equity in higher education. *Dissertation Abstracts International, 46*, 3314A. (University Microfilms No. DA8601699)

Triandis, H. C. (1980). A theoretical framework for the study of bilingual-bicultural adaption. *International Review of Applied Psychology, 29*, 7–16.

Trimble, J. (1981). Value differentials and their importance in counseling American Indians. In P. Pedersen (Ed.), *Counseling across cultures* (pp. 203–226). Honolulu: University of Hawaii Press.

Van Den Bergh, N. (1991). Managing biculturalism at the workplace: A group approach. In K. L. Chau (Ed.), *Ethnicity and biculturalism* (pp. 71–84). New York: Haworth Press.

Vasquez, M. J., & McKinley, D. L. (1982). Supervision: A conceptual model—reactions and extension. *The Counseling Psychologist, 10*, 59–63.

Vogt, E. Z. (1957). The acculturation of American Indians. *Annals of the American Academy of Political and Social Science, 311*, 137–146.

Weatherford, J. (1988). *Indian givers: How the Indians of the Americas transformed the world.* New York: Fawcett Columbine.

Williams, C. L., & Berry, J. W. (1991). Primary prevention of acculturative stress among refugees: Application of psychological theory and practice. *American Psychologist, 46*, 632–641.

Young, M. C., & Gardner, R. C. (1990). Modes of acculturation and second language proficiency. *Canadian Journal of Behavioural Science, 22*, 59–71.

Zane, N., Sue, S., Hu, L., & Kwon, J. (1991). Asian-American assertion: A social learning analysis of cultural differences. *Journal of Counseling Psychology, 38*, 63–70.

Zuniga, M. E. (1988). Assessment issues with Chicanas: Practice implications. *Psychotherapy, 25*, 288–293.

This article was prepared at the request of the National Center for American Indian and Alaska Native Mental Health Research and was partially supported by the National Institute of Mental Health Grant 1R01MH42473. We are indebted to the following colleagues: Clifford Barnett, Raphael Diaz, Martin Ford, Amado Padilla, and Wayne Rowe for their constructive feedback on earlier versions of this article.

THINKING CRITICALLY AND APPLYING YOUR KNOWLEDGE

1. Review the five models of biculturalism that LaFromboise and her associates discuss: assimilation, acculturation, alternation, multiculturalism, and fusion. Identify the positive and negative features of each model. How do they differ from each other and how are they similar? (You may want to refer back to Table 1.)

2. How do LaFromboise and her associates define cultural competence? Using their definition, would you say that you are a culturally competent person? A biculturally competent person?

3. LaFromboise and her associates argue that bicultural competence grows out of the alternation model, namely the assumption that it is possible for an individual to know and understand two different cultures and to alter his or her behavior to fit a particular social context. Do you think the alternation model is necessary for bicultural competence to occur? Why or why not?

4. LaFromboise and her associates argue that, far from creating marginality and a divided self, biculturalism may actually produce a life experience more beneficial than living a monocultural life-style. What arguments do they offer for this idea? Can you think of others? Do you agree with their conclusion?

5. Think about some of the ethnic groups in the United States, such as African Americans, Latinos/Hispanics, or Native Americans. How easy do you think it would be for members of these different groups to develop bicultural competence? Do you think there are barriers or facilitating factors that might enable one group to develop bicultural competence more easily than another?

❖ CHAPTER 11 ❖

Negotiating Social Identity When Contexts Change: Maintaining Identification and Responding to Threat

Kathleen A. Ethier and Kay Deaux

How does attending a predominantly Anglo college affect the identity and self-esteem of ethnic minority students? Ethier and Deaux conducted a longitudinal study of Hispanic students during their first year at predominantly Anglo universities. They found that the students' adjustment to the new environment depended heavily on how invested they were in their Hispanic identity. Those with initially strong identification with their ethnicity became involved in cultural activities, maintaining and even increasing their commitment to their Hispanic background. Those with initially weak identification, however, found the new environment to be threatening and actually experienced loss of self-esteem in the new context. This study is important because it shows how ethnic identity may falter or thrive in a new environment where one is in a minority. It also shows the importance of the cultural context for making sense of one's self and one's personal identifications.

ABSTRACT: *The impact of change in context on identity maintenance, the implications of maintenance efforts for group identification, and the effects of perceived threats to identity on self-esteem associated with group membership are examined in a longitudinal study of Hispanic students during their first year at predominately Anglo universities. Whereas ethnic identity is initially linked to the strength of the students' cultural background, maintenance of ethnic identity is accomplished by weakening that link and remooring the identity to the current college context. Results suggest two distinct paths by which students negotiate their ethnic identity in a new context. Students with initially strong ethnic identity become involved in cultural activities, increasing the strength of their identification. In contrast, students with initially weaker identification perceive more threat in the environment, show decreases in self-esteem associated with group membership, lowering identification with their ethnic group. The findings both support social identity theory and illustrate the need for more contextual analyses of identity processes.*

Source: Reprinted from *Journal of Personality and Social Psychology, 67*(2), (1994), 243–251. Copyright © 1994 by the American Psychological Association. Reprinted by permission.

Identification of oneself with other people who share common attributes is an important aspect of self-definition. Theories of social identity, developed by Tajfel (1981), Turner (1987), and others, emphasize the importance of collective membership and the significant effects that group membership can have on behavior. These behaviors include feelings of attraction toward members of the in-group, stereotypic judgments of out-group members, social influence, and preferential treatment toward the in-group (Abrams & Hogg, 1990; Hogg & Abrams, 1988; Turner, 1987).

As a number of investigators have shown, the need for and expression of social identity is not static. Brewer (1991), for example, found that the motivation to claim group membership depends on the competing needs for inclusiveness and uniqueness, whereby people seek an optimal level of distinctiveness in their choice of a collective. What particular identity is claimed can depend on situational cues that make an identity salient or that fit with one's own priorities (Deaux & Major, 1987; Oakes, 1987).

Although the presentation of self may be quite variable, it can also be argued that the self-concept is generally stable across time. Individuals not only view themselves and others in consistent terms, but they actively create social situations that support their views of themselves (Swann, 1983). Across the life span, however, there are transitions that can have significant effects on self-definition (Hormuth, 1990; Ruble, 1994). During these transitions, individuals may find it necessary to adapt in some way to changes in environmental opportunities and demands. These adaptations may involve more than momentary responses to situational pressures; rather, the new situation may elicit fundamental changes in the meaning, importance, or support that a central identity has (Deaux, 1993).

These issues of redefinition and change are particularly interesting when one considers social identity categories that are ascribed to the person, such as ethnicity or gender, and might be thought to be particularly resistant to change. The importance of ethnic identity is well documented. Within the United States, the majority of people who are demographically designated as ethnic group members subjectively claim this identity as well (Waters, 1990). Ethnic identity is embedded in a multidimensional context, related to factors such as language, cultural background, geographic region, social class, and political conflict (Christian, Gadfield, Giles, & Taylor, 1976; Giles, Llado, McKirnan, & Taylor, 1979; Giles, Taylor, & Bourhis, 1977; Giles, Taylor, Lambert, & Albert, 1976; Phinney, 1990). The importance of these links is suggested by Ethier and Deaux's (1990) finding that the strength of ethnic identity is significantly predicted by such factors as the language spoken in the home, the ethnic composition of the neighborhood, and the percentage of a student's friends who were in the same ethnic group.

If a person's group identification is supported by a particular context (Abrams, 1992; Ethier & Deaux, 1990), what happens when the person leaves that context and moves into another? According to social identity and self-categorization theories, contextual change that increases the salience of a particular identity leads to an increase in group identification (Emler & Hopkins, 1990; Oakes, 1987; Waddell & Cairns, 1986). Thus, in a study of Welsh identity, Christian et al. (1976) found that when group conflict was made salient by having subjects write essays about Welsh–English conflict, group identification was stronger.

Studies of the effect of contextual change on social identity have generally been focused on short-term situational changes (Christian et al., 1976; Haslam, Turner, Oakes, & Mc-Garty, 1992; Waddell & Cairns, 1986). Are the issues the same for long-term contextual change? By *change in context*, we do not mean a temporary shift in situation or place (e.g., having to perform a task that has some relation to a particular social identity, or a temporary move from one environment to another). Instead, our question concerns the effects on social identity of a complete change of environment, where the former supports of an identity (e.g., contact with group members) no longer exist as the person has known them. Because we are interested in looking at long-term change, the issues may be more complex, and the predictions of social identity theory and self-categorization theory may need to be expanded.

Salience and Identity Change

Social identity theory and self-categorization theory posit that when identity is made salient, as for example by a change in context, a person will become increasingly identified with his or her group. The concept of salience can be elusive, however, particularly when dealing with long-term changes in context.

There are at least three bases on which one might make predictions about the influence of salience on group identification. First, one might posit that chronic levels of group identification would predict identity salience. Thus, those individuals who are more highly identified with their group would be more likely to experience that identity as salient, independent of situational context. In the specific context of Hispanic students entering college, we would then predict that students with a strong cultural background would be more likely to engage in activities relevant to their ethnic identification.

A second saliency prediction is based on the contrast between a student's self-definition and the current context. Thus, as the research of McGuire and his colleagues shows, people whose status (e.g., ethnicity, gender, or hair color) is a minority in their group are more likely to be aware of that characteristic than those whose status is a majority (McGuire, McGuire, Child, & Fujioka, 1978). This position would suggest that ethnicity would be equally salient for all Hispanic students entering primarily Anglo universities.

A third model of salience would consider the contrast between a student's past background and current context. If these two contexts were markedly different, salience should be greater than if there were no change. By this line of reasoning, students from primarily Hispanic neighborhoods and schools should find ethnicity more salient in the new primarily Anglo environment than students whose previous background more closely resembled their current context.

Thus, although each of these positions is consistent with the prediction from social identity theory that salience increases group identification, each proposes a different basis for determining when identity will be salient. When the change involves large-scale environments studied over an extended period of time, it must also be recognized that considerable variation exists. One specific situation within the general context (e.g., attending a relevant group meeting) may make an identity salient, whereas others (e.g., going to a history class) may not. These variations are in part dependent on individual choices and in part are a function of the opportunity structure available. Because of the possible variation in the natural environment, we would predict that individual differences in salience and identification should be particularly noticeable. As Abrams (1990) has argued, people often make choices about which course of action to follow, and social identity theory needs to take individual variation into account when considering the identity–salience relationship. Group involvement, both before the transition and in the new context, should be an important factor in determining whether an individual experiences increased salience in the new environment.

Identity Maintenance and Change

Social identity, as manifested in natural group memberships, cannot be conceptualized only as a cognitive categorization process. Rather, social identities are supported and sustained by a network of social relationships (Abrams, 1992). During times of transition, the relationship between the individual and his or her environment changes, and the person must adapt to those changes in some way (Hormuth, 1990). If a social identity is supported by a network of relationships, then one would anticipate that a change in context, for example, a change in physical location or a change in the social environment, would have some impact on identity. The ways in which the person had previously maintained the identity are no longer valid or useful in the new context, and the person must change the way in which he or she maintains the identity. Thus, in a new context, maintaining a social identity must include a process of remooring the identity to new social supports. Specifically, we hypothesize that to successfully maintain an identity in a new environment, a person must develop new bases for supporting that identity and, in the process, detach the identity from its supports in the former environment.

Because any activity expended in developing these new links implies commitment to the identity, one could also predict that the process of remooring would in turn strengthen identification with the group (Aronson & Mills, 1959). Thus, although remooring is assumed to imply a decrease in the links to previous bases of identification, it should not result in any decrease in the strength of identification itself.

Responses to Identity Threat

New environments may challenge the meaning or value of an identity. Breakwell (1986) describes a variety of situations, including the loss of employment, the loss of a spouse, and cultural conflicts, that pose threats to identity. If severe enough, threats can call into question the very existence of an identity. In other cases, the existence of the identity may not be threatened, but rather the meanings or value associated with the identity are questioned. The latter process is particularly likely when an identity is associated with membership in an ascribed category, for example, race, ethnicity, or gender. When experiencing threat to these identities, individuals are unlikely to consider abandoning the identity but may well alter the way that they feel about that identity. In other words, one's identification with the group does not change, but the self-esteem associated with that group becomes more negative. Consistent with this line of reasoning, Frable, Wortman, Joseph, Kirscht, & Kessler (1994) found that gay men who perceive more stigmatization of their group have lower self-esteem.

There has been disagreement within social identity theory concerning the consequences of lowered self-esteem. According to social identity theory, the "need for positive self-esteem" (Turner, 1982, p. 33) is a fundamental human motivation. When an identity is made salient, this need is satisfied by positive evaluation of one's own group. However, what if a positive evaluation is not possible? Tajfel (1981) would predict that, if possible, the individual would leave the group; however, a person cannot easily leave an ascribed category. Hogg and Abrams (1990) pointed out the difficulty in finding support for the self-esteem hypothesis and suggested that other self-related motives (e.g., self-consistency) might override the motive for positive self-esteem. They argued that individuals are motivated to categorize themselves in the most meaningful way as dictated by the context. This process may result in a number of behaviors, including intergroup discrimination, acquiescence, intragroup normative competition, elevated self-esteem, or depressed self-esteem, and these behaviors should be dictated by the "sociocultural and contextual factors" (p. 47). Thus, if it is not realistic to derive positive self-esteem from group membership, then other motives, such as the need to maintain a coherent and stable self-concept, could keep the individual from discarding the group membership. In other words, it might be more beneficial to live with depressed self-esteem than to lower group identification, especially if that group identification is difficult to forsake. On the other hand, if group identification is not strong, then the need for stability of the identity should also be weaker. In this case, the individual would be more likely to lower group identification to avoid further experiences of low self-esteem. In other words, the social identity theory prediction that lowered self-esteem will cause an individual to leave the group would be supported in a psychological sense, even if actual group membership could not be changed. Thus, we suggest that the relationship between self-esteem and group identification will vary depending on the importance of group membership.

In minimal group situations, like those often used in social identity research, there is probably less variation in group identification than is found in natural groups. Although individuals may respond as members of the minimal group, these reactions do not mean that their identification with the group is strong or that group membership is central to the person. Thus, in these situations it would not be detrimental to the need for stability for the person to leave the group as a result of low self-esteem. By examining natural groups such as ethnic or racial groups in which individuals have spent their lives as group members, lived in communities with other group members, and spoken the same language as other group members, we can examine a situation in which different goals may have priority. In sum, we suggest that prior group involvement is an important factor in determining whether an individual experiences chronic salience, whether he or she becomes involved in the group in the new context, and whether he or she experiences the new context as threatening to his or her identity.

Research Questions

Ethier and Deaux (1990) explored both identity supports and perceptions of threat to ethnic identity in a study of Hispanic students who had begun their first year of university at primarily Anglo colleges. The present study extends those initial findings with a longitudinal investigation over the course of the students' first full year of college, investigating the relationships among threat, maintenance efforts, and change in a specific social identity. By interviewing the students at three times during their first year at college, we could examine the consequences for social identity in a naturally occurring situation that involves major contextual change. In so doing, we extend the range of investigation for social identity theories.

We expected these students to adapt to their new environment in several ways. First, we expected to see general trends of remooring, that is that students would change the way they supported their Hispanic identity, moving from family and home culture to group involvement at school. Second, we expected that the students would make efforts to maintain stability, so that those students who were more involved in their ethnic group would be more likely to join Hispanic groups and have Hispanic friends at the university. We also expected that group involvement would be positively related to changes in ethnic identity. Third, we considered the possibility that students would react in different ways to the new environment as a function of the strength of their ethnic identification and prior background variables and that the relationship between threat, involvement, and self-esteem would be influenced by identification and cultural background.

METHOD

Sample and Recruitment Procedure

Hispanic[1] first-year students at two Ivy League universities were identified through lists provided either by the Dean of Students office at the university or through the university telephone directory. Sixty-five students were telephoned and asked to participate in a study about Hispanic students in their first year of college. All students who were contacted resided on the campus. Four students declined to participate; 16 agreed but did not appear for their first scheduled interview.

Students who agreed to participate were scheduled for a first interview during late November or early December of their first semester at university. Two additional interviews were scheduled during the academic year. The second interview took place in February, shortly after students returned from the holiday break; the third was conducted in May as the students were completing their first year in college. All interviews took place in university buildings; each interview lasted approximately 45 min and was conducted in Eng-

---

[1] Those students who did claim this identity used a variety of terms to label themselves including *Latino, Chicana, Puerto Rican,* and *Mexican-American* in addition to *Hispanic.* Without attempting to resolve the political issues involved here, we use *Hispanic* as the more inclusive term.

lish. Students were paid $5 for their participation in each interview. Although the repeated testing necessitated keeping a record of names and questionnaires, these lists were confidential and kept separate from the data.

A total of 45 students (28 men and 17 women) participated in the first interview. Of this total, 39 students (87%) participated at both Time 1 and Time 2 and 36 students (80%) were interviewed on all three occasions. The modal age of the students was 18 years, with a range of 17 to 19 years. All of the students were of Hispanic background, but there was a mixture of nationalities. Twenty-seven of the students classified themselves as Mexican-American. Most of these students were born in the United States; however, 6 were born in Mexico and moved to the United States before the age of 16. Seventeen students classified themselves as Puerto Rican. Of this number, 11 were born on the mainland and 6 were from Puerto Rico. One student was of Spanish descent.

Measures

The key concepts measured were identity, self-esteem associated with group membership, and perceptions of threat. Each of these variables was assessed at each of the three interviews. In addition, questions concerning past and present context for ethnic identity were included at each interview.

Identity. Identity was assessed through a combination of qualitative and quantitative methods. First, to assess the pattern of identities by which individuals defined themselves, we asked each student to name all of the identities that were important to him or her. In the instructions for this task, they were given possible examples (e.g., age, gender, relationships to other people, and race or ethnicity). If any of a preestablished set of identities (Hispanic, student, son or daughter, family member, and friend) was not named voluntarily, the interviewer specifically asked the student whether he or she had these as part of the self-concept.[2] Students were then asked to list the attributes or characteristics that they associated with each identity to understand the subjective meaning that students attached to their identities. The personal significance or importance of an identity was assessed in quantitative terms with two measures. First, students were asked to rate the importance of each identity that they named on a scale of 1 (*not at all important*) to 7 (*very important*). The second measure of group identification was the identity subscale of the Collective Self-Esteem Scale (Luhtanen & Crocker, 1992), with items written to refer to Hispanic identity specifically. This scale consists of four items, including "Being Hispanic is an important reflection of who I am," and "Being Hispanic is an important part of my self-image." As reported in Ethier and Deaux (1990), coefficient alpha for this scale at Time 1 was .92. Similar alpha coefficients were obtained for Times 2 and 3 (.91 and .91, respectively).

---

[2] Although this probe increases the frequency with which a given identity is mentioned, it by no means results in universal endorsement. In our sample, 13% of the students did not claim this identity, even after being prompted.

Collective self-esteem. Self-esteem can be conceptualized in terms of *personal self-esteem*, referring to a general evaluation of one's individual self, or *collective self-esteem*,[3] referring to one's membership in collective groups. In this study, we define self-esteem in collective terms, referring to one's evaluation of one's ethnic group membership. Self-esteem was assessed using the Private Acceptance subscale of Luhtanen and Crocker's (1992) Collective Self-Esteem Scale. Again, items were phrased in terms of Hispanic identity, specifically. This subscale consists of four items, including "In general, I'm glad that I'm Hispanic" and "I often regret that I am Hispanic." As reported in Ethier and Deaux (1990), coefficient alpha for this scale at Time 1 was .66. Identical alpha coefficients were obtained for Times 2 and 3.

Perceptions of threat. Perceptions of threat to one's ethnic identity were assessed by a six-item scale developed by us. This scale included items such as "I feel that my ethnicity is incompatible with the new people I am meeting and the new things I am learning" and "I cannot talk to my friends at school about my family or my culture."[4] Students answered each item on a 7-point scale, indicating whether they had experienced that feeling or situation (1 = *not at all*, 7 = *a great deal*). The possible range of scores was 6 to 42; the obtained range was 6 to 41. Coefficient alpha for Times 1, 2, and 3 were .66, .82, and .72, respectively.

Ethnic involvement. At each interview, a variety of questions were asked to assess the extent of involvement with family, friends, and Hispanic culture. In the initial interview, these questions were directed at community and family background. Responses to six questions were combined to form an index termed *Strength of Cultural Background* (SCB; α = .80). Items included in this index referred to mother's and father's birthplace, language spoken in the home, percentage of home community that was Hispanic, and percentage of Hispanic high school friends.

At the second and third interviews, questions were directed at the level of students' involvement in ethnic culture at school. At Time 2, these questions referred to involvement during the first semester, and at Time 3, they referred to involvement during the second semester. Again, composite indexes were developed. Hispanic activity consisted of two items, $rs(38)$ = .70 at Time 2 and .74 at Time 3, that asked about participation in Hispanic activities at college and percentage of current friends who were Hispanic.

RESULTS

Stability of Measures

Table 1 presents the means and standard deviations for each of the major variables in the study at each of the three occasions. Table 2 shows the correlations of each measure across the three occasions of testing. In the case of the identities, common element correlations

---

[3] We use the term *collective self-esteem* to refer to self-esteem associated with group membership. Luhtanen and Crocker's Collective Self-Esteem Scale actually measures four different dimensions of feeling associated with group membership (membership, private acceptance, public acceptance, and identification). In the present study, we use the Private Acceptance subscale, which refers to personal feelings about the group, to index collective self-esteem.

[4] See Ethier and Deaux (1990, p. 433) for a full listing of the items of the Perceived Threat scale.

TABLE 1
Means and Standard Deviations of Major Variables

Variable	Time		
	1	2	3
Number of identities			
M	7.6	6.8	7.4
SD	2.4	1.8	1.6
Hispanic importance			
M	4.4	4.4	4.6
SD	2.5	2.5	2.3
Identification			
M	19.5	20.4	19.3
SD	6.4	5.6	5.5
Self-esteem			
M	24.1	23.9	23.8
SD	3.6	3.2	3.3
Perceptions of threat			
M	12.1	13.1	12.7*
SD	5.4	7.9	5.8

*$p < .06$.

TABLE 2
Stability of Variables Across Testing Occasions

Variable	Testing occasions		
	1–2	1–3	2–3
Identities named	.69	.70	.79
Hispanic importance	.75	.70	.96
Identification	.72	.82	.74
Self-esteem	.59	.42	.74
Perception of threat	.78	.58	.70

Note: $N = 39$ for the Occasion 1–2 comparison and $N = 36$ for the other comparisons.

(McNemar, 1962) were used to determine the repetition of elements across time for qualitative data. High correlations in this case indicate that students were naming a similar set of identities on the different occasions.

As Table 1 shows, there were no mean changes in the number of identities that students mentioned, the importance that they attached to their Hispanic identity, or the level of self-esteem associated with ethnic identity. Perceptions of threat to the Hispanic identity did change during the course of the year, however, $F(2, 70) = 2.91$, $p < .06$. A trend analysis shows a significant curvilinear trend in the data, $F(1, 102) = 31.25$, $p < .01$. As the means in Table 1 show, perceived threats were the strongest at Time 2, soon after students had returned from holiday break and were beginning the second semester, but threat did not diminish substantially over the course of the second semester.

As evident in Table 2, all of the measures were highly stable with the exception of self-esteem associated with group membership and, to a lesser extent, perceptions of threat. In both cases, the correlations are lowest for the longest interval of time, from early fall to late spring, as would be expected. In the case of collective self-esteem, the low correlation suggests considerable individual variation despite a constant mean level of collective self-esteem within the sample.

Characteristics of Hispanic Identity

The vast majority of the students mentioned Hispanic as one of their important identities (87%, 83%, and 86% at Times 1, 2, and 3, respectively). Although not surprising, given the explicit focus of the study, it does verify the central role that ethnicity plays for many people. Ethnicity was among the most important identities, although several others were similar in frequency of mention (e.g., student, friend, and daughter or son). In fact, both student and friend were mentioned as an identity by 100% of the students at Times 2 and 3, whereas ethnicity was still not endorsed by some students. Furthermore, although the rated importance of Hispanic identity was stable and high, it was not as high as the rated importance of either the student identity (Ms = 5.3, 5.7, and 5.6, respectively) or the friend identity (Ms = 5.3, 5.9, and 6.0, respectively). As expected, the rated importance of Hispanic identity was significantly related to the identity subscale of the Collective Self-Esteem Scale, $r(45) = .79$, $p < .01$, at Time 1; $r(38) = .59$, $p < .01$, at Time 2; and $r(34) = .73$, $p < .01$, at Time 3.

Students used many different terms to describe their Hispanic identity. As shown in Table 3, at all three times, positive feelings about the group (e.g., proud, aware, and loyal) and background characteristics (e.g., culture, language, family, and tradition) were mentioned most often. Background became significantly less prominent over time (Cochran's Q = 7.05, $p < .03$), dropping from 63% and 71%, at Times 1 and 2, to 48% by the end of the year.

There is also a significant decrease (Cochran's Q = 14.0, $p < .001$) in negative feelings as well as in the use of personality attributes to characterize Hispanic identity (Cochran's Q = 18.3, $p < .001$). These qualitative changes support our view that although objective membership in the group remains stable, the subjective meaning associated with the identity is open to change.

Maintaining Identity Through Remooring

We predicted that in response to the changes in environment that the students experienced, they would change the ways in which they maintained their Hispanic identity, remooring the identity within the new context. These expectations were supported. At the beginning of the year, the importance of the student's ethnic identity was significantly related to family background, both in terms of degree of Hispanic influence, $r(43) = .42$, $p < .01$, and to the spe-

TABLE 3
Categories of Attributes Most Often Associated With Hispanic Identity

Category	Percentage of students		
	Time 1	Time 2	Time 3
Positive feelings about the group (e.g. proud, loyal)	57.9	51.6	51.6
Positive feelings because of membership (e.g., happy, lucky)	12.2	25.8	19.4
Others' negative reactions (e.g., prejudice)	36.8	32.3	25.8
Negative feelings (e.g., resentment, doubt)	44.7	12.9	25.8**
Active reactions (e.g., educate others)	15.8	29.0	29.0
Background (e.g., language, family)	63.2	71.0	48.4*
Personality characteristics (e.g., caring, strong)	47.4	12.9	16.1**
Identification with the group (e.g., "who I am")	21.1	38.7	32.3
Change (e.g., learning, growing)	23.7	12.9	12.9

Change over time: *$p < .05$. **$p < .001$.

cific importance of their identity as a son or daughter, $r(43) = .30$, $p < .05$.[5] In contrast, at the second and third interviews, the link between cultural background and the strength of ethnic identification was no longer significant ($rs = .26$ and $.19$, respectively), suggesting that ethnic identity had been detached from its previous cultural context. The link between the importance of the identity as a son or daughter and Hispanic identity also loses its significance, although this detachment takes longer. At Time 2, ethnic identification and the importance of one's identity as a son or daughter remains important, $r(38) = .34$, $p < .05$. By Time 3, however, this relationship is no longer significant, $r(34) = .14$, $p < .25$.

Involvement with Hispanic activities on the campus appears to take the place of family background as a support for ethnic identity. At Time 2, the correlation between strength of identification and involvement in Hispanic activities during the preceding semester is significant, $r(38) = .55$, $p < .01$. This relation shows increased strength at Time 3, when ethnic identity is correlated with Hispanic activities during the second semester, $r(34) = .62$, $p < .01$.

Ethnic Involvement and Perceived Threat

Ethnic involvement played a powerful but shifting role across the students' first year at university. As a prior condition, ethnic involvement was measured by the Strength of Cultural Background index. Initially, this background served to buffer students from perceived threats to their ethnic identity. Thus, SCB was negatively related to Perceived Threat ($r(43)$

---

[5] As reported in Ethier and Deaux (1990), the pattern of these relationships differed for men and women. General Hispanic background was the more significant predictor for men, whereas the specific parent-daughter link was more influential for women.

= −.39, $p < .01$), such that the stronger the students' cultural background, the less likely they were to perceive the new environment as threatening. Past ethnic involvement, as assessed by SCB, also predicted a student's tendency to become involved in Hispanic activities on the campus ($r(38) = .41$, $p < .01$). The more involved the students were in their ethnic group before the transition to college, the more likely they were to become involved in ethnic activities on campus.

The importance of these indexes of ethnic involvement to group identification is evidenced in the results of regression analyses, used to determine the influence of involvement on changes in the strength of identification. In all of the regression analyses presented here, the initial value of the dependent variable (e.g., identification at Time 2) was entered into the equation first to control for any variance in the change score that could be explained by the initial value of the variable itself. These analyses show, first, that ethnic involvement before college (as measured by SCB) was a significant predictor of changes in identification from Time 1 to Time 2 ($b = −.28$, $p < .05$): The stronger the students' ethnic background, the stronger the identification with the group became during the student's first semester at college. Second, ethnic involvement at the university (as measured by the Hispanic activities index) was a significant predictor of changes in identification from Time 2 to Time 3 ($b = −.65$, $p < .001$): The more involved the students were with their ethnic group at college, the stronger their ethnic identity became in the second semester of the year. In fact, after controlling for the initial value of identification, Hispanic activities, by itself, explained 30% of the variance in changes in identification from Time 2 to Time 3.

When ethnic involvement was not strong, the processes of identity negotiation were quite different. As suggested above, students whose ethnic involvement before college was low perceived the college environment as more threatening. Perceptions of threat, in turn, had negative effects on self-esteem. Perceived threat at Time 1 was a significant predictor of changes in self-esteem both from Time 1 to Time 2 ($b = .36$, $p < .01$) and from Time 2 to Time 3 ($b = .42$, $p < .05$). (There was no association between ethnic involvement and self-esteem.)

In support of the prediction made by social identity theory, we find that collective self-esteem at Time 2 predicts changes in identification from Time 2 to Time 3 ($b = −.32$, $p < .05$). Thus, if students experience low self-esteem associated with their group membership, the strength of that identification decreases. Ethnic involvement before college moderates this relationship between collective self-esteem and identification. The interaction between SCB and private acceptance significantly predicts change in identification from Time 2 to Time 3 ($b = .15$, $p < .05$), such that students who had lower cultural background before college and who had lower self-esteem associated with group membership showed more negative changes in identification.

Two Paths of Identity Negotiation

These results suggest that there are two quite different processes occurring as students negotiate their ethnic identity in a changed context. For students who come in with a strong ethnic background, choices are made that continue ethnic involvement and result in a strengthening of the group identification. In contrast, students with a weak ethnic background show more signs of stress with resultant lower self-esteem and negative changes in identification.

To explore this possibility further, we divided the sample into two groups, based on the initial strength of their ethnic involvement, as assessed by the SCB. Because the distribution of scores on this measure was essentially bimodal, we divided the sample at the point of separation. High ethnic involvement subjects scored between 6 and 12 on the SCB measure; low involvement subjects scored between 16 and 22.

As would be expected on the basis of the previous findings, these two groups differed significantly on their involvement in Hispanic activities at school ($t = -2.50$, $p < .01$) and in the degree of threat they perceived in the college environment ($t = 2.54$, $p < .01$). Students who were more ethnically involved before the transition were more likely to become involved in ethnic activities at school and were less likely to experience threats to their identity, as compared with those students who were less ethnically involved before the transition.

More interesting in terms of supporting a position that there are two distinct paths of identity negotiation is the fact that SCB group (high vs. low) moderates the relationship between perceived threat and changes in self-esteem. The interaction between SCB group and perceived threat is a significant predictor of changes in private acceptance from Time 2 to Time 3 ($b = .20$, $p < .03$). Thus, those students with lower ethnic involvement before college and higher perceived threat were more likely to show negative changes in self-esteem later in the year.

DISCUSSION

This study provides several unique insights on the process by which people negotiate a social identity when the context for enacting that identity has substantially changed. By focusing on an identity of considerable importance, that is, ethnic identity, and by tracking the students over the course of more than 6 months, we gained a measure of ecological validity that studies of social identity rarely attain.

One key aspect of maintaining an identity when confronted with a new environment is a process we term *remooring*. In a general sense, ethnic identity is quite stable, particularly when one considers the frequency with which the category is endorsed by the individual. (Stability is not invariant, however, as Waters [1990] has shown.) What allows this stability to be maintained, however, is the process of remooring the identity to supportive elements in the new environment. Initially, a strong ethnic identity was supported by family background, by high school friends, and by neighborhood context. With the movement to a new locale, students who wished to maintain a strong ethnic identity needed to develop a new base of support for that identity, much as Hormuth (1990) has suggested. Students in the present study did this by linking their identity to people and activities on the campus that were consistent with a Hispanic identity. It is striking that these new links did not act as a supplement to cultural background but actually replaced the earlier basis of support. We suspect that this process is particularly characteristic of identities, like ethnicity, that are not directly tied to specific role relationships.

A second important finding concerns the way in which previous group involvement shapes the individual's approach to an altered context. In this study, the students' history of ethnic involvement predicted the degree to which they made efforts to maintain their group membership. Students who came from communities with high concentrations of Hispanics, who spoke Spanish in their homes, and who had a high percentage of Hispanic friends in high school were more likely to join Hispanic organizations at college and to make friends with other Hispanic students. The students who made these efforts showed an increase in Hispanic identification; those who did not make these efforts showed a decrease in Hispanic identification.

Social identity and self-categorization theory posit that an increase in salience will lead to an increase in identification. As discussed earlier, a clear statement about salience is not easily made. One might assume that Hispanic identity would be salient for all students in this study, given their clear minority status within the college population. If so, however, not all students responded to this salience with increased group identification. Only those students for whom ethnic involvement was high initially showed the increase in identification that social identity theory would predict. The obtained pattern of results would also be consistent with an assumption of salience based on the contrast between past context and current context. From this perspective, it would again be the students from the most Hispanic backgrounds for whom ethnic identity would be most salient on the college campus.

One hesitates to infer, however, that ethnic identity was not salient for those students whose ethnic background was weaker. For these students, however, the awareness of ethnicity appears to have had negative effects, rather than the increased identification predicted by social identity theory. These findings are consistent with Abrams's (1990) contention that there may be considerable variation in people's actions once an identity is made salient. Whereas social identity theory has traditionally given little attention to individual variation, preferring to stress the common response to conditions of salience, the present results stress the need to consider more agentic possibilities by people acting in their natural environments. We have shown clearly, and indeed the finding makes a great deal of intuitive sense, that variations in the level of previous group involvement determine the effect of contextual change on ethnic identity.

A third key finding from this study involves the reaction of students to their perception that the new environment was threatening to their identity. Our results suggest that in the face of threats, evaluations associated with the identity are particularly vulnerable to negative change. Students who perceived substantial threat and ambivalence about their identity as Hispanics showed subsequent drops in self-esteem associated with that identity. Thus, perceptions of threat to ethnic identity assessed in November correlated with negative changes in collective self-esteem from early in the year to midyear and from midyear to the end of the year.

We also find strong support for Tajfel's (1981) prediction that low self-esteem associated with a particular group membership will lead the individual to move away from the group.

Self-esteem associated with Hispanic identity was significantly correlated with changes in identification: Those students who evaluated their group negatively lowered their identification with the group, whereas those students who felt positively about their group showed an increase in identification.

The observation that students take one of two paths in the new environment on the basis of previous group involvement is a particularly intriguing one. As discussed earlier, these students varied in the degree to which they were involved in their ethnic group before the transition. Students with a strong cultural background were more likely to become involved in their ethnic group at college and, subsequently, to show increases in identification with that group. In contrast, students without a strong cultural background were more likely to perceive threats to their identity, to have lower self-esteem associated with that identity, and to lower their identification with the group. There could be a number of underlying reasons for this pattern. One possibility is that the students with a strong cultural background are simply continuing to manage their ethnicity in the same ways they had before. They may be responding to the upheaval of leaving home and going to college by seeking out others with similar backgrounds as a way of making themselves more comfortable. Indeed several of the students in open-ended interviews conducted at the end of the year mentioned that having a group of people who spoke the same language and had similar experiences was a benefit of being Hispanic and made adjustment to college easier for them. These highly identified students might also be more likely to use the supportive services made available by the university for minority students, such as ethnic counselors, cultural houses, and special orientations. In taking advantage of these opportunities, the highly identified students may have strengthened their identification and minimized perceptions of threat and consequent loss of self-esteem associated with group membership.

The contrasting case of students who did not come from a strong ethnic background suggests quite different events and processes. It seems quite likely that these students felt conflict about being categorized as Hispanic by the university when they themselves did not strongly identify with their ethnic group. Because they are less likely to speak the language or to come from areas densely populated by other Hispanics, they may not feel accepted by other ethnic group members, thus failing to gain the support that the group might offer. Similarly, these students might be less likely to use the ethnically oriented services that the university provides. The end result is a decrease in ethnic group identification but a drop in self-esteem associated with group membership as well. Whatever the underlying dynamics, it is quite significant that students who are more strongly identified with their ethnic group fare better during this transition than the students who are less strongly identified with the group. This finding speaks to the protective nature of group identity in situations in which the group is a numerical minority and is possibly faced with discrimination from the majority group.

Although our sample is small, the patterns are sufficiently strong to warrant confidence in the results. At the same time, we do not know how specific these phenomena are to elite private institutions in which a particular ethnic group, such as Hispanics, is such a numerical minority. When one's group is in the majority or even a substantial minority, environmental demands and opportunities could be quite different. Ethnicity might be less salient in such situations, creating fewer threats for those with weak ethnic identification and less perceived need to get involved in specific ethnic activities for those with high ethnic identification.

Beyond the specific results, this study attests to the importance of studying identity-related experience in a natural field setting over the course of time (Deaux, 1993). This approach allows us to examine the dynamics of identity work—the reinterpretation, reevaluation, and reconnection that allow identities to maintain seeming consistency over time. It also shows how theories of social identity play out with natural groups in realistic environments and how existing theories about social identity can be enriched and extended.

REFERENCES

Abrams, D. (1990). How do group members regulate their behavior? An integration of social identity and self-awareness theories. In D. Abrams & M. A. Hogg (Eds.), *Social identity theory: Constructive and critical advances* (pp. 89–112). New York: Springer-Verlag.

Abrams, D. (1992). Processes of social identification. In G. M. Breakwell (Ed.), *Social psychology of identity and the self-concept* (pp. 57–99). London: Surrey University Press.

Abrams, D., & Hogg, M. A. (1990). *Social identity theory: Constructive and critical advances.* New York: Springer-Verlag.

Aronson, E., & Mills, J. (1959). The effect of severity of initiation on liking for a group. *Journal of Personality and Social Psychology, 59,* 177–181.

Breakwell, G. (1986). *Coping with threatened identities.* London: Methuen.

Brewer, M. B. (1991). The social self: On being the same and different at the same time. *Personality and Social Psychology Bulletin, 17,* 475–482.

Christian, J., Gadfield, N. J., Giles, H., & Taylor, D. M. (1976). The multidimensional and dynamic nature of ethnic identity. *International Journal of Psychology, 11,* 281–291.

Deaux, K. (1993a). Enacting social identity: Maintaining stability and dealing with change. In S. Stryker (Eds.), *Self and affect in society.*

Deaux, K. (1993b). Reconstructing social identity. *Personality and Social Psychology Bulletin, 19,* 4–12.

Deaux, K., & Major, B. (1987). Putting gender into context: An interactive model of gender-related behavior. *Psychological Review, 94,* 369–389.

Emler, N., & Hopkins, N. (1990). Reputation, social identity and the self. In D. Abrams & M. A. Hogg (Eds.), *Social identity theory: Constructive and critical advances* (pp. 113–130). New York: Springer-Verlag.

Ethier, K. A., & Deaux, K. (1990). Hispanics in ivy: Assessing identity and perceived threat. *Sex Roles, 22,* 427–440.

Frable, D. E. S., Wortman, C., Joseph, J., Kirscht, J., & Kessler, R. (1994). *Predicting self-esteem, well being, and distress in a cohort of gay men: The importance of cultural stigma and personal visibility.* Manuscript submitted for publication.

Giles, H., Llado, N., McKirnan, D. J., & Taylor, D. M. (1979). Social identity in Puerto Rico. *International Journal of Psychology, 14,* 185–201.

Giles, H., Taylor, D. M., & Bourhis, R. Y. (1977). Dimensions of Welsh identity. *European Journal of Social Psychology, 7,* 165–174.

Giles, H., Taylor, D. M., Lambert, W. E., & Albert, G. (1976). Dimensions of ethnic identity: An example from northern Maine. *Journal of Social Psychology, 100,* 11–19.

Haslam, S. A., Turner, J. C., Oakes, P. J., & McGarty, C. (1992). Context-dependent variation in social stereotyping: I. The effects of intergroup relations as mediated by social change and frame of reference. *European Journal of Social Psychology, 22*, 3–20.

Hogg, M. A., & Abrams, D. (1988). *Social identifications*. London: Routledge.

Hogg, M. A., & Abrams, D. (1990). Social motivation, self-esteem and social identity. In D. Abrams & M. A. Hogg (Eds.), *Social identity theory: Constructive and critical advances* (pp. 28–47). New York: Springer-Verlag.

Hormuth, S. E. (1990). *The ecology of the self: Relocation and self-concept change*. Cambridge, England: Cambridge University Press.

Luhtanen, R., & Crocker, J. (1992). A collective self-esteem scale: Self-evaluation of one's social identity. *Personality and Social Psychology Bulletin, 18*, 302–318.

McGuire, W. J., McGuire, C. V., Child, P., & Fujioka, T. (1978). Salience of ethnicity in the spontaneous self-concept as a function of one's ethnic distinctiveness in the social environment. *Journal of Personality and Social Psychology, 36*, 511–520.

McNemar, Q. (1962). *Psychological statistics*. New York: Wiley.

Oakes, P. J. (1987). The salience of social categories. In J. C. Turner (Ed.), *Rediscovering the social group: A self-categorization theory* (pp. 117–141). Oxford, England: Basil Blackwell.

Phinney, J. S. (1990). Ethnic identity in adolescents and adults: Review of research. *Psychological Bulletin, 108*, 499–514.

Ruble, D. (1994). A phase model of transitions: Cognitive and motivational consequences. In M. Zanna (Ed.), *Advances in social psychology* (pp. 163–214). San Diego, CA: Academic Press.

Swann, W. B. (1983). Self-verification: Bringing social reality into harmony with the self. In J. Suls & A. G. Greenwald (Eds.), *Psychological perspectives on the self* (pp. 33–66). Hillsdale, NJ: Erlbaum.

Tajfel, H. (1981). *Human groups and social categories*. Cambridge, England: Cambridge University Press.

Turner, J. C. (1982). Towards a cognitive redefinition of the social group. In H. Tajfel (Ed.), *Social identity and intergroup relations* (pp. 15–40). Cambridge, England: Cambridge University Press.

Turner, J. C. (1987). *Rediscovering the social group: A self-categorization theory*. Oxford, England: Basil Blackwell.

Waddell, N., & Cairns, E. (1986). Situational perspectives on social identity in Northern Ireland. *British Journal of Social Psychology, 25*, 25–31.

Waters, M. (1990). *Ethnic options: Choosing identities in America*. Berkeley: University of California Press.

Portions of these data were presented at the 98th Annual Convention of the American Psychological Association, Boston, 1990. Preparation of this article was facilitated by a grant from the National Science Foundation (BNS-9110130) to Kay Deaux. We thank Michelle Fine, Tracey Revenson, and members of the Identity Research Seminar at the City University of New York Graduate Center for their advice and comments on a draft of this article.

THINKING CRITICALLY AND APPLYING YOUR KNOWLEDGE

1. Ethier and Deaux found that students with initially weak ethnic identities perceived the environment to be threatening to their ethnic identity, lowered their identification with their ethnic group, and showed decreases in self-esteem. It is important to remember, though, that the study was conducted during a one-year period only. Do you think the results would hold up after junior year? Following graduation? Would these individuals still perceive more threat and would they still have low self-esteem? Why or why not?

2. Ethier and Deaux refer to the process of *remooring*. What do they mean by this? When you came to college, did you find you had to go through a remooring process with respect to your ethnic, political, or religious identity? How did you go about doing this?

3. Ethier and Deaux conducted a longitudinal study and interviewed the Hispanic students in November/December, again in February, and a third time in May. What are the advantages of repeating the measurement three times? Can you think of any disadvantages of a six-month longitudinal study?

4. Ethier and Deaux used social identity theory as the theoretical context for understanding shifts in identification and self-esteem over time among these Hispanic college students. Social identity can have positive effects on individual self-esteem because it involves positive valuations of one's own social group. Can you think of any adverse consequences of a positive social identity involving one's ethnic or racial group?

PART IV

RELATING TO OTHERS

COLLECTIVISM–INDIVIDUALISM IN EVERYDAY SOCIAL LIFE: THE MIDDLE KINGDOM AND THE MELTING POT

Ladd Wheeler, Harry T. Reis, and Michael Harris Bond

How do cultural variations in individualism versus collectivism affect everyday social contacts with friends and family? In this cross-cultural study, college students in the United States (an individualist culture) and Hong Kong (a collectivist culture) kept detailed records of all their social interactions for two weeks. They recorded who they interacted with, how long each interaction lasted, how much each person revealed about himself or herself, and the nature of the interaction. As predicted, the Americans had nearly twice as many different interactions each day as did the Chinese, but Americans' interactions were of shorter duration. Americans (especially American men) disclosed relatively less in their interactions than did the Chinese. Clearly, cultural norms and values are associated with different patterns of socializing.

ABSTRACT: *Used the Rochester Interaction Record (RIR) to investigate the effects of individualism–collectivism on everyday social interaction. Triandis (in press) defined collectivism as placing great emphasis on (a) the views, needs, and goals of the in-group rather than of oneself, (b) social norms and duty defined by the in-group rather than behavior to get pleasure, (c) beliefs shared with the in-group rather than beliefs that distinguish oneself from in-group, (d) great readiness to cooperate with in-group members, and (e) intense emotional attachment to the in-group. University students in the United States, an individualistic country, and in Hong Kong, which is highly collectivistic, maintained the RIR for two weeks. Consistent with predictions, the Hong Kong students had longer but fewer interactions (half as many) with fewer people, had a higher percentage of group and task interactions, and indicated greater self- and other-disclosure.*

One of the most tantalizing questions for cross-cultural psychology concerns the manner in which cultures can be distinguished on the basis of their social activities. Two cultures that should differ markedly in this regard are the American and the Chinese. In discussing differences to be expected in the social life of Chinese and Americans, several theories should be examined. Hsu (1981) noted that in American life, emphasis is put on

Source: Reprinted from *Journal of Personality and Social Psychology, 57*(1), (1989), 79–86. Copyright © 1989 by the American Psychological Association. Reprinted by permission.

the predilections of the individual, a pattern he termed *individual-centered*. In contrast, the Chinese emphasis is on an individual's appropriate place and behavior among others, a pattern he termed *situation-centered*.

Yang (1981) has articulated a similar position, describing the traditional Chinese pattern as a *social orientation*, as opposed to an *individual orientation*. Social orientation represents a tendency for people to act in accordance with external expectations or social norms, rather than with internal wishes or personal integrity, so that they are able to protect their social selves and function as an integral part of the social network. As a result, they are more likely to pursue group activities. More individualistically oriented Americans, in contrast, are more likely to follow personal desires.

Although not directed specifically toward differences between Chinese and Americans, the work of Hofstede (1980) is clearly relevant. His work-related value survey, distributed to comparable populations of employees in 53 cultural units of one company, produced two dimensions important to this discussion: collectivism–individualism and large versus small power distance. Compared with westerners, the Chinese samples (from Hong Kong, Singapore, and Taiwan) were highly collective and moderately high in power distance. *Individualism* stands for a preference for a loosely knit social framework in society wherein individuals are supposed to take care of themselves and their immediate families only. Its opposite, *collectivism*, represents a preference for a tightly knit social framework in which individuals can expect their relatives, clan, or other in-group to look after them in exchange for unquestioning loyalty. *Power distance* refers to the extent to which the members of a society accept that power in institutions and organizations is distributed unequally. People in large power distance societies accept a hierarchical order in which everybody has a ranking that needs no further justification. People in societies characterized by small power distance strive for power equalization and demand justification for power inequalities. It is not surprising that the Chinese, with their emphasis on filial piety, should accept a larger power distance.

The concepts of situation centeredness (Hsu, 1981), social orientation (Yang, 1981), and collectivism (Hofstede, 1980) are quite similar. Cross-cultural psychologists have concentrated on collectivism, and so shall we. Triandis and his associates, in particular, have articulated the concept (Hui & Triandis, 1986; Triandis, in press; Triandis et al., 1986; Triandis, Bontempo, Villareal, Asai, & Lucca, 1988). Triandis (in press) defined collectivism as great emphasis on (a) the views, needs, and goals of the in-group rather than of oneself, (b) social norms and duty defined by the in-group rather than behavior to get pleasure, (c) beliefs shared with the in-group rather than on beliefs that distinguish oneself from the in-group, (d) great readiness to cooperate with in-group members, and (e) intense emotional attachment to the in-group.

An analysis of collectivism includes (a) the number of in-groups, (b) the extent of the sphere of influence of each in-group, and (c) the depth of this influence. These are related in that as the number of in-groups increases, each in-group has a narrower sphere and less depth of influence. Extreme collectivism exists when one group completely determines all aspects of one's life. One must conform to the norms of this group because there is nowhere else to go. Extreme individualism exists when there are so many in-groups that none of them has an overriding influence on one's life.

Generally, collectivist societies are characterized by one or two in-groups, and in the case of the Chinese, the two groups are family and close friends. Of the five cardinal relationships of the Confucian tradition, four deal with family and friends (only that between sovereign and subject is an exception). Family and friends are also in-groups for individualists, but additional in-groups may include the work group, the neighbors, the poker group, the club, and so forth.

Triandis (in press) noted that it is not at all clear how different levels of collectivism–individualism are linked to social phenomena. He and his colleagues have provided some observations, however, about this linkage:

> People in individualistic cultures often have greater skills in entering and leaving new social groups. They make "friends" easily, but by "friends" they mean nonintimate acquaintances. People in collectivist cultures have fewer skills in making new "friends" but "friend" in their case implies a life-long intimate relationship with many obligations. So the quality of the friendships is different. This difference in quality may complicate our understanding of the construct of collectivism, since people in individualistic cultures are likely to appear more sociable, while intimacy is not a readily observable attribute. (Triandis et al., 1988, p. 325)

Triandis (personal communication, February 22, 1988) has no systematic data supporting these statements, but he observed that at cocktail parties, for example, individualists will circulate easily while collectivists will find someone they know and stick with that person.

Hofstede (1980) reported a positive relationship (Spearman rank-order correlation = .46 across 22 countries) between the Individualism Index and McClelland's need affiliation. He commented, "In the most individualist countries, affective relationships . . . must be acquired by each individual personally. Thus, making friendships becomes more of an issue for the individual" (Hofstede, 1980, p. 228). Several reviews have suggested a prominent theme of *fear of rejection* as inherent in the need affiliation construct (Boyatzis, 1973; McAdams, 1982; Stewart & Chester, 1982), and McAdams (1980) derived and cross-validated a Thematic Apperception Test scoring system for a new construct termed the *intimacy motive*. McAdams and Constantian (1983) characterized the affiliation motive as an "agentic," active, striving orientation toward relationships that is rooted in a fear of rejection, and the intimacy motive as a more communal orientation. Using the experience sampling technique (Csikszentmihalyi, Larson, & Prescott, 1977), McAdams and Constantian concluded that those high in need affiliation desire relationships but do not find them particularly fulfilling and pursue more relationships to fill the perceived lack. Those high in need intimacy find their relationships satisfactory and do not mind being alone. Our view is that individualists are relatively high in need affiliation and that collectivists are relatively high in need intimacy.

It is the purpose of the present research to provide empirical tests of these notions.

Relating Collectivism to Social Interaction

This portrayal of the Chinese as oriented toward in-groups and low in need affiliation but perhaps high in need intimacy—though theoretically interesting—is based upon cross-cultural value surveys and personality data. Whether it actually translates into ongoing patterns of social participation in everyday life has not been tested. There have been laboratory studies of such things as aggression, conformity, and resource allocation (see Bond & Hwang, 1986, for a review) but no studies of naturally occurring interaction.

The Rochester Interaction Record (RIR) is a fixed-format diary technique in which subjects record all of their social interactions of ten minutes or more over a period of time (Nezlek, Wheeler, & Reis, 1983; Reis, Nezlek, & Wheeler, 1980; Reis & Wheeler, 1988; Reis, Wheeler, Kernis, Spiegel, & Nezlek, 1985; Reis et al., 1982; Wheeler & Nezlek, 1977; Wheeler, Reis, & Nezlek, 1983). As will be described below, a number of different indices may be obtained, but the basic dimensions on which the respondent provides information are number and length of interactions, sex and number of others involved in the interaction, disclosure by self and others, quality (unpleasant–pleasant), satisfaction (less or more than expected), initiation, influence, and nature of the interaction. These indices seem well suited to characterize with concrete variables the general interaction notions described earlier.

The following hypotheses, derived from our earlier discussion, will be tested:

1. The Chinese will have fewer social interactions than Americans.
2. The Chinese will have relatively more group interactions than Americans.
3. The Chinese will have longer interactions than Americans.
4. In that collectivism focuses on in-groups, the Chinese will have fewer interaction partners than Americans.
5. The Chinese will be more likely to have task interactions and less likely to have recreational interactions. This is because greater feelings of responsibility to the group should lead to preferences for productive activities.
6. The Chinese will disclose more to one another than will the Americans, a prediction made on the basis of Triandis's (Triandis et al., 1988) view of greater intimacy in collective cultures.
7. Because power distance concerns are more salient for the Chinese, initiation and influence should reveal greater variance among the Chinese than among Americans. That is, higher status persons should claim more control (initiation and influence) and lower status persons less control, relative to more equalitarian Americans (Lin Yi Cheng, personal communication, September 3, 1988).

We are unable to offer predictions about quality and satisfaction because the Chinese appear to stress harmonious interactions, whereas Americans appear to focus on meeting their personal needs. We just do not know how these different motives will affect quality and satisfaction.

METHOD

Subjects

The American subjects were 43 male and 53 female seniors enrolled in the University of Rochester. These data were already reported by Wheeler et al. (1983). The Chinese subjects were 27 male and 41 female juniors and seniors enrolled in the Chinese University of Hong Kong. The American and Hong Kong universities were approximately the same size. The American subjects were recruited from a student directory, and the Chinese subjects were recruited from two sections of a social psychology course. The American subjects completed the RIR for an average of 14.5 days; the Chinese subjects, for an average of 15.8 days. All records were adjusted by computing indices on a per day or per interaction basis. The American subjects were paid $20 for their participation, and the Chinese subjects received extra course credit.

Whereas all of the American students lived in campus dormitories, 42% of the Hong Kong sample lived off campus. To ensure that this factor would not confound cross-cultural comparisons, a series of Sex × Residence analyses of variance (ANOVAs) were conducted. One hundred fifty-nine variables were examined, including all of this study's central variables and various other secondary variables. Only five significant ($p < .05$) main effects of residence and two Sex × Residence interactions appeared. This is well below chance and indicates that residence location did not meaningfully affect the interaction data.

Procedure

During a brief meeting, the importance of understanding interaction patterns was explained and the students' role as collaborators in this naturalistic research was stressed.

The interaction record, a sample of which is shown in Figure 1,[1] was to be completed for every interaction that lasted 10 min or longer. An interaction was defined as any encounter with another person(s) in which the participants attended to one another and adjusted their behavior in response to one another. Examples were provided (e.g., sitting silently next to someone in a lecture was not an interaction, whereas talking during the lecture for 10 min was), and the various categories were discussed until everyone felt comfortable with the forms. A more detailed description may be found in Wheeler and Nezlek (1977) and Reis and Wheeler (1988). We suggested to subjects that they fill out the records as soon as possible after an interaction. A scratch sheet was provided to facilitate memory. To encourage daily recording, subjects were asked to return their completed forms and pick up blank ones every few days. Throughout the study, a collaborative, nondeceptive atmosphere was maintained, which we believe aided the gathering of valid data. Confidentiality of the records was emphasized and closely guarded throughout.

---

[1] Although all the Chinese subjects read English, Chinese translations of all the terms were given below the English terms. There were some slight differences between the versions of the RIR given to the two ethnic groups. On the Chinese version, *conversation* was changed to *chatting*, and *pastime* was changed to *recreation*.

```
Date _____ Time _____ AM _____ Length: _____ Hrs _____ Mins
                                       PM _____
Initials _____ _____ _____    If more than 3 others:

Sex      _____ _____ _____    # of Females _____ # of Males _____

Intimacy:              Superficial   1 2 3 4 5 6 7   Meaningful
I disclosed:           Very little    1 2 3 4 5 6 7   A great deal
Other disclosed:       Very little    1 2 3 4 5 6 7   A great deal
Quality:               Unpleasant    1 2 3 4 5 6 7   Pleasant
Satisfaction:  Less than expected    1 2 3 4 5 6 7   More than expected
Initiation:              I initiated  1 2 3 4 5 6 7   Other initiated
Influence:      I influenced more    1 2 3 4 5 6 7   Other influenced more

Nature:     Work     Task     Pastime     Conversation
```

FIGURE 1 Sample copy of the Rochester Interaction Record.

At the conclusion of the record-keeping period, a brief interview with one of the researchers was held. During that session, the interviewer probed for difficulties, ambiguities, and potential sources of inaccurate data. In particular, subjects were urged to inform us of anything that might have impeded their accuracy.

Construction and Nomenclature of Interaction Variables

From the raw interaction records, composite indices were created in the following manner: *number per day*—total number of interactions divided by the number of days the interaction records were kept; *time per day*—mean number of minutes per day spent socializing (to avoid disproportionate influence, the maximum length of any single interaction was truncated at 360 min); *number of others*—total number of different individuals interacted with during the entire record-keeping period; and *percentage*—percentage of all interactions falling into a given category. *Self-disclosure, other-disclosure, pleasantness, satisfaction, initiation*, and *influence* were all computed as the mean value reported across all interactions. *Nature* was scored as the proportion of all interactions classified in each category.

In order to simplify data presentation, the six adjective dimensions listed above were summed into three composites: *disclosure* (sum of self- and other-disclosure), *control* (initiation and influence), and *quality* (pleasantness and satisfaction). The variables within each composite were highly correlated both in these data and in our prior studies using the RIR. Separate analyses of the individual scales produced results very similar to those using the composites.

Each of these indices was then subdivided in accordance with the sex composition of the encounter: *same sex*—interactions including up to three other persons of the same sex; *opposite sex*—interactions including up to three members of the opposite sex; *mixed sex*—interactions including up to three others, at least one of each sex; and *group*—interactions including more than three other people. *Overall* measures incorporated all interactions.

A small number of the categories listed above contained no observations for some subjects. These entries were treated as missing data in the analysis.

RESULTS

Quantitative Indices of Social Activity

Hypothesis 1 proposed that Chinese students would have fewer interactions than would American students. This hypothesis was confirmed for interactions per day: U.S. $M = 6.98$, Hong Kong $M = 3.43$, $F(1, 162) = 111.76$, $p < .0001$. There were no significant sex differences or interactions between sex and culture.

To test our second hypothesis (concerning cultural differences in the relative frequency of different types of interaction), 2 (culture) × 2 (sex) ANOVAs were conducted on the percentage of all interactions that fell into the same-sex, opposite-sex, mixed-sex, and group categories.[2] Mean values are reported in Table 1. As predicted, all categories differed by culture, with U.S. subjects demonstrating considerably more same-sex and opposite-sex interaction and Hong Kong subjects showing somewhat more mixed-sex interactions and substantially more group interactions. The only sex effect was a tendency of men to interact more in groups regardless of culture: male $M = 25.1$, female $M = 20.7$, $F(1, 162) = 5.60$, $p < .02$. No significant interactions appeared.

This pattern was corroborated by the number of interactions, examined in 2 (culture) × 2 (sex) × 4 (composition) ANOVAs, with repeated measures on the final variable. The expected Composition × Culture interaction was obtained, $F(3, 486) = 36.09$, $p < .001$. Follow-up simple effects tests (Winer, 1962) were conducted to locate the source of this interaction. As shown in Table 2, American subjects had more same-sex and opposite-sex interactions per day than Chinese subjects did, whereas mixed-sex and group interactions did not differ significantly by culture. In other words, Chinese and American students had approximately the same amount of mixed-sex and group interaction, but because Chinese students interacted much less on the whole, these categories constituted a greater proportion of the total. There were no significant sex effects or interactions.

TABLE 1
Percentage of Interaction by Composition

Culture	Same sex	Opposite sex	Mixed sex	Group
United States	45.8	27.5	9.9	16.7
Hong Kong	36.4	22.6	11.9	29.2
Culture F	14.69	4.71	3.97	45.30
p	.001	.05	.05	.0001

Note: Culture Fs are one-way ANOVAs with 1, 62 *df*s.

---

[2] A repeated measures analysis could not be used here because the fourth category is necessarily correlated perfectly and negatively with the other three.

TABLE 2
Frequency and Time Spent Interacting

Culture	Same sex	Opposite sex	Mixed sex	Group
Number of interactions per day				
United States	3.19	1.90	0.70	1.18
Hong Kong	1.19	0.84	0.42	0.98
Culture *F*	195.61	54.95	3.83	1.96
p	.0001	.0001	.06	*ns*
Time per day (in minutes)				
United States	132.70	103.31	34.86	77.71
Hong Kong	53.24	51.64	22.20	74.81
Culture *F*	96.76	40.91	2.46	0.12
p	.0001	.0001	*ns*	*ns*

Note: Culture *F*s are simple effects tests with 1,486 *dfs.*

Similar effects were obtained for the amount of time per day spent interacting. As documented in Table 2, a significant Composition × Culture interaction, $F(3, 486) = 18.74$, $p < .001$, indicated that American students reported spending more time in same-sex and opposite-sex interaction, whereas there were no differences in the mixed-sex and group categories.

Interaction length. Hypothesis 3 predicted that Chinese students' interactions would last longer than those of American students. Analysis of overall length per interaction confirmed this prediction, such that Chinese students' interactions averaged 61.0 min versus 52.6 min among Americans, $F(1, 162) = 8.24$, $p < .005$. A repeated-measures analysis examining the four composition categories separately did not reveal any significant culture effect, however, although the means in each category differed in the predicted direction. Thus, Hypothesis 3 received mixed support.

Number of interaction partners. Our fourth hypothesis was that the Chinese would have fewer interaction partners. As expected, American students reported interacting with significantly more same-sex ($M = 22.4$) and opposite-sex ($M = 16.7$) partners than did Hong Kong students ($Ms = 14.8$ and 10.0, respectively), same-sex $F(1, 162) = 27.86$, $p < .0001$; opposite-sex $F(1, 162) = 29.53$, $p < .0001$. There were no reliable sex differences, but a significant Culture × Sex interaction, $F(1, 162) = 10.39$, $p < .002$, indicated that American women reported more opposite-sex partners than did men, $F(1, 162) = 16.43$, $p < .001$, whereas there was no sex difference among Hong Kong students, $F(1, 162) < 1$; see Table 3 for mean values. The number of same-sex partners did not yield a significant interaction.

Nature. The final analysis in this section deals with Hypothesis 5, concerning the relative proportion of different types of interactions. These data were examined in 2 (culture) × 2 (sex) × 4 (activity) ANOVAs, with repeated measures on the final factor. Because the fourth nature category is necessarily correlated perfectly and negatively with the other three, ob-

TABLE 3
Number of Interaction Partners

Culture	Same sex		Opposite sex	
	Men	Women	Men	Women
United States	22.8	22.0	13.7	19.7
Hong Kong	14.6	15.1	11.1	9.7

viating full repeated measures analyses, we decided to drop work from the analysis. Work constituted only 3.8% of the interactions on average; if it is included and other categories are dropped, the results do not change meaningfully. The data were considered separately for same-sex, opposite-sex, mixed-sex, and group interactions to enhance interpretability.

Across all four composition categories, significant Culture × Activity interactions appeared, all $Fs(2, 324) > 7.71$, $p < .001$. In each instance, this was because Chinese students were more likely to engage in tasks (overall compositions, 30.0% vs. 14.6%), whereas American students were more likely to socialize in recreation (overall, 22.4% vs. 11.8%). The only other significant effect occurred in same-sex interactions, and this was a Sex × Activity interaction, $F(2, 324) = 8.79$, $p < .0002$. Both sexes participated in chats more than in recreation, but the discrepancy was greater for women (66.7% vs. 10.3%) than for men (54.8% vs. 19.9%).

Subjective Features of Social Participation

Disclosure. Hypothesis 6, concerning disclosure levels, was evaluated in separate 2 (culture) × 2 (sex) ANOVAs within each of the four composition categories.[3] Mean values and F statistics are reported in Table 4 to enhance clarity. As predicted, Chinese students reported significantly higher mean levels of disclosure than American students did in all four categories. The culture mean differences were 1.02, 0.82, 1.24, and 1.54 for same-sex, opposite-sex, mixed-sex, and group interactions, respectively, consistently supporting Hypothesis 6.

Significant sex differences were found for same-sex and mixed-sex interactions. In each instance, and consistent with prior research (Reis, 1986; Wheeler et al., 1983), women reported higher levels of disclosure than men. This effect was moderated in the same-sex category by a Culture × Sex interaction, which also emerged in groups. In both cases, simple effects tests indicated that American men and women differed significantly from each other, $Fs(1, 162) = 27.52$ and 10.03, both $ps < .01$, whereas Chinese men and women did not differ, $Fs(1, 162) < 1.17$, ns.

[3] These four categories were analyzed separately rather than in repeated measures analyses for clarity. In computing culture and sex effects, repeated measures analysis would weight each category equally. This is inappropriate, because they occur with very disproportionate frequency.

TABLE 4
Mean Values and F Statistics for Disclosure Levels

Measure	Same sex	Opposite sex	Mixed sex	Group
United States *M*				
Men	6.51	7.68	6.09	5.32
Women	8.21	8.06	7.20	6.46
Hong Kong *M*				
Men	8.23	8.90	7.80	7.66
Women	8.52	8.48	7.97	7.20
Culture *F*	16.01***	9.23**	17.25****	
Sex *F*	15.48****		4.60*	
Culture × Sex *F*	7.68**			7.99**

*$p < .05$. **$p < .01$. ***$p < .001$. ****$p < .0001$.

Quality. Similarly, 2 (culture) × 2 (sex) ANOVAs were conducted on the interaction quality composite within each of the four composition categories. As Table 5 indicates, the only reliable culture effects were Culture × Sex interactions in mixed-sex and group interaction. American men enjoyed these interactions more than Hong Kong men, $Fs(1, 162) = 5.95$ and 7.62, $ps < .05$ and .01, respectively, but there was no difference between American and Chinese women, both $Fs(1, 162) < 1$. The only other significant result in these analyses was a sex effect in same-sex interaction. Women enjoyed these interactions more than did men.

Control. Analyses of the control variable yielded significant results only for opposite-sex interactions. As predicted, the variance of mean control ratings was greater in Hong Kong than in the United States (1.45 vs. 0.86), Levene's $F(1, 162) = 5.13$, $p < .05$. Control ratings in opposite-sex interactions also revealed mean differences. American subjects reported exerting less personal control than did Chinese subjects ($Ms = 8.10$ vs. 7.58), $F(1, 160) = 9.99$, $p < .002$. In addition, regardless of culture, men felt that they controlled such interactions more than did women ($Ms = 7.62$ vs. 8.05), $F(1, 160) = 6.86$, $p < .01$.[4]

[4] Although not part of our hypotheses, the interaction records allow us to isolate interactions involving the subject's closest partners. To see if American and Chinese students differed in their reliance on close partners, two sets of analyses were conducted. First, a reliance index was computed by dividing the number of dyadic interactions per day with their most frequent same-sex or opposite-sex partner (separately) by the total number of dyadic interactions of that gender composition. Second, the primary interaction variables were examined in repeated measures ANOVAS that contrasted dyadic interactions involving closest partners with dyadic interactions not involving those persons. These analyses revealed no culture main effects of interactions beyond chance and will therefore not be reported.

TABLE 5
Mean Values and F Statistics for Interaction Quality

Measure	Same sex	Opposite sex	Mixed sex	Group
United States M				
Men	9.09	9.56	9.97	8.93
Women	9.65	9.72	9.56	9.48
Hong Kong M				
Men	9.16	9.57	9.18	9.03
Women	9.38	9.27	8.93	8.73
Culture F	8.77****			3.71*
Culture × Sex F			3.91**	6.26***

*$p < .06$. **$p < .05$. ***$p < .02$. ****$p < .005$.

DISCUSSION

We will begin our discussion with a summary of the evidence bearing on our hypotheses.

1. As predicted, the Chinese had fewer interactions than the Americans. This was true for the same-, opposite-, and mixed-sex interactions. Combining these three categories, the Americans had 5.99 interactions per day, compared with 2.45 for the Chinese. The two cultures did not differ on the number of group interactions.

2. A higher percentage of the Chinese interactions were group interactions, as predicted. In addition, the Chinese had a larger percentage of mixed-sex interactions (those involving two to three interaction partners).

3. We hypothesized that the Chinese would have longer interactions than the Americans. For each composition category, there were small but insignificant differences in the predicted direction. Combining the four composition categories, the prediction was confirmed.

4. The Chinese, as hypothesized, had fewer interaction partners, both same- and opposite-sex. There was, however, a Culture × Sex interaction on the number of opposite-sex interaction partners. American women, but not men, had more opposite-sex partners than did their Chinese counterparts.

5. The Chinese had more task interactions and fewer recreational interactions, as predicted.

6. Regardless of the composition of the interaction, the Chinese were higher than the Americans on disclosure. For same-sex and group interactions, however, there was a Culture × Sex interaction, indicating that the men in the two cultures differed more than did the women. American men were particularly low on disclosure.

7. We predicted that the Chinese would show higher variance in control ratings than would Americans. In fact, this was true only for opposite-sex interactions.[5]

We were unable to make predictions about the quality (pleasantness and satisfaction) of interactions, and the only difference that emerged was that American men enjoyed mixed-sex and group interactions more than did Hong Kong men. In addition, women of both cultures enjoyed their same-sex interactions more than did men.

But if this article is to make a lasting contribution, what will it be? It will show that the Chinese interact less frequently with fewer people, incline toward groups, and disclose more. These are very strong results and have not been demonstrated previously. Nor are they obvious. The prototypical American individualist is often portrayed as the cowboy, a largely solitary creature. Our data suggest that a very different picture is more accurate. Triandis et al. (1988), in discussing paper-and-pencil measures of allocentrism (collectivism) and idiocentrism (individualism), noted,

> Thus, it seems appropriate to *change* our view of collectivism. It is not that people are less sociable in individualistic cultures—in fact it seems that they are more sociable in individualistic countries than they are in the collectivistic because they have to work hard to get into and remain in their ingroups. (p. 333; emphasis added)

One of the distinguishing characteristics of collectivists is that they delineate sharply between the in-group and out-groups. For example, Leung (1988) found that Chinese were more likely than Americans to pursue a conflict with a stranger but less likely with a friend. Harmonious relationships with members of the in-group are essential, but the out-groups can be damned. Individualists, in contrast, do not make such a sharp distinction because who is "in" depends more on what is up (the activity or situation).

If collectivists have a defined in-group, it follows more or less logically that they would interact with fewer people. That a larger percentage of these interactions would be group interactions also follows, because there would be a tight network of people who know one another well and depend upon one another, all members of one in-group.

Our results strongly supported the hypothesis that self- and other-disclosure would be greater in collectivist Chinese subjects than in individualistic American subjects. At first blush, this finding would appear to contradict stereotypic portrayals of the Chinese as private and emotionally reserved, at least in contrast to Americans, who are sometimes de-

---

[5] There is some possibility that the 10-min criterion might have slightly biased our results. If, as predicted, Americans have shorter interactions, then a relatively greater share of American's daily social activity would be excluded by this criterion. Frequency distributions revealed that 10.5% of American interactions lasted 10 min, in contrast to only 5.6% of Chinese interactions. If shorter interactions had been included, however, our results for interaction frequency, length, and intimacy, would in all likelihood have been stronger, because a greater number of shorter (and presumably less intimate) interactions by Americans would adjust the obtained means further in the expected direction.

scribed as exhibitionistic and immodest about personal facts. Nevertheless, our hypothesis was derived from a central component of Triandis's (in press; Triandis et al., 1988) theory of collectivism, namely that in a collectivist culture, friendships are closer and longer lived because the sense of emotional attachment to the in-group is greater. In individualistic cultures, a greater proportion of one's social network is likely to be composed of superficial acquaintances, so that, in essence, the mean level of interactional intimacy is lowered not because the most intimate interactions are less intimate but rather because of the greater prevalence of relatively nonintimate interactions. These data therefore corroborate an important, not obvious prediction of Triandis's framework.

There is, however, a potential alternative explanation for this finding. It might be argued that if Chinese norms dictate greater personal reserve, the same self-disclosures should seem more revealing to a Chinese subject than to an American. Thus, it is possible that our data were produced by contrast effect—the identical content (or even less intimate material) being viewed as relatively more disclosing in Hong Kong by virtue of differential norms. This alternative cannot be ruled out from the present data, and we are currently conducting research to examine its viability. At the same time, it must be remembered that intimacy is a subjective quality whose meaning depends on the value and interpretations of the perceiver. Extraordinarily revealing information will probably have little impact if perceived as shallow by discloser and listener, whereas minimally revealing information may be important if experienced as intimate. Thus, even if our disclosure data reflect cultural differences in the perception of similar content, rather than actual content differences, the fact that Chinese subjects experienced their interactions as more intimate than did Americans is no less valid or important.

Consistent with our results on self-disclosure, Gudykunst et al. (in press) found that students from Hong Kong and Taiwan reported more self-disclosure to in-group than to out-group members, whereas students from the United States and Australia reported no difference in disclosure to the two groups. Moreover, there was also a main effect showing that the Chinese subjects disclosed more to in-group members than did the Australians and Americans. However, a fifth group in this study, the collectivistic Japanese, reported less disclosure to the in-group than to the out-group and indeed less disclosure to the in-group than any other of the cultures. Barnlund (1975), using the technique of Jourard and Lasakow (1958), also found that the Japanese claimed to have disclosed less even to best friends than did Americans. Neither Gudykunst et al. nor Barnlund used the interaction-by-interaction measure of self-disclosure used here, but the fact that both found low self-disclosure by the Japanese is troublesome for the argument that collectivists are necessarily high self-disclosers to in-group members. The obvious fact is that cultures differ on more dimensions than just individualism–collectivism. Barnlund (1975) suggested that the extraordinary homogeneity of Japanese culture could play a part: "The greater the cultural homogeneity, the greater the meaning conveyed in a single word, the more that can be implied rather than stated" (p. 162). And on two of Hofstede's (1980) dimensions, masculinity and uncertainty avoidance, Japan ranks very high in comparison with Chinese cultures.

These are the sorts of variables that might override intimacy differences based on collectivism. At the moment, all we can say is that this is an area ripe for further investigation.

In general, sex differences in disclosure were larger among Americans than among the Chinese. Disclosure was greater in American women than men, a finding that has emerged in many other studies as well (see, for example, Reis, 1986), and that can be handled by the individualism–collectivism notion. The personality scale that seems most directly related to individualism–collectivism is the Swap and Rubin (1983) Interpersonal Orientation (IO) scale (Triandis, in press). American female college students do score higher (more collective) than do male students. Furthermore, Swap and Rubin reported that if men and women are equated in IO, they both respond with increased liking of a self-disclosing other, a result in contrast to the usual finding that only women respond with increased liking (Ehrlich & Graeven, 1971; Worthy, Cary, & Kahn, 1969). This argument implies that sex differences in IO should be smaller in Hong Kong than in the United States (we know of no data testing this hypothesis). It is important to note that the IO scale is essentially unrelated to sociability (Swap & Rubin, 1983), so it would not predict sex differences on such variables as interaction frequency.

The IO Scale is also related to reward allocation, with high scorers more likely to use equality than equity, just as women are, and just as Chinese are when dealing with in-group members (Leung & Bond, 1984). Eagly (1987), in her recent meta-analytic study of sex differences, used the terms *communal* and *agentic* to refer to the different orientations of women and men, and there seems to be a similarity between this distinction and the collectivism–individualism distinction. Another similar distinction between communal and exchange relationships has been drawn by Mills and Clark (1982). Perhaps a theoretical rapprochement is in the making.

Are the Chinese and American samples truly comparable? The major way in which they are not comparable is that there are only two universities in Hong Kong, most prospective undergraduates want to stay in Hong Kong, and, consequently, only 10% of applicants to the Chinese University are admitted. Only 2% of age-eligible people attend either of the universities. All of these numbers are, of course, much higher at the University of Rochester and in the United States in general. Thus, the Chinese students are a more elite group. What effect this might have on social interaction patterns is unclear. We have not observed that the students at the most elite American universities socialize more or less than those at the University of Rochester. In fact, there is remarkable consistency in RIR data reported to us from other universities. Furthermore, the amount of work required of the Chinese students seems comparable with that of our students. Nevertheless, the possibility remains that the habit of hard work learned by the Chinese students accepted into the university may partially explain their lower level of socializing.

In a constructive critique of cross-cultural psychology, Wheeler and Reis (1988) argued that mainstream social psychologists will not be particularly interested in cross-cultural research unless the cultures involved differ on some important theoretical dimension relevant to the research. For example, comparison of resource allocation in two cultures wouldn't be very interesting unless those two cultures were known to differ on a dimension that predicts different kinds of resource allocation. The contribution of this article is an attempt to link the dimension of collectivism–individualism to some aspects of social interaction. Although the attempt seems to be successful, we cannot be sure that the differences we found between the cultures are actually due to collectivism and individualism.

REFERENCES

Barnlund, D. C. (1975). *Public land private self in Japan and the United States.* Tokyo: Simul Press.

Bond, M. H., & Hwang, K. K. (1986). The social psychology of Chinese people. In M. H. Bond (Ed.), *The psychology of the Chinese people* (pp. 213–264). Hong Kong: Oxford University Press.

Boyatzis, R. E. (1973). Affiliation motivation. In D. C. McClelland & R. S. Steele (Eds.), *Human motivation: A book of readings* (pp. 252–278). Morristown, NJ: General Learning Press.

Csikszentmihalyi, M., Larson, R., & Prescott, S. (1977). The ecology of adolescent activity and experience. *Journal of Youth and Adolescence, 6,* 281–294.

Eagly, A. H. (1987). *Sex difference in social behavior: A social-role interpretation.* Hillsdale, NJ: Erlbaum.

Ehrlich, H. J., & Graeven, D. B. (1971). Reciprocal self-disclosure in a dyad. *Journal of Experimental Social Psychology, 7,* 389–400.

Gudykunst, W. B., Ge, G., Schmidt, K. L., Nishida, T., Bond, M. H., Leung, K., Wang, G., & Barraclough, R. A. (in press). The influence of individualism–collectivism, self-monitoring, and predicted outcome value on communication in ingroup and outgroup relationships. *Journal of Cross-Cultural Psychology.*

Hofstede, C. (1980). *Culture's consequences: International differences in work-related values.* Beverly Hills, CA: Sage.

Hsu, F. L. K. (1981). *American and Chinese: Passage to differences* (3rd ed.). Honolulu: University of Hawaii Press.

Hui, C. H., & Triandis, H. C. (1986). Individualism–collectivism: A study of cross-cultural researchers. *Journal of Cross-Cultural Psychology, 17,* 222–248.

Jourard, S. M., & Lasakow, P. (1958). Some factors in self-disclosure. *Journal of Abnormal and Social Psychology, 56,* 91–98.

Leung, K. (1988). Some determinants of conflict avoidance. *Journal of Cross-Cultural Psychology, 19,* 125–136.

Leung, K., & Bond, M. H. (1984). The impact of cultural collectivism on reward allocation. *Journal of Personality and Social Psychology, 47,* 793–804.

McAdams, D. P. (1980). A thematic coding system for the intimacy motive. *Journal of Research in Personality, 14,* 413–432.

McAdams, D. P. (1982). Intimacy motivation. In A. J. Stewart (Ed.), *Motivation and society* (pp. 133–171). San Francisco: Jossey-Bass.

McAdams, D. P., & Constantian, C. A. (1983). Intimacy and affiliation motives in daily living: An experience sampling analysis. *Journal of Personality and Social Psychology, 45,* 851–861.

Mills, J., & Clark, M. S. (1982). Exchange and communal relationships. In L. Wheeler (Ed.), *Review of personality and social psychology* (Vol. 3, pp. 121–144). Beverly Hills, CA: Sage.

Nezlek, J., Wheeler, L., & Reis, H. T. (1983). Studies of social participation. In H. T. Reis (Ed.), *Naturalistic approaches to studying social interaction* (pp. 57–73). San Francisco: Jossey-Bass.

Reis, H. T. (1986). Gender effects in social participation: Intimacy, loneliness, and the conduct of social interaction. In R. Gilmour (Ed.), *Personal relationships* (pp. 91–105). London: Academic Press.

Reis, H. T., Nezlek, J., & Wheeler, L. (1980). Physical attractiveness in social interaction. *Journal of Personality and Social Psychology, 38,* 604–617.

Reis, H. T., & Wheeler, L. (1988). *The Rochester Interaction Record*. Unpublished manuscript.

Reis, H. T., Wheeler, L., Kernis, M. H., Spiegel, N., & Nezlek, J. (1985). On specificity in the impact of social participation on physical and psychological health. *Journal of Personality and Social Psychology*, *48*, 456–471.

Reis, H. T., Wheeler, L., Spiegel, N., Kernis, M., Nezlek, J., & Perri, M. (1982). Physical attractiveness in social interaction: II. Why does appearance affect social experience? *Journal of Personality and Social Psychology*, *43*, 979–996.

Stewart, A. J., & Chester, N. L. (1982). Sex differences in human social motives: Achievement, affiliation, and power. In A. J. Stewart (Ed.), *Motivation and society* (pp. 172–218). San Francisco: Jossey-Bass.

Swap, W. C., & Rubin, J. Z. (1983). Measurement of interpersonal orientation. *Journal of Personality and Social Psychology*, *44*, 208–219.

Triandis, H. C. (in press). Collectivism vs. individualism: A reconceptualization of a basic concept in cross-cultural social psychology. In C. Bagley & C. K. Verma (Eds.), *Personality, cognition and values: Cross-cultural perspectives of childhood and adolescence*. London: Macmillan.

Triandis, H. C., Bontempo, R., Betancourt, H., Bond, M., Leung, K., Brenes, A., Georgas, J., Hui, C. H., Marin, G., Setiadi, B., Sinha, J. B. P., Verma, J., Spangenberg, J., Touzard, H., & de Montmollin, G. (1986). The measurement of the etic aspects of individualism and collectivism across cultures. *Australian Journal of Psychology*, *38*, 257–267.

Triandis, H. C., Bontempo, R., Villareal, M. J., Asai, M., & Lucca, N. (1988). Individualism and collectivism: Cross-cultural perspectives on self-ingroup relationships. *Journal of Personality and Social Psychology*, *54*, 323–333.

Wheeler, L., & Nezlek, J. (1977). Sex differences in social participation. *Journal of Personality and Social Psychology*, *35*, 742–754.

Wheeler, L., & Reis, H. (1988). On titles, citations, and outlets: What do mainstreamers want? In M. H. Bond (Ed.), *The cross cultural challenge to social psychology* (pp. 36–40). Beverly Hills, CA: Sage.

Wheeler, L., Reis, H. T., & Nezlek, J. (1983). Loneliness, social interaction, and sex roles. *Journal of Personality and Social Psychology*, *45*, 943–953.

Winer, B. J. (1962). *Statistical principles in experimental design*. New York: McGraw-Hill.

Worthy, M., Cary, A. L., & Kahn, B. M. (1969). Self-disclosure as an exchange process. *Journal of Personality and Social Psychology*, *13*, 59–63.

Yang, K. S. (1981). Social orientation and individual modernity among Chinese students in Taiwan. *Journal of Social Psychology*, *113*, 159–170.

The authors wish to express their appreciation to Associate Editor Eliot Smith for his assistance as well as his constructive suggestions about the manuscript. This research was supported by sabbatical and research funds provided by the University of Rochester and the Chinese University of Hong Kong. Preparation of this article was aided in part by Grant BNS 8416988 from the National Science Foundation to Harry T. Reis. We are grateful to Kwok Leung for help with translation and to Arthur Aron, Garth Fletcher, Lee Hamilton, Yi Cheng Lin, Kuni Miyake, Harry Triandis, and Kuo-shu Yang for helpful comments on earlier drafts of this article.

THINKING CRITICALLY AND APPLYING YOUR KNOWLEDGE

1. Based on Figure 1, create your own version of the Rochester Interaction Record. Make multiple copies of the form and use it to record every interaction you have that lasts for ten minutes or more. Keep records for at least one full day (preferably longer). Then

summarize your results using simple tables similar in format to Tables 1–4 in the article. What did you learn from this activity?

2. The Rochester Interaction Record (RIR) provides detailed information about specific interactions. An alternative method for studying interaction is to ask people to respond to more general questions about their relationships. For instance, people might indicate "In general, how much do you disclose to your friends" using a rating scale from 1 (not at all) to 9 (very much). Or people might indicate whether they usually spend more time with one other person or in a group. Discuss the advantages and disadvantages of the fine-grained data provided by the RIR versus more global, overall ratings of one's social interactions.

3. Wheeler and his associates find higher levels of self-disclosure among Chinese students than among American students. How did they assess self-disclosure? What are the strengths and weaknesses of this method? What are possible alternative interpretations of the Chinese versus American difference in disclosure?

4. Studies of Americans often find that women disclose more to their women friends than men disclose to their men friends. Wheeler et al. replicate this finding for Americans. However, as shown in Table 4, the Chinese women and men in their sample did *not* differ in self-disclosure to same-sex friends. What factors might contribute to the sex difference often found in the United States? And why might this sex difference not be found in China?

❖ CHAPTER 13 ❖

Individualistic and Collectivistic Perspectives on Gender and the Cultural Context of Love and Intimacy

Karen K. Dion and Kenneth L. Dion

Although love and romance may seem the most personal of human experiences, they are strongly influenced by cultural beliefs and norms. American lovers insist on the right to follow their heart in selecting a mate. In some cultures, however, marriages arranged by parents or matchmakers are considered preferable. In this paper, Karen and Kenneth Dion consider how the differences between individualistic and collectivistic cultures may affect the experience of romantic love and emotional intimacy. Their literature review finds support for several fascinating cultural differences in love and marriage.

ABSTRACT: *Individualism and collectivism help explain culture-related differences in romantic love and in the importance of emotional intimacy in marriage. Three propositions are suggested: (a) Romantic love is more likely to be an important basis for marriage in individualistic than in collectivistic societies; (b) psychological intimacy in marriage is more important for marital satisfaction and personal well-being in individualistic than in collectivistic societies; and (c) although individualism fosters the valuing of romantic love, certain aspects of individualism at the psychological level make developing intimacy problematic. Evidence pertaining to these propositions is considered based on conceptual and empirical accounts of romantic love and psychological intimacy in marriage in two individualistic societies (Canada and the United States) and three collectivistic societies (China, India, and Japan). In addition, we suggest that consideration of individualism and collectivism as these constructs pertain to gender provides a framework for interpreting gender differences in the reported experience of love and intimacy in North American society.*

They met, fell in love, decided to marry (or cohabit), and hoped to live happily ever after. To many North Americans, this depiction of the development of an intimate relationship between a woman and a man has been an enduring prototype, and its features seem very familiar and self-evident. This depiction, however, reflects several assumptions about the nature of intimate, opposite-sex relationships that are culturally based. These as-

Source: Reprinted from *Journal of Social Issues*, 49(3), (1993), 53–69. Copyright © 1993 by The Society for the Psychological Study of Social Issues. Reprinted by permission.

sumptions are by no means universally shared, particularly in non-Western societies; even in Western societies, this view of love, intimacy, and marriage has not always prevailed.

We have contended that a cultural perspective is needed to understand the factors contributing to the development of close relationships (Dion & Dion, 1979, 1988). The first step in theory building in this area is to identify conceptual dimensions that have the potential to provide an integrative framework. We believe that the dimensions of individualism and collectivism are key constructs with this potential for the topic of close relationships. These dimensions have been acknowledged by scholars from diverse cultural backgrounds to be of conceptual relevance for understanding the social structuring of relationships. We have previously suggested that there are cultural differences in views of self and that these differences in self-construal have implications for understanding the experience of romantic love and intimacy in heterosexual relationships (Dion & Dion, 1988).

In the present article, we present a more fully elaborated conceptual framework linking individualism and collectivism to culture-related and gender-related differences in close relationships and consider the evidence relevant to three conceptual propositions. We discuss the contrasts in the social construction of love and intimacy in two societies where individualism has been a dominant value orientation (the United States and Canada) and three Asian societies in which a collectivistic orientation has prevailed (China, India, and Japan). Our analysis is therefore most directly applicable to the manifestations of individualism and collectivism in these societies. Moreover, although we focus on the contrasts between individualism and collectivism in this article, as work in this area develops, additional conceptual and empirical analysis of culture and close relationships will be needed to compare different individualistic societies and different collectivistic societies, respectively.

INDIVIDUALISM AND COLLECTIVISM: CULTURAL PERSPECTIVES

The constructs of individualism and collectivism concern the relation between the individual and the group as reflected across many domains of social functioning (Hofstede, 1984). Individualism has been defined as "the subordination of the goals of the collectivities to individual goals" while collectivism involves the opposite, namely, "the subordination of individual goals to the goals of a collective" (Hui & Triandis, 1986, pp. 244–245). These constructs have been conceptualized at the cultural level and at the personal level, and it is important to distinguish these two levels (Kim, 1993). Societies are labeled as "individualistic" or "collectivistic" when these value orientations characterize the majority of individual members (Hui & Triandis, 1986). Within a given society, however, individual differences exist in adherence to the prevailing orientation. We have proposed using the terms *societal individualism* and *societal collectivism* to refer to these constructs at the cultural level and *psychological individualism* and *psychological collectivism* to designate these constructs at the individual level (Dion & Dion, 1991).

In his seminal work in this area, Hofstede (1984) proposed that the following features distinguished individualistic as compared to collectivistic societies. In societies characterized by individualism, the emphasis is on promoting one's self-interest and that of one's immediate family. The individual's rights rather than duties are stressed, as are personal autonomy, self-realization, individual initiative, and decision making. Personal identity is defined by the individual's attributes. Prototypic examples of individualistic societies in Hofstede's study were the United States, Australia, Great Britain, and Canada. At the personal level, individualism is characterized by valuing one's independence and showing less concern for other persons' needs and interests (Hui & Triandis, 1986).

In contrast, collectivistic societies, according to Hofstede, are characterized as stressing the importance of the individual's loyalty to the group, which in turn safeguards the interests and well-being of the individual. Other features include reduced personal privacy, a sense of personal identity based on one's place in one's group, a belief in the superiority of group compared to individual decisions, and emotional dependency on groups and organizations. Among the Asian countries and city states in Hofstede's sample characterized by the above features were Taiwan, Singapore, Hong Kong, and Pakistan. At the personal level, collectivism is manifested by concern about interpersonal bonds, greater awareness of and responsiveness to the needs of others reflecting a sense of interconnectedness, and interdependence (Hui & Triandis, 1986).

These contrasts between individualism and collectivism are reflected in the psychological concepts underlying North American compared to Asian analyses of personal and interpersonal functioning. For example, concepts that have been salient in North American personality and social psychology, such as locus of control, self-actualization, and self-esteem, can be regarded as different manifestations of individualism (Waterman, 1984). As a result of her or his personal choices across the diverse areas of life, the individual can "realize a variety of inherent potentialities and capabilities" and organize personal identity based on these choices (Roland, 1988, p. 330). In this context, a sense of self as independent is likely, characterized by features such as valuing personal uniqueness, self-expression, and the realization of personal goals (Markus & Kitayama, 1991).

Asian scholars have contended that psychological concepts emerging from an individualistic orientation constrain a full understanding of human functioning. (Western scholars, too, have been critical of the pervasive impact of individualism as shown by Bellah et al., 1985; Hogan, 1975; Sampson, 1977, 1985). Asian and some Western behavioral scientists have identified psychological constructs pertaining to interpersonal functioning that are derived from a collectivistic social structure. Based on these analyses, there is evidence that the social construction of self and other differs greatly in individualistic as contrasted with collectivistic societies. Specifically, many important concepts in Asian societies, such as *amae*, are inherently relational (Ho, 1982). They reflect a sense of self as interdependent, rather than independent (Hsu, 1971; Markus & Kitayama, 1991).

To illustrate the emphasis on interdependence that characterizes many constructs from Asian psychology, the Japanese construct of *amae*, which has been discussed extensively by Doi (1962, 1963, 1977, 1988) provides a good example. The verb form of this noun is *amaeru*, which is defined as "to depend and presume upon another's benevolence" (Doi, 1962). A Japanese person who wishes to *amaeru* seeks to be a passive love object and to be indulged by another. The psychological prototype of *amae* is the mother–infant relationship (Doi, 1988). According to Doi (1988) and other scholars (Morsbach & Tyler,

1986), the expression of *amae* is aimed at psychologically denying the fact of one's separation from the mother.

Doi (1988) has used the *amae* concept as a single, sovereign principle for understanding Japanese personality as well as Japanese society. The people one can *amaeru* with impunity define insiders and include one's parents, relatives, close friends, and others with whom one stands in an hierarchical relationship. According to Doi, among outsiders, one must exhibit restraint or *enryo* and suppress the expression of any dependency needs, which Japanese find unpleasant.

A second example of cultural contrasts can be found in Roland's (1988) discussion of the *familial self* in India, which he compared with the North American *individualized self*. In his analysis, the Indian conception of self is basically relational rather than autonomous. Roland suggested that the familial self developed in hierarchical relationships within the extended family in which the following qualities were present: strong emotional interdependence, reciprocal demands for intimacy and support, mutual caring, and a high degree of empathy and sensitivity to another's needs and desires within the family structure.

INDIVIDUALISM AND COLLECTIVISM: GENDER PERSPECTIVES

There are some conceptual parallels between the above discussion of cultural differences in the social construction of self–other relationships and analyses of gender differences in self–other construal within North American society. The characteristics of the relational self hypothesized to be prevalent in various Asian societies are similar to some aspects of self-construal suggested as characterizing many North American women. Various scholars have proposed that the social construction of self for many North American women is relational, while for many men, it is autonomous. Before discussing this hypothesized contrast, it should be acknowledged that individual differences in self-construal *within* gender also seem likely. Nonetheless, hypothesized gender differences in self-construal provide a provocative analytical framework. The following two examples illustrate this viewpoint. (See also Lykes, 1985, and Markus & Kitayama, 1991, for an additional example and discussion of this issue.)

Chodorow (1978) analyzed the relation between the role of women as primary care givers in the family and the development of a sense of personal identity in their daughters and sons. She argued that primary parenting by women fostered the emergence of a "sense of self . . . continuous with others" for girls, while boys were encouraged to develop a more autonomous and distinct sense of self (Chodorow, 1978, p. 207). She suggested that this autonomous orientation ultimately made satisfying the emotional needs of others more problematic for men than for women.

Bardwick (1980) suggested that the predominant mode of self-construal for women has been either a dependent or an interdependent mode, both of which involve the self defined in the context of relationships. The former involves a sense of dependency, both psychologically and economically, as would be the case in a traditional marriage. The latter type involves both a "sense of self" but at the same time an awareness of the reciprocal aspects of an intimate relationship. With reference to Levinson's (1978) theory of adult development in which individuation is a key developmental task, Bardwick commented that this particular view of development was "very American and very male" and contrasted markedly with a view of adulthood as a time for "meeting responsibilities within relationships" (p. 40). She suggested that an individualistic, egocentric view of self characterized only a small minority of women.

Considered together, the above conceptual analyses suggest that in some individualistic societies there are gender differences in self-construal that in turn may be related to the experience of romantic love and the capacity for intimacy in close relationships. Although the focus here is on gender differences, there are other important individual difference dimensions that also are related to the experience of love and intimacy for both women and men (see Dion & Dion, 1985; Worell, 1988).

Finally, this perspective raises some intriguing questions about the relation between gender and the experience of love and intimacy in collectivistic societies. Specifically, if the mode of self-construal is interdependent for women and for men, this social construction of self should facilitate the capacity for intimacy for both sexes. As will be evident, however, in collectivistic societies both gender and cultural factors are related to the expression of intimacy in particular close relationships, such as marriage.

In the remainder of this article, we propose that individualistic societies (the United States and Canada) differ from collectivistic ones (China, India, and Japan) in the social construction of love and intimacy. Moreover, we suggest that gender and cultural differences in the reported experience of love and intimacy in heterosexual relationships are related in part to differences in self-construal.

LOVE AND INTIMACY

Proposition 1: Romantic love is more likely to be considered an important basis for marriage in societies where individualism as contrasted with collectivism is a dominant cultural value.

As noted at the start of this article, marriage based on romantic love may seem like a description of the natural progression of intimacy to many North Americans. It has been suggested, however, that romantic love is most likely to emerge in particular societal contexts. For example, Averill (1985) suggested a relation between aspects of romantic love such as idealization of the lover for his or her unique qualities and "individuation of the self" (Averill, 1985, p. 101). Both during earlier periods of Western history and in some Asian societies, Averill argued that since personal identity was not highly differentiated from the group, the social context did not provide the conditions in which romantic idealization could develop.

The conceptual link between the presence of romantic love and societal individualism has been commented on by other scholars. Bellah and his colleagues discussed the pervasive impact of individualism in both the public and the private domain of American life (Bellah et al., 1985). They used the term "expressive individualism," referring to the need for self-expression and self-realization, to describe the role of individualism in the private domain of life, including intimate relationships. In this context, romantic love provided the chance for exploring and revealing dimensions of oneself, with each member of the couple seeking to share their "real selves" with one another (Bellah et al., 1985).

Interestingly, although undertaken from a very different theoretical perspective on love, similar themes emerged in Sternberg and Grajek's (1984) research on the core components of love, based on adults' completion of several psychometric measures of love across different types of relationships. Among the features of love identified as central by Sternberg and Grajek were several which pertain to intimate self-expression and personal fulfillment such as "sharing of deeply personal ideas and feelings" and "personal growth through the relationship."

In more collectivistic societies, such as China, traditionally, love and intimacy between a woman and a man were less important than other factors as a basis for marriage. Hsu (1981) suggested that the concept of romantic love did not fit particularly well with traditional Chinese society since the individual was expected to take into account the wishes of others, especially one's parents and other family members, when choosing a spouse. The Western ideal of romantic love characterized by intense feelings, disregard of others' views of one's lover, and complete mutual absorption would be regarded as disruptive. Indeed it can be argued that in many collectivistic societies, romantic love as a basis for marriage would be dysfunctional.

Consistent with this line of reasoning, family structure has been found to be related to the occurrence of romantic love as a basis for marriage and autonomous selection of one's marital partner (Lee & Stone, 1980). Analyzing cross-cultural data from 117 nonindustrial societies, Lee and Stone found that marriage based on love and choice of one's own spouse was *less* likely to occur in societies characterized by extended family systems compared to those with nuclear family structures. An extended family system can be viewed as one manifestation of greater societal collectivism.

Among recent cohorts of young adults in some Asian societies, there are signs of change toward greater valuing of love as a basis for marriage. For example, in Japan, the number of "love marriages" has increased over the past four decades. However, traditional values in the parents' generation have persisted (Fukada, 1991). As of the early 1980s, Buruma (1984, p. 40) reported that up to 50% of all marriages in Japan were still arranged ones. Survey data for the latter part of the 1980s presented by De Mente (1989), however, seem to indicate stronger pressure for "love" or "love-based" marriages among young Japanese women today. Specifically, 70% of unmarried women in Japan were said to prefer to find their own husband, and an "overwhelming majority" (the exact percentage was not stated) of young Japanese women were described as preferring a love-based marriage. Similarly, in the 1980s (prior to 1989), there were signs of individualistic trends pertaining to choice of spouse in the People's Republic of China (Honig & Hershatter, 1988; Xiaohe & White, 1990).

It is intriguing to speculate about the factors that may contribute to the importance assigned romantic love as a basis for marriage in the People's Republic of China in the future. As a function of the "one child per family" policy, there are now large numbers of families in which there is only one child, and this child occupies a special and favored place in a household where traditionally the needs of the family unit were dominant. It would seem that a sense of personal uniqueness, a desire for personal gratification and fulfillment—in essence a highly individualized sense of self—are likely to develop in many of these children. Paradoxically, in a society where a relational sense of self traditionally has been the cultural norm, the family structure resulting from the "one-child" policy may ultimately foster a generation of individualists who may attach greater importance than earlier cohorts to self-discovery and personal fulfillment in their relationships with opposite-sex peers.

Proposition 2: Psychological intimacy in a marital relationship is more important for marital satisfaction and personal well-being for adults in individualistic societies than for those in collectivistic societies.

Much conceptual analysis and research on dating and marital relationships has been undertaken by researchers in the United States and in Canada. This interest in understanding what factors contribute to satisfaction and to stability in these types of relationships reflects the cultural value placed on marriage or similar types of committed relationships as an important source of personal well-being. The social support, especially the emotional support provided by one's spouse, has been suggested as one important contributor to physical and psychological health (Ross, Mirowsky, & Goldsteen, 1990).

Moreover, gender is related to societal expectations about the responsibility for fostering this desired intimacy in marriage. Based on a content analysis of articles pertaining to marriage in U.S. women's magazines from 1900 to 1979, Cancian and Gordon (1988) found that despite a shift toward emphasizing the importance of self-fulfillment in marriage, the advice given to women still conveyed the expectation that the woman was responsible for the emotional tenor of the marital relationship. It was her role to keep the relationship functioning smoothly.

This valuing of emotional intimacy with one's spouse found in some individualistic societies contrasts with expectations about emotional intimacy in marriage occurring in some traditionally collectivistic societies, such as China, Japan, and India. In the following discussion, we are *not* suggesting that in collectivistic societies couples do not develop affection and caring for each other. We are suggesting that for married couples in collectivistic societies, personal well-being is not as strongly related to psychological intimacy in marriage when compared to married couples in individualistic societies. In China, even after marriage, the primary ties of intimacy in which the individual's psychological well-being was rooted were the family relationships with parents, siblings, and other relatives (Hsu, 1985). Dependency on the family and the virtues of filial piety and devotion were emphasized across the life span (Ho, 1975).

Based on definitions of intimacy provided by North American behavioral scientists, Perlman and Fehr (1987) suggested three major components: degree of self-disclosure, interdependence, and emotional warmth. Interestingly, in Hsu's (1981) description of the traditional Chinese marriage, intimacy, as defined by reciprocal self-disclosure, sharing of activities, and revealing strong personal feelings, was not emphasized. Hence, there was little, or at least, less concern with issues such as happiness or satisfaction in the marriage since the bond between spouses was not their most important relationship. The man's primary responsibility was to his parents; the woman's primary responsibility after her marriage was to her husband's family.

There is, however, evidence suggesting some change. In Xiaohe and Whyte's (1990) study, the predictors of marital satisfaction among Chinese women were examined. The measure of marital satisfaction mostly assessed different facets of reported psychological intimacy (such as mutual disclosure of thoughts and feelings, affection given to and received from spouse, spouse's concern for wife's problems). The findings indicated that after controlling for a number of other background and family-related variables, degree of freedom of choice was the strongest positive predictor of marital satisfaction. In addition, reflecting the continuing importance of family relationships, parental approval of respondent's marriage, and having a good current relationship with husband's family also positively predicted marital satisfaction. This pattern of findings suggested the importance of individualistic factors (choice) and collectivistic factors (relations with other members of the family system) as correlates of Chinese women's satisfaction with their marital relationship.

According to Honig and Hershatter (1988), the depiction of the Chinese wife's role has begun to change from passive compliance and obedience to her husband and in-laws to a more active role in maintaining good family relations. For example, popular articles advised women that once married, they were expected to be a "skilled emotional manager," responsible for dealing with any friction with in-laws and for the emotional aspects of the relationship with their spouse. This portrayal of the wife's role in maintaining marital and familial harmony has its parallels in Cancian and Gordon's (1988) analysis of women's responsibility for maintaining intimacy, as depicted in advice to North American women in popular magazines throughout several decades of the 20th century.

Traditional Japanese society also illustrated the lesser importance of psychological intimacy in marriage in a collectivistic society. Marriages were generally arranged based on the two families' similarity of rank, occupation, and/or status (Fukada, 1991). Upon marriage, the bride was incorporated and effectively assimilated into her husband's *ie* (i.e., extended household), where she began a lengthy and demanding apprenticeship under the tutelage of her mother-in-law and, to a lesser extent, any sisters-in-law. Given the almost completely separate social spheres of women and men in the *ie* household, the married woman's primary relationships of emotional intimacy were focused primarily upon her children and secondarily with the other married women in the hierarchically structured, extended household (Roland, 1988). Fulfillment of needs for intimacy and nurturance were realized by a feeling of belonging in the context of the family group rather than by "sharing one's intimate self in companionship and communion" with one's spouse (DeVos, 1985, p. 165).

Among contemporary middle-class Japanese couples, it has been suggested that there continues to be relatively little psychological intimacy in the marital relationship for many couples (Roland, 1988). Although the influence of the *ie* extended household weakened in the post–World War II period, for many middle-class men, emotional and psychological needs are grounded in the intricate social relationships of their occupational context. The desire for a more intimate marital relationship on the part of some more educated Japanese women is difficult to realize given their spouse's long hours at work combined with the men's extensive postwork socializing. Thus for many middle-class Japanese women, the relationship with their children and to a lesser extent, long-standing friendships with women who were former classmates, are the principal sources of intimacy (Roland, 1988).

When considering the importance of psychological intimacy with one's spouse in Indian cultural contexts, the existence of religious and regional diversity in India must be kept in mind. In much of India, though there are some exceptions, the family structure is patriarchal, with age and gender defining one's position in the social hierarchy (Desai & Krishnaraj, 1990). A relational sense of self, although applicable to both sexes, has been suggested as more strongly descriptive of Indian women's self-construal (Kumar, 1991). For Hindu women, the complex family system structured women's relationships first in their family of origin, where they were prepared for their eventual roles as wife and mother. After an arranged marriage, they entered their husband's family where their relationships with the husband's mother and other female relatives became important. These relationships with the female relatives were traditionally a major source of concern and attention for married women, rather than the relationship with the spouse. Another source of emotional intimacy was the mother–child, especially the mother–son, relationship (Kumar, 1991).

Derlega (1984) suggested that to develop intimacy, it was important for individuals to accept each other's "true self," which involved in part a willingness to reveal negative as well as positive information about oneself. From this perspective, the findings of a study comparing marital satisfaction and communication in three types of marriages, Indian arranged marriage, Indian "love marriage," and American "companionate" marriage, are of interest (Yelsma & Athappilly, 1988). The data for the American couples were from a previous study and were used for comparison purposes with the Indian sample. For the Indian couples, most marriages were arranged by parents, but in urban areas, there were some "love matches," in which the individuals chose their own partners, sometimes from different religious, caste, or socioeconomic backgrounds. In the case of arranged marriages, both members of the proposed match could decline the choice made by the parents.

Individuals completed a measure of marital satisfaction (the Dyadic Adjustment Scale developed by Spanier, 1976) and a measure of reported interaction with their spouse in three domains (verbal, nonverbal, and sexual). In the North American sample, many aspects of reported marital communication were related to marital satisfaction, while among the Indian couples in arranged marriages, very few reported behaviors were correlated with marital satisfaction. Yelsma and Athappilly (1988) interpreted their findings as suggesting that while "a desire for emotional excitement" contributed to satisfaction in companionate marriages, other variables such as "a sense of life-long commitment and cultural tradition" were more likely to be related to satisfaction in arranged marriages. Their observation raises an important issue—namely, the criteria for defining a "successful marriage" may well differ for persons from individualistic and collectivistic societies.

Examination of the specific reported behaviors that were correlated with marital satisfaction among the American respondents reveals that many items pertained to psychological intimacy, such as sharing feelings and personal concerns, including discussing personal problems as well as positive topics. Among Indian respondents, some aspects of psychological intimacy, such as "talk about intimate matters" and "can tell what kind of day spouse has had," were related to marital satisfaction for those in love-based marriages but not for those in arranged marriages. However, compared to the American companionate marriages, the pattern of findings suggested that the type of intimacy reported by Indian respondents in the love-based marriages involved less extensive self-disclosure.

This pattern of findings raises an intriguing question about the nature of intimacy in close relationships. What is the role of verbal self-disclosure in the development of a sense of intimacy? Perhaps verbal disclosure is especially important in societal contexts where close relationships must be constantly negotiated, and a sense of mutual dependence and positive regard cannot be assumed, even after the initial formative phases of the relationship. This suggestion leads to our final proposition.

Proposition 3: Although individualism fosters the valuing of romantic love as a basis for marriage, certain aspects (or types of) individualism at the psychological level make developing intimacy problematic.

Problems with developing intimacy in a relationship should be most likely to occur among those persons characterized by "self-contained individualism" described by Sampson (1977), in which the emphasis is on valuing autonomy, personal control over one's life outcomes, and disliking any form of dependency. Attempting to reconcile the needs of two people in a relationship, each of whom is striving for intimacy, yet at the same time trying not to sacrifice personal control, is difficult (see also Bellah et al., 1985).

In our own research, we recently examined the relation between psychological individualism—valuing individualism at the personal level—and romantic love among Canadian respondents (Dion & Dion, 1991). This study illustrates a point made earlier: namely, that within an individualistic society, there are differences in the degree to which people endorse the prevailing value orientation. We reasoned that one component of psychological individualism was a desire to maintain one's personal autonomy, as illustrated by endorsing the following types of items: "My freedom and autonomy mean more to me than almost anything else" or "The best way to avoid trouble is to be as completely self-sufficient as possible." If psychological individualism partly reflects the valuing of personal autonomy, there might be ambivalence about emotional dependence in an intimate relationship. This ambivalence was hypothesized to manifest itself in less reported affective involvement with one's partner and in a less satisfying experience of romantic love.

We found, as predicted, that "self-contained individualism" was negatively related to reported caring, need, and trust of one's partner. "Self-contained" individualists were also less prone to describe their experience of romantic love as rewarding, deep, and tender. They were more likely to view "love as a game," as a test of their skills and power in a love relationship. In essence, our study suggested that psychological individualism, at least the "self-contained" type, was related to emotional detachment in romantic relationships.

Given the above pattern of findings, it is plausible that psychological individualism may be one factor contributing to a high rate of divorce in the United States and in Canada. Cherlin (1981) speculated that an individualistic view of relationships that specifies that a relationship end when either party is dissatisfied, might well contribute to a greater likelihood of divorce. Consistent with this speculation, we found that university students scoring high on psychological individualism indicated a less positive attitude toward marriage and were less opposed to divorce (Dion & Dion, 1993).

There is a marked difference in the evaluation of interpersonal dependency in individualistic vs. collectivistic societies. For example, *amae* psychology in Japan affirms an essentially positive and constructive attitude toward dependency upon others, especially in familial and pseudofamilial social arrangements. *Amae* has generally positive connotations to the Japanese, who use it to describe a variety of positively toned and sentimentalized relationships between parent and child, wife and husband, where one partner depends upon the other to provide indulgent gratification and considerate affection. In contrast, the term "dependency" has primarily negative or ambivalent connotations in Western cultures, such as the United States, which value autonomy and individuality. There is no equivalent word to *amae* or *amaeru* in Western languages, a fact that apparently astonishes Japanese (Doi, 1988).

Research on gender and relationships is also consistent with the proposition that some aspects of individualism may create problems for intimacy in relationships. As noted earlier, it has been suggested that women's construal of self is more relational (that is, more collectivistic) than men's views of self. Hui (1988) found some support for gender differences on his measure of individualism–collectivism in a cross-cultural study comparing university students from the United States and from Hong Kong. Women from both cultural groups scored higher on collectivism with regard to parents and friends than did their male peers.

Gender differences in reported social skills are also consistent with hypothesized gender differences in self-construal. Riggio (1986) found that women reported greater emotional expressivity and sensitivity as well as greater social expressivity and social sensitivity than men, qualities consistent with a relational view of self. Men in contrast reported greater emotional control and social manipulation than did women, qualities consistent with a view of self as autonomous. On another type of social skill that is consistent with a relational view of self, namely, the capacity to take one's partner's perspective, women were perceived both by themselves and by their spouse as more capable on this dimension (Long & Andrews, 1990).

In our research on the relation between gender and the reported experience of romantic love, the pattern of findings indicated that college-age women from the United States and from Canada expressed greater pragmatism than their male peers in their beliefs about love and more caution in their readiness to "fall in love." Once involved in a romantic relationship, however, women reported more intense positive emotions and described their experience as more emotionally involving and rewarding than did men (Dion & Dion, 1985, 1991). We have suggested that these gender differences might reflect greater responsiveness and adeptness on the part of the women in relationships involving psychological intimacy, described by Shaver and Buhrmester (1983) as involving reciprocal self-disclosure, emotional supportiveness, and a low level of defensiveness. All of these qualities are those that one would expect to be associated with a relational sense of self.

After marriage, however, some North American studies on the correlates of marital satisfaction have found greater dissatisfaction reported by wives compared to husbands (see Dion, 1985; Worell, 1988). Of interest here, much of the greater reported dissatisfaction appears to center around the issue of psychological intimacy (e.g., Locksley, 1980; Thurnher, 1976). In an individualistic society, both women and men may expect psychological intimacy in marriage. However, gender-related differences in how self is viewed in relation to others may in turn be related to the capacity for providing psychological intimacy to one's spouse. In a recent review of North American research, Ross et al. (1990) suggested that marriage was related to greater physical and psychological health benefits for men than for women. One of the key factors they proposed as underlying the relation between marriage and personal well-being was providing emotional intimacy and support to one's partner.

CONCLUSIONS

In conclusion, the purpose of this paper is to draw attention to the need to take into account the cultural context in which women's and men's experience of love and intimacy is based. Most theoretical accounts of close relationships in the social psychological literature have not explicitly considered this issue. As we can attest from writing this article, there is relatively little empirical research on close relationships in other cultural contexts, especially non-Western societies. Much of the research that does exist is in other disciplines such as psychological anthropology, family sociology, or comparative family studies.

We have presented three propositions suggesting a relation between individualism and collectivism, on the one hand, and romantic love and emotional intimacy in marriage, on the other. Considered together, these propositions lead to the following paradox: In societies where individualism is prevalent, greater emphasis is placed on romantic love and on personal fulfillment in marriage. However, some features of individualism at the psychological level make the likelihood of realizing these outcomes more difficult. In contrast, collectivism (as illustrated by the examples from three Asian societies) fosters a receptiveness to intimacy, but at the psychological level, this intimacy is likely to be diffused across a network of family relationships.

What are the implications of this conceptual analysis? It can be argued that in some respects, the marital relationship in individualistic societies is under greater pressure than in collectivistic societies because marriage is expected to fulfill a diverse array of psychological needs. It is not coincidental that at both the level of professional services and popular advice, there are numerous individuals and groups proffering advice on how to maintain and improve marriage. Given the high expectations for personal fulfillment in marriage, the rate of divorce is likely to increase as individualism, especially the self-contained type of individualism, increases. It may be that other types of individualism are not as problematic, but this possibility remains to be empirically documented.

We have suggested that some of the gender differences in the reported experience of romantic love and satisfaction with emotional intimacy in marriage within North American society may reflect gender differences in self-construal. It should not, however, be assumed that differences in self-construal are inherent in gender per se. Instead, it seems more plausible that a sense of self as relational or autonomous develops within a particular context of social relationships. Accordingly, cohort differences in self-construal for women and for men, respectively, might well be expected if there were changes in the structure of social relationships at both the personal and the societal levels. One can speculate, for example, that within North American society, there has been a trend for cohorts maturing in the 1970s and 1980s toward more individualistic self-construal. If so, we would expect that this trend might ultimately be related to greater reported dissatisfaction with emotional intimacy in marriage and similar relationships for both sexes compared to earlier cohorts.

Finally, although in recent years individualistic features (most notably, greater freedom of choice of one's spouse) have been present in some collectivistic societies, this particular trend should not necessarily be assumed to be a harbinger of the self-contained type of individualism. More collectivistic factors (such as parental approval of one's choice and maintaining a network of family and kin relationships after one's marriage) continue to be important. However, the analysis in this paper suggests that if some aspects of traditionally collectivistic societies change in the direction of greater individualism, the importance of psychological intimacy in marriage for marital satisfaction and personal well-being will increase.

REFERENCES

Averill, J. R. (1985). The social construction of emotion: With special reference to love. In K. J. Gergen & K. E. Davis (Eds.), *The social construction of the person* (pp. 89–109). New York: Springer-Verlag.

Bardwick, J. (1980). The seasons of a woman's life. In D. McGuigan (Ed.), *Women's lives: New theory, research and policy* (pp. 35–55). Ann Arbor: University of Michigan Press.

Bellah, R. N., Madsen, R., Sullivan, W. M., Swidler, A., & Tipton, S. M. (1985). *Habits of the heart: Individualism and commitment in American life.* Berkeley: University of California Press.

Buruma, I. (1984). *A Japanese mirror: Heroes and villains of Japanese culture.* New York: Viking Penguin.

Cancian, F., & Gordon, S. L. (1988). Changing emotion norms in marriage: Love and anger in U.S. women's magazines since 1900. *Gender and Society, 2,* 308–342.

Cherlin, A. J. (1981). *Marriage, divorce and remarriage.* Cambridge, MA: Harvard University Press.

Chodorow, N. (1978). *The reproduction of mothering: Psychoanalysis and the sociology of gender.* Berkeley: University of California Press.

De Mente, B. (1989). *Everything Japanese.* Lincolnwood, IL: Passport Books.

Derlega, V. J. (1984). Self-disclosure and intimate relationships. In V. J. Derlega (Ed.), *Communication, intimacy, and close relationships* (pp. 1–9). Orlando, FL: Academic.

Desai, N., & Krishnaraj, M. (1990). *Women and society in India.* Delhi, India: Ajanta Publications.

DeVos, G. (1985). Dimensions of the self in Japanese culture. In A. J. Marsella, G. DeVos, & F. L. K. Hsu (Eds.), *Culture and self: Asian and Western perspectives* (pp. 141–184). London, England: Tavistock.

Dion, K. K. (1985). Socialization in adulthood. In G. Lindzey & E. Aronson (Eds.), *Handbook of social psychology* (Vol. II, pp. 123–148). New York: Random House.

Dion, K. K., & Dion, K. L. (1985). Personality, gender, and the phenomenology of romantic love. In P. R. Shaver (Ed.), *Self, situations and behavior: Review of Personality and Social Psychology* (Vol. 6, pp. 209–239). Newbury Park, CA: Sage.

Dion, K. K., & Dion, K. L. (1991). Psychological individualism and romantic love. *Journal of Social Behavior and Personality, 6,* 17–33.

Dion, K. L., & Dion, K. K. (1979). Personality and behavioural correlates of romantic love. In M. Cook & G. Wilson (Eds.), *Love and attraction* (pp. 213–220). Oxford, England and New York: Pergamon.

Dion, K. L., & Dion, K. K. (1988). Romantic love: Individual and cultural perspectives. In R. J. Sternberg & M. L. Barnes (Eds.), *The psychology of love* (pp. 264–289). New Haven, CT: Yale University Press.

Dion, K. L., & Dion, K. K. (1993). *Correlates of psychological individualism and collectivism.* Manuscript in preparation.

Doi, T. (1962). AMAE: A key concept for understanding Japanese personality structure. In R. J. Smith & R. K. Beardsley (Eds.), *Japanese culture: Its development and characteristics* (pp. 132–139). Chicago, IL: Aldine.

Doi, T. (1963). Some thoughts on helplessness and the desire to be loved. *Psychiatry, 26,* 266–272.

Doi, T. (1977). The structure of amae. In M. Hyoe & E. G. Seidensticker (Eds.), *Guides to Japanese culture* (pp. 84–88). Tokyo: Japan Cultural Institute.

Doi, T. (1988). *The anatomy of dependence.* Tokyo and New York: Kodansha International.

Fukada, N. (1991). Women in Japan. In L. L. Adler (Ed.), *Women in cross-cultural perspective* (pp. 205–219). Westport, CT: Praeger.

Ho, D. Y. F. (1975). Traditional approaches to socialization. In J. W. Berry & W. J. Lonner (Eds.), *Applied cross-cultural psychology* (pp. 309–314). Amsterdam, Holland: Swets und Zeitlinger.

Ho, D. Y. F. (1982). Asian concepts in behavioral science. *Psychologia, 25,* 228–235.

Hofstede, G. (1984). *Culture's consequences: International differences in work-related values.* Newbury Park, CA: Sage.

Hogan, R. (1975). Theoretical egocentrism and the problem of compliance. *American Psychologist, 30,* 533–540.

Honig, E., & Hershatter, G. (1988). *Personal voices: Chinese women in the 1980's.* Stanford, CA: Stanford University Press.

Hsu, F. L. K. (1971). Psychosocial homeostatis and Jen: Conceptual tools for advancing psychological anthropology. *American Anthropologist, 73,* 23–44.

Hsu, F. L. K. (1981). *Americans and Chinese: Passage to differences* (3rd ed.). Honolulu, HW: The University Press of Hawaii.

Hsu, F. L. K. (1985). The self in cross-cultural perspective. In A. J. Marsella, G. DeVos, & F. L. K. Hsu (Eds.), *Culture and self: Asian and Western perspectives* (pp. 24–55). London, England: Tavistock.

Hui, C. H. (1988). Measurement of individualism–collectivism. *Journal of Research in Personality, 22,* 17–36.

Hui, C. H., & Triandis, H. C. (1986). Individualism–collectivism: A study of cross-cultural researchers. *Journal of Cross-Cultural Psychology, 17,* 225–248.

Kim, U. (1993). *Introduction to individualism and collectivism: Conceptual clarification and elaboration.* Unpublished manuscript.

Kumar, U. (1991). Life stages in the development of the Hindu woman in India. In L. L. Adler (Ed.), *Women in cross-cultural perspective* (pp. 142–158). Westport, CT: Praeger.

Lee, G. R., & Stone, L. H. (1980). Mate-selection systems and criteria: Variation according to family structure. *Journal of Marriage and the Family, 42,* 319–326.

Levinson, D. (1978). *The seasons of a man's life.* New York: Knopf.

Locksley, A. (1980). On the effects of wives' employment on marital adjustment and companionship. *Journal of Marriage and the Family, 42,* 337–346.

Long, E. C. J., & Andrews, D. W. (1990). Perspective taking as a predictor of marital adjustment. *Journal of Personality and Social Psychology, 59,* 126–131.

Lykes, M. B. (1985). Gender and individualistic vs. collectivist bases for notions about the self. *Journal of Personality, 53,* 356–383.

Markus, H. R., & Kitayama, S. (1991). Culture and the self: Implications for cognition, emotion, and motivation. *Psychological Review, 98,* 224–253.

Morsbach, H., & Tyler, W. J. (1986). A Japanese emotion. In R. Harré (Ed.), *The social construction of emotions* (pp. 289–307). New York: Blackwell.

Perlman, D., & Fehr, B. (1987). The development of intimate relationships. In D. Perlman & S. Duck (Eds.), *Intimate relationships: Development, dynamics, and deterioration* (pp. 13–42). Newbury Park, CA: Sage.

Riggio, R. E. (1986). Assessment of basic social skills. *Journal of Personality and Social Psychology, 51,* 649–660.

Roland, A. (1988). *In search of self in India and Japan.* Princeton, NJ: Princeton University Press.

Ross, C. E., Mirowsky, J., & Goldsteen, K. (1990). The impact of the family on health: The decade in review. *Journal of Marriage and the Family, 52,* 1059–1078.

Sampson, E. E. (1977). Psychology and the American ideal. *Journal of Personality and Social Psychology, 35,* 767–782.

Sampson, E. E. (1985). The decentralization of identity: Toward a revised concept of personal and social order. *American Psychologist, 40,* 1203–1211.

Shaver, P., & Buhrmester, D. (1983). Loneliness, sex-role orientation and group life: A social needs perspective. In P. B. Paulhus (Ed.), *Basic group processes* (pp. 259–288). New York: Springer–Verlag.

Spanier, G. B. (1976). Measuring dyadic adjustment: New scales for assessing the quality of marriage and similar dyads. *Journal of Marriage and the Family, 38,* 15–25.

Sternberg, R. J., & Grajek, S. (1984). The nature of love. *Journal of Personality and Social Psychology, 47,* 312–329.

Thurnher, M. (1976). Midlife marriage: Sex differences in evaluation and perspectives. *International Journal of Aging and Human Development, 7,* 129–135.

Waterman, A. S. (1984). *The psychology of individualism.* New York: Praeger.

Worell, J. (1988). Women's satisfaction in close relationships. *Clinical Psychology Review, 8,* 477–498.

Xiaohe, X., & Whyte, M. K. (1990). Love matches and arranged marriages: A Chinese replication. *Journal of Marriage and the Family, 52,* 709–722.

Yelsma, P., & Athappilly, K. (1988). Marital satisfaction and communication practices: Comparisons among Indian and American couples. *Journal of Comparative Family Studies, 19,* 37–54.

Preparation of this article was facilitated by a Social Sciences and Humanities Research Council of Canada (SSHRCC) grant to the first author. The authors would like to express their appreciation to Arthur Aron, Val Derlega, Susan Sprecher, and Barbara Winstead for their helpful and constructive comments on earlier versions of this article.

THINKING CRITICALLY AND APPLYING YOUR KNOWLEDGE

1. Dion and Dion propose a distinction between two levels of analysis, the societal and the psychological. Explain the concepts of societal individualism, societal collectivism, psychological individualism, and psychological collectivism. Give examples of how these

concepts might apply to the relations between workers and employers in a large business or factory.

2. Linda, an American college sophomore, has fallen in love with Minoru, an exchange student from a Japanese university. Based on the analysis by Dion and Dion, what issues or problems might arise if Linda and Minoru's relationship becomes closer?

3. In recent years, young adults in some Asian societies have shown a greater desire to select a marriage partner based on romantic love. What factors do you think may contribute to this change? What impact might an increase in "love-based" marriages (rather than arranged marriages) have for marital happiness and divorce in these Asian cultures?

4. Dion and Dion suggest that American couples may find it difficult to reconcile their desire for emotional intimacy with their desire for independence and psychological individualism. Do you agree or disagree with this proposition? Evaluate the evidence that Dion and Dion present to support their assertion.

5. Although Americans value freedom of choice in the selection of a mate, our choices are often influenced by cultural norms about "acceptable" or "desirable" partners. Think about your own cultural or ethnic background. What qualities are considered desirable in a boyfriend or husband? in a girlfriend or wife?

❖ CHAPTER 14 ❖

COOPERATION–COMPETITION AND SELF-ESTEEM: A CASE OF CULTURAL RELATIVISM

Spencer Kagan and George P. Knight

Why do some people feel good about themselves and their worth as a person while other people feel worthless and inadequate? Kagan and Knight show that our self-esteem tends to be high when we live up to the norms and values of our culture. In this study of Anglo-American and Mexican-American schoolchildren in the United States, the researchers investigated cultural values about competition versus cooperation. American culture tends to value competitiveness, and so more competitive Anglo-American children tend to have higher self-esteem than their less competitive Anglo peers. In contrast, Mexican culture places a premium on cooperation, and so the more cooperative Mexican-American children tend to have higher self-esteem than their less cooperative Mexican-American peers. In other words, competitiveness predicts high self-esteem in one cultural context (American values) and low self-esteem in another cultural context (Mexican values). In general, we feel good about ourselves when we have qualities valued by our cultural group.

ABSTRACT: *Several empirical studies have demonstrated that among Black and White U.S. children high self-esteem is associated with competitiveness. To test the generality of that relationship, the correlation of self-esteem and cooperation–competition was assessed among two generations of Mexican-American children and an Anglo-American comparison group. Among second-generation Mexican-American children, who display a cultural norm of cooperativeness, high self-esteem was significantly correlated with cooperativeness; among Anglo-American children, who display a cultural norm of competitiveness, high self-esteem was associated with competitiveness; among third-generation Mexican-American children, who do not demonstrate clear cooperation–competition norms, no clear relationship between self-esteem and cooperation–competition was found. Results do not support the generality of a self-esteem cooperation–competition relationship; rather, they are consistent with the interpretation that self-esteem is partially a function of the extent to which children live up to their cultural norms.*

In his pioneering work on self-esteem, Rosenberg (1965) noted a strong relationship between self-esteem and competition. Rosenberg used a stratified random sampling

---

Source: Reprinted from *Journal of Cross-Cultural Psychology*, *10*(4), (1979), 457–467. Copyright © 1979 by Western Washington University. Reprinted by permission of Sage Publications, Inc.

technique to ensure that his subjects were representative of public high school students in New York State. He noted that although a broad geographical range was sacrificed, his over 5,000 high school students represented various social classes, races, religious groups, rural and urban communities, and nationality groups. In presenting the strong systematic relationship between high self-esteem and competitiveness, data were not presented separately for the various subsamples. Nevertheless, Rosenberg noted that the relationship was not due to social class, grades, sex, or religion. The results of Rosenberg's study, therefore, suggest that the positive association of high self-esteem and competitiveness might be quite general, at least within the United States. The results of Rosenberg's study, however, remain only suggestive, because preference for competition was assessed by a single verbal question which asked respondents to indicate preference for a job involving competition or one involving little or no competition. No validity or reliability data are presented for the Rosenberg competition question, although increased self-esteem was extremely consistently related to increased preference for competition across seven levels of self-esteem.

Recently two additional empirical investigations also have demonstrated that high self-esteem is related to competitiveness (DeVoe, 1977; Vance & Richmond, 1975). The studies sampled over 500 children in both urban and rural elementary schools in the southeastern United States. Using the Kagan and Madsen (1971) Circle Matrix Game cooperation–competition measure, both studies found pairs of children high in self-esteem were more competitive than pairs containing one or both children with low self-esteem as assessed by the Piers-Harris Children's Self-Concept Scale (Robinson & Shaver, 1973). Together with the Rosenberg (1965) study, these two additional studies support the possibility of a culturally universal relationship between self-esteem and competitiveness; as a group the studies have employed two distinct self-esteem measures, two distinct competition measures, and have sampled a large number of subjects of diverse cultural backgrounds, with similar results in all cases.

The positive relationship of competitiveness to self-esteem, however, may not be a manifestation of a cultural universal, but rather may hold only among cultural groups in which competitiveness is highly valued. That is, self-esteem may be partially a function of the extent to which children live up to cultural norms, and so a positive relationship of self-esteem to competitiveness might be expected only among groups for which competition is the modal response. Although competition is the modal response among most Anglo-American children (Kagan, 1977; Knight & Kagan, 1977a), it is not the modal response among all cultural groups living within the United States. For example, among early generations of Mexican-American children cooperation rather than competition is the modal response (Knight & Kagan, 1977a). If self-esteem is indeed partially a function of the extent to which children live up to cultural norms, then among early generations of Mexican-American children the relation between competitiveness and self-esteem might be negative rather than positive. To test this hypothesis, the relationship of cooperation-competition to self-esteem was examined among two generations of Mexican-American children and an Anglo-American comparison group.

METHOD

Subjects

Data for the present analysis were generated by two previous studies of generational differences among Mexican-American children (Knight & Kagan, 1977a; Knight et al., 1978). Children in these studies were almost the entire population of fourth-, fifth-, and sixth-grade children in a predominantly Mexican-American school. The community from which the children were sampled is of particular interest because it strongly maintains traditional Mexican-American cultural values; it has been described in some detail by Ramirez and Castañeda (1974) as "traditional" because it is a stable community with little in- or outmigration and because many individuals within the community maintain many aspects of Mexican-American culture, including Spanish language and cultural ties with Mexico. Children in the community are approximately evenly divided among second-generation Mexican-Americans, third-generation Mexican-Americans and Anglo-Americans; and parents of the three groups of children do not differ significantly in income level. For the present analysis, 41 second-generation Mexican-American children, 50 third-generation Mexican-American children, and 45 Anglo-American children were sampled. The subjects were all children for whom both self-esteem and cooperation–competition scores were available.

Cooperation–Competition

The cooperation–competition measure employed in the present experiment, the Social Behavior Scale, has been described in some detail (Knight & Kagan, 1977a, 1977b). It is a measure derived from a theoretical framework described by Kagan (1977). The Social Behavior Scale is a behavioral choice card which assesses total amount of rewards given to a peer as well as the frequency of four separate behavioral choices, each of which satisfied distinct social motives, as follows: (1) altruism/group enhancement; (2) equality; (3) superiority; and (4) rivalry/superiority. The scale was administered in the present experiment as an individual measure. Previous work has established a .72 lower limit of reliability for this measure administered in this fashion (Knight & Kagan, 1977b). The Social Behavior Scale differs in several ways from the measures used in previous studies of the competition–self-esteem relationship. It is more appropriate for use with young children than the Rosenberg competition question, which involves job preference. For the present study the Social Behavior Scale also has some important advantages over the Kagan and Madsen (1971) Circle Matrix Game cooperation–competition measure employed by DeVoe (1977) and Vance and Richmond (1975) because that competitive measure was designed for assessing dyadic social interaction patterns; it does not directly assess individual differences in cooperative and competitive motivation and does not distinguish distinct motives.

Self-Esteem

Self-esteem was assessed by the short form of the Coopersmith Self-Esteem Inventory (SEI; Coopersmith, 1967). Although the reliability of the short form SEI has not been established, it correlates over .95 with the long form SEI, which has a test-retest reliability of

.88 over five weeks and .70 over three years for a sample of fifth- and sixth-grade children (Coopersmith, 1967). The SEI is more appropriate for use with children than is the ten-item Rosenberg Self-Esteem Scale (1965), which was developed for use among adolescents, but the two scales correlate .60 among college students (Robinson & Shaver, 1973). The 50-item SEI is similar in format to the 80-question Piers-Harris Children's Self Concept Scale; both scales sample a variety of domains, including school, relations with parents, and relations with peers.

RESULTS

Cooperation–Competition

The modal response of Anglo-American children in the present sample is the most competitive response possible, rivalry/superiority. The modal response of the second-generation Mexican-American children is equality, closely followed by altruism/group enhancement. The third-generation Mexican-American children have no clear modal response; their choices are bimodally distributed almost equally between equality and rivalry/superiority. As previously reported (Knight & Kagan, 1977a), linear trend analyses indicate that second-generation Mexican-American children make significantly more altruism/group enhancement responses than third-generation Mexican-American children, who make more than Anglo-American children. In contrast, Anglo-American children make significantly more rivalry/superiority choices than do third-generation Mexican-Americans, who, in turn, make more rivalry/superiority choices than second-generation Mexican-Americans.

Self-Esteem

The cultural and generational differences in self-esteem are not significant and the generational differences do not follow a linear pattern. As previously reported (Knight et al., 1978), a quadradic trend approaches significance, indicating that second-generation Mexican-American children tend to be more similar to Anglo-American children than are third-generation Mexican-Americans; second-generation Mexican-Americans and Anglo-Americans tend to be higher in self-esteem than third-generation Mexican-Americans.

Self-Esteem and Cooperation–Competition

All previous research on the self-esteem cooperation–competition relationship (DeVoe, 1977; Rosenberg, 1965: Vance & Richmond, 1975) has divided subjects into groups of high and low self-esteem and then tested their levels of cooperation–competition. To determine the extent to which the present results replicated those findings, high/low median splits were calculated and differences in cooperation–competition for the groups were analyzed by a $3 \times 2 \times 2 \times 3$ (cultural group × self-esteem group × sex × grade) analysis of variance. Given the hypothesis that early generation Mexican-American children might show a self-esteem cooperation–competition relationship reversed from that of the Anglo-American children, additional a priori contrasts were computed specifying that high self-esteem children would make more rivalry/superiority and superiority choices and fewer equality and altruism/group enhancement choices than low self-esteem children in the Anglo-American sample, while high self-esteem children would make more equality and altruism/group enhancement choices and fewer superiority and rivalry/superiority choices than low self-esteem children in the second-generation Mexican-American sample.

The analysis of variance revealed that among second-generation Mexican-American children high self-esteem was related to higher levels of equality responses but that among Anglo-American and third-generation Mexican-Americans the reverse was true: high self-esteem was related to less frequent choice of the equality alternatives, as illustrated in Figure 1. This interaction was statistically significant $F (2,110) = 3.37$, $p < .05$ as was the a priori contrast, $F (1,110) = 5.63$, $p < .05$. Culture interacted with self-esteem in determining frequency of rivalry/superiority choices as well. For the Anglo-American children high self-esteem was related to greater rivalry/superiority, whereas it was related to lower rivalry/superiority for the second-generation Mexican-American children. This interaction approached significance in the analysis of variance $F (2,110) = 2.76$, $p < .10$, and was significant in the a priori contrast, $F (1, 110) = 4.23$, $p < .05$. The only other significant differences revealed by these analyses were the cultural group differences indicating that

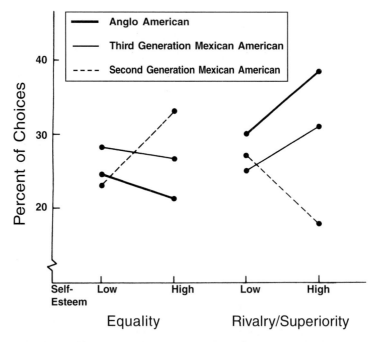

FIGURE 1 Self-esteem and percentage of equality and rivalry/superiority choices among Anglo-American, third-generation Mexican-American, and second-generation Mexican-American children (sex and grade collapsed).

Anglo-American children were most competitive, second-generation Mexican-American children were most cooperative, and third-generation Mexican-American children scored between the other two groups, as presented previously (Knight & Kagan, 1977b).

DISCUSSION

The results indicate that the relationship of self-esteem to cooperation–competition is partially culturally determined. Among Anglo-American children, who have very competitive cultural norms (Kagan, 1977; Knight & Kagan, 1977a), competitive children are relatively higher in self-esteem. Among third-generation Mexican-American children, for whom there is no clear modal response on the cooperation–competition measure, there is no clear relationship between cooperation–competition and self-esteem. Among second-generation Mexican-American children, who have clearly cooperative cultural norms (Knight & Kagan, 1977a) cooperative children are relatively higher in self-esteem. Interestingly, the modal response of second-generation Mexican-American children is equality, and it is that response which shows the highest relationship to self-esteem. This pattern of results is consistent with the conclusion that self-esteem is partially a function of the extent to which children live up to culturally determined cooperation–competition norms.

The culturally relative nature of the self-esteem cooperation–competition relationship indicates a need to reconsider the conclusions of previous researchers. For example, DeVoe (1977) indicates that high self-esteem students are likely to seek out and create competitive situations. The present results indicate that quite the opposite may be true among early generations of Mexican-Americans. Vance and Richmond (1975) indicate that the individual in American society who is seeking growth in self-concept may be impelled toward a competitive approach to others. For children of at least some cultural groups, growth of self-concept may not depend on a competitive social comparison process. Thus, the generality of the self-esteem cooperation–competition relationship suggested by the results of previous studies does not meet an important cross-cultural test. It appears that self-evaluation occurs within a cultural context. Self-esteem is probably a product of the evaluation of different variables and even different evaluation processes among various cultural groups. The present study provides further support for the need to evaluate psychological relations within specific cultures.

The present results also do not support the causal model assumed in previous research. The three previous research studies on the self-esteem cooperation–competition relationship have suggested that the direction of causality flows from self-esteem to cooperation–competition. That is, self-esteem differences are seen as causing individuals to either approach or avoid competition (DeVoe, 1977; Rosenberg, 1965) or self-esteem needs are seen as demanding that the individual enter the competitive social comparison process (Vance & Richmond, 1975). The pattern of the present results, however, suggests that the direction of causality may be reversed. That is, cultural norms for cooperation or competition are probably determined by long-standing cultural responses to the social ecology (Kagan, 1977), and therefore must be antecedent to self-evaluations based on those norms.

A common assumption among psychologists and educators has been that minority cultural groups in the United States have a substantially lower self-esteem than Anglo-American groups. That assumption is not supported in the present study; neither was it supported in previous studies. No significant differences between minority children and the Anglo-American comparison groups were observed in the present study, nor in the studies by DeVoe (1977) and Vance and Richmond (1975). A tendency for Blacks to score somewhat lower than Whites in the Rosenberg (1965) study was observed, but Rosenberg noted that the cultural differences were small and considerably smaller than expected. In contrast to the absence of cultural differences in self-esteem, the present study as well as those of DeVoe (1977) and Vance and Richmond (1975) consistently found minority children to be significantly more cooperative than their Anglo-American counterparts. Thus, across all studies the between-group differences in self-esteem are either small or not significant and so cannot account for the between-group differences in cooperation–competition which are consistently larger and significant.

Although the present study indicates an important exception to the high self-esteem competitiveness relationship, it also indicates that that relationship may be quite general. Given the four studies on that relationship to date, a wide range of methods and samples have revealed a positive relationship of high self-esteem and competitiveness in Black and White children and adolescents in urban and rural communities across the United States. It is only among recently immigrated Mexican-American children that the relationship does not hold. This pattern of results is consistent with the conclusion that in the mainstream United States culture, in which competitiveness is pervasively valued, individuals learn to feel good about themselves in part by living up to the cultural competition norm.

One final implication of the present findings is worth noting: The present results provide an important challenge to those who speak of "healthy" competition with the implied assumption that minority children who are less competitive are somehow deficient. The culturally relative nature of the present findings indicates noncompetitive minority children are not necessarily deficient; quite in contrast, they appear to be realizing important cooperative cultural values, increasing their self-esteem in the process.

REFERENCES

Coopersmith, S. (1967). *The antecedents of self-esteem*. San Francisco: W. H. Freeman.

DeVoe, M. W. (1977). Cooperation as a function of self-concept, sex, and race. *Educational Research Quarterly, 2,* 3–8.

Kagan, S. (1977). Social motives and behaviors of Mexican American and Anglo American children. In J. L. Martinez (Ed.), *Chicano psychology*. New York: Academic Press.

Kagan, S., & Madsen, M. (1971). Cooperation and competition of Mexican, Mexican-American, and Anglo-American children of two ages under four instructional sets. *Developmental Psychology, 5,* 32–39.

Knight, G. P., & Kagan, S. (1977a). Acculturation of prosocial and competitive behaviors among second- and third-generation Mexican American children. *Journal of Cross-Cultural Psychology, 8,* 273–284.

Knight, G. P., & Kagan, S. (1977b). Development of prosocial and competitive behaviors in Anglo American and Mexican American children. *Child Development, 48,* 1385–1394.

Knight, G. P., Kagan, S., Nelson, W., & Gumbiner, J. (1978). Acculturation of second- and third-generation Mexican American children: Field independence, locus of control, self-esteem, and school achievement. *Journal of Cross-Cultural Psychology, 9,* 87–97.

Ramirez, M., & Castaneda, A. (1974). *Cultural democracy, bicognitive development, and education.* New York: Academic Press.

Robinson, J. P., & Shaver, P. R. (1973). *Measures of social psychological attitudes.* Ann Arbor: Institute for Social Research, University of Michigan.

Rosenberg, M. (1965). *Society and the adolescent self-image.* Princeton, NJ: Princeton University Press.

Vance, J. J., & Richmond, B. O. (1975). Cooperative and competitive behavior as a function of self-esteem. *Psychology in the Schools, 12,* 225–259.

THINKING CRITICALLY AND APPLYING YOUR KNOWLEDGE

1. Kagan and Knight compare second-generation Mexican-American children (whose parents were born in Mexico) to third-generation Mexican-American children (whose parents were born in the United States). What similarities and differences did the researchers find? Why is this comparison useful?

2. The authors describe American culture as highly competitive. Evaluate this assertion. Think of specific examples from your own experiences that illustrate an American emphasis on competition. Can you think of counterexamples, that is, situations or contexts in which American culture actually encourages or rewards cooperation rather than competition?

3. American classrooms tend to be competitive environments, with students vying for attention and approval from the teacher. For example, grading students "on a curve" so that only a fixed proportion of students can get top grades creates competition for grades. Based on Kagan and Knight's research, how might this competitive approach to education affect students from more cooperative cultures? What might educators do to help all students succeed in school?

4. Kagan and Knight studied how a cultural emphasis on competition versus cooperation can affect self-esteem. What other aspects of personality, attitudes, or behavior might also be affected by this cooperation–competition dimension of culture?

❖ CHAPTER 15 ❖

Violence and U.S. Regional Culture

Richard E. Nisbett

A country as large and diverse as the United States encompasses many distinctive cultural groups. In this provocative paper, Nisbett examines the culture of Whites living in the southern United States. According to Nisbett, White southerners adhere to a "culture of honor" that endorses the use of violence to protect one's home or family or in response to insults. Nisbett traces the origins of this culture of honor to the early European settlers in the South, whose dependence on herding for a livelihood fostered certain attitudes toward violence. Nisbett believes that the legacy of this cultural tradition is the persistence of regional differences in attitudes toward violence and in actual violent behavior. He supports his argument with a wide range of data including national opinion polls about violence, crime statistics on rates of homicide, and experiments comparing the behavior of college students from different regions of the United States. Nisbett's program of research illustrates how a sociocultural perspective can help to identify connections among economic and historical factors, cultural values, and individual behavior.

ABSTRACT: *The U.S. South, and western regions of the U.S. initially settled by Southerners, are more violent than the rest of the country. Homicide rates for White Southern males are substantially higher than those for White Northern males, especially in rural areas. But only for argument-related homicides are Southern rates higher. Southerners do not endorse violence more than do Northerners when survey questions are expressed in general terms, but they are more inclined to endorse violence for protection and in response to insults. Southern subjects responded with more apparent anger to insults than did Northerners and were more likely to propose violent solutions to conflicts presented in scenarios after being insulted. The social matrix that produced this pattern may be the culture of honor characteristic of particular economic circumstances, including the herding society of the early South. Consistent with this possibility, the herding regions of the South are still the most violent.*

Phenomena involving regional, ethnic, or cultural differences in patterns of behavior often prompt heated disputes among historians, sociologists, anthropologists, and economists who seek to account for such phenomena using the particular analytic tools of their disciplines. For the most part, social psychologists have chosen to stand apart from such controversies, although such differences seem to have a psychological component and to

Source: Reprinted from *American Psychologist*, 48(4), (1993), 441–449. Copyright © 1993 by the American Psychological Association. Reprinted by permission.

be susceptible to examination by social psychological methods. Indeed, because of the diversity of methods and theoretical approaches used by social psychologists, the field may be well positioned to act as a kind of broker for questions about differences in collective patterns of behavior. The question of regional differences in violence is one of this sort.

Throughout the history of the United States, Southerners have been regarded—by Northerners, by travelers from Europe, and by themselves—as being more violent than Northerners. The *Encyclopedia of Southern Culture* devotes 39 pages to the topic of violence, beginning with the sentence "Violence has been associated with the South since the time of the American Revolution" (Gastil, 1989, p. 1473). The subsequent pages are replete with accounts of feuds, duels, lynchings, and bushwhackings—events that are held to have been relatively commonplace in the South and relatively rare in the North. Less lethal forms of violence are also reputed to have characterized the South. Autobiographies of Southerners, more than of Northerners, report severe beatings by parents (Fischer, 1989, p. 689). Pastimes that seem inconceivable on a New England village green or a Middle Atlantic town square were commonplace in the old South. For example, there was a sport called "purring," in which two opponents grasped each other firmly by the shoulders and began kicking each other in the shins at the starting signal. The loser was the man who released his grip first (McWhiney, 1988, p. 154).

Assuming the accuracy of the historical evidence, why should there be such strong regional differences in preference for violence? Historians, anthropologists, and other social scientists have offered five different explanations.

One explanation calls on the temperature difference between North and South. There is a reliable relationship between temperature and violence; homicides (Anderson, 1989) and other violent acts, such as injuries from misthrown baseball pitches (Reifman, Larrick, & Fein, 1991), are more common in hot weather than in cooler weather.

A second explanation is poverty. The South is poorer than the rest of the country, and poverty is associated with crimes of all kinds, including crimes of violence. Hence, greater Southern rates of violence might be attributable to greater poverty (Blau & Blau, 1982).

A third explanation, and one of the oldest, attributes Southern violence to the institution of slavery. Tocqueville (1835/1969) traveled down the Ohio River and contrasted the industrious farmers on the Ohio side with the boisterous layabouts he found on the Kentucky side. He noted that the institution of slavery made it both unnecessary and demeaning for the Whites to work and that the resulting idleness allowed them to turn to exciting, dangerous pastimes.

But the Kentuckian scorns not only labor but all the undertakings that labor promotes; as he lives in an idle independence, his tastes are those of an idle man; money has lost a portion of its value in his eyes; he covets wealth much less than pleasure and excitement; and the energy which his neighbor devotes to gain turns with him to a passionate love of field sports and military exercises; he delights in violent bodily exertion, he is familiar with the use of arms, and is accustomed from a very early age to expose his life in single combat. (p. 379)

A fourth explanation is that the violence of the Whites was the result of imitating the violence of African Americans (Cash, 1941). The violence of that group might be due to an originally violent culture or a reaction to ill treatment at the hands of Whites, but whatever its cause, Whites may have been unconsciously mimicking it (see Hackney, 1969).

HERDING ECONOMIES AND THE CULTURE OF HONOR

A fifth explanation, and the one that I argue for, is that the South is heir to a culture, deriving ultimately from economic determinants, in which violence is a natural and integral part. New England and the Middle Atlantic states were settled by sober Puritans, Quakers, and Dutch farmer–artisans. In their advanced agricultural economy, the most effective stance was one of quiet, cooperative citizenship with each individual being capable of uniting for the common good. In contrast, the South was settled initially by swashbuckling Cavaliers of noble and landed gentry status, who took their values not from the tilling of the soil and the requirements of civic responsibility but from the knightly, medieval standards of manly honor and virtue. The major subsequent wave of immigration, and a much larger and ultimately more influential one, was from the borderlands of Scotland and Ireland (Fischer, 1989; McWhiney, 1988). These Celtic peoples had long had an economy based on herding, primarily pig herding. At the time of the Puritan migrations, they were "isolated from and hostile to their English neighbors, and they remained tribal, pastoral and warlike" (McWhiney, 1988, p. xxxiv). Upon arrival in America, during the 17th and 18th centuries, they moved inland from the northeast coast (usually from the entry port of Philadelphia) to the southern and western frontiers, especially to the hill country regions. There they continued and even intensified the hunting and herding practices at the base of their economy.

Herding, even when carried out in less isolated circumstances than the American frontier, predisposes people to a violent stance toward their fellows (Lowie, 1954; Peristiany, 1965). This is so because pastoralists are extraordinarily vulnerable economically. Their livelihoods can be lost in an instant by the theft of their herds. To reduce the likelihood of this occurring, pastoralists cultivate a posture of extreme vigilance toward any act that might be perceived as threatening in any way, and respond with sufficient force to frighten the offender and the community into recognizing that they are not to be trifled with. In writing of the Mediterranean herding culture, similar in many ways to traditional Celtic cultures of Europe and the American South, Campbell (1965) described the task confronting young shepherds:

> The critical moment in the development of the young shepherd's reputation is his first quarrel. Quarrels are necessarily public. They may occur in the coffee shop, the village square, or most frequently on a grazing boundary where a curse or a stone aimed at one of his straying sheep by another shepherd is an insult which inevitably requires a violent response. . . . It is the critical nature of these first important tests of his manliness that makes the self-regard (*egoismos*) of the young shepherd so extremely sensitive. It is not only the reality of an obvious insult which provokes him to action, but even the finest of allusions on which it is possible to place some unflattering construction. (p. 148)

Young White Southern men were taught to create a similar impression of themselves as being ferocious in defense of their reputations.

> From an early age, small boys were taught to think much of their own honor, and to be active in its defense. Honor in this society meant a pride of manhood in masculine courage, physical strength and warrior virtue. Male children were trained to defend their honor without a moment's hesitation—lashing out against their challengers with savage violence. . . . These backcountry child ways were . . . transplanted from the borders of North Britain, where they were yet another cultural adaptation to the endemic violence of that region. . . . This system of child rearing flourished in its new American environment. (Fischer, 1989, p. 690)

The socialization of Andrew Jackson, the first U.S. president raised in a herding region (the hills of Tennessee), was very much in this culture-of-honor tradition. In advice to the young Jackson, his mother made it clear how he was to deal with insults: "Never tell a lie, nor take what is not yours, nor sue anybody for slander or assault and battery. Always settle them cases yourself" (McWhiney, 1988, p. 169). Jackson, a true representative of his culture, was involved in more than 100 violent quarrels in his lifetime, including one in which he killed a political opponent.

Southern society seems to have retained aspects of the culture of honor even in this century, resulting in very different views about violence there than are common in the rest of the country. Hodding Carter, a Mississippi journalist, reported that in the 1930s he served on a jury in a homicide case. The accused was an irritable man who lived next to a gas station. Day after day, the workers at the station made jokes at the man's expense until one morning the man emptied his shotgun into the crowd, maiming one of the jokers, wounding another, and killing an innocent customer. Carter was the only juror for conviction. As one of the 11 jurors voting for acquittal put it, "He ain't guilty. *He wouldn't of been much of a man if he hadn't shot them fellows*" (Carter, 1950, p. 50). Brearley (1934) wrote that in much of the South of his time it was impossible to obtain a conviction for murder if the perpetrator had (a) been insulted and (b) had warned the victim of his intention to kill if the insult were not retracted or compensated. Lundsgraade (1977) has maintained that the same pattern holds in modern Houston, Texas. And until the 1970s, Texas law held that there was no crime if a man killed his wife's lover caught in *flagrante delicto* (Reed, 1981).

REGIONAL DIFFERENCES IN HOMICIDE

There is abundant historical and anecdotal evidence supporting the view that the South is more violent and other such evidence linking this violence to the herder–warrior culture of honor. What is the status of statistical evidence of the sort likely to convince a social scientist? Most research to date has focused on homicide, both because of its obvious importance and because excellent, relatively error-free data are available. It is a simple matter to determine whether homicide rates are higher in one region than another, and in fact most investigators find that they are higher in the South. Linking this difference to the nature of traditional Southern White culture has proved to be a matter of great dispute. Some investigators (e.g., Blau & Blau, 1982) have maintained that Southern homicide rates are no higher than Northern rates once one "corrects" for the facts that the South is poorer, has greater income inequality, and has more African Americans—three factors associated with higher homicide rates. However, the elimination of differences among regions through statistical adjustment obscures potentially important differences among regions. In my view, the data have been analyzed at too high a level of aggregation, examining homicides from all races and all city sizes (another variable with a heavy positive effect on homicide rates) and then trying to pull race, city size, and other effects out statistically.

It seems to make more sense to examine the rates for Whites separately, at each city size separately, and see whether the rates are different between North and South. This is what Gregory Polly, Sylvia Lang, and I did (Nisbett, Polly, & Lang, 1993). We looked at both male offender rates and victim rates, because they have different sources of error. Offender rates could be wrong about the race of some of the perpetrators because the wrong person was arrested. Victim data would rarely be wrong about the race of the victim, but in a small fraction of cases the perpetrator is not of the same race as the victim (Hackney, 1969). We examined White, non-Hispanic offender and victim data for small cities (10,000–50,000 inhabitants), medium sized cities (50,000–200,000 inhabitants), and large cities (more than 200,000 inhabitants) for the period 1976–1983. We included in our analysis every variable found by any investigation we have read to be significantly associated with homicide rates in the United States, including an index of poverty, an index of income inequality (the "Gini" index; U.S. Bureau of the Census, 1983), population density, and percentage of the population who are males between the ages of 15 and 29. Instead of just examining North versus South as a two-level dummy variable, we followed the recommendation of Gastil (1971) and used a continuous variable of degree of "Southernness" of the state in which the offense ocurred. This variable reflects the fact that some non-Southern states, including several Western and southern Midwest states, were settled primarily by Southerners. In fact, in the mid to late 19th century, the great majority of the residents of some non-Southern states, such as Oklahoma and Arizona, had been born in the South. Gastil's scheme assigns a score to each state reflective of the proportion of the population descended from Southerners.

We may examine first the data just for cities with 90% or more residents who are White and non-Hispanic. This means that population density, poverty, and income inequality data are derived primarily from the White population. There are no cities of more than 200,000 people having 90% or more White non-Hispanic populations, but there are sufficient numbers of smaller cities like that in our sample to make an analysis meaningful. Table 1 presents regression coefficients (from an analysis in which variables were entered simultaneously) for these cities for White male offender rates and for victim rates. It may be seen that the only variables that predict homicide rates consistently across both measures and both city sizes are poverty and Southernness. Although poverty is an important predictor of homicide, Southernness is also important and remains important even when poverty differences among regions are taken into account.

TABLE 1
Standardized Regression Coefficients for White Non-Hispanic Homicide Rates for Cities That Are 90% or More White and Non-Hispanic

	City size			
	10,000–50,000 (*n* = 101)		50,000–200,000 (*n* = 60)	
Measure	Male offender rate	Victim rate	Male offender rate	Victim rate
Gini index	−.03	.15	.26*	.14
Population density	−.05	−.08	−.11	−.14
Poverty index	.38***	.25*	.42 ***	.46***
% Males 15–29	−.10	−.06	−.22*	−.20*
Southernness index	.37***	.43***	.52**	.64**
*r*²	.29	.33	.49	.57

*p ≤ .05. **p ≤ .01. ***p ≤ .001.

The unadjusted rates for White, non-Hispanic homicide in the major census regions are presented in Table 2. The regions of the country are ordered in terms of increasing Southernness, defined as percentage of the current population descended from Southerners. It may be seen in Table 2 that the regional differences are really quite large in absolute terms. For the smaller cities, the ratio of homicides in the South to homicides in New England, the least Southern region, is about three to one. For the medium-size cities, the ratio is more than two to one. It is important to note that the rates for Southern regions are higher than for comparable, more Northern regions even when one takes into account poverty differences between regions. For example, the small cities of the plains region of Texas having the lowest poverty rates produce much higher homicide rates than the small cities of the plains region of Nebraska having the highest poverty rates (and substantially higher than the poverty rates of the low-poverty-rate Texas cities).

Essentially the same picture as in Tables 1 and 2 can be found by examining the White homicide rates for cities of all kinds, including those with high non-White and Hispanic populations. Again, the ratio of White homicides for a random sample of all small cities is three times higher for the South than for New England, and twice as high for medium-size cities. For cities of more than 200,000, however, the regional difference is very slight. A regional difference for large cities emerges in regression analyses because poverty rates for Northern large cities are actually higher than for Southern large cities. Because poverty rates in large cities are heavily influenced by the rates for non-Whites, the adjustment for poverty probably gives a misleading picture for the White population. It seems more likely

TABLE 2
White Non-Hispanic Homicide Rates for Cities That Are 90% or More White and Non-Hispanic

	City size					
	10,000–50,000			50,000–200,000		
Region	Male offender rate	Victim rate	n	Male offender rate	Victim rate	n
New England	2.62	1.77	22	3.16	1.63	11
Middle Atlantic	1.90	1.02	10	3.35	2.49	7
Midwest	2.92	1.97	45	3.37	2.20	24
Pacific	4.62	2.64	8	6.10	4.26	5
Mountain	4.67	3.26	14	4.56	3.14	8
Southwest	5.13	4.69	4	4.47	2.84	2
South	8.23	4.85	9	6.63	4.49	4
Ratio of South to New England	3.14	2.74		2.10	2.74	

that regional differences are indeed smaller for the White population in large cities than in smaller cities.

The pattern of greater regional differences for smaller cities has two important implications. First, it shows that the South is not uniform with respect to homicide. It is the smaller communities of the South—and West—that have elevated homicide rates. This pattern suggests that the phenomenon is primarily rural in nature, consistent with the historical argument about the importance of type of agricultural economy in producing the cultural differences in the first place. Second, it indicates that temperature differences between regions are not the basis of regional differences in homicide, because regional temperature differences are as great for large cities as for small ones.

REGIONAL DIFFERENCES IN ATTITUDES TOWARD VIOLENCE

Of course, the argument to this point is what sociologists call a merely *residual* one. Southernness may be correlated with something not yet measured that no one would want to call culture. It would be good to have some positive indication that there are regional differences in attitudes or other psychological variables between North and South that could plausibly explain the homicide differences. As many investigators have pointed out, there just are not that many documented differences between Southerners and non-Southerners in attitudes toward violence (e.g., Reed, 1981). (It is customary, though, to find Southerners more in favor of whatever war the United States is fighting at the time of the survey, more approving of spanking as a discipline technique for children, and more opposed to gun control.)

Dov Cohen and I (in press) have recently begun a review of the major national surveys that have covered topics of violence and have conducted our own survey of White men in the most rural counties of the South and the western portion of the Midwest. The national surveys include the National Opinion Research Council (NORC; Davis & Smith, 1989) items of the past 20 years that have dealt with questions of interpersonal violence and the classic study by Blumenthal, Kahn, Andrews, and Head (1972) on American males' attitudes toward violence. I report the data for White men only from each of these surveys.

The NORC and Blumenthal et al. (1972) data sets contained numerous questions about violence in the abstract, but few produced regional differences. For example, respondents from different regions proved equally willing to endorse items such as, "An eye for an eye and a tooth for a tooth is a good rule for living"; "Many people only learn through violence"; and "When someone does wrong, he should be paid back for it." Although there were a few abstract questions for which Southerners were more inclined to endorse violence (e.g., "It is often necessary to use violence to prevent violence"), there were just as many for which Southerners were less inclined to endorse violence (e.g., "When a person harms you, you should turn the other cheek and forgive him"). Even when the questions were made more concrete, specifying the settings or participants, Southerners were not necessarily more likely than Northerners to endorse violence. For example, Southerners were no more likely to agree that police may sometimes have to beat suspects or that it might be right for a man to punch another adult male.

Despite these null results Cohen and Nesbitt (in press) found three specific categories of survey items that differentiate Southerners from non-Southerners—items that relate to self-protection, to the proper response to an insult, and to the role of violence in the socialization of children.

Attitudes Toward Violence for Self-Protection

The protection items show a difference relating both to protection of property and to the protection of human life, including one's own. For example, when asked whether a man has the right to kill to defend his home, 36% of White Southern men agreed a great deal, compared with 18% of non-Southern White men. (There is a North Carolina proverb saying that "Every man is a sheriff on his own hearth.") Southern men were also more likely to agree that "a man has the right to kill a person to defend his family" (80% vs. 67%). Similarly, Southern men were more likely to say that police should shoot, or even shoot to kill, to protect against rioters, whether the rioters are Blacks, gangs of hoodlums, or students (all examples are from Blumenthal et al., 1972.)

In our survey of rural counties, we found White Southern men to be twice as likely to report having guns for purposes of protection as rural Midwestern White men, although they were no more likely to report owning them. It seems not to be a stretch to explain both the customary Southern opposition to gun control and the customary Southern endorsement of the war of the moment in terms of the greater importance of protection. If protection of life and property by violent means is a necessity, then ownership of guns is required, and gun control imperils self-protection. Wars are usually defended (at least in this century) in terms of the need for self-protection, which might be expected to appeal to Southerners.

Attitudes Toward Violence in Response to Insults

The second major difference we find has to do with the appropriate response to insults. A pair of NORC questions presented in Table 3 is revealing. Respondents were asked if they thought it could ever be right for an adult male to punch another male and whether it could ever be right for a man to hit a drunk who bumped into the man and his wife. Although there were no regional differences in approval of the notion that it could ever be right for a man to punch another adult male, there were differences when it was specified that the other man was a drunk who bumped into the man and his wife, a situation that many would regard as an insult. Cohen and Nisbett (in press) included the insult item in their survey of rural respondents and found similar results. Other concrete scenarios, which did not involve insults, produced no regional differences in endorsement of a man punching another man, either in the NORC data or in Cohen and Nisbett's data.

TABLE 3
Percentage Endorsing 1990 NORC Questions on Violence as a Function of Region

Region	NORC national data[a]		Cohen & Nisbett rural country survey[b]
	Ever approve of a man punching adult male	Approve of hitting a drunk who bumped into a man and his wife	Approve of hitting a drunk who bumped into a man and his wife
New England	73	7	—
Middle Atlantic	68	7	—
Midwest	69	8	6
Pacific	73	8	—
Mountain	72	10	—
Southwest	70	14	—
South	73	15	16

Note: NORC = National Opinion Research Council.

[a] Davis & Smith, 1989. [b]"Self-Protection and the Culture of Honor" by D. Cohen and R. E. Nisbett, in press. *Personality and Social Psychology Bulletin.*

Cohen and Nisbett (in press) presented their subjects with a series of scenarios in which an insult occurs and asked them whether a violent response—either fighting or shooting the person who does the insulting—would be justified, extremely justified, or not at all justified. For example, they described a situation in which "Fred fights an acquaintance because that person looks over Fred's girlfriend and starts talking to her in a suggestive way" and another situation in which "Fred shoots another person because that person sexually assaults Fred's 16-year-old daughter." In addition, they asked those subjects who felt that the violence would be justified whether they thought that the insulted person "would not be much of a man" if he failed to respond violently.

White Southern men were more likely than White Midwestern men both to feel that the violent response to the insult is extremely justified (12% vs. 6%) and to say that a failure to respond violently would indicate that the insulted person was not much of a man (19% vs. 12%; both regional differences are significant at the .01 level). It is important to note that these results cannot be explained by differences in either educational or economic status, both of which were nearly identical for the Northern and Southern samples.

Socialization for Violence

The third major area in which Southern attitudes differ from Northern ones has to do with socialization for violence. Anthropologists point out that an adult male cannot be expected to respond with violence to insults and to be prepared to defend himself and his family and property with violence when threatened unless he has a long-time familiarity with violence. Thus, his own youthful infractions may have been dealt with violently—by spankings or beatings—and he may have been encouraged to respond with violence, from an early age, to the insults of his peers (e.g., Cambell, 1965; Lowie, 1954; Peristiany, 1965).

Cohen and Nisbett (in press) have found that these patterns of socialization for violence are characteristic of modern Southern White men. They asked their subjects whether they thought spankings in general were justified and whether they thought that a spanking for a specific infraction, such as shoplifting, was justified. About 49% of their Southern subjects strongly agreed that spanking was an appropriate discipline policy, whereas only 31% of their Midwestern subjects thought so. Similarly, 67% of their Southern subjects thought spanking was appropriate for shoplifting, whereas only 45% of their Northern subjects thought so. These differences are comparable to others reported in the literature on regional differences in attitudes toward spanking.

Cohen and Nisbett (in press) also presented their subjects with two scenarios in which a young child was bullied. Respondents were asked to imagine that a 10-year-old boy named James is confronted with "a boy a year younger who picks a fight with him. James tries to talk the other boy out of fighting, but it doesn't work. The boy gives James a black eye and bloody nose in front of a crowd of other children." They were also asked to imagine that "every day another boy pushes James down and steals his lunch money. One time, James tries to talk to the other boy to get him to quit. But the other boy still continues to bully and steal from him every day." Subjects were asked what they thought most fathers would expect James to do—"take a stand and fight the other boy" or avoid fighting. For both questions, Southern respondents were more likely than Northern respondents to think that most fathers would expect fighting (39% vs. 25%).

Thus, there appears to remain today a difference between Southern and Northern White men in attitudes toward children and violence. More Southern than Northern respondents believe in spanking as a means of discipline, and more Southerners than Northerners believe that fathers would expect their bullied child to fight.

REGIONAL DIFFERENCES IN BEHAVIORAL RESPONSES TO INSULTS

If Northern and Southern cultures differ so much in the meaning and importance they attach to insults, then it ought to be possible to show that Southerners have different reactions to insults than do Northerners—for example, that they respond to insults with more anger, that they see more aggressiveness and hostility in their environment, or that insults prime violent imagery. Norbert Schwarz, Brian Bowdle, and I decided to examine these possibilities in the laboratory (Bowdle, Nisbett, & Schwarz, 1993). This is a tricky business if one wishes to avoid damaging people's sense of well-being or making them feel quite unhappy, but we believe we have hit on a way of insulting people in the laboratory with little risk of such damage.

Male out-of-state undergraduate students at the University of Michigan were screened for their permanent addresses and randomly called and asked to participate (for $5) in a study in which they would be performing a variety of cognitive tasks under time pressure. We oversampled Southern students so as to invite an equal number (40 of each) of Southerners (students from the South and Southwestern census regions) and Northerners (from any non-Southern or non-Southwestern state except Michigan) to the lab. Subjects filled out a brief questionnaire on arrival and were asked to take it to a table at the end of a long, narrow hall. On the way to the table, they had to crowd past a male undergraduate confederate working at an open file cabinet. The confederate was required to close the file cabinet and press himself against it to allow the subject room to pass. When the subject returned a few seconds later, the confederate, who had just reopened the file drawer, slammed it shut, pushed his shoulder against the shoulder of the subject, and said, loudly enough to be clearly heard by the subject, "Asshole." The confederate then quickly entered a room with a locked door at the end of the hall. (The locked door was a needed precaution. One angry subject actually pursued the confederate and rattled the door knob.) Two confederates were posted at opposite ends of the narrow hall to observe the subject's reaction and record their impressions of the anger, amusement, and other emotions expressed by the subject. (The confederate near the locked door was prepared to intervene to announce that the provocation was part of the experiment if this had been necessary, but it never was.)

Upon their return to the laboratory, subjects were presented with two apperception tasks allowing for assessment of their level of hostility. They were asked to complete words from a series of letters including a blank, for example, __ight, gu__, __ill. Each letter series could be completed to form words with hostile connotations (e.g., fight, gun, kill) or non-hostile ones (e.g., light, gum, hill). Immediately following that task, subjects were asked to rate a series of photographs of male faces for the degree to which they expressed several emotions, including anger. Finally, subjects were asked to provide completions for three different written scenarios. Although two of the scenarios were intended to be neutral, the third involved a clear insult to the protagonist. In this scenario, which takes place at a party, a man's fiancée tells him that an acquaintance, who knows them to be engaged, has made two clear passes at her during the course of the evening. Following the collection of some background data, subjects were gently debriefed, including an apology by the experimenter for the deception and an explanation of the reasons for it and a reconciliation session with the confederate. (Only 1 of the 65 subjects and pretest subjects exposed to the manipulation to date has verbally expressed any unhappiness with the treatment afforded him. Two others were silent and unresponsive during the debriefing. The great majority of subjects responded to the debriefing with interest and amusement.)

The various assessment procedures in the experiment allow us to compare the emotional response of Southerners and Northerners to an insult. We can determine whether such a provocation differentially causes Southerners versus Northerners to see hostility in pictures of faces, to complete word fragments in a manner reflective of violence, or to provide aggressive completions to the scenarios.

The results concerning the subjects' immediate emotional response to the insult were quite clear. We subtracted the observers' ratings of subjects' amusement from their ratings of subjects' anger. The reaction patterns were remarkably different for the two groups of subjects. For 65% of the Northern subjects, but only 15% of Southern subjects, the amusement ratings were higher than the anger ratings.

It seems equally clear, however, that the insult did not cause Southern subjects to spend the rest of their time in the experiment in a state of hostility or paranoia. Their word fragment completions did not yield more hostile words than those of either noninsulted Southerners or Northerners, whether insulted or not. Nor did the insulted Southerners see more anger (or fear, or any of the other emotions rated) in the male faces they saw. Nor did they offer more violent completions to the two neutral scenarios. However, in reacting to the third scenario, involving affront and sexual challenge, the insulted Southerners were far more likely to respond with violent imagery. Seventy-five percent of insulted Southerners completed the affront scenario with events in which the protagonist physically injured, or threatened to injure, his antagonist, whereas this was true for only 25% of Southerners who were not insulted—a highly significant difference. Northerners were unaffected by the manipulation, being equally likely to conclude the scenarios with violence whether insulted or not.

In summary, the results indicate that Southerners are more sensitive to a given provocation, one interpretable as an insult, than are Northerners—in two respects. First, the provocation makes them angrier. It seems not to be something they can brush off as easily as Northerners can. Secondly, it seems to prime violent responses to subsequently encountered insult stimuli. The implications of these results seem clear. Southerners, by virtue of the emotional meaning that the insult has for them, are more likely to display anger in certain situations in which escalation is dangerous and are more susceptible to considering violent responses in those situations. (See Huesmann, 1988, for a treatment of the role of script accessibility in aggressive behavior.)

ARGUMENTS AND REGIONAL DIFFERENCES IN HOMICIDE

Much of the evidence presented above suggests that it might only be certain types of homicide, and not homicide in general, that should be more common in the South. Situations in which an affront occurs should be disproportionately likely to trigger violent responses. There is little reason to expect the rates of other kinds of homicide, such as those occurring in the context of robbery or burglary, to be elevated. To examine this possibility, I compared the rates for homicide committed in the context of another felony with the rates for homicide that seemed likely to be argument-related (e.g., lovers' triangles, barroom quarrels, and acquaintance homicide). The data were obtained from Fox and Pierce's (1987) supplementary homicide reports for 1976–1983. The two types of homicide are not exhaustive of all homicides because some were ambiguous as to whether they were argument-related or felony-related (e.g., "drug-related" homicides).

It may be seen in Table 4 that White male homicide rates in small cities are much higher in the South and Southwest than in other areas for argument-related cases but not for felony-related cases. In larger cities, the homicide rates again are higher in the South and Southwest for argument-related cases, but they are actually smaller for felony-related cases (ps for the interaction between homicide type and region are highly significant for the raw frequencies for both city sizes). Similar conclusions have been reached by other investigators, who have found that only homicides involving people personally known to the perpetrator are elevated in the South (Reed, 1981; Simpson, 1985; Smith & Parker, 1980).

TABLE 4
White Male Homicide Rates for Felony-Related and Argument-Related Murders as a Function of Region and City Size

Homicide type	City size	
	Less than 200,000	200,000 or more
Felony-related murders		
South & Southwest	1.16	2.25
Other regions	0.88	3.22
Argument-related murders		
South & Southwest	4.77	7.66
Other regions	2.13	6.51

Note: Data are adopted from *Uniform Crime Reports United States: Supplementary Homicide Reports 1976–1983* by J. A. Fox and G. L. Pierce, 1987, Boston: Northeastern University, Center for Applied Research.

HOMICIDE AND HERDING VERSUS FARMING SUBREGIONS OF THE SOUTH

The data presented to this point are more consistent with the hypothesis that Southern violence has its origin in a culture of honor than with the other hypotheses that have been suggested over the years (although it must be admitted that no argument from contemporary data to a long-term historical process can be as tight as one would like). The attitudinal differences relating to self-protection, insults, and socialization of children; the behavioral differences in response to insults; and the elevation of argument-related rather than felony-related homicides make sense in terms of a culture of honor deriving from a herding economy. This pattern of findings could not be predicted readily on the basis of temperature, poverty, the institution of slavery, or observation of violence by African Americans. Another unique implication of the culture-of-honor hypothesis is that those regions of the South today that still have a herding economy might be particularly prone to violence. One would expect this to be true not because herding today involves a significant risk of rustling and a realistic need for self-defense but because the agricultural uses of the land today would obviously be similar to those in the past, and those uses influenced past culture and hence present culture.

In an attempt to link homicide rates to agricultural practices, Andrew Reaves and I (1993) have examined the homicide rates of different physiographic regions of the South. We studied the most rural counties of the South—all those having no town with a population of more than 2,500—looking at homicide rates (White, non-Hispanic male offender rates), per capita income of the White population, population density, mean July temperature, percent of the population that is African American, and percentage of the population that was slave in 1860. We have categorized the counties of the South into two kinds on the basis of their likely use for farming or herding. In general, the moist plains areas of the South allow for farming and cash crops whereas the hills (average slope of land 8% or more) and the dry plains (precipitation rate of 24 inches or less) are more appropriate for herding.

In addition to the Southern counties, we examined White, non-Hispanic male homicide rates for all comparably rural counties in New England, the Middle Atlantic states, and the states of the nonindustrial, western Midwest (North Dakota, South Dakota, Nebraska, and Kansas). The homicide rates are far higher for the southern counties (8.77 per 100,000) than for the northern (2.13 per 100,000). This is a ratio of slightly more than four to one.

It may be seen in Table 5, which presents data for the Southern counties, that the counties of the moist plains in fact have a higher percentage of their farmland developed for crop purposes than the hills and dry plains, and a lower percentage of their farmland is undeveloped pasture. As would be expected by the herding–culture-of-honor hypothesis, White male homicide rates are substantially higher in the hills and dry plains regions (12.27 per 100,000) than in the farming regions (4.98 per 100,000). It may also be seen that, although differences in poverty rate remain a conceivable explanation of the homicide differences (because White per capita income is higher in the moist plains than in the other counties), three other factors—temperature, history of slavery, and high proportion of

TABLE 5
White Male Homicide Offender Rate and Demographic and Land Use Variables as a Function of Land Type in the South

Variable	Moist plains	Hills and dry plains
Percent of farmland developed	26.1	17.5
Percent farmland undeveloped pasture	38.7	53.9
White male homicide rate	4.98	12.27
White per capita income (dollars)	4,649	4,095
Population density (persons/square mile)	25.2	24.6
July temperature	80.7	78.2
Percent slave in 1860	44.8	10.4
Percent black in 1980	32.4	2.1

Note: All differences are significant at the .0001 level except for population density, which does not differ across groups.

African Americans—can effectively be excluded as explanations. Differences for each of these latter variables are in the wrong direction to explain the results. Mean temperatures are slightly higher in the farming areas than the herding areas, and the slavery and African-American population indices are dramatically higher in the farming areas. (Slavery of course was more common in the wet plains regions of the South because it was there that intensive cultivation of cash crops, notably cotton, made slavery economically viable, and the percentage of African Americans in these regions has remained high.)

REGIONAL DIFFERENCES IN VIOLENCE: PAST, PRESENT, AND FUTURE

The evidence suggests several conclusions, with more clarity than one expects for historical and cultural questions.

1. There is a marked difference in White homicide rates between regions of the United States, such that homicide is more common in the South and in regions of the country initially settled by Southerners.

2. There is solid negative evidence against a temperature interpretation of the difference in homicide rates. Regional differences are larger for smaller towns and more rural areas than for large cities, although regional differences in temperature are obviously just as great in the small-population towns and counties. In addition, the warmest areas of the South have the lowest homicide rates.

3. There is also good evidence against two of the traditional cultural interpretations of Southern violence. Appealing to a history of slavery to explain current regional differences in violence seems doomed because the regions of the South that had the highest concentrations of slaves in the past are those with the lowest homicide rates today. Similarly, imitation of African-American violence seems an implausible explanation, because the counties with small African-American populations have the highest White homicide rates.

4. Although differences in poverty are associated with higher homicide rates, regional differences in homicide are by no means completely explained by poverty, because Southernness remains a predictor of homicide even when poverty differences between regions are taken into account; and because in microregions of North and South that are highly comparable from the standpoint of ecology, population density, economy, and other variables, the richest Southern towns have higher homicide rates than even the poorest Northern towns.

5. There is positive evidence of cultural differences between North and South in attitudes toward violence and in responses to insults. These differences are not explainable as a consequence of Southern poverty. The behavioral data were obtained from college students, and the attitudinal differences were found for rural samples that did not differ in income.

6. The most theoretically interesting but inherently hardest to establish proposition is that the South has a culture of honor with historical roots that underlies its preferences for violence. Southerners do not endorse violence in the abstract more than do Northerners, nor do they endorse violence in all specific forms of circumstances. Rather, they are more likely to endorse violence as an appropriate response to insults, as a means of self-protection, and as a socialization tool in training children. This is the characteristic cultural pattern of herding societies the world over. Consistent with the culture-of-honor interpretation, it is argument-related and not felony-related homicide that is more common in the South.

Finally, it should be noted that what is referred to as Southern violence, in the historical and anthropological literature, as well as in this article for purposes of brevity, is actually a much more complicated regional phenomenon. It is the rural counties and smaller towns of the South and West, especially those with a herding economy, that have elevated homicide rates.

This localized pattern of violence may indicate something about the future and the likelihood that regional differences will persist. Already, the biggest urban regions of the South and West show only a trace of the elevation in White homicide rates found in other population units. This may be due in part to the manifest irrelevance of the culture of honor to the conditions of urban life, and it may be due in part to the admixture of Northern culture to these centers in the form of immigration from other regions of the country. A purely material interpretation of the Southern attitude toward violence indicates that it will not persist. It is already long since an anachronism. Few people today live in any realistic danger of having their entire livelihood taken irrevocably away from them by outlaws, not even current American pastoralists.

On the other hand, the material interpretation of the culture of honor may not be a complete explanation for its existence. Certain cultural stances may take on a life of their own because they are embedded in a matrix of behavioral patterns that sustains them. If individuals believe that they must own and even carry weapons for protection, and if they respond to insults with sufficient anger to occasionally cause them to use those weapons, this will tend to affect the entire local community. Its members may respond with heightened consciousness of the need for protection, more vigilance concerning threats, and a consequent greater likelihood of violence.

There is another sense in which the culture of honor might turn out to be self-sustaining or even capable of expanding into mainstream culture. The culture is a variant of warrior culture the world over, and its independent invention countless times (Gilmore, 1990), combined with the regularities in its themes having to do with glorification of masculine attributes, suggests that it may be a particularly alluring stance that may be capable of becoming functionally autonomous. Many observers (e.g., Naipaul, 1989; Shattuck, 1989) have noted that contemporary Southern backcountry culture, including music, dress, and social stance, is spreading beyond its original geographical confines and becoming a part of the fabric of rural, and even urban, working-class America. Perhaps for the young males who adopt it, this culture provides a romantic veneer to everyday existence. If so, it is distinctly possible that the violence characteristic of this culture is also spreading beyond its confines. An understanding of the culture and its darker side would thus remain important for the foreseeable future.

REFERENCES

Anderson C. A. (1989). Temperature and aggression: Ubiquitous effects of heat on occurrence of human violence. *Psychological Bulletin, 106,* 74–96.

Baron, L., & Straus, M. A. (1988). Cultural and economic sources of homicide in the United States. *The Sociological Quarterly, 29,* 371–390.

Blau, J. R., & Blau, P. M. (1982). The cost of inequality: Metropolitan structure and violent crime. *American Sociological Review, 47,* 114–129.

Blumenthal, M. D., Kahn, R. L., Andrews, F. M., & Head, K. B. (1972). *Justifying violence: Attitudes of American men.* Ann Arbor, MI: Institute for Social Research.

Bowdle, B., Nisbett, R. E., & Schwarz, N. (1993). *Regional differences in responses to insults.* Unpublished manuscript, University of Michigan.

Brearley, H. C. (1934). The pattern of violence. In W. T. Couch (Ed.), *Culture in the south* (pp. 221–238). Chapel Hill: University of North Carolina Press.

Campbell, J. K. (1965). Honour and the devil. In J. G. Peristiany (Ed.), *Honour and shame: The values of Mediterranean society* (pp. 112–175). London: Weidenfeld & Nicolson.

Carter, H. (1950). *Southern legacy.* Baton Rouge: Louisiana State University Press.

Cash, Wilbur J. (1941). *The mind of the South.* New York: Knopf.

Cohen, D., & Nisbett, R. E. (in press). Self-protection, insults and the culture of honor: Explaining southern homicide. *Personality and Social Psychology Bulletin.*

Davis, J. A., & Smith, T. W. (1989). *General social surveys, 1972–1990.* Storrs, CT: National Opinion Research Center.

Fischer, D. H. (1989). *Albion's seed: Four British folkways in America.* New York: Oxford University Press.

Fox, J. A., & Pierce, G. L. (1987). *Uniform crime reports United States: Supplementary homicide reports 1976–1983.* Boston: Northeastern University, Center for Applied Social Research.

Gastil, R. D. (1971). Homicide and a regional culture of violence. *American Sociological Review, 36,* 416–427.

Gastil, R. D. (1989). Violence, crime and punishment. In C. R. Wilson & W. Ferris (Eds.), *Encyclopedia of Southern culture* (pp. 1473–1476). Chapel Hill: University of North Carolina Press.

Gilmore, D. D. (1990). *Manhood in the making: Cultural concepts of masculinity.* New Haven, CT: Yale University Press.

Hackney, S. (1969). Southern violence. *The American Historical Review, 74,* 906–925.

Huesmann, L. R. (1988). An information-processing model for the development of aggression. *Aggressive Behavior, 14,* 13–24.

Lowie, R. H. (1954). *Indians of the plain.* New York: McGraw-Hill.

Lundsgraade, H. P. (1977). *Murder in space city: A cultural history.* New York: Oxford University Press.

McWhiney, G. (1988). *Cracker culture: Celtic ways in the old South.* Tuscaloosa: University of Alabama Press.

Naipaul, V. S. (1989). *A turn in the South.* New York: Knopf.

Nisbett, R. E., Polly, G., & Lang, S. (1993). *Homicide and regional U.S. culture.* Unpublished manuscript, University of Michigan.

Peristiany, J. G. (Ed.). (1965). *Honour and shame: The values of Mediterranean society.* London: Weidenfeld & Nicolson.

Reaves, A. L., & Nisbett, R. E. (1993). *Ecology, agriculture, and homicide rates in the southern United States.* Unpublished manuscript, University of Michigan.

Reed, J. S. (1981). Below the Smith and Wesson line: Reflections on southern violence. In M. Black & J. S. Reed (Eds.), *Perspectives on the American South: An annual review of society, politics, and culture* (pp. 9–22). New York: Cordon & Breach Science.

Reifman, A. S., Larrick, R. P., & Fein, S. (1991). Temper and temperature on the diamond: The heat-aggression relationship in major league baseball. *Personality and Social Psychology Bulletin, 17,* 580–585.

Shattuck, R. (1989, March 30). The reddening of America. *New York Review of Books,* pp. 3–5.

Simpson, M. E. (1985). Violent crime, income inequality, and regional culture: Another look. *Sociological Focus, 18,* 199–208.

Smith, M. D., & Parker, R. N. (1980). Type of homicide and variation in regional rates. *Social Forces, 59,* 136–147.

Tocqueville, A. de. (1969). *Democracy in America* (J. P. Mayer, Ed., G. Lawrence, Trans.). Garden City, NY: University of Chicago Press. (Original work published 1835)

U.S. Bureau of the Census. (1983). *Characteristics of the U.S. population: Vol. I.* Washington, DC: U.S. Government Printing Office.

I am indebted to Brian Bowdle, Dov Cohen, James Hilton, Rowell Huesmann, Sylvia Lang, Greg Polly, Andrew Reaves, Lee Ross, and Norbert Schwarz for advice and assistance.

THINKING CRITICALLY AND APPLYING YOUR KNOWLEDGE

1. What are the basic elements in the "culture of honor"? Write a 10-item questionnaire that could be used to assess individual differences in endorsement of the culture of honor among college students.

2. Nisbett's analysis of the culture of honor focuses on the attitudes and behaviors of southern white men. How might this cultural tradition affect the attitudes and experiences of southern white women, or African Americans of both sexes from the southern United States?

3. A careful researcher always considers alternative explanations for an empirical finding. In addition to the "culture of honor," what other explanations for regional differences in

violence does Nisbett consider? How convincing are Nisbett's reasons for rejecting these alternatives? Are there additional explanations that should be considered?

4. Nisbett studied regional differences in violence, but there may also be regional differences in other attitudes and social behaviors as well. Identify one other domain of attitudes and/or behavior where you think there may be regional differences. What predictions would you make? How could you test these predictions empirically?

5. Nisbett argues that cultural traditions are affected by economic and historical factors. Today, Americans are increasingly coming to rely on computers to assist in performing work activities and to communicate with others through electronic mail. What new cultural norms and values may be encouraged by this new computer technology?

PART V

SOCIAL PSYCHOLOGY IN LIFE

❖ CHAPTER 16 ❖

Race and the Schooling
of Black Americans

Claude M. Steele

> In this thoughtful essay, psychologist Claude Steele describes in poignant detail his despair at watching talented African-American college students fall by the wayside as the full weight of racial stigma becomes evident to them. More than half of African-American college students fail to complete their college degrees for reasons having little to do with ability. Steele draws on empirical findings and examples to show how the stigma of race leads Black students to disidentify with their college and to see intellectual achievement as increasingly irrelevant to their self-esteem. He shows that when school atmospheres reduce racial stigma, achievement among African Americans is enhanced.

My former university offered minority students a faculty mentor to help shepherd them into college life. As soon as I learned of the program, I volunteered to be a mentor, but by then the school year was nearly over. Undaunted, the program's eager staff matched me with a student on their waiting list—an appealing nineteen-year-old black woman from Detroit, the same age as my daughter. We met finally in a campus lunch spot just about two weeks before the close of her freshman year. I realized quickly that I was too late. I have heard that the best way to diagnose someone's depression is to note how depressed you feel when you leave the person. When our lunch was over, I felt as gray as the snowbanks that often lined the path back to my office. My lunchtime companion was a statistic brought to life, a living example of one of the most disturbing facts of racial life in America today: the failure of so many Black Americans to thrive in school. Before I could lift a hand to help this student, she had decided to do what 70 percent of all Black Americans at four-year colleges do at some point in their academic careers—drop out.

I sense a certain caving-in of hope in America that problems of race can be solved. Since the sixties, when race relations held promise for the dawning of a new era, the issue has become one whose persistence causes "problem fatigue"—resignation to an unwanted condition of life.

This fatigue, I suspect, deadens us to the deepening crisis in the education of Black Americans. One can enter any desegregated school in America, from grammar school to high school to graduate or professional school, and meet a persistent reality: Blacks and Whites in largely separate worlds. And if one asks a few questions or looks at a few records,

Source: Reprinted from *The Atlantic Monthly*, *69*(4), (1992, April), 68–78. Copyright by C. S. Steele. Reprinted by permission.

another reality emerges: these worlds are not equal, either in the education taking place there or in the achievement of the students who occupy them.

As a social scientist, I know that the crisis has enough possible causes to give anyone problem fatigue. But at a personal level, perhaps because of my experience as a Black in American schools, or perhaps just as the hunch of a myopic psychologist, I have long suspected a particular culprit—a culprit that can undermine Black achievement as effectively as a lock on a schoolhouse door. The culprit I see is *stigma*, the endemic devaluation many Blacks face in our society and schools. This status is its own condition of life, different from class, money, culture. It is capable, in the words of the late sociologist Erving Goffman, of "breaking the claim" that one's human attributes have on people. I believe that its connection to school achievement among Black Americans has been vastly underappreciated.

This is a troublesome argument, touching as it does on a still unhealed part of American race relations. But it leads us to a heartening principle: If Blacks are made less racially vulnerable in school, they can overcome even substantial obstacles. Before the good news, though, I must at least sketch in the bad: the worsening crisis in the education of Black Americans.

Despite their socioeconomic disadvantages as a group, Blacks begin school with test scores that are fairly close to the test scores of Whites their age. The longer they stay in school, however, the more they fall behind; for example, by the sixth grade Blacks in many school districts are two full grade levels behind Whites in achievement. This pattern holds true in the middle class nearly as much as in the lower class. The record does not improve in high school. In 1980, for example, 25,500 minority students, largely Black and Hispanic, entered high school in Chicago. Four years later only 9,500 graduated, and of those only 2,000 could read at grade level. The situation in other cities is comparable.

Even for Blacks who make it to college, the problem doesn't go away. As I noted, 70% of all Black students who enroll in four-year colleges drop out at some point, as compared with 45% of whites. At any given time nearly as many Black males are incarcerated as are in college in this country. And the grades of Black college students average half a letter below those of their White classmates. At one prestigious university I recently studied, only 18% of the graduating Black students had grade averages of B or above, as compared with 64% of the whites. This pattern is the rule, not the exception, in even the most elite American colleges. Tragically, low grades can render a degree essentially "terminal" in the sense that they preclude further schooling.

Blacks in graduate and professional schools face a similarly worsening or stagnating fate. For example, from 1977 to 1990, though the number of Ph.D.s awarded to other minorities increased and the number awarded to Whites stayed roughly the same, the number awarded to American Blacks dropped from 1,116 to 828. And Blacks needed more time to get those degrees.

Standing ready is a familiar set of explanations. First is societal disadvantage. Black Americans have had, and continue to have, more than their share: a history of slavery, segregation, and job ceilings; continued lack of economic opportunity; poor schools; and the related problems of broken families, drug-infested communities, and social isolation. Any of these factors—alone, in combination, or through accumulated effects—can undermine school achievement. Some analysts point also to Black American culture, suggesting that, hampered by disadvantage, it doesn't sustain the values and expectations critical to education, or that it fosters learning orientations ill suited to school achievement, or that it even "opposes" mainstream achievement. These are the chestnuts, and I had always thought them adequate. Then several facts emerged that just didn't seem to fit.

For one thing, the achievement deficits occur even when Black students suffer no major financial disadvantage—among middle-class students on wealthy college campuses and in graduate school among Black students receiving substantial financial aid. For another thing, survey after survey shows that even poor Black Americans value education highly, often more than Whites. Also, as I will demonstrate, several programs have improved Black school achievement without addressing culturally specific learning orientations or doing anything to remedy socioeconomic disadvantage.

Neither is the problem fully explained, as one might assume, by deficits in skill or preparation which Blacks might suffer because of background disadvantages. I first doubted that such a connection existed when I saw flunk-out rates for Black and White students at a large, prestigious university. Two observations surprised me. First, for both Blacks and Whites the level of preparation, as measured by Scholastic Aptitude Test scores, didn't make much difference in who flunked out; low scorers (with combined verbal and quantitative SATs of 800) were no more likely to flunk out than high scorers (with combined SATs of 1,200 to 1,500). The second observation was racial: whereas only 2% to 11% of the Whites flunked out, 18% to 33% of the Blacks flunked out, even at the highest levels of preparation (combined SATs of 1,400). Dinesh D'Souza has argued recently that college affirmative-action programs cause failure and high dropout rates among Black students by recruiting them to levels of college work for which they are inadequately prepared. That was clearly not the case at this school; Black students flunked out in large numbers even with preparation well above average.

And, sadly, this proved the rule, not the exception. From elementary school to graduate school, something depresses Black achievement *at every level of preparation, even the highest.* Generally, of course, the better prepared achieve better than the less prepared, and this is about as true for Blacks as for Whites. But given any level of school preparation (as measured by tests and earlier grades), Blacks somehow achieve less in subsequent schooling than Whites (that is, have poorer grades, have lower graduation rates, and take longer to graduate), no matter how strong that preparation is. Put differently, the same achievement level requires better preparation for Blacks than for Whites—far better: among students with a C+ average at the university I just described, the mean American College Testing Program (ACT) score for Blacks was at the 98th percentile, while for Whites it was at only the 34th percentile. This pattern has been documented so broadly across so many regions of the country, and by so many investigations (literally hundreds), that it is virtually a social law in this society—as well as a racial tragedy.

Clearly, something is missing from our understanding of black underachievement. Disadvantage contributes, yet Blacks underachieve even when they have ample resources, strongly value education, and are prepared better than adequately in terms of knowledge and skills. Something else has to be involved. That something else could be of just modest importance—a barrier that simply adds its effect to that of other disadvantages—or it could be pivotal, such that were it corrected, other disadvantages would lose their effect.

That something else, I believe, has to do with the process of identifying with school. I offer a personal example:

I remember conducting experiments with my research adviser early in graduate school and awaiting the results with only modest interest. I struggled to meet deadlines. The research enterprise—the core of what one does as a social psychologist—just wasn't *me* yet. I was in school for other reasons—I wanted an advanced degree, I was vaguely ambitious for intellectual work, and being in graduate school made my parents proud of me. But as time passed, I began to like the work. I also began to grasp the value system that gave it meaning, and the faculty treated me as if they thought I might even be able to do it. Gradually I began to think of myself as a social psychologist. With this change in self-concept came a new accountability; my self-esteem was affected now by what I did as a social psychologist, something that hadn't been true before. This added a new motivation to my work; self-respect, not just parental respect, was on the line. I noticed changes in myself. I worked without deadlines. I bored friends with applications of arcane theory to their daily lives. I went to conventions. I lived and died over how experiments came out.

Before this transition one might have said that I was handicapped by my Black working-class background and lack of motivation. After the transition the same observer might say that even though my background was working-class, I had special advantages: achievement-oriented parents, a small and attentive college. But these facts alone would miss the importance of the identification process I had experienced: the change in self-definition and in the activities on which I based my self-esteem. They would also miss a simple condition necessary for me to make this identification: treatment as a valued person with good prospects.

I believe that the "something else" at the root of Black achievement problems is the failure of American schooling to meet this simple condition for many of its Black students. Doing well in school requires a belief that school achievement can be a promising basis of self-esteem, and that belief needs constant reaffirmation even for advantaged students. Tragically, I believe, the lives of Black Americans are still haunted by a specter that threatens this belief and the identification that derives from it at every level of schooling.

THE SPECTER OF STIGMA AND RACIAL VULNERABILITY

I have a good friend, the mother of three, who spends considerable time in the public school classrooms of Seattle, where she lives. In her son's third-grade room, managed by a teacher of unimpeachable good will and competence, she noticed over many visits that the extraordinary art work of a small Black boy named Jerome was ignored—or, more accurately perhaps, its significance was ignored. As genuine art talent has a way of doing—even in the third grade—his stood out. Yet the teacher seemed hardly to notice. Moreover, Jerome's reputation, as it was passed along from one grade to the next, included only the slightest mention of his talent. Now, of course, being ignored like this could happen to anyone—such is the overload in our public schools. But my friend couldn't help wondering how the school would have responded to this talent had the artist been one of her own, middle-class white children.

Terms like *prejudice* and *racism* often miss the full scope of racial devaluation in our society, implying as they do that racial devaluation comes primarily from the strongly prejudiced, not from "good people" like Jerome's teacher. But the prevalence of racists—deplorable though racism is—misses the full extent of Jerome's burden, perhaps even the most profound part.

He faces a devaluation that grows out of our images of society and the way those images catalogue people. The catalogue need never be taught. It is implied by all we see around us: the kinds of people revered in advertising (consider the unrelenting racial advocacy of Ralph Lauren ads) and movies (Black women are rarely seen as romantic partners, for example); media discussions of whether a Black can be president; invitation lists to junior high school birthday parties; school curricula; literary and musical canons. These details create an image of society in which Black Americans simply do not fare well. When I was a kid, we captured it with the saying "If you're White you're right, if you're yellow you're mellow, if you're brown stick around, but if you're Black get back."

In ways that require no fueling from strong prejudice or stereotypes, these images expand the devaluation of Black Americans. They act as mental standards against which information about Blacks is evaluated: that which fits these images we accept; that which contradicts them we suspect. Had Jerome had a reading problem, which fits these images, it might have been accepted as characteristic more readily than his extraordinary art work, which contradicts them.

These images do something else as well, something especially pernicious in the classroom. They set up a jeopardy of double devaluation for Blacks, a jeopardy that does not apply to Whites. Like anyone, Blacks risk devaluation for a particular incompetence, such as a failed test or a flubbed pronunciation. But they further risk that such performances will confirm the broader, racial inferiority they are suspected of. Thus, from the first grade through graduate school, Blacks have the extra fear that in the eyes of those around them their full humanity could fall with a poor answer or a mistaken stroke of the pen.

Moreover, because these images are conditioned in all of us, collectively held, they can spawn racial devaluation in all of us, not just in the strongly prejudiced. They can do this even in Blacks themselves: A majority of Black children recently tested said they like and prefer to play with White rather than Black dolls—almost fifty years after Kenneth and Mamie Clark, conducting similar experiments, documented identical findings and so paved the way for *Brown v. Topeka Board of Education*. Thus Jerome's devaluation can come from a circle of people in his world far greater than the expressly prejudiced—a circle that apparently includes his teacher.

In ways often too subtle to be conscious but sometimes overt, I believe, Blacks remain devalued in American schools, where, for example, a recent national survey shows that through high school they are still more than twice as likely as White children to receive corporal punishment, be suspended from school, or be labeled mentally retarded.

Tragically, such devaluation can seem inescapable. Sooner or later it forces on its victims two painful realizations. The first is that society is preconditioned to see the worst in them. Black students quickly learn that acceptance, if it is to be won at all, will be hard-won. The second is that even if a Black student achieves exoneration in one setting—with the teacher and fellow students in one classroom, or at one level of schooling, for example—this approval will have to be rewon in the next classroom, at the next level of schooling. Of course, individual characteristics that enhance one's value in society—skills, class status, appearance, and success—can diminish the racial devaluation one faces. And sometimes the effort to prove oneself fuels achievement. But few from any group could hope to sustain so daunting and everlasting a struggle. Thus, I am afraid, too many Black students are left hopeless and deeply vulnerable in America's classrooms.

"DISIDENTIFYING" WITH SCHOOL

I believe that in significant part the crisis in Black Americans' education stems from the power of this vulnerability to undercut identification with schooling, either before it happens or after it has bloomed.

Jerome is an example of the first kind. At precisely the time when he would need to see school as a viable source of self-esteem, his teachers fail to appreciate his best work. The devalued status of his race devalues him and his work in the classroom. Unable to entrust his sense of himself to this place, he resists measuring himself against its values and goals. He languishes there, held by the law, perhaps even by his parents, but not allowing achievement to affect his view of himself. This psychic alienation—the act of not caring—makes him less vulnerable to the specter of devaluation that haunts him. Bruce Hare, an educational researcher, has documented this process among fifth-grade boys in several schools in Champaign, Illinois. He found that although the Black boys had considerably lower achievement-test scores than their White classmates, their overall self-esteem was just as high. This stunning imperviousness to poor academic performance was accomplished, he found, by their de-emphasizing school achievement as a basis of self-esteem and giving preference to peer-group relations—a domain in which their esteem prospects were better. They went where they had to go to feel good about themselves.

But recall the young student whose mentor I was. She had already identified with school, and wanted to be a doctor. How can racial vulnerability break so developed an achievement identity? To see, let us follow her steps onto campus: Her recruitment and admission stress her minority status perhaps more strongly than it has been stressed at any other time in her life. She is offered academic and social support services, further implying that she is "at risk" (even though, contrary to common belief, the vast majority of Black college students are admitted with qualifications well above the threshold for Whites). Once on campus, she enters a socially circumscribed world in which Blacks—still largely separate from Whites—have lower status; this is reinforced by a sidelining of minority material and interests in the curriculum and in university life. And she can sense that everywhere in this new world her skin color places her under suspicion of intellectual inferiority. All of this gives her the double vulnerability I spoke of: She risks confirming a particular incompetence, at chemistry or a foreign language, for example; but she also risks confirming the racial inferiority she is suspected of—a judgment that can feel as close at hand as a mispronounced word or an ungrammatical sentence. In reaction, usually to some modest setback, she withdraws, hiding her troubles from instructors, counselors, even other students. Quickly, I believe, a psychic defense takes over. She *disidentifies* with achievement; she changes her self-conception, her outlook and values, so that achievement is no longer so important to her self-esteem. She may continue to feel pressure to stay in school—from her parents, even from the potential advantages of a college degree. But now she is psychologically insulated from her academic life, like a disinterested visitor. Cool, unperturbed. But, like a pain-killing drug, disidentification undoes her future as it relieves her vulnerability.

The prevalence of this syndrome among Black college students has been documented extensively, especially on predominantly White campuses. Summarizing this work, Jacqueline Fleming, a psychologist, writes, "The fact that Black students must matriculate in an atmosphere that feels hostile arouses defensive reactions that interfere with intellectual performance. . . . They display academic demotivation and think less of their abilities. They profess losses of energy." Among a sample of Blacks on one predominantly White campus, Richard Nisbett and Andrew Reaves, both psychologists, and I found that attitudes related to disidentification were more strongly predictive of grades than even academic preparation (that is, SATs and high school grades).

To make matters worse, once disidentification occurs in a school, it can spread like the common cold. Blacks who identify and try to achieve embarrass the strategy by valuing the very thing the strategy denies the value of. Thus pressure to make it a group norm can evolve quickly and become fierce. Defectors are called "oreos" or "incognegroes." One's identity as an authentic Black is held hostage, made incompatible with school identification. For Black students, then, pressure to disidentify with school can come from the already demoralized as well as from racial vulnerability in the setting.

Stigmatization of the sort suffered by Black Americans is probably also a barrier to the school achievement of other groups in our society, such as lower-class Whites, Hispanics, and women in male-dominated fields. For example, at a large midwestern university I studied, women match men's achievement in the liberal arts, where they suffer no marked stigma, but underachieve compared with men (get lower grades than men with the same ACT scores) in engineering and premedical programs, where they, like Blacks across the board, are more vulnerable to suspicions of inferiority.

"WISE" SCHOOLING

> When they approach me they see . . . everything and anything except me. . . . [this] invisibility . . . occurs because of a peculiar disposition of the eyes. (Ralph Ellison, *Invisible Man*)

Erving Goffman, borrowing from gays of the 1950s, used the term "wise" to describe people who don't themselves bear the stigma of a given group but who are accepted by the group. These are people in whose eyes the full humanity of the stigmatized is visible, people in whose eyes they feel less vulnerable. If racial vulnerability undermines Black school achievement, as I have argued, then this achievement should improve significantly if schooling is made "wise"—that is, made to see value and promise in Black students and to act accordingly.

And yet, although racial vulnerability at school may undermine Black achievement, so many other factors seem to contribute—from the debilitations of poverty to the alleged dysfunctions of Black American culture—that one might expect "wiseness" in the classroom to be of little help. Fortunately, we have considerable evidence to the contrary. Wise schooling may indeed be the missing key to the schoolhouse door.

In the mid-seventies Black students in Philip Uri Treisman's early calculus courses at the University of California at Berkeley consistently fell to the bottom of every class. To help, Treisman developed the Mathematics Workshop Program, which, in a surprisingly short time, reversed their fortunes, causing them to outperform their White and Asian counterparts. And although it is only a freshman program, Black students who take it graduate at a rate comparable to the Berkeley average. Its central technique is group study of calculus concepts. But it is also wise; it does things that allay the racial vulnerabilities of these students. Stressing their potential to learn, it recruits them to a challenging "honors" workshop tied to their first calculus course. Building on their skills, the workshop gives difficult work, often beyond course content, to students with even modest preparation (some of their math SATs dip to the 300s). Working together, students soon understand that everyone knows something and nobody knows everything, and learning is speeded through shared understanding. The wisdom of these tactics is their subtext message: "You are valued in this program because of your academic potential—regardless of your current skill level. You have no more to fear than the next person, and since the work is difficult, success is a credit to your ability, and a setback is a reflection only of the challenge." The Black students' double vulnerability around failure—the fear that they lack ability, and the dread that they will be devalued—is thus reduced. They can relax and achieve. The movie *Stand and Deliver* depicts Jaime Escalante using the same techniques of assurance and challenge to inspire advanced calculus performance in East Los Angeles Chicano high schoolers. And, explaining Xavier University's extraordinary success in producing Black medical students, a spokesman said recently, "What doesn't work is saying, 'You need remedial work.' What does work is saying, 'You may be somewhat behind at this time but you're a talented person. We're going to help you advance at an accelerated rate.'"

The work of James Comer, a child psychiatrist at Yale, suggests that wiseness can minimize even the barriers of poverty. Over a fifteen-year period he transformed the two worst elementary schools in New Haven, Connecticut, into the third and fifth best in the city's thirty-three-school system without any change in the type of students—largely poor and Black. His guiding belief is that learning requires a strongly accepting relationship between teacher and student. "After all," he notes, "what is the difference between scribble and a letter of the alphabet to a child? The only reason the letter is meaningful, and worth learning and remembering, is because a *meaningful* other wants him or her to learn and remember it." To build these relationships Comer focuses on the overall school climate, shaping it not so much to transmit specific skills, or to achieve order per se, or even to improve achievement, as to establish a valuing and optimistic atmosphere in which a child can—to use his term—"identify" with learning. Responsibility for this lies with a team of ten to fifteen members, headed by the principal and made up of teachers, parents, school staff, and child-development experts (for example, psychologists or special-education teachers). The team develops a plan of specifics: teacher training, parent workshops, coordination of information about students. But at base I believe it tries to ensure that the students—vulnerable on so many counts—get treated essentially like middle-class students, with conviction about their value and promise. As this happens, their vulnerability diminishes, and with it the companion defenses of disidentification and misconduct. They achieve, and apparently identify, as their achievement gains persist into high school. Comer's genius, I believe, is to have recognized the importance of these vulnerabilities as barriers to *intellectual* development, and the corollary that schools hoping to educate such students must learn first how to make them feel valued.

These are not isolated successes. Comparable results were observed, for example, in a Comer-type program in Maryland's Prince Georges County, in the Stanford economist Henry Levin's accelerated-schools program, and in Harlem's Central Park East Elementary School, under the principalship of Deborah Meier. And research involving hundreds of programs and schools points to the same conclusion: Black achievement is consistently linked to conditions of schooling that reduce racial vulnerability. These include relatively harmonious race relations among students; a commitment by teachers and schools to seeing minority-group members achieve; the instructional goal that students at all levels of preparation achieve; desegregation at the classroom as well as the school level; and a deemphasis on ability tracking.

That erasing stigma improves Black achievement is perhaps the strongest evidence that stigma is what depresses it in the first place. This is no happy realization. But it lets in a ray of hope: Whatever other factors also depress Black achievement—poverty, social isolation, poor preparation—they may be substantially overcome in a schooling atmosphere that reduces racial and other vulnerabilities, not through unrelenting niceness or ferocious regimentation but by wiseness, by *seeing* value and acting on it.

WHAT MAKES SCHOOLING UNWISE

But if wise schooling is so attainable, why is racial vulnerability the rule, not the exception, in American schooling?

One factor is the basic assimilationist offer that schools make to Blacks: You can be valued and rewarded in school (and society), the schools say to these students, but you must first master the culture and ways of the American mainstream, and since that mainstream (as it is represented) is essentially White, this means you must give up many particulars of being Black—styles of speech and appearance, value priorities, preferences—at least in mainstream settings. This is asking a lot. But it has been the "color-blind" offer to every immigrant and minority group in our nation's history, the core of the melting-pot ideal, and so I think it strikes most of us as fair. Yet nonimmigrant minorities like Blacks and Native Americans have always been here, and thus are entitled, more than new immigrants, to participate in the defining images of the society projected in school. More important, their exclusion from these images denies their contributive history and presence in society. Thus, whereas immigrants can tilt toward assimilation in pursuit of the opportunities for which they came, American Blacks may find it harder to assimilate. For them, the offer of acceptance in return for assimilation carries a primal insult: It asks them to join in something that has made them invisible.

Now, I must be clear. This is not a criticism of Western civilization. My concern is an omission of image-work. In his incisive essay "What America Would Be Like Without Blacks," Ralph Ellison showed Black influence on American speech and language, the themes of our finest literature, and our most defining ideals of personal freedom and democracy. In *The World They Made Together*, Mechal Sobel described how African and European influences shaped the early American South in everything from housing design and land use to religious expression. The fact is that Blacks are not outside the American mainstream but, in Ellison's words, have always been "one of its major tributaries." Yet if one relied on what is taught in America's schools, one would never know this. There Blacks have fallen victim to a collective self-deception, a society's allowing itself to assimilate like mad from its constituent groups while representing itself to itself as if the assimilation had never happened, as if progress and good were almost exclusively Western and White. A prime influence of American society on world culture is the music of Black Americans, shaping art forms from rock-and-roll to modern dance. Yet in American schools, from kindergarten through graduate school, these essentially Black influences have barely peripheral status, are largely outside the canon. Thus it is not what is taught but what is *not* taught, what teachers and professors have never learned the value of, that reinforces a fundamental unwiseness in American schooling, and keeps Black disidentification on full boil.

Deep in the psyche of American educators is a presumption that Black students need academic remediation, or extra time with elemental curricula to overcome background deficits. This orientation guides many efforts to close the achievement gap—from grammar school tutoring to college academic-support programs—but I fear it can be unwise. Bruno Bettelheim and Karen Zelan's article "Why Children Don't Like to Read" comes to mind: Apparently to satisfy the changing sensibilities of local school boards over this century, many books that children like were dropped from school reading lists; when children's reading scores also dropped, the approved texts were replaced by simpler books; and when reading scores dropped again, these were replaced by even simpler books, until eventually the children could hardly read at all, not because the material was too difficult but because they were bored stiff. So it goes, I suspect, with a great many of these remediation efforts.

Moreover, because so many such programs target Blacks primarily, they virtually equate Black identity with substandard intellectual status, amplifying racial vulnerability. They can even undermine students' ability to gain confidence from their achievement, by sharing credit for their successes while implying that their failures stem from inadequacies beyond the reach of remediation.

The psychologist Lisa Brown and I recently uncovered evidence of just how damaging this orientation may be. At a large, prestigious university we found that whereas the grades of Black graduates of the 1950s improved during the students' college years until they virtually matched the school average, those of Blacks who graduated in the 1980s (we chose only those with above-average entry credentials, to correct for more liberal admissions policies in that decade) worsened, ending up considerably below the school average. The 1950s graduates faced outward discrimination in everything from housing to the classroom, whereas the 1980s graduates were supported by a phalanx of help programs. Many things may contribute to this pattern. The Jackie Robinson, "pioneer" spirit of the 1950s Blacks surely helped them endure. And in a pre-affirmative-action era, they may have been seen as intellectually more deserving. But one cannot ignore the distinctive fate of 1980s Blacks: A remedial orientation put their abilities under suspicion, deflected their ambitions, distanced them from their successes, and painted them with their failures. Black students on today's campuses may experience far less overt prejudice than their 1950s counterparts but, ironically, may be more racially vulnerable.

THE ELEMENTS OF WISENESS

For too many Black students school is simply the place where, more concertedly, persistently, and authoritatively than anywhere else in society, they learn how little valued they are.

Clearly, no simple recipe can fix this, but I believe we now understand the basics of a corrective approach. Schooling must focus more on reducing the vulnerabilities that block identification with achievement. I believe that four conditions, like the legs of a stool, are fundamental.

- If what is meaningful and important to a teacher is to become meaningful and important to a student, the student must feel valued by the teacher for his or her potential and as a person. Among the more fortunate in society, this relationship is often taken for granted. But it is precisely the relationship that race can still undermine in American society. As Comer, Escalante, and Treisman have shown, when one's students bear race and class vulnerabilities, building this relationship is the first order of business—at all levels of schooling. No tactic of instruction, no matter how ingenious, can succeed without it.
- The challenge and the promise of personal fulfillment, not remediation (under whatever guise), should guide the education of these students. Their present skills should be taken into account, and they should be moved along at a pace that is demanding but

doesn't defeat them. Their ambitions should never be scaled down but should instead be guided to inspiring goals even when extraordinary dedication is called for. Frustration will be less crippling than alienation. Here psychology is everything: Remediation defeats, challenge strengthens—affirming their potential, crediting them with their achievements, inspiring them.

But the first condition, I believe, cannot work without the second, and vice versa. A valuing teacher–student relationship goes nowhere without challenge, and challenge will always be resisted outside a valuing relationship. (Again, I must be careful about something: In criticizing remediation I am not opposing affirmative-action recruitment in the schools. The success of this policy, like that of school integration before it, depends, I believe, on the tactics of implementation. Where students are valued and challenged, they generally succeed.)

• Racial integration is a generally useful element in this design, if not a necessity. Segregation, whatever its purpose, draws out group differences and makes people feel more vulnerable when they inevitably cross group lines to compete in the larger society. This vulnerability, I fear, can override confidence gained in segregated schooling unless that confidence is based on strongly competitive skills and knowledge—something that segregated schooling, plagued by shortages of resources and access, has difficulty producing.

• The particulars of Black life and culture—art, literature, political and social perspective, music—must be presented in the mainstream curriculum of American schooling, not consigned to special days, weeks, or even months of the year, or to special-topic courses and programs aimed essentially at Blacks. Such channeling carries the disturbing message that the material is not of general value. And this does two terrible things: It wastes the power of this material to alter our images of the American mainstream—continuing to frustrate Black identification with it—and it excuses in Whites and others a huge ignorance of their own society. The true test of democracy, Ralph Ellison has said, "is . . . the inclusion—not assimilation—of the Black man."

Finally, if I might be allowed a word specifically to Black parents, one issue is even more immediate: Our children may drop out of school before the first committee meets to accelerate the curriculum. Thus, although we, along with all Americans, must strive constantly for wise schooling, I believe we cannot wait for it. We cannot yet forget our essentially heroic challenge: To foster in our children a sense of hope and entitlement to mainstream American life and schooling, even when it devalues them.

Thinking Critically and Applying Your Knowledge

1. Steele clearly argues against the customary explanation for African-American students dropping out of college, namely that their disadvantaged background fails to prepare them adequately for college work. What evidence does he provide to suggest that this is not the reason why African-American students disproportionately drop out? What does he suggest is the reason?

2. Imagine that you are a high school principal, and your job is to create a climate that will enable African-American students to achieve at their full potential. Would you create special programs, and if so, what would be their important components?

3. According to Steele, what factors lead African-American students to "disidentify" with their colleges and universities? Can you think of additional aspects of college that might have this effect?

4. Imagine that you are an African-American parent whose child is doing increasingly badly in school. You know that your child is bright, and so the deterioration in grades has nothing to do with ability. What would you do to try to change the situation? How would you try to help your child?

❖ CHAPTER 17 ❖

THE SOCIOCULTURAL CONTEXT OF AFRICAN-AMERICAN AND WHITE AMERICAN WOMEN'S RAPE

Gail Elizabeth Wyatt

There is growing public awareness of the high rate of rape in the United States and the harmful consequences experienced by victims of rape. In this paper, Gail Wyatt compares the experience of rape among African-American and White American women. During the time of slavery, White men were seldom punished for raping Black women and even today, Wyatt suggests, Black women may fear that their reports of rape will not be taken seriously. Using a community sample of women from Los Angeles, Wyatt finds that Black and White women are equally likely to have been raped and to experience negative physical and psychological effects. However, a much smaller percentage of African-American women (36%) than of White women (64%) disclosed their rape to friends, family, or the police. Wyatt discusses the sociocultural factors that may discourage Black women from revealing their victimization.

ABSTRACT: *This paper examines historical factors related to African-American women's rape and their disclosure patterns. It compares similarities and differences in incidents of attempted or completed rape in a community sample of 55 African-American and White women. The possibility that African-American women may not perceive themselves as rape victims or their experiences as meeting the criteria of "real rape" has implications for the disclosure of incidents, as well as the initial and lasting effects of sexual victimization. Researchers are urged to include ethnicity as a factor contributing to women's self-perceptions as rape survivors.*

Research has documented societal attitudes about rape (Brownmiller, 1975; Burt, 1980; Burt & Katz, 1987), the prevalence and circumstances of its occurrence, and its initial and lasting effects on women's sexual and psychological well-being (Kilpatrick, Veronen, & Best, 1985; Koss & Gidycz, 1985; Koss, Gidycz, & Wisniewski, 1987; Meyer & Taylor, 1986; Notham & Nadelson, 1976; Russell, 1983; Wyatt, Newcomb, & Notgrass, 1990). The effects of sexual victimization can be influenced by perceptions of the experience, attributions of blame, and expectations of how victims will be judged by those around them.

Source: Reprinted from *Journal of Social Issues, 48*(1), (1992), 77–91. Copyright © 1992 by The Society for the Psychological Study of Social Issues. Reprinted by permission.

Definitions of rape vary by culture and national origin. The variety of historical and political issues related to rape and gender in America have inspired feminist contributions to current definitions of rape (see Donat & D'Emilio, this issue) in American culture, rape and sexual vulnerability have a unique history because of the sexual exploitation of slaves for over 250 years. Economic and legal factors have influenced cultural definitions of sexual assault for American women, and especially for women of African descent.

This paper asserts that, because of the historical context of rape, African-American women may be somewhat cautious about accepting changes in societal attitudes about their right to be protected from rape. This may complicate their postassault adjustment, help-seeking behaviors, and attitudes about those who attempt to control their sexual behavior. Reasons for nondisclosure of rape experiences may differ by racial and ethnic group. In some cases women may not perceive the assault as "real rape" by societal standards; in others they may perceive themselves as unlikely to be seen as rape victims, though they are well aware of current definitions of rape (Williams & Holmes, 1981).

Research has also not taken into consideration the historical factors related to African-American women's rape and their disclosure patterns, nor examined similarities and differences in rape incidents compared with those of White women of similar demographic characteristics. Attitudes about rape, and the effects of these experiences upon women's adjustment years later, may be influenced by the sociocultural context in which the experiences of sexual abuse were initially defined. If African-American women perceive that society does not consider that they can be raped, and that they would not be believed if they disclosed their assault, the chances are minimal that they will disclose or seek help from authorities that represent societal views regarding "real rape."

This paper presents a brief discussion of the history of sexuality and rape in Colonial America, and then describes a study designed to understand ethnic and cultural factors that may be associated with disclosure, consequences, and expectations of rape among African-American and White women.

Sexuality and Rape in Colonial America

As early as the 15th century, even before the African slave trade began, the sexual practices of Africans were described by Christian missionaries, who dramatized the need for some control over their "sexual appetites" (Getman, 1984). These descriptions also reinforced assumptions that African sexual behavior could be brought under control if Africans were enslaved. In some of the American colonies a variety of economic factors also created a need for a more cost-effective labor force than that provided by White servitude.

Consequently, laws were enacted to institutionalize access to this labor force and discourage racial mixing that would allow future generations of slave descendants to be free (Getman, 1984). Sexual oppression was viewed as a means of enhancing the labor force. By 1660 in the American South, there were laws that encouraged sex between Black women and White men, but sex between White women and Black men was strongly discouraged, in order to ensure that interracial unions would produce children who were also slaves (Getman, 1984; Wriggins, 1983). Historically, children were considered to be the property of their fathers (LaFree, 1989), but during slavery, they were the property of their mothers, who in turn belonged to slave masters.

There were marked differences in the consequences of sexual assault on White vs. Black women, especially when the alleged assailant was a Black male. For example, free or enslaved Black men convicted of an incident of attempted or completed rape of a White woman were often castrated or sentenced to death (Jordan, 1968). However, regardless of fornication statutes and antimiscegenation laws, there were no penalties for the rape of Black women by White men. The reasons are apparent in the following quote:

> Abuse had only positive economic and social ramifications for the slave owners—an increase in the slave population and the further subjugation of the Black community through the sexual tyranny of White men over slaves (Getman, 1984, p. 126)

In spite of the wealth of literature written by Black female slaves about the deleterious effects of not being considered worthy of being protected, prevalent stereotypes held that Black women, because of their sexual "nature," could not be raped (Getman, 1984). Little attention was given to the sexual oppression of women of African descent, because legal sanctions were unavailable to them (Hines, 1989). Throughout American history, the legal system has overlooked or has considered the rape of Black women less seriously than similar assaults on White women (Wriggins, 1983).

As a result of the slavery period in American history, the sexualization of men and women of African descent has been fostered in our culture and has remained as a component of racial oppression (Williams, 1984). While stereotypes about the sexual abilities of African-American men often emphasize their male prowess, stereotypes about African-American women continue to stress negative characteristics such as sexual promiscuity (Wyatt, 1982). It is well established that, historically in our society, sexual assault on African-American women has been perceived and treated with little concern. Although not all African-American women today may be aware of their ancestors' maltreatment, there is reason to believe some African-American women may be convinced that rape is not treated any differently today than it was in the past.

Rape as a Hidden Crime: Barriers to Disclosure

In spite of increasingly sophisticated research on sexual assault, and improvement in the treatment of rape victims by legal and health professionals, there are numerous reasons that victims/survivors still tend not to disclose their assaults. Rape is often unacknowledged or hidden due to societal definitions and the circumstances under which sexual assault occurs (Koss & Burkhart, 1989). However, nondisclosure is a multifaceted issue; another reason for it is the influence of racial/ethnic group membership upon societal definitions of rape. Because many victims/survivors do not perceive that their experience meets the criteria for a "real rape" (Burt, 1980; Estrich, 1987), they tend not to disclose assaults, even to police, and to blame themselves for the incidents' occurrence. Although open discussions of sexual victimization have been described as important to the recovery process (Davis & Friedman, 1985; Wyatt, Newcomb, & Notgrass, 1990), victims/survivors often experience emotional and physical problems that are not only untreated but not understood by those around them (Pennebaker & Herron, 1984; Wyatt, Newcomb, & Notgrass, 1990).

Long-established patterns of nondisclosure of rape have often been reinforced by historical, societal, and legal attitudes about racial and ethnic groups. Ironically, given the history of Blacks in America, research has not focused upon the effects of rape on Black women (Williams & Holmes, 1981), nor have studies examined women's perceptions of the likelihood of their rape incidents being considered "real" if they are members of an ethnic group at high risk for rape (Hines, 1989). Furthermore, little attention has been given to ethnic or racial stereotypes concerning African-American women's sexual practices that are thought to disqualify them as rape victims (Williams, 1979). There is evidence to suggest that minorities are more likely to agree that "a girl's reputation is ruined if she is raped" than are nonminorities (Williams, 1979). It is possible that American minority groups may perceive and experience consequences of rape for their group differently than do nonminorities (Borque, 1980).

This paper attempts to broaden our understanding of why rape is hidden, especially for African-American and White American women. These two groups may have been socialized differently regarding the history of rape in America and stereotypes about who meets the societal criteria for rape victims today. The paper investigates initial effects of rape, including attributions of victimization, as well as lasting effects of rape on women's intimate relationships and sexual functioning. A community sample of 55 women who had experienced sexual assault was interviewed to identify ethnic and cultural factors affecting women's reactions and adjustments to sexual assault. These data were the first to include two ethnic groups that were comparable in their distribution of demographic characteristics such as education and income. The study also allowed for an examination of all incidents of attempted or completed rape, in order to assess the effects of repeated victimization.

METHOD

Sample Selection

For a large study of women's sexual experiences, multistage stratified probability sampling was used with quotas to recruit comparable samples of African-American and White American women 18–36 years of age in Los Angeles County. The age criteria were established to include women who had had an opportunity to develop a number of adult heterosexual relationships. The quotas used for the study were based upon the population of African-American women 18–36 years of age with various levels of education, marital status, and numbers of children. The categorization of African-American and White American women in the sample was based upon their own ethnic identification. In this study the terms "African-American" and "Black" were used interchangeably to indicate women of African descent, whose parentage might also include a variety of other ethnic and racial groups in

America. White women were of Caucasian background and included women of Jewish heritage. Both groups of women had spent at least 6 of the first 12 years of their childhood in the United States. (See Wyatt, 1985, for further discussion of the sampling.)

The participants were located by random digit dialing of 11,834 telephone numbers in Los Angeles County, combining prefixes with four randomly generated numbers. Women were recruited over the telephone, and of those eligible, 27% refused to participate. The first 248 women meeting the desired quotas were interviewed: 126 African-American women and 122 White American women. Both samples were compared with women in Los Angeles County between the ages of 18 and 36, and were found to be representative of the demographic characteristics of their ethnic group in the larger population (Wyatt, 1985). The two samples were also comparable with each other on the demographic characteristics noted above, including most income levels. Where discrepancies were noted, they reflected income differences between ethnic groups in the county (Wyatt, 1985).

Procedure

Each participant was interviewed face-to-face at the location of her choice by a trained female interviewer of the same ethnicity. This was one of the first studies that matched the gender and ethnicity of respondent and interviewer in a sex-related study. Participants were reimbursed for their time and expenses. Interviews were usually conducted in two sessions and ranged in total length from 3 to 8 hours. At the completion of the interview, referrals for mental health services were provided upon request (for less than 5% of the sample).

The Wyatt Sex History Questionnaire (WSHQ), a 478-item structured interview, was used to obtain both retrospective and current data regarding women's consensual and abusive sexual experiences, and the effects on their intimate relationships, and psychological and sexual functioning. The internal consistency and construct validity of the WSHQ are high, and have been described elsewhere (Wyatt, 1985; Wyatt et al. 1990).

At the end of the interview that covered a range of sex-related topics, respondents were asked four questions about whether they had experienced, since age 18, any of the several types of sexual abuse most commonly reported. If the respondent answered "yes" to any of these questions, she was asked a series of more detailed questions about each incident.

Definition of Rape

In this study, rape was defined as the involuntary penetration of the vagina or anus by the penis or another object. After this definition was read to each person, they were asked about sexual experiences that may have occurred since age 18 without their consent, and may have involved a friend, a relative, or a stranger.

The women's responses showed that, regardless of ethnicity, they were often uncertain about whether a particular experience constituted sexual abuse. This type of hesitancy was particularly common in cases of attempted or completed rapes committed by persons known to them. Consequently, while such incidents were sometimes not considered by these women to be a typical rape, as other studies have also found (Burt, 1980), they were counted as rapes in this study.

Although this approach differs from recent studies that have used behavioral descriptions and excluded the term *rape* (Koss & Gidycz, 1985), it appeared to be optimal with women who ranged substantially in literacy and educational levels. Information was obtained regarding the circumstances of each incident of attempted and completed rape. The questions pertaining to rape were asked after rapport was well established, 1–2 hours into a structured interview. Discrepancies between the woman's usage and research definitions of rape and other terms such as *anus* (a word about which 9% were unfamiliar), *vagina*, and *other objects used for penetration* were clarified. It was also found to be particularly useful to discuss the definition of rape before women described their experiences. After the completion of the interview, it was not uncommon for women to recontact the interviewer and report additional incidents, once they understood the definition of rape.

RESULTS

Prevalence and Type of Sexual Assault

There were 55 women who reported 146 incidents of attempted or completed rape—25% of African-American women and 20% of White women experienced at least one such incident since age 18, a nonsignificant difference between the ethnic groups. Of the 146 separate incidents of attempted or completed rapes, 81 were reported by African-American women and 65 by White women.

Although a Fisher's exact test was not significant, African-American women tended to report a higher proportion of attempted rape incidents (27% vs. 17% for White women). Consistent with other reports (Koss & Burkhart, 1989; Russell, 1983; Wriggins, 1983), most of the incidents were perpetrated by someone known to them (54% of incidents reported by African-American and 48% of incidents reported by White women). Black women, however, reported slightly more incidents by strangers (33% of incidents vs. 24% of incidents for White women).

Disclosure of Sexual Assault

A chi-square test assessed the relationship between women's disclosure patterns and ethnicity. Of those incidents that were not disclosed to anyone until years later, 64% involved African-American women as compared to 36% for White women; $\chi^2(5) = 13.09$, $p < .02$. Only 23% of incidents for Black women, as compared to 31% for White women, were reported to police or a rape center. Only 3 of 20 incidents reported only to the police resulted in perpetrators being arrested and jailed. Of those incidents not reported at the time they occurred, for Black women 58% involved attempted rape, whereas for White women only 42% involved attempted rape.

As a result of their disclosure to a confidant, African-American women were slightly but nonsignificantly less likely to receive support. In 26% of African-American women's incidents and 12% of White women's the confidant to whom the abuse was disclosed was either nonsupportive or failed to offer any reaction at all.

The Impact of the Assault

Three dimensions of the immediate impact of the abuse were assessed—effects on the victim's physical and psychological well-being, and sexual functioning. Physical effects were identified in over 39% of incidents involving African-American women and 46% of those involving White American women, a nonsignificant difference. These effects included injuries of varying degrees of severity, sleep or appetite disturbances, becoming infected with sexually transmitted diseases, and becoming pregnant. Negative psychological effects including fear, anger, anxiety, depression, and preoccupation with the abuse incident were identified in 85% of African-American women's incidents and 86% of White women's reports. Problems in women's sex lives were identified in 48% of incidents reported by African-American women and 55% of those reported by White women, a nonsignificant difference. These effects included avoidance of sex, decreased frequency of sexual activity, diminished enjoyment, the development of specific sexual problems, and avoidance of men resembling the perpetrator.

Long-term effects on sexual functioning did not display significant ethnic differences, but 28% of incidents for African-American women and 17% of incidents for White American women involved long-lasting negative effects, which were similar in nature to the types of sexual difficulties reported as immediate effects. Long-term psychological effects, including mistrust of men, negative attitudes toward men, chronic depression, and specific fears of being left alone and being out at night, were reported by 62% of White women and 60% of African-American women.

Participants' responses to the question "Why do you think that you were victimized (abused)?" were grouped into two categories: primarily self-oriented or attributed to external events. Self-oriented responses included both global statements ("I was stupid") and specific references to the woman's behavior or judgment ("I'd been flirting with him earlier"; "I was wearing a sexy dress and that gave him the wrong idea"; "I shouldn't have let him into my apartment"). Externally oriented responses referred to the characteristics of the perpetrator ("he was a sick man"), the riskiness of the situation ("I was living in a bad neighborhood"), or simply bad luck, being in the wrong place at the wrong time. A Fisher's exact test revealed that African-American women were significantly more likely than White women to offer explanations about their victimization that involved the riskiness of their living circumstances (76% vs. 24%, $p < .04$).

Other aspects of women's relationships that could have been affected by rape were also examined. An analysis of variance was conducted with the number of times respondents had been married as the dependent variable, and ethnicity and abuse in adulthood as the independent variables. The results were significant for the main effect of ethnicity [F (1,247) = 5.27, $p < .05$] and of abuse [F (2,247) = 2.97 p = .05]. Women who experienced incidents of attempted or completed rape were married an average of 1 time, compared to .8 times for women who did not report abuse and .6 times for women who experienced abuse that did not involve body contact (e.g., observing exhibitionists or masturbators). On the average, White women tended to be married more times than African-American women, but the ethnicity by abuse interaction was not significant.

Women's responses to a variety of questions regarding their sexual patterns were also assessed. An analysis of variance with high variety and frequency of sexual behaviors as dependent variables, and ethnicity and type of abuse as independent variables, was significant overall $[F(2,231) = 9.29, p < .0001]$. In comparison to women with no abuse histories, women with rape histories reported high frequencies of sexual behaviors, including fellatio, cunnilingus, vaginal intercourse, anal sex, extramarital affairs, higher numbers of partners, and shorter-term sexual relationships since age 18. Ethnic differences were also noted, with White women more likely to exhibit this pattern of sexual behavior than Black women $[F(1,231) = 35.94, p < .0001]$. However, ethnicity by abuse interaction effects were not significant. Furthermore, female rape survivors were more likely than women with no rape histories to have unintended and aborted pregnancies, and histories of prostitution $[F(2,231) = 9.43, p < .0001]$. No ethnic differences or interaction effects were noted here.

Women were also asked whether they had heard 15 sex-related statements, one of which was "Some women are more likely to be raped than others." African-American women were more likely to have heard this statement $[84\%$ vs. 60% for White women—$\chi^2(1, n = 105) = 8.24, p < .01]$, and they also reported that Black women were at greatest risk for rape $[36\%$ vs. 17% for White women—$\chi^2(1, n = 104) = 20.46, p < .001]$. These findings illustrate the extent to which stereotypes about who is at risk for being raped are conveyed in society.

DISCUSSION

This study examined historical and sociocultural factors that influence African-American and White American women's sexual assault experiences and postassault adjustment. The findings indicate that, contrary to surveys based upon police reports, which identify Black women as most at risk for rape (Katz & Mazur, 1979), no significant ethnic differences in the prevalence of rape incidents were noted. The discrepancy between those reports and the present data is probably a result of the demographic characteristics of the samples. In this study, women of both ethnic groups reported an average of thirteen years of education, and their income was comparable except for women below the poverty level. Most rapes reported to police involve women of lower socioeconomic status who tend to be single (Williams, 1979; Wriggins, 1983). Thus, when other variables were controlled, Black women in Los Angeles County were not more at risk for rape than White women.

While the finding that African-American women reported more rape incidents per person was not significant, it emphasizes the importance of learning more about the effects of revictimization for these two ethnic groups. Recent evidence suggests that multiple incidents of attempted or completed rapes are associated with women's later psychological and intimacy problems (Wyatt et al., 1990). It is possible, however, that the effects may be manifested not only in areas such as psychological adjustment, relationships, or sexual functioning, but also in women's perceptions of the world and their role in it. Measures assessing ethnically related perceptions of women's roles and their value as women should be included in future rape research.

Because incidents of attempted and completed rape for Black women were slightly more likely to be repeated, their victimization may have a more severe effect on their understanding of the reasons that these incidents occurred, and some of these reasons may be beyond their control. As a consequence, they may be less likely to develop coping strategies to facilitate the prevention rather than the recurrence of such incidents (Koss & Burkhart, 1989; Summit, 1983; Wyatt 1990). Black women are also more likely than White women to be single, to be without transportation, to be dependent upon public facilities, to have jobs that demand long and inflexible working hours, and to live in high crime areas (Williams, 1979). These environmental and economic realities are often difficult to overcome when attempting to develop coping strategies that will prevent rape or attempted rape from occurring. All too often, Black women drop out of therapy because they perceive that the therapeutic plan ignores aspects of their environment that they cannot change. Rape crisis treatment centers often fail to address these realities that Black rape survivors continue to face as they move through the recovery process.

Some of the findings in this study differed for the two ethnic groups. African American women were significantly less likely to disclose incidents involving sexual assault. There are many reasons that women do not disclose their abuse to anyone, including the police. One important factor is the anticipation of lack of community and societal support as a victim/survivor. The credibility of Black women as rape victims has never been established as firmly as it has for White women. Current legislation regarding rape and the prosecution of rapists notwithstanding, racial discrimination in the identification of cases that can be successfully prosecuted still exists (Wriggins, 1983). According to LaFree (1989, p. 4), "Black or poor defendants receive harsher sanctions than others in criminal cases." Acknowledging that most cases of rape that are prosecuted involve Black males and White victims, there is some question about how rigorously Black–Black rape is prosecuted in the legal system.

Public reactions to rape are still mediated not only by sex and age, but also by race/ethnicity (Borque, 1989). These realities become a part of the rape and revictimization experience (Williams & Holmes, 1981). Women who do not perceive their experiences as "real rape" are also more likely not to disclose their least credible incidents and to cautiously discuss only the most severe incidents that approximate culturally sanctioned rape—incidents where strangers were perpetrators, or where physical violence or weapons were involved (Burt, 1980). In this study, African American women may have perceived attempted rape incidents as least credible, and consequently reported such incidents less often than completed rapes.

Rape victims may not perceive the police as supportive because of their recollections of past racial incidents where race/ethnicity mediated police responses to other crimes or to rape incidents in the Black community (Wyatt et al., 1990). There is also evidence that the sociocultural orientation of the police often incorporates the offender's rather than the victim's viewpoint. Police are more cautious about intervening in cases of rape because it is, according to Feild (1978), "a private crime." This reaction follows traditional viewpoints that women are the property of men, and consequently family matters are left to be resolved by the persons involved (LaFree, 1989). The credibility of the victim is often the only basis that the police have upon which to build a case against a perpetrator. If the victim's credibility is not established on factors other than her race/ethnicity or the type of crime committed, an African-American woman may have good reason not to expect equitable treatment from police or other authorities, and consequently she may not report incidents of rape.

The concern about how others will perceive their credibility as rape victims is an issue that few treatment centers address with ethnic minority victims/survivors. In the present study, African-American women were significantly more likely than White women to recognize the danger in their living environments that placed them at risk of being victimized by men if the opportunity presented itself. This finding appears a realistic assessment of barriers to their safety which need to be conveyed to young Black children and adults on an ongoing basis.

That more African-American women had heard that they were more likely to be rape victims and believed this statement to be true suggests that rape is perceived as a likely rather than an unlikely occurrence in their lives. Such an assumption can complicate male-female relationships where feelings of trust and sexual vulnerability are at issue. If women's rights to be protected are contingent upon the color of their skin, perceptions of the likelihood of rape occurring may also lower women's efforts to prevent its occurrence.

In contrast to other findings, there were aspects of sexual assault experiences that were similar for women, regardless of their ethnicity. The immediate effects of incidents of rape were similar for both groups. Many of the symptoms that victims described in the areas of postassault physical, sexual, and psychological functioning were similar to descriptions of posttraumatic stress disorder.

In addition to the immediate impact of abuse incidents, many women also indicated that they experienced lasting effects. Most of the fifty-five women who had experienced sexual assaults reported effects that had lasted, on average, fifty-one years. This was particularly true for the psychological impact of sexual assault, where long-term effects were reported in connection with almost two thirds of the incidents involving women of either ethnic group. These lasting effects included mistrust of men or of people in general, continued emotional distress in connection with the abuse, specific fears such as being left alone or being out at night, and chronic depression. Although rape cannot be implicated as the sole contributing factor in these effects, some of these findings are consistent with other studies of effects of rape on women's later sexual functioning (Feldman-Summers, Gordon, & Meagher, 1979).

Other findings regarding the effects of rape on sexual behaviors were also similar for both ethnic groups. The pattern included increased involvement in sexual behaviors, perhaps in an effort to gain mastery over past sexual encounters where the women may have felt powerless (Rutter, 1983; Summit, 1983). This pattern, however, also included high-risk sexual behaviors that increased the risk of transmission of diseases including the human immunodeficiency virus (HIV). These women were less likely to use contraceptives to prevent pregnancy or disease transmission, or to request that their partners use condoms.

Their profile of sexual behaviors and decision making about sex and contraception is similar to that of women who report sexual abuse in childhood (Wyatt, 1991).

Furthermore, difficulties in male–female relationships that may also lead to marital problems and divorce were suggested for both ethnic groups of women. As a result of their victimization, rape survivors may feel stigmatized and powerless to develop coping strategies and behaviors that will prevent another form of victimization from occurring (Finkelhor & Browne, 1985; Koss & Burkhart, 1989; Summit, 1983). Their behavior and decision making may resemble that of women who perceive themselves as having been "ruined" because of rape. However, the interpretation may vary for each ethnic group. African-American rape victims whose experiences do not meet the criteria for "real rape" may not find support in their own community because they did not "fight" or resist their perpetrators, and by doing so, avoid assumptions and stereotypes about being someone's "sexual property." Consequently, perceptions of being "ruined" may be more salient for them.

It is possible that African-American women's awareness of rape stems not only from their personal experience, but also from membership in an ethnic group that lived through a period of American history where their incidents of sexual assault were not considered crimes. In the present study, some women recalled incidents that renewed memories of the historical treatment of Black women who were raped during the slavery era. For example, one African-American woman recalled hearing about a relative who was abducted, beaten, raped, and killed while her family was living in the South. Even though the family moved West following the incident, all of the women in the family were told about the incident, seemingly as part of a "rite of passage" into womanhood. Rape was described as something that could happen to you just because you were Black and female. This vignette appears to contradict the view that all women initially feel invulnerable, and see the world as "kind and just" (Janoff-Bulman, 1985; Taylor, 1983). Indeed, African-American women may seem more vulnerable to crime because they do not anticipate that they will be protected by traditional authorities and institutions. There is no historical basis for women of color to grow up with that assumption.

These findings, some subtle and others highly significant, illustrate the need to broaden the current focus on gender issues, and to examine the effects of both gender and ethnicity on the aftermath of rape. It is also important to assess the prevalence of rape among community samples. Furthermore, research should investigate the reasons for nondisclosure of rape incidents, including survivors' perceptions of not fitting the criteria as a rape victim because of race or ethnic group membership. While the current research focus on acquaintance rape of college students has generated invaluable information regarding definitions of rape among educated populations (Koss & Gidycz, 1985), the agenda for rape prevention should not lose sight of ethnic differences in the occurrence of rape in community groups who experience both stranger and acquaintance rapes.

Although it is difficult to separate respondents' awareness of historical treatment of rape from their personal experience, failure to assess what Black women anticipate, as well as what they have experienced, may result in a less comprehensive understanding of the effects of rape among women of color.

Strategies for Rape Prevention

Unfortunately, there is little rape education information available to specific ethnic groups that specifies who is most likely to be at risk, and under what circumstances. This kind of community-based information would convey to the public that certain individuals are most at risk in certain environments. The specific identification of risky environmental circumstances should reduce the global threat, in which women of color perceive themselves as potential rape victims in a dangerous world regardless of other factors that may affect the risk of being raped.

In efforts to empower African-American women, and to confirm their right to be protected from rape and to control what happens to their bodies, a different strategy needs to be included among rape prevention efforts. It is important first to acknowledge the efforts of female slaves and African-American writers, along with feminists in the 1960s and 1970s, as the catalysts who redefined America's perception of rape. These historical figures serve as appropriate models for African-American women who may be likely to feel that reporting their sexual assault will not be supported and believed. Rape prevention information also needs to acknowledge that, although many women of African descent have been victims of unreported sexual assault, there have always been efforts within the Black community to prevent rape and to obtain equitable treatment for rape survivors, regardless of their gender or ethnicity. Victims' individual disclosure of rape incidents continues those efforts. Finally, it is critical to convey that risk factors for rape differ according to local and national trends in crime rates. Unreported rape still occurs in every neighborhood, but especially in areas where crime rates are high. Furthermore, stranger rape is less likely to occur among Black women than sexual assaults perpetrated by acquaintances. A knowledge of these and other risk factors for sexual assault, such as having to use public transportation or walking unescorted in poorly lit neighborhoods, should be included in information targeted for the Black community. Though it is important to assert that attitudes toward Black women's rape are slowly changing, their continued hypervigilance in high-risk circumstances is still required.

There are many reasons for unacknowledged and unreported rapes. We must continue to educate both the public and the professional community, emphasizing that these reasons may include the historical context of rape, which is still incorporated into the definition of "real rape," as well as stereotypic images of women of color being sexual victims. Incidents of rape and their effects on survivors need to be investigated within the sociocultural and environmental context of their occurrence. And within that context, strategies for recovery and the prevention of revictimization should evolve.

REFERENCES

Borque, L. B. (1989). *Defining rape*. Durham, NC: Duke University Press.

Brownmiller, S. (1975). *Against our will: Men, women and rape*. New York: Simon & Schuster.

Burt, M. R. (1980). Cultural myths and supports of rape. *Journal of Personality and Social Psychology, 38,* 217–230.

Burt, M. R., & Katz, B. J. (1987). Dimensions of recovery from rape. Focus on growth outcomes. *Journal of Interpersonal Violence, 2*, 57–82.

Davis, R. C., & Friedman, L. N. (1985). The emotional aftermath of crime and violence. In C. R. Figley (Ed.), *Trauma and its wake: The study and treatment of post-traumatic stress disorder* (pp. 90–111). New York: Brunner/Mazel.

Estrich, S. (1987). *Real rape.* Cambridge, MA: Harvard University Press.

Feild, H. S. (1978). Attitudes toward rape: A comparative analysis of police, rapists, crisis counselors, and citizens. *Journal of Personality and Social Psychology, 36*, 156–179.

Feldman-Summers, S., Gordon, P. E., & Meagher, J. R. (1989). The impact of rape on sexual satisfaction. *Journal of Abnormal Psychology, 88*, 101–105.

Finkelhor, D., & Browne, A. (1985). The traumatic impact of child sexual abuse: A conceptualization. *American Journal of Orthopsychiatry, 55*, 530–541.

Getman, K. (1984). Sexual control in the slaveholding South: The implementation and maintenance of a racial caste system. *Harvard Women's Law Review, 7*, 115–153.

Hines, D. C. (1989). Rape and the inner lives of Black women in the Middle West. *Signs: Journal of Women in Culture and Society, 14*, 912–920.

Janoff-Bulman, R. (1985). The aftermath of victimization: Rebuilding shattered assumptions. In C. R. Figley (Ed.), *Trauma and its wake: The study and treatment of post-traumatic stress disorder* (pp. 15–35). New York: Brunner/Mazel.

Jordan, W. (1968). *White over Black: American attitudes toward the Negro* (pp. 1550–1812). Williamsburg, VA: University of North Carolina Press.

Katz, S., & Mazur, M. A. (1979). *Understanding the rape victim.* New York: Wiley.

Kilpatrick, D. G., Veronen, L. J., & Best, C. L. (1985). Factors predicting psychological distress among rape victims. In C. R. Figley (Ed.), *Trauma and its wake: The study and treatment of post-traumatic stress disorder* (pp. 113–141). New York: Brunner/Mazel.

Koss, M., & Burkhart, B. (1989). A conceptual analysis of rape victimization. *Psychology of Women Quarterly, 13*, 27–40.

Koss, M. P., & Gidycz, C. A. (1985). Sexual experiences survey: Reliability and validity. *Journal of Consulting and Clinical Psychology, 42*, 162–170.

Koss, M. P., Gidycz, C. A., & Wisniewski, N. (1987). The scope of rape: Incidence and prevalence of sexual aggression and victimization in a national sample of higher education students. *Journal of Consulting and Clinical Psychology, 55*, 162–170.

LaFree, G. (1989). *Rape and criminal justice: The social construction of sexual assault.* Belmont, CA: Wadsworth.

Meyer, C. B., & Taylor, S. D. (1986). Adjustment to rape: *Journal of Personality and Social Psychology, 50*, 1226–1234.

Notman, M. T., & Nadelson, C. (1976). The rape victim: Psychodynamic considerations. *American Journal of Psychiatry, 133*, 408–413.

Pennebaker, J. W., & O'Herron, R. C. (1984). Confiding in others and illness rate among spouses of suicide and accidental-death victims. *Journal of Abnormal Psychology, 93*, 473–476.

Russell, D. E. H. (1983). The prevalence and incidence of forcible rape of females. *Victimology: An International Journal, 7*, 81–93.

Rutter, M. (1983). Stress, coping, and development. In N. Garmezy & M. Rutter (Eds.), *Stress, coping, and development in children* (pp. 1–41). New York: McGraw-Hill.

Summit, R. (1988). Hidden victims, hidden pain: Societal avoidance of child sexual abuse. In G. E. Wyatt & G. J. Powell (Eds.), *The lasting effects of child sexual abuse* (pp. 39–59). Newbury Park, CA: Sage.

Taylor, S. E. (1983). Adjustment to threatening events: A theory of cognitive adaptation. *American Psychologist, 38*, 1161–1173.

Williams, J. E. (1979, Winter). Sex role stereotypes, women's liberation and rape: A cross-cultural analysis of attitudes. *Sociological Symposium*, No. 25, p 61–97.

Williams, J. E. (1984). Secondary victimization: Confronting public attitudes about rape. *Victimology: An International Journal, 9*, 66–81.

Williams, J. E., & Holmes, K. A. (1981). *The second assault: Rape and public attitudes*. Westport, CT: Greenwood.

Wriggins, J. (1983). Rape, racism, and the law. *Harvard Women's Law Journal, 6*, 103–141.

Wyatt, G. E. (1982). Identifying stereotypes of Afro-American sexuality and their impact upon sexual behavior. In B. Bass, G. E. Wyatt, & G. Powell (Eds.), *The Afro-American family: Assessment, treatment and research issues* (pp. 333–346). New York: Grune & Stratton.

Wyatt, G. E. (1985). The sexual abuse of Afro-American and White American women in childhood. *Child Abuse and Neglect, 9*, 507–519.

Wyatt, G. E. (1991). Child sexual abuse and its effects on sexual functioning. *Annual Review of Sex Research, 1*, 249–266.

Wyatt, G. E., Newcomb, M., & Notgrass, C. (1990). Internal and external mediators of women's rape experiences. *Psychology of Women Quarterly, 14*, 153–176.

This research was funded by the Center for Prevention and Control of Rape, NIMH Grant R01 MH33603, and a Research Scientist Career Development Award, K01 MH00269. The author wishes to thank the Women's Staff for data collection, Gwen Gordon for data analysis, Dafna Brook for editorial assistance, and Sarah Lowery for manuscript preparation.

THINKING CRITICALLY AND APPLYING YOUR KNOWLEDGE

1. According to Wyatt, the reactions of friends, family, and the police to a woman who reports being raped may differ for African-American and White women. Propose specific hypotheses about potential differences in reactions to rape reports by White versus Black women. Design a study to test at least one of your hypotheses.

2. Wyatt notes that definitions of rape may vary by culture and change over time. Consider the case of "marital rape." In some places, a husband cannot be charged with raping his wife because the legal definition of rape specifies that the act must occur between people who are not legally married. In other places, a husband who forces his wife to have sex against her will can be charged with rape. Discuss these differing definitions of rape. Which definition do you endorse and why?

3. When Wyatt asked women why they thought they had been raped, some emphasized external factors, such as living in a bad neighborhood or the perpetrator's being "sick." Other women gave explanations that focused on their own personal actions, such as flirting with the perpetrator or wearing provocative clothes. How might a woman's reactions to the experience of rape be affected by whether she primarily attributes the rape to external factors or to things about herself?

❖ CHAPTER 18 ❖

THE PACE OF LIFE

Robert V. Levine

Is the general pace of life faster in New York than in Los Angeles, or in Tokyo than in Rome? Psychologist Robert Levine has devised ingenious ways to measure the pace of life in cities around the globe. In this article, he describes cross-cultural differences in the tempo of daily activities. By documenting this fascinating cultural dimension, Levine highlights an important way in which the norms and values of a culture shape individual behavior. Levine also finds differences among cities within the United States in the pace of life. Finally, Levine shows that the pace of life in U.S. cities is related to physical health: The rate of death from heart disease is higher in fast-paced cities than in more leisurely locales. Levine speculates about the role that a particular behavior pattern, known as Type A personality, may have in explaining the link between health and the pace of life.

When I was teaching in Brazil some years ago, I noticed that students there were more casual than those in the United States about arriving late for class. I was puzzled by their tardiness, since their classroom work revealed them to be serious students who were intent on learning the subject. I soon found, however, that they were likely to be late not only in arriving for class but also in leaving it afterward. Whatever the reason for the students' lateness, they were not trying to minimize their time in the classroom.

In my classes in the United States I do not need to wear a watch to know when the session is over. My students gather their books at two minutes before the hour and show signs of severe anxiety if I do not dismiss them on time. At the end of a class in Brazil, on the other hand, some students would slowly drift out, others would stay for a while to ask questions, and some would stay and chat for a very long time. Having just spent two hours lecturing on statistics in broken Portuguese, I could not attribute their lingering to my superb teaching style. Apparently, staying late was just as routine as arriving late. As I observed my students over the course of a year, I came to realize that this casual approach to punctuality was a sign of some fundamental differences between Anglo-American and Brazilian attitudes toward the pace of life.

My experience in Brazil inspired an ongoing research program whose aim is to devise ways of measuring the tempo of a culture and to assess peoples' attitudes toward time. Every traveler has observed that the pace of life varies in different parts of the world, and even from place to place within a single country, but it is not obvious how to quantify these differences. We could question individuals about their concern with time and about the

Source: Reprinted from *American Scientist, 78,* (1990), 450–459. Copyright © 1990 by R. V. Levine. Reprinted by permission.

course of their days, but this method yields subjective descriptions that do not allow for systematic comparisons between groups. Without a suitable basis for comparison, it be comes difficult to gauge the meaning of "fast" or "slow."

In the past few years my colleagues and I have attempted to develop reliable, standardized measures of the pace of life. Our measurement techniques are based on simple observations that require no equipment more elaborate than a stopwatch. Much of the field work has been done by students in the course of their travels on summer vacation or during breaks between semesters.

PACE AND CULTURE

There is value in describing and appreciating another culture's sense of time. We might, for example, begin to understand the source of some of the difficulties we experience when we are exposed to another culture. Adjusting to an alien pace of life may present almost as many difficulties as learning a foreign language. This was revealed most dramatically in an investigation into the roots of culture shock among Peace Corps volunteers returning from overseas assignments. James Spradley of Macalester College and Mark Phillips of the University of Washington found that two of the three greatest adjustment difficulties were the "general pace of life" and the "punctuality of the people." Only the "language spoken" proved to be a more stressful change. The temporal aspects of life may even be thought of as a silent language. As the American anthropologist Edward Hall has noted, these informal patterns of time "are seldom, if ever, made explicit. They exist in the air around us. They are either familiar and comfortable, or unfamiliar and wrong."

Misinterpreting this silent language may lead to serious difficulties in communication. In 1985, for example, a group of Shiite Muslim terrorists hijacked a TWA jetliner, holding 40 Americans hostage with the demand that Israel release 764 Lebanese Shiite prisoners being held in Israeli prisons. The terrorists handed the hostages over to Shiite Muslim leaders who assured the American negotiators that nothing would happen to the hostages if all demands were met. At one point during the delicate negotiations one of the leaders of the Shiite militia Amal said that the hostages would be returned to the hijackers in two days if there were no movement toward meeting their demands. The American negotiators knew that neither they nor the Israelis would be able to forge a settlement in such a short time. By setting a limit of two days, the Shiites made a compromise unlikely and elevated the crisis to a very dangerous level. But when the Shiite leader realized how his statement was being interpreted, he quickly backed off: "We said a couple of days but we were not necessarily specifying 48 hours" (United Press International, June 23, 1985). Forty lives were put in jeopardy by a misinterpretation of the word *day*.

A society's pace of life may have consequences for the health of the inhabitants as well. This idea has been widely publicized in the wake of the observation that individuals with a constant sense of time urgency, described as Type-A behavior, may be more susceptible to heart disease than individuals who have a more relaxed attitude toward time.

With these considerations in mind, my colleagues and I have carried out a series of studies across and within cultures over the past 15 years. Our results indicate that differences in the pace of life exist not only between the Northern and Southern hemispheres but also between the Eastern and Western worlds; indeed, important differences can be perceived between the regions of a single country.

THE PACE OF WORLD CITIES

In collaboration with Kathy Bartlett of California State University–Fresno, I have attempted to extend and refine our understanding of cross-cultural differences in the perception of time. Rather than focus on some single dimension such as punctuality, we used several objective measures that assessed the more general issue of the pace at which people live their lives. We collected our data from six countries: Japan, Taiwan, Indonesia, Italy, England and the United States. The selection of these countries allowed for comparisons between Eastern and Western cultures with varying degrees of economic development. In each country we collected data from the largest city and from one medium-size city (the populations ranged from 415,000 to 615,000).

We examined three indicators of tempo in each city. First, we measured the accuracy of a sample of outdoor bank clocks in the main downtown area. Fifteen clocks were checked and their times compared to that reported by the telephone company; deviations from the "correct time" were measured to the nearest minute.

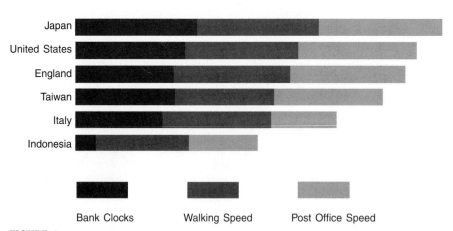

FIGURE 1
Three readily measured quantities were used to gauge the overall pace of life in six countries: the walking speed of pedestrians on downtown streets, the speed at which postal clerks fulfilled a standard request, and the accuracy of outdoor clocks on bank buildings. In each country the same measurements were made in the largest city and in one other, medium-size city. The results indicate that the pace is fastest in Japan and slowest in Indonesia. In the graph a longer bar corresponds to greater accuracy in public clocks, faster pedestrians, and faster postal clerks.

Second, we measured the average walking speed of randomly chosen pedestrians over a distance of 100 feet. The measurements were made on clear summer days during business hours in at least two locations on main downtown streets. We avoided crowded or congested areas, so that the pedestrians could potentially walk at their own preferred maximum speed. In order to control for the effects of socializing, only pedestrians walking alone were timed. Subjects with obvious physical handicaps, and those who appeared to be window shopping, were excluded from the survey.

Third, as an indicator of working pace, we measured the speed with which postal clerks fulfilled a standard request for stamps. In each city we presented clerks some paper money (the nearest equivalent of a five-dollar bill) and a note in the native language requesting a common denomination of stamp. We then measured the elapsed time between the passing of the note and the completion of the request.

Our results revealed a number of significant differences between the six countries. The Japanese cities rated the highest on all three measures: They had the most accurate bank clocks, the pedestrians there walked the fastest, and their postal clerks were the quickest to fulfill our request. In contrast, the Indonesian cities had the least accurate public clocks and the slowest pedestrians. The distinction of having the slowest postal clerks went to the Italian cities, where buying a stamp took nearly twice as long as it did in Japan.

There were also a number of differences between the large and the medium-size cities within each country. In particular, we found that people in the larger cities walked faster than those in the smaller communities. The difference was greatest in the least-developed countries in our sample, namely Indonesia and Taiwan. This may reflect the persistence of a traditional village life style among people in the smaller cities of those countries. (It would be interesting to investigate the pace of life in rural areas and small towns, but a different set of measures would be needed; there are few bank clocks in farming villages.)

What impressed us most about these findings was the high correlation between the three pace-of-life measures for each city. The accuracy of the bank clocks is strongly correlated with walking speed; the correlation coefficient, r, is .82. (An r value of 1 indicates perfect correlation.) There is also a strong correlation between clock accuracy and the speed of the postal clerks ($r = .71$). Finally, walking speed is positively correlated with postal-clerk speed ($r = .56$). The high correlation between these distinct measures supports the notion that a city has a definable overall pace, which manifests itself in the behavior of the inhabitants. It appears reasonable, then, to speak of a characteristic pace of life for a particular area and to distinguish between cultures on the basis of this characteristic.

THE PACE OF U.S. CITIES

Intrigued by our findings that various world cities have a particular pace of life, we decided to take a closer look at the cities of the United States. Are Californians really more laid-back than people in other parts of the country? Do New Yorkers live up to their reputation of living in the fast lane? What we learned confirmed many of our general preconceptions, but we also found some surprises.

Our methods were similar to those we employed in our studies of world cities. We examined nine cities in each of four regions of the United States: the Northeast, Midwest, South, and West. Within each region, we studied three large metropolitan areas (population greater than 1,800,000), three medium-size cities (population between 850,000 and 1,300,000) and three smaller cities (population between 350,000 and 550,000).

Within each city we measured four indicators of the pace of life. First, we determined the walking speed of pedestrians over a distance of 60 feet. The speeds were measured during business hours on a clear summer day along a main downtown street. We applied the same restrictions on the selection of subjects and locations as in our international study.

Second, in order to gauge the speed of working life, we measured how long it took bank clerks to complete a simple request: We asked a teller in each of at least eight downtown banks to make change for two $20 bills or to give us two $20 bills for change.

Our third indicator of pace was talking speed. We asked postal clerks to explain the difference between regular mail, certified mail and insured mail; we recorded their responses and calculated their speaking rate by dividing the total number of syllables by the total time of their response.

Fourth, as a measure of the population's concern with time, we counted the proportion of men and women in downtown areas during business hours who were wearing a wristwatch.

Each of these measures considered individually has certain quirks. The number of people wearing a watch, for example, reflects not only a society's preoccupation with time but also its sense of fashion and perhaps its level of affluence. Basing measurements on interactions with postal clerks and bank tellers puts undue emphasis on these rather specialized subpopulations; furthermore, the performance of the clerks and tellers depends on their skill and knowledge as well as on their general tendency to hurry or tarry. To compensate for these distortions we combined the scores from the four sets of measurements, creating an overall index of the pace of life in each city. First we normalized the scores, so that they all extended over the same range (an operation that has the effect of assigning equal weight to all four factors); then we added the normalized values.

In general, our results confirmed the widespread impression that the Northeastern United States is fast-paced, whereas the West Coast is a little more relaxed. We found that people in the Northeast walk faster, make change faster, talk faster, and are more likely to wear a watch than people in other parts of the country. In fact, seven of the nine fastest cities are in the Northeast. Boston, Buffalo, and New York are the fastest overall; a big surprise was that New York does not lead the list. (Manhattan residents might be excused a couple of steps, however, in order to watch the local events; during an interval of an hour and a half, our observer on one New York street corner reported an improvised concert, an attempted purse-snatching and a capsized mugger.)

The slowest pace is on the West Coast, and the slowest city overall is Los Angeles. The residents of that city scored 24th out of 36 in walking speed, next to last in speech rate, and far behind everyone else in the speed of the bank tellers. The Los Angelenos' only concession to the clock was to wear one: the city was 13th highest in the proportion of the population wearing a watch.

PACE AND CONSEQUENCES

These temporal measures serve not only to inform us of differences between peoples, but they may also be used to examine relations between the pace of life and other traits of a population. One trait that has long been suspected of being associated with the pace of life is psychological and physical health. Of particular note is the reported association between a fast-paced life and a high incidence of heart disease.

In 1959 Meyer Friedman and Ray Rosenman reported that men who exhibit a behavior pattern characterized by a sense of time urgency, hostility and competitiveness are seven times more likely than others to have evidence of heart disease and are more than twice as likely to have a heart attack. People who exhibit this behavior pattern, which Friedman and Rosenman called Type A, tend to walk quickly, eat quickly, do two things at once, and take pride in always being on time. The study seemed to support suspicions that behavior patterns can affect the incidence and course of a disease.

Since that first report, however, the association between type-A behavior and heart disease has become increasingly controversial. A number of authors have not been able to reproduce the results found by Friedman and Rosenman. The nature of our own studies suggested that we might be able to shed some light on this issue by investigating the relationship between the pace of life and the incidence of heart disease for particular populations. We were especially struck by the similarities between type-A behavior and those traits that we measured as indicators of a fast pace of life. Our research provides a unique perspective on the question, since most studies linking heart disease with a sense of time urgency have focused on individuals, not on geographic areas.

We began with the hypothesis that the faster a city's overall pace of life, the higher will be its rate of death from heart disease. To test the hypothesis we compared the overall pace of life measured in our 36 American cities with the death rate in each city from ischemic heart disease (a decreased flow of blood to the heart). The death rates were those reported by the Department of Health and Human Services for the year 1981. Since age is positively correlated with the incidence of heart disease, we statistically adjusted the death rates for the median age of each city's population. In this way we hoped to isolate the effects of social factors on heart disease.

Briefly, our results reveal a significant correlation between the pace of life and the rate of death from ischemic heart disease. The magnitude of the correlation ($r = .50$) is higher than that usually found between heart disease and measures of Type-A behavior in individuals. In other words, our data suggest that the pace of a person's environment is at least as good a predictor of heart disease as his or her score on a Type-A personality test. This was true whether we corrected for age or not.

Why are people in fast environments more prone to heart disease? In large part, we suspect that fast environments attract fast-moving, Type-A people. The psychologist Timothy Smith and his colleagues at the University of Utah have shown that Type-A individuals both seek and create time-urgent environments. The fastest cities in our study may represent both the dreams and the creations of people who live under a sense of urgency.

The development of a fast-paced city could be explained by the following scenario. First, Type-A people are attracted to fast-paced cities. In turn, the greater proportion of Type-A residents serves to maintain and further promote a fast-paced way of life. Meanwhile, slower, Type-B individuals tend to migrate away from fast-paced cities to environments more compatible with their temperament. Smith's research suggests that the temporal expectations of fast-paced cities demand time-urgent behavior in all people—Type As and Type Bs alike. The result is that Type-B individuals act more like Type As, and Type As strive to accelerate the pace still more.

The precise mechanism linking time-urgent behavior to heart disease is not known. Nevertheless, some recent statistics from the Department of Health and Human Services hint at one possibility: The incidence of cigarette smoking follows the same regional pattern as that of ischemic heart disease and the pace of life. That is, the rates for cigarette smoking and ischemic heart disease are highest where the pace of life is fastest: the Northeastern United States. The Northeast is followed by the Midwest, the South and then the West on all three variables.

Cigarette smoking has been identified as the single most important preventable cause of heart disease. It is also well documented that cigarette smoking is often related to psychological stress. These correlations suggest, but do not confirm, the possibility that a causal relation exists between these variables. One possibility is that stressful, time-pressured environments lead to unhealthy behaviors such as cigarette smoking and poor eating habits, which in turn increase the risk of heart disease. Our model of the fast-paced "Type-A city" may provide a basis for examining this hypothesis.

The pace of modern life offers an interesting perspective on our way of living, but a caveat is also in order here. Although we have come to view the choice between rushing and leisurely activity as a trade-off between accomplishment and peace of mind, we should note that time pressure is not always stressful; it may also be challenging and energizing. The optimal pressure seems to depend on the characteristics of the task and the personality of the individual. Similarly, what we have characterized as a Type-A environment will affect different people in different ways. What may be most important is fitting people to their environment. Although a Type-A setting may be stressful to a Type-B individual, a Type-A person may experience more distress in a Type-B environment. Given that heart disease remains the single largest cause of death in the United States, the search for a healthy person–environment fit takes on great importance.

REFERENCES

Amato, P. R. (1983). The effects of urbanization on interpersonal behavior. *Journal of Cross-Cultural Psychology, 14*, 153–367.

Booth-Kewley, S., & Friedman, H. (1987). Psychological predictors of heart disease: A quantitative review. *Psychological Bulletin, 101*, 343–362.

Bornstein, M. H. (1979). The pace of life: Revisited. *International Journal of Psychology, 14*, 83–90.

Chernoff, H. (1973). The use of faces to represent points in k-dimensional space graphically. *Journal of the American Statistical Association, 68*, 361–368.

Cohen, J. B., Syme, S. L., Jenkins, C. D., Kagan, A., & Zyzanski, S. J. (1975). The cultural context of Type A behavior and the risk of CHD. *American Journal of Epidemiology, 102*, 434.

Freedman, J., & Edwards, D. (1988). Time pressure, task performance, and enjoyment. In J. E. McGrath (Ed.), *The social psychology of time: New perspectives* (pp. 113–133). Newbury Park, CA: Sage.

Friedman, A. P., & Rosenman, R. H. (1974). *Type A behavior and your heart.* New York: Knopf.

Hall, E. T. (1959). *The silent language.* New York: Doubleday.

Lauer, R. H. (1981). *Temporal man: The meaning and uses of social time.* New York: Praeger.

Levine, R. (1988). The pace of life across cultures. In J. E. McGrath (Ed.), *The social psychology of time: New perspectives* (pp. 39–62). Newbury Park, CA: Sage.

Levine, R., & Bartlett, K. (1984). Pace of life, punctuality and coronary heart disease in six countries. *Journal of Cross-Cultural Psychology, 15*, 233–255.

Levine, R., Lynch, K., & Lucia, M. (1989). The Type A city: Coronary heart disease and the pace of life. *Journal of Behavioral Medicine, 12*, 509–524.

Levine, R., West, L., & Reis, H. (1980). Perceptions of time and punctuality in the United States and Brazil. *Journal of Personality and Social Psychology, 38*, 541–550.

Marmot, M. G., & Syme, S. L. (1976). Acculturation and coronary heart disease in Japanese Americans. *American Journal of Epidemiology, 104*, 225–247.

Matthews, K. (1988). Coronary heart disease and Type A behaviors: Update on an alternative to the Booth-Kewley and Friedman (1987) quantitative review. *Psychological Bulletin, 104*, 373–380.

McGrath, J. E. (1989, July). The place of time in social psychology: Some steps toward a social psychological theory of time. Paper presented at the Seventh Conference of the International Society for the Study of Time, Glacier Park, Montana.

Reid, D. D. (1975). International studies in epidemiology. *American Journal of Epidemiology, 102*, 469–476.

Smith, T., & Anderson, N. (1986). Models of personality and disease: An interactional approach to Type A behavior and cardiovascular risk. *Journal of Personality & Social Psychology, 50*, 1166–1173.

Spradley, J. P., & Phillips, M. (1972). Culture and stress: A quantitative analysis. *American Anthropologist, 74*, 518–529.

Werner, C. M., Altman, I., & Oxley, D. (1985). Temporal aspects of homes: A transactional perspective. In I. Altman & C. M. Werner (Eds.), *Home environments: Human behavior and environment. Advances in theory and research* (Vol. 8, pp. 1–32). New York: Plenum.

Wright, L. (1988). The Type A behavior pattern and coronary heart disease. *American Psychologist, 43*, 2–14.

THINKING CRITICALLY AND APPLYING YOUR KNOWLEDGE

1. Levine developed standardized measures of the "pace of life" such as the walking speed of pedestrians and the accuracy of public clocks. What are the advantages and disadvantages of Levine's measures? Describe at least two new measures not used by Levine that could be employed to assess the pace of life on a college campus.

2. Levine reports a strong statistical association (correlation) among his three cross-cultural measures of the pace of life. What does this mean? Why is it important?

3. Cross-cultural differences in the pace of life suggest that each culture develops its own norms (group rules) and values about the use of time. What messages about the pace of life have you learned from your family, at school, or at work? How might cultural dif-

ferences in the pace of life lead to mutual misunderstandings between individuals from different countries—for example, a foreign exchange student or a business consultant working abroad?

4. Levine reports that the pace of life in a city is related to the rate of death from heart disease in that city. How does Levine explain this link? What role does he believe Type A and Type B personality may play in the association between a city's pace of life and heart disease?

5. Describe the pace of life on your campus or in your city. Ideally, would you prefer to live in a fast-paced or slow-paced environment? Why?

❖ CHAPTER 19 ❖

CULTURAL PERSPECTIVES
ON INTERNATIONAL NEGOTIATIONS

Paul R. Kimmel

When diplomats from different cultures meet to try to resolve disputes and avoid international conflicts, they often bring quite different assumptions to the negotiating table. Americans and other diplomats from the West tend to view bargaining as an impersonal business activity designed to solve problems. They emphasize the efficient use of time, direct communications among participants, and adherence to international law. In contrast, negotiators from the Middle East often emphasize a more slow-paced approach based on continued personal interaction. A failure to understand the implicit assumptions and values of each side can lead to miscommunication and unsatisfactory outcomes. In this paper, Paul Kimmel outlines typical American assumptions and values about negotiation and then argues in favor of a more intercultural approach. Kimmel illustrates his perspective by describing unsuccessful negotiations between the United States and Iraq in 1991 about the Iraqi invasion of Kuwait, a situation that eventually lead to the deployment of American troops in the Gulf War. Kimmel believes that greater intercultural understanding can enhance our ability to negotiate successfully with other nations.

ABSTRACT: *The traditional Western diplomatic approach to international negotiation is compared with an intercultural approach. The implicit assumptions underlying the universal "culture" of diplomacy and the American values in which these assumptions are grounded are discussed. Individual levels of cultural awareness including cultural chauvinism, ethnocentrism, tolerance, minimization, and cultural understanding are described, and their influence on the interpersonal processes of international negotiation are illustrated through a consideration of the Iraq/U.S. diplomatic meetings in Geneva in 1991. Finally, the potential of the intercultural approach is discussed.*

M any misunderstandings and breakdowns in important international meetings and negotiations have resulted from the expectations about negotiation that the representatives brought to these encounters—expectations that were not shared by representatives from other societies (Adler, 1986; Cohen, 1991, 1992; Fisher, 1972, 1980, 1988; Weiss, 1993). A variety of implicit assumptions about the processes of negotiation—learned through being reared and

---

Source: Reprinted from *Journal of Social Issues, 50*(1), (1994), 179–196. Copyright © 1994 by the Society for the Psychological Study of Social Issues. Reprinted by permission.

educated in different common cultures—affect how individuals will behave in international meetings. One's own assumptions appear to be normal and realistic, because they are familiar and unquestioned when negotiating domestically. Most people believe that other negotiators should share their "common sense" assumptions, so it is natural for them to assume that those who do or say the unexpected in these international meetings are not as committed to and forthright about the negotiations as they are.

To develop a less presumptive, more empathic approach to international negotiation requires insights into one's own and others' subjective cultures (Triandis, 1972), those cognitive, perceptual, and communication habits individuals acquire as a result of their socialization. In essence, improving communication in international negotiations is a process of learning how to learn in intercultural encounters. A good place to begin this process is with an explication of one's own implicit assumptions about negotiations and the common cultural values in which these assumptions are grounded. It is very difficult to improve intercultural communication if the communicators remain oblivious to their own cultural assumptions and values. Let us examine some U.S. assumptions and values associated with negotiation.

U.S. ASSUMPTIONS ABOUT NEGOTIATING

Listed below are 11 topic areas that have been used to describe international meetings and negotiations (Weiss & Stripp, 1985). I have used these dimensions to categorize some of my observations of typical U.S. assumptions about negotiation based on my work with international negotiators (Kimmel, 1989) and business persons (Kimmel, in press). While I will allude to other cultural perspectives on negotiation in the latter parts of this section, I prefer to focus primarily on the implicit assumptions and values that I have firsthand (emic) knowledge about as a citizen, trainer, and researcher in the United States. There are pitfalls in any study of cultural variables and their influence (Weiss, 1987, 1993). These are multiplied when trying to describe the assumptions and values of a common culture other than one's own. Throughout this discussion, I will distinguish between *common culture*—the externalized, mutually shared perceptions of a people's symbolic environment—and *subjective culture*—the internalized, cognitive, perceptual and communication habits unique to the individual.

> *Conception of the negotiation process.* For the U.S. negotiator, negotiation is a business, not a social activity. The objective of a negotiation is to get a job done, which usually requires a mixture of problem-solving and bargaining activities. Most negotiations are adversarial with other parties seen as opponents who are trying to get as much as possible. The flow of a negotiation is from pre-negotiation strategy sessions to opening positions to give and take (bargaining) to final compromises to signing and implementation of agreements. All parties are expected to give up some of their original demands in the process of reaching an agreement. Success can be measured in terms of how much each party achieves its bottom line objectives.

Type of issues. Substantive issues are more important than social and emotional issues. Differences in positions among negotiators are seen as problems to be solved or overcome. The substantive issues that are the basis of each party's position and that are the focus of the negotiation are worked on in the give and take of the negotiation process.

Protocol. Negotiations are scheduled occasions that require face-to-face interactions among the involved parties. Effective use of time (efficiency) on substantive tasks is valued over ceremony and social amenities. During the give and take of formal negotiation processes, standardized procedures such as Robert's Rules of Order should be followed. Other social interactions are informal and should take place outside the scheduled negotiation meetings.

Reliance on verbal behaviors. Communication is direct and verbal. There is little deliberate or intentional use of nonverbal behaviors in the communication process. What is said is more important than how it is said, or what is not said. Honesty and frankness are valued. Communications tend to be spontaneous and reactive after the presentation of initial positions.

Nature of persuasive arguments. Tactics, such as bluffing, are acceptable in the bargaining process. Current information and ideas are more valid than historical or traditional opinions and information. Expert opinions and data are most persuasive; theory is not important. Timing is important in the presentation of positions and concessions.

Individual negotiators' latitude. The representatives at the table have a great deal of latitude in reaching acceptable agreements for their sponsors. Negotiators may not have a firm idea of their final positions (bottom line) until the negotiation process is well along. Whatever is not expressly forbidden by the negotiator's sponsor or the standardized procedures of the negotiation process is possible. A maximum of options is kept open.

Bases of trust. Negotiators trust the other parties until they prove untrustworthy. Trust is judged by the behaviors of others. Fair play, principled behavior, equity, and objective thinking are valued. Deception, coercion, elitism, unresponsiveness, and bribery are not valued. Past experience with the other parties is an important consideration in trusting.

Risk-taking propensities. Negotiators are open to different or novel approaches to problem issues. Brainstorming is good. Avoiding uncertainty is not important in the negotiation process. Fixed ideological positions and approaches are not acceptable. Negotiators are able to go beyond sponsors' directives on some occasions.

Value of time. Time is very important. Punctuality is expected. A fixed time is allotted for concluding a negotiation. There may be rescheduling and a decision to work longer hours to finish a negotiation on time or the clock may be stopped. Negotiators may skip over difficult points and return to them later to keep a negotiation on schedule.

Decision-making system. Majority voting and/or authoritative decisions are the rule. Certain team members are expected to be authorized to make binding decisions. Those who disagree with major decisions are expected to express themselves at the time (e.g., a minority report), but to abide by the decisions of the majority.

Forms of satisfactory agreement. Oral commitments are not binding. Written contracts that are exact and impersonally worded are binding. There is the expectation of contractual finality. Lawyers and courts are the final arbitrators in any arguments after contracts have been signed.

U.S. VALUES RELATED TO NEGOTIATION ASSUMPTIONS

If most of these implicit assumptions about the processes of international negotiation seem familiar and sound reasonable, it is because they reflect dominant procedures in many Western nations and especially within the U.S. These procedures are based on some of our basic values, values that represent our ideals, goals, and norms. Some of the important U.S. values (Stewart, 1972; Stewart & Bennett, 1991) that underlie these implicit assumptions about negotiations include the following:

1. Time is a precious commodity. It should be used efficiently to accomplish goals, make plans, set deadlines, chart progress, and schedule activities. There is an emphasis on the near future.
2. Specialization is desirable in work and social relationships. One has different friends and colleagues for different occasions. There is little emphasis on being harmonious or consistent.
3. Individuals control their destinies. One should do something about his life, environment, and social activities.
4. There are few absolute truths; what works is good. Problems can be solved and differences resolved through compromises.
5. Conflicts should be resolved through democratic processes. Everyone with an interest in an issue should have some say in how things are done.
6. Everyone should have an equal opportunity to develop their abilities.
7. Authority is resisted, independence valued. Everyone has a right to privacy.
8. One must compete with others to get ahead. Achievements are rewarded through upward mobility and income. Nepotism and welfare are disliked.

Table 1 shows the connections between these eight values and the implicit assumptions U.S. negotiators make about international negotiations. Some of the connections between the selected U.S. cultural values and implicit assumptions about negotiations are obvious, such as seeing time as a commodity and the value of time in international negotiations. Precise scheduling of a negotiation and punctuality are more important in a common culture like ours in which time is considered precious than in a common culture in which time is experienced as a natural succession of day and night or the seasons and thus considered plentiful. For those with these more polychronic beliefs and values about time (see Hall, 1959), scheduling and punctuality are not as likely to characterize negotiations. Such negotiators are also likely to have a different temporal focus than the American emphasis on the near future. They may pay more attention to the past with its history, precedents, and traditions, or may think in terms of the more distant future, considering the consequences of a negotiation for their descendents.

TABLE 1
U.S. Assumptions and Values Relating to Negotiation

Assumptions	Values							
	Time as commodity	Individual control	Specialization	Pragmatism	Democracy	Equal opportunity	Independence	Competition
Process		X		X				X
Issues	X		X					X
Protocol			X		X	X		
Verbal behavior		X					X	
Persuasion							X	
Latitude					X		X	
Trust					X	X		
Risk taking		X		X	X			X
Time	X		X				X	
Decisions				X		X		
Agreements				X		X		

Negotiators who value time as a precious commodity are not as likely to "take" the time needed to develop relationships in their negotiations. They will focus instead on substantive issues and tasks. Our norm of different friends for different occasions is also relevant to forming relationships in negotiations. This approach to friendship is part of our time-conscious, fast-paced, and mobile society. U.S. negotiators have too many obligations and other commitments to allow them to "spend" much time socializing or getting acquainted with the other negotiators—especially those they do not need to influence—hence, a general lack of amenities and a more impersonal approach to socializing during negotiations.

The U.S. approach of getting down to business in a negotiation is related to the values of personal control and pragmatism. Believing that it is possible and important to do something about one's situation and that one can affect the near future makes it obligatory for our negotiators to see the job at hand as the reason for the negotiation. Solving a problem and/or reaching an agreement are why they are there. Knowing that problems are to be solved and differences to be resolved, it is not surprising that our negotiators feel there is little time for anything but the task at hand, which is usually "tackled" with great enthusiasm whether it is to reach a compromise, strike a deal, or find a solution.

This task-oriented approach to negotiation has ramifications for the processes that take place during the negotiations themselves. With no cultural emphasis on harmony and a belief that all with an interest in an issue should have a voice in the discussion, it is not surprising that U.S. negotiators favor honesty and frankness in their negotiations. They prefer face-to-face interactions among the involved parties and engage in spontaneous and reactive communications. Their preference is for what Hall (1976) calls low-context communication in which what is said (the message) is more important than how it is said or what is not said. The less direct, face-saving approaches characteristic of other negotiators who value harmony and cordial communication in such situations are not well understood by our negotiators. In their efforts to get down to "brass tacks," it is not surprising that they often appear brusque, insensitive, and even arrogant to those who rely more on nonverbal behaviors and paralinguistic signals in their "high-context" (Hall, 1976) communications.

Following impersonal rules of procedure and law, taking votes, working out deals and compromises, and signing contracts are other procedures that our egalitarian, task-oriented negotiators use to facilitate the negotiation processes they favor. These rules ensure that everyone gets heard, that power and influence are tempered by routinized procedures (e.g., one negotiator, one vote), that the majority rules, and that everyone understands what they are agreeing to. The values of equal opportunity and democracy are important to these negotiators. What they would see as elitism, favoritism, nepotism, and injustice may be viewed differently, however, by other negotiators who come from cultures that value differences in rank and status more than equality. These negotiators expect to rely on authority, to honor past debts and acquire new allies, and to follow orders from their superiors. Their values do not predispose them to the legal procedures or the democratic behaviors favored by the U.S. negotiators.

The U.S. negotiators' beliefs in the values of individual control, personal independence, and pragmatism combine to promote risk taking. They are willing, even eager to take responsibility for new ideas and initiatives in negotiations. Rather than avoiding uncertainty, as do other negotiators who are more concerned with authority and tradition, the U.S. negotiators enjoy brainstorming, using tactics such as bluffing, keeping their options open, and trying out novel solutions. These risk-taking behaviors are well served by their spontaneous and reactive communication styles and the individual latitude they expect in the negotiations.

These U.S. values and the implicit assumptions about negotiation that result from them promote a problem-centered, competitive approach to international meetings for U.S. negotiators. Other negotiators are seen as adversaries who are trusted only as long as their behavior merits such trust by Western standards. Behaviors such as honoring commitments, keeping confidences, playing fair, and being reasonable merit trust. Behaviors such as deception, breaking promises, using coercion and bribery, and being unresponsive destroy trust. Negotiators who hold other values and implicit assumptions about negotiating will have different approaches to international negotiations. They may prefer meetings in which the emphasis is on building interpersonal relationships through a more cooperative social approach. They might see other negotiators as strangers who cannot be trusted until they become well known through lasting reciprocal relationships.

THE CULTURE OF DIPLOMACY

Becoming more cognizant of the U.S. values and implicit assumptions that affect communication in international negotiations involving non-Western negotiators is an important first step in facilitating such negotiations. It is also necessary to understand that there are other values and implicit assumptions that influence other international negotiators' perceptions and behaviors in international meetings. A number of Western students and practitioners of negotiation, however, do *not* believe this. The following statement is typical of their thinking: "Cultural factors are peripheral to the understanding of the basic negotiating process" that is "universal" (Zartman & Berman, 1982, p. 226). These scholars believe that a universal, international diplomatic "culture" has been established that supersedes the idiosyncrasies of ethnographic cultures. "It is difficult to maintain . . . that the Western system of diplomacy and negotiation worked out over the centuries is in danger of imminent destruction. . . . To the contrary, the new nations have learned the Western ways well and are using them to their own purposes" (Zartman & Berman, 1982, p. 226). Since these scholars are usually members of the Western societies in which the current rules and traditions of international diplomacy were developed, it is not surprising that they find them to be reasonable and "culture free."

These scholars claim that the Western system of diplomacy, which embodies many of the assumptions about negotiation listed above, is the operative reality in international negotiations. They point out that protocol, diplomatic courtesy, international law, and other Western diplomatic inventions have enabled international negotiators to deal with each other in a variety of bilateral situations over the last century. But these diplomatic procedures and the implicit assumptions and values on which they are based are becoming increasingly less effective in enabling negotiators to reach common ground and creatively problem solve in today's more complex world of multilateral relations (Touval & Rubin, 1987). Examples of problematic international meetings appear weekly in the U.S. press: a diplomat in a problem-solving workshop on the Palestinian/Israeli conflict who left complaining of being treated like a "guinea pig"; a negotiator in the Iraq/U.S. meetings prior to the Gulf War saying, "I never thought you Americans could be so arrogant"; the Japanese coining the word *kenbei* to express their feelings about the perceived arrogance and self-righteousness of Western negotiators; and the head of the Canadian free-trade negotiation team telling the *Toronto Star*, "The Americans are bastards. They are behaving like real thugs these days in protecting their interests." The list goes on.

The key to success in any negotiation, and especially in international negotiations, lies in the successful exchange of meanings among the negotiators. At the international level, both verbal and nonverbal exchanges become increasingly complex as intended (and unintended) and perceived meaning varies, sometimes in highly subtle ways. International negotiators who are unaware of (or unconcerned about) the influence of their own cultural values and implicit assumptions in negotiating situations are prone to expect all other qualified negotiators to share their values and assumptions about negotiations and international meetings. When the communications and behaviors of these other negotiators overtly belie this assumption, untutored parties usually attribute these "inappropriate" acts and messages to undesirable character traits (such as arrogance) and motivations (such as protecting interests) of the "misbehaving" or "unreasonable" negotiators, instead of attributing them to cultural differences (Jones et al., 1972).

THE INTERCULTURAL APPROACH TO NEGOTIATION

I believe that a more intercultural, less ethnocentric approach to negotiation, especially by the more powerful Western nations, is crucial in today's multicultural, multilateral world of business and politics where the communication contexts and the cognitions of negotiators vary more widely than they do in domestic situations. "Multilateral negotiation is more difficult than domestic policy making because the relevant actors come from very different backgrounds, and they represent nations that have occasionally worked out very different procedures for handling similar problems" (Winham, 1979, p. 196). An intercultural approach to negotiation is more relevant to multilateral negotiations than the traditional bargaining approach. In such negotiations, situations are more likely to be *new* (without familiar meanings), *complex* (with a great number of meanings to be taken into account), and *contradictory* (with different actors having different interpretations).

Multilateral negotiations put a premium on the ability to find integrative solutions by defining situations in ways that include and are responsive to the perspectives and needs of all the parties. Verbal persuasion replaces bargaining from strength, and consensus supplements compromise. Negotiators who can mutually define and redefine the problems being dealt with, overcome enmity and misunderstandings among themselves and their constituencies, and create interpersonal relationships and procedures that lead to creative solutions of their problems are most successful in such multilateral negotiations. To facilitate this process, Saunders (1987) recommends that nations focus on their relationships. He advocates a change in the perceptions of policymakers in bilateral situations from "us and them" to "we." To make such changes requires that policymakers and negotiators have the experience and training to achieve a level of cultural awareness and skill in intercultural communication that allows them to collaborate effectively, developing what Saunders calls mature relationships.

Those who have developed such awareness and skills can take account of their cultural assumptions and values in their interactions and communications with other negotiators. They have learned how to learn in international meetings. I have suggested that the process of intercultural exploration (Kimmel, 1989) is particularly effective for such negotiators. In this process the negotiators consciously identify the major cultural assumptions and values that are affecting their own perceptions and behaviors in the negotiations; communicate these assumptions and values clearly as an explicit part of their negotiations; encourage and help other negotiators identify and communicate clearly their major cultural assumptions and values; and then move toward creative and collaborative problem solving. Intercultural exploration will avert or clarify misunderstandings and misperceptions by creating new meanings and relationships. It is possible that the intercultural exploration process can also help produce solutions to problems that combine the ideas and approaches of individuals with different subjective cultures into something new that none of them could have conceived alone.

Negotiations involving intercultural exploration are better suited to a world in which longer-term relationships and multicultural problem solving are becoming increasingly important (Fisher, 1989; Winham, 1977). To use this intercultural approach effectively requires special training and experience to discover and get beyond one's own cultural blinders (Kimmel, 1989, in press). Without such training, international negotiators are likely to rely on their own subjective cultural assumptions and the culture of diplomacy. They will minimize rather than take account of cultural differences, attribute motivations typical in their common culture rather than empathizing with other cultures, ignore rather than explore values and assumptions, and essentially "negotiate with themselves."

Cultural awareness is one measure of the level of intercultural skills an individual has available. I have observed several different levels of individual subjective cultural awareness in working with thousands of international business people in intercultural training programs, ranging from the ethnocentric balance of power approach typified by a trainee who told me, "I'm representing America, I'll just tell them what to do," to very perceptive and sophisticated intercultural negotiators.

INDIVIDUAL LEVELS OF CULTURAL AWARENESS

We are born culturally illiterate. We learn our folk psychology and our common sense from those who socialize us. The subjective cultures of individuals are constructions based on their history of symbolic exchanges with others and with their environment (Stryker & Gottlieb, 1981). Through these exchanges, individuals develop deep-seated implicit assumptions about human beings that underlie their understanding of and behavior in future exchanges (Avruch & Black, 1991). The wider the variety of symbolic exchanges we have in our lives, the richer our subjective cultures become. Our subjective cultures provide a highly selective screen between us and our environment, which enables us to interpret our world and act purposefully in it (Hall, 1976). Subjective cultures characterize both the participants in a negotiation and the analysts and mediators who try to understand them.

I have noted five different levels of cultural awareness that can be used to categorize the complexity of an individual's subjective culture:

1. In the narcissistic and egocentric world of early childhood, individuals are unaware of other cultures. Since young children are only beginning to learn the rules of the common culture into which they are being socialized, any behaviors or communications that differ from these rules are attributed to others' ignorance and bad intentions. This egocentric approach to human behavior leads individuals to try to get any "nonconforming" individuals they encounter to do things their way; the right way. This level of awareness I have termed *cultural chauvinism*. Individuals at this level of awareness have little knowledge of or interest in people with different subjective cultures. This level is not typical of international negotiators.

2. With more socialization (a wider range of symbolic interactions), individuals move from cultural chauvinism to *ethnocentrism*, a level of awareness in which differences in important behaviors and communications among peoples are linked to observed ethnic, religious, racial, and/or national differences of the individuals involved. Since individuals at this level of awareness have learned many elements of their common culture, these different actions are compared to their own cultures'. Given the human readiness to favor the groups to which we belong (Brewer, 1986), it is likely that most differences will be labeled as undesirable and those exhibiting them avoided or treated in an unfriendly manner. Those whose level of cultural awareness is primarily ethnocentric are utterly convinced of the superiority of their ways of doing and thinking about things. They communicate most easily with those who share and favor their own common culture. Thus, communication among ethnocentric individuals from different common cultures is not likely to be mutually satisfying or productive. Their differences are apt to be too great, their emotional attachments too strong, and their adaptability too little. Recent episodes of American and Japanese "bashing" are examples of ethnocentric negotiation behaviors.

3. The next level in the development of cultural awareness is that of *tolerance*. Reaching this level requires a wider range of interactions and a greater understanding of cultural differences. At this level, the different behaviors and communications of foreigners are usually attributed to their socialization in a different society or country rather than being seen as inherent. These differences are not necessarily labeled as undesirable, as they are by those at the more ethnocentric level of awareness, but the practices of one's own society or nation are still regarded as more realistic and effective. Individuals who are tolerant will make some efforts to understand and be sympathetic to the differences that they experience in others and often disapprove of the more chauvinistic and eth-

nocentric members of their own and other cultures. However, these "tolerant" individuals will try to educate, legislate, "develop," or coerce those with whom they differ into adopting their own ways of thinking and behaving. International meetings among individuals who are tolerant of each other may be moderately successful, although often frustrating, as each tries to educate, control, or seduce the others to a more realistic way of doing things: namely, their own. The Camp David meetings provide many examples of tolerant negotiation behavior among diplomats.

4. The fourth level of cultural awareness is that of *minimization*. Bennett (1986) states that individuals who minimize cultural differences overtly acknowledge them and do not see them as something to denigrate or change. However, they trivialize (minimize) the significance of these differences and emphasize what they believe are more basic universal patterns of behavior—religious, economic, political, historical, or psychological "laws" that suggest all adult humans are in some ways basically alike. Individuals who "attempt to 'bury' [cultural] difference under the weight of cultural similarities" see such differences "as either superficial or even obstructive to the pursuit of communication. This is because communication is assumed to rest necessarily on the common ground of universal rules or principles" (Bennett, 1986, pp. 183–184). The practitioners of international negotiation or mediation who have this minimalist conception of cultural differences are the ones who are most surprised by the "idiosyncrasies" of other diplomats and negotiators (whom they thought they understood) when they do or say something unexpected.

Learning to minimize cultural differences may be culturally based. As Stewart and Bennett (1991) note, "Americans typically believe that everyone is basically alike, and other people have the same basic needs that they have themselves. Since the important differences among people are believed to be individual, not cultural or social, Americans are sensitive to similarities in others rather than to differences" (p. 151). U.S. social scientists who study or popularize negotiation processes often minimize cultural differences in their quest for universal human behaviors and generalizable findings.

5. The fifth level of cultural awareness and communication is that of *understanding*. Individuals at this level have discovered (usually through mediated intercultural experiences) that some of their own categories, plans, and rules are cognitively and perceptually arbitrary and that "appropriate" behavior and feelings and "realistic" thinking in intercultural situations are not necessarily givens. Those who understand that their common sense and the common sense of those from other cultures are different rather than normal and abnormal, realistic and unrealistic, have learned to be culturally understanding. They often try to put themselves in the other parties' shoes (this is called intentional empathy by Tyler, 1987) when communicating, realizing that their approaches to interpreting the world and acting purposefully in it are likely to diverge.

Few students or practitioners of international negotiation operate consistently at the level of cultural understanding because cultural understanding runs counter to human inclinations to define self and reality in a more or less permanent way. It also exposes the understanding individuals to charges of cultural relativity and disloyalty to their own groups, and to suspicion by members of other groups who are uncomfortable with "being understood." Being conscious of one's own implicit assumptions and motives and reflecting on one's communications to see if they are as empathetic as possible is hard work intellectually, but the potential of cultural understanding for empowering all parties and finding intercultural solutions to international conflicts is worth the effort.

To provide a more concrete sense of how subjective cultural understanding and common cultural value differences are related to intercultural communication and conflict in international negotiations, I will examine the meetings between the representatives of the U.S. and Iraq in Geneva in January, 1991. Some of the American assumptions and values related to negotiation discussed above will be highlighted and contrasted with those of the Iraqis.

IRAQ AND THE U.S., GENEVA 1991

Prior to the Geneva meeting between Secretary of State Baker and Foreign Minister Aziz, the U.S. and Iraqi officials behaved in ways that were not expected by their counterparts in Baghdad and Washington. For example, the U.S. appointed a woman, April Glaspie, as its ambassador. In many Middle Eastern common cultures the American value of gender equality is not well accepted. The ambassador's gender and her status as a "Westerner" made her a very weak representative in Iraq. Even if she had delivered a clearer (from the Western point of view) message, it would not have been treated as seriously as if it had come from a male. The ambiguity of the message, of course, complicated the issue and signaled to Hussein that the U.S. was not concerned with his "retaking of Iraq's territory." To him, what was not said by the U.S. was more important than what was said (high-context communication).

The meeting between U.S. Secretary of State Baker and the Iraqi Foreign Minister Aziz in Geneva was plagued by several common cultural differences (see Halverson in Olsson, 1985). The U.S. approach was as follows: (1) task oriented—demanding Iraq withdraw from Kuwait; (2) abstract—appealing to international law; (3) impersonal—sending a letter from president to president with no personal meetings; (4) definite—demanding Hussein respond or else; and (5) fast paced—setting short time deadlines. According to Halverson, Easterners such as the Iraqis prefer a different approach to meetings, one that is more holistic, long term, and relational. The Iraqis in Geneva were more as follows: (1) group oriented—wanting to get to know the U.S. negotiators; (2) experiential—appealing to past history; (3) personal—asking for direct meetings between the leadership; (4) indefinite—making no commitments without more interaction with the U.S. representatives; and (5) slow paced—rejecting early deadlines. Indeed, some have argued that the U.S. could not have done a better job of alienating the Iraqis had they tried. And yet the Associated Press (AP) reported that Baker was "genuinely stunned" when Aziz said, "I am sorry, I cannot receive this letter." Why?

Obviously, part of Baker's reaction was surprise at the audacity of a small nation flaunting a U.S. ultimatum. But equally important was the attribution process. Attributions are judgments about the causes of behavior (self or situation). An individual's attributions reflect those prevalent in his or her common culture. Baker knew that as the U.S. representative, he would have accepted such a letter in a similar circumstance. For the Iraqis not to do so was therefore inconceivable. Attributing American thought processes to the Iraqis, the U.S. decided that this behavior indicated that the Iraqis did not want to negotiate and thus must be dealt with through force. The possibility that they might have a very different approach to international negotiation and communication in conflict situations was apparently not entertained.

What might Aziz's reasons have been for refusing to accept the Bush letter? He is reported by the AP to have said, "If we had met several months ago we might have been able to reach some understanding." His emphasis was not on the task at hand, but on the building of a relationship. In many parts of the world, including Iraq, one does not conduct negotiations or do business with a stranger. Unless there is a well-cultivated relationship involving the establishment of trust, no understandings or agreements can be reached. Such relationships are between individuals as people, not as representatives of their organizations or nations. It is likely that Aziz was suggesting to Baker that he did not know him well enough to negotiate.

In addition, Aziz said that the letter contained "language that is not compatible with language between heads of state." Notice his emphasis on the form of the letter rather than its content. I believe that the foreign minister of Iraq was alluding to two important aspects of his common culture—saving face and proper protocol—when he judged the letter to be unacceptable. In common cultures that emphasize relationships and an intimate knowledge of those you deal with, much interpersonal communication is nonverbal or high context (Hall. 1976). That is, what is said is often not as important as how it is said, who says it, and what is left unsaid. In more impersonal common cultures, like the U.S., communication is more explicit; the contents of a letter or the spoken words of a conversation carry more of the meaning. Aziz judged the Bush letter too explicit to be presented to Hussein. Although we do not know the contents, the odds are high that they were blunt and unequivocal. Such communications are not acceptable to high-status officials who expect room to maneuver so that they and their constituents are not embarrassed (lose face).

For Aziz, proper protocol required the right kind of message to be sent in the right way by the right person. Written communications are less acceptable than spoken ones in high-context situations. Conversations provide more possibilities for nonverbal signaling. Also, people in high-context situations often prefer to use intermediaries or go-betweens to communicate so that any misunderstandings can be corrected without the principal parties losing face. An explicit written statement from one head of state directly to another was the wrong kind of message sent in the wrong way to the wrong person. The American deadlines and ultimatums compounded the disrespect inherent in this very low-context approach. Attributing Iraqi thought processes to the Americans, the Iraqis decided that these behaviors indicated that the Americans were not serious about negotiating and were insulting them.

Support for the theory that the Iraqi delegation felt insulted by the behavior of the U.S. delegates in Geneva is provided by another quote in the AP news story. One Iraqi delegate said in a "quaking voice" as he left the meeting, "I never thought that you Americans could be so arrogant. Such a free and open country you have and still you refuse to see our viewpoint." The emotions expressed here are those of an individual who has been condescended to and made to look bad in public, the very essence of losing face. In cultures where public appearance is of ultimate importance, the worst insult is to be shamed before one's peers. Humiliating an individual from a face-saving common culture can create an enemy for life. Rather than persuading him or her to change their behaviors or beliefs, such humiliation will stiffen their resolve and reduce the possibilities for change. The shame-oriented statements made by the U.S. officials (from comparisons of Hussein to Hitler to the lack of acknowledgment of the Iraqi viewpoint in Geneva) contributed to the Iraqi refusal to modify or apologize for their actions or to take part in the proposed negotiation framework of the U.S.

CONCLUSIONS

As the Iraq situation illustrates, egalitarian relationships are crucial in today's world of multilateral negotiations and consensual agreements. Without good faith and trust, negotiations will break down. Trust and good faith will only develop when negotiators treat each other as equals. The recognition and respect that emerge when negotiators genuinely feel they are equals provide a foundation upon which they can begin to debate and collaborate regardless of major differences in their subjective and common cultures.

There were few egalitarian relationships and little intercultural understanding evident in the Iraq illustration. All of the parties ethnocentrically believed they had the most realistic approach and the other side was not as wise as they. No one felt there was much to be learned or achieved through collaborating with all the others as equals, especially if they had to be more forthcoming and flexible in their own behaviors. The perceived arrogance and disrespect that comes from a lack of intercultural understanding will continue to frustrate their efforts to negotiate.

Progress will come in these and similar negotiations when the negotiators gain the modesty and graciousness that come with cultural understanding and self-awareness. A great deal of effort has gone into getting nations that are in conflict to negotiate. Persuading them to recognize and talk to each other has not been easy (Saunders, 1983). Similar amounts of effort are required to develop and implement programs to train their representatives and the leadership they represent in the cognitive and communication skills necessary to make those negotiations more successful.

It is my hope that future policymakers will correct the current imbalance in our approaches to international diplomacy and invest in the research and development work and the training programs needed to produce negotiators who can learn how to learn interculturally. We are reaching impasses in our political, economic, and diplomatic negotiations on more and more occasions. Using the same ethnocentric, tolerant, or minimalist diplomatic approaches will not build international or interpersonal relationships. Coercion, force, and violence do not create acceptable "solutions." It is past time to begin improving our intercultural awareness and communication abilities.

The intercultural approach to international meetings will be especially effective in permanent multilateral negotiations such as those sponsored by the United Nations (which includes most such negotiations). Because their agreements are all recommendatory, U.N. negotiators require consensus in their negotiations. They have found that agreements are only effective if all parties feel a moral commitment to carry them out. When negotiating is secondary to other, more political goals, as it was in Iraq, agreements will break down. Moreover, the chances of gaining the support of important political groups in each country for any agreements that might be achieved at the U.N. are much less when the traditional, adversarial approach to negotiations is used. Diplomats from Wilson to Sadat have suffered the domestic consequences of the power politics approach to negotiation.

In an article in the *Los Angeles Times* magazine, Jonathan Rauch (1992) imagines the willingness to work of the Japanese public being combined with the flexible and open social and political institutions of the Americans: "Then what a country you'd have!" (p. 36). He laments that we will have to make do with the hope that the two countries will drag each other bumpily in the right direction. I believe we can do better than that. With more appropriate training of our international representatives, and through them the intercultural education of our leadership, we can build international relationships that will help create the kind of global village we need—a village in which we can all learn how to learn from and with each other.

REFERENCES

Adler, N. J. (1986). *International dimensions of organizational behavior*. Boston, MA: Kent Publishing Co.

Avruch, K., & Black, P. (1991). The culture question and conflict resolution. *Peace & Change, 16*, 22–45.

Bennett, M. (1986). A developmental approach to training for intercultural sensitivity. *International Journal of Intercultural Relations, 10*, 179–196.

Brewer, M. (1986). The role of ethnocentrism in intergroup conflict. In W. G. Austin & S. Worchel (Eds.), *The social psychology of intergroup relations* (2nd ed., pp. 88–102). Monterey, CA: Brooks/Cole.

Cohen, R. (1991). *Negotiating across cultures: Common obstacles in international diplomacy*. Washington, DC: The U.S. Institute of Peace Press.

Cohen, R. (1992). Deadlock: Israel and Egypt negotiate. In F. Korzenny & S. Ting-Toomey (Eds.), *International and intercultural communication annual: Vol. 14. Communicating for peace: Diplomacy and negotiation across cultures* (pp. 136–153). Newbury Park, CA: Sage.

Fisher, G. (1972). *Public diplomacy and the behavioral sciences*. Bloomington: Indiana University Press.

Fisher, G. (1980). *International negotiation: A cross-cultural perspective*. Yarmouth, ME: Intercultural Press.

Fisher, G. (1988). *Mindsets: The role of culture and perception in international relations*. Yarmouth, ME: Intercultural Press.

Fisher, G. (1989). Diplomacy. In M. Asante & W. Gudykunst (Eds.), *Handbook of international and intercultural communication* (pp. 407–422). Newbury Park, CA: Sage.

Hall, E. T. (1959). *The silent language*. Garden City, NY: Doubleday & Company.

Hall, E. T. (1976). *Beyond culture*. Garden City, NY: Anchor Books.

Jones E., Kanouse, D., Kelley, H., Nisbett, R., Valins, S., & Weiner, B. (Eds.). (1972). *Attribution: Perceiving the causes of behavior*. Morristown, NJ: General Learning Press.

Kimmel, P. R. (1989). *International negotiation and intercultural exploration: Toward cultural understanding*. Unpublished manuscript, The U. S. Institute of Peace, Washington, DC.

Kimmel, P. R. (in press). Using the culture contrast method. In S. M. Fowler & M. Mumford (Eds.), *Intercultural sourcebook: Cultural styles training methodologies*. Yarmouth, ME: Intercultural Press.

Olsson, M. (1985). *Meeting styles for intercultural groups*. (Occasional Papers in Intercultural Learning, No. 7). New York: American Field Service International.

Rauch, J. (1992, March 8). Just another ordinary different place. *Los Angeles Times Magazine*, p. 36.

Saunders, H. H. (1983). *The "Peace Process": The importance of the pre-negotiation phases*. Unpublished manuscript, The Brookings Institution, Washington, DC.

Saunders, H. H. (1987). *Beyond "US and THEM": Building mature international relationships*. Unpublished manuscript, The Brookings Institution, Washington, DC.

Stewart, E. (1972). *American cultural patterns: A cross-cultural perspective*. Yarmouth, ME: Intercultural Press.

Stewart, E., & Bennett, M. (1991). *American cultural patterns: A cross-cultural perspective* (rev. ed.). Yarmouth, ME: Intercultural Press.

Stryker, S., & Gottlieb, A. (1981). Attribution theory and symbolic interactionism: A comparison. In J. Harvey, W. Ickes, & R. Kidd (Eds.), *New directions in attribution research* (Vol. 3, pp. 425–458). Hillsdale, NJ: Lawrence Erlbaum.

Touval, S., & Rubin, J. (1987). *Multilateral negotiation: An analytic approach*. Cambridge, MA: Working Paper Series, Program on Negotiation, Harvard Law School.

Triandis, H. (1972). *The analysis of subjective culture*. New York: John Wiley & Sons.

Tyler, V. L. (1987). *Intercultural interacting*. Provo, UT: Brigham Young University, David Kennedy Center for International Studies.

Weiss, S. (1993). *Negotiating with "Romans": A range of culturally-responsive strategies* (Working Paper No. 5). Toronto: Faculty of Administrative Studies, Business Negotiations Across Cultures, York University.

Weiss, S. (1987, September). Negotiation and cultures: Some thoughts on models, ghosts and options. In *Dispute Resolution Forum* (pp. 3–6). Washington, DC: National Institute for Dispute Resolution.

Weiss, S., & Stripp, W. (1985). *Negotiating with foreign businesspersons: An introduction for Americans with propositions on six cultures* (Working Paper No. 85–86). New York: Graduate School of Business Administration, New York University.

Winham, G. (1977). Negotiations as a management process. *World Politics, 30*, 87–114.

Winham, G. (1979). The mediation of multi-lateral negotiations. *Journal of World Trade Law, 13*, 193–208.

Zartman, W., & Berman, M. (1982). *The practical negotiator*. New Haven, CT: Yale University Press.

Much of the research that is presented in this article was undertaken at the U.S. Institute of Peace in Washington, D.C. when the author was a Peace Fellow in 1988–89.

Thinking Critically and Applying Your Knowledge

1. Summarize the 11 assumptions that American negotiators tend to make about the process of international diplomacy. Do these assumptions also influence how people try to resolve more personal conflicts? Based on this article, how might two college roommates—one American and the other from a Middle Eastern culture like Iraq—try to resolve their disagreements about such things as quiet time for studying, keeping their dorm room clean, or entertaining guests?

2. Kimmel presents 8 important U.S. values that he believes influence the negotiation process. Relate Kimmel's discussion of U.S. values to the characterizations of the United

States found in at least 3 other articles you have read in this book. What are the commonalities—and differences—in the descriptions of U.S. culture that you have read?

3. Kimmel asserts that "the key to success in any negotiation, and especially in international negotiations, lies in the successful exchange of meanings among the negotiators." Explain what Kimmel means by the exchange of meanings. Then, evaluate this assertion and present your personal view on the topic.

4. Kimmel suggests that there are five levels of cultural awareness ranging from cultural chauvinism to understanding another culture. Consider the situation of an elementary schoolteacher with a class of children from diverse cultural backgrounds who largely socialize with classmates from their own ethnic group. How might the teacher use Kimmel's analysis to try to improve social relations among children from different backgrounds? Describe 3 specific activities the teacher might use and explain the rationale for each.